Adult Biliteracy
in the
United States

Adult Biliteracy
in the
United States

David Spener, Editor

A co-publication of
the Center for Applied Linguistics and Delta Systems Co., Inc.
prepared by the National Clearinghouse on Literacy Education,
an adjunct ERIC Clearinghouse

Language in Education

Theory & Practice

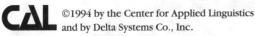
Printed in the United States of America

10 9 8 7 6 5 4 3 2 1

Language in Education: Theory and Practice 83

Editorial/production supervision: Joy Peyton and Fran Keenan
Editorial assistance: Amy Fitch
Cover design and production: Julie Booth

ISBN 0-937354-83-X

This publication was prepared with funding from the Office of Educational Research and Improvement, U.S. Department of Education, under contract No. RI 89166001. The opinions expressed in this report do not necessarily reflect the positions or policies of OERI or ED.

Library of Congress Cataloging-in-Publication Data

Adult biliteracy in the United States / David Spener, editor.
     p. cm.
     "A publication of the Center for Applied Linguistics prepared by
the National Clearinghouse on Literacy Education."
     Papers presented at a conference entitled Biliteracy—theory and
practice held Jan. 1991, Washington, DC.
     Includes bibliographic references.
     ISBN 0-937354-83-X : $19.95
     1. Language planning—United States—Congresses. 2. Bilingualism—
United States—Congresses. 3. United States—Languages—
Congresses. 4. Literacy—United States—Congresses. I. Spener,
David, date. II. Center for Applied Linguistics. III. National
Clearinghouse on Literacy Education. IV. Title: Biliteracy—theory
and practice.
P40.5.L352U613 1994
306.4'46'0973—dc20   93-45622

CONTENTS

INTRODUCTION   **1**
David Spener

CHAPTER 1
Inheriting Sins While Seeking Absolution: Language
Diversity and National Data Sets   **15**
Reynaldo F. Macías

CHAPTER 2
Sociolinguistic Considerations in Biliteracy Planning   **47**
Arnulfo G. Ramírez

CHAPTER 3
Bidialectal Literacy in the United States   **71**
Walt Wolfram

CHAPTER 4
Biliteracy in the Home: Practices Among *Mexicano*
Families in Chicago   **89**
Marcia Farr

CHAPTER 5
Literacy and Second Language Learners:
A Family Agenda   **111**
Gail Weinstein-Shr

CHAPTER 6
¿*Guariyusei?* Adult Biliteracy in Its Natural Habitat   **123**
Tomás Mario Kalmar

CHAPTER 7

**Literacy as Cultural Practice and Cognitive Skill:
Biliteracy in an ESL Class and a GED Program** 147

Nancy H. Hornberger & Joel Hardman

CHAPTER 8

**Putting a Human Face on Technology:
Bilingual Literacy Through Long-Distance Partnerships** 171

Dennis Sayers & Kristin Brown

CHAPTER 9

**Discourse and Social Practice: Learning Science
in Language Minority Classrooms** 191

Beth Warren, Ann S. Rosebery, & Faith Conant

CHAPTER 10

**Engaging Students in Learning: Literacy, Language,
and Knowledge Production with Latino Adolescents** 211

Catherine E. Walsh

ACKNOWLEDGMENTS

In addition to the authors of individual chapters in this volume, I owe thanks to a number of people whose contributions to its successful completion were crucial. First, I would like to thank G. Richard Tucker and JoAnn Crandall, former CAL president and vice president, respectively, for their support and encouragement for putting together a book on the critical issue of adult biliteracy in the United States. Second, Jeannie Rennie, Fran Keenan, and Amy Fitch of the National Clearinghouse on Literacy Education performed the laborious tasks of copyediting and overseeing the layout and made sure that the errors missed by this editor did not make their way into the final text. Finally, I would like to express special thanks to Joy Peyton, NCLE Publications Coordinator. Without her diligence in shepherding this book through the editorial process, from beginning to end, it would not be in your hands today.

INTRODUCTION

David Spener
University of Texas at Austin

One of the primary purposes of this introduction is to give readers a sense of the contents of this book by more clearly defining and establishing parameters for the topic contained in its title, *Adult Biliteracy in the United States.* Another purpose is to provide a sociopolitical framework within which to place the discussions contained in individual chapters. A third purpose is to introduce readers to issues that individual authors discuss. In attempting to accomplish the first two purposes, I have simplified some important issues in the interest of presenting a clear and readily comprehensible overview for the book. It must be noted, however, that adult biliteracy in this country is a complex matter, and any attempt to simplify important issues leads inevitably to distortions in the picture one develops. I hope that any perceived distortions in this summary will be cleared up as one reads subsequent chapters in this volume.

Defining the Parameters of Adult Biliteracy in the United States

Put in the simplest way possible, the term *biliteracy* refers to reading and writing in two languages. Because two languages are involved, biliteracy is inseparably linked to the term *bilingualism*, which *The American Heritage Dictionary of the English Language* defines as "habitual use of two languages, especially in speaking" (Morris, 1973). With regard to modern, living languages (as opposed to certain classical languages such as Latin), it is typically the case that reading and writing a given language presupposes some proficiency in speaking it and understanding it when it is spoken. As a result, it is practically impossible to discuss the phenomenon of bi*literacy* in a sensible way without at the same time discussing bi*lingualism* and the many issues surrounding oral language use that bilingualism implies. With regard to how the term biliteracy is used in this book, we can go further and say that what is implied by the term bilingualism is contained within the term biliteracy. In other words, biliteracy is bilingualism *plus* reading and writing in both languages.

Biliteracy may be discussed with reference to individuals, communities and their institutions, or educational approaches. It can refer to the abilities of individual people to speak, read, and write in two different languages. It can also be used to refer to communities (from villages to nations to multinational or global communities) where materials are read and written in two different languages, whether or not many individuals in those communities are themselves biliterate. With regard to educational approaches, biliteracy can be used to describe attempts to develop literacy in two different languages either simultaneously or sequentially. All three of these aspects of biliteracy are discussed in this volume, though not necessarily by each author in each chapter.

A book on adult biliteracy in the United States could potentially deal with virtually any adult or group of adults who read and write any two languages in any setting in the country, no matter how small the group or how limited the use of the languages. As is often the case, however, both more and less are meant by the term biliteracy than immediately comes to mind. This book does not, for example, address itself to biliteracy among native English speakers. Instead, the biliteracy discussed in this book refers to second language literacy[1] in English *plus* literacy in the mother tongue of one of the many ethnolinguistic minority groups residing in the United States. While it may be true that biliteracy has considerable potential value to native speakers of English in the United States, these native English speakers are not often particularly disadvantaged by being literate only in English. Adult members of linguistic minorities, on the other hand, frequently are substantially disadvantaged in U.S. society if they are not literate in English, even if they are literate in their mother tongue. The chapters in this book are all, to varying degrees, written with this fact as the backdrop and generally portray biliteracy as at least part of a remedy to this disadvantage. At the same time, the book not only discusses language issues related to biliteracy, but also considers those issues within the broader contexts in which they occur.

A Sociopolitical Framework for Biliteracy

A combination of demographic, economic, linguistic, and educational factors have led to increased interest in adult biliteracy in the United States and have presented many challenges for policy makers and educators.

Demographic diversity: A fact of life in the United States

The United States today is a multiracial, multicultural, and multilingual nation. It has been so since its inception and will continue to be so for the foreseeable future. Though English is thoroughly established as the language of commerce, government, and cross-cultural communication, it has always interfaced with a plethora of other languages spoken, read, and written both by newcomers and by the peoples who occupied the North American continent since before Anglo settlers arrived. Massive immigration to the United States has been a constant of 20th-century life in spite of various legislative attempts to curtail or control it, and 1990 census data indicate that this phenomenon has greatly intensified as the country prepares to enter the 21st century (see Macías, this volume). Racial, cultural, and linguistic diversification of the U.S. population is fast on the rise. While the preeminence of English inside the country is most assuredly not threatened in any immediate way by this process, the question of oral and written communication among residents of the United States becomes more problematic.

The competitive stance of the United States in the world economy: Adult literacy in the context of new concerns about the workforce

Also more problematic in recent years has been the world economic standing of the United States. As a truly global economy has evolved since the end of World War II, the United States has faced increasing competition from rival industrialized nations in Europe and Asia, and the ability of U.S. firms to dominate trade in many markets has flagged. While this relative economic decline of the United States in the world economy can be attributed to a variety of causes, business and government leaders have pointed to one cause in particular that concerns us here: the relatively low literacy levels of large numbers of workers and potential workers in the national economy. (See, e.g., Johnston & Packer, 1987; Mississippi Literacy Foundation, 1989.) These leaders believe that it will be necessary to raise the literacy levels of millions of adult and young adult workers if U.S. firms are to reach the higher levels of productivity and efficiency made possible by new technologies and made necessary by foreign competition. President Bush made the advancement of adult literacy one of the cornerstones of his education policy, and the educational establishment began working during his administration to make the achievement of this goal possible.

Literacy education and the linguistic diversity of the workforce

The literacy picture, however, is complicated by the demographic factors discussed above, particularly by the increasing linguistic diversity of the United States population. A substantial percentage of those adults identified by the U.S. Departments of Education and Labor as being insufficiently literate to function effectively with government and business institutions are not fully proficient speakers of English. Since literacy in a modern language typically requires some degree of spoken proficiency, educational programs designed to promote literacy and basic skills in English must either (a) assume that learners already possess a minimum threshold of spoken proficiency in English or (b) promote the acquisition of spoken English and its communicative functions. Clearly, English as a second language (ESL) classes will play a major role in advancing the literacy of a growing number of immigrant adults and youth in the U.S. labor force.

If providing ESL classes were a sufficient answer to the question, "How can educators best advance literacy among language minority adults and their families?", the title of this book would probably be *ESL in the United States*, instead of *Biliteracy in the United States*. More and more literacy researchers and educators, however, are finding that the answer is not quite that simple. For one thing, while it is known that many nonnative English speakers seem not to be functionally literate in English, it is not known how literate they are in other languages. Typical ESL classes assume limited spoken proficiency in English; they also typically assume some minimum ability to use reading and writing skills to learn English in a classroom situation, even when the emphasis of instruction is on the acquisition of oral language. In other words, to take full advantage of ESL instruction, adult learners must already be literate to some extent in their native language. What, then, is to be done about the student enrolling in an ESL class who does not meet this minimum requirement? A few years prior to President Bush's announcement of his adult literacy goals, implementation of the educational provisions of the 1986 Immigration Reform and Control Act (IRCA) brought this question into sharp relief for adult ESL educators nationwide.

IRCA offered undocumented immigrants and refugees who had resided in the United States continuously since before January 1, 1982, the opportunity to become legal permanent residents of the United States through participation in what came to be known as the amnesty program. With some specific exceptions (see Terdy & Spener, 1990), legal permanent residence status would be awarded only to those previously undocumented persons who demonstrated either (a) the ability to speak and write English and a knowledge of U.S. history and civics (as measured by a test) or (b) *progress* toward acquiring that ability and knowledge. Satisfactory progress came to be defined as completion of 40 hours of a 60-hour course of instruction in ESL and U.S. history and civics that had been certified by the Immigration and Naturalization Service. Hundreds of thousands of students enrolled in these amnesty classes all over the United States, the majority having never previously enrolled in adult ESL classes.

In many cities, adult basic education systems suddenly found themselves swamped with a new student population they were not adequately prepared to serve. Not only were they faced with the daunting tasks of establishing administrative procedures, developing curricula, and recruiting qualified teachers in a short amount of time, they were also faced with the new challenge of how best to transmit specific content knowledge about the United States to students who did not speak, read, write, or understand English. This was the first time that adult education systems were required to teach specific subject area content to limited-English-proficient adults on a massive scale. One obvious option was to design courses that were bilingual in nature, with ESL instruction offered in conjunction with content area instruction in the students' native language. Here, however, the question of literate ability in the adult students' native language came into play.

In the state of California, for example, where 1.6 million potential participants in the amnesty program resided (by far the largest number of any state), an assessment of the English ability and educational background of 265,000 amnesty students was conducted at the time of their initial enrollment in amnesty classes.[2] The assessment found, among other things, that 85% of those students assessed in English would have difficulty in "reading basic warning or safety signs or filling out a simple job application," and that the median level of formal education completed in the native language in the country of origin was only 6.5 years (Comprehensive Adult Student Assessment System, 1990). The number of years of formal education completed is only an indirect measure of literate ability, yet this finding came as no surprise to many educators in amnesty programs who had already learned from difficult experience that large numbers of students in their amnesty classes had extremely limited literacy skills in their native language as well as in English. Thus, the bilingual solution was turning out to be inadequate as well, since the formal learning of subject area content was also dependent to a large extent on students already having a minimum threshold of reading and writing skills in their native language. More and more adult ESL teachers and administrators were coming to believe that the extent to which students were literate in their native language played a large role in determining their educational future in the United States.

Regardless of its quality, 60 hours of instruction—the maximum number of hours for the above-described amnesty classes—is an impossibly short amount of time to achieve significant gains in spoken English proficiency, much less in English literacy; neither does it allow for any but the most superficial treatment of the history and government of the United States. The importance of the instructional approach and language of instruction used in these classes should therefore not be exaggerated. The long-term importance of instructional approach and medium of instruction became evident later, as many "amnestied" students continued to enroll in adult education courses even after they had fulfilled the educational requirements IRCA had imposed for obtaining legal permanent residence. Administrators of adult education programs began to find that their amnesty students wished to continue their education both in ESL classes and through other kinds of training, such as vocational education and computer classes. How to make instruction in these classes accessible to immigrant students with low levels of both spoken English proficiency and literacy in their native language continued to preoccupy adult educators in many locales.

In fairness to the ESL profession, it must be noted that methods and materials have been developed for combining the teaching of initial literacy and oral language in ESL classrooms without depending on literacy ability in the native language or on use of the native language in class (see, e.g., Bell & Burnaby, 1984; Haverson & Haynes, 1982). Methods and materials have also been developed for K-12 instruction that promote the acquisition of spoken and written English by limited-English-proficient pupils through instruction in specific content areas such as math, science, and social studies (see, for example, Mohan, 1986; Crandall, 1987). It would thus be inaccurate to state that using students' native language to teach initial literacy and specific subject content was or is the only option available to adult educators.

It must also be said, however, that although ESL literacy and content-area methods and materials do exist, there does not exist sufficient research evidence to suggest that these methods and materials are superior to some combination of ESL and native language instruction. Research evidence with both school children and adults does suggest, however, that the stronger the language and literacy abilities of learners in their native language, the more likely it is that they will develop similarly strong language and literacy abilities in English (Burtoff, 1985; Collier, 1989; Cummins, 1981, 1984; Robson, 1982). It is this evidence that has led a growing number of literacy practitioners and researchers to look at ways of promoting literacy in the native language (or, to use an alternate term, the mother tongue) of language minority adults living in the United States. (For a synopsis of trends in native language literacy for adults, see Rivera, 1990.)

If an individual who is literate in his or her mother tongue is more likely to become a proficient speaker, reader, and writer of English than one who is illiterate in the mother tongue, and if in turn such proficiency and literacy in the English language increases that individual's potential to be a skilled and productive worker in the U.S. economy, then a rationale for biliteracy as both an educational goal and an instructional approach for language minority adults can be conscientiously made. We must speak of biliteracy even if learning to read and write in the native language is thought to serve no other purpose than to promote the subsequent goal of acquiring English literacy. One presumably does not cease to be literate in one's native language upon becoming literate in English—one arrives at a state of biliteracy; that is, being simultaneously, though not necessarily equally, literate in two languages.

Biliteracy education, job training, and promoting the social mobility of language minority adults

There is a growing realization in adult education that language minority adults have educational needs and interests that go beyond the acquisition of spoken and written English (see, e.g., Kalmar, 1992). Bilingual education programs were put in place for non-English-speaking children in the public schools so that they could be taught other subjects, such as math, in their native language while they were learning English. Why not do the same for adults who, as things now stand in many cities across the country, must postpone their participation in job training programs until that "someday" when their English literacy and spoken proficiency have developed sufficiently to allow them to benefit from training provided only in English?

Despite their high levels of motivation to learn English, that someday never comes for many language minority adults. Spoken proficiency and literacy in a second language take many years to develop even under ideal conditions; for many immigrant adults, the conditions are far from ideal and may tend toward the inadequate. In addition to the difficulty of finding time to study English each day after family and work responsibilities are taken care of, both immigrants and U.S.-born limited English speakers too often find themselves working low-skill, low-wage jobs where they either work primarily alongside other immigrants (with whom they interact in their shared native language or in their limited English) or at jobs where they are required to engage in only limited verbal communication with anyone. The potential for them to acquire English informally through interaction with native English speakers is thus limited as well. Denying access to job-related training by making it available only to literate, proficient English speakers (native or not) only compounds the problem of lack of contact with English by making it more difficult for language minority adults to break into higher skilled jobs where they are more likely to interact with native English speakers. It also runs counter to the stated goals of U.S. government and business leaders to improve the competitiveness of U.S. firms in the world market by increasing the skill levels of the nation's workers.

The economic value of fluency and literacy in non-English languages

In describing how it has come to be that biliteracy has gained some currency at the level of setting educational policy, I have focused on the economic value to U.S. society of a skilled, English-literate workforce, and how educational programs for language minorities have attempted to contribute to that value. This focus ignores the practical value of native language literacy in and of itself, not just as a bridge to English. In the United States, many language minority communities in numerous cities and regions are sufficiently large that governmental, commercial, and cultural activities involving literacy are conducted in non-English languages; so to some extent, at least, literacy in those languages constitutes a marketable commodity within those communities. In addition, as economic production becomes increasingly globalized, we should witness a growing demand for U.S. workers who are literate in the languages of countries with which the United States trades or in which U.S. companies produce goods. The value in the world economy of being fluent and literate in a language other than English cannot be denied. In fact, its value has not historically been denied in the United States if the individual possessing that ability is a native speaker of English. Perhaps the time has come for native speakers of other languages to have the value of their non-English language abilities recognized.

Non-economic aspects of literacy

The economically focused picture I have painted above presents literacy as highly functional for overall society, but ignores questions of the many non-economic purposes to which individuals and specific groups within society might wish to put literacy. It also fails to take into account how literacy learners might participate in setting their own agendas for becoming more literate, including deciding what kinds of educational programs involving which languages could best serve their interests (which may in fact conflict at times with the interests of the business, government, and educational establishments). A number of authors in this volume (e.g., Walsh and Weinstein-Shr) address these non-economic issues.

Moreover, the picture I have presented glosses over some key aspects of the nature of literacy itself. From the way I have used the term throughout this introduction, it might be assumed that (a) being literate is a plus or minus condition for any given individual; (b) literacy is a single set of reading and writing skills, acquired through schooling, that may be used equally well in a multitude of unrelated situations; and (c) literacy is generally comparable from language to language, so that it means the same thing to be literate in Spanish, Arabic, or English. These assumptions, in the view of many researchers today, are gross distortions of the nature of literacy in human society. Literacy (and, by extension, biliteracy) is now recognized as a complex continuum of skills and abilities acquired and practiced in a variety of sociolinguistic contexts (not just school contexts), involving a number of distinct types of texts tied to these contexts (see, e.g., Heath, 1983; Hornberger, 1989; Kirsch, 1990; Street, 1984). The authors of the remaining chapters in this book dedicate themselves to the challenge of investigating and illuminating this complexity. It is hoped that the knowledge and experiences they share will inform policies affecting the education of language minority adults in such a way that these policies will be consonant with the real-life experiences and aspirations of language minority adults and their families.

Chapters in This Book

The essays in this volume constitute the proceedings of a two-day research symposium—*Biliteracy: Theory and Practice*—convened in Washington, DC in January 1991 by the National Clearinghouse on Literacy Education and made possible by a grant from the William and Flora Hewlett Foundation. The authors approach the theme of adult biliteracy from a variety of theoretical, research, and practice-based perspectives. It is hoped that readers of this volume will include theorists, researchers, and practitioners, as well as others with a more general interest in the topic. While most of the chapters limit their discussions to biliteracy as it relates to adults, some chapters describe learning situations involving adolescents and school-age children. Authors of these chapters were invited to contribute to this volume based on the belief that the situations they describe have strong implications for the education of language minority adults as well.

Chapters 1, 2, and 3 address primarily the question of linguistic diversity in the United States and its implications for the education of language minority adults. In Chapter 1, Reynaldo Macías of the University of California, Santa Barbara discusses the history of collecting data on language diversity and literacy in this country, including a description of the design and methods of the most current effort at data collection, the National Adult Literacy Survey, conducted by the National Center on Education Statistics. In Chapter 2, Arnulfo Ramírez of Louisiana State University examines biliteracy from a language-planning perspective and emphasizes the importance of biliteracy planners taking into account such sociolinguistic factors as language variety, language style and register, language attitudes, and language choice. Walt Wolfram of North Carolina State University, in Chapter 3, discusses *bidialectalism* in the United States, examining the case of Standard and Black Vernacular Englishes and the teaching of reading to African-American children in the public schools.

In Chapters 4 and 5, Marcia Farr of the University of Illinois–Chicago and Gail Weinstein-Shr of San Francisco State University, respectively, discuss biliteracy with regard to the cultural practices and life concerns of language minority immigrant families. Farr places her description of the family literacy practices of a Mexican social network in Chicago within a theoretical framework defining literacy. Weinstein-Shr presents her recommendations for a research and practice agenda for family literacy as she shares vignettes from the experiences of people involved in Project LEIF, an educational project serving Philadelphia's Southeast Asian refugee community.

The remaining chapters focus, to greater or lesser extents, on the experiences of different groups of people learning literacy in differing contexts. Chapter 6, by Tomás Mario Kalmar of Lesley College in Cambridge, MA, relates the work of 19th-century British philologist Henry Sweet and a 9th-century medieval glossary to both the nascent biliteracy of 20th-century Mexican migrant workers in the orchards of southern Illinois and the role that Christian missionaries played in a post-revolutionary biliteracy campaign in the Tarascan region of Mexico's Michoacán state in the 1930s. Not incidentally, the Mexican migrant workers discussed in this chapter were largely ethnic Tarascans from Michoacán who were in the process of writing their own biliterate glossaries.

In Chapter 7, Nancy Hornberger and Joel Hardman of the University of Pennsylvania present elements of their ethnographic research on the instructional practices followed in a Cambodian ESL class and a Puerto Rican GED program. They analyze their findings with respect to Hornberger's theoretical model for examining the various dimensions of biliteracy (Hornberger, 1989) and with respect to two competing models characterizing the nature of literacy: the autonomous and ideological models (Street, 1984).

Chapter 8 describes Project *Orillas*, a project linking geographically dispersed classes of language minority schoolchildren and their parents through the use of satellite computer networking technology. Authors Dennis Sayers of New York University and Kristin Brown of University of San Francisco describe the effectiveness of the approach in terms of increasing parental involvement in their children's schooling, improving the self-esteem of members of language minority families, changing language attitudes, and engaging both parents and children in meaningful writing activities in two languages.

The authors of Chapter 9, Beth Warren, Ann Rosebery, and Faith Conant of the Technical Education Research Center in Boston, see the process of becoming literate as the successive appropriation of different thematic discourses, irrespective of the language in which these discourses take place. In this chapter they describe the experiences of a group of language minority students in a high school basic skills class as they struggle to master scientific discourse, that is, learning to think about and explore the world as professional scientists do.

In the final chapter, Catherine Walsh of the University of Massachusetts–Boston examines her own beliefs about literacy with regard to her work with Latino high school students labeled "at risk" of dropping out by their Boston-area school. Her account describes the efforts of these students to come to grips with their own identity and to express themselves as they collectively write a "photonovel" based on their school experiences. In concluding, she points to the importance of critical pedagogy for making evident, to teacher and student alike, "the complex significance of language and literacy, and the conditions, relationships, and practices that surround their use and development."

Notes

[1] Throughout this volume, we use terms such as "English as a second language learners," "Second language literacy," and so on, recognizing that for some speakers English may be a second, third, or fourth language.

[2] According to the Comprehensive Adult Student Assessment System (CASAS), these 265,000 students were "predominantly Hispanic (98%) and between the ages of 25 and 44 (70%). . . . Men and

women were represented almost equally (51% and 49%). . . . Most students were from Mexico (85%) and spoke Spanish as their native language (98%)" (CASAS, 1990, p. 2).

References

Bell, J., & Burnaby, B. (1984). *A handbook for ESL literacy.* Toronto, Ontario: OISE Press.

Burtoff, M. (1985). *Haitian Creole literacy evaluation study: Final report.* Washington, DC: Center for Applied Linguistics. (ERIC Document Reproduction Service No. 277 273)

Collier, V.P. (1989). How long? A synthesis of research on academic achievement in a second language. *TESOL Quarterly, 23,* 509-531.

Comprehensive Adult Student Assessment System (CASAS). (1990). *Amnesty education report: IRCA preenrollment appraisal results.* San Diego: Author. (ERIC Document Reproduction Service No. 321 605)

Crandall, J. (Ed.). (1987). *ESL through content-area instruction: Mathematics, science, social studies.* Englewood Cliffs, NJ and Washington, DC: Prentice Hall and Center for Applied Linguistics.

Cummins, J. (1981). The role of primary language development in promoting educational success for language minority students. In *Schooling and language minority students: A theoretical framework* (pp. 3-50). Los Angeles: California State University, Evaluation, Dissemination, and Assessment Center.

Cummins, J. (1984). *Bilingualism and special education: Issues in assessment and pedagogy.* San Diego: College Hill.

Haverson, W.W., & Haynes, J.L. (1982). *ESL/literacy for adult learners.* Washington, DC: Center for Applied Linguistics.

Heath, S.B. (1983). *Ways with words: Language, life and work in communities and classrooms.* Cambridge: Cambridge University Press.

Hornberger, N. (1989). Continua of biliteracy. *Review of Educational Research, 59*(3), 271-296.

Johnston, W.B., & Packer, A.H. (1987). *Workforce 2000: Work and workers for the 21st century.* Indianapolis, IN: Hudson Institute.

Kalmar, T. (1992). Drawing the line on minority languages: Equity and linguistic diversity in the Boston Adult Literacy Initiative. *Journal of Adult Basic Education*, 2(2), 84-112.

Kirsch, I. (1990). Measuring adult literacy. In R. Venezky, D. Wagner, & B. Ciliberti (Eds.), *Towards defining literacy* (pp. 40-47). Newark, DE: International Reading Association.

Mississippi Literacy Foundation. (1989). *State literacy strategies: A policy primer.* Jackson, MS: Author.

Mohan, B.A. (1986). *Language and content.* Reading, MA: Addison-Wesley.

Morris, W. (Ed.). (1973). *The American Heritage dictionary of the English language.* New York: American Heritage.

Rivera, K. (1990). *Developing native language literacy in language minority adults. ERIC Digest.* Washington, DC: Center for Applied Linguistics, National Clearinghouse on Literacy Education. (ERIC Document Reproduction Service No. ED 358 747)

Robson, B. (1982). *Hmong literacy, formal education, and their effects on performance in an ESL class.* In B.T. Downing & P.O. Dougleas (Eds.), *The Hmong in the West—Observations and reports: Papers of the 1981 Homg Research Conference, University of Minnesota* (pp. 201-225). Minneapolis, MN: University of Minnesota, Center for Urban and Regional Affairs. (ERIC Document Reproduction Service No. ED 299 829)

Street, B. (1984). *Literacy in theory and practice.* New York: Cambridge University Press.

Terdy, D., & Spener, D. (1990). *English language literacy and other requirements of the Amnesty Program. ERIC Q&A.* Washington, DC: Center for Applied Linguistics, National Clearinghouse on Literacy Education. (ERIC Document Reproduction Service No. 321 616)

CHAPTER 1
Inheriting Sins While Seeking Absolution: Language Diversity and National Statistical Data Sets

Reynaldo F. Macías
University of California, Santa Barbara

Understanding the literacy of the U.S. population has been a struggle for researchers, educators, and policymakers for most of the 20th century. Despite several national surveys over the last 20 years, our knowledge is skimpy at best and limited to English literacy. Complicating the literacy situation is the increased linguistic diversity of the nation.

Measuring Literacy in a Linguistically Diverse Population

In 1980, there were 28 million people age 5 years and older who lived in households where a non-English language (NEL) was spoken. About 23 million of them actually spoke a non-English language themselves, and about half of these people spoke Spanish (see Table 1). In the subsequent 10 years, the Hispanic and Asian population (with large numbers of speakers of non-English languages) increased by much greater percentages than the general population: 53% and 108% respectively, compared to 10% for the general population (see Table 2). The number of people age 5 years and older who spoke languages other than English increased 38.6% from 22,973,410 to 31,844,979, between 1980 and 1990 (see Tables 1 and 3). The total population 5 years and older increased 9.6% during that time. The number of Spanish speakers 5 years and older increased 56%, from 11,117,606 to 17,345,064 (see Table 4). Over four fifths of this growth was in the adult, not the school-age population.

I would like to thank several people for providing helpful comments on an earlier draft of this essay: David Spener, Douglas Rhodes, Irwin Kirsch, Ann Jungeblut, and Hannah Fingeret.

Table 1
Bilingual Abilities of Selected Language Groups by Age, for the U.S., 1980

	Total NEL Speakers		Bilinguals		NEL Monolinguals	
	N	%(Col/Row)	N	%(Col/Row)	N	%(Col/Row)
5-17 yrs						
All non-English Languages	4,529,098	100.0% 100.0%	3,875,536	100.0% 85.6%	653,562	100.0% 14.4%
Spanish	2,947,051	65.1% 100.0%	2,474,619	63.9% 84.0%	427,432	72.3% 16.0%
Other NEL	1,582,047	34.9% 100.0%	1,400,917	36.1% 88.6%	181,130	27.7% 11.4%
18+ yrs						
All NEL	18,444,312	100.0% 100.0%	14,801,370	100.0% 80.2%	3,642,942	100.0% 19.8%
Spanish	8,170,555	44.3% 100.0%	5,879,301	39.7% 72.0%	2,291,254	62.9% 28.0%
Other NEL	10,273,757	55.7% 100.0%	8,922,069	60.3% 86.8%	1,351,688	37.1% 13.2%
5+ yrs						
All NEL	22,973,410	100.0% 100.0%	18,676,906	100.0% 81.3%	4,296,504	100.0% 18.7%
Spanish	11,117,606	48.4% 100.0%	8,353,920	44.7% 75.1%	2,763,686	64.3% 24.9%
Other NEL	11,855,804	51.6% 100.0%	10,322,986	55.3% 87.1%	1,532,818	35.7% 12.9%

Source: Data are from U.S. Bureau of the Census, (1982, March), Provisional social and economic estimates from the 1980 Census. (PHC-80-S1). Washington, DC: USGPO. Table P-2.

Note: Bilinguals were constructed by taking those who "speak a language other than English at home" and also "speak English well or very well." Non-English monolinguals were constructed by taking those who "speak a language other than English at home" and also "speak English not well or not at all."

Table 2
Population Change Between 1980 & 1990 by Race & Ethnicity, U.S.

	1980		1990		Change		
	N	%	N	%	N	Increase	% of change
Total Population	226,545,805	100.0%	248,709,873	100.0%	22,164,068	9.8%	100.0%
White	188,371,622	83.1%	199,686,070	80.3%	11,314,448	6.0%	51.0%
Black	26,495,025	11.7%	29,986,060	12.1%	3,491,035	13.2%	15.8%
AmerIndian	1,420,400	0.6%	1,959,234	0.8%	538,834	37.9%	2.4%
Asian & Pacific Isl.	3,500,439	1.5%	7,273,662	2.9%	3,773,223	107.8%	17.0%
Other	6,758,319	3.0%	9,804,847	3.9%	3,046,528	45.1%	13.7%
Hispanic	14,608,673	6.4%	22,354,059	9.0%	7,745,386	53.0%	34.9%

Sources: Data are from the 1990 Census Summary Tape file, 1A. The data were obtained from the U.S. Census Bureau Regional Office, Los Angeles, CA. Also see U.S. Bureau of the Census 1991, April.

Table 3
Bilingual Abilities of Non-English-Language Speakers, by Age, for U.S., 1990

	Total NEL Speakers		Bilinguals		NEL Monolinguals	
	N	%(Col/Row)	N	%(Col/Row)	N	%(Col/Row)
5-17 yrs	6,322,934	19.9% 100.0%	5,415,371	21.5% 85.6%	907,563	13.6% 14.4%
18+ yrs	25,522,045	80.1% 100.0%	19,757,407	78.5% 77.4%	5,764,638	86.4% 22.6%
5+ yrs	31,844,979	100.0% 100.0%	25,172,778	100.0% 79.0%	6,672,201	100.0% 21.0%

Source: Data are from U.S. Bureau of the Census, 1992, Special tabulation 1990 CPH-L-96. Tables ED90-3, 4, and 5: Language use and English ability, Persons 5 years and over; 5-17 years; and 18 years and over, by state: 1990 Census. Washington, DC: Author.

Note: Bilinguals were constructed by taking those who "speak a language other than English at home" and also "speak English well or very well." Non-English monolinguals were constructed by taking those who "speak a language other than English at home" and also "speak English not well or not at all."

	1980		1990		Change		
	N	%	N	%	N	Increase	% of change
5-17 yrs.	2,947,051	26.5%	4,167,653	24.0%	1,220,602	41.4%	19.6%
18+ yrs.	8,170,555	73.5%	13,177,411	76.0%	5,006,856	61.3%	80.4%
5+ yrs.	11,117,606	100.0%	17,345,064	100.0%	6,227,458	56.0%	100.0%

Source: Data for 1980 are from U.S. Bureau of the Census, 1982, March. Provisional social and economic estimates from the 1980 Census. (PHC-80-S1). Washington, DC: USGPO. Table P-2. Data for 1990 were taken from U.S. Bureau of the Census. (1992). Special tabulation 1990 CPH-L-96. Tables ED90-3, 4, and 5: Language use and English ability, Persons 5 years and over; 5-17 years; and 18 years and over, by state: 1990 Census. Washington, DC: Author.

Literacy, and particularly English literacy, is so important for success in this society that we should have the best possible description of the distribution of these abilities for the nation. But, despite the number of literacy surveys undertaken in this country over the last two decades, very little data have been produced or released on language minority adult literacy. In most instances, the sponsors have not taken the nation's ethnic or linguistic diversity into account in designing the studies or analyzing the data, other than to distinguishing between White and Black races. This leaves us with a skewed picture of the nature of literacy and its distribution within the national population. When these studies have supplemental samples of ethnic minorities and there are language and literacy data related to these subsamples, these data are often not analyzed or studied, so they yield little of what they could contribute. A more specific focus on cultural/racial/linguistic diversity in the design and analysis of the studies would provide for a more detailed, accurate, and textured picture of literacy in the nation. Support for specific language and literacy analyses of extant data sets would also be useful in advancing our knowledge.

This country is changing rapidly as a result of internal migration, external migration, and the differential rates of natural increase (births over deaths) among racial and cultural groups. National surveys monitor these changes and others. Descriptions of language and literacy characteristics are important in several ways, not the least of which is that they help us define our national cultural identity. The recent debates over cultural literacy and common culture present different value positions and should be informed by survey data (see especially the debates around Hirsch, 1987). Furthermore, national statistical studies very often inform (not determine) national policies and programs. If language minority diversity is absent from these studies or is presented in a distorted manner, the policies and programs may not address the needs of these groups.

One of the results of a distorted picture of the national diversity in languages and literacy is that we tend to fill the gaps in our knowledge and understanding with ideological content, particularly with what I have called the English language ideology (Macías, 1985a). This is manifested in adult literacy programs and services by the refusal of literacy providers to serve adequately the needs of language minority adults, and sometimes their refusal to allow them entry into adult literacy programs. Very often these programs refer language minority adults seeking literacy instruction to English as a second language (ESL) classes, without understanding that most of these classes teach oral English rather than English literacy. School districts often provide confusing reasons to justify the distinction that is often made between adult basic education (ABE) and adult ESL programs (Kalmar, 1992).

Finally, it is important to recognize the relationship of the national data sets to local and qualitative research. In the past several years, major qualitative studies have reported on language and literacy abilities and use among particular groups within the nation. These have helped advance our knowledge of literacy functions and uses as well as the relationship between community and school definitions of literacy. Yet, we do not have much information about how these community literacy functions and definitions of literacy are distributed across different communities or particular states in the nation. Large-scale, national quantitative research studies can provide some of this information, but large-scale surveys are not better than local or qualitative studies. Both are needed, and each can contribute answers to questions that the other cannot. We should keep these qualitative studies in mind as we discuss the values of national data sets.

Overview of National Surveys and Data Sets

At least 15 national surveys were conducted between 1975 and 1990 and several between 1990 and 1992 that have contributed to our knowledge of language minorities, literacy, and biliteracy. These studies, however, vary in their quality and detail. They each provide us with part of the national linguistic diversity and literacy picture (and we should keep in mind each of these parts as we attempt to piece together the broader picture), but they vary on several key dimensions: the types of measures of language and literacy used, the kinds of information gathered in background questionnaires, and the sample sizes. (See Table 5 for a summary of the differences among studies.)

Measures of language and literacy

The surveys have used three different types of measures of English oral language proficiency and literacy: direct measures (e.g., performance on a test), indirect measures (usually self-reported assessment of literacy ability or non-English language abilities), and surrogate or substitute measures (often the number of years of school completed in the United States as a surrogate for literacy). Each of these types of measures must be clearly understood in order to appreciate the value of the data sets for our purposes. Even the direct measures have varied widely in how they define literacy (Kirsch, 1990). Almost all of them implicitly or explicitly assume *English* literacy as the focus of the surveys.

Types of information gathered in background questionnaires

The data collection instruments for the surveys have usually included a household screener to identify eligible households and individuals, a background questionnaire, and a literacy measurement instrument. Several of these surveys have collected information about both the English and non-English language and literacy abilities of the respondents through background questionnaires that have been translated into Spanish, providing some information on bilingual and biliterate abilities as well as on bilingual survey methodology. However, the information provided by these background questionnaires is often ignored by researchers and policymakers. When the sample size for a survey is small or the measures narrow, it is important to look at the background questionnaire for possible additional information on language diversity.

Table 5
Selected Summary Characteristics of National
Language Data Sets, 1975-1992

Survey	Sample Size	Language Background Variable	LEP Variable	Literacy Data	Literacy Measure
1975 Current Pop. Survey— Survey of Languages Supplement (CPS-SLS)	42,000 HH	yes	no	no	surrogate
1976 Survey of Income & Education (SIE)	440,000	yes	no	no	surrogate
1978 Children's English & Services Study (CESS) 1 & 2	2,200	yes	yes	yes	direct
1979 National Chicano Survey (NCS)	1,000	yes	no	yes	indirect
1980 Projections Study—5-14 yr olds	N A	yes	yes	no	surrogate
15+ yr olds	N A	no	no	surrogate	
1980 Census	33 Million	yes	no	no	surrogate
1982 English Language Proficiency Study (ELPS)	9,000 HH	yes	yes	yes	direct
1986 Young Adult Literacy Survey (YALS)	3,600	yes	yes	yes	direct
1990 Census	41 Million	yes	no	no	surrogate
1990 DOL Workplace Literacy Survey (DOL-WLS)	5,800	yes	yes	yes	direct
1992 National Adult Literacy Survey (NALS)	13,000	yes	yes	yes	direct
1992 State Option to NALS	1,000+ per state	yes	yes	yes	direct

HH = households

Sampling limitations

All of these studies have been based on samples. Even the decennial census collects data from a sample of the population that fills out what is termed the "long questionnaire." The size of the samples for all other surveys is much smaller than the 16% sample in the 1980 and 1990 censuses (giving sample sizes of 33 million and 40 million, respectively) and, in some instances, so small that only two-way cross tabulations can be done for analysis. This means that when we are interested in three variables, like ethnicity, language background, and literacy (or gender, place of birth, age), the cell sizes are often too small to provide a stable picture or description.

Another concern, besides the sample size of these surveys, is the composition of the samples. Many of these samples were selected based on general population characteristics, like gender, age, and race, as well as geographic location—rural, urban, or suburban. Rarely have the sample selection criteria included language or literacy backgrounds. These variables may have been afterthoughts or added as the result of a supplemental sample to the survey. Where they have been included, they make the study and its results very special. In addition, because almost all of these surveys were designed to assess English literacy, samples may have excluded individuals with little or no proficiency in English from being respondents, or from the direct measure data, or from the analyses. So even if there is a substantial representation of language diversity in the sample, some subjects may be excluded from selection or from analyses because of their limited English proficiency.

Even with these variations and shortcomings in mind, many of the national data sets provide valuable stop-gap information. Of the studies described below, seven were part of a systematic attempt at developing language minority information for bilingual education policy needs, and so reflect consistent definitions and concepts with slight variations: (1) 1975 Current Population Survey—Survey of Languages Supplement (CPS-SLS); (2) 1976 Survey of Income and Education (SIE); (3) 1978 Children's English and Services Study (CESS); (4) 1980 Projections Study; (5) 1980 Census; (6) 1990 Census; and (7) the 1982 English Language Proficiency Study (ELPS). Three others were developed with a literacy policy mandate and provided for similar direct measures of English literacy, but included language minority data in their designs: (1) 1986 Young Adult Literacy Survey

(YALS); (2) 1990 Department of Labor Workplace Literacy Survey (DOL-WLS); and (3) the 1992 National Adult Literacy Survey (NALS). Only one was specifically designed to survey a national language minority sample, using bilingual, biliterate survey methodology: 1979 National Chicano Survey (NCS) (see Figure 1). The combined data wealth generated in these surveys is impressive.

Figure 1.
Developmental Relationship of Selected National Surveys

Bilingual Education	Literacy Policy	Ethnic/Language Minority
1975 CPS-SLS		
1976 SIE		
1978 CESS		1979 NCS*
1980 Projections Study		
1980 Census		
1982 ELPS	1984 NAEP	
	1986 NAEP	
	1986 YALS	
1990 Census	1990 DOL-WLS	
	1992 NALS	

*There are other such surveys, but none which has matched the developmental work of the NCS to assure the validity of the bilingual research methodologies and design. The federal government's preferred mode for reaching language minorities, principally the Latino population, over the last decade has been supplemental samples and questionnaires to existing surveys. A National Survey of Issues, undertaken in 1989 by the Institute for Survey Research at Temple University and the Center for Mexican American Studies at the University of Texas, Austin included a Latino Questionnaire that was specifically designed to collect data on the national Latino population in English and Spanish, but I have little other information on it at this time.

Selected National Studies

Selected surveys and studies are discussed below, including the National Adult Literacy Survey, which collected data in the Spring and Summer of 1992. They are reviewed in chronological order to indicate the developmental nature of some of the key concepts and the overlap of some of the efforts.[1]

1975 Current Population Survey—Survey of Languages Supplement (CPS-SLS)

In response to debates and amendments surrounding the 1974 Bilingual Education Act, the federal government initiated a series of studies that resulted in a rather dramatic shift in language-related national data collection. These studies were designed to answer the question, "How many students in the nation are in need of bilingual education?" As a result of reviewing the national legislation, several key concepts and operational definitions were developed for "non-English language background" (NELB) or "language minority" (LM), and "limited-English-proficient" (LEP). These were not new concepts to the educational field or in the research literature, but to the U.S. data-gathering agencies, they were new.

A second question was also asked: "How can this estimate be derived from a national study?" The answer came from several quarters, including the Center for Applied Linguistics, which developed a Measure of English Language Proficiency (MELP) under contract to the National Center for Education Statistics (NCES) (Macías & Spencer, 1983, Chapter 1). The MELP was a series of survey questions correlated with data on elementary school language minority children who had been classified as needing bilingual services because their English proficiency was limited. The idea was to identify the pool of language minority individuals from which non-English-proficient and limited-English-proficient students could be identified, and then to assess their English proficiency to arrive at the estimate.

These non-English language background questions were field tested in the July 1975 Current Population Survey (CPS), a 42,000-household survey conducted monthly by the Census Bureau. The results of the CPS-Survey of Languages Supplement were reported in Chapter 4 of the *The Condition of Bilingual Education in the Nation* (U.S. Commissioner of Education, 1976). A shorter list of questions was identified as useful for surveys and valid for obtaining the non-English language background pool.

1976 Survey of Income and Education (SIE)

In 1976, the U.S. Census Bureau undertook one of the largest national surveys under congressional mandate to produce an estimate of poverty at the state level, in order to reformulate several national programs whose funding depended on this information. Other agencies took advantage of this survey by adding items to the questionnaire and supplemental samples for particular analyses, in what was informally touted as a mid-decennial census because of its size. The survey collected information from 151,000 households and 440,000 individuals. The NCES and U.S. Office of Bilingual Education added the language background questions developed and field tested with the 1975 CPS. They also worked to assure an adequate sample for the survey so that it would yield language information that could be used to draw a subsequent sample stratified by language characteristics for the Children's English and Services Study (discussed below), which would include a direct measure of English language proficiency. The survey also used a more specific list than previous surveys of racial and ethnic identifiers, especially for the Latino subgroups, which provided for better national coverage of racial and ethnic groups.

The results of the SIE were published by the National Center for Education Statistics (1978a, 1978b, 1978c, 1979) and represented the first major description of the current (as opposed to retrospective) language abilities of the national population. The SIE also produced a major data set that has been heavily analyzed (see López, 1982; Macías, 1985b; Veltman, 1983, for several such studies looking at language issues). With the completion of the SIE, we could describe the language minority diversity of the national population—including those who did not speak English at all—by state, language, and age. However, we could not provide an estimate of those who were limited in their English proficiency except in a gross indirect manner and with no indication of literacy ability.

1978 Children's English and Services Study 1 and 2 (CESS)

The Children's English and Services Study was designed as a follow-up to the SIE to determine the size of the national language minority population and the proportion of individuals in this population between the ages of 5 and 14 years of age who were limited in their English proficiency (including speaking, listening, reading, and writing). A direct measure of English proficiency that correlated with schooling classification practices, the Language Measurement and Assessment Inventory, was developed as a survey instrument. The CESS 1 screened 35,000 households and tested 2,200 school-age non-English language background individuals. CESS 2 followed a subset of those individuals into the schools to see what kinds of educational services they were receiving.

An important methodological contribution of the CESS was an index of the proportion of LEP individuals 5-14 years of age by language background within four regions of the country that could be linked with the SIE to get more detailed information about the national LEP population (which was later used with the 1980 Projections Study below).

The CESS data were not as widely analyzed as other data sets, although the National Institute of Education published a two-volume report on the data and the analyses that were done by the government (O'Malley, 1981).

1979 National Chicano Survey (NCS)

This survey was principally funded by the National Institute of Mental Health, with supplemental funding from other agencies and foundations. It was designed to draw a nationally representative sample of the adult Mexican-origin population and describe demographic and social characteristics and behaviors. The data collection instruments were in English and Spanish, and the data collection procedures were designed for a bilingual population, with extensive training of the bilingual field personnel. The language data included language background questions, language use questions, literacy ability questions, and language use case histories. This survey allowed researchers to develop a profile of the Chicano population's literacy abilities in English and Spanish (see Wiley, 1988, for a study on these biliteracy data).

1980 Projections Study

The Projections Study was not designed to collect data. It was designed to synthetically derive estimates and projections of the language minority and limited-English-proficient population of the nation. It continued the federal government's attempt to profile the language minority and limited-English-proficient characteristics of the national population for bilingual education policy needs. The LEP rates from the CESS were applied to the population characteristics of the SIE and linked with the national population projections developed by the Census Bureau to the year 2000 in five-year intervals. This study yielded LEP estimates by age for the 5- to 14-year-old population by state and language background, and language minority data by language and states for all ages (see Oxford-Carpenter et al., 1984).

1980 Census

The 1980 Census provided the opportunity to collect language background data for the nation that would surpass the SIE in detail and coverage. The Census dropped the mother tongue question it had included since 1890. This mother tongue question (What was the language spoken in the home of the head of household when he was a child?) was actually a household language question and was initially used as a surrogate measure of the number of immigrants and their immediate progeny in the country and their rate of assimilation. The question was replaced with questions on current language ability. These three questions were slightly modified from those developed and used in the CPS Survey of Languages and the SIE.

13a. Does this person speak a language other than English at home?
- yes   - no, only speaks English—skip to 14
13b. What is this language? _____
13c. How well does this person speak English?
- very well   - not well
- well   - not at all

(U.S. Bureau of the Census, 1980)

There were no specific direct or indirect literacy items on the Census.[2]

This was also the first Census that included the Latino origin question on the 100% "short form" questionnaire, which goes to the total population:

7. Is this person of Spanish/Hispanic origin or descent?
- no, not Spanish/Hispanic
- yes, Mexican, Mexican American, Chicano
- yes, Puerto Rican
- Cuban
- other Spanish/Hispanic

(U.S. Bureau of the Census, 1980)

In prior decennial counts, a question on being Latino may have been asked only in certain states, or not at all, using surname and other techniques to arrive at estimates of this population. Language data were published by the Census Bureau and made available for secondary data analyses in 1983 and 1984.

1982 English Language Proficiency Study (ELPS)

The English Language Proficiency Study was designed as a follow-up study to the Census, using a language minority sample of the 1980 Census, that would collect language and literacy data using two direct measures—the Language Measurement and Assessment Inventory and the Measure of Adult English Proficiency (MAEP)—developed to identify the English literacy abilities needed by the adult population to access social services and benefits, especially from government agencies. The LEP rates for the school-age and adult populations derived from these two measures of English proficiency would then be applied to the 1980 Census to yield much more comprehensive and detailed information on the language and literacy characteristics of the national population, including updating the answer to the question of how many LEP individuals there were in the nation. This technique was similar to the one that applied the CESS LEP rate to the SIE. Unfortunately, this survey was caught in political infighting between different parts of the newly created U.S. Education Department, in a federal administration that was openly hostile to bilingual education and that politicized the educational research efforts of the federal government.

The ELPS was linked with the 1980 Census in limited ways. It was linked in 1987, in a special tabulation by the Education Department, to provide synthetic estimates of the school-age limited-English-proficient population (U.S. Department of Education, 1987). In 1986, limited (il)literacy results from the ELPS were released with no linkage to any other data set or systematic presentation of the data. No separate analyses have been made linking the ELPS and the 1980 Census for adults or specifically to answer questions related to literacy. There has also been no independent study or analysis of the MAEP used in this survey (Macías & Spencer, 1983). Despite these limitations, there was discussion during the Summer and Fall of 1991 about applying the ELPS in some fashion to the 1990 Census, to update these LEP estimates.

The 1986 Young Adult Literacy Survey (YALS)

The Young Adult Literacy Survey was undertaken by the Educational Testing Service using a new conceptual approach to literacy assessment named the "profiles approach" by the developers (see Kirsch, 1990; Kirsch & Jungeblut, 1986; U.S. Department of Education, 1990). The YALS framework for literacy included reading and writing tasks using real-world materials, and the analyses of the data derived three scales of literacy proficiency: prose, document, and quantitative. These scales reflected a move away from a single score distinguishing between literacy and illiteracy and from grade equivalents as in previous literacy surveys. Analyses of the items by text types also reflected a more complex notion of literacy assessment.[3] The document scale, for example, involved

> the number of features or categories of information in the question or directive that had to be matched to information in the document, the degree to which the wording in the question or directive corresponded to that in the document, and the number of distractors or plausible correct answers in the document. (Kirsch, 1990, p. 45)

The YALS background questionnaire (which was translated into Spanish) also included 32 items related to the language background of the respondents. About 80 persons used the Spanish questionnaire.

The YALS sample consisted of 3,600 persons 21 to 25 years old. Latinos and Blacks were oversampled at twice their rate of occurrence in the population in order to derive data that could be reported by race and Latino ethnicity, although the sample was not large enough to report by Latino subgroups. The survey included a seven-item screener for identifying individuals who had no literacy skills and for whom taking the assessment would be nonproductive, and individuals who were not proficient enough in English to be assessed. Approximately 1% of the sample fell into each of these two categories and so were excluded from the analyses of the data.

Several reports were published on the YALS, but limited data could be published on the limited-English-proficient or language minority part of the sample. The influence on the field of this approach to measuring literacy, however, was significant. One of its basic conclusions was that the youth of the United States were not illiterate, but had some literacy problems; most could perform well on the prose scale but not well on the high end of the prose scale or on the document or quantitative scales (see Kirsch & Jungeblut, 1986).

1990 Census

The 1990 Census included the same current language ability and ethnicity questions as the 1980 Census. The language ability questions were on the sample (long) form, which, again, included about 16% of the population. The race/ethnicity questions were also replicated from the previous Census.[4] The ethnic data were released in 1991, while the language data were made available in mid-1992 (see Macías, 1993, for discussion of the ethnic and new language classifications used for reporting these data).

There were significant problems with the undercount of specific groups for the 1990 Census. Although other decennial census counts have had differential population undercounts for ethnic groups and the poor, the 1990 Census may be the first Census that did not improve over previous efforts at counting the population.

1990 Department of Labor Workplace Literacy Survey (DOL-WLS)

This survey was conducted by the Educational Testing Service for the U.S. Department of Labor. It used basically the same framework and direct measure of literacy as the Young Adult Literacy Survey, augmented with additional, new items. The background questionnaire included eight questions related to the subjects' language background.

It surveyed about 2,500 persons who were enrolled in a Job Training Partnership Act (JTPA) program and about 3,300 persons applying for jobs through the Employment Service or filing for Unemployment Insurance benefits. The results were compared to data collected through the 1986 Young Adult Literacy Survey and the 1992 National Adult Literacy Survey. The results were released in Fall 1992.

The 1992 National Adult Literacy Survey (NALS)

The NALS is the most current federal attempt at measuring literacy abilities and distribution of those abilities across the national population. This survey builds on the YALS and the Department of Labor study in its direct measure of literacy, the oversampling of Blacks and Latinos, and the language background questions. It is unique in that it included an option for states who wanted to purchase a state-level sample to augment their national sample and in that it allowed for state-level analyses and reports. Since it is the most recent of the literacy studies, a more detailed discussion of NALS is warranted.

Definition of literacy

The following definition was developed.

[Literacy involves] using printed and written information to function in society, to achieve one's goals, and to develop one's knowledge and potential. (Educational Testing Service, 1990, p. 5; U.S. Department of Education, 1990)

This definition was operationalized along three scales: prose, document, and quantitative literacy. Prose literacy tasks involved the knowledge and skills needed to understand and use information from texts that include editorials, news stories, poems, and fiction. Document literacy tasks involved the knowledge and skills required to locate and use information contained in job applications or payroll forms, transportation schedules, maps, tables, and indices. Quantitative literacy tasks involved the knowledge and skills needed to apply arithmetic operations, either alone or sequentially, that are embedded in printed materials, such as balancing a checkbook, figuring out a tip, completing an order form, or determining the amount of interest from a loan advertisement. This framework and definition included reading and writing across each of the three scales (despite argument from some members of the Literacy Definition Committee that writing was not part of literacy; see U.S. Department of Education, 1990, p. 13).

Methods and measures

The survey was conducted by interviewers who used a household screener for selecting eligible households and respondents, a background questionnaire, and assessment booklets for the direct measure of literacy proficiencies. The background questionnaire took an average of 15 minutes to complete, was available in English and Spanish versions, and included the following 14 language background items:

A-4. When you were growing up, what language or languages were usually spoken in your home?

A-5. What language or languages did you learn to speak before you started school?

A-6. What language did you first learn to read and write?

A-7. How old were you when you learned to speak English?

A-8. With regard to [the non-English language, NEL], how well do you: understand it when it is spoken to you; speak it; read it; write it?

A-9. With regard to [NEL], how often do you: listen to radio programs, tapes, or records in [language]; watch television programs or video tapes in [language]; read newspapers, magazines, or books in [language]; write or fill out letters or forms in [language]?

A-10. Tell me what language you use in each of the following situations: at home; at work; while shopping in your neighborhood; when visiting relatives or friends?

A-11. Have you ever taken a course to learn how to read and write English as a second language?

A-12. Did you complete this course?

A-13. Have you ever taken a course to learn how to speak and understand English as a second language?

A-14. Did you complete this course?

A-15. Which language do you usually speak now?

A-16. What other language do you often speak now?

A-17. With regard to the English language, how well do you: understand it when it is spoken to you; speak it; read it; write it; do arithmetic problems when you have to get the numbers from written materials?

The race/ethnicity questions included the following:

F-9. Which of the groups on this card best describes you?
   A. White
   B. Black, African American
   C. American Indian
   D. Alaskan Native
   E. Pacific Islander
   F. Asian (Specify: _____)
   G. Other (Specify: _____)

F-10. Are you of Spanish or Hispanic origin or descent?

yes

no

F-11. Which of the groups on this card best describes your Hispanic origin?

A. Mexicano, Mexican, Mexican American, Chicano

B. Puerto Rican

C. Cuban

D. Central/South American

E. Other Spanish/Hispanic (Specify: _____)

(Educational Testing Service, 1991)

Other questions covered family background; respondent demographic data; schooling experiences; labor market status; self-perceptions of literacy needs; and literacy practices at home, on the job, and in the community.

The literacy assessment took an average of 45 minutes to administer. All of the three scales involved reading, writing, arithmetic/computational, and problem-solving/reasoning tasks focused on simulated text stimuli taken from actual, popular publications—mainly newspapers, magazines, and commonly used forms.

Sample

The sample consisted of 13,000 adults, 16 years of age and older, residing in households and federal and state prisons within the United States. The sample was drawn using the 1990 Census and was stratified by region and race. Blacks and Latinos were oversampled within large urban areas to obtain reasonable sample sizes for reporting by race and ethnicity, although, again, the size of the Latino sample did not allow reporting by subgroups. The sample was weighted to the 1990 national population, adjusting for the estimated undercount.

State options

Since the national sample size did not allow for state-level analyses, the NALS had a state option. This option allowed states to purchase an additional sample of 1,000 respondents within the state that would augment that state's portion of the national sample in order to report at the state level.[5] The states were also given the opportunity to add five additional questions to the background questionnaire.

This option was important for several reasons. We have already noted some of the limitations in reporting by subgroups because of the sample size. There are other limitations dictated by the national scope of the survey and the costs involved. The sins of the national survey ought not to be uncritically inherited by the states. Some of the states (California, New York, Illinois, Texas, Florida) have large numbers and proportions of language minorities, and these characteristics should have been taken into account in the data collected for that state, especially in non-English literacies. Although there was no modification of the direct measure of English literacy, the background questionnaire should have been translated into Chinese, Navajo, and other major local languages in addition to Spanish. The states and jurisdictions that signed up for the NALS state option were California, New York, Illinois, Texas, Florida, Washington, Louisiana, Indiana, Iowa, New Jersey, Ohio, and Pennsylvania.[6] This state option was an important opportunity to redress some of the limitations of national surveys, and participation in similar options to national surveys should be advocated heartily by those interested in biliteracy questions that are not easily studied within small national sample frameworks.

Implications of National Survey Research for Understanding Language Diversity, English Literacy, and Biliteracy in the Nation

The definitions and concepts of literacy developed in the United States since 1975 are useful for future studies of language proficiency and literacy. However, our institutional memory regarding these surveys is close to being lost, with history repeating itself. Out of the Bilingual Education Act research, we have the two core notions of "non-English language background/language minority (NELB/LM)" and "non- or limited-English-proficient." The NELB/LM designation was designed to be an inclusive category that would be the pool from which, or within which, all individuals (not just school-age youngsters) who were limited in their English could be found. It was also an upper limit of the number of limited-English-proficient individuals. This pool of individuals was identified through surrogate (probability) characteristics, like foreign birth, living in a community or household where a language other than English was spoken, or speaking a non-English language. The CESS used current household languages as the primary indicator of non-English-language background (excluding mother tongue and nativity).

Using these household language identifiers, there is quite an overlap with some ethnic groups (e.g., Chinese-speaking households tend to be occupied by persons who are ethnically Chinese), but not a 100% overlap. It has become an easy surrogate identification, however, over the last few years, to use ethnic identifiers for language minorities. This confuses the two categories. If we define language minorities by non-English household languages, then English monolinguals who are members of ethnic minority groups are excluded. The size of this excluded group may be significant. On the other hand, if we define language minorities as the same as ethnic groups within which there are large numbers of NELB speakers, then this should also be made clear. It is important for new studies to be clear how such a category as language minority or non-English-language background is being used or could be used.

The limited-English-proficient (and non-English-proficient) category was a subgroup of language minority. The term "limited English speaking ability" was taken from the bilingual education legislation of 1968 and referred only to understanding and speaking English. The CESS Advisory Committee in 1977 and the Bilingual Education Act in 1978 added reading and writing to the definition, and the term became "limited-English-proficient" (LEP). The CESS also determined that English proficiency would be the exclusive criterion for the LEP population, irrespective of the person's proficiency in the non-English language (comparing a person's ability in one language to another is an attempt at identifying the person's language dominance).[7] In many ways, this standard has survived and expanded, with the Office of Civil Rights, for example, moving from a language dominance standard to an English proficiency standard during the 1980s (U.S. Department of Education, 1991).

The prevalence of the English proficiency standard is useful because it focuses on the critical characteristic that drives bilingual education programs for K-12 schooling, that of students acquiring English proficiency so they can participate effectively in an all-English classroom. It minimizes, however, the existence of the non-English language, with the result that school and program personnel ignore the non-English language resources of the learner. This is a particularly grievous position when it comes to adult English literacy programs serving language minority populations.

Background questions, especially those in the NALS, recognized these two core concepts of non-English-language background and limited English proficiency and were designed to distinguish: (a) between oral bilingualism and biliteracy; (b) between environmental (group) bilingualism and individual bilingualism; and (c) among acquisition, ability, and use of more than one language. The first distinction is reflected in questions regarding the four modalities (also called channels, skill areas, or components): speaking, listening, reading, and writing.

The second distinction is reflected in questions about household languages (regardless of whether or not the respondent speaks them) and languages of the community. In bilingual communities, individuals range in their knowledge and ability to use the two languages from monolingualism in one of the languages, to varying degrees of bilingualism, to monolingualism in the other language, yet almost everyone shares the speech norms of the community.

The third distinction involves questions about when and in what order the respondents acquired each language,[8] how well they believe they know the languages, and when, where, and for what purposes they use the languages.

Each of these distinctions has been previously used as a definition of language proficiency, but they represent quite different notions. These distinctions have also been central to debates about literacy definitions (see Macías, 1988, p. 3; Venezky, 1990). They have not only been staples of sociolinguistic work, but have also been woven into the development of national (language) surveys over the past couple of decades.

In addition to these core definitions or notions, several others come to mind, but only tangentially from these surveys. The language of initial literacy is the language of the first literacy acquired, regardless of the pattern of (oral) language acquisition of the individual. When we refer to native language literacy, we refer to literacy in the native (first) language of the individual. Second language literacy refers to literacy in the second language of the (sequential) bilingual individual, implying no native language literacy. Biliteracy reflects literacy in two languages.[9] The distinctions between environmental/community/household bilingualism and individual bilingualism, acquisition patterns, ability, use/functions, can also be applied to literacy.

While these terms do not all come specifically from the surveys, they are useful in guiding survey instrument development and the conceptualization of what information is needed in biliteracy research.

The information about this nation's linguistic diversity generated by these surveys has been great. Language surveys were not new to the world in 1975. But the number and quality of language surveys undertaken in this nation between 1975 and 1990 were impressive. Yet, the need for broader and more in-depth descriptions of the NELB population, especially their (bi)literacy characteristics, is still high.

The information we derived and can derive on English literacy from these data sets varies. Obviously, if there is no literacy measure, the data set is not useful for this purpose. However, as we analyze the data sets that do have an English literacy measure, we should keep in mind the coverage of ethnic and linguistic minorities within the sample. We know that in some cases exclusion of non- and limited-English-proficient respondents from the survey or from the analyses has skewed the results toward higher English literacy rates. The questions generated by this exclusion have to do with "how much?" and "is this significant?" While the impact may not be significant for the national population, it certainly plays a heavier role in subgroup analyses. This is particularly important when we compare the results across data sets.

A case in point is the 1984 and 1986 National Assessment of Educational Progress (NAEP). The NAEP changed hands from the Education Commission of the States to the Educational Testing Service in 1983. As part of this change a number of modifications in the design of the assessment and the instruments also took place. One new instrument was the *Excluded Student Questionnaire*, which indicated how many students were excluded from the NAEP and why. One of the reasons for exclusion was limited English proficiency.[10] In 1984, and again in 1986, the U.S. Office of Bilingual Education and Minority Languages Affairs (OBEMLA) funded a language minority supplemental sample to the NAEP, and also included additional language background items to the questionnaires, in order to obtain educational achievement data for language minority students and, if possible, LEP students.

While we received additional information from the sample supplement, and certainly better information on when and why schools excluded students from the NAEP, we were left with difficult data to analyze, and we realized that the NAEP results were not reflecting the total national enrollment of students. The decision to exclude or include LEP individuals from a survey or assessment should be made with consideration of the impact on the overall purpose of the study. In the 1992 NALS, for example, it was more important to get a good profile of the total national population on English literacy scales, and be able to indicate how that profile was influenced by the inclusion of limited-English-proficient adults in the sample. It was also important to get self-report data on non-English language and literacy abilities, even though the direct measure of literacy was in English. The design options for national surveys have to be widened to include items on language and ethnic backgrounds, for better understanding English literacy as well as biliteracies.

We already have the ethnic and language data in the 1990 Census allowing stratification of the sample frames on these variables. These surveys should also take into account the undercount of minorities in the 1990 Census, as the NALS did. In addition, the NALS, with the state option, has given us information on some aspects of biliteracy from the background questionnaires. It is not only possible, but very desirable, to pursue another National Chicano Survey or similar activity, with a greater focus on biliteracy, that would extend coverage to other ethnolinguistic minority groups.

Sampling frames need to reflect the linguistic diversity of the nation. Data collection instruments and procedures need to accommodate language minority populations in securing bilingual and biliteracy data. Surveys in Spanish and other non-English languages should be part of the mandates and capabilities of the various national data collection agencies. The NALS for 1996 (if pursued) should include a direct Spanish literacy measure as well as an English one.

There is a need for linking national surveys with local quantitative and qualitative studies. Not every aspect of linguistic diversity can be addressed through national surveys. They are also time-consuming and very expensive. These surveys should be complemented with a generous set of grant competitions on various issues related to biliteracy, supporting local and university-generated research. In addition, the Current Population Survey should include a Survey of

Languages Supplement on a regular basis (it already includes a regular supplement on education, for example). Alternatively, language questions could be added to the special supplement on Latinos included in the CPS every March. Such questions could be added to special supplements on other ethnic minorities as well, if and when such supplements are included in the CPS in the future.

Finally, in state options to national surveys, the ethnic/racial categories should be standardized and made detailed enough to allow for state-level and ethnic subgroup analyses, rather than be limited to a set of general categories rationalized by small national samples, but lost for the states.

Conclusion

As this nation becomes more like the rest of the world in terms of racial, ethnic, and linguistic diversity, the need for reflecting that diversity in the literacy data we collect increases. The development of national language and literacy surveys since 1975 has given us a better picture of language diversity and bilingualism in both non-English languages and English. Key concepts and definitions to conceptualize part of this diversity have proven useful for descriptive, analytic purposes and for policymaking. Yet more can and should be done.

Literacy surveys are providing better information about ethnic and racial diversity and language background, but not better information about biliteracy. NALS bears close watching and deserves secondary analysis. There is much more we can do to improve biliteracy surveys and bilingual survey methodologies as well.

The challenges are before us. Let us not merely inherit the sins of the previous surveys while seeking absolution from their shortcomings. Language survey efforts from 1975 through 1982, followed by similarly important developmental work in the 1980s in defining and measuring literacy, indicate that we can do much in a short period of time with the will to do so. Let us not ignore these developmental phases so that we are not condemned to repeat them.

Notes

[1] For a more detailed analysis of those studies specifically addressing the estimate of language minority and limited-English-proficient populations, see Macías & Spencer, 1983.

[2] The 1965 Voting Rights Act provided for the use of ethnicity, voting, and literacy rates to identify possible violations of the Act. In 1975, Congress added the language minority amendments to the Act, which added non-English language background of Latinos, Asians, AmerIndians, and Alaskan natives as an additional factor that triggered coverage of the Act. In 1982, Congress revised the definition of language minority and added limited or no oral/comprehensive ability in English to narrow the coverage of the Act quite a bit. The definition of illiteracy was "less than a fifth grade education." The Director of the Census Bureau was instructed to identify the jurisdictions covered by the Act using the 1980 Census data. The Director did so in 1984 and attempted to validate this procedure with the use of the English Language Proficiency Study.

[3] During the developmental phase of the instruments, a suggestion was made to include two questions for every item on the assessment, designed to find out if the person was familiar with the task on the item and whether or not they had a need to perform that task in their daily life. This suggestion was made because other research indicated the differential uses of literacy across class, race, and ethnic groups. These items were included in the field test. As important as this information is to understand and interpret performance on the assessment, especially across racial and ethnic groups, answering them became so repetitive and boring that they became distractors for the respondents and interrupted the assessment. They also lengthened the time for the assessment, leading to less time for the performance tasks, and thus the number of performance items that could be included or completed. This kind of information should be pursued through other types of literacy research and linked, if possible, with these survey data.

[4] The comparability of the language and ethnic data between the 1980 and the 1990 Censuses allows us to analyze changes in language abilities of the United States population in very detailed ways.

[5] This is similar to the 1990 and 1992 NAEP experiments that also allowed for states to buy an option to increase the sample of students

assessed within a particular state in order to get state-level reporting. The state option for the NAEP was, in part, motivated by the accountability movement in public schooling. The state option may become a more familiar part of national surveys in the future, making these considerations of sample all the more important.

[6] There apparently were federal resources available that could be used to pay for this state option, although it was not clear that all states knew this, wanted, or were able to access these monies. ETS identified at least one federal source of funds that could be used by the states and communicated this to all of them, including some of the nonstate jurisdictions, like the District of Columbia and Puerto Rico. The federal government should subsidize this state option, much as it does for the National Assessment of Education Progress, which had almost 100% state participation in 1990.

[7] This contrasted with the U.S. Department of Health, Education, and Welfare's Office of Civil Rights (OCR) definitions of "national origin" and "language discrimination" under *Lau v. Nichols* (1974). OCR used a relative language proficiency (or language dominance) standard to identify the different categories of students needing educational services regardless of their English proficiency. A student or group of students needed to be dominant in a non-English language and a member of a national origin group, and be discriminated against, to trigger this civil rights law protection.

[8] The usual distinctions in language acquisition patterns of bilinguals include whether the individual acquired the languages simultaneously (simultaneous or dual language acquisition) or sequentially (sequential bilingual). The latter type of bilingual can further be sub-categorized as an early sequential bilingual (acquired the second language before puberty) or late sequential bilingual (acquired the second language after puberty). In addition, if the second language is taught with the intention of replacing the native language, very often it is called subtractive bilingualism, while teaching a second language for enrichment purposes is generally referred to as additive bilingualism. If the individuals learned the languages informally, they are generally referred to as circumstantial bilinguals, while those who learned the second language formally are generally referred to as elective bilinguals.

[9] One of the results of the dominance of the ESL field in the polemics and terminology of school bilingualism is the over-generalization that the first language (L1) is the non-English language, and the second language (L2) is English. This is reflected in the school term "primary language" referring to the non-English language, even when there are no data or need to refer to relative language proficiencies or dominance. This lack of precision and specificity led to convoluted terms in 1980, when the Department of Education attempted to promulgate rules related to the *Lau v. Nichols* decision. One of the sets of classification terms used in these proposed rules was "limited-English-proficient, primary language other than English, English superior." These terms lead to a minimalization of simultaneous or dual language bilingual acquisition for individuals, and to a predominance of instructional models based on sequential bilingualism, rather than simultaneous bilingualism.

[10] One of the more critical questions in not only these surveys but also state and district achievement testing is what to do with LEP students, since all of these testing programs are conducted in English. There is often a wholesale exclusion of LEP students from the testing. A report from the National Education Goals Panel (1991, p. 19) recommended inclusion of LEP students in these assessments and assessments in non-English languages:

> *Examining in foreign languages.* The Resource Group considers it essential that children of limited-English-proficiency (LEP) be included in systems of nationwide assessment. They recommend that all children (including the limited-English-proficient) be examined for oral and written communication skills in English. In subjects other than English the group wants consideration to be given to testing LEP children in their language of instruction. The Resource Group also recommends that to encourage the foreign language competencies of native English speakers as well as to preserve the native language capacity of immigrant children, communication competencies of all children should be assessed in two languages, beginning in elementary school. (National Education Goals Panel, 1991, p. 19)

A responsible position on this issue cannot separate these two points.

References

Educational Testing Service. (1990). [The brochure for the National Adult Literacy Survey]. Princeton, NJ: Author.

Educational Testing Service. (1991). *The English background questionnaire. National Adult Literacy Survey.* Princeton, NJ: Author.

Hirsch, E.E. (1987). *Cultural literacy: What every American needs to know.* Boston: Houghton-Mifflin.

Kalmar, T.M. (1992). Drawing the line on minority languages: Equity and linguistic diversity in the Boston Adult Literacy Initiative. *Journal of Adult Basic Education, 2*(2), 84-112.

Kirsch, I. (1990). Measuring adult literacy. In R. Venezky, D. Wagner, & B. Ciliberti (Eds.), *Towards defining literacy* (pp. 40-47). Newark, DE: International Reading Association.

Kirsch, I., & Jungeblut, A. (1986). *Literacy: Profiles of America's young adults.* Princeton, NJ: Educational Testing Service, National Assessment of Educational Progress.

López, D. (1982). *Language maintenance and shift in the U.S. today: Basic patterns and social implications.* Los Alamitos, CA: National Center for Bilingual Research.

Macías, R.F. (1985a). Language and ideology in the U.S. *Social Education, 49*(2), 97-100.

Macías, R.F. (1985b). National language profiles of the Mexican-origin population in the United States. In W. Connor (Ed.), *Mexican Americans in comparative perspective* (pp. 238-308). Washington, DC: The Urban Institute.

Macías, R.F. (1988). *Latino illiteracy in the U.S.* Claremont, CA: The Tomás Rivera Policy Center.

Macías, R.F. (1993). Language and ethnic classification of language minorities: Chicano and Latino students in the 1990s. *Hispanic Journal of Behavioral Sciences 15*(2), 230-257.

Macías, R.F., & Spencer, M. (1983). *Estimating the number of language minority and limited-English-proficient persons in the U.S.: A comparative analysis of the studies.* Los Alamitos, CA: National Center for Bilingual Research.

National Center for Education Statistics. (1978a, July). *Bulletin: The educational disadvantage of language minority persons in the U.S., Spring 1976.* (NCES-78-121). Washington, DC: Author.

National Center for Education Statistics. (1978b, August). *Bulletin: Geographic distribution, nativity, and age distribution of language minorities in the U.S., Spring 1976.* (NCES-78-134). Washington, DC: Author.

National Center for Education Statistics. (1978c, October). *Bulletin: Place of birth and language characteristics of persons of Hispanic origin in the U.S., Spring 1976.* (NCES-78-135). Washington, DC: Author.

National Center for Education Statistics. (1979, May). *Bulletin: Birthplace and language characteristics of persons of Chinese, Japanese, Korean, Filipino, and Vietnamese origin in the U.S., Spring 1976.* (NCES-79-144). Washington, DC: Author.

National Education Goals Panel. (1991, March). *Measuring progress toward the national education goals: Potential indicators and measurement strategies.* [Discussion document]. Washington, DC: Author.

O'Malley, J.M. (1981). *Children's English and services study: Language minority children with limited English proficiency in the United States.* Rosslyn, VA: National Clearinghouse on Bilingual Education.

Oxford-Carpenter, R., Pol, L., López, D., Stupp, P., Gendell, M., & Peng, S. (1984). *Demographic projections of non-English-language-background and limited-English-proficient persons in the U.S. to the year 2000, by state, age, and language group.* Rosslyn, VA: National Clearinghouse for Bilingual Education.

U.S. Bureau of the Census. (1980). *Official 1980 U.S. Census form.* Washington, DC: U.S. Department of Commerce, Bureau of the Census.

U.S. Commissioner of Education. (1976). *The condition of bilingual education in the nation.* Washington, DC: U.S. Department of Health, Education and Welfare, Office of Education.

U.S. Department of Education. (1987). *Numbers of limited-English-proficient children: National, state, and language-specific estimates. Based on the 1982 English Language Proficiency Survey and special tabulations of the 1980 Census.* Washington, DC: Office of Planning, Budget and Evaluation. Unpublished paper.

U.S. Department of Education. (1990, July). *Report to the Congress on defining literacy and the National Adult Literacy Survey.*

Washington, DC: Author. (Available from the Division of Adult Education and Literacy)

U.S. Department of Education. (1991, June). *U.S. Department of Education: Elementary and secondary school civil rights compliance report, Fall 1992 district summary.* Draft. Washington, DC: Author. (Available from the Office of Civil Rights)

Veltman, C. (1983). *Language shift in the U.S.* Amsterdam: Mouton.

Venezky, R. (1990). Definitions of literacy. In R. Venezky, D. Wagner, & B. Ciliberti, (Eds.). *Towards defining literacy* (pp. 2-16). Newark, DE: International Reading Association.

Wiley, T. (1988). *Literacy, biliteracy, and educational achievement among the Mexican-origin population in the United States: A secondary analysis of the National Chicano Survey.* Doctoral dissertation, Department of Education, University of Southern California.

CHAPTER 2
Sociolinguistic Considerations in Biliteracy Planning

Arnulfo G. Ramírez
Louisiana State University

The creation of effective literacy education programs to meet the needs of language minority adults in a multilingual society like the United States requires addressing a broad range of sociolinguistic questions that can be approached from a language planning perspective. As a problem-solving activity, language planning is the realization of the language policy that a government adopts with respect to such issues as language diversity, minority language treatment, language standardization, or the national language question. Language planning stresses the social nature of language and its functions in society. It also takes into account both the attitudes of society's different ethnolinguistic groups toward different languages or speech varieties and the need for members of these groups to master different languages and dialects (Cooper, 1984). Thus, a language planning perspective is a useful one to bring to bear on the discussion of adult biliteracy.

Language planning is typically, though not necessarily, seen as the task of national governments seeking to accomplish broad social and political goals. García (1982) notes that countries can implement different kinds of language or literacy programs depending upon what they hope to accomplish. These can include educational programs designed to promote one or more of the following:

1. *Vernacularization*, the restoration of an indigenous language to establish it as a national standard (e.g., Tagalog in the Philippines);

2. *Internationalization*, the development of proficient bilinguals who can function effectively in the international community (e.g., English for Greek and Dutch students);

47

3. *Assimilation,* the incorporation of immigrant groups or ethnolinguistic minority groups into the mainstream culture (e.g., English programs for immigrant groups to Australia, or Hebrew for immigrants to Israel);

4. *Pluralization,* bilingual programs that enable different language and cultural groups to co-exist within a nation (e.g., Basque and Catalán language programs in Spain; Navajo language programs in the American Southwest).

Biliteracy programs, that is, educational programs that foster mastery of literacy skills in both the mother tongue and a second language, can serve to promote any one or more of the goals in García's framework, depending upon the extent to which literacy is developed in each language and for what purposes. Looking at Spanish and English in the United States, for example, one can find biliteracy programs that teach only initial mother tongue literacy skills to Spanish-speaking adults so that these skills might then be applied to the learning of English (serving the goal of assimilation), as well as programs that seek to develop literacy to the fullest extent possible in both languages (serving the goal of pluralization and, if Spanish literacy were developed to a level sufficient for conducting transnational exchanges, internationalization).

Ornstein-Galicia (1979) has developed a language planning model that takes into account sets of sociopolitical and linguistic factors. In terms of planning for biliteracy, the model can be used as a heuristic device for predicting the favorability of bilingual literacy education for a particular ethnolinguistic group. The model's sociopolitical dimension includes eight factors:

1. the demographic strength of the group,

2. the group's territoriality, or the specific geographic area(s) of residency it claims,

3. the cultural-religious distance that separates the ethnic group from the mainstream,

4. the ethnicity or ethos tending to promote intra-group solidarity to greater or lesser extents,

5. the relative socioeconomic status of the group, determining to varying degrees the needs of group members to become bilingual to survive or conduct business,

6. the level of political mobilization among members of the group,

7 & 8. the degree of congruence between local needs or aspirations and the national climate and federal policies, at the micro and macro levels.

The linguistic dimension of the model encompasses six factors:

1. the vitality of the minority language,

2. the history or formal, written tradition of the language,

3. the degree to which the language has been standardized with usage norms,

4. the linguistic distance from the dominant, national language with respect to alphabet, grammatical structure, and vocabulary,

5. language attitudes—the group's perceptions of its own language and that of other groups, and its commitment to using and studying the language,

6. the national language situation in terms of linguistic diversity, tolerance, and implicit or explicit language policies.

Sociopolitical factors can override linguistic considerations, but both linguistic and sociopolitical issues should be examined using this model to identify situations where biliteracy education is both warranted and likely to succeed for a given group of language minority adults.

Agents of Biliteracy Planning and Promotion in the United States

Literacy planning as a sociolinguistic activity is not the exclusive domain of state or federal governments. Individuals or groups of individuals can also engage in community literacy efforts designed to serve the needs of ethnolinguistic minority groups. In the United States, biliteracy language programs designed for adults are highly diverse in terms of sponsorship, learner characteristics, and focus. In addition to federal and state government support, sponsorship for literacy programs may come from city and county governments, community-based and religious organizations, and private businesses. The programs can be found in such places as community centers, libraries, prisons, churches, synagogues, factory lunchrooms, and housing projects. The adult learners may be immigrants, refugees, newly naturalized citizens, or native-born residents. They may differ widely with respect to personal background, educational experiences in the first language, professional training, and interest in becoming literate in a second language. Some literacy programs may focus exclusively on the development of English language oral and written skills, while others may devote considerable attention to the maintenance of literacy traditions in the students' native language. While many programs strive to be learner-centered, with students themselves setting their own literacy-learning agendas, these same programs are also called upon to serve the agendas of outside parties. Shifts in sources of finding, in particular, can require changes in a program's official goals and objectives for literacy learning (Wrigley, 1991).

The Sociolinguistic Perspective: What It Has to Offer for Biliteracy Planning

Regardless of the institutions or organizations leading them, effective biliteracy planning efforts at the local, regional, and national levels must take as their starting point the existing patterns of language use in the communities to be affected by the planning effort. Examination of these language use patterns in the fact-finding phase of literacy planning can best be undertaken from a sociolinguistic perspective (Rubin, 1973). Achieving a true (as opposed to an idealistic) understanding of the complex language use patterns of an ethnolinguistic minority group can be difficult. This may be the case whether the fact finding for biliteracy planning is being conducted at the macro (national) or micro (local) level. Nonetheless, taking into account certain sociolinguistic phenomena, such as language varieties, sociolinguistic domains, language choice, and language attitudes, is particularly important to ensuring that biliteracy programs in the United States address the real needs of members of the ethnolinguistic communities they serve, as well as the sociopolitical goals of their sponsoring agencies. Understanding the ways members of an ethnolinguistic minority group actually use or might reasonably use different language varieties in their everyday lives can help prevent biliteracy planners from initiating projects that are likely to fail because they seek to develop literacy skills that are incongruent with the real-life literacy tasks confronted by learners in their communities.

At this point in our discussion of biliteracy planning, it is useful to look at the case of a particular ethnolinguistic minority to illustrate more concretely some of the complex sociolinguistic issues that biliteracy planners in the United States have to confront as they develop educational programs. As diverse as this country's language and ethnic situation is today, we have many possibilities from which to choose. In the United States, one finds minority ethnolinguistic communities identified with indigenous American languages (e.g., Navajo, Hopi, Cherokee, Mohawk), European colonial languages (e.g., Spanish, French, German), and immigrant languages (e.g., Chinese, Italian, Greek, Japanese, Russian, Tagalog, Urdu). Languages like Spanish, French, German, and Chinese, to name a few, also exhibit variation reflecting the differing geographical origins and social backgrounds of their speakers. In the case of some languages, this variation may reflect the existence of distinct subcommunities within the larger ethnolinguistic group, reflecting the many layers of diversity in the U.S. language situation.[1]

The selection of Hispanics residing in the United States as a case-in-point offers several advantages. First, the sociolinguistic issues involving this group have been extensively studied, and there exists a body of literature to which we may refer. Second, language use among members of this group is exceptionally diverse and complex, given the multiplicity of national origins of U.S. Hispanics—including many whose families have lived in the United States for generations—and the dispersed regions of the country where they reside. Finally, Hispanics are the largest single ethnolinguistic minority group in the United States, and many readers of this volume will find a discussion of Hispanic issues to be directly relevant to their own literacy work. Let us, then, look at the case of Hispanics with regard to language varieties, language choice, language styles, and the distribution of written text types across languages.

Language Varieties

A number of varieties of Spanish have been identified as being spoken by Hispanics living in the United States. These include Mexican Spanish, particularly in the Southwest and large urban centers of the Midwest (Detroit, Cleveland, and Chicago); Puerto Rican Spanish, principally in the Eastern states (New York, New Jersey, Pennsylvania, and Connecticut); Cuban Spanish, in Miami, Boston, and New Orleans (Cárdenas, 1970); and Peninsular Spanish, spoken in Newark, New Jersey. Isleño, a dialect from the Canary Islands, still survives in Bayou Lafourche, Louisiana (Craddock, 1981). Within the

Southwest, four dialectal zones with some degree of overlapping are noticeable: (a) Texas Spanish, with considerable influence due to Mexican migration; (b) New Mexican and Southern Coloradan Spanish, which includes a number of archaisms due to its relative isolation, until recently, from the rest of the Spanish-speaking world; (c) Arizonan Spanish, with a number of linguistic features in common with New Mexican Spanish, but with a significant influence of northern Mexican Spanish due to its proximity to Sonora; and (d) Californian Spanish, an extension of Arizonan Spanish greatly influenced by borrowing from English (Cárdenas, 1970).

Sánchez (1983) argues that there are basically two principal varieties of Spanish in the Southwest. One is the standard and the other the popular. The popular can be further divided into urban and rural subcodes in many cases. Within each subcode of popular Spanish, there are special varieties such as Caló, which is an urban subcode. Differences among the standard and popular Spanish varieties occur primarily at the morphosyntactic level (the formation of word within sentence construction), although variation can exist at the level of words in the case of archaic terms, English loanwords, or rural vocabulary.

The language varieties used among Hispanics in the Southwest have also been described in terms of an English–Spanish continuum ranging from Standard (formal) Mexican Spanish to Standard (formal) English with several dialects or speech styles blending into each other between the two standard varieties (Elías-Olivares & Valdés, 1982). The continuum is illustrated in Figure 1.

Figure 1
Language Varieties Among Hispanics in the Southwest

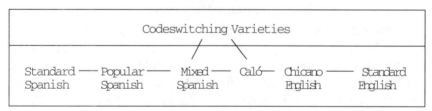

Adapted by permission from Elías-Olivares & Valdés, 1982, p. 155.

Differences among these Southwest varieties can be established on the basis of linguistic criteria. Popular Spanish, for example, contains a number of nonstandard features with respect to vowel and consonant changes, verb tenses and conjugations, and gender/number agreement rules. Mixed Spanish and Caló (also called Pachuco) contain elements of both English and Spanish, maintaining basic Spanish word order and using English pronunciation (*londri* for "laundry," *escrín* for "screen," and *esquipiar* for "skip"). Mixed Spanish can serve for informal speaking and sometimes is used by children who have not been exposed to either English or Spanish as a separate code. Mixed Spanish and Caló make extensive use of codeswitching, which involves the alternating use of the two languages at the word, phrase, clause, or sentence level. For example, while speaking Spanish, a speaker may say:

1. No voy a ir al gym.
(I'm not going to the gym.)

2. Estoy muy cansado, so I'm going to bed.
(I'm very tired, so I'm going to bed.)

In the case of codeswitching at the word level (1) and codeswitching at the clause level (2), English pronunciation and morphology are maintained with no attempt to adapt to Spanish.

The language situation among Puerto Ricans living in the New York City area, on the other hand, has been described in terms of a polyglossic model for English, codeswitching, and Spanish (Pedraza, Attinasi, & Hoffman, 1980). The verbal repertoire of Puerto Rican speakers may sustain several influences different in both content and kind, depending on their participation in different social networks and how they are influenced by the mass media, both electronic and print. Figure 2 illustrates the potential verbal repertoires of different members of this speech community with respect to the range of language varieties in active use.

Figure 2
A Polyglossic Model for English, Codeswitching,
and Spanish in El Barrio

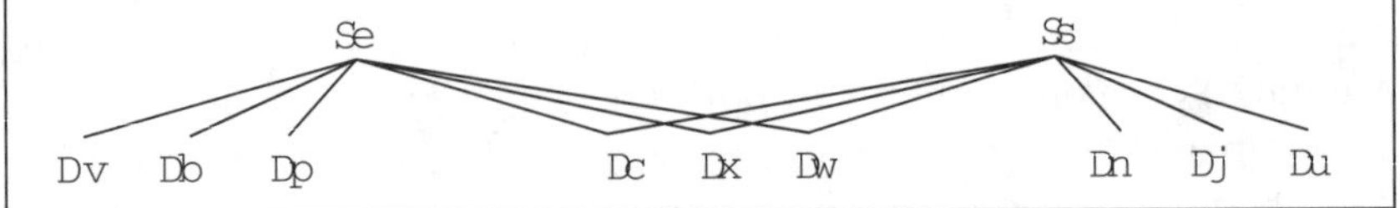

Se	= Standard English
Ss	= Standard Spanish
Dv	= New York local English vernaculars
Db	= Black English speech
Dp	= Puerto Rican English
Dc, Dx, Dw	= Varieties involving different types/levels of codeswitching in English and Spanish
Dn	= New York City Spanish
Dj	= Rural variety of Puerto Rican Spanish
Du	= Urban variety of Puerto Rican Spanish

Adapted by permission from Pedraza, Attinasi, & Hoffman, 1980, p. 90.

The polyglossic model hypothesizes that for Puerto Ricans living in New York the standard written forms of English and Spanish (Se, Ss) and their corresponding formal spoken dialects are set in dynamic relation with a number of spoken vernaculars. Puerto Rican speakers have varying abilities to use the different spoken varieties and written styles present in their speech community, some of which are presented in the figure. Varieties shown in Figure 2 include the following: (Dv) New York English or other local English vernaculars; (Db) the speech of African-Americans in New York; (Dp) the speech of Puerto Ricans raised speaking English; (Dn) the Spanish of Puerto Ricans born in New York City; (Dj) a more rural style of Puerto Rican speech; and (Du) urban Puerto Rican Spanish. (Dc), (Dx), and (Dw) are potential varieties of codeswitching between Spanish and English. Other language varieties not illustrated in this figure may also influence the verbal repertoires of Puerto Ricans in New York. These might include standard and vernacular varieties of both Spanish and English heard on television and radio, as well as the different Spanish vernaculars spoken by immigrants from other Spanish-speaking countries such as Colombia and the Dominican Republic.

Language Choice

The particular variety of language chosen for use in a specific communicative event may be influenced by a number of individual variables or combinations of variables associated with the situation itself, the participants, the topic, and the purpose of the interaction. Table 1 summarizes some of the salient factors that have been noted to influence language choice in bilingual communities.

Table 1
Factors Influencing Language Choice
in a Communicative Event

Characteristics of the participants	Situation
Language proficiency	Location/setting
Language preference	Presence of monolinguals
Socioeconomic status	Degree of formality
Age	Degree of intimacy
Gender	Topic
Occupation	Type of vocabulary
Education	
Ethnic background	Function of interaction
History of speakers' linguistic interaction	To raise status
	To create social distance
Kinship relationships	To exclude someone
Attitude toward languages	To request or command
Outside pressures	

Source: Grosjean, 1982, p. 136. Reprinted by permission.

In examining the patterns of English and Spanish use among Chicanos in the United States, Sánchez (1983) noted that language choice in a given sociolinguistic domain seemed to be strongly correlated with the degree of formality or informality of that domain. English was found to be used most typically in the formal societal domains such as work, government, and media, while Spanish was more often used in the informal contexts of home and neighborhood. At the same time, there are differences among Hispanics attributable to variables such as socioeconomic status and number of generations a given speaker's family has resided in the United States.

Table 2									
Language Use Among Hispanics in the Southwest									

	Working Class								
	Middle Class			Rural			Urban		
Generation	1	2	3	1	2	3	1	2	3
Language Domain									
Home	S	B	E	S	B	B	S	B	E
Neighborhood	E	E	E	S	B	B	B	B	B
Recreation	B	E	E	B	B	B	B	B	E
Work	E	E	E	B	B	B	B	E	E
Media	B	E	E	B	B	B	B	B	E
Government	E	E	E	E	E	E	E	E	E

S = Spanish   E = English   B = Both languages/bilingual

Adapted by permission from Sánchez, 1983, p. 63.

Table 2 illustrates some of the dynamics of language choice among Hispanics in the Southwest.

All first-generation Spanish speakers use Spanish in the home domain regardless of their social class and the part of the country they live in. The middle class shifts to English entirely by the third generation, while the working class employs both languages in at least the neighborhood domain (among urban dwellers) and in other domains such as recreation, work, and media (among rural residents).

A variety of language use patterns can be found within a single sociolinguistic domain as well. At the level of the home, Zentella (1988) identified four distinct language use patterns among Puerto Rican families living in New York City.

1. The parents/caretakers speak only Spanish to each other and to the children; the children respond to their parents in Spanish but speak Spanish and English to each other. (This accounted for 26% of the 19 families in the study.)

2. The parents/caretakers speak Spanish to each other and to the children, but one of them sometimes speaks English to them. The children respond in both languages, preferring Spanish for the adults and English for their siblings (47% of the families studied).

3. The parents usually speak English to each other and to the children; one parent speaks some Spanish to them. The children understand Spanish but respond in English and speak English to each other (16% of the families studied).

4. The parents codeswitch frequently among themselves and when speaking to their infants, who are just learning to speak (11% of the families studied).

These patterns were observed over a period of time using an ethnographic research approach. According to Zentella, in the majority of families in patterns one and two, Spanish is used among the parents, and at least one caretaker uses Spanish while speaking to the children. Parents in these two groups have emigrated to the United States usually after having spent their adolescent years in Puerto Rico. Children from these families tend to be more fluent bilinguals, often demonstrating a greater competence in English than in Spanish. Parents in pattern three include those born and raised in New York City and those who left Puerto Rico before late adolescence or who married a monolingual English speaker, who would speak mainly English to the children. Young couples born or raised in New York frequently codeswitch between English and Spanish with each other, and the children from these homes have some limited knowledge of Spanish, at least in the area of vocabulary.

Ramírez (1991) documents the relative use of Spanish and English among Hispanic adolescents (N=549: 250 males and 299 females) in 10 urban centers involving Mexican-Americans (216=39.3%), Puerto Ricans (119=21.7%), Cubans (51=9.3%), and members of other ethnic groups. The results presented in Figures 3 and 4 differentiate between the uses of English and Spanish with respect to generation and domain. Spanish only is most frequently used when speaking to one's grandparents, mostly Spanish is used when talking with parents, and both languages or mostly English are used when interacting with siblings. Usage patterns according to domains indicate that the church context is the only other area outside the home where Spanish plays a major role among these adolescents. There are other observable differences in language use patterns associated with the particular locations where samples were drawn. These differences can be attributed to characteristics of the sample (e.g., place of birth, home language environment, proficiency in Spanish).

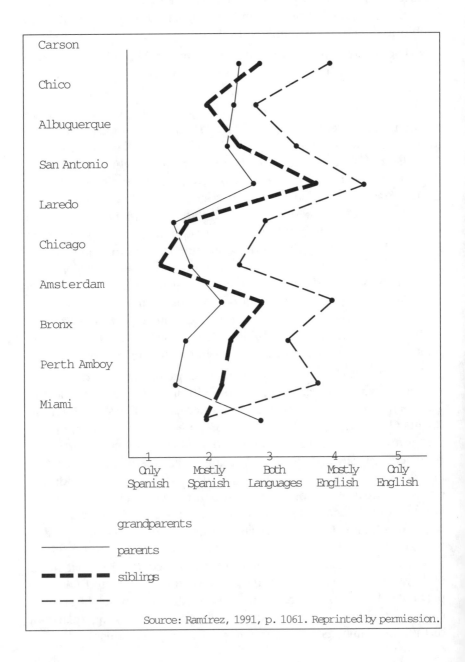

Figure 3
Use of Spanish and English to Communicate with Different Family
Members in Ten Localities

Carson

Chico

Albuquerque

San Antonio

Laredo

Chicago

Amsterdam

Bronx

Perth Amboy

Miami

1	2	3	4	5
Only	Mostly	Both	Mostly	Only
Spanish	Spanish	Languages	English	English

.... grandparents

——————— parents

━ ━ ━ ━ siblings

– – – –

Source: Ramírez, 1991, p. 1061. Reprinted by permission.

Figure 4
Relative Use of Spanish and English in Different Sociolinguistic Domains of Ten Localities

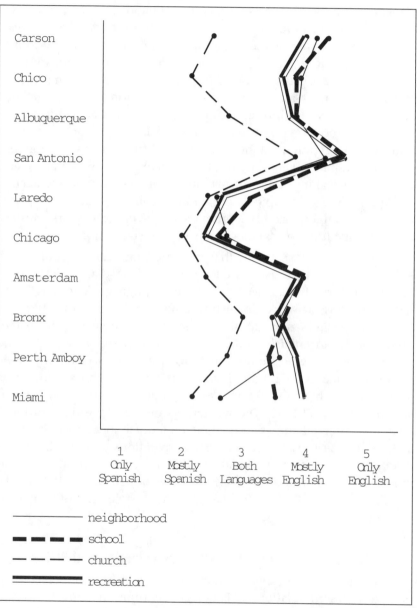

	1 Only Spanish	2 Mostly Spanish	3 Both Languages	4 Mostly English	5 Only English
Carson					
Chico					
Albuquerque					
San Antonio					
Laredo					
Chicago					
Amsterdam					
Bronx					
Perth Amboy					
Miami					

———————— neighborhood

▬ ▬ ▬ ▬ ▬ school

— — — — — church

═══════════ recreation

Source: Ramírez, 1991, p. 1062. Reprinted by permission.

Language Styles

In addition to language variation that is reflected in regional dialects and social dialects, speakers adopt different styles of speaking depending on the circumstances. Formal situations like lectures, newscasts, and public announcements call for careful speech, often based on prepared scripts that are read and sound like written discourse. Informal situations like casual conversations among friends involve unplanned speech that evolves through the course of the interaction. Some conversations involve the use of intimate language such as the talk between husband and wife or parents and children. In the work cited previously with regard to language variety and the codeswitching practiced by Hispanics in the Southwest, Sánchez (1983) found that even more frequently than switching codes, speakers shifted speaking styles (formal, informal, and intimate) to accommodate a change in topic (food, family, religion, sports), addressee (relative, stranger, friend), context (home, church, work, street), and language function (apology, reprimand, suggestion, advice).

Other studies have found that in some bilingual communities, a shift in style can be associated with a shift in dialect (e.g., rural Spanish to formal Spanish) or a switch in language (e.g., English to talk to the boss at work; Spanish to interact with coworkers). Some bilingual speakers may be able to shift from casual to formal to literary styles in English, while in Spanish their repertoire might be more limited, ranging from intimate to casual due to lack of schooling experience in the textbook variety of Spanish. This situation was found by Teschner (1981) among Hispanic students at the University of Texas at El Paso. The written Spanish compositions of these students reflected the style of their colloquial speech due to their lack of familiarity with the standard conventions of Spanish written discourse. Other bilingual speakers, such as some of those described in *Bilingualism in the Barrio* (Fishman, Cooper, & Ma, 1971), may be able to shift from informal to formal style in both Spanish and English.

Distribution of Text Types Across Varieties and Styles

Of particular importance to literacy planners is an understanding of text types in relation to language distribution patterns in the communities to be served by a biliteracy program. Among Hispanics, some text types may be associated with English, others with

Spanish, and still others with both languages. Following Ferguson's (1959) depiction of "high" and "low" varieties in a diglossic language situation, one might find the distribution of text types shown in Table 3 in a given Spanish/English bilingual community.

Table 3
Types of Written Texts Associated with English and Spanish

Written Text Types	English	Spanish	Both
Church bulletins			+
Personal letters		+	
Newspapers	+		
Magazines			+
Business correspondence	+		
TV guides	+		
Visual with texts (novelas with comic illustration)		+	
Warnings/signs			+
Labels	+		

Source: Original

The formal/informal distinction, in terms of both sociolinguistic domain and style, sheds light on the distribution of text types in this table. Spanish seems to be associated with the home domain (personal letters) and the domain of recreation (reading comic books for pleasure), both of which can be regarded as informal. The style in which texts such as personal letters and comic books are written is also informal. English seems to be associated with the domain of work and commerce (business correspondence), as well as with the domain of the mass media (newspapers), both generally formal domains. Business correspondence and newspapers, accordingly, are written in a formal style. The distribution of other text types in the figure does not fit easily into the formal/informal framework, and may have to be explained in terms of some combination of the multiple factors affecting language choice (Grosjean, 1982) listed in Table 1 of this chapter. Also important to consider in understanding the distribution of text types is the *availability* of certain kinds of texts in each language. Questions of choice of language variety and style become moot when some text types are available in one language but not the other.

After Fact Finding: Subsequent Stages of Biliteracy Planning

As we can see from looking at the case of Hispanics in the United States, the patterns of language use among members of an ethnolinguistic minority group in a multilingual setting can be exceedingly complex. In addition to collecting information about such language-use patterns (the fact-finding stage of language planning), it is the job of literacy planners to apply knowledge of these patterns in a sensible way as they proceed with subsequent stages of the biliteracy planning effort. According to Rubin (1973), the subsequent stages of such a language or literacy planning effort would include the following:

Selection Phase: Identify literacy goals, including the role of native language literacy skills in relation to the second language. Specify literacy skills in terms of both individual and societal needs, and suggest strategies for reaching the various goals.

Development Phase: Prepare materials needed for biliteracy instruction, perhaps obtain materials used in other projects, and consider the incorporation of authentic texts as used in different social situations—workplace, health care, social services, and cultural activities. Curriculum planning efforts should take into account research findings on such topics as the development of reading and writing skills among bilinguals, the role of learner differences, differences between oral and written language, and the cognitive processes associated with the various text types.

Implementation Phase: Provide information to the members of the speech community, solicit support from different agencies or groups to disseminate information to the broader community about the literacy goals, and offer an instructional program that centers on the needs of the adult learner.

Evaluation Phase: Examine the degree to which the different literacy goals and objectives have been met; revise, if necessary, making modifications in objectives, teaching methods, and learner/workplace needs.

Types of Literacy to be Developed

Planning for biliteracy involves making decisions about what role different languages and dialects should play in society. In many countries these questions do not arise, because the choices are not open to revision. With regard to the selection stage described above, important questions regarding the types of literacy to be promoted, and in which languages, need to be answered. Educators have recognized three broad categories of literacy: functional, cultural, and critical (Williams & Capizzi Snipper, 1990). These categories may be related to the ability to read text types corresponding to levels of reading proficiency. Table 4, based on the ACTFL (American Council on the Teaching of Foreign Languages) Proficiency Guidelines, provides a tool for seeing this relationship.

Table 4
Parallel Hierarchies of Text Types and Sample Reading Materials According to Proficiency Levels

Proficiency Level	Text Type	Sample Texts
0/0+	Enumerative	Numbers, names, street signs, money denominations, office/shop designations, addresses
1	Orientational	Travel and registration forms, plane and train schedules, TV/radio program guides, menus, memos, newspaper headlines, tables of contents, messages
2	Instructive	Ads and labels, newspaper accounts, instructions and directions, short narratives and descriptions, factual reports, formulaic requests on forms, invitations, introductory and concluding paragraphs
3	Evaluative	Editorials, analyses, apologia, certain literary texts, biography with critical interpretation
4	Projective	Critiques of art or theater performances, literary texts, philosophical discourse, technical papers, argumentation

Adapted by permission from Lee and Musumeci, 1988, p. 174.

Functional literacy is usually related to basic writing (encoding) and reading (decoding) simple texts, which corresponds to the enumerative, orientational, and instructive text types shown in Table 4 and described by Child (1987). Cultural literacy encompasses the cultural schemata necessary for fully comprehending texts in the social sense (Level 3 in Table 4). Critical literacy involves an understanding of the ideology of written texts (Level 4). Deciding what texts in what languages are to be produced or comprehended at what literacy levels would correspond to the selection stage of literacy planning.

Importance of Language Attitudes and Learner Motivation to the Success of the Planning Effort

Biliteracy offers some adult learners the possibility of fully living their bicultural lives and participating in literacy events associated with each language that they know. At the same time, higher literacy levels (Levels 3 and 4 in Table 4) may not be possible to the same degree in both languages given the distribution of the two languages in society and the speakers' attitudes toward each variety of each language. Language attitudes not only influence the language use patterns of ethnolinguistic minorities, they also may be a significant obstacle to the success of biliteracy programs if they are ignored or left unchanged by the biliteracy effort.

The attitudes of ethnolinguistic minorities toward different varieties of their mother tongue are especially important in guiding the selection of teaching approaches and materials for mother tongue literacy. Returning to Spanish as an example, Ramírez, Milk, and Sapiens (1985) found that among adolescent Hispanic pupils in Texas and California, attitudes toward four varieties of Spanish (Standard Mexican Spanish, local Spanish, ungrammatical Spanish, and Spanish/English codeswitching) were hierarchical in nature, ranging from standard Spanish (rated most acceptable) to codeswitching (rated least acceptable). These ratings were made with respect to acceptability in the classroom, degree of correctness, and the speaker's academic potential. Judgments about the four varieties were influenced by the language use, location, place of birth, and gender of the rater. Teachers in Texas reacted in a similar way to the four varieties on the basis of a standard language continuum: Standard Spanish was rated higher than the two nonstandard varieties (local and ungrammatical) and codeswitching. The two nonstandard varieties were evaluated more favorably than codeswitching, a common feature of bilingual communication (Ramírez & Milk, 1986). Some approaches to literacy education emphasize reading texts that students have spoken or dictated or that use language reflecting students' spoken dialect. Students holding the language attitudes presented in this example might show little enthusiasm for learning to read and write their own dialect, especially if it includes a large amount of codeswitching. (Editor's note: See Wolfram's chapter for a description of African-American parents' objections to the use of dialect readers in their children's schools.) Of course, language attitudes may change, and it is also possible for effective biliteracy programs to contribute to increasing students' pride in their own dialect.

It is also important for biliteracy planners to consider the role that individual learner motivation plays in language and literacy acquisition. The concept of motivation has been studied closely in relation to language attitudes, especially by researchers studying second language acquisition. Findings on the role of learner motivation in the acquisition of a second language can be applied to the acquisition of mother tongue literacy skills as well as oral proficiency and literacy in a second language in a biliteracy program. Brown (1981) points out that a learner may study a (second) language initially for instrumental purposes (an interest in occupational uses of the language) and later manifest an integrative motivation (a desire to associate with speakers of that language). Brown (1981) has also noted that there are at least three basic types of motivation: (a) global motivation, associated with the general orientation to the goal of learning; (b) situational motivation, which can vary according to the context in which the learning takes place (e.g., in a classroom or naturalistic setting); and (c) task motivation, which corresponds to the motivational drive for performing different learning tasks. Ely (1986), on the other hand, suggests that some learners may have a desire to learn a second language that is not related to either instrumental or integrative motives—as a means of promoting social respect, developing a better understanding of the world, or gaining a well-rounded education.

The relationship between attitudes and motivation is not always clear. Attitudes can be used to refer to the set of beliefs that a learner holds of the community and people who speak the language to be learned. The term can also be used to refer to the language-learning act itself ("Learning French is interesting/not interesting at all") or the learning task ("I find studying English is dull/exciting; hard/easy"). Some investigators use the term attitudes to refer to motivational tendencies. Others use the concept of motivation for describing course-related attitudes and opinions about specific learning tasks. Given the abstractness of the two concepts and types of relationships that can exist between the two constructs, it is difficult to establish precisely how attitudes and motivation affect language and literacy acquisition. There can be no doubt, however, that both motivation and attitudes are powerful factors that help to determine the level of proficiency attained by different learners (Gardner, 1980; Gardner & Lambert, 1972). Savignon (1976), in fact, believes that attitude is the single most important variable in second language learning. According to Savignon, it may be possible to foster a more favorable language attitude and motivational orientation by the selection of appropriate learning tasks based on the learner's motives, interests, and needs. Clearly, biliteracy planners will need to take learner motivations and language attitudes seriously as they enter the third phase of the planning effort, where decisions regarding oral proficiency or literacy levels in each language will be incorporated into the developing curriculum.

In developing curricula to promote biliteracy, planners may find that ethnographic approaches to literacy study and learner-centered approaches to literacy education provide valuable insights into the ways individuals think about their literacy experiences and needs within a particular community. Cisneros and Leone (1990) describe how, among a group of Mexican-Americans from San Antonio, Texas, it was possible to learn from the individuals themselves (a) their motivations for literacy learning, (b) their strategies for literacy learning, (c) their literacy experiences and needs at work, and (d) their literacy experiences in school. Literacy learners can also pose literacy problems and offer solutions for these problems in the work setting and other domains such as health, housing, education, legal matters, and cultural concerns (Auerbach, 1992; Spener, 1990).

Conclusion

The language planning situation in the United States can be characterized in terms of both linguistic and cultural diversity. The development of biliteracy skills among adults appears to be a complex phenomenon. The various steps used in language planning efforts may prove to be essential in addressing biliteracy issues that are social, political, and psychological in nature. Efforts in planning biliteracy programs for adults can benefit from considering the sociopolitical and linguistic factors that can influence the literacy prospects for the various ethnolinguistic groups in society. Finally, literacy learners themselves can offer valuable insights about their literacy goals, their strategies for literacy acquisition, and the roles that biliteracy plays or could play in their daily lives.

Notes

[1] With regard to Chinese, for example, immigrants from Taiwan are likely to speak Ming-nan; those from Hong Kong typically speak Cantonese; immigrants from the mainland might speak Mandarin if they are from the north or Wu if they are from the south. Ethnic Chinese immigrants from Vietnam might speak any of these or other dialects, depending on their geographic origins within China. While these dialects share a common set of written characters, they differ significantly in vocabulary, phonology, and, to a lesser extent, grammar. See Yuen-ren (1976).

References

American Council on the Teaching of Foreign Languages. (1986). *ACTFL proficiency guidelines*. Hastings-on-Hudson, NY: Author.

Auerbach, E. (1992). *Making meaning, making change: Participatory curriculum development for adult ESL literacy*. Washington, DC and McHenry, IL: Center for Applied Linguistics and Delta Systems.

Brown, H.D. (1981). Affective factors in second language learning. In J.E. Alatis, H.B. Altman, & P.M. Alatis (Eds.), *The second language classroom: Directions for the 1980s* (pp. 113-129). New York and Oxford: Oxford University Press.

Cárdenas, D.N. (1970). *Dominant Spanish dialects spoken in the United States*. Washington, DC: Center for Applied Linguistics. (ERIC Document Reproduction Service No. ED 042 137)

Child, J.R. (1987). Language proficiency levels and the typology of texts. In H. Byrnes & M. Canale (Eds.), *Defining and developing proficiency: Guidelines, implementations and concepts* (pp. 97-106). Lincolnwood, IL: National Textbook.

Cisneros, R., & Leone, E. (1990). Becoming literate: Historias de San Antonio. In J.J. Bergen (Ed.), *Spanish in the United States: Sociolinguistic issues* (pp. 86-109). Washington, DC: Georgetown University Press.

Cooper, R.L. (1984). Language planning, language spread and language change. In C. Kennedy (Ed.), *Language planning and language education* (pp. 17-36). London: George Allen & Unwin.

Craddock, J.R. (1981). New World Spanish. In C.A. Ferguson & S.B. Heath (Eds.), *Language in the USA* (pp. 196-211). New York: Cambridge University Press.

Elías-Olivares, L., & Valdés, G. (1982). Language diversity in Chicano speech communities: Implications for language teaching. In J.A. Fishman & G.D. Keller (Eds.), *Bilingual education for Hispanic students in the United States* (pp. 151-166). New York: Columbia University, Teachers College.

Ely, C.M. (1986). Language learning motivation: A descriptive and causal analysis. *The Modern Language Journal, 70*(1), 28-35.

Ferguson, C.A. (1959). Diglossia. *Word, 15*, 325-40.

Fishman, J.A., Cooper, R.L., & Ma, R. (1971). *Bilingualism in the barrio*. Bloomington: Indiana University Press.

García, R.L. (1982). *Teaching in a pluralistic society*. New York: Harper and Row.

Gardner, R. (1980). On the validity of affective variables in second language acquisition: Conceptual, contextual and statistical considerations. *Language Learning, 30*, 255-270.

Gardner, R.C., & Lambert, W.E. (1972). *Attitudes and motivation in second language learning*. Rowley, MA: Newbury House.

Grosjean, F. (1982). *Life with two languages: An introduction to bilingualism.* Cambridge, MA: Harvard University Press.

Lee, J.F., & Musumeci, D. (1988). On hierarchies of reading skills and text types. *Modern Language Journal, 72*(2), 173-187.

Ornstein-Galicia, J.L. (1979). Comparative ethnic factors in bilingual education: The United States and abroad. In R.V. Padilla (Ed.), *Ethnoperspectives in bilingual education research: Bilingual education and public policy in the United States* (pp. 461-482). Ypsilanti, MI: Eastern Michigan University, Bilingual Bicultural Education Programs.

Pedraza, P., Attinasi, J., & Hoffman, G. (1980). Rethinking diglossia. In R.V. Padilla (Ed.), *Ethnoperspectives in bilingual education research: Theory in bilingual education, Vol. II* (pp. 75-97). Ypsilanti, MI: Eastern Michigan University, Bilingual Bicultural Education Programs.

Ramírez, A.G. (1991). Sociolingüística del español-inglés en contacto entre adolescentes hispanos de Estados Unidos. *Hispania, 74,* 1057-1067.

Ramírez, A.G., & Milk, R.D. (1986). Notions of grammaticality among teachers of bilingual pupils. *TESOL Quarterly, 20,* 495-513.

Ramírez, A.G., Milk, R.D., & Sapiens, A. (1985). Intragroup differences and attitudes toward varieties of Spanish among bilingual pupils from California and Texas. *Hispanic Journal of Behavioral Sciences, 5,* 417-429.

Rubin, J. (1973). Language planning: Discussion of some current issues. In J. Rubin & R.W. Shuy (Eds.), *Language planning: Current issues and research* (pp. 1-10). Washington, DC: Georgetown University Press.

Sánchez, R. (1983). *Chicano discourse: Sociohistoric perspectives.* Rowley, MA: Newbury House.

Savignon, S.J. (1976). On the other side of the desk: Teacher attitudes and motivation in second language learning. *Canadian Modern Language Review, 32,* 295-304.

Spener, D. (1990). *The Freirean approach to adult literacy education. ERIC Q&A.* Washington, DC: Center for Applied Linguistics, National Clearinghouse on Literacy Education. (ERIC Document Reproduction Service No. ED 321 615)

Teschner, R.V. (1981). Spanish for native speakers: Evaluating twenty-five Chicano compositions in a first-year course. In G. Valdés, A.G. Lozano, & R. García-Moya (Eds.), *Teaching Spanish to the Hispanic: Bilingual issues, aims, and methods* (pp. 115-139). New York: Teachers College Press.

Williams, J.D., & Capizzi Snipper, G. (1990). *Literacy and bilingualism*. New York: Longman.

Wrigley, H.S. (1991). Language and literacy teachers: Diverse backgrounds, common concerns. *TESOL Adult Education Newsletter, 16*(1), 1, 4.

Yuen-ren, C. (1976). *Aspects of Chinese sociolinguistics: Essays.* Stanford, CA: Stanford University Press.

Zentella, A.C. (1988). The language situation of Puerto Ricans. In S.L. McKay & S.C. Wong (Eds.), *Language diversity: Problem or resource?* (pp. 140-165). New York: Newbury House.

CHAPTER 3
Bidialectal Literacy in the United States

Walt Wolfram
William C. Friday Professor
North Carolina State University

The question of dialect diversity and literacy among native English speakers in the United States represents a unique challenge to those considering the issue of biliteracy, particularly as it compares with the kinds of bilingual situations that are the focus of other papers in this volume. As a straightforward language issue, the question of bidialectal literacy can be reduced to a relatively simple question: Does the spoken language of dialectally divergent groups create a linguistic mismatch that is responsible for creating problems in the acquisition of literacy skills? The correlation of low literacy skills with membership in groups that speak a nonstandard dialect is indisputable, but the question of causation is another matter. In this respect, of course, some of the language issues that relate to the role of dialect differences in literacy contrast clearly with bilingual situations, where relative language *proficiencies* in the mother tongue and second language always have to be a main consideration.

From a broader sociocultural perspective, however, it is indisputable that dialect differences enter the sociolinguistic equation, whether or not there is a significant linguistic mismatch between the language of the speaker and the written language. The stark reality of literacy education in bidialectal situations is that language differences are rarely ignored, and that these differences may strongly influence the perceptions, expectations, and even practical instructional strategies in literacy education. For example, suppose a teacher of literacy skills assumes that a vernacular dialect speaker cannot hope to access the Standard English of written English text without a knowledge of spoken Standard English. As a result of this understanding, literacy education may combine instruction in spoken Standard English with other literacy skills related to reading and writing. Thus, inordinate amounts of time might be assigned to skills with questionable bearing on the actual acquisition of literacy skills per se.

By the same token, vernacular dialect speakers themselves are likely to be socialized into the American mythology that vernacular dialects are simply unworthy approximations of the standard variety with little linguistic validity in their own right. Given this attitude, they may feel that their "broken" or "corrupted" English precludes them from ever acquiring a full range of literacy skills. Thus, their acquisition of literacy skills is impeded by a self-fulfilling prophecy about their literacy potential. These cases are not far-fetched scenarios; in fact, I believe that there are probably many literacy education encounters that follow these scenarios quite closely, and I have observed some of these cases firsthand.

In the following, I discuss the critical need for an informed perspective on language variation in approaching literacy in a bidialectal context. I approach this first by reliving an old controversy in the language planning of bidialectal literacy—the case of "dialect readers." This case is instructive because it points to some of the broad sociopolitical and sociolinguistic issues that surround bidialectal literacy, particularly as they are similar to and different from the issues surrounding bilingual literacy. At the same time, this case underscores the need for practical information about the nature of language variation for literacy practitioners and vernacular dialect speakers themselves.

It is now two decades since the dialect reader controversy erupted, and yet we still reap the effects of the phobia that it engendered in many educational and popular circles. Applied social dialectologists are still often reminded by an unforgetting and unforgiving educational establishment and general public that a few of us once attempted to convince educators that it was at least worthwhile to experiment with dialect readers to see if they helped incipient readers gain access to the literate world.

The lesson of dialect readers is a worthy one to review here, as it places the issue of bidialectal literacy in its true sociopolitical context. For the record, a so-called dialect reader is a text that incorporates the nonstandard grammatical forms typical of a vernacular-speaking community. As a brief illustration of how a dialect reader looked, we may compare two versions of the same text, one in Standard English and one in a vernacular dialect.

Standard English Version

"Look down here," said Suzy.
"I can see a girl in here.
That girl looks like me.
Come here and look, David!
Can you see that girl?"

Vernacular Black English Version

Susan say, "Hey, you-all, look down here!"
"I could see a girl in here.
That girl, she look like me.
Come here and look, David!
Could you see the girl?"

(Source: Wolfram & Fasold, 1974, p. 198. Reprinted by permission.)

The second passage is a deliberate attempt to incorporate the features of vernacular dialect into a basal reader—in this case, a primer for children. The aim of such dialect primers, which typically use a standard English orthography rather than a modified, dialect spelling, was never to develop a dualistic reading system as some opponents contended, but simply to use a familiar language system in the initial steps of the reading process. This beginning phase was then to be followed by a transition stage which would lead students into materials written in the standard written variety. Although the use of dialect readers seemed like a radical departure from traditional approaches and materials in reading, this was not the only example of specially adapted reading materials designed for the incipient stages of developmental reading. The use of a special, invariant phonetic alphabet such as the Initial Teaching Alphabet for teaching initial decoding skills certainly departed to some extent from traditional reading primers. So we can conclude that it was not the specially adapted materials themselves that were at the heart of the matter, but the nature of the materials.

Although other kinds of alternative strategies in teaching reading may have engendered some debate as well, the controversy over dialect readers still stands in a class of its own. There seem to be several major reasons for this controversy. One involves the deliberate use of socially stigmatized language forms in written material.

This tactic is viewed by some as a reinforcement of nonstandard dialect patterns, and thus it flies in the face of traditional mainstream institutional values endorsing standard dialects. After all, educational tolerance of socially stigmatized forms in spoken language is in itself a significant departure from a tradition committed to stamping out such forms; to confront them in written text designed to teach people how to read was simply too much. The potential readers for whom the materials were designed found these stigmatized forms objectionable as well, even when these forms were shown to be in common use in their everyday language. For example, N.H. Stokes (personal communication, April 16, 1990), using a cloze passage technique, showed that beginning readers tended to substitute standard forms in reading even when such forms were not regularly used in their spoken style.

It is quite clear that vernacular dialects have been defined in our society as inappropriate vehicles for literacy, and it is apparent that children are socialized regarding this functional differentiation from the onset of their socialization regarding literacy. In this respect, the U.S. situation is akin to some third-world situations, in which unwritten minority languages are considered inappropriate for literacy vis-a-vis official state languages even when knowledge of the official language is minimal or nonexistent.

Another reason that these dialect primers were considered so objectionable was that this approach singled out particular groups of readers for special materials—namely, those who spoke vernacular dialects. In this case, it was Vernacular Black English speakers. This selective process was viewed as patronizing—and ultimately racist and classist—educational differentiation. This may have been unfortunate and even unfair, but the perception could not be denied. In fact, targeting particular materials for special dialect groups was considered so patronizingly offensive that one mother declared that she would rather not have her child learn how to read at all than to learn to read such unsightly language (reported to the author by William A. Stewart, personal communication).

A Sociolinguistic Perspective

From the viewpoint of educational sociolinguistics, the use of dialect readers is based on three assumptions: (a) that there is a sufficient mismatch between a potential reader's linguistic system and the Standard English text to warrant distinct materials, (b) that the benefits from reading success will outweigh any negative connotations associated with the use of a socially stigmatized variety, and (c) that the use of vernacular dialects in reading will promote reading success.

From the standpoint of simple linguistic processing, it is reasonable to hypothesize that the greater the mismatch between the spoken and written word, the greater the likelihood of processing difficulties in reading. But the real issue is whether dialect differences are great enough to become a significant barrier to linguistic processing. At this point, there still remain no carefully designed experimental studies that have examined this important research question in the United States in detail, but several observations are germane to this issue. First of all, there is some indication that vernacular dialect speakers do have receptive capability to process most spoken Standard English utterances whether or not they use this variety productively. Although receptive and productive capability in language may not transfer to the reading process in the same way, we would certainly expect considerable carryover from this receptive capability in spoken Standard English to the reading process, which is itself a receptive language activity.

Writing, a productive process, may be more transparently influenced by dialect divergence, and a number of different studies have documented the influence of spoken language differences on writing (Farr & Janda, 1985; Whiteman, 1981; Wolfram & Whiteman, 1971). Even with the productive medium of writing, however, it should be noted that the influence of spoken language is not isomorphic. Generalized strategies affecting both Standard English and vernacular dialect speakers account for some types of divergence, and not all predicted influence from spoken vernacular dialects is realized for various sociolinguistic reasons, so that the picture of written language divergence for vernacular speakers is somewhat more complicated than we might expect at first glance (Farr & Daniels, 1986; Farr & Janda, 1985; Whiteman, 1981).

It is, of course, erroneous to assume that Standard English speakers confront written language that is identical to the way they speak, and vernacular speakers do not. In reality, all readers encounter written text that differs from spoken language to some extent. Even in early reading, sentences with an adverbial complement moved to the beginning of the sentence (e.g., Over and over rolled the ball; Up the hill he ran) represent a written genre that differentiates written from spoken language for all speakers. So the problem of mismatch between written and spoken language is a matter of degree rather than kind. [Editor's note: See also Ramírez, this volume, for a discussion of the need to take style and register variation into account in literacy planning.]

Admittedly, the gap between written and spoken language is greater for vernacular dialect speakers than it is for speakers of standard varieties. But is this gap wide enough to cause problems on the basis of linguistic differences alone? Again, carefully controlled experimentation on this issue is lacking, although I am reminded of the fact that there are situations in the world where the gap between spoken dialect and written text is quite extensive without resulting in significant reading problems. In northern Switzerland, for example, texts are written in standard German although much of the population speaks Swiss German, yet the Swiss population does not reveal significant reading failure. Although it is difficult to measure "degree of dialect difference" in a precise way, Swiss German is certainly as different from standard written German as many vernacular dialects of English are from standard written English (Fishman, 1969, p. 1109). Pointing to linguistic mismatch as a primary variable in reading failure among vernacular speakers thus seems suspect. As we shall see, differences in the written and spoken language may have to be taken into account by an aware reading instructor, but it is doubtful that the neutralization of these differences in reading material would alleviate the reading problems associated with various vernacular-speaking populations. Given children's socialization into mainstream attitudes and values about dialects at an early age, there is also little reason to assume that the psychosocial benefits of using a vernacular dialect would outweigh the disadvantages. In fact, the opposite seems to be the case, as children reject nonstandard forms in reading, and parents and community leaders rail against their use in dialect readers. A positive relationship between reading success and the use of vernacular dialect readers also has not been firmly established. Some initial investigation of dialect readers reported slight gains for children given these materials (Leaverton, 1973), but substantive research in favor of dialect readers is lacking. Due to the continuing controversy surrounding the use of dialect primers, this alternative now has been largely abandoned.

To say that dialect readers do not hold promise does not, however, suggest that the representation of dialect can never be used advantageously in literacy. In fact, there is a sustainable vernacular language literature which may have merit in its own right. Vernacular dialects are written in two main contexts. One is dialogue sequences in novels and short stories, where the dialect captures the indigenous community character of the speaker. In fact, it would be quite unreal and inappropriate for writers to represent speakers from these communities in any other way, and these passages make speakers authentic representatives of their communities. Another literate tradition for vernacular dialects is the poetry of well known and respected African-American writers who selectively write poetry in the community vernacular. Writers such as Langston Hughes, Paul Laurence Dunbar, and Maya Angelou all use this technique to great advantage. In fact, Paul Laurence Dunbar wrote approximately one-third of his poetry in vernacular dialect. Consider, for example, the following portion of a poem by Dunbar (1941, p. 60):

DISCOVERED

Seen you down at chu'ch las' night,
  Nevah min', Miss Lucy.
What I mean? oh, dat's all right,
  Nevah min', Miss Lucy.
You was sma't es sma't could be,
But you could n't hide f'om me.
Ain't I got two eyes to see!
  Nevah min', Miss Lucy.

Guess you thought you's awful keen;
  Nevah min', Miss Lucy.
Evahthing you done, I seen;
  Nevah min', Miss Lucy.
Seen him tek yo' ahm jes' so,
When he got outside de do'—
Oh, I know dat man's yo' beau!
  Nevah min', Miss Lucy.

It is important to note that these writers coupled the selective use of verse written in vernacular dialect with standard English, showing their bidialectal facility. Vernacular verse seems to be contextualized as a "literature of the heart." As Fasold (1990) notes, the literature of Vernacular Black English may have a place, but "its use is circumscribed and the settings considered appropriate have been quite consistent at least the past half century or so" (p. 3).

In retrospect, then, one of the major problems of dialect readers was their sociolinguistic insensitivity to the appropriate setting for the use of African-American dialect. As it turns out there is a reading curriculum that uses a version of dialect materials, namely, *Bridge: A Cross-Cultural Reading Program* (Simpkins, Simpkins, & Holt, 1977). This program is not designed for beginning readers but for older junior high and high school students who have experienced reading difficulty. The program limits the dialect text to passages representative of students' cultural background experiences so that the use of vernacular is placed in an appropriate community context. It also makes a sincere effort to provide positive motivation and successful reading experiences for students as the major component of the program. While this program has hardly been free of controversy, its limitation of dialect passages to culturally appropriate contexts has made it less offensive than other approaches which use dialect passages without regard for their culturally appropriate setting. By contextualizing dialect use in reading so that it fits into appropriate cultural contexts, these materials have avoided a major flaw of some of the decontextualized dialect primers. In fact, in many respects, the use of dialect passages in the *Bridge* program falls in line with a well established, fairly secure tradition of representing dialect in literature. In this instance, the intent is to seize upon this literary tradition of dialect representation for the benefit of a reader who may identify with the dialect rather than the representation of a dialect assumed to be different from that of the reader. Rigorous measurement of the outcomes of this program has not been undertaken, but its authors claim that it is an approach to reading that capitalizes in a more positive, appropriate way on the use of a literate vernacular dialect. So, the selective literary uses of vernacular dialect in literacy programs may not be completely dead, after all.

Since the 1970s, a number of approaches to literacy education have come into vogue that build literacy skills using students' own spoken language as a starting point. The language experience approach comes to mind in particular. In the language experience approach, stories dictated by learners themselves are used as reading texts. These dictated stories are not typically corrected by instructors on the premise that keeping the discrepancy between written language and student speech to a minimum fosters reading success in the early stages of acquiring literacy. (See, e.g., Davidson & Wheat, 1989; Richardson, 1981; Rigg & Taylor, 1979; Taylor, in press). Dialogue journals are another tool being promoted by some educators as a way to develop writing proficiency in particular. (See e.g., Peyton & Staton, 1990.) In dialogue journals, students write to their teachers or to other partners about topics of personal interest to them, and the partners write back. As the writing continues back and forth, an ongoing dialogue develops. The focus of dialogue journals is on the content of the messages exchanged, not their form, and student language use is not subject to teacher correction. Thus, while dialogue journals may not actively promote the reading and writing of vernacular dialects, they do offer a nonjudgmental context for the use of vernacular dialects encoded into writing. Finally, whole language approaches to literacy emphasize the importance of readers being able to select which texts they are going to read and write. One of the important roles of literacy educators in the whole language approach is to provide learners with a rich and diverse print environment that includes texts written in a variety of styles and dialects. (See, e.g., Newman, 1985; Rigg & Kazemek, 1985, in press.)

Applying Sociolinguistic Knowledge to the Current Situation

Although there are some ways in which dialect may affect reading, most current approaches to literacy for vernacular dialect speakers play down simple linguistic differences as a primary factor in the high levels of reading failure found among vernacular-speaking populations. Instead, cultural values about reading (Labov, 1972), the technological conditions for reading instruction (Dreeban & Gamoran, 1986), the process of socialization into the social activity of reading, the mismatch between readers' interests and the content of reading material, and interactional dynamics during reading instruction (Washington & Miller-Jones, 1989) have been considered more essential factors in accounting for high failure rates among nonmainstream populations (see also García, Jiménez, & Pearson, 1989). Focus on these other variables does not, however, excuse those involved in providing literacy for such populations from understanding the ways in which dialectal differences may impact on the reading process and from taking these factors into consideration in instruction. This was, in fact, the major point of the much heralded Ann Arbor Decision (Center for Applied Linguistics, 1979), where it was decreed that educators had a responsibility to take into account sociolinguistic differences in their teaching of reading.

A Perspective on Language Variation for Practitioners

First of all, it seems to be essential for those involved in literacy on all levels to understand the kinds of reading processes that may be affected by dialect differences. (For more detail, see Farr & Daniels, 1986; Wolfram & Christian, 1989). For example, one process in reading that may be affected by dialect is *decoding*. Whereas different approaches to reading rely on decoding skills to varying degrees, and many current approaches deemphasize a basic decoding model of reading, the systematic sounding out of letters still appears to be a skill that readers should be familiar with.

A literacy worker engaged in decoding tasks with students must recognize that there are systematic differences in the symbol-sound relationships from dialect to dialect. For example, consider how a reader of a vernacular dialect might decode orally the passage "There won't be anything to do until he finds out if he can go without taking John's brother." A modified orthography is used below to indicate the pronunciation differences for the vernacular speaker.

D̲e̲u̲h̲ won't be anything to do until he fin̲ʼ out if he can go wi̲f̲out takin̲ʼ John_ bro̲v̲uh.

Systematic decoding differences may affect a number of symbol-sound relationships in the example, such as the final consonant of find, the th of without, the th and final r of brother, and so forth. These differences are no more severe than variant regional decodings of the vowel au of caught (e.g., [ɔ] or [a]) or the s of greasy (e.g., [s] or [z]), except that they involve a couple of heavily stigmatized variants. The variant decoding becomes a problem only if an instructor does not recognize dialectally appropriate sound-symbol relationships and classifies these differences as errors in decoding. Imagine the confusion that might be created for a dialect speaker if an accurate dialect decoding such as th —> [f] in without or th —> [v] in brother is treated as a problem comparable to the miscoding of b as [d] or sh as [s]. To avoid this confusion and potential misdiagnosis of reading problems, literacy practitioners need to be able to separate dialect differences from actual reading disabilities. The potential impact of dialects on the decoding process can be minimized if reading instructors have this information.

It is also important to recognize that dialect differences may lead to reading miscues that derive from grammatical differences, as indicated in the following vernacular dialect rendering of the passage given above.

It won't be nothing to do till he find_ out can he go without taking John_ brother.

The use of existential it for there, multiple negation, the absence of inflectional -s, and the inverted question order of can he go are all instances of mismatch between the spoken vernacular variety and the written word. Given the potential for dialect influence in processing written text, it seems imperative that literacy instructors familiarize themselves with the linguistic structure of vernacular varieties.

Similar application can be made to the writing process, where spoken vernacular dialect features may influence the written form. It is not difficult to document cases of vernacular spoken language influence on the writing process similar to those cited for reading above. However, as Whiteman (1981) and Farr and Janda (1985) point out, dialect features are not reflective of spoken language in a simple isomorphic relationship. We need to appeal to general developmental principles with respect to the writing process (e.g., inflectional suffixes may be omitted) and to principles related to the social evaluation of language (e.g., highly stigmatized, stereotyped features are less likely to be used in writing) to account for the observed patterning of dialect features in the written language of vernacular dialect speakers.

The preceding paragraphs point to a need for literacy practitioners to know something about the structural details of the dialects of their vernacular-dialect-speaking clientele in order to distinguish genuine language processing difficulties from dialectally appropriate renditions. This discussion also suggests that information about the social evaluation of forms needs to be acquired as a basis for understanding the nature of dialect manifestations in reading and writing, since different forms may be expected to manifest themselves at different points in the progression of literacy skills.

Another area of language variation to consider in the reading process involves the broader sociolinguistic base of language, including background cultural differences. In most current models of the reading process, the application of background knowledge is essential for comprehension. Readers need such background in order to derive meaning by inference; they may also need to apply knowledge about the world in order to process some of the literal content. For example, imagine the differences in how a third grader from California and one from New York City might interpret the following passage on the age of giant redwood trees. Incidently, this item appeared in the *Metropolitan Achievement Test*.

They are so big that roads are built through their trunks. By counting the rings inside the tree trunk, one can tell the age of the tree. (Meier, 1973, p. 15)

Meier (1973) reports that some readers in New York conjured up fairy tale interpretations of this passage that included, among other things, pictures of golden rings lying inside trees. The fairy tale interpretation was certainly fostered by images of cars driving through giant holes in trees. On the other hand, those who live near the Redwood Forest in California would interpret the passage quite differently, since its literal content would match their knowledge of the world. There is certainly the potential for students to expand their range of experience through reading, but background information is critical for comprehension, and the reality of real-world differences in experiential backgrounds must be confronted as part of the consideration of the broader sociolinguistic setting of reading. Different community language and culture experiences may, in fact, actually affect reading comprehension in both obvious and subtle, yet important ways.

In the above paragraph, we see a need for literacy practitioners to know more than simply the structural details of vernacular speaking communities. Their knowledge of language variation must include the broader base of cultural background and experience that vernacular dialect speakers bring to the literacy situation.

Finally, we need to remember that dialect differences may have an effect on some of the metalinguistic tasks often associated with literacy skills. Beginning-level reading assessment measures are particularly susceptible to the impact of dialect because they often rely on metalinguistic tasks that are sensitive to dialect-specific decoding differences. For example, the use of minimal-word-pair tasks or rhyming tasks to measure decoding skills might result in misclassifying cases of dialect-appropriate symbol-sound relationships as incorrect responses. Consider test items (taken from an actual reading achievement test) that include the following word pairs as part of an attempt to determine early readers' specific decoding abilities.

Choose the words that sound the same:
pin/pen
reef/wreath
find/fine
their/there
here/hear

For speakers of some vernacular varieties, all of these items might legitimately sound the same. The "correct" response, however, would be limited to there/their and hear/here, based upon the Northern standard dialect norm. An informed perspective on language variation must therefore consider the ways in which literacy skills are measured, including narrowly based metalinguistic skills and broader based inferencing that bring background knowledge into play in the acquisition of literacy skills.

Language Variation for Vernacular Dialect Speakers

We have seen that there are several types of fundamental knowledge about language variation that are essential for literacy practitioners to acquire to adequately serve the vernacular-speaking community. But what about the speakers themselves who are acquiring literacy skills? Is there a need for them to know something about the nature of language variation? I would maintain that it is also essential for those acquiring literacy skills to be exposed to some fundamental notions about language variation. We must remember that speakers of vernacular dialects, like mainstream dialect speakers, have been socialized into the American prejudice against nonstandard dialects. Operating on erroneous assumptions about language differences, it is easy for these learners to feel that since "they can't talk right," they can't learn literacy skills either. Such learners need to know that dialect divergence is natural and neutral linguistically, that the linguistic discrimination and prejudice they have been subjected to is unjustified, and that their own dialect is systematically patterned with a linguistic history as viable as any other variety. The honest, open discussion of language prejudice, a brief examination of the legitimate history of the vernacular dialect, and even an examination of the development of several exemplary structures may well be worth the time and effort in terms of moving learners to a less shameful view of their dialect. For example, showing the video *American Tongues* (available through the Center for New American Media, 524 Broadway, 2nd floor, New York, NY 10012-4408) or the *Black on White* program from McNeil's *Story of English* series (available through Films Incorporated, 5547 N. Ravenwood, Chicago, IL 60640-1199) tends to get adult literacy students to talk much more openly and honestly about the unjustified prejudices about Vernacular Black English and to confront its legitimate history. Even a brief discussion of the relationship of the current-day aks pronunciation in Vernacular Black English to the older, mainstream English form (axian) from which it was derived can help learners view their own dialect in a less shameful light. In this context, exposing readers to some of the vernacular dialect verse of prominent African-American writers might provide tacit support for the legitimacy of the dialect. Since we hypothesize that speakers who feel good about the way they speak are more likely to take the kinds of learning risks needed to acquire literacy skills than those who feel shameful about their spoken language, we may reason that there is an important educational benefit to be derived from the introduction of such material apart from our moral conviction to provide accurate information about dialects.

I have accumulated several enthusiastic testimonials from adult literacy programs about the benefits of such information for learners, both in terms of the atmosphere surrounding the context of literacy instruction and the learners' willingness to engage in literacy instructional encounters. While this evidence is still anecdotal, it offers a reasonable working hypothesis to guide those who teach literacy skills to vernacular dialect speakers. Even if it doesn't prove beneficial when examined within the framework of a tightly controlled experimental design, we can be assured that people are ultimately better off knowing the truth about dialects. This goes for specialists in social dialectology, literacy practitioners, and vernacular dialect speakers acquiring basic literacy skills.

Language Variation for ESL Students

As perplexing as language variation sometimes is for native speakers of English, it is even more mystifying for students of English as a second language (ESL). The standard version of English provided in most ESL curricula aims unrealistically at a dialect-neutral variety of English identified as General American Standard. And yet the majority of ESL learners are surrounded by a rich variety of dialects, including vernacular dialects of English for those who live in economically impoverished conditions. It is not surprising for speakers living in these communities to report that, while they comprehend the neutral variety of English they are taught in the ESL classroom, they cannot comprehend the vernacular dialects surrounding them.

Along the way, many ESL learners' socialization in American culture may lead them to adopt the same uncharitable, biased opinion of vernaculars as that so often found among native speakers of English. Furthermore, many ESL learners may, in fact, speak vernacular varieties of their native languages that are comparable in status to the vernacular dialects of English. It thus seems appropriate to incorporate dimensions of language variation into the ESL curriculum so that such learners may share in the full, realistic range of language variation as offered ideally to their native-English-speaking peers. In fact, the absence of a sociolinguistic perspective in most ESL programs robs them of their full educational potential. Theoretically, it deprives students of an honest understanding of the nature of language variation—a perspective that can lead to an authentic sociolinguistic appreciation for the natural basis of variation in both their native and their second language. Practically, it deprives students of the benefits of learning about everyday English—the real-world varieties of English that they will actually face in their everyday sociolinguistic interaction. In the real world, sociolinguistic success is determined by the ability to carry out everyday affairs with a wide range of English speakers—speakers who speak different dialects, including vernacular ones. ESL programs have much to gain from adopting a curriculum that includes a healthy understanding of language variation.

Despite the obvious correlation between low levels of literacy and membership in a vernacular-speaking dialect group, there does not appear to be substantive evidence for concluding that dialect per se is a major variable in explaining this relationship between illiteracy and speaking a vernacular dialect. At the same time, however, this fact does not let literacy practitioners off the language variation hook. I have stressed that there are several reasons why knowledge of language variation is critical for such practitioners, as knowledge about dialect differences affects numerous activities related to literacy, including the interpretation of reading behavior, teaching procedures, metalinguistic activities related to literacy, and attitudes about those who do not speak standard varieties of English. In addition, I have suggested that vernacular dialect speakers themselves have nothing to lose and much to gain from exposure to some basic, fundamental notions about language variation.

References

Center for Applied Linguistics. (1979). *The Ann Arbor decision: Memorandum, opinion, and order and the educational plan.* Washington, DC: Author.

Davidson, J.L., & Wheat, T.E. (1989). Successful literacy experiences for adult illiterates. *Journal of Reading, 32,* 342-346.

Dreeban, R., & Gamoran, A. (1986). Race, instruction, and learning. *American Sociological Review, 51,* 660-669.

Dunbar, P.L. (1941). *The complete poems of Paul Laurence Dunbar.* New York: Dodd, Mead, and Company.

Farr, M., & Daniels, H. (1986). *Language diversity and writing instruction.* Urbana, IL: National Council of Teachers of English.

Farr, M., & Janda, M.A. (1985). Basic writing students: Investigating oral and written language. *Research in the Teaching of English, 19*(1), 62-83.

Fasold, R.W. (1990). *Sustainable vernacular language literacy illustrated by U.S. Vernacular Black English.* Unpublished manuscript, Georgetown University, Washington.

Fishman, J. (1969). Literacy and the language barrier [Review of *Teaching black children to read*]. *Science, 165,* 1108-1109.

García, G.E., Jiménez, R.T., & Pearson, P.D. (1989). *Annotated bibliography of research related to reading of at risk children* (Tech. Rep. No. 482). Urbana, IL: Center for the Study of Reading.

Labov, W. (1972). The relation of reading failure to peer-group status. In W. Labov (Ed.), *Language in the inner city: Studies in the Black English Vernacular* (pp. 241-254). Philadelphia: University of Pennsylvania.

Leaverton, L. (1973). Dialect readers: Rationale, use, and value. In J.L. Laffey & R.W. Shuy (Eds.), *Language differences: Do they interfere?* Newark, DE: International Reading Association.

Meier, D. (1973). *Reading failure and the tests*. New York: The Workshop Center for Open Education.

Newman, J. (Ed.). (1985). *Whole language: Theory in use*. Portsmouth, NH: Heinemann.

Peyton, J., & Staton, J. (Eds.). (1990). *Writing our lives: Reflections on dialogue journal writing with adults learning English*. Englewood Cliffs, NJ and Washington, DC: Regents Prentice Hall and Center for Applied Linguistics.

Richardson, J.S. (1981). Language experience for adult beginning readers: Sometimes it works. *Lifelong Learning: The Adult Years*, *4*(8), 12-13.

Rigg, P., & Kazemek, F. (1985). For adults only: Reading materials for adult literacy students. *Journal of Reading*, *28*, 726-731.

Rigg, P., & Kazemek, F. (1993). Whole language in adult literacy instruction. In J.A. Crandall & J.K. Peyton (Eds.), *Approaches to adult ESL literacy instruction* (pp. 35-46). Washington, DC and McHenry, IL: Center for Applied Linguistics and Delta Systems.

Rigg, P., & Taylor, L. (1979). A twenty-one-year-old begins to read. *English Journal*, *68*(3), 52-56.

Simpkins, G.C., Simpkins, C., & Holt, G. (1977). *Bridge: A cross-cultural reading program*. Boston: Houghton Mifflin.

Taylor, M. (1993). The language experience approach. In J.A. Crandall & J.K. Peyton (Eds.), *Approaches to adult ESL literacy instruction* (pp. 47-58). Washington, DC and McHenry, IL: Center for Applied Linguistics and Delta Systems.

Washington, V.M., & Miller-Jones, D. (1989). Teacher interaction with nonstandard English speakers during reading instruction. *Contemporary Educational Psychology*, *14*, 280-312.

Whiteman, M.F. (1981). Dialect influence in writing. In M.F. Whiteman (Ed.), *Writing: The nature, development, and teaching of written communication: Vol. 1* (pp.153-165). Hillsdale, NJ: Erlbaum.

Wolfram, W., & Christian, D. (1989). *Dialects and education: Issues and answers.* Englewood Cliffs, NJ and Washington, DC: Prentice Hall Regents and Center for Applied Linguistics.

Wolfram, W., & Fasold, R.W. (1974). *The study of social dialects in American English.* Englewood Cliffs, NJ: Prentice Hall.

Wolfram, W., & Whiteman, M. (1971). The role of dialect interference in composition. *The Florida FL Reporter, 9,* 34-38.

CHAPTER 4
Biliteracy in the Home: Practices Among *Mexicano* Families in Chicago

Marcia Farr
University of Illinois, Chicago

Many scholars have struggled in recent years to define precisely what literacy is. Clearly literacy cannot be reduced to one definition (Graff, 1986, 1987); "a plurality of literacies" (Szwed, 1981, p. 16) more accurately reflects literacy practices that vary from context to context. Definitions of literacy, then, range rather widely, but usually cluster around two concepts: One is referred to as functional (or basic) literacy and the other as essayist (often meaning text-level) literacy (Olson, 1977; Scollon & Scollon, 1981). Heath (1987) has suggested the terms *literacy skills* and *literate behaviors* to refer to the cognitive and linguistic processes behind these two general conceptions of literacy. Distinguishing literacy skills (the encoding and decoding of a writing system, or basic reading and writing) from literate behaviors (using problem-solving and knowledge-creating abilities) may have clarified some problems in defining literacy, particularly in providing terms for common conceptions of literacy, but it has led to other problems.

Ethnographic research on literacy among particular groups of people (Heath, 1983; Scribner & Cole, 1981; Shuman, 1986; Street, 1984; Tannen, 1982) has countered effectively the earlier assertion of some scholars that literacy and orality represented an essential dichotomy (Olson, 1977; Ong, 1982), and that entire groups of people, even in complex literate societies, had oral cultures and thus were unable to think abstractly (Farrell, 1983). Ethnographic research on literacy has shown clearly that oral and written language (in societies that use a writing system) overlap in subtle ways and are often used within the same communication event. Recently,

89

however, some have taken this finding even further and have argued that literacy can be an entirely oral activity; that is, rather than using oral language to discuss or otherwise converse about a piece of print (Heath, 1983), some have argued that literacy can mean using oral language in ways that are considered literate without involving any print at all (Gee, 1989; Vasquez, 1989).

One problem with this view is that it doesn't allow for distinctions between languages or cultures with no writing system (i.e., nonliterate societies) and those with writing. It has been argued with both historical and ethnographic evidence that, over time, writing does make a difference in cultures (Goody, 1986, 1987a), although it does not represent the "great leap" that was originally claimed by some scholars (Goody & Watt, 1963; Olson, 1977; Ong, 1982). Finnegan (1988), in a careful synthesis of anthropological work that bears on the orality-literacy debate, concludes that the invention of writing acts as an enabling factor, which, along with other social factors (e.g., the development of paper from trees), can stimulate significant changes in a culture.

Ultimately, one arena in which change may occur is in the use of oral language as feedback from literacy to oral language (Goody, 1987b); thus, the oral language of those who are immersed in written texts begins to resemble the written language of their culture. Because of this feedback, some oral language use can be quite literate in the sense that it reflects characteristics of literate traditions of a particular culture. In my view, however, this phenomenon doesn't justify claiming that using solely oral language (e.g., in the construction of personal narratives) is a literacy activity, even though it may involve, for example, some analytic thinking. Finnegan's (1988) synthesis provides abundant evidence that nonliterate peoples engage in the kinds of thinking that in our culture are termed literate, but they do not do so with writing. To say, then, that what these peoples, or other groups, do solely with oral language constitutes a kind of literacy, eliminates this distinction between literate and nonliterate societies. We then would have to claim that the invention of writing in various cultures around the world was relatively insignificant in human history. Clearly, although no great leap, writing is not an insignificant development, primarily because of its ability to extend communication over space and time.

Undoubtedly, something very important is at stake when so much energy is spent on—and such controversy surrounds—defining a phenomenon such as literacy. What is at stake here are the political implications of various definitions. Depending on the definition, entire groups of people can be labeled illiterate. For example, if literacy is defined as using higher order critical thinking (i.e., analytic logic and other abstract cognitive processes) in written language, then those who use written language only in functional ways (i.e., to function pragmatically in daily life) can be said to be illiterate.

In fact, recent research has shown that relatively few adults in the United States can be said to be *non*literate (Kirsch & Jungeblut, 1986), although those who use literacy skills but, supposedly, not literate behaviors (at least not with writing), have been termed semiliterate (Miller, 1988). In this way, the economic problems of the so-called underclass, or of the working classes more generally, can be seen as their own problem; members of these groups are not literate enough to perform jobs that would yield them more money. Wilson (1987), however, has shown that the economic problems of what he termed the underclass (and has revised to "the ghetto poor") are the result of structural changes in the economy, not group or individual factors. Moreover, some research has shown that literacy often is used to screen potential employees, even when it is not actually needed on the job (Levine, 1986). Thus it does not seem to be clear that, even if everyone were fully literate, everyone could be fully employed.

Workforce 2000 (Johnson & Packer, 1987), a report of the U.S. Department of Labor, claims that there soon will be numerous jobs, but that many people will not have the skills (including literacy—or perhaps the cognitive style associated with literate behaviors) to perform these jobs. This claim is based on an expectation that jobs in an increasingly automated workplace will require new kinds of abilities and skills. As increasing numbers of women and minorities are entering the workforce, it is apparently these groups in particular who may need further training. Researchers may be skeptical, as I am, about these predictions, but we have limited evidence about the actual uses of literacy in a variety of work situations with which to argue with those who make the claims.

What do we actually know of the role of literacy in the workplace? This question is central to the controversy over how literacy is defined, since defining literacy will affect what kinds of literacy are taught in school, and one (though not the only) justification for a particular kind of literacy instruction is that it prepares students for the workplace. Reviews of work in this area have indicated that:

- Literacy demands can vary greatly from one place of work to another.
- Many blue as well as white collar jobs involve almost daily literacy activity.
- Much of this literacy activity (especially for blue collar work) involves the filling out of forms.
- More research is needed in a variety of settings to determine the range of variation in the level of literacy from one place of work to another and to provide an in-depth view of writing processes, functions, and social contexts (Jacob, 1982; Mikulecky, 1982).

In my own ethnographic research with Mexican-origin families in Chicago, I have found the demand for literacy at work to vary widely. In some of the jobs family members hold, no literacy is required at all (e.g., in a poultry processing plant where a workforce of virtually all Mexican women debone, weigh, and pack chicken breasts and other parts), whereas in others, women with as few as two years of formal schooling in Mexico, in Spanish, are struggling to write reports in English as part of a quality control process in a factory. As researchers have noted, people in such jobs often perform beyond their apparent level of literacy skills (Cintron, 1989; Crandall, 1981; Diehl & Mikulecky, 1980), using contextual information to complete tasks that they probably would be unable to complete under experimental, out-of-context conditions.

It is not totally clear, then, what role(s) literacy plays, or doesn't play, in all settings across the workplace domain. While initial work in this area has shown literacy activity to be involved in many jobs, we need more in-depth, on-site ethnographic studies to describe workplace literacy activity more fully and, importantly, to compare employer and employee perceptions of this activity (Gundlach, Farr, & Cook-Gumperz, 1989). Finally, we have insufficient generalizable evidence at this point to determine conclusively how important literacy is in the employability of people, although we do know that this seems to vary greatly from context to context, even within the same job level in the same industry (Jacob, 1982).

Our knowledge gaps, in addition to the variation in literacy activity researchers already have found, thus lend limited clarity to the controversy over how literacy should be defined, or whose literacy should provide the model for this definition. Graff (1981) has pointed out, however, that only functional literacy skills can be considered universal, since what people do with these skills varies from culture to culture and throughout history. Also, functional literacy may be the most widely and frequently used by many segments of the population in this country, whether or not essayist literacy is used as well by some of them. Virtually everyone has to deal with forms (i.e., the literacy of bureaucratic institutions) in one aspect or another of their lives, whether at work or at home. The teaching of essayist literacy, in both oral and written activities at school, then becomes a separate question, justified not just on economic, but on civic— including political—grounds. My working definition of literacy, then, like Graff's, is that of Heath's literacy skills: communication which involves encoding (writing) or decoding (reading) with a writing system. My choice of functional literacy as the working definition of literacy itself is supported by the fact that this definition generally reflects the view of literacy held by the Mexican families with whom I have been working. That is, the members of these families generally view literacy as the decoding and encoding of language with a writing system, in this case either the Spanish or English alphabet.[1]

The Mexican-Origin Language and Literacy Project[2]

The Mexican-origin Language and Literacy Project at the University of Illinois, Chicago has as its overall goal the description of oral and written language patterns in the Mexican-origin community of Chicago. Our preliminary work in the two (contiguous) most concentrated Mexican-origin neighborhoods in Chicago indicated at least three major subgroups in this community: *mexicanos* (immigrants raised in Mexico), Mexican-Americans raised in Chicago (who generally prefer the terms Mexican or Mexican-American to Chicano), and Mexican-Americans raised in Texas (who often refer to themselves as *tejanos*). The first phase of this project has investigated language and literacy among *mexicanos* in this community (Elías-Olivares,

1990; Farr, 1989, in press; Guerra, 1991). We hope that future studies will provide a closer look at the two groups of Mexican-Americans.

For several years I have participated in the lives of families within one social network of *mexicanos* in the heart of the Mexican-origin community in Chicago. A social network, a conceptual tool of anthropology (see review in Hannerz, 1980), is comprised of one center person or one center family and all immediate kin and close friends. In methodological terms, a researcher starts by getting to know the center person or family and works his or her way out to the other people or families close to the center. For Mexicans this involves both kin and *compadrazco* (godparent-like) relationships, and the network itself, like the family, is of central importance in all facets of social life. Approximately 11 families (about 75 people) comprise the inner circle of this particular network, and, in keeping with the gender-based activity patterns of these culturally conservative families, my participant-observation has been primarily, but by no means exclusively, with the women and children. I am continuing to gather data on the literacy practices in both Spanish and English of these families and on female verbal performances, in all-female contexts, of jokes, stories, and arguments (what I am calling "oral folk texts").

This work is being carried out within the framework of the ethnography of communication as conceptualized by Hymes (1974) and as extended by Hymes (1981) and Bauman (1977). Within this framework, speaking and reading and writing are viewed as ways of communicating that are characteristic of a particular cultural group; context is crucial to the interpretation of behavior; and linguistic behavior is inextricably connected to and reflective of social meaning. Thus the women's jokes, for example, reflect social meanings to insiders of the group, and it is only through long-term participant-observation that an outsider can discern these meanings.

In this chapter I will provide a partial description of the literacy practices of the families in whose lives I have participated. In analyzing my data, I have chosen to focus on domains in which literacy is used, rather than the functions of each literacy activity, as have other researchers (Heath, 1983; Taylor & Dorsey-Gaines, 1988), because so many literacy activities serve multiple functions. For example, a particular use of written Spanish or English (e.g., reading a letter from a government agency) may serve both instrumental and social-interactional functions. In contrast, viewing literacy activities as occurring in broad domains within the lives of family members allowed a more social, and less individual, perspective on my data.

In focusing on domains, I adapted a framework provided by Goody (1986), which synthesizes anthropological and historical studies of writing in societies all over the world. Goody posits four large domains ("along the lines of the frequently accepted subsystems of society," p. xvi) in which writing has been central historically: religion, economy, politics (the state), and law. The families I am studying, like many families living in the United States, regularly interact with print issued from large institutions in these four domains: the church, commerce, the state, and the law.

As Goody points out, these domains can and often do overlap, and for the purposes of my analysis I collapsed two of his domains: those of the state and the law. I did so because the recent U.S. amnesty process for undocumented workers, in which these families participated, essentially combined the interests of these two domains, and the written forms encountered and responded to during this process represented both the state and the law. In addition, however, my data show literacy practices in these families extending beyond Goody's four societal domains; thus in my analysis I have added to his framework two additional domains: that of education (both large institutional and personal) and that of the family/home (as the only private, rather than public, institution). My revision of Goody's framework, then, results in a description of literacy practices among Mexican immigrant families within five primary domains: the church, commerce, the state/the law, education, and family/home.

Particularly relevant to the concerns of this book is the domain of family/home, especially in light of current policy concerns: Not only is this domain the only one of the five that is exclusively private (education as a domain includes both private/informal and public/formal activities, and the three remaining domains—the church, commerce, and the state/the law—entirely represent public institutions), but there is much contemporary controversy over whether or not, and if so, how government agencies should intervene in family literacy practices, given that it is a private domain (Auberbach, 1989; Szwed, 1981). Elsewhere (Farr, in press), I provide a fuller description of all five domains, representing both public and private institutions.

Family Literacy Practices

During the first 1½ years of fieldwork, literacy practices seemed to us minimal and infrequent, possibly because these activities were not made evident to us by participants themselves, but were inconspicuously interwoven with daily activities. Another reason that the literacy activities of these families seemed so minimal to us was the fact that literacy materials are generally stored away, out of sight. Magazines, for example, are kept neatly inside the compartments below the top of the coffee table in the living room; they are brought out only when they are to be used. A complete set of hardback religious books is also stored away, for example, up in a cupboard in a back bedroom. Finally, all meaningful papers (certificates, records, and other papers seen as important) are stored in a special place like the parents' bedroom, in either a box, a valise, or a bag. It is worth noting that many papers seen as important enough to be stored away by members of these families seemed to me unimportant (e.g., receipts from telephone calls placed to or from Mexico through commercial long distance offices); it may be that virtually all pieces of writing are viewed as potentially having importance (and the amnesty provisions of the 1986 Immigration Reform and Control Act may have proven these families right).

In spite of the surface invisibility of literacy artifacts, however, a recent computer search through my field notes from the first year of the project revealed a very different picture from that of our initial impression. Theme words involving literacy occurred continuously throughout the field notes; the following list should indicate the regular presence of literacy in the lives of these families:

read/reading	map
write/writing/written/wrote	library
draw	literate/literacy
copy/copied	form(s), application(s)
list, note	contract(s)
print	certificate(s), record(s)
telegram, mail, letter(s)	advertisement
bill(s), receipt(s)	worksheet
invitation(s)	homework, study(ing), test
page, word(s), paper(s)	checking account
book(let), TV guide, magazine	sign(ature)
catalogue	*doctrina*/catechism

Literacy activities are woven into the ongoing stream of family life. Print, in both Spanish and English, is omnipresent both within the neighborhood and within homes. Outside, in the neighborhood, stores display a multitude of signs primarily in Spanish (e.g., *Discolandia* for a music store, *Abarrotes* for a grocery store), less frequently in English (e.g., McDonald's—although there are both English and Spanish menus inside on the wall behind the counter), and sometimes in both languages together (e.g., a bar that advertises *Tenemos Via Satellite* to indicate they have cable television). Within homes, print also abounds in both Spanish and English:

- Labels on cans of food—usually in English, but in Spanish on items imported from Mexico.
- Wall calendars—same type as in Mexico, and in Spanish.
- Audiotapes—the music is usually Mexican or Mexican-American, so the packaging print is usually in Spanish.
- Magazines—either religious or with a focus on health and beauty for women, and usually in Spanish; *TV Guide* is the exception in English.
- Newspapers—the *Chicago Sun Times* in English and *La Raza* and *El Diario*, local weeklies, in Spanish.
- Invitations printed especially for a formal event (and addressed and signed by hand), usually at the church—to baptisms; *quinceañeras,* which celebrate daughters turning 15; or special masses and parties that celebrate major birthdays such as the 50th.
- Letters—personal ones to and from Mexico are in Spanish; official ones from government agencies are usually in English, although deportation notices are printed in both languages; other official letters, e.g., from a school, are in Spanish or both languages.
- Documents, certificates, and other records—in both Spanish and English, depending primarily upon country of origin, Mexico or the United States.
- Books—those children use for their schoolwork (which are in English and Spanish, depending on whether the child is in bilingual education or in English-only classes) and those that are religious in nature, either for catechism class or more general purposes.

- Television—because the families have cable television, three of the several dozen channels are entirely in Spanish, so when print is displayed on the screen, which it frequently is, it is in Spanish as well.

In short, there is an abundance of print in the home environment, and much of it is in Spanish. This is not surprising, since these are immigrant families in which the parents were raised in Mexico; literacy artifacts printed in English are more common in the homes where there are other family members, especially teenagers or young adults, who are fluent in English (having been raised, if not born, in Chicago).

As should be clear from the above list, there is substantial literacy activity within the family/home domain in these Mexican families. Much of this activity is similar to that found in studies of other populations: rural working-class white and black families, as well as black and white middle-class townspeople in the southeast (Heath, 1983); white middle-class families in the northeast (Taylor, 1983); and black inner-city families in the northeast (Taylor & Dorsey-Gaines, 1988). I haven't, however, observed frequent literacy activity in the realm of literature (fiction and nonfiction books and poetry) that Taylor and Dorsey-Gaines (1988) describe among the inner-city black families they studied, or the reading and joint discussion of newspaper and other printed items that Heath (1983) describes for the rural black families she studied.

Within the Mexican families I have come to know, literacy is not viewed as something to be taken for granted, something that children will acquire naturally, in contrast to what Taylor (1983) found with her white, middle-class families (and, possibly, as can be inferred from the studies of black families by Heath and by Taylor and Dorsey-Gaines). Taylor's white, middle-class families, like those studied by Gundlach, McLane, Stott, and McNamee (1985), were even playful with literacy in their interactions with their children because they assumed all of their children would become literate, and it was not something they, the parents, needed to work on. While this no doubt doesn't characterize all middle-class parents (e.g., there are those who are so anxious about their children learning to read or write that it causes problems for the children in doing so), many working-class parents, depending on the state of schools in their neighborhoods, cannot take literacy for granted at all. McLane and

McNamee (1990), in fact, describe black inner-city mothers in Chicago who explicitly teach literacy skills to their children in an attempt to ensure that they become literate, with or without the public school.

Similarly, I have observed Mexican parents explicitly teaching literacy skills to their children. In one case, a mother held her youngest child (about 4 years old) on her lap, grasped his hand in hers, and carefully guided him in making the letters of the alphabet, one by one. Like the parents in Delgado-Gaitán's study (1989), these parents provide strong support for, and belief in, formal education, insisting children do homework before watching television or playing with other children. They also assist with the homework when they can, especially if it is in Spanish, from a child's bilingual education program. Another mother regularly insists that her children practice their multiplication tables, especially when I arrive, at which times she directs them to do whatever lesson I teach them. Clearly (being a *maestra*, or teacher), I am a resource that this mother doesn't want to waste. To oblige, I improvise writing lessons on the spot and do the best with mathematics that I can.

Although literacy is not always accompanied by schooling (Farr, 1989, in press; Scribner & Cole, 1981; Taylor & Dorsey-Gaines, 1988), it is generally seen in these Mexican families as connected to schooling; even those who learned it informally, or *liricamente*,[3] outside of school insist that it must be taught explicitly. It is not something one can learn oneself; one needs to learn from someone else who already knows the writing system, that is, the letters of the alphabet—usually someone who has learned them in school. Both literacy and schooling, then, are taken seriously and as something that cannot be taken for granted as developing in the natural course of events. In many of the lives of the adults in this network, schooling and literacy were privileges not afforded to everyone.

An illustration of the high regard these network members have for schooling was revealed during the first amnesty class we held in one family's home. (In exchange for their participation in our research, we offered to help them through the amnesty process.) I was struck by how serious and earnest everyone was; in a flurry of ardent activity, extra chairs were brought into the living room and lined up in rows, pencils were located and sharpened, notebooks readied, children quieted, and expectant faces turned toward the *maestros*. Most surprising to me was that everyone participated, including children of all ages, in spite of the fact that only the adults would undergo the amnesty process. Moreover, other adults in the network sometimes participated in our weekly class, even when they already had green cards. The message was clear: Schooling was very important, and one should use every opportunity to learn what one could.

Many of these adults had little opportunity during their childhoods in Mexico to go to school, often attending only a few years. Most of the older adult members (in their 30s and 40s), in fact, have had fewer than 5 or 6 years of formal schooling, all of which were in Mexico, in Spanish. A number of the middle-aged men from one particular village in Mexico had almost no formal schooling, yet are functionally literate in their current lives because they learned how to write outside of school, after migrating to the United States, in order to write letters back home (Farr, 1989, in press). Many of the younger adults (in their 20s) finished *secundaria* in Mexico (the equivalent of U.S. middle school); a common view in these families is that one doesn't go on to *preparatoria* (the equivalent of U.S. high school) unless one intends to go on to college or to a specific career.

Although these individuals would be counted in this country as dropouts because they have not graduated from the equivalent of U.S. high school, it is clear to me that they don't consider themselves dropouts. Moreover, their education has prepared them to meet many of the literacy demands in their lives, and network members more proficient in literacy help those who are less proficient with more demanding literacy tasks. Literacy, like other resources (e.g., knowledge of automobile repair or of health remedies) is shared. Other studies of Mexican social networks (Horowitz, 1983; Velez-Ibañez & Greenberg, 1989) have found a similarly extensive sharing of resources. Within these Chicago families, those who are more literate tend to be those who have had more schooling, and those who have had more schooling tend to be younger. The youngest generation (those in their teens and younger), having been raised almost entirely in Chicago, are finishing high school here, and some of them are going on to college or other schools. Proficiency in literacy, then, is primarily a matter of childhood opportunity, with a clear trend toward more literacy across the generations in these families.

Even the older adults in the network, regardless of the level of schooling they were able to reach, indicate a great deal of interest in some written texts. During a month I spent in the Mexican state of Michoacán with some of the family members on the *ranchos*[4] where they were born or grew up, I shared books I had located at El Colegio de Michoacán, nearby in Zamora. Many network members showed intense interest in two books in particular: *Más Allá de los Caminos: Los Rancheros del Potrero de Herrera* (*Far Beyond the Roads: The Rancheros of Potrero of Herrera*) by Esteban Barragán López (1990), and *La Villa de Tingüindin de Argandar* (*The Village of Tingüindin of Argandar*) by Ramón Pardo Pulido (1957).

The former, *Más Allá de los Caminos*, was recognized by some network members who had heard of it before. It is a study of *ranchos* in a nearby, more isolated area (the local *tierra caliente*, a hotter and drier region than their own, which is closer to the cooler sierra area of Michoacán, as well as closer to paved roads). One woman, in fact, pointed out the author (currently on the faculty at El Colegio de Michoacán) in one of the photographs in the book, saying he had grown up in one of the *ranchos* he studied. Another network member was so excited about the book that he began reading it immediately and finally agreed to my suggestion that he keep it awhile, to read at his leisure. When I left the *rancho* a week or so later, he offered to return the book to me, but I declined, having bought another copy for myself. Now my second copy is in demand by yet other families in the network; clearly, I could have given many copies of this book to interested people. Later I was told by various people that it was "an important book" because it had many important things to say about the people of the *tierra caliente*, who are reputed to be very tough *rancheros* (small landowners).

The second book that stirred great interest among network members was a local history of the municipality (Tingüindin) and its nearby *ranchos*, including their own. Before I located this book, one man had told me a story that had been handed down in his family about their ancestors from Spain; when I told him of the book, he asked for it (and for his daughter to get his reading glasses) and began reading immediately. I waited 45 minutes that evening at the kitchen table with him while he read. At one point he called my attention to a passage in the book that contained his family name, seeming to corroborate his family's story. Subsequently, there was so much interest in this book as well (I was unable to obtain another copy, as it is out of print) that I photocopied the entire book before leaving the *rancho*. Upon returning to Chicago, I encountered yet more interest in this book, like the other one.

Conclusion

In this chapter I have reviewed briefly the controversy surrounding the definition of literacy, a complex matter since literacy varies so from context to context. I also have discussed what is known about workplace literacy (not enough) in light of how it might inform attempts to define literacy. I have argued that the controversy over definition stems from the political implications inherent in any attempts at definition, concluding that it seems more sensible at this time to use the only universal definition of literacy, knowledge and use of a writing system, as a working definition. My own choice in doing so is further supported by the fact that this is the conception of literacy generally held by the members of the social network of Mexican families with whom I have been working.

These families, especially as a social network, have considerable expertise with literacy. They routinely handle literacy demands from a variety of domains in their lives. In this chapter I have provided descriptions of their literacy practices in one of these domains, that of the family/home. In the other four domains (church, commerce, the state, and the law), large public institutions that require the use of a writing system for their very existence regularly provide additional literacy demands—the church in a variety of religious events; factories and other businesses where network members work; large corporations (e.g., Tupperware), which sustain network members' small businesses; and finally, government agencies like the Immigration and Naturalization Service (INS) and the Internal Revenue Service (IRS).

Families in this network cope very well with the literacy demands confronting them, in spite of the fact that virtually all adult members have less than a high school education. Their preparation in literacy, from relatively scant formal schooling, has nonetheless enabled them to participate in modern urban life. From their point of view, life in Chicago may have its drawbacks (it's awfully cold in the winter, for one thing), but they are making more money here than they currently could in Mexico, and their lives are materially better than they would have been had they not migrated.

To say, however, that these family members are functioning well with the literacy demands in their lives is not to say that there is no interest among them in becoming more literate, that is, in reading or writing more extended texts and becoming more proficient and fluent with literacy, as is evident in their intense interest in the books I shared with them. Literacy programs that attempt to build on the interests of learners clearly could be effective with members of these families.

A number of scholars have worked to broaden traditional education, for both adults and children, by using information gathered (often through ethnographic research) in community and home contexts (Auberbach, 1989; Heath, 1983; Moll & Díaz, 1987; among others). Undoubtedly, these kinds of approaches would be appropriate and welcomed by the network members with whom I have been working, since they would encourage already expressed interest in literate texts particularly relevant to their lives.

A word of caution, however, is in order. First, a group's own perceptions of phenomena such as literacy cannot be ignored if a literacy program is to be effective. In this case, network members share a perception of literacy as something apart, as something generally linked to formal schooling, as a technology to learn for use in their own lives. This runs counter to many descriptions of literacy in the research literature, which focus on its humanistic, creative, or consciousness-raising aspects (e.g., Freire, 1973; Taylor & Dorsey-Gaines, 1988; Walsh, 1990). Such descriptions, in fact, parallel those used in other research literatures (e.g., literary criticism, ethnography of communication, even psychotherapy) as characteristic of human language itself, either oral or written. None of these descriptions, however (in a laudable attempt to avoid the restrictions of a limited skills-centered approach to literacy instruction), allow for an alternative conception of literacy as a valuable cultural technology (Coulmas, 1989; Sampson, 1985). Neither view of literacy, either as cultural technology or as humanistic discourse, is sufficient alone; rather, both are necessary for a fully adequate understanding of what literacy is and what it means to people.

A second caution involves an aspect of education that is troubling to many researchers: literacy instruction as a cultural invasion (Delgado-Gaitán, 1989). This danger is presumed to be avoided with an emphasis on Freirean dialogue with learners, a dialogue that draws out the life concerns of learners and organizes literacy learning around these concerns. True dialogue can be egalitarian, but, as Stotsky (1991) has argued, sometimes a teacher's political zeal can replace true dialogue with political consciousness raising along the lines of the teacher's beliefs. When this happens, it is cultural invasion as surely as when school discourse and linguistic practices are imposed on people (although in both cases resistance exists as well). Even in true dialogue, however, in which learning and change occur, a kind of cultural invasion transpires. That is, education involves change, and developing new ways of thinking, reading, and writing within a group is a significant change, one that by definition is culturally embedded. As long as we teach essayist literacy, then, we cannot avoid a type of cultural invasion (see Scollon & Scollon, 1981 for a clear explication of this point).

Nonetheless, if it is the learners' (or their parents') choice that such new linguistic and cognitive ways be learned, then, whether or not others believe—and argue quite convincingly—that these choices are constrained by external, structural factors, those choices should be respected. Not to respect them leads to a patronizing stance that certainly undermines the principle of true dialogue and can undercut effective learning as well (Gundlach, 1991).

As Walsh (1990) has pointed out, much of the rhetoric in the contemporary "literacy crisis" is, in fact, patronizing, at times even forthrightly denigrating. This rhetoric labels Mexican immigrants, among others, as illiterate even when they demonstrate functional literacy skills. Why should such people be deemed illiterate or even semiliterate because they don't read or write extended text in their (scant) leisure time, or for a living? They use literacy, and they use the critical thinking processes that people all over the world use, whether or not their languages have a writing system. They think critically in oral language, and they do so when dealing with the functional literacy demands of large institutions. The question is not whether a particular group of people can think (all human beings do); the question is whether or not they do a specific kind of thinking with written language that is characteristic of one discourse strand of Western civilization (Farr, 1993).

I would argue that most of the members of this social network don't currently practice such essayist literacy because it makes no sense in their lives to do so. There are exceptions, of course, in the younger generation, who are going to high school, college, and even graduate school; for these members of the network, practicing academic literacy does make sense in their lives. Those continuing beyond high school are making a choice for themselves, and academic literacy is a part of that choice. For most of the adults, however, there is little time in their hard-working lives for the reading of novels or for attendance in classes at night for long periods of time.

To call people semiliterate because they are doing what it makes sense to do in their own lives is to privilege a particular kind of literacy—essayist literacy. On the other hand, to define literacy so as to include oral language activities in totally nonliterate peoples makes no sense at all. I would argue, instead, that we (i.e., literacy researchers) use the only common definition of literacy that endures across cultures and throughout history—knowledge and use of a writing system—and grant that anyone who knows and uses written language adequately in their own lives is literate. This means, of course, that we must give up a (felt) position of superiority, either one of arrogance (we are fully literate; others are less so) or one that is patronizing (everyone is literate, either in oral or written language; or, we are literate and must save those who are not). A stance that seems to me to be more truly egalitarian allows for differences, for example, between literate and *non*literate, or among different kinds of literacy, like essayist and "form-filling" literacy, without privileging one kind as being superior in all contexts for all people. The literacy practices of the families I have come to know are neither to be pitied nor exalted; they are quite simply the active and energetic responses of a very resourceful group of people to the demands of a changing and challenging world. As Dinerman (1982) has noted:

> I regard rural agriculturalists and their decisions as neither politically ineffective nor inconsequential to the interests and decisions of more powerful groups. The decision of millions of persons from Mexico to migrate to the United States and to destinations within Mexico has forced these more powerful groups in both societies to take account of them. If it is true that peasants vote with their feet, and that their number now makes a deafening din, then in the broadest sense migration has surely become a political action. (p. 120)

Notes

[1] Many of the parents have remarked to me on various occasions that literacy is "easier" in Spanish than in English, since the Spanish alphabet matches spoken sounds more closely than English letters do; that is, you really can sound out printed words fairly accurately. In addition, I have observed both adults and children sounding out printed words in Spanish, syllable by syllable. In one incident, a young boy won an argument with his cousin over the writing of someone's name (and other words) because the cousin had left out crucial sounds, and thus letters.

[2] My colleague, Lucia Elías-Olivares, and I are grateful to the National Science Foundation, Linguistics Program, for providing a grant to support the first 1½ years of this study. Juan Guerra, a Ph.D. student of mine, worked as a co-ethnographer with us during that time. I am also grateful to the Spencer Foundation for providing a grant to fund another 2 years of the study through August 1992.

[3] The concept of "lyrical" learning (learning informally, orally, without books, about practical things) is shared throughout this social network and by their friends and relatives with whom I talked in Michoacán and Guanajuato. Farr (in press) discusses it more fully.

[4] I am very grateful to Gail Mummert and others at El Colegio de Michoacán for suggesting references to recent and ongoing studies of the region and for help in locating census data and a history of the area from which the social network discussed in this chapter originated.

References

Auberbach, E. (1989). Toward a social-contextual approach to family literacy. *Harvard Educational Review, 59*(2), 165-181.

Barragán López, E. (1990). *Más allá de los caminos: Los rancheros del Potrero de Herrera*. Zamora, Michoacán, México: El Colegio de Michoacán.

Bauman, R. (1977). *Verbal art as performance*. Prospect Heights, IL: Waveland.

Cintron, R. (1989). *Striving for literacy: Oral and written language acquisition among some mexicano families.* Unpublished doctoral dissertation, University of Illinois, Chicago.

Coulmas, F. (1989). *The writing systems of the world.* Cambridge, MA: Basil Blackwell.

Crandall, J. (1981). *A sociolinguistic investigation of the literacy demands of clerical workers.* Unpublished doctoral dissertation, Georgetown University, Washington, DC.

Delgado-Gaitán, C. (1989). Mexican adult literacy: New directions for immigrants. In S. Goldman & H. Trueba (Eds.), *Becoming literate in English as a second language* (pp. 9-32). Norwood, NJ: Ablex.

Diehl, W., & Mikulecky, L. (1980). The nature of reading at work. *Journal of Reading, 24,* 221-228.

Dinerman, I. (1982). *Migrants and stay-at-homes: A comparative study of rural migration from Michoacán, México.* La Jolla, CA: Center for U.S.-Mexican Studies.

Elías-Olivares, L. (1990, August). *Hablar con sinceridad: Variedad discursiva del español méxico-americano.* Paper presented at the international conference of ALFAL, Campinas, Brazil.

Farr, M. (1989, November). *Learning literacy lyrically: Informal education among mexicanos in Chicago.* Paper presented at the annual meeting of the American Anthropological Association, Washington, DC. (ERIC Document Reproduction Service No. ED 321 598)

Farr, M. (1993). Essayist literacy and other verbal performances. *Written Communication, 10*(1), 4-38.

Farr, M. (in press). *En los dos idiomas*: Literacy practices of *mexicano* families in Chicago. In B. Moss (Ed.), *Literacy across communities.* Cresskill, NJ: Hampton.

Farrell, T.J. (1983). IQ and standard English. *College Composition and Communication, 34,* 470-484.

Finnegan, R. (1988). *Literacy and orality.* New York: Blackwell.

Freire, P. (1973). *Education for critical consciousness.* New York: Continuum.

Gee, J. (1989). *What is literacy?* (Tech. Rep. No. 2). Cambridge, MA: Education Development Center, The Literacies Institute.

Goody, J. (1986). *The logic of writing and the organization of society*. New York: Cambridge University Press.

Goody, J. (1987a). *The domestication of the savage mind*. Cambridge: Cambridge University Press.

Goody, J. (1987b). *The interface of the written and the oral*. New York: Cambridge University Press.

Goody, J., & Watt, I. (1963). The consequences of literacy. *Comparative Studies in Society and History, 5*(3), 304-345.

Graff, H.J. (Ed.). (1981). *Literacy and social development in the West*. New York: Cambridge University Press.

Graff, H.J. (1986). *The legacies of literacy: Continuities and contradictions in Western culture and society*. Bloomington: Indiana University Press.

Graff, H.J. (1987). *The labyrinths of literacy: Reflections on literacy past and present*. London: Falmer.

Guerra, J. (1991). *The literacy practices of an extended Mexican immigrant family*. Unpublished doctoral dissertation, University of Illinois, Chicago.

Gundlach, R. (1991). What it means to be literate. In R. Beach, J. Green, M. Kamil, & T. Shanahan (Eds.), *Multidisciplinary perspectives on literacy research* (pp.365-372). Urbana, IL: National Council of Teachers of English.

Gundlach, R., Farr, M., & Cook-Gumperz, J. (1989). Writing and reading in the community. In A. Dyson (Ed.), *Writing and reading: Collaboration in the classroom?* (pp. 91-130). Urbana, IL: National Council of Teachers of English.

Gundlach, R., McLane, J., Stott, F., & McNamee, G. (1985). The social foundations of children's early writing development. In M. Farr (Ed.), *Advances in writing research: Children's early writing development* (pp. 1-58). Norwood, NJ: Ablex.

Hannerz, U. (1980). *Exploring the city: Inquiries toward an urban anthropology*. New York: Columbia University Press.

Heath, S.B. (1983). *Ways with words: Language, life and work in communities and classrooms*. New York: Cambridge University Press.

Heath, S.B. (1987). Foreword. In H. Graff, *Labyrinths of literacy* (pp. vii-ix). New York: Cambridge University Press.

Horowitz, R. (1983). *Honor and the American dream: Culture and identity in a Chicano community*. New Brunswick, NJ: Rutgers University Press.

Hymes, D. (1974). *Foundations in sociolinguistics*. Philadelphia: University of Pennsylvania Press.

Hymes, D. (1981). *In vain I tried to tell you: Essays in Native American ethnopoetics*. Philadelphia: University of Pennsylvania Press.

Jacob, E. (1982). Research on practical writing in business and industry. In L. Gentry (Ed.). *Research and instruction in practical writing* (pp. 37-50). Los Alamitos, CA: SWRL Educational Research and Development.

Johnson, W.E., & Packer, A.H. (1987). *Workforce 2000: Work and workers for the 21st century*. Indianapolis: Henson Institute.

Kirsch, I.S., & Jungeblut, A. (1986). *Literacy: Profiles of America's young adults*. Princeton, NJ: Educational Testing Service, National Assessment of Education Progress.

Levine, K. (1986). *The social context of literacy*. London: Routledge and Kegan Paul.

McLane, J., & McNamee, G. (1990). *Early literacy*. Cambridge, MA: Harvard University Press.

Mikulecky, L. (1982). Functional writing in the workplace. In L. Gentry (Ed.), *Research and instruction in practical writing* (pp. 51-72). Los Alamitos, CA: SWRL Educational Research and Development.

Miller, G. (1988). The challenge of universal literacy. *Science, 241*, 1293-1299.

Moll, L., & Díaz, S. (1987). Teaching writing as communication: The use of ethnographic findings in classroom practice. In D. Bloome (Ed.), *Literacy, language, and schooling* (pp. 193-221). Norwood, NJ: Ablex.

Olson, D. (1977). From utterance to text: The bias of language in speech and writing. *Harvard Educational Review, 41*, 257-281.

Ong, W.J. (1982). *Orality and literacy*. New York: Methuen.

Pardo Pulido, R. (1957). *La villa de Tingüindin de Argandar*. Zamora, Michoacán, México: Ramirus Vargas Cacho.

Sampson, G. (1985). *Writing systems: A linguistic introduction.* Stanford, CA: Stanford University Press.

Scollon, R., & Scollon, S.B. (1981). *Narrative, literacy and face in interethnic communication.* Norwood, NJ: Ablex.

Scribner, S., & Cole, M. (1981). *The psychology of literacy.* Cambridge, MA: Harvard University Press.

Shuman, A. (1986). *Storytelling rights: The uses of oral and written texts by urban adolescents.* New York: Cambridge University Press.

Stotsky, S. (1991). On literacy anthologies and adult education: A critical perspective. *College English, 52,* 916-923.

Street, B. (1984). *Literacy in theory and practice.* New York: Cambridge University Press.

Szwed, J. (1981). The ethnography of literacy. In M. Farr Whiteman (Ed.), *Variation in writing: Functional and linguistic-cultural differences* (pp. 13-23). Hillsdale, NJ: Erlbaum.

Tannen, D. (Ed.). (1982). *Spoken and written language: Exploring orality and literacy.* Norwood, NJ: Ablex.

Taylor, D. (1983). *Family literacy: Young children learning to read and write.* Portsmouth, NH: Heinemann.

Taylor, D., & Dorsey-Gaines, C. (1988). *Growing up literate: Learning from inner-city families.* Portsmouth, NH: Heinemann.

Vasquez, O. (1989). *Connecting oral language strategies to literacy: Ethnographic study among four Mexican immigrant families.* Unpublished doctoral dissertation, Stanford University, Stanford, CA.

Velez-Ibañez, C., & Greenberg, J. (1989, November). *Formation and transformation of funds of knowledge among U.S. Mexican households in the context of the borderlands.* Paper presented at the annual meeting of the American Anthropological Association, Washington, DC.

Walsh, C. (1990). Preface. In C. Walsh (Ed.), *Literacy as praxis: Culture, language, and pedagogy* (pp. 1-22). Norwood, NJ: Ablex.

Wilson, W.J. (1987). *The truly disadvantaged: The inner city, the underclass, and public policy.* Chicago: University of Chicago Press.

CHAPTER 5

Literacy and Second Language Learners: A Family Agenda

Gail Weinstein-Shr
San Francisco State University

Imagine this scenario. There is a people's revolution. Academics are all forced to leave the United States with our families. Somehow, we end up in Laos. Glad for our lives, we take what we can get. The only work available is in the lowland rice farms. Our academic training has not prepared us well. Because of flabby upper arms and inexperience, we plant slowly and get very low wages. We can only hope that things will get better when we learn some Lao, so we can get better jobs.

I imagine my daughter Hannah going to school. Of course, Lao is the language of instruction. There are times when she doesn't understand the school assignment. Neither do I. After long outdoor days, I am lucky to have a slot in overcrowded adult classes for LLP (limited-Lao-proficient) adults, where I learn the essential vocabulary of farm implements. Hannah hangs out with some Lao kids. She wants to fit in. Soon she talks to me in Lao. She teases that she doesn't understand English anymore.

What would I want for Hannah, for my husband, and for me in this new life? How could my adult classes and Hannah's school classes contribute to making that new life? What would any of us want? This paper is an attempt to explore that question.

I am grateful to the tutors and students at Project LEIF, through whom I learned about how the world looks through other eyes. And hugs to Hannah, who helped me learn about family issues in the first person.

Defining the Problem of School Perspective

Experience

> *I feel so bad for these kids. The parents don't come to parent-teacher conferences. I've never seen any at open house either. I don't think they really try to help the kids with school. I wonder—maybe in their culture, education isn't as important.*

(secondary school teacher in refugee concerns discussion group, TESOL, 1989)

The teacher quoted above does not know very much about the families or the communities of the children in her classroom. She only knows that they are poor. She does not have the time, she feels, or the adequate means to find out more.

> *I visit them (the Cambodians) in their homes. I explain why it's important for them to come. I even call them the night before to remind them. "Yes," they say. "I'm coming." Then, next morning, I wait, no one comes. So I call them.*

(U. Thiem, personal communication)

Thiem knows quite a bit about the families of the children she teaches. She is a native speaker of Khmer. Her commitment to helping Cambodian children succeed is reflected in the long hours she puts in and in her persistent (though often fruitless) efforts to convince parents to come to the school for parent events. Teachers and administrators are frustrated. The solution, it seems, is to help these parents to get involved and to provide them with the skills they need to do the kinds of things that the parents of successful school achievers do.

Research

The evidence is convincing. Educational research from several domains indicates the importance of parents in the school achievement of their children. Scholars of emergent literacy point to evidence that conceptual development happens during the earliest years in life (Teale & Sulzby, 1986), leading to emphasis on parents as the first teacher. Children's achievement in school has been demonstrated to be directly correlated with the mother's level of education (Sticht, 1988). In addition, it is clear that parent behaviors, such as ways of "scaffolding" or constructing conversations, ways of talking about pictures in books, ways of telling bedtime stories, and other ways of interacting around print, are important factors in predicting children's school achievement (Heath, 1982).

The impact of parents and home environment has also been a recent focus of scholars interested in language minority children. Attempts to understand school achievement have focused on early literacy and language at home (Cochran-Smith, 1984) and on other school-home differences (Cummins, 1981; Moll & Díaz, 1987). Results of these studies have been aimed at helping educators understand differences in order to sensitize teachers and to facilitate academic learning.

Practice

"Family literacy" is the response in practice for working with parents to improve the school achievement of children. Among the new intitiatives are the Barabara Bush Family Literacy Foundation, the Even Start Legislation, and the Family English Literacy Program of the Office of Bilingual Education and Minority Languages Affairs, which funds family literacy programs around the country.

One set of goals for family and intergenerational programs has been improving the school achievement of children by promoting parental involvement in their children's education. Programs aimed primarily at increasing parental involvement are constituted by activities that encourage or teach parents (a) to provide a home environment that supports children's learning needs; (b) to volunteer in the schools as aides or in other roles; (c) to monitor children's progress and communicate with school personnel; and (d) to tutor children at home to reinforce work done in school (Simich-Dudgeon, 1986).

A second set of goals often found in family literacy programs is "to improve skills, attitudes, values, and behaviors linked to reading" (Nickse, 1990, p. 5). Models that aim at these goals are often made up of a variety of reading activities. Some of these may involve teaching parents to imitate behaviors that occur in the homes of successful readers, such as reading aloud to children and asking them specific types of questions as they read. Parents of young children may practice in adult groups on books that they may then read to their children. This approach is possible for parents of very young children, who have some hope of learning enough English to be able to keep linguistically one step ahead of their children.

The Social Context of Literacy: Literacy and Everyday Lives

Over the past five years, I have had the opportunity to learn about the lives and the concerns of refugees and immigrants in Philadelphia through Project LEIF, Learning English through Intergenerational Friendship,[1] and more recently through work in the Cambodian community in western Massachusetts. The concerns of adults I have spoken with revolve around three themes: survival, communication, and power.

Survival

Soldiers come we run always run. I have my baby inside. I run. Baby come out I can't rest. My family we hear guns. I run with baby. When we not run baby dead. Five my children die from Khmer Rouge in my country.

(as told to Patrice Lopatin, a project LEIF tutor, 1990)

The stories of the Hmong, Khmer, and Vietnamese that I know reveal a common characteristic: These people are survivors. The families we have worked with made it here despite unbelievable odds, and they continue to use their survival resources to manage in difficult conditions with limited resources. The families we know have been ingenious in their strategies for dealing with problems.

Families divide the language and literacy labor. In one Cambodian home, the kids read the English mail, the mother reads Khmer letters aloud to the family, and the eldest daughter, who was able to get her license, has become the family driver. In several homes, every phone call is answered by two people—an adult native language speaker and a younger English speaker. The superfluous interlocutor then hangs up.

Adults without a history of literacy or of schooling have come up with some very creative strategies for supporting their children's education. Poor Khmer farmers in Cambodia often sacrificed their most valued resource by selling a parcel of their own farmland to send one child to school (Samien Nol, Director of the Cambodian Association of Philadelphia, personal communication). Likewise, in Philadelphia, many adults miss their own language classes to earn money from seasonal blueberry picking, but rarely pull their children from school for the same purpose (Andrew Atzert, Project LEIF tutor, personal communication). One Hmong family has separate hooks on the walls for their children's book bags and a study table in the common room that automatically gets priority for use for homework. The father attends clan meetings in Nebraska to discuss, among other things, strategies for supporting children's school success. One decision, for example, was for clan elders (most of whom are not themselves literate) in cities across the country to throw a party in which all children of the clan were given a quarter for every "A" received (Weinstein-Shr, 1992).

Our experience at Project LEIF confirms the research of others that refugees are excellent problem solvers. Like the native speakers of English that we learn about from Fingeret (1983), many refugees who have limited experience with print rely on social networks and their own wits to solve a wide variety of problems. When older adults were asked why they wanted to learn English, they rarely brought up survival concerns (Weinstein-Shr & Lewis, 1991). Rather, most reported that they wanted to learn English to be able to communicate with children or grandchildren. The second theme, then, is communication.

Communication

Cambodia was more fun. I had friends there, and they all spoke Khmer. We'd all talk about things, then we'd go get something to eat.

(S. Yi to A. Atzert, 1990)

This is the response of an elder Cambodian woman as translated by her grandson. She had just been asked what the difference was between Philadelphia's open air market and the market where she shopped in Cambodia. Atzert confesses that this was the first time he actually pictured his language-learning partner as the talkative, bubbly, competent, and sociable person that he now imagined from her answer.

For uprooted adults, there are important consequences of changes in the "communicative economy" (Hymes, 1974) when they enter a setting in which new codes (languages) as well as new channels (writing) are used. One Puerto Rican woman reports that she feels like an outsider in her own children's homes when her grandchildren speak English. A Hmong woman speaks of her fear that her grandchildren will not know what life was like in Laos, and that as their linguistic repertoire changes, she will have no way to tell them.

For parents of school-age children, the change in the communicative economy means that they often have to rely on children to decipher communications from school. One Cambodian man tearfully reported that his son had been expelled from school six months earlier. The boy left every morning at 8:00, returning at 4:00, so the man did not know about the expulsion until six months later when a neighbor told him. He had, until then, depended on the boy to decipher messages from school. This raises the third theme that repeatedly arises in the tales of our neighbors—the theme of power.

Power

I have ears but I am deaf! I have a tongue but I am mute!

(Chinese elder on life in his English-speaking neighborhood)

What happens when children are the translators, the decoders, the messengers for adults? One tutor noted in his log that he wondered who was in charge when he went to tutor his older Khmer partner and found heavy metal posters displayed in every room in the house. One Lao boy sabotages his mother's efforts to learn English; he disrupts her English lessons and repeatedly tells her that she is too stupid and too old to learn. Another tutor reports that when she calls her Vietnamese partner on the phone, the woman's son hovers on the line, as if English has become his domain to supervise and control. When this woman can't solve a problem, she lets it go unsolved rather than ask her children.

The issues of power have an important impact on issues of schooling. Several parents report their frustration that they are unable to help with homework. Many Asian parents we work with report their fear of looking stupid to their children. Even when kids are willing to be helpful, parents report their shame in having to depend on them.

The discomfort caused by power shifts in communication is as uncomfortable for children as it is for adults. When I asked Asian teens for advice to teachers, one response was particularly poignant— "Please, if I translate for you when you talk to my mother, don't look at me, look at her when you speak" (at Penn TESOL, 1989). This Chinese youth told us of his embarrassment when his own mother was marginalized and when he was treated like an authority in front of her.

These examples show that literacy events (Heath, 1983) and speech events (Hymes, 1974) can be structured in ways to ascribe roles that are empowered or powerless for the interlocutors. The consequences of shifts in power positions have consequences for all who are involved in the shift.

Redefining the Problem: A Family Perspective

If I were to find myself in Laos, I would certainly want my daughter Hannah to succeed in school. Her achievement would be one source of our concern and, hopefully, of our pride. However, that is not all that I would want. I would want her to see me as a competent and loving parent. Despite my limited Lao proficiency, I would want her to see me as a person with authority and with the wisdom of life experience. The way that she was taught in school could have a great impact on the degree to which this would be the case. Would teachers and resettlement workers tell Hannah to learn Lao as quickly as possible and ask us to stop using English in the home because it would be bad for her? Would Hannah have to tell her teacher with shame that she hadn't done her homework because we were unable (too ignorant or stupid) to help her? Would Hannah learn only Lao history, concluding indirectly that our past life in America had nothing to do with her and was thus of no use or consequence? If the goal were only to make Hannah into a successful student, to what degree could the mission succeed under these conditions? If it did, what would the price be for us and for Hannah?

I propose an educational agenda in which family strength and joyful interdependence is the goal, and where schooling is a variable with profound consequences for the prospects of realizing that goal. With a family agenda, the issues and questions shift.

Research

Educational research for a family agenda would explore issues of survival, communication, and power such as those in the three sets of questions posed below:

1. How do refugees, immigrants, or any families served by schools solve or fail to solve problems that require literacy skills? (This requires seeking to discover existing resources in addition to those that are lacking.)

2. What are the functions and uses of literacy (both native and second language) in the lives of people that are served? Who uses what language to whom and under what circumstances? What are the consequences of this particular communicative economy? What are the implications for home-school communications (including the *parents'* experience of those communications)?

3. What is the significance of language in the negotiation of new roles and relationships in a new setting? How have authority and power shifted in families? What is the role of language in intergenerational relationships? What are the ways in which schools influence the process in which these relationships are negotiated?

Experience

With a family agenda, teachers and administrators will continue to share their perspectives. However, channels will also be created for documenting the experiences of mothers, fathers, grandmothers, grandfathers, and children themselves about their lives in school and at home with one another.

Research like that of Twymon (1990) shows the price that parents can sometimes pay for taking on behaviors in the home to help their children do well in school. This research showed that when parent-child interaction became centered around school-like tasks such as the reenactment of reading lessons, the children initially did well in school. However, over time, children began to experience tension, anger, hostility, resistance, and alienation in their relationships at home (Willett & Bloome, 1993). Delgado-Gaitán (1987) provided another example in her documentation of the hopes and frustrations of Mexican parents who desperately want something better for their children. She demonstrated the ways that these adults provide supports within the limits of their resources in a system that does not tap into their potential for more substantial involvement.

The hopes and the frustrations of teachers and administrators are one part of the tale that needs to be told. However, parents' experiences with their children's schools and schooling, the experiences of elders as unique and irreplaceable sources of cultural transmission, and the experiences of children who make sense of the world through lived experiences at school and at home also need to be part of the story on the record that shapes research, decision-making, and policy.

Practice

Research on the experience of children and adults in families can inform practice that aims at supporting the educational achievement of children without undermining the family as a crucial resource for making sense of a new life in a new setting. The Foxfire experiment provided a strong sense of the possibilities for enabling children to strengthen their literacy skills while documenting and valuing the collective knowledge and experience of their families and communities (Wigginton, 1985). In this project, children from the hills of Appalachia collected recipes, folktales, instructions for making banjos, and so forth, by interviewing elders and creating documents that would preserve this information for their future children and their children's children. Innovative educators are beginning to rediscover the power of acknowledging these resources. Navajo parents who are unable to read in any language are often wonderful storytellers who can captivate their children with tales, and who can listen to their children tell or read stories (Gray & Murphy, 1986). Latino adults in the Pajaro Valley have become more interested in learning to read and in sharing literacy experiences with their children because of an emphasis on Spanish literature in addition to English (Ada, 1988).

When schools can capitalize on these resources, literacy skills are developed and relationships are nurtured in synergy. As emphasis is placed on what can be done and what can be shared rather than on what isn't done or what isn't shared, children and adults can develop ways of being together in which they both stretch, learn, and profit from one another. One experiment showed that children who read to their parents improved their reading skills as much as a control group who received equal hours of academic tutoring in reading (Tizard, Schofield, & Hewison, 1982). If I were in Laos, I would imagine feeling pretty foolish trying to struggle through a Lao story, with Hannah looking on in contempt. But I can imagine listening with pleasure as Hannah read proudly to me!

While steps have been taken to use insight into the family for improving school achievement, the next logical step is to use knowledge of schooling and learning processes to strengthen families and communities as resources for their members. With a family perspective, the consequences of educational practice will be measured not only by achievement test scores, but also by measures of success for families and communities as sources of cooperative problem solving, mutual support for learning, and respect for the resources of the generations. With the challenges that our children will face for solving global problems, teamwork and cooperation between the generations are our best hope.

Note

¹ Project LEIF, Learning English through Intergenerational Friendship, is a model program developed at Temple University Institute on Aging's Center for Intergenerational Learning. Through Project LEIF, over 1,000 college-age volunteers have been trained to tutor English as a second language (ESL) to elder refugees and immigrants at community centers throughout the city; these include a Cambodian Buddhist temple, a Chinese community center, a Latino senior center, and a multicultural neighborhood center. For information about Project LEIF, see Weinstein-Shr, 1989.

References

Ada, A.F. (1988). The Pajaro Valley experience: Working with Spanish-speaking parents to develop children's reading and writing skills in the home through the use of children's literature. In T. Skutnabb-Kangas & J. Cummins (Eds.), *Minority education: From shame to struggle* (pp. 223-238). Philadelphia: Multilingual Matters.

Cochran-Smith, M. (1984). *The making of a reader.* Norwood, NJ: Ablex.

Cummins, J. (1981). The role of primary language development in promoting educational success for language minority students. In *Schooling and language minority students: A theoretical framework* (pp. 3-50). Los Angeles: California State University, Evaluation, Dissemination, and Assessment Center.

Delgado-Gaitán, C. (1987). Mexican adult literacy: New directions for immigrants. In S.R. Goldman & H. Trueba (Eds.), *Becoming literate in English as a second language* (pp. 9-32). Norwood, NJ: Ablex.

Fingeret, A. (1983). Social network: A new perspective on independence and illiterate adults. *Adult Education Quarterly, 33*, 133-146.

Gray, V.M., & Murphy, B. (1986). *Report on the Navajo parent-child reading program at the Chinle Primary School.* Chinle, AZ: Chinle School District.

Heath, S.B. (1982.) What no bedtime story means: Narrative skills at home and at school. *Language in Society, 2*(2), 49-76.

Heath, S.B. (1983). *Ways with words.* New York: Cambridge University Press.

Hymes, D. (1974). *Foundations of sociolinguistics: An ethnographic approach* (pp. 3-28). Philadelphia: University of Pennsylvania Press.

Moll, L., & Díaz, R. (1987). Teaching writing as communication: The use of ethnographic findings in classroom practice. In D. Bloome (Ed.), *Literacy and schooling* (pp. 195-222). Norwood, NJ: Ablex.

Nickse, R. (1990). Foreword. In C. McIvor (Ed.), *Family literacy in action: A survey of successful programs* (pp. 4-5). Syracuse: New Readers Press.

Simich-Dudgeon, C. (1986). *Parent involvement and the education of limited English proficient students. ERIC Digest.* Washington, DC: ERIC Clearinghouse on Languages and Linguistics. (ERIC Document Reproduction Service No. ED 279 205)

Sticht, T.G. (1988). Adult literacy education. In E. Roth (Ed.), *Review of research in education 1988-89* (pp. 59-96). Washington, DC: American Educational Research Association.

Teale, W., & Sulzby, E. (Eds.). (1986). *Emergent literacy: Writing and reading.* Norwood, NJ: Ablex.

Tizard, J., Schofield, W., & Hewison, J. (1982). Symposium: Reading collaboration between teachers and parents in assisting children's reading. *British Journal of Educational Psychology, 5*(1), 1-15.

Twymon, S. (1990). *Early reading and writing instruction in the homes and schools of three five-year-old children from black working class families.* Unpublished doctoral dissertation, University of Michigan, Ann Arbor.

Weinstein-Shr, G. (1989). Breaking the linguistic and social isolation of refugee elders. *TESOL News, 13*(5), 9, 17.

Weinstein-Shr, G. (1992). Literacy and social process: A community in transition. In B. Street (Ed.), *Cross-cultural approaches to literacy* (pp. 279-293). Cambridge: Cambridge University Press.

Weinstein-Shr, G., & Lewis, N. (1991). Language, literacy, and the older refugee in America: Research agenda for the nineties. *College ESL, 1*(1), 53-65.

Wigginton, E. (1985). *Sometimes a shining moment: The Foxfire experience*. Garden City, NY: Anchor Press/Doubleday.

Willett, J., & Bloome, D. (1993). Literacy, language, school and community: A community-centered view. In A. Carrasquillo & C. Hedley (Eds.), *Whole language and the bilingual learner* (pp. 35-57). Norwood, NJ: Ablex.

CHAPTER 6

¿*Guariyusei?* Adult Biliteracy in Its Natural Habitat

Tomás Mario Kalmar
Lesley College
Cambridge, Massachusetts

> *One often forgets that the translator is a frontiersman in more than one sense: He creates the very frontier over which he brings his booty. He is like a ferryman whose boat turns the wild beyond of the barbarous babble into the "other" bank.*

(Illich & Sanders, 1988, p. 52)

The neologism *adult biliteracy* was coined to give value to a topic of public discourse that seems to want legitimacy. You always risk halving rather than doubling the legitimacy of anything when you add *bi* to it. As Tove Skuttnabb-Kangas (1983) says:

> Those who are bi-something are the ones without power: minorities, women, blacks, working class, those who have become bi-something in order to survive. The ones who rule us, white middle class males from the majority groups, have never been forced to look at things from somebody else's perspective. If they are to have the slightest chance to understand anything, they must have mediators, people with whom they in some respects can identify because they share the same cultures, languages, and people. The group who could function as mediators are the migrants—if we gave them a chance. (pp. 326-327)

Philip Bouwsma taught me to look closely at the actual letters, Rip Keller to listen closely to the actual sounds. Hanna Arlene Fingeret taught me to pay close attention to the logic, rhetoric, and irony of my argument, Bridget Suarez O'Hagin to pay close attention to *la primera voz*. My heartfelt thanks to Philip, Rip, Hanna, and Bridget for their invaluable help.

123

In the United States, *native language literacy* and *bilingual education* put together do not enjoy even half the legitimacy of *adult literacy*. Hence, it seems to some of us worth trying to legitimize the value of *adult biliteracy*. (See, e.g., the *Language Policy Recommendation* of the Literacy Network's 1989 National Forum on Literacy Issues and Policy, reprinted in Kalmar, 1990.) For some, adult biliteracy can never be more than "real" literacy minus native literacy; the subtractive paradigm. For others, adult biliteracy is at least "literacy times two"—the additive paradigm. And for those of us who are ourselves biliterate, adult biliteracy is often experienced as a field of complex variables rather than scalar quantities, biliteracy as "literacy squared"—a multiplicative or even a transcendental paradigm.

To complement the perspective of other chapters in this volume, I offer a sort of parable of the laborers in the vineyard from the Bible (Matthew 20:1-16), a case history of adult biliteracy, not in the publicly funded urban classroom, but in its natural habitat, the no-man's-land between two languages, two orthographies, two economies. Theorizing around a single document (the *Cobden Glossary*, Exhibit B below), I propose to investigate what it would mean to circumscribe adult biliteracy as a legitimate field of academic inquiry and cast it in a theoretical mold.

The Idea of an International Phonetic Alphabet

The paradigm shift that transformed 19th-century philology into 20th-century linguistics is commonly perceived as a Copernican revolution which put script into orbit as a satellite governed by the primacy of speech. As a corollary, the 19th-century question of how two scripts may rotate around each other becomes, for 20th-century linguistics, a mere epiphenomenon, since all scripts may, in principle, be mapped onto one canonical script, represented by the IPA, the International Phonetic Alphabet.

The IPA could reasonably be described as the scientific canonization of what was already functioning as an international phonetic alphabet. The IPA is but the Roman alphabet "writ large." But the Roman is the Greek alphabet writ large, the Greek is the Phoenician alphabet writ large, and so on. Start with present-day Roman, Cyrillic, Arabic, or Devanagari alphabets, each of which has spread and bifurcated from language to language, and go back upstream to their common origin, to the "unique and once-and-for-all-invention" (Illich, 1987, p. 10), and in each generation of the genealogy you find that right from the start every alphabet is always already saturated with biliteracy. A homogeneous speech community of competent but monoglot native speakers, as envisioned in the enabling fiction of 20th-century linguistics, would have no need for, and no idea of, a phonetic transcription. The protoCanaanite script, ancestor of all phonetic alphabets now used around the world, was itself a strategic political and economic response to heteroglossia, a heterography rather than an orthography. (For a detailed, linguistically informed account of the way adult biliterates have ferried each alphabet over from one language to the next, see Coulmas, 1989.)

Each expansion of the domain of an existing orthography to take possession of new linguistic facts nourishes and is nourished by the idea of an international or universal phonetic alphabet. What is of interest here is the intellectual labor—the conscious, biliterate, adult labor—that must be invested in producing and reproducing a single orthography fit to serve two tongues. The theoretical vision of the IPA, of a language-free generic orthography, is best regarded as a guiding fiction. In practice, in the real world, language-specific values must always enter into an exchange, favorable or unfavorable, with educational, social, political, and economic values. It is this trade-off between values that my parable seeks to illuminate.

A Kind of Algebraic Notation

The canonical status of an institutionalized International Phonetic Alphabet need not prevent us from seeing it as "an alphabet among the alphabets."

The pretence that one is being presented with a description strictly of spoken language begins to wear thin as soon as it occurs to the reader that the real discovery procedure being employed is invariably: "Assume that standard orthography identifies all the relevant distinctions, until you are forced to assume otherwise." It is as if the two basic principles of geographical surveying were taken to be (1) that an existing map is always accurate until it is proved inaccurate, and (2) that no existing map can be totally inaccurate. The consequence of these two principles would be that the surveyor should never start from scratch making a new map of an area already charted, but make only the minimum adjustments to the existing map. This corresponds roughly to the rule of thumb modern linguistics has adopted, whereby an existing orthographic map is made wherever possible to serve as a guide to the topography of speech. (Harris, 1980, p. 9)

Harris's metaphor illuminates every biliterate generation in the genealogy of all actually existing alphabets including the IPA. Coulmas (1989) has shown, in greater linguistic detail than some might have realized necessary, how the creation of every practical orthography is always a variation on the topographical theme articulated by Harris. Coulmas's account ends, however, at the birth of the IPA, which he has no need to include among the (practical) scripts of the world. To sketch out, for present purposes, what such a coda or postscript to Coulmas might look like, it will suffice to focus on the pivotal work of Henry Sweet, the advocate of Broad Romic, which in turn begat the IPA.

Henry Sweet (1845-1912), who "taught phonetics to Europe" (Wrenn, 1946, 1967, p. 154; Howatt, 1984, p. 181), is today best known through his reincarnation as Henry Higgins in Shaw's *Pygmalion* (1941). The original Henry Sweet was a meticulous historian of European speech sounds who understood that the letter killeth but the spirit giveth life. The sounds of speech, which he could discriminate and notate in the minutest detail, were to him always alive with human breathing. He could hear the speech sounds of 9th-century Europe as vividly and precisely as those of 19th-century Europe. In order to write down the history of English speech sounds, he first developed a normalized orthography for the 9th-century West Saxon speech of King Alfred the Great, preserved in surviving 9th-century manuscripts, and then systematically expanded this into a generic orthography for all speech sounds. The generic orthography he called Romic, to distinguish it from Glossic, a rival orthography proposed by his colleague Ellis.

Letter by letter, phoneme by phoneme, language by language, Sweet hammered out his claim that Glossic, which assigned English values to Roman letters, was less useful than Romic, which restored the Roman alphabet's Continental or Late Latin values, the phonemes of what Whorf was to call Standard Average European (Whorf, 1941). Both Glossic and Romic were designed to lower illiteracy through rational spelling reform. Glossic was an early version of today's phonics, an essentially monolingual reform. Romic was essentially biliterate.

Sweet was an energetic phonetic enthusiast (Shaw, 1941). Only prejudice and sloth could favor the barbaric system of traditional spelling:

There can, of course, be no doubt that in the end truth and reason will triumph over those arch-enemies of progress, prejudice and sloth, and it is certain that the longer reform is delayed, the more sweeping it will be when it comes. (Wyld, 1913, pp. 87-88)

He was sure that social inequities would be reduced if everyone spelled English in Romic, not Glossic. He therefore distinguished between a Narrow and a Broad version of Romic: Narrow Romic as a scientifically accurate system for professional linguists, Broad Romic as a practical orthography for the laity.

Although the neologism *phoneme* was actually coined by Sweet's East European contemporary Baudouin de Courtenay (see Wrenn, 1967), what it circumscribes was the controlling principle of all Sweet's work, and especially of his distinction between Narrow and Broad speech transcription: between *phonetic* and *phonemic* analysis. "It will be observed that I use the less accurate 'Broad Romic' as *a kind of algebraic notation* [italics added], each letter representing a group of similar sounds" (Sweet, 1888, p. x; see also Wrenn, 1946, 1967, p. 159). Broad Romic letters represent not constants but variables. The algebraic structure of Broad Romic is invoked by saying, in effect: Let there be a one-to-one correspondence between the set of letters {a,b,c, ...} and the segments of speech such that each letter is mapped onto a group of segments which differ from the viewpoint of phonetic taxonomy but which share a single phonological *function*. (This formulation draws on Abercrombie, 1967.)

The mathematization of the phoneme, now thoroughly elaborated by Soviet and East European linguists (see Kortlandt, 1972), began as a formalization of the chain of biliterate transformations which brought us the Roman alphabet in the first place. "The important part of phoneme theory is that two segments may be in complementary distribution in one language, but in parallel distribution in another" (Abercrombie, 1967, p. 87). Sweet's Broad Romic initiated the paradigm shift that Saussure completed: the algebraic axiomatization of the generic vernacular.

But in the 20th century, Broad Romic has forked into (a) the International Phonetic Alphabet used by pure and applied linguists to meet their own professional biliteracy needs and (b) the large family of practical orthographies designed and disseminated by Christian missionaries to meet the biliteracy needs of "Bible-less natives" speaking unwritten tongues.

What Henry Sweet meant by "a kind of algebraic notation" can be illustrated by scrutinizing the following two documents.

Exhibit A

PEDES	FOOZI
FIGIDO	LEPARA
PULLI	HONIR
PULCINS	HONCHLI
CALLUS	HANO
GALINA	HANIN
PRIDIAS	UUANTI
MUFFLAS	HANTSCOH
IMPLENUS EST FOL	IST
MANNEIRAS	PARTA
MARTEL	HAMAR
PUTICLA	FLASCA
FIDELLI	CHALPIR
FOMERAS	UUAGANSO
RADI MEO PARBA	SKIR MINAN PART

AHORITA REGRESO	AVIVAK
VOLVER	CAMVAK
DEMASIADO	TUMACH
MUCHO	MACH
DEJAME VER	LIMISI
YO NO SE	AIDONO
QUE DICE USTED	GUARIYUSEI
ROTO	BROUKEN
TENGO	AIJEF
DEME	GIMI
NO AY	NODER
POQUITO	LRERO
EL	JIT
ALEGRE	JAPI
POBRE	POR
ALGUNAS	SAM
VECES	TAIMS
ALGUNA COSA	ENI TENK
FIESTA	PARI/PARTI
SIESTA	NEP
CUANTO	JAMACH
GANAS	DU YOU ORN
NECESITO	AI NID
AIRE	SAM ER
COMPROMETIDO	ENGEICH(D)
YO FUI	AI GUENT
AL PUEBLO	TU TAON
PODEMOS IR	GUIQUEN GOU
AHORA	NAU
NO PODEMOS IR	GUIKENT GOU

Artificial and Natural Contexts for Adult Biliteracy

In the United States, adult biliteracy is entangled in a host of controversial pedagogical, social, political, and economic issues (Kalmar, 1988a, 1988b, 1988c, 1992). Precisely because Exhibits A and B can be regarded as pure texts with no context (other than each other), they function effectively as catalysts in workshops designed to help educators talk to one another about the transfer of literacy from language to language and from the classroom to the community.

In some workshops I use Exhibit A as an icebreaker and then introduce Exhibit B. In others I use just Exhibit B. Experience has taught me to expect an interesting difference in the group dynamics set in motion by these alternative opening moves, a difference in how the ice breaks, what people do to make sense out of the text, what they bring to the task, what contexts they imagine, what contexts they recreate for themselves, and, above all, the range of negative and positive *feelings* people express toward the use of Broad Romic to transcribe English speech sounds in the classroom and the community.

Responses to Exhibit A

When I begin a workshop by inviting participants to see what sense they can make out of Exhibit A and to note the strategies they come up with in the process, the first phase usually lasts a couple of minutes. During this phase individuals tend to stare at the document, silent and alone. (This phase reproduces in microcosm the habitat of individual students reading in a generic classroom.)

After a couple of minutes of silence, people start declaring that the text makes no sense whatever. They want to know who wrote it, what use it is, what language it's in, *where it comes from.* The tension that builds up is invariably resolved when small groups start forming to share their frustrations, pool their insights, and make sense of things. (This second phase reproduces in microcosm the natural habitat of a community of scholars, especially 19th-century philologists collaborating on the joint interpretation of a newly discovered text.)

It has never taken the small groups more than about 15 minutes to convince one another that

- Exhibit A is some sort of dictionary;
- The left-hand column records some sort of Romance language;
- The right-hand column records some sort of Germanic language;
- The words appear simultaneously in Romance and Germanic.

Many groups guess (correctly) the meaning of at least some words in the list (e.g., MARTEL = HAMAR = *hammer*) and quite a few guess (again correctly) that the document is an authentic early medieval European text.

The discussions that result always identify as a critical turning point in the small group dynamics the moment when people start listening to one another read aloud various items in the text. (This moment reproduces in microcosm the moment when philologists give voice to hitherto dead languages.) For it is only after people hear rather than read silently the speech sounds represented by, for example, CALLUS and GALINA, HANO and HANIN, that they make the connection with what they already know and exclaim, "Aha! GALINA is the feminine of CALLUS. It's gotta be *hen*." And then someone else will exclaim, "Aha! So HANIN is the feminine of HANO," and someone will butt in, "I get it! They're the same thing, they're both *hen*."

The interesting point, for present purposes, is that my workshop participants by no means claim to be pronouncing the words in question correctly. The precise allophones or speech-segments that would have been used by native speakers of the languages in question remain unknown. But this doesn't matter. Near enough turns out to be good enough. Which goes to show that a knowledge of Broad Romic as a kind of algebraic notation is, in some nontrivial sense, part of our common culture today, at least among the kind of people who attend my kind of workshops.

Only through speculation can we reconstruct the environment in which Exhibit A was originally produced. It does indeed come from an authentic early medieval European document, the unique 9th-century manuscript known to philologists as the *Kassel Glossary* (Elcock, 1960; Marchot, 1895; Titz, 1923). The hermeneutic strategies spontaneously simulated in microcosm by the small groups in my workshops are the ones used by 19th-century philologists who imagined the manuscript being written in a small community at the margins of the former Roman Empire, where illiterate speakers of two different languages joined in some sort of give and take. The Barbarians spoke a vernacular now identified as Old Bavarian. The Romans spoke something now identified as between Late Vulgar Latin and Early Protoromance. (For an engaging and illuminating account of the interplay between Germanic and Romance languages and literacies in 9th-century Europe, see Illich & Sanders, 1988.) Philologists of Sweet's calibre could prove that it was not the Romans but the Barbarians who decided to broaden the Roman alphabet with its Late Latin values into a biliterate phonetic transcription system in order to map words spoken by one group onto words spoken by the other. The unvoicing of initial voiced consonants (e.g., GALLUS > CALLUS or BARBA > PARBA), which sounds like Romance spoken with a thick German accent, actually represents how the Barbarians heard what the Romans said. The unvoiced phoneme is in the ear of the scribe, not the mouth of the speaker.

Exhibit A is therefore a specimen of adult biliteracy in its natural habitat, and if we can read it today, it is thanks to the continuity of naive or popular Broad Romic from the 9th century to the present.

From A to B

Small groups that have cut their teeth on Exhibit A and are then shown Exhibit B usually burst out laughing. But not everyone gets the joke. As the shock of recognition spreads, the small groups rapidly decide, collectively, that A and B are variations on a common genre, that

- B is some sort of dictionary;
- The left-hand column records a Romance language, namely Spanish;
- The right hand column records a Germanic language, namely English; and
- The same word appears in both Spanish and English.

The laughter is provoked, I believe, by experiencing the transvaluation of the *Container and the Thing Contained*, an inversion of legitimized hierarchies. For some people this is no joke (Cottom, 1989). The sight of actual English vernacular speech-sounds transcribed in a version of Broad Romic, which would have warmed the heart of Henry Sweet, seems to be particularly disturbing to educators who earn their living as professional gatekeepers of traditional English literacy. So while some laugh, others frown.

Responses to Exhibit B

When, on the other hand, I begin a workshop by inviting participants to see what sense they can make out of Exhibit B, the results are far more dramatic. It is as if opening the workshop with Exhibit A releases a sort of disinfectant, in the absence of which Exhibit B strikes many people as pathological. Those who frown are offended by those who laugh. Since the frowners tend to be monolingual English speakers while the laughers tend to be biliterate Latinos, the dialectic is usually mediated by broad-minded English speakers who respect the Spanish language. This results in a ritual drama of strong and contradictory feelings, attitudes, ideologies, definitions, and re-definitions of linguistic, pedagogic, social, political, and economic values. What this reproduces in microcosm is the ritual drama of communities struggling to cope with communicating in a situation where separate ethnolinguistic groups do not speak or understand each other's languages.

In equating "dramatic" with "dialectic," we automatically have also our perspective for the analysis of history, which is a "dramatic" process, involving dialectical oppositions. And if we keep this always in mind, we are reminded that every document bequeathed us by history must be treated as a *strategy for encompassing a situation*. (Burke, 1973, p. 109)

Whether Exhibit B is a good or a bad strategy for encompassing a situation depends, of course, on who gets to define the situation in question. Biliterate Latinos call it good. The situation they imagine (and try to recreate in my workshops) is not the ESL classroom. It is a diglossic community on the margins of literacy, very much like the medieval community imagined by philologists as the natural habitat of the *Kassel Glossary*, Exhibit A—in short, a community in which people who speak different tongues are engaged in the give-and-take of everyday life and are trying to make speech-sounds intelligible to one another. Exhibit B records—with wit, logic, and panache—what gringos really sound like to monolingual Spanish speakers.

Let's take LRERO, for example. Monolingual English speakers need considerable phonetic instruction before they can be persuaded that LRERO is English. To them it is "obviously Spanish." ERO is a Spanish, not an English, ending. And no English word could possibly begin with the strange-looking LR. (Actually, nor could any Spanish word. But this they don't realize, not knowing Spanish.) The beauty that biliterates see in words like LRERO is inevitably inaudible to monoliterates. *Little* is a poor guide to the way the English word is pronounced with a Southern twang. The traditional dialect spelling *li'l* is not much better, since the one letter *l* represents two very different speech-sounds. Coupling the Roman letters L and R (with their Spanish values) records to a large extent the way the tongue really moves in pronouncing the initial *l* of *li'l*. ERO captures beautifully the vowels, the intonation, and the rhythm of the word as actually spoken by Southerners. The mathematical elegance of Exhibit B is evident only to those who have themselves tried to use the Roman alphabet as a kind of algebraic notation in Henry Sweet's sense.

The frowners in my workshops are ESL teachers who assume (quite mistakenly) that Exhibit B was written by ESL students, in an ESL classroom, under the authority of a legitimate ESL teacher like themselves. They imagine (and try to reproduce in my workshops) a situation in which Exhibit B is, at best, a dubious strategy and, at worst, no strategy at all. "I'd never be allowed to let my students get away with this sort of thing," is a typical response. "This isn't English, it isn't Spanish, it's nothing, it's worse than nothing, it's not bilingual, it's zero-lingual," is another. The most negative feelings are those directed at me personally: "You are condemning these people to second-class citizenship."

"These people" are all too familiar to ESL teachers in publicly funded programs. They are the adult speakers of minority languages, especially Spanish, who "can't even write their own language" (de Tal, 1988). They are the target population referred to in some adult literacy circles as "zero-zero people"—zero English, zero literacy (Kalmar, 1988a, 1992). Meeting their needs has always been a nagging headache to overworked, underpaid part-time ESL and Adult Basic Education (ABE) teachers throughout the United States. The headache won't go away; it's getting worse. Thanks to the 1986 Immigration Reform and Control Act amnesty program, formerly illegal aliens are raising the percentage of "zero-zero people" enrolling in publicly funded programs. In this context, Exhibit B looks like the cause of the headache, not the cure for it.

Caught in the middle are the progressive ESL teachers who want to empower their students by problem-posing in the ESL classroom. The situation they imagine (and try to recreate in my workshops) is that of a community-based learning environment that simulates the conflicts of languages and cultures in the real world, a classroom in which, under certain circumstances, they may permit their students to talk to one another in languages other than English. The native language phonics or invented spellings on the right hand side of Exhibit B strikes these teachers as an attractive solution to a recalcitrant problem—how to move people from native language literacy to ESL literacy. I have demonstrated elsewhere (Kalmar, 1988a) that this is a problem posed by administrators and funding sources, not by students.

What this group reproduces in microcosm can be illustrated by Nina Wallerstein's ground-breaking book, *Language and Culture in Conflict: Problem-Posing in the ESL Classroom* (1983). Wallerstein cites items taken from Exhibit B as examples of a teaching technique that she calls "eye dialect." For her, such words as JUARUYUSEI [sic], LIMISI, and JAMACH are not English. They are "eye dialect." They require a teacher to translate them into English. (Note that JUARUYUSEI must be Wallerstein's misreading of either JAURUYUSEI = *how do you say* or GUARIYUSEI = *whaddayasay*. See Kalmar, 1983, pp. 37, 94). This technique, which she says "excited students to learn as they eagerly compiled a daily dictionary of phrases they wanted to know," solves the problem of teachers who "may often wonder what students are trying to say or write" (Wallerstein, 1983, p. 37).

Wallerstein goes on to suggest how teachers true to a Freirean approach might experiment with the effectiveness of this technique in their own classrooms, "although the underlying linguistic assumptions for this new method are not clear yet" (p. 38). The above pages have demonstrated, however, that Exhibit B shares with the *Kassel Glossary* (Exhibit A) a biliterate strategy for encompassing a diglossic situation, which, far from being a new method, is as old as the alphabet itself, a strategy whose underlying linguistic assumptions were made abundantly clear a hundred years ago by the "founding genius of applied linguistics," Henry Sweet himself (Howatt, 1984, p. 181).

Exhibit B in Its Natural Habitat: Biliteracy in Cobden, Illinois

I have no quarrel with the problem-posing method. However, who poses the problem? Who decides whether the problem has been solved? And, above all, is the problem posed in the ESL classroom by a publicly funded teacher or in its natural habitat by a community free to assemble and speak in a diversity of human tongues and voices? It is a Christian question (The Bible, 1 Corinthians 14; Kalmar, 1983); it is also a Marxist question (Giroux, 1988; Kalmar, 1974; Mackie, 1981).

The angle of vision of a professional ESL teacher seems to render occult what from a different perspective appears obvious. This, I think, is the controlling paradox of discourse on adult biliteracy in the United States today. As mentioned above, the idea of Broad Romic is, in a nontrivial sense, part of common culture. It was at the very center of the language teachers' reform movement led by Henry Sweet (Howatt, 1984). Why it is nonetheless occult to ESL teachers is an interesting sociology-of-knowledge question worth pursuing elsewhere. Here, however, I concentrate on the even more interesting question of how this obvious or occult idea was invented, reinvented, or inherited by the original authors of Exhibit B.

Just as the text displayed in Exhibit A is copied from an authentic 9th-century manuscript, so that in Exhibit B is copied from a 20th-century manuscript, which I have hitherto (Kalmar, 1983) called *el diccionario mojado* (*mojado* = wetback, illegal alien, undocumented worker, zero-zero, second-class citizen) but which, from now on, I will refer to as the *Cobden Glossary*, because it is so like the *Kassel Glossary*.

Cobden, Illinois, the natural habitat of the *Cobden Glossary*, is a tiny rural community consisting of "a thousand people and two thousand Mexicans" (to quote the local phraseology). In 1980, the "people" spoke no Spanish, the Mexicans no English. To encompass this situation, the strategy embodied in the *Cobden Glossary* was collectively conceived and put into practice by a group of undocumented Mexican migrant workers, most of whom were Tarascan Indians from Cherán, Michoacán.

Between 1978 and 1982, I lived and worked among the original authors of the glossary, of which Exhibit B is a sample. In 1980, I witnessed them composing biliterate texts; I saw and heard them transcribing the speech of their neighbors, and I compiled field notes.

Between 1980 and 1982, I reproduced samples of these texts and field notes in a series of 10 working papers. These circulated through a national network for Hispanic adult education programs. In 1983, Alfred Schenkman published the full series as *The Voice of Fulano: Working Papers from a Bilingual Literacy Campaign* (Kalmar, 1983). To answer the question of how the biliterate use of Broad Romic was "invented, re-invented, or inherited by the original authors of Exhibit B," I am currently writing up a full-fledged ethnography of the *Cobden Glossary*. Could it be the case that the monolingual Mexicans in Cobden learned the use of Broad Romic from the bilingual Tarascans, who learned it from Christian missionaries, who learned it from Henry Sweet? To support this possible answer, I offer in the following pages a series of seven field notes not included in *The Voice of Fulano*, highlighting the need to interpret native theories of biliteracy and exploring historical parallels and possible sources for the native discourse recorded in Cobden in 1980. Look at these notes as snapshots of the ecology and evolution of a hybrid alphabet.

Field Note 1

Alfredo Fabian's slogan is *La lengua tiene que doblarse donde uno la maneja* (Kalmar, 1983, p. 25). In other words, you tell your tongue where to go, it doesn't tell you where to go. (Cobden, June 24, 1980)

Field Note 2

Un sólo alfabeto, pero dos abecedarios distintos (A single *alfabeto*, but two different *abecedarios*)

Constantino took me aside two weeks ago and said, "*Por favor, don Tomacito, enséñame el abecedario de inglés* (Tomacito, please teach me the *abecedario* of English)." I explained that the *abecedario* of English and the *abecedario* of Spanish were the same. A week ago he made the same request and I gave him the same response. Today he explained to me that I was mistaken; the *alfabeto* is the same, but the *abecedario* is very different. He gave me a crash course on the difference between letters and sounds. He explained that when you recite *las letras del alfabeto* (the letters of the alphabet) in Spanish you are simultaneously saying *los sonidos del abecedario* (the sounds of the *abecedario*), but that this is not so in English. (He seemed to be asking for the phonemes of English along with some allophones.) I told him that he was quite right, that the *abecedario* of English had some 40 distinct sounds, but that, even though I'd been to university I couldn't stand there and recite them in lexical order and I didn't know anyone who could. He was very surprised and seemed to think that I was politely telling him that he was too stupid to master the *abecedario* of English. He simply cannot believe that literate gringos cannot recite the *abecedario*. (Cobden, July 18, 1980)

Field Note 3

El diccionario no sirve.

The group decided today to write down English *como de veras se oye*—the way it really sounds. Constantino led the discussion. His recurrent motif was *no podemos aprender la escritura y la pronunciación de un solo golpe*—we should stop trying to figure out the script system and the speech sounds both at the same time. Everyone reached an agreement that you do have to focus on one or the other, *o la una o la otra*. Some balked at the pressure to decide which they wanted to work on first, but in the end the consensus was *primero la pronunciación y después la escritura* (pronunciation first, spelling later).

They've gone through all the paperback Spanish/English dictionaries they could find and have resolved that *el diccionario no sirve*—the dictionary is useless. Even if you find the Spanish word you're looking for, you can't figure out how to say it in English. And if you hear a common English word and do know how to say it, but don't know what it means, you can't find it in the dictionary.

Before reaching this conclusion, they divided the dictionaries into three types: those (surprisingly many) that have no pronunciation guide at all, those that use the IPA, and those that use their own phonetic alphabet. The group sees no point in learning an alphabet (*una escritura*) used only in a given dictionary and nowhere else. They believe me that scientists claim to be able to write any language in the IPA. But they figure that for their own, less ambitious purposes, the ordinary alphabet can probably do the trick.

They decided to work together to produce their own dictionary of *inglés como de veras se oye, en el sistema de ortografía mexicana* (How English really sounds, according to the Mexican system of orthography). (Cobden, August 11, 1980)

Field Note 4

Tongue-doubling

La lengua tiene que doblarse (The tongue must double itself)

This relates to the ability of a human tongue to "double itself," the axiom that every tongue has an *abecedario*, the principle that there is no such thing as "a nonphonetic language" (Wallerstein, 1983, p. 37), the empirical fact that two *abecedarios* may share a common *alfabeto*, the project of transcribing accurately but economically the actual flow of English speech-sounds *como de veras se oye*. The Mexican discourse on adult biliteracy conducted by the authors of the *Cobden Glossary* matches, point by point, the subtlety and rationality of the scientific discourse inaugurated by Henry Sweet. Examples:

Phonology without comparison is a sheer impossibility, and the disadvantages of being a foreigner are partly counterbalanced by the advantage of being forced to observe and systematize, and also of having a special knowledge of individual sounds. (Sweet, 1877, pp. 542-543, reprinted in Wyld, 1913, pp. 446-447)

Our existing dictionaries err in trying to satisfy too many requirements at once. . . .

[A short word-list in Broad Romic] would enable anyone to express himself on most of the ordinary topics of life with far greater accuracy than is now attainable, even after years of floundering about in the pages of unwieldy and unpractical dictionaries and grammars. . . .

The first great step will be to discard the ordinary spelling entirely in teaching pronunciation, and substitute a purely phonetic one, giving a genuine and adequate representation of the actual language, not, as is too often the case, of an imaginary language, spoken by imaginary "correct speakers". . . .

The success of the phonetic method is largely dependent on the notation employed. It is a great step to discard the English values of the vowels. (Sweet, 1884, pp. 582-585, reprinted in Wyld, 1913, pp. 39-42)

Field Note 5
La ortografía mexicana as a version of Broad Romic

The difference between the official orthography of the Royal Academy of Spain and the Mexican orthography developed in the *Cobden Glossary* lies in the fact that since the 1930s—one might almost say since the Spanish Conquest—the Roman alphabet has been systematically extended in Mexico to create practical biliterate orthographies for indigenous native languages. (For an excellent account of the ups and downs of adult biliteracy campaigns in Mexico from the Conquest to the present, see Heath, 1972b, esp. Chapters 6 and 7, pp. 99-150. For those who read Spanish, I recommend the Spanish version, Heath, 1972a, pp. 151-222.)

In the 1930s the intellectual labor of producing and disseminating these biliterate orthographies was shared between socialists and Christian missionaries, in close collaboration. The socialists, influenced by Stalinist policies on linguistic minorities, provided the ideology, and the Christian missionaries, influenced by Sweet's policies on phonetic transcriptions, provided the Broad Romic biliterate alphabets.

Field Note 6
How shall I write this language?

Adult biliteracy has always been central, not marginal, to the work of Christian missionaries. To be acceptable and useful, a new orthography devised by a missionary for a hitherto unwritten language must maximize its "biliteracy quotient," that is, its transferability to the legitimate orthography of the dominant colonial or trade language in the region. In his article aptly entitled, "How Shall I Write This Language?", the Rev. William Smalley (1963) codified a wealth of experience shared by Christian missionaries grappling with the trade-off between language-specific values and competing educational, social, political, and economic values. (The article, first published in 1959, was reprinted along with many detailed, fascinating studies of specific cases in Smalley, 1963.)

Smalley analyzes and lists in order of importance five criteria[1] that govern the production of optimal new writing systems by missionaries:

1. Maximum motivation for the learner and acceptance by his society and controlling groups such as the government. Occasionally maximum motivation for the learner conflicts with government acceptance, but usually the learner wants most what is considered standard in the area.

2. Maximum representation of speech. The fullest, most adequate representation of the actual spoken language is, by and large, the ideal. There are a few points of exception here.

3. Maximum ease of learning. Many writing systems have failed as a missionary tool because they were essentially too complicated for a learner.

4. Maximum transfer. Here we refer to the fact that certain letters of the alphabet or other written symbols will, when learned, be applicable to the more rapid learning of the trade or colonial languages in the area. Thus, if a new learner learns a certain pronunciation of a certain symbol in his native language, and if he can use that same pronunciation with the same symbol in the trade or national language, this is a case of transfer. If, however, the same symbol is used with different value in the other writing system, that transfer cannot be made.

5. Maximum ease of reproduction. Typing and printing facilities are a consideration, although they are not of first importance. (Smalley, 1963, p. 34)

Smalley's criteria 1, 3, 4, and 5 are variations on what I call "maximum biliteracy quotient."

Field Note 7

A Marxist-Christian dialogue

At the top of Smalley's list is the criterion he calls "maximum motivation" but that might more aptly be described as "maximum legitimacy." Christian missionaries do not, by and large, devise or advocate orthographies that question or threaten the legitimacy of the dominant power structures in their host countries. (If and when the power structure changes, especially after a revolution, the orthographies thus given to linguistic minorities may then be criticized as reactionary by the ideologues of the new regime.) This willingness to accept the prevailing ideology of the host government explains the paradoxical and spectacularly successful collaboration between the founder of the Summer Institute of Linguistics, William Cameron Townsend, and the leader of the Mexican socialist reform movement of the 1930s, President Lázaro Cárdenas. (On the fruitful results of the close personal friendship between Townsend and Cárdenas, see Brend & Pike, 1977, and the works cited in Heath, 1972a, pp.154-184 or 1972b, pp. 99-150.)

Cárdenas was himself from Michoacán and valued his Tarascan heritage. Under his presidency, the Tarascan Project began its ascent to stardom. In 1936, three young missionaries from the newborn Summer Institute of Linguistics conducted ground-breaking biliteracy campaigns in Mexico, along with their leader Townsend. One was Kenneth Pike, who began his illustrious career as a phonetician among the Mixtec of Oaxaca armed with little more than a crash course on vowels and consonants. Pike (1981) recalls with affection "ordering sight unseen" the writings of Sweet and other phoneticians in a Mexico City bookstore. The other two young missionaries were Maxwell and Elizabeth Lathrop, who chose Tarascan and settled in Cherán, Michoacán. (In 1980, Tarascans in Cobden, Illinois, would fondly describe "don Max" to me as an old gringo who had lived in Cherán forever and who, they all agreed, spoke a purer and more correct variety of Tarascan than any indio. He had read the old books, the Tarascan/Spanish glossaries compiled by Vasco de Quiroga at the time of the Conquest.)

The Tarascan Project, including Carapan and Patzcuaro as well as Cherán (see Friedrich, 1986, p. 61 for a useful map), became the showpiece of adult biliteracy campaigns, first on a national level, then, after 1937, on an inter-American (i.e., Latin American) level (Heath, 1972a, 1972b), finally becoming, after 1951—through Jaime Torres Bodet's leadership in UNESCO—a paradigmatic "exemplary program" worldwide (Heath, 1972a, p. 208; 1972b, p. 139). The virtues of Tarascan culture and the poetic "metaphonological awareness" of Tarascan linguistic theorizing (Friedrich, 1975, 1986) would need to be taken into account in a full analysis of the unusual success of this project, which simultaneously launched the Mexican adult biliteracy movement and the Summer Institute of Linguistics.

For 50 years, Tarascans in Cherán have been used to producing and reproducing various Tarascan/Spanish wordlists or glossaries written *en el sistema de ortografía mexicana*: that is, in a version of Broad Romic with maximum biliteracy quotient. And it was bilingual Tarascans from Cherán who showed their monolingual Hispanic and Anglo companions in the orchards around Cobden how to catch the local lingo *como de veras se oye*, how to play it by ear, learn it by heart, *liricamente*, how to make their own Spanish/English glossary by stretching—*¡otra vez la misma!*—the biliteracy quotient of *la ortografía mexicana*—the working alphabet of the teacherless campesino. One letter, one sound. One man, one vote. Each one teach one.

Conclusion

This completes my sketch of a tradition of adult biliteracy, which could, I believe, be traced from the authors of the 9th-century *Kassel Glossary* to the authors of the 20th-century *Cobden Glossary*, an apostolic tradition codified and canonized by Henry Sweet and his followers at the turn of the 19th century, transplanted to Cherán, Michoacán by the Christian founders of the Summer Institute of Linguistics and the socialist leaders of the Cardenista reform movement in the 1930s, and imported into the heartland of the United States by "the group who could function as mediators if we gave them a chance," the illegal migrants who labor in our vineyards.

Note

[1] Secular and Marxist writers on the production and distribution of orthographies continue to draw on Smalley's five criteria. Smalley (1963) is cited as an authority, for example, by Donaldo Macedo in his doctoral thesis on the phonology and orthography of Cape Verdean Creole (Macedo, 1979), by Joshua Fishman in a long section on the creation of writing systems in *Current Trends in Linguistics 12* (Fishman, 1974), and by Coulmas, 1989, along with a detailed commentary.

References

Abercrombie, D. (1967). *Elements of general phonetics*. Edinburgh: Edinburgh University Press.

Brend, R.M., & Pike, K.L. (Eds.). (1977). *The Summer Institute of Linguistics: Its works and contributions*. The Hague: Mouton.

Burke, K. (1973). *The philosophy of literary form*. Berkeley and Los Angeles: University of California Press.

Cottom, D. (1989). *Text and culture: The politics of interpretation*. Minneapolis: University of Minnesota Press.

Coulmas, F. (1989). *The writing systems of the world*. Oxford: Basil Blackwell.

de Tal, F. (1988). *Even in my own tongue*. Lawrence, MA: Lawrence Literacy Coalition. (ERIC Document Reproduction Service No. ED 326 085)

Elcock, W.D. (1960). *The Romance languages*. New York: Macmillan.

Fishman, J.A. (1974). The sociology of language: An interdisciplinary social science approach to language in society. In T.A. Sebeok (Ed.), *Current trends in linguistics 12* (pp. 1829-1884). The Hague: Morton.

Friedrich, P. (1975). *A phonology of Tarascan*. Chicago: University of Chicago Press.

Friedrich, P. (1986). *The language parallax: Linguistic relativism and poetic indeterminacy*. Austin: University of Texas Press.

Giroux, H. (1988). Border pedagogy in the age of postmodernism. *Journal of Education, 170*(3), 162-181.

Harris, R. (1980). *The language-makers*. Ithaca, NY: Cornell University Press.

Harris, R. (1986). *The origin of writing*. LaSalle, IL: Open Court.

Heath, S.B. (1972a). *La política del lenguaje en México de la colonia a la nación*. Mexico, D.F.: Instituto Nacional Indigenista.

Heath, S.B. (1972b). *Telling tongues: Language policy in Mexico, colony to nation*. New York and London: Teachers College Press.

Howatt, A.P.R. (1984). *A history of English language teaching*. Oxford: Oxford Univesity Press.

Illich, I. (1987). A plea for research on lay literacy. *Interchange, 18*(1-2), 9-22. Toronto: The Ontario Institute for Studies in Education.

Illich, I., & Sanders, B. (1988). *ABC: The alphabetization of the popular mind.* San Francisco: North Point.

Kalmar, T.M. (1974). *Learning community.* Sydney: Action for World Development and Education Commission of Australian Yearly Meeting of Society of Friends.

Kalmar, T.M. (1983). *The voice of Fulano: Working papers from a bilingual literacy campaign.* Cambridge, MA: Schenkman. (ERIC Document Reproduction Service No. ED 326 082)

Kalmar, T.M. (1988a). Do we need a linguistic minority task force? In T.M. Kalmar & F. de Tal (Eds.), *Working papers from the Lawrence Literacy Coalition.* Lawrence, MA: Northeast Consortium of Colleges and Universities in Massachusetts. (ERIC Document Reproduction Service No. ED 326 085)

Kalmar, T.M. (1988b). *A five-year literacy plan for the Lower Merrimack Valley.* Lawrence, MA: Northeast Consortium of Colleges and Universities in Massachusetts. (ERIC Docu- ment Reproduction Service No. ED 326 085)

Kalmar, T.M. (1988c). *Who requests ESL? A preliminary study on linguistic minority applicants to community colleges in Northeastern Massachusetts.* Lawrence, MA: Northeast Consortium of Colleges and Universities in Massachusetts. (ERIC Document Reproduction Service No. ED 326 083)

Kalmar, T.M. (1990). *Adult biliteracy: Testimony delivered before a public forum on issues in Hispanic education.* Boston: Adult Literacy Resource Institute. (ERIC Document Reproduction Service No. ED 324 983)

Kalmar, T.M. (1992). Drawing the line on minority languages: Equity and linguistic diversity in the Boston Adult Literacy Initiative. *Journal of Adult Basic Education, 2*(2), 84-112.

Kortlandt, F.H.H. (1972). *Modeling the phoneme: New trends in East European phonemic theory.* The Hague: Mouton.

Macedo, D.P. (1979). *A linguistic approach to the Capeverdean language.* Unpublished doctoral dissertation, Boston University.

Mackie, R. (Ed.). (1981). *Literacy and revolution: The pedagogy of Paulo Freire*. New York: Continuum.

Marchot, P. (1895). *Les gloses de Cassel: Le plus ancien texte réto-roman*. Fribourg: Libraire de l'Universite.

Pike, K.L. (1981). An autobiographical note on phonetics. In R.E. Asher & E.J.A. Henderson (Eds.), *Towards a history of phonetics* (pp.181-185). Edinburgh: Edinburgh University Press.

Shaw, G.B. (1941). *Pygmalion*. Harmondsworth: Penguin.

Skutnabb-Kangas, T. (1983). *Bilingualism or not: The education of minorities* (L. Malmberg & D. Crane, Trans.). Clevedon: Multilingual Matters.

Smalley, W.A. (1963). How shall I write this language? In W.A. Smalley (Ed.), *Orthology studies: Articles on new writing systems*. London: United Bible Society.

Sweet, H. (1877). *A handbook of phonetics including a popular exposition of the principles of spelling reform*. Oxford: Clarendon.

Sweet, H. (1884). The practical study of language. *Transactions of the Philological Society 1882*, 4, 577-99.

Sweet, H. (1888). *A history of English sounds from the earliest period with full word-lists*. Oxford: Clarendon.

Titz, K. (1923). *Glossy Kasselske*. Prague: Rozpravy České Akademie Věd a Umění Třída III, Číslo 55.

Wallerstein, N. (1983). *Language and culture in conflict: Problem-solving in the ESL classroom*. Reading, MA: Addison-Wesley.

Whorf, B.L. (1941). The relation of habitual thought and behavior to language. In L. Spier (Ed.), *Language, culture, and personality: Essays in memory of Edward Sapir* (pp. 134-159). Menasha, WI: Sapir Memorial Publication Fund.

Wrenn, C.L. (1946). Henry Sweet. *Transactions of the Philological Society, 1946*, 177-201.

Wrenn, C.L. (1967). *Word and symbol: Studies in English language*. London: Longman, Green.

Wyld, H.C. (Ed.). (1913). *Collected papers of Henry Sweet*. Oxford: Clarendon.

CHAPTER 7

Literacy as Cultural Practice and Cognitive Skill: Biliteracy in an ESL Class and a GED Program

Nancy H. Hornberger
Joel Hardman
Graduate School of Education
University of Pennsylvania

Literacy is often regarded as a neutral and technical tool, identified in terms of discrete elements of reading and writing skills, and seen as autonomous and independent of context. Under this view, literacy, once acquired, brings not only positive cognitive, social, and economic consequences to the literate individual, but also social and economic development to the literate society (Wagner, 1990, pp. 8-9). Problems with this view include the implication that illiteracy necessarily precludes abstract reasoning and the attribution of a cause-and-effect relationship between literacy and development (cognitive, social, and economic), where research evidence at best supports only a correlational one.

Street (1993) has suggested that an alternative to this "autonomous" model of literacy is the "ideological" model, in which literacy is seen as "inextricably linked to cultural and power structures in society" and attention is on "the variety of cultural practices associated with reading and writing in different contexts" (p. 7) rather

We would like to thank the students and staff of *Abriendo Caminos* and the SEAMAAC ESL classes for welcoming us as participant observers in their midst. We gratefully acknowledge support from a National Academy of Education Spencer Fellowship, which enabled Hornberger to devote full time to this research during 1989; and from the Dean's Fellowship of the Graduate School of Education of the University of Pennsylvania, which enabled Hardman's participation in the research. We also thank David Spener, Brian Street, and participants at the National Clearinghouse on Literacy Education's Colloquium on Biliteracy (January 1991) for helpful comments on earlier versions of this paper.

than on reading and writing in and of themselves. While the autonomous model focuses on "how literacy affects people," the ideological model takes note of "how people affect literacy" (Kulick & Stroud, 1993, p. 31).

Some suggest that these two approaches to literacy are irreconcilable, that the autonomous and ideological models of literacy are polarized (see Street, 1993), that literacy as cognitive skill is at odds with literacy as cultural practice. This paper aims to resolve perceived conflicts between cognitive and cultural (or autonomous and ideological) approaches to literacy, by using Hornberger's (1989) nine continua of biliteracy as a framework for examining two specific situations of biliteracy and biliterate development. By doing so, we hope to show that the two approaches should not be viewed as opposing beliefs of what literacy is, but different ways of looking at literacy. To understand any particular instance of (bi)literacy from the participants' point of view, both perspectives need to be understood by the observer. A generous understanding of the notion of literacy as cultural practice allows for the possibility that the cognitive or autonomous aspects of literacy are themselves part of a culturally circumscribed activity.

Hornberger (1989) uses the notion of intersecting and nested continua to demonstrate both the multiple and complex interrelationships between bilingualism and literacy, and the importance of the contexts and media through which biliteracy develops. Biliteracy refers to "any and all instances in which communication occurs in two (or more) languages in or around writing" (Hornberger, 1990, p. 2), and the continua framework suggests that the development of biliteracy occurs:

1) simultaneously along (a) the first language–second language transfer continuum, (b) the reception–production continuum, and (c) the oral language–written language continuum;

2) through the medium of two (or more) languages and literacies that vary along (a) the similar–dissimilar linguistic structures continuum, (b) the convergent–divergent scripts continuum, and (c) the simultaneous–successive exposure continuum; and

3) in contexts—including every level of context from the face-to-face interactions involving individuals who are becoming biliterate to the global politico-economic situations and the

national policy settings in which they are doing so—that are defined by being situated along (a) the micro–macro continuum, (b) the oral–literate continuum, and (c) the monolingual–bilingual continuum.

From this framework, Hornberger argues that in order to understand any particular instance of biliteracy, be it a biliterate individual, situation, or society, we need to take account of all dimensions represented by the continua. At the same time, the advantage of the framework is that it allows us to focus on one or selected continua and their dimensions without ignoring the importance of the others.

The two concrete situations of biliteracy and biliterate development examined here are part of a larger long-term comparative ethnographic study on biliteracy in two communities in Philadelphia. Each of the authors of this chapter has been involved in the study for two years or more, and intensively for several months in the situation we describe.

The first situation is an adult ESL (English as a second language) class for recent Cambodian refugees (all women) taught by a young Cambodian woman who has been in the United States through high school and a few years of community college and vocational school. It is the assumption of this paper that the teacher and students in this class, as members of an urban Cambodian refugee community, share norms of behavior and language use and also share attitudes toward learning and what it means to know a language. Therefore, their work together reflects a culture of literacy. When their class is read using the continua of biliteracy, it will be shown that a cognitive-skills approach to literacy (emphasizing mechanical encoding and decoding skills) coexists comfortably with a cultural-practice approach characterized by student-initiated, teacher-supported social learning strategies.

The second specific biliteracy situation is ASPIRA's[1] *Abriendo Caminos* (Creating Opportunities) program, serving approximately 60-80 Puerto Rican adolescents (ages 16-21) per year in parallel Spanish-medium and English-medium GED (General Educational Development) classes. The program includes not only GED instruction, but also cultural and self-awareness training and work orientation and experience. An examination of this program using the continua of biliteracy reveals how the program approaches literacy as cognitive skill while at the same time embedding it as cultural practice.

Each biliteracy situation in turn will be briefly described and analyzed using the continua; Hardman will describe the Cambodian adult ESL class, and Hornberger the Puerto Rican GED program. A concluding section will return to consideration of the coexistence of the two models.

A Cambodian Adult ESL Class

The ESL class for Cambodians was founded in the mid 1980s by the Southeast Asian Mutual Assistance Associations Coalition, Inc. (SEAMAAC) in Philadelphia. SEAMAAC is made up of Cambodian, Chinese, Hmong, Lao, and Vietnamese associations. It was formed in 1979 to address important issues and concerns common to the newly arriving Southeast Asian refugees. The founders of the coalition were especially concerned with issues such as gangs and fighting, drugs, and joblessness (interview, director of SEAMAAC, July 27, 1990).

The ESL program is a part of SEAMAAC's program in adult basic education. The director of SEAMAAC sees its primary goal as basic or survival English skills: reading the gas bill, reading street signs, and so forth. And, because the students are almost all mothers of school-age children, the director sees it as important for them to be able to communicate with their children's teachers (interview, July 27, 1990). The 1989-1990 class described here was held in the basement of a rowhouse in West Philadelphia that is owned by the Greater Philadelphia Overseas Chinese Association, a member of SEAMAAC. The Chinese Association provided space and supplies for this class as well as for other ESL classes for Chinese.

The Cambodian ESL class was held four afternoons a week for two hours each. The teacher for three of those classes was a Cambodian woman in her 20s, Sarah Lim. She has been in the United States since high school, has been through two years of college, and is just finishing a vocational program for laboratory technicians. She is nearly fluent in English. The students were almost all women between 25 and 35 years old who had come to the United States in the last five years.

Most of the students had received little formal education in Cambodia or in the refugee camps. As there were no entrance requirements for the class, the students were quite diverse in their English proficiencies and levels of literacy. Most were literate in Khmer, though some were not. Most of them knew the English alphabet and were familiar with reading and writing English words, though a few were not. Some could carry on a basic conversation in English, but most could not. There were no graduation requirements for the class, and all the students received a formal certificate from SEAMAAC at the end of the course.

On any given day, between 5 and 10 students showed up for class somewhere between 2:00 and 2:15 in the afternoon. They often brought their children, who played in or outside the classroom. Often, in the middle of class, students would yell at their children to be quiet or to go home. They would leave class to attend to crying children, give someone a key, or just go home. Some students seldom participated in class activities, but would instead just sit quietly and watch what their neighbors were doing. All through class the students chatted comfortably in Khmer and laughed.

Despite the above description, the class was not informal or learner-centered in the current pedagogical sense. Sarah, the teacher, was quite formal. In the classroom she seemed to create a great distance between herself and the students. She was very serious and rarely joked. She tried to speak entirely in English. To the outside observer, she seemed to make little effort to be interesting, to entertain, to excite, or to be friendly. Her role as teacher caused her to behave in extremely formal ways—more formal than American ESL teachers who commonly try these days to break down traditional barriers between teachers and students.

What I perceived as formality and informality did not lead to observable conflict in the classroom; the students and the teacher did not seem to be working at cross-purposes. Together they appeared to have created a context for learning appropriate to their desires and goals as language learners. Somehow, what I (as educational researcher) saw as a conflict between literacy-as-cognitive-skill and literacy-as-cultural-practice approaches to literacy acquisition, the students and teacher experienced smoothly as their way of learning. One classroom activity that demonstrates some of the tensions I perceived surrounding literacy acquisition will be described using

Hornberger's three continua of biliterate development: L1–L2 (first language-second language) transfer, reception-production, and oral-written.

The L1–L2 transfer continuum: Formal L2 emphasis with informal L1 support

Sarah's nearly exclusive use of English in the classroom suggests a belief that using her students' first language, Khmer, was of no use to her instruction or the students' development of English. At the time, I read this as a formal approach to second language instruction reflective of certain approaches, such as audio-lingualism, which view the second language as a discrete set of skills to be learned and practiced in a controlled, formal environment. Sarah's avoidance of Khmer might indicate a fear of L1 interference in L2 acquisition. However, as shown below, the students relied on Khmer to respond to Sarah's questions and to help each other understand what was going on. Also, though not reported below, some of the students wrote in Khmer in their notes, mostly to help with vocabulary by writing down the meanings of English words, indicating that the students did believe that their L1 was an appropriate tool to use in learning English.

February 22, 1990; 2:26-2:34 p.m.

The students have finished copying a dialogue from the board and a list of new words with blanks after them which Sarah wrote on the board before the beginning of class.

Feb. 22, 1990

AT THE DENTIST

(continue from Tuesday)

Dr.:   Do you have any pain?

Kim: Yes. A little (pointing) in this tooth here in back.

Dr.:   Let me see. Open your mouth, please . . . wider . . . . Does this hurt?

Kim: A little.

Dr.:   I can see you have a big cavity there. I would also like to take an X-ray today to see if you have any other cavities.

Kim: Oh. O.K.

Dr.: After we take the X-ray, we'll clean up your teeth. Then we'll make an appointment for you to come back next week.

Kim: O.K. Thank you.

Give the meaning of:

1) patients _____

2) cavity _____

3) appointment _____

4) reminder note _____

Sarah asks the students to write the meanings of the new words.

Sarah: O.K., does anybody remember what this means? (She points to *patient* on the board. We talked about it on Tuesday. If you remember, write it down. (She stands silently for two minutes.)

Sarah: Finished? Just give the main . . . meaning? The meaning of the word, like, patient means something else. Another word for patient? (no response) What is appointment? (A student answers in Khmer.) O.K., in English.

A student: You make appointment.

Sarah: Set up time and date. (She writes that on the board.)

Sarah: What is reminder note? (She waits a long time for answers. There are a few answers in Khmer. Sarah writes on the board after patients: *People visit doctor or dentist.*) What is cavity?

A student: Cavity is when teeth hurt.

Sarah: Right. (She writes on the board: *Big holes.*) O.K., reminder note. Anybody think of it yet? (long pause) Reminder note. (There is some scattered Khmer. Sarah explains reminder note in English, writes on the board: *short letter.*) A short letter is called a reminder note. O.K., is everybody finished copying down from the board?

(She walks around and checks a student's work.)

The reception–production continuum: Repeating, copying, and reading aloud

I did not perceive any conflict between the formal and informal along this continuum. Both Sarah and the students were most comfortable with what are usually considered the more passive receptive skills: repeating, copying, listening, and reading aloud. Reading aloud, especially, seemed to be a ritual that brought Sarah and the students together. Interestingly, however, repeating and copying are skills that draw on both ends of the reception–production continuum simultaneously; reproduction (repeating, copying) has both receptive and productive aspects. It is likely that Sarah and her students saw these activities as more productive than I did; that is, literacy as cultural practice may shape particular definitions of literacy as cognitive skill. The same is true for reading aloud, which draws not only on both ends of the reception–production continuum, but also on both ends of the written–oral continuum discussed next. Below is a description of their reading routine.

February 22, 1990; 2:35-2:50 p.m.
Sarah: O.K., let's read over.

Sarah reads a line of the dialogue written on the board, and the students repeat each line twice. They even repeat the word "pointing," which is a parenthetical stage direction written in the dialogue. Everyone reads together, loudly. When they are finished, they repeat the procedure. Next, the students read as a group, without prompting or instruction from Sarah. It seems very routine. Sarah points to words on the board often as they read. When they are finished, Sarah asks them to repeat. Again, they read "Yes . . . a little, pointing in this tooth. . . ."

Sarah next nominates students to read. She says, "O.K., who wanna be a doctor and who wanna be the patient?" Then she nominates two students who had not raised their hands. The student playing Kim reads "pointing." They read through, with Sarah having to prompt only on "cavities" and "little," then they switch parts and read again.

While another pair of students is reading the dialogue, it is clear that one of them is barely literate in English. She needs prompting every other word or so. She also gets prompts from students next to her. Over and over, Sarah asks her to repeat "little." The typical prompting pattern goes something like this: prompt from a student, attempt at repetition, prompt from Sarah, a second attempt.

The oral language–written language continuum:
The authenticity of reading aloud

Both formal and informal modes in this classroom embedded the written within the oral, and vice-versa. Sarah almost never spoke about anything that wasn't written down or soon to be written down, and the students never said anything that wasn't written or about something written. Also, as shown above, they read aloud most of what they wrote. While neither their oral nor written language use in English was what would be called "authentic" in Edelsky's (1986) sense of the word, there is the possibility that there was more meaning to their reading, writing, and speaking activities than an outsider could readily see. The question of authenticity is a complex one, and I believe the degree of authenticity of certain literacy events (such as reading aloud, repeating, or copying) varies cross-culturally—another instance of literacy as cultural practice shaping definitions of literacy as cognitive skill.

The ability of students in this class to read aloud far exceeded their ability to speak or even to understand what they were reading. Even when reading a dialogue aloud, as shown above, their commitment to reading a stage direction indicated that they saw the dialogue simply as written language, with no relation to what might be a real conversation. Below is another example of how what might look like a listening and speaking activity is really another chance to practice reading aloud in chorus.

February 22, 1990; 2:50 p.m.
After students read the dialogue aloud, Sarah reviews the vocabulary. The answers to her vocabulary questions were written on the board earlier. Students answer her as a group, reading from the board.

Sarah:	Students:
O.K. what is "cavity"?	big hole
How do you get "cavity"?	hurt your teeth
What is "patient"?	people visits doctor or dentist
What is "appointment"?	set up time and date
What is "reminder note"?	a short letter

The episodes described above exhibit the combination of a cognitive skills approach with a cultural practice approach to literacy instruction. By cognitive skills approach, I refer to those teacher-directed activities—emphasizing mechanical encoding and decoding skills (particularly decoding) through copying, reading aloud, and vocabulary drills—that reflect an autonomous model of literacy. By cultural practice approach, I refer to social learning strategies that are student-directed, though implicitly supported by the teacher—including prompting, collaboration, and using the L1 to answer questions and talk with other students—and that reflect an ideological model of literacy. Not shown in the examples above is the rather fluid movement of students and their children in and out of activities and in and out of the classroom, illustrating how, in fact, the formal literacy-learning activity of these students is not truly autonomous from their other life activities—activities that taken as a whole constitute their cultural practice.

As stated above, though I perceived these differences in the teacher's and students' approaches to literacy acquisition, there was in fact no conflict in the classroom. Both teacher and students were living up to the others' expectations of behavior. The continua show that there was actually a good deal of common ground between teacher and students in the area of biliterate development, though at first I only noticed the great difference in their use of L1 and L2. The two approaches described above are complementary parts of a larger whole—the larger culture of teaching, learning, and literacy in the Cambodian community.

A Puerto Rican GED Program

The *Abriendo Caminos* (Creating Opportunities) program was founded in 1986 by ASPIRA, Inc. of Pennsylvania and was designed "to help what has been regarded as the most difficult of populations—Hispanic high school dropouts with dead-end futures" (ASPIRA, correspondence, April 27, 1990). The program has been housed since 1988 in the heart of Philadelphia's Puerto Rican community in a spacious two-story former firehouse donated by the city and refurbished by ASPIRA. The program runs from September to May, enrolling 60-80 Puerto Rican adolescents, ages 16-21, each year. To enroll in the program, the student must be able to read at a sixth-grade level or higher. English-dominant students are assigned to the English-medium class and Spanish-dominant students, most of them recently arrived from Puerto Rico, are assigned to the Spanish-medium class. Placement is generally done on the basis of whether students' previous schooling has been mostly in English or in Spanish; only in cases where students have had fairly equal exposure and appear to be equally at ease in both languages are they asked about their language preference in reading (interview with program director,

June 7, 1989). During the 1989-1990 year, there were four classes: two English-medium GED classes, one Spanish-medium GED class, and one pre-GED class, each class meeting in either the morning or afternoon session. In each three-hour session, two hours were devoted to GED work and the third hour to a "reinforcement" time, taught by the program's counselors and focused on cultural and self-awareness training.

Abriendo Caminos receives funds through the federal Job Training Partnership Act (JTPA), which, among other things, aims to provide avenues to employment for low-income youth. Under this act, the program must place a certain percentage of its students in jobs; and the students must stay on the job for at least 30 days to be counted a successful placement. Toward fulfillment of this goal, the *Abriendo Caminos* staff not only seek to establish on-going partnerships with employers in the Philadelphia area for placement of their students, but also emphasize work orientation in their instruction.

In the following paragraphs, I will consider some aspects of the *Abriendo Caminos* program from the perspective of the continua of biliteracy, concentrating on the continua of biliterate contexts. A consideration of the program context in the light of the macro–micro continuum will bring out the ways in which the program approaches literacy as a cognitive skill while simultaneously embedding it as cultural practice; the monolingual–bilingual continuum will reveal the significance of the cultural awareness training for both the English- and the Spanish-medium groups; and the oral–literate continuum will suggest that powerful English literacy is embedded in Spanish oral language use and that changes in biliteracy configurations may entail significant social disruption.

The macro–micro continuum: Traditional teaching in a non-traditional environment

The overriding goal of the *Abriendo Caminos* program is for all of its students to pass the GED test, and they have succeeded at a 70% rate in the three years of operation (interview with program director, March 20, 1991). For those students who enter the program speaking only or mostly Spanish, the program's concomitant goal is for them to learn English. There is a clear cognitive skill approach to both GED and ESL literacy; both the GED and the ESL curricula are structured around discrete reading and writing skills that must be mastered.

In the GED classes, the students work out of the English and Spanish versions of the GED preparation books. The books are organized around the areas tested on the examination—math, science, social studies, writing, and reading comprehension—and include diagnostic tests, sample problems, exercises for developing skills, some reference information (charts, glossaries), and practice tests. The students work at their own pace, area by area, testing regularly until they pass.

The program director keeps the focus on mastering the GED exam. In some cases, due to funding constraints, this focus must be more narrowly defined than the participants would like. For example, students are tested regularly, despite the fact that the practice tests can be very discouraging when students repeatedly fail to pass. In addition, the director had to put a stop to a play that the Spanish GED teacher had been working on with her students to both build up their skills in English and contribute to their motivation, because the students were too far behind in their GED work (personal observation, November 30, 1989).

Abriendo Caminos has found that the GED preparation books it must use are deficient in many ways. Inadequacies identified by students and teachers include gaps in information, confusing instructions, linguistic and sociolinguistic differences, and sociopolitical assumptions. In the science area of the Spanish GED book (Serrán-Pagán, Acosta, & Márquez, 1987), for example, topics are tested but not covered; the teacher will have to use the local library to supplement the book's inadequate information. In the writing area, instructions to correct the spelling of a list of words are misleading, because in fact some of the words are already correctly spelled. Furthermore, as a student pointed out, in the case of homonyms, you can't tell which one is intended, since no context is given. The program director notes that the Spanish GED book causes some problems for the students because it reflects a variety of Spanish different from the Puerto Rican variety they speak. (Editors' note: See Ramírez, this volume, for a discussion of the different language varieties spoken by Hispanics in the United States.) In addition, for these bilingual students, certain points at which the English and Spanish languages, orthographies, or spelling conventions differ may cause trouble: For example, students complain that, according to the book, the words *Incas*, *Mayas*, and *Aztecs* are not capitalized, whereas they should be because they are proper names. Furthermore, some exercises carry rather strong sociopolitical messages that remain unquestioned; for example, two sentences for which students were asked to identify and correct errors of article usage were: a) *Estados Unidos son una nación económicamente fuerte* (The United States is an economically strong nation); and b) *Los Estados Unidos es un gran potencia militar* (The United States is a great military power).

These inadequacies raise legitimate doubts and provide opportunities for further questioning and intellectual inquiry. The overall approach to them in the class and in the program, however, is not to take them as starting points for investigation, but rather to determine what would be the correct answer in terms of the GED book and proceed from there. In this sense, the approach to GED literacy is one of mastering these discrete pieces of reading and writing, independent of contextual meaning and variation.

In 1989-1990, *Abriendo Caminos* adopted a new ESL curriculum for use in its GED program,[2] the Comprehensive Competencies Program (CCP). The CCP is described by its creator, U.S. Basics of Alexandria, VA, as a "learning management system designed to deliver individualized, self-paced, competency-based instruction using print, audio-visual and computer-assisted instruction combined with one-on-one teaching." This computerized program includes both academic and functional components; *Abriendo Caminos* is emphasizing the latter (interview with program director, September 18, 1989).

The CCP curriculum is organized hierarchically within each component, such that a given lesson is to be found within a given unit within a given level, in a given subject, at a certain tier in the program that corresponds to a student's general level of ability. Each lesson is filed in a separate binder and labeled; in each binder are the core print lesson, an audiocassette, language cards for use on a language card reader, references to print and computer-assisted instruction supplements, tutorial activities, lesson assignments, mastery tests, and forms for tracking learner progress. The use of this program involves extensive record-keeping, including a computerized database on each student, with information such as personal information, years of school, assistance programs (food stamps, housing assistance, etc.), test scores, number of hours completed in each of various CCP units, and entry and exit dates.

As with the GED program, students work individually, proceeding in order through the lessons, units, and levels, with regular testing to assess their progress. As with the GED program as well, emphasis is on the students' mastery of the discrete pieces of reading and writing as presented by the materials, independent of contextual meaning or variation. For example, sequencing of the discrete pieces of language from one level to the next seems, in some cases, to leave the lowest level learner with the least amount of significant meaningful content. In the sequence from 2.1.3.2.1 (Functional Foundations) to 2.1.3.3.1 (Functional Frameworks) to 2.1.3.4.1 (Functional Bridges), for example, students proceed from sounds (at the beginning, middle, and end of words) to vocabulary (extended family) to topics (the social security system and making phone calls). Further, scoring procedures on the tests do not allow for sensitivity to students' biliterate or sociolinguistic knowledge: When Lourdes succeeds in identifying the object pictured and the name and position of the vowel sound in it (for five different objects), missing only because she calls *e* /e/ instead of /i/ and *i* /i/ instead of /ai/, she nevertheless must be marked wrong for the whole question simply because of confusion between the Spanish and English names for vowels; when Nilsa completes a personal information writing task perfectly except for spelling Pennsylvania as Pensilvania, she too must be marked wrong for the entire task; when José's test asks who should use the designation Ms. in filling out a form and José answers, with considerably more sociolinguistic sensitivity than the "correct" answer (unmarried female), "single female or married female who doesn't wish to state her marital status," he too must be marked wrong. Program staff are aware that the tests and the scoring procedures may not accurately reflect students' knowledge: The director says she feels the scoring is too subjective, while one of the staff members comments that he doesn't know "what [the test] tells you." Yet, there appears to be a consensus in the program that these skills are the literacy these students need to succeed, and the program must do all it can to help them learn them.

At the same time, however, the *Abriendo Caminos* program embeds this literacy as cultural practice at every level of context from the macro level of Puerto Ricans as Latin Americans to the micro level of interaction in the classroom. Consider the following, taken from my field notes.

October 19, 1989

Lilliam tells the Spanish GED class that she saw a program on TV last night that gave her an idea. She tells them that though we are all poor here, we know there are people in Latin America who are much worse off, and she proposes that the class adopt a Latin American child through a reliable agency like the church. They will send a certain amount of money each month (about $21, or $2 a piece) to provide the child with clothing, food, medicine, books. They will correspond with the child. They will really make a difference in the life of the child. The class is immediately in favor of the idea. Marilyn asks what will happen when they graduate; Lilliam assures her that she and her next year's class will follow through with the child. Nilsa wonders if they could support two; Lilliam suggests they start with one to see how it goes. As the discussion continues, Nilsa eventually starts to wipe her eyes. She has been moved to gentle tears (these are genuine, and she suffers some good-natured teasing about it). After the class approves the plan, Sonia, as class secretary, agrees to call the agency. The class prepares a poster announcing their decision and posts it around the building.

October 12, 1989

The first thing I notice upon entering the building today is an election poster for Minitza, one of the students in the Spanish GED class. Neida tells me that the students are campaigning this week for their elections next week; each class elects its officers, who in turn elect the representatives to sit on the ASPIRA Club Federation board, who in turn elect a representative to sit on the ASPIRA board. Officers participate in conferences and retreats focusing on developing leadership skills.

When I arrive at the class, the students are preparing posters for the election. They have written a rap song, which they perform for me; Nilsa speaks and others provide the back-up. Although it doesn't appear rhythmic or rhymed as written, when performed it is.

The words of the rap are as follows (exactly as written by the students, with my translation):

Let's Rap

Dejé la escuela	I left school
a los Quince años	at age fifteen
y vine a Aspira a	and I came to Aspira to
Terminar el cuarto	finish my senior
año.	year.
Coro: Aspira, Aspira	Chorus: Aspira, Aspira
Yo soy Lourdes y te	I am Lourdes, and I
digo a tí que mi	say to you that my
presidencia Te	presidency
conviene a tí.	is to your advantage.
Coro: Aspira, Aspira	Chorus: Aspira, Aspira
Y ahora yo le digo	And now I say to
a jóvenes como yo,	young people like me,
Que día a día le	that day after day
gusta el vacilón, que	enjoy wasting time, that
vayas a la escuela y	you better go to school and
aprovechen la ocación.	take advantage of the
	opportunity.
Coro: Aspira, Aspira	Chorus: Aspira, Aspira
y terminando este	and once finished
rapeo y empezando	this rap, and starting
aquí, ahora yo te	from here, now I
pido que votes por mí.	ask you to vote for me.

Subsequently, before the election, another verse was added:

Llegué a Aspira	I arrived at Aspira
y empecé a saludar	and started greeting everybody
La maestra me dijo	The teacher told me to
ponte a trabajar.	get to work.

After the election, the program director asked the students to revise the rap, removing the verses about the election, and keeping the rest as an ASPIRA rap.

October 26, 1989
This Saturday, the GED classes will have a workshop at Edison High School, in which the GED students will meet in small groups with Puerto Rican professionals to learn what their professions are like.

November 30, 1989
While Lilliam is out of the classroom for a moment, Marinés, who is working on the science test, asks me which is the largest bird in America: the *águila real* or the *cóndor*. I say I think the *cóndor* is, but she seems quite sure it's the *águila*. Then Liberto and Lourdes get into the discussion, too; Liberto is saying *cóndor*, and Lourdes is not sure. When Lilliam comes back, they ask her, and she authoritatively answers, "cóndor," whereupon Lourdes and Marinés correct their answers, grinning sheepishly as they do so.

Each of these is representative of the way in which the *Abriendo Caminos* program not only affords its students opportunities to use the literacy skills they are acquiring, but also embeds the whole of their GED and ESL literacy learning in a cultural, institutional, and interactional context that recognizes and validates their identity as Puerto Ricans. The first case represents an opportunity for the class to act in solidarity with other Latin Americans; the second shows the *Abriendo Caminos* program's connection to a network of ASPIRA-sponsored organizations and programs that support the Puerto Rican community; the third exemplifies how the program draws on the Puerto Rican community to support the students' development; and the fourth reveals how the students accommodate the highly individualized competency-based program to the more collaborative learning approach they seem to prefer.

The monolingual–bilingual continuum: Reinforcement of cultural identity in two languages
Entry from my field notes:

October 5, 1989
After observing the very lively discussion in today's reinforcement session, I express some surprise to the teacher that most of these young people had never visited *Taller Puertorriqueño* (a Puerto Rican cultural arts center a few blocks away from where the GED program is housed) until yesterday. This leads to a discussion with him about how, growing up here, with the media coverage of their community, the young people's Puerto Rican identity in some ways

comes to reflect the external rather than the internal point of view. That is, they take on the identity portrayed in the media (drugs, violence, dropping out), rather than the identity within the community, represented, for example, by *Taller*.

Thus, when they first are acquainted with *Taller*, it really is an eye-opening experience, because they begin to realize that many of the things they know and live with are part of their culture, not just odd stray things (e.g., the way their mothers cook and care for them; the music; the fact that Puerto Rican women are "good to their men"; Puerto Rican good looks; the shared history; and so on), and they begin to feel some pride in being Puerto Rican.

Beyond embedding literacy as cultural practice, the *Abriendo Caminos* program explicitly teaches cultural awareness to its students in the reinforcement session, which meets during the third hour (alternating with ESL and work-orientation sessions) and is taught by the counselors. There are three counselors on the staff, who meet individually with each student for a half hour each week in addition to teaching the reinforcement sessions. The counselors take these sessions seriously; one counselor commented that once you give the students an opening and they begin to talk about values, goals, and so on, you must be conscientious about following through with them (personal communication, September 18, 1989).

As the counselor's comment indicates, the sessions are directed toward self-awareness, toward helping students explore their own values and goals. For example, I observed sessions on the emotional and practical issues surrounding leaving home (September 28, 1989), on personal attributes (September 18, 1989), and on a self-directed search for career possibilities (October 19, 1989). The core of the sessions, however, is the validation and promotion of the students' Puerto Rican identity. The counselors feel that one reason that students do well in the *Abriendo Caminos* program, despite having dropped out of school, is that here it is O.K. to be Puerto Rican, while at school it's as if everything they are is working against them from the first day they show up (personal communication, September 18, 1989).

Of course, the *Abriendo Caminos* program as a whole reinforces the students' Puerto Rican identity. The program administrators, teachers, and counselors are all Puerto Rican. The center is named for Antonia Pantoja, Puerto Rican educator and founder of ASPIRA. The walls of the center are decorated with posters portraying scenes from Puerto Rico and famous Puerto Ricans such as actress Rita Moreno and former baseball player Roberto Clemente; tables display brochures printed in English, Spanish, or both, advertising, for example, a concert by the *Asociación de Músicos Latinos* (Latino Musicians' Association, AMLA) or workshops and colloquia sponsored by the Arts of Social Change/*Las Artes del Cambio Social*. Nevertheless, it is in the reinforcement sessions that students have the opportunity to explore their Puerto Rican identities, as exemplified in the note quoted above.

What is particularly significant when the program context is considered in terms of the monolingual–bilingual continuum is that Puerto Rican identity reinforcement is seen as crucial for both the English-medium and Spanish-medium GED classes. Both groups take up exactly the same issues and explorations in their reinforcement sessions. The counselors prepare materials in both languages; for example, during the discussions after the students' visits to *Taller Puertorriqueño*, it became clear that the counselor had prepared both an English and a Spanish version of the questionnaire that they were using as the basis for discussion. On another occasion, José explained to me that he takes care to do a good job whenever he prepares written material in Spanish, because he feels it conveys an important message to the students. However, the crucial content of the sessions, from the participants' point of view, is not the language in which they are conducted, but the exploration of Puerto Rican identity that they pursue. For this case, anyway, language is apparently separable from ethnic identity.[3]

The oral–literate continuum: Some tensions regarding language use

Well, we have to report to our funding source, and they're not bilingual, so all of the documents that we leave behind, other than the curriculum and the course lesson plans for the Spanish GED class . . . mostly we gear toward English. Now you'll find when the staff sits together that we talk Spanish. The Spanish-dominant staff will naturally write in Spanish, but when they submit reports they're submitted in English, because, again, if we're audited, and we usually are at the end of the program year, they will send people down to review files.

(interview with program director, June 7, 1989)

Entry from my field notes:

October 12, 1989

As the Spanish GED class discusses the mock interviews to be held tomorrow with all the classes, it comes out that some of the students in this class are very unhappy with the way some of the students in the English GED classes have been behaving toward them, and in general. Nilsa and Marinés go on at length, in very rapid Spanish, about the rudeness of these other girls, even to the guest speaker yesterday.

A look at the program context from the perspective of the oral–literate continuum, however, reveals that there are some tensions between the languages and their speakers, despite their shared Puerto Rican ethnic identity. For one thing, it becomes clear that there is an unequal relation between the two languages: The predominant pattern in the program is that of powerful English literacy embedded in Spanish oral language use. Spanish is of course used most extensively in the Spanish GED class, yet even there it is often used primarily to embed English literacy; for example, students use Spanish to ask for clarification during their CCP ESL diagnostic test (field observation, October 5, 1989). In the English GED class, the use of Spanish is even more restricted: Magda conducts their entire reinforcement session in English, the handout is in English, everything she writes on the board is in English, and her discussion is in English, with a very few codeswitches into Spanish to issue a directive to the students (field observation, September 18, 1989). Again, what oral Spanish use there is embeds English literacy.

Secondly, there are differences between the Spanish- and English-medium students, differences that at times flare up in intergroup tensions. While the English-medium students tend to be those born or at least mostly raised on the mainland, the Spanish-medium students tend to be island-born and raised. This means not only that the schooling of the two groups has been in different languages, but also that they likely reflect slightly different sets of values and behaviors associated with the mainland and island settings, respectively. The program director comments, for example, that the program has a hard time convincing the English GED students to accept help, while the Spanish GED students are very open to help and tutoring. The excerpt quoted above shows how the Spanish GED group gets upset with the English GED group for what appears to them as lack of politeness. These are little tensions which seem to reflect a larger underlying tension accompanying the changing biliteracy configuration as both groups acquire English literacy. It is to the program's credit that it acknowledges and addresses these tensions, making it possible for both groups to graduate at year's end.

Conclusion: The Autonomous Model Is Not Truly Autonomous

The GED program owes its success at least in part to the fact that it manages to embed literacy as a cultural practice even while it approaches teaching it as a cognitive skill. Ferdman (1990) notes that

at the individual level . . . the process of becoming and being literate involves becoming and being identified with a particular culture. . . . When there is a mismatch between the definition and significance of literacy as they are represented in a person's cultural identity and in the learning situation, the individual is faced with making a choice that has implications for his or her acquisition of reading and writing skills. (pp. 189-195)

Recognizing this, the program attempts to foster its students' success by making it possible for them to acquire the discrete reading and writing skills they need for attaining high school graduation credentials and employment in U.S. society, while at the same time representing and reinforcing a cultural identity that they can accept. Indeed, we suggest that it is the very fact that the program emphasizes and reinforces literacy as cultural practice that enables the students to obtain the GED credential and thus demonstrate their mastery of literacy as a cognitive skill.

In the Cambodian adult ESL class, many of the students (excluding the few who are not literate in Khmer) are engaged in learning a second literacy. They bring to this task both Khmer language skills and previous literacy acquisition experience. They are building a bridge to a new language and culture using the materials and skills from a familiar one. As the students are becoming adept at handling two very different cultures, it should not be surprising that they can handle, even depend on, a language learning environment (a culture of literacy) built upon a fusion of two different approaches to language learning and literacy acquisition: cognitive skills and cultural practice.

While the autonomous model of literacy arises from a peculiarly monocultural notion of a single, standardized, schooled literacy (see Cook-Gumperz, 1986), the ideological model reflects a pluralistic view. It is hardly surprising, then, that it is in these situations of *bi*literacy, where participants are daily involved in negotiating the coexistence of languages and cultures, that we find evidence of the coexistence of the two models, specifically of the autonomous model circumscribed by the ideological model.

Notes

[1] ASPIRA is a private, non-profit, Puerto Rican organization, founded in 1961 in New York City. One of its primary aims is to promote education among Puerto Rican youth. The name of the organization refers to its unique message to youth—"Aspire to a better and more fulfilling life" (Micheau, 1990, p. 547). The Pennsylvania branch of ASPIRA was founded in 1969.

[2] The Spanish GED contains a section testing students' English abilities; this section of the test must also be passed for students to be awarded their high school equivalency certificates.

[3] Micheau (1990) found language to be only one of seven defining characteristics of "Puerto Ricanness" in the Philadelphia Puerto Rican community, the others being island ancestry, mixed ethnic and racial heritage, knowledge of/pride in culture, Puerto Rican values, political consciousness, and community responsibility and sacrifice.

References

Cook-Gumperz, J. (1986). *The social construction of literacy*. Cambridge: Cambridge University Press.

Edelsky, C. (1986). *Writing in a bilingual program: Había una vez*. Norwood, NJ: Ablex.

Ferdman, B. (1990). Literacy and cultural identity. *Harvard Educational Review, 60*(2), 181-204.

Hornberger, N. (1989). Continua of biliteracy. *Review of Educational Research, 59*(3), 271-296.

Hornberger, N.H. (1990). Creating successful learning contexts for biliteracy. *Penn Working Papers in Educational Linguistics* 6(1), 1-21. (ERIC Document Reproduction Service No. ED 335 930)

Kulick, D., & Stroud, C. (1993). Conceptions and uses of literacy in a Papua New Guinean village. In B. Street (Ed.), *Cross-cultural approaches to literacy* (pp. 30-61). Cambridge: Cambridge University Press.

Micheau, C. (1990). *Ethnic identity and ethnic maintenance in the Puerto Rican community of Philadelphia*. Unpublished doctoral dissertation, University of Pennsylvania, Philadelphia.

Serrán-Pagán, G., Acosta, A., & Márquez, A. (1987). *Examen de equivalencia de la escuela superior en español*. New York: Arco.

Street, B. (Ed.). (1993). *Cross-cultural approaches to literacy*. Cambridge: Cambridge University Press.

Wagner, D.A. (1990). *World literacy in the year 2000: Introductory thoughts on research and policy*. Paper prepared for the Conference on World Literacy in the Year 2000, Philadelphia.

CHAPTER 8

Putting a Human Face on Technology: Bilingual Literacy Through Long-Distance Partnerships

Dennis Sayers
New York University
Kristin Brown
University of San Francisco

This chapter describes an effort to foster intergenerational bilingual literacy by setting up technology-mediated partnerships between parents of school-age children over long distances. The ethnic and linguistic minority parents who participated in this effort were from San Diego, California and Denver, Colorado in the United States, and from Caguas in Puerto Rico. This partnership between distant parents is part of a larger computer-based communications network of teacher partnerships coordinated by two Schools of Education, the first at Brooklyn College of the City University of New York and the second at the University of Puerto Rico. The network's name, *De Orilla a Orilla* (Spanish for "From Shore to Shore," and usually shortened to *Orillas*) was chosen to reflect the reality of collaborations that span oceans and continents.

However, the Spanish name *Orillas*, while highlighting the network's origin in Puerto Rico, nevertheless obscures its multilingual identity, because teachers and students (and recently, parents) communicate in, among other languages, French, Haitian Creole, English, Spanish, various English-based Caribbean Creoles, and American and French Canadian Sign Languages. *Orillas* is most definitely multinational; indeed, 100 team-teaching partnerships have been formed, principally among educators in Puerto Rico, Quebec, and the United States, but also including teachers in English-speaking Canada, Costa Rica, France, Japan, Mexico, and several French- and English-speaking islands in the South Pacific.

While *Orillas* teacher partnerships began in 1985, partnerships between parents and between parent-child dyads within *Orillas* have been initiated only in the last few years. The network has been overwhelmingly concerned with distance team-teaching projects, often employing computer-based electronic mail. That is, partner teachers communicate regularly to plan and implement jointly executed, collaborative teaching projects between their classes. Typical projects have included (a) shared student journalism and publishing; (b) comparative research, including dual community surveys, joint science investigations, and contrastive geography projects; and (c) both traditional and modern folklore compendia, extending from oral histories and collections of proverbs to children's rhymes and riddles, lullabies and game songs, and fables and folktales.

To coordinate their collaborative works-in-progress, teachers use electronic mail to stay in frequent contact and to transmit their students' work. While using up-to-date technology, *Orillas* has employed an educational networking model first developed by the French pedagogue Célestin Freinet in 1924 (Clandfield & Sivell, 1990; Lee, 1980, 1983; Sayers, 1988b). Following Freinet's model, *Orillas* is not a student-to-student penpal project, but rather a class-to-class collaboration designed by partner teachers who have been matched according to common teaching interests and their students' grade level.

Given the class-to-class focus of *Orillas*, it is not surprising that teacher collaborations and student projects, rather than parent partnerships, have received the greatest share of attention from the educational research community. For example, *Orillas* has been described as an exemplary curricular project for bilingual education programs (Cummins, 1986, 1988; Cummins & Sayers, 1990; Faltis & DeVillar, 1990; Figueroa, Sayers, & Brown, 1990; Sayers & Brown, 1987), English as a second language programs (Cazden, 1985), foreign language programs (Green, 1990; Willetts, 1989), and writing programs (Figueroa, 1988). The network was also cited as a noteworthy project for linguistic minority students by the U.S. Congress Office of Technology Assessment (Roberts & staff, 1987):

Long-distance networking capabilities of computer-based technologies are being used to encourage [these] students to write and communicate more effectively in highly functional contexts, both in their native language and in English. When used in this context, the computer can provide a means for students to break out of the traditional mode of thinking, to enhance their sense of mastery, and to enrich the learning experience by providing access to role models and speakers from their native culture. (p. 96)

Finally, DeVillar and Faltis (1991) judged *Orillas* "certainly one of the more, if not the most, innovative and pedagogically complete computer-supported writing projects involving students across distances" (p. 116).

In addition, there have been several research studies of *Orillas* teacher partnerships, encompassing both qualitative (Sayers, 1988a, 1989, 1991) and quantitative research designs (Sayers, in press). To date, no formal research study has centered on long-distance parent collaborations mediated by technology. However, we have conducted an informal study (based on observations completed over the course of a full academic year, together with interviews of teachers, parents and their children, and numerous videotapes) at an after-school parent-child computer course offered at Sherman School in San Diego, California, one of the *Orillas* sites that formed a parent partnership with similar after-school groups in Denver, Colorado and Caguas, Puerto Rico. We believe that the results of our informal investigation of parent partnerships illustrate many of the findings of the more formal studies of teacher collaborations in *Orillas*, with intriguing implications for family literacy programs for minority language parents and children.

The Sherman School After-School Computer Course for Parents and Their Children: A Portrait

Sherman School is located in Barrio Sherman in San Diego, California, in a neighborhood principally composed of African-American, Latino, Cambodian, and Euro-American communities. There have been many attempts by educators from Sherman School to involve parents in school activities and to establish literacy classes for the parents of the children at this school. However, owing to a number of factors familiar to all who have worked with low-income immigrant adults, many difficulties have been confronted. For example, heads of single-parent families often work long hours or during second or third shifts and have little time to devote to school-based activities, such as the Parent Teacher Organization or parent-teacher conferences. Teachers affirm that in spite of high expectations and great concern expressed by most parents for their children's success in school, few parents actually get involved in school-community outreach efforts.

Language differences and wide language variation pose barriers between school professionals and parents; not only do parents have limited proficiency in Standard English, they are from a number of language and dialect backgrounds, including Spanish, Khmer, and Black Vernacular English (BVE). Inside the family unit, most parents are devoted to improving the quality of life for their own family; but within Barrio Sherman, sharp divisions among community members are revealed in the frequent strife between gangs, which pits the Cambodians and the African-Americans in an uneasy alliance against the larger Latino community. Drug abuse in the community is also a major destabilizing force, and an overriding concern of both teachers and parents is to make Barrio Sherman a safer place to live through confronting the drug problem.

At the start of the 1989-1990 school year, a new attempt was made by the Sherman School to establish literacy classes for adults in the community. Both the teacher of this literacy class, Maria de Lourdes Bouras, and the school contact person, Laura Parks-Sierra, had worked extensively with students in the *Orillas* Project in previous years and had discovered the effectiveness both of using computers with a variety of communication activities and of having students work in teams. Together, they made the decision to design their literacy class for students *and* their parents. The design of the literacy course would be similar to the approach they had already used in *Orillas*: Local partners would work on the computer, learning to use it both as a writing tool (word processing) and as a communication tool (telecommunications). Next, the many partners who made up the Sherman School literacy course would form another kind of partnership with distant sister classes, using electronic mail. Finally, what they wrote would eventually be published locally in a newsletter distributed in the community. The only difference between previous *Orillas* projects and this literacy course would be that this time the local partnerships would be made of a parent and his or her child.

This decided, an evening computer class was announced during regular school hours to all second- through sixth-grade students. There would be no cost to join, but it was clearly stipulated that students had to be accompanied by one or more parents for each computer class. The teachers reported that, unlike other messages designed to reach parents (often "lost" due to language differences or incorrect addresses given by worried parents with uncertain immigrant status), this announcement was efficiently delivered to their parents by Sherman's students, for whom computer time was a favorite school activity. On the first night, dozens of parents appeared, and even more unaccompanied students; however, the teachers maintained their parent-child partnership policy and turned away those students who had not brought parents. Parents who enrolled commented that they were tired after long days at work and of caring for families and would not have attended except for their children's insistence.

Teachers said that parents were intrigued with the prospect of learning how to use computers with their children, and particularly with the idea of communicating with other parents and children in far-off places like Colorado and Puerto Rico. They were especially interested to hear that other parents were involved in similar projects, and many who had seen little of the United States were curious about life in these distant places. They liked the idea of helping their children in school and also of helping them acquire technology skills. Students who attended the parent-child computer class received a certificate with the name of the parent and child printed on it to deliver to their regular classroom teachers the following day; classroom teachers had agreed to announce the names of parents and children who had participated in the initial literacy classes to encourage continued attendance.

At the outset, participants had some difficulties just in learning to use word processing and other software. Explanations to the group seemed labored: The teacher was bilingual (English-Spanish), but English speakers initially expressed some impatience at having to wait during translations, at the time thus taken from more important, computer-related tasks. Parents were at very different levels of English proficiency. Moreover, Ms. Bouras reported her sense that, during initial computer projects, whoever was at the keyboard assumed control, creating barriers for others to join in as full participants.

Two emerging themes: Communication and teamwork based on sharing of skills

Once communications from the distant parent groups began to arrive, some interesting changes seemed to take place in parents' and students' attitudes, both toward engaging in computer-based collaborations and toward language use. The teacher and school contact person reported that parents and students began to see the computer as a tool for communication. They began to evidence more comfort with the new technology, because communication was something everyone understood and felt competent at. The group, faced with the task of representing and describing San Diego in response to the initial questions of the distant groups, became more cohesive.

To help introduce themselves to their partner groups in Colorado and Puerto Rico, the Sherman School parents and children decided to make and send a "cultural package" that featured a book to which everyone could contribute, regardless of their level of literacy in their mother tongue or in English. For example, the Cambodian family in which parents could not speak, read, or write in English, brought in the most magazine articles and pictures. Together, parents and their children elaborated a clear picture of the book they wanted to send; the parents and children worked in teams to create the different sections and then shared their writing and the pictures they had gathered with the rest of the group. By the time the parents had helped one another and the children had helped their parents, the cultural package book had become a seamless group product where the individuality usually expressed in the concept of authorship had become unimportant.

Moreover, the status of the Spanish speakers changed when the majority of the text began arriving in Spanish. Ms. Parks-Sierra captured on videotape the first night the group logged on to the electronic mail system to read messages. Parents and children were pulling their chairs as close as possible to the computer, waiting for the phone call to go through. Soon the electronic messages from Colorado and Puerto Rico began to appear letter by letter on the screen as though the computer had become a teletype machine. When Ms. Bouras translated the messages from Spanish, the English-speaking parents started questioning her and other Spanish-speaking parents to make sure that they understood everything; in Ms. Parks-Sierra's words, "These discussions really seemed to bring the group together."

Suddenly, proficiency in Spanish became highly prized as the texts that everyone was so interested in reading were written in Spanish. The English speakers, rather than relying exclusively on the teacher for information, would turn instead to Spanish speakers. As text arrived in Spanish, English speakers saw the importance of devoting time to translation, even insisting that translation be done carefully to ensure that everyone understood the messages. English-speaking parents who previously had worked on their own sought seats next to Spanish speakers and were active in assuring that the teacher had translated every detail (at times double-checking with their local bilingual expert).

Unlike previous literacy courses sponsored by the Sherman School, attendance at the parent-child computer course justified continuing the class for the entire academic year. Parents and children attributed this, in large part, to the communications with the faraway parent groups. There was great curiosity about what the distant partner classes would write. Parents and students said that they did not want to miss class in case any electronic mail might have arrived from the other groups. Evidently, their distant correspondents felt similarly, as shown in this message from Denver:

> *Hi! My name is Guadalupe and I have a sister her name is Claudia. Colorado is a very nice place to live in. We're here tonight because we came to write back to you!*
>
> > *Sincerely,*
> > *Guadalupe and Claudia Ortiz*
> > *(February 12, 1990)*

Another factor may have been the prestige associated with working in a project that focused on long-distance communication. Ms. Bouras reported that several parents told her that when they got together with friends and family over the weekend and they had mentioned their using the computer to write to parents in Puerto Rico and Colorado, their friends had been very impressed. The Sherman School parents seemed honored that people from so far away would be interested in what they had to say, and therefore they worked hard both on their electronic messages and on the book for their cultural package, in order to give the distant parents the clearest impression of Barrio Sherman, Sherman School, and San Diego.

Before the end of the academic year, the Sherman School parents had collaborated in the production of numerous highly literate publications. A description of these publications, followed by sample writings, illustrates the range of emergent literacy skills being shared between parents and their children. Please note that original spellings have been maintained throughout and that, except where indicated, translations are those provided by parents and children. The Sherman School Computer Class published the following:

• A bilingual booklet of parent-teacher conference guidelines distributed to all of Sherman School's parents and teachers—an outcome of close consultation with several teachers.

Tu participación es importante:
¿Qué es una conferencia familiar?

Una conferencia familiar es cuando nos reunimos con los maestros de nuestros hijos para hablar sobre su aprovechamiento escolar y su comportamiento en la escuela. Es el momento de aprender más acerca de nuestros hijos y sus maestros . . . .

Let's Lead the Way: What is a Family Conference?

A family conference is an update on your child's progress and to discuss their future goals. It is a network between teacher, student, and parents.

• Bilingual books, including a parent-child guidebook to San Diego for the Sherman School Library's permanent collection and for the Puerto Rico and Colorado parent groups, describing interesting places for families to visit in San Diego—the result of collaboration between children and their parents.

The San Diego Zoo

I like the San Diego Zoo because it is a very nice place to go and you can see a big snake and a tall giraffe. In the San Diego Zoo you can find a lot of animals like rabbits, polar bears, big brown bear, and the eagles in the trees. The tallest animal of all is the giraffe and the fattest animal of all is the elephant.

There are huge bears also. The animal I like most is the giraffe because it is tall. My mom likes the monkey the most... The tigers like meat and they are very big. The best thing I like about the tiger is that it runs fast and has sharp teeth because I would like to have sharp teeth like that too. My mom hates the tiger because it kills animals and people. The San Diego Zoo is like the San Diego Wild Animals Park because they have almost the same numbers of animals. The trolleys look the same.

(Keovong Sar and Eam, Cambodian son and mother)

• An international *refranero,* or book of proverbs, for which parents consulted their extended families to create lists of proverbs (and how they are used) that were shared with the parent partner groups as well as with all the other teacher partnerships in *Orillas*— a consequence of sharing among families, the local community, and the wider world of *Orillas* participants.

Proverbio: Dios aprieta pero no ahorca.
[Translation: God may squeeze you but he won't choke you.]

Explicación: Por que cuando tiene uno algun problema siempre ay alguna forma para resolberlo con la bolunta de dios. [Because when one has some problem there is always some way to solve it, God willing.]

Situación: Un día andabamos tres amigas en un carro y tubimos un acidente con un troque de la Cuidad y quedamos atrapadas, y una de nosotros dijo no te preocupes dios aprieta pero no ahorca, i fue sierto porque no nos paso nada todos salimos bien porque nadie salio golpeado gracias dios. [One day two friends and I were driving and we had an accident with a City truck and we were trapped. One of us said not to worry "Dios aprieta pero no ahorca," and that was true, because none of us were hurt, thank God.]

(Emely Guzman E. and Isabel García, Mexican-American mothers)

• An international collection of articles on self-esteem and technology, for which the Sherman School computer class worked with professors and graduate students from Harvard University Education School as well as with psychologists, teachers, and other parents and children from Argentina, Mexico, Puerto Rico, Quebec, and the United States.

I think that a computer is good for children as well as adults because it let you put down your thoughts and feelings and express your opinions. . . . I thing it's great that the children are learning about computers and how they work and how to use them and write their own stories and to read what they have written. I think it gives them a good feeling inside to know that they did it and that they are as important as we are.

(Christyl McCorley, African-American with 2 children in computer class)

In respons to the question, on learning by thecnology, it is my personal belive, that it is a good way to prepare are children and owr selfs, to meet the future for it is chainging dayly, it is nothing to be afreid of, it is like turning on your television or dialing you'r, phone the deferance is that here you are apon samething new, and if you do not have similiarity with the equipment, it natural to feel unease about thecnology.

1. In the case of computers, at first you may feel not capable to be able, to manipulate it's sistem, as you start plaing the key board, you begun to gett amuch better feeling about wath you are doing, it then becomes a chalange betweing you and the sestem, until you are able master it.

2. It is also useful in teaching, for it helps to support a subjet, by bringing in graffic suport to the teacher, to esplain better, and helping the students to understand better the subjet.

(Hector Reynoso, Mexican-American parent)

Why I like Computers

When I use the computer I fill nervous inside my body because when you start to use a computer you really have to get ready. I think computers help students because if they do not know how to read the computer help him or her to say it. I think computers are important because if someone does not have a phone and they only have a computer and they could use the computer to call the people they want to call. The computer was after all made for children to help them learn. I like computers and I wand to know more about computers.

(Keovong Sar and Eam, Cambodian son and mother)

- A community newspaper, the product of collaboration with teachers and administrators and children at Sherman School.

Exemplary Mother

Eam is originally from Cambodia, she is medium high has a beautiful black hair and is always smiling. She started coming to the computer class almost from the beginning She never missed a class and she always had a positive attitude toward everybody. Eam looks so young that you will never beleive she is thirty six years old. She was a mother of nine children, but three of them died in the war in Batanbag, in Cambodia.

Eam was 15 when she got married, eventhough this sounds too young, this is normal for Cambodians. . . . Eam didn't want to have children right away but contraceptive methods were not very advance in Cambodia so she got pregnat right away. Her new family grew fast and she had to work harder and harder, since in Cambodia your children depend very much from the mother's care. It was fascinating talking with Eam and getting to know such a different culture, but what makes this story more facinating is the fact that no matter where in the world we are or where do we come from the importance of being a caring and loving parent is always the key for our future generations. And Eam is one of this great mothers that has helped six children grow up with an incredible future in front of them.

(anonymous article written by other parents)

In a very real sense, these publications by parents and children would not have been possible without their electronic partnerships, since each formal publication was preceded and accompanied by informal dialogues, among themselves and with distant classes, to identify issues and topics for writing, to test developing ideas, and to elaborate drafts.

Throughout the 1989-1990 academic year, parents and children in the computer class worked in teams. To be sure, all teams did not function identically. Some parents and their children shared equally all stages of writing (prewriting, drafting, and revising and editing) and translating (from their home language to English and back).

Other teams divided the writing task in a variety of effective ways, with some parents playing the key role of topic "definers" in the home language while their children acted as keyboardists and language interpreters and "refiners" in English. Certainly, all parents and children, while working in teams, showed evidence of moving toward greater independence; as an example, for the year's final project, the community newspaper, every parent submitted articles for publication. Perhaps the term "teamwork" does not adequately convey the complex literacy activities that developed among the Sherman School parents and children as a result of their collaboration with distant *Orillas* parent-child groups.

These occasions provided by *Orillas* for displaying literacy may better be viewed as sequences of nested, interlocking collaborations. Let us take as an example an introductory letter written early in the year to distant parent groups by Eam (the Khmer-speaking 36-year-old Cambodian "Exemplary Mother"), Keovong (her bilingual son), and Maria (his Spanish-English bilingual schoolmate).

> *Dear Parents and children,*
>
> *Our names are Keovong, Maria and Eam. I am Keovong the one that is typing because I am good at typing. I was born in Phillipines and my parents are from Cambodia. My mom come to computer class. My mom is writing in Cambodian and someone will translate it in English or Spanish. My dad used to come with me to the computer. Many of my people had died in Cambodia. My land has been taken by the bad people. But now I am far away from my home land and I am safe in San Diego.*
>
> > *Your new friend,*
> > *Keovong Sar, [October 1990]*

Clearly, this text has evolved from a rich, intergenerational learning situation with great potential for fostering biliteracy skills—a mother and her son (and in the first writing, a Spanish-speaking friend) seated together at a computer, using two languages to plan what they will coauthor, and sharing linguistic, cultural, or technical talents at which one or another is more skilled.

This was the first stage in the sequence of nested collaborations. Next, the writing had to be rendered into Spanish by Maria so that it could be shared with other Spanish-dominant parents for discussion prior to sending it over the electronic mail system. This involved a focused collaboration between the bilingual (English-Khmer) child and other bilingual (Spanish-English) parents and children. Of course, the second collaboration had a clear goal—the linguistically accurate and culturally faithful rendering of what the original collaboration had set out in writing. Other nested collaborations followed in interlocking sequence once the San Diego group had sent their message out. For example, parents and children in San Diego and the other *Orillas* sites often sent messages out only in the original Spanish or English; that is, they did not copy into the computer their translations of writings, using them strictly for internal discussion. Therefore, whenever a message was received, a further occasion for translation naturally arose, leading to new sequences of nested and interlocking collaborations.

Previous Formal Research into *Orillas* Teacher Partnerships

All four studies on *Orillas* Teacher Partnerships, three qualitative studies (Sayers, 1988a, 1989, 1991) and a quantitative study (Sayers, in press), have involved bilingual program students of Puerto Rican heritage who used computer-based telecommunications to build literacy skills in both their mother tongue, Spanish, and their second language, English. The three qualitative studies were conducted in a New England urban school district with a long record of advocacy for the educational rights of language minority students. The studies underscored the heterogeneous character of bilingual classes. In this city, the typical composition of a fourth- or fifth-grade bilingual class is 25% Spanish-dominant new arrivals, and 75% bilingual and English-dominant students who are frequently in their last year of bilingual schooling. The Spanish-dominant children were all born in Puerto Rico, while most of the English-dominant children were born in the United States. All students in the pilot studies, regardless of their language dominance, were from Puerto Rican families and spoke Spanish in their homes.

The qualitative studies also revealed that instructional delivery in bilingual classrooms at this level was predominantly in English, which placed the Spanish-dominant students at a marked disadvantage vis-à-vis their bilingual and English-dominant classmates. Spanish was principally used by bilingual teachers for quick summaries and to ask students if they had questions on material previously covered in

English. The negative language attitudes of the English-dominant students toward their Spanish-dominant classmates was revealed in direct commands ("Talk English!"), deprecatory comments ("I can't understand you when you talk that Spanish") and through critical remarks upon hearing Spanish spoken by Spanish-dominant classmates ("I wish they wouldn't talk so fast that way"). Negative attitudes toward Puerto Rican culture were exemplified by one English-dominant U.S.-born Puerto Rican student when the topic was raised of *personas ilustres puertorriqueñas* (famous Puerto Rican historical figures): "What' she talkin' about? We don' got none of those 'round here" (Sayers, 1988a).

All three qualitative studies focused on student-directed small group activities as a vehicle for promoting the simultaneous development of literacy in both the home and second languages. The small group activity that was studied involved student-directed editorial boards. In this activity structure, students in both partner classes are nominated for joint editorial boards, which plan, coordinate, and supervise the production of a common bilingual newsletter.

In the initial study (Sayers, 1989), the partner class exchanges were between a fifth-grade bilingual class in New England and another bilingual class of the same grade level in California. All the students in the New England class were from Puerto Rican families who spoke Spanish at home, but for most of these students the dominant language for school activities was English. The California students were in a two-way bilingual program, where half the students were Anglos and half were from Mexican-American families who spoke Spanish at home; like their New England counterparts, most of these students interacted easily in English during school hours. Students in both the New England and California classes had been nominated for the joint editorial boards by their teachers, without regard for their relative proficiency in English and Spanish. Thus, it is not surprising that the amount of written communication in Spanish that resulted from the exchanges between these particular partner classes was minimal; there was little reason to tap the relatively weak, emerging Spanish skills of the Anglo students in California or the declining Spanish language skills of the English-dominant Latino students in both partner classes.

In the other qualitative studies (Sayers, 1988a, 1991), the same New England teacher was teamed with a teacher from Puerto Rico;

moreover, in the New England classroom, all Spanish-dominant students were assigned to the joint editorial board and matched with another student nominated by the teacher. A major finding of the second study was that, in the context of editorial board exchanges with a Puerto Rican partner class conducted entirely in Spanish, the prestige of the Spanish-dominant editorial board members increased, both in their own estimation and in that of their bilingual and English-dominant peers. The Spanish-dominant students became language and cultural experts whose skills were much sought after by their English-speaking classmates.

The quantitative study (Sayers, in press) focused on change in language attitudes among 89 students in four elementary school bilingual classrooms toward speakers of their home language, Spanish. Once more, the students participated in technology-based long-distance exchanges in partnership with students in Puerto Rico. The research contrasted two instructional approaches, one centering on student-led small group work and another emphasizing teacher-facilitated whole group work. The study sought to determine under which of these two conditions increased status and prestige are conferred upon speakers of the minority language. Students were identified as Spanish-dominant, bilingual, or English-dominant on the basis of holistically rated translation tasks, teacher assessments, and their performance on reading comprehension tests in both languages. Both sociometric and stereotypic measures of language attitude change were employed.

Two measures of the dependent variable, change in language attitude, were employed. For the cross-language dominance group inventory, students employed photographs of classmates as markers and individually rated, using a four-point continuum, her or his classmates on five attributes: how hard-working, how friendly, and how easy to work with they are, as well as how helpful they are to the evaluating student, and how helpful they are to the teacher. For the matched guise task, two guises (a Spanish and an English version of a short narrative) were read onto an audiotape by a bilingual Puerto Rican girl unknown to the subjects. Students listened to the tape in groups and evaluated the Spanish and English recordings on a four-point scale for four constructs: correctness, the listener's personal identification with the speaker, appropriateness of the language for school, and the speaker's likelihood of achievement.

Analysis of Variance (ANOVA) by regression yielded results that confirmed the research hypothesis that improvement in students' language attitudes toward Spanish speakers would occur in all classes, suggesting that technology-mediated exchanges with distant colleagues from the students' home culture indeed constitute an intervention that can produce language attitude changes even over a brief period of five months. Results from the sociometric cross-language dominance group inventory supported the prediction that greater improvement would occur in small-group-work classes, while the stereotypic matched guise indicated greater improvement in the whole-group-work classes.

Implications for intergenerational bilingual literacy projects

One implication of this research into teacher partnerships that also appears relevant for parent-child partnerships is the importance of between-class variables, that is, of finding a productive match between classes involved in distant collaborations. This is seen clearly in the very different outcomes of the initial qualitative study of an *Orillas* exchange and the remaining qualitative investigations. Partnerships between teachers of a New England bilingual class and a California two-way bilingual class did not create a context conducive to the promotion of Spanish and English simultaneously, since English was the majority language in both communities, as well as the home language of many of the California students. This situation changed when a match was formed between the New England bilingual class and a class in Puerto Rico, where Spanish was the dominant language used both at school and in the children's homes.

In this latter situation, namely involving partnerships between a U.S. teacher and a Puerto Rican colleague, a learning context was established that privileged both Spanish language competence and awareness of Puerto Rican culture. The prestige of the Spanish-dominant new arrivals was enhanced in the eyes of their classmates as they became cultural experts who were in a particularly advantaged position to help interpret and clarify messages from their Puerto Rican partner class. At the same time, the balanced bilinguals played a special role as translators, in the most profound sense, of both linguistic and cultural knowledge, working to mediate communications between English-dominant classmates, on the one hand, and both their Spanish-dominant classmates and the distant students in Puerto Rico, on the other.

In this fashion, *Orillas* provided the students with multiple opportunities to display and share their changing linguistic competencies and varied cultural experiences within their classrooms, thus fostering genuine bilingualism and the creation of authentic cross-cultural knowledge between distinct subgroups of Puerto Rican language minority students. Similarly, the partnerships formed by the Sherman School computer class underscore how important the language used by the distant partner class can be in prompting closer collaboration between linguistic minority groups, fostering (indeed, almost forcing) repeated occasions for parents and children to translate for one another and thus share their differing cultural and linguistic skills.

A related implication of the quantitative research on *Orillas* teacher partnerships concerns the importance of within-class collaborations. That study established that pairs and small groups of students offer more opportunities for the kinds of interactions that can lead to significant attitude change toward classmates (Sayers, in press). Because we have not conducted a formal study of the Sherman School computer class, it is impossible to isolate what specific factors account for the evident success of these long-distance parent-child partnerships as settings for building literacy. However, the parent-child dyads and triads that were formed at Sherman School clearly lent themselves to the type of productive sequences of nested and interlocking collaborations to which we previously referred.

What the experience of the Sherman School parent-child computer class does suggests to us is that technology-mediated exchanges like *Orillas* can serve as intergenerational learning contexts, which make parents partners in the building of their children's literacy, and which help them to become more active agents in the promotion of their own literacy skills. By sharing linguistic, literacy, and cross-cultural skills, they are forging tools to empower themselves as they shape their own communities.

References

Cazden, C. (1985, April). *The ESL teacher as advocate.* Plenary paper presented at the annual conference of Teachers of English to Speakers of Other Languages, New York, NY.

Clandfield, D., & Sivell, J. (1990). *Cooperative learning and social change: Selected writings of Célestin Freinet.* Toronto: Our Schools/Our Selves.

Cummins, J. (1986). Cultures in contact: Using classroom microcomputers for cultural exchange and reinforcement. *TESL Canada Journal/Revue TESL du Canada, 3*(2), 13-31.

Cummins, J. (1988). From the inner city to the global village: The microcomputer as a catalyst for collaborative learning and cultural interchange. *Language, Culture, and Curriculum, 1,* 1-13.

Cummins, J., & Sayers, D. (1990). Education 2001: Learning networks and educational reform. In C. Faltis & R. DeVillar (Eds.), *Language minority students and computers* (pp. 1-29). New York: Haworth.

DeVillar, R., & Faltis, C. (1991). *Computers and cultural diversity: Computers, cooperation, and communication for classroom socioacademic achievement.* Albany: State University of New York Press.

Faltis, C., & DeVillar, R. (1990). Computer uses for teaching Spanish to bilingual native speakers. In C. Faltis & R. DeVillar (Eds.), *Language minority students and computers* (pp. 257-269). New York: Haworth.

Figueroa, E. (1988). *Efectos del adiestramiento en redacción computadorizada en las actitudes del personal de Tecnología Educativa hacia la enseñanza de la redacción.* (The effects of staff development on attitudes toward the teaching of writing among the Educational Technology Office Staff of the Department of Public Transportation of Puerto Rico). Unpublished manuscript, University of Puerto Rico, Río Piedras.

Figueroa, E., Sayers, D., & Brown, K. (1990). Red multilingüe para el aprendizaje: De Orilla a Orilla. [A multilingual learning network: From Shore to Shore]. *Micro-Aula: El Maestro y la Computadora, 8,* 27-30.

Green, C. (1990). *An implementation of Project "De Orilla a Orilla": A cultural exchange program in a fourth-grade English immersion class in Mayagüez, Puerto Rico.* Unpublished master's thesis, University of Puerto Rico, Mayagüez.

Lee, W.B. (1980). Ecole Moderne Pédagogie Freinet: Educational bonesetters. *Phi Delta Kappan, 61*(5), 341-45.

Lee, W.B. (1983). Célestin Freinet, the unknown reformer. *Educational Forum, 48*(1), 97-114.

Roberts, L., & staff. (1987). *Trends and status of computers in schools: Use in Chapter 1 programs and use with limited English proficient students.* Washington, DC: U.S. Congress Office of Technology Assessment.

Sayers, D. (1988a). *Editorial boards between sister classes.* Unpublished manuscript. Harvard Graduate School of Education, Cambridge, MA.

Sayers, D. (1988b). *Interscholastic correspondence exchanges in Célestin Freinet's Modern School Movement: Implications for computer-mediated student writing networks.* Unpublished manuscript. Harvard Graduate School of Education, Cambridge, MA.

Sayers, D. (1989). Bilingual sister classes in computer writing networks. In D. Johnson & D. Roen (Eds.), *Richness in writing: Empowering ESL writers* (pp. 120-133). New York: Longman.

Sayers, D. (1991). Cross-cultural exchanges between students from the same culture: A portrait of an emerging relationship mediated by technology. *The Canadian Modern Language Review/La Revue Canadienne des langues vivantes, 47,* 678-696.

Sayers, D. (in press). Bilingual teacher partnerships over long distances: A technology-mediated context for intra-group language attitude change. In C. Faltis & R. DeVillar (Eds.), *Successful cultural diversity: Classroom practices for the 21st century.* Albany: State University of New York Press.

Sayers, D., & Brown, K. (1987). Bilingual education and telecommunications: A perfect fit. *The Computing Teacher, 17,* 23-24.

Willetts, K. (1989). Computer networking applications. *Athelstan Newsletter on Technology and Language, 2*(2), 1-3, 10.

CHAPTER 9

Discourse and Social Practice: Learning Science in Language Minority Classrooms

Beth Warren, Ann S. Rosebery, and Faith Conant
Technical Education Research Center (TERC)
Cambridge, Massachusetts

This chapter is broadly about literacy or, more properly, literacies. Taking as our starting point the discussions of biliteracy in many of the chapters in this volume, we hope to contribute to the elaboration of the meaning of biliteracy by exploring the pluralistic and socially embedded nature of literacy. In these chapters biliteracy has been explored from linguistic, cognitive, pedagogical, political, and sociocultural perspectives. We will extend the focus on language—first and second languages—expressed in these chapters to a focus on discourse as the unit of analysis needed to understand the complexity of the task facing bilingual students.

Knowing a language, any language, means knowing more than the English language, or the Spanish language, or any other language for that matter. Each language is really many languages, a set of possible discourses people use to communicate with one another in their daily activity (Bakhtin, 1981). Each of these discourses in turn constitutes a set of beliefs and values in terms of which one speaks, thinks, and acts (Gee, 1989). The particular discourse worlds we inhabit will depend on our history, the books we have read, the people with whom we have talked and from whom we have learned, the social circles in which we have moved, our economic class, our generation, our epoch, the institutions (church, political party, schools, societies) to which we have belonged, and so forth (Booth, 1986). As the Soviet theorist Mikhail Bakhtin (1981) explains:

> At any given moment of its historical existence, language . . . is heteroglot from top to bottom: it represents the co-existence of socio-ideological contradictions between the present and the

past, between differing epochs of the past, between different socio-ideological groups in the present, between tendencies, schools, circles and so forth, all given a bodily form. These "languages" of heteroglossia intersect each other in a variety of ways, forming new socially typifying "languages." (p. 291)

The idea that language is heteroglot poses some difficulties for both our common sense and technical uses of the term "literacy." In both senses, the term is often used to suggest a capability that is unitary and univocal rather than pluralistic and multivocal (although the varied definitions of literacy that abound in the literature are perhaps a clue to its inherent diversity). In the same vein, literacy often is defined in terms of mastery of certain general skills—reading, writing, arithmetic skills—rather than in terms of mastery of whole systems of meaning and practices, each involving a set of beliefs and values or, in Bakhtin's term, an ideology.

From this perspective, the task facing the second language learner—specifically, in this culture, the learner of English—is enormously complex. Learning English in school really means appropriating whole systems of meaning involved in such school tasks as reading and answering questions about stories, talking to the teacher, taking tests, playing with other students in the schoolyard, doing mathematics, doing science, doing history, and so on. But in many, if not most, schools this pluralistic perspective is not enacted; English—that is, grammar and vocabulary—is the real subject of instruction, whether in ESL, science, or social studies. It is presented as a ready-made and neutral system that the learner is meant to assimilate through practice and memorization.

In our work, we are trying to understand how language minority students begin to appropriate a new discourse, specifically *scientific discourse* (Rosebery, Warren, & Conant, 1990; Rosebery, Warren, & Conant, 1992; Warren, Rosebery, & Conant, 1989). In collaboration with bilingual teachers, we are working to create communities of authentic scientific practice in language minority classrooms; that is, communities in which students do science in ways that practicing scientists do. In this context, science is organized as a socially embedded activity in which students pose their own questions, plan and implement research to explore their questions, collect, analyze, and interpret data, build and argue theories, draw conclusions and, in some cases, take actions based on their research. We stress the notion of appropriation because we see the learner as essentially finding ways to take the sense-making practices of science and make them his or her own, tuning them to his or her own intention, his or her own sense-making purposes.

The complexity of the appropriation process cannot be overstated, as Bakhtin (1981) explains:

[The word in language] becomes "one's own" only when the speaker populates it with his own intention, his own accent, when he appropriates the word, adapting it to his own semantic and expressive intention. Prior to this moment of appropriation, the word . . . exists in other people's mouths, in other people's contexts, serving other people's intentions: it is from there that one must take the word, and make it one's own. And not all words for just anyone submit equally easily to this appropriation, to this seizure and transformation into private property: many words stubbornly resist, others remain alien, sound foreign in the mouth of the one who appropriated them and who now speaks them; they cannot be assimilated into his context and fall out of it; it is as if they put themselves in quotation marks against the will of the speaker. Language is not a neutral medium that passes freely and easily into the private property of the speaker's intentions; it is populated— overpopulated—with the intentions of others. Expropriating it, forcing it to submit to one's own intentions and accents, is a difficult and complicated process. (pp. 293-294)

For language minority students, the appropriation process can be even more arduous than for other students, for the distance they must travel between discourse worlds is often far greater. They keenly feel the conflict between American viewpoints, values, and beliefs and those of their own culture; perhaps the most well researched example of this is the emphasis in American schools on individual as opposed to collective action (Au, 1980; Au & Jordan, 1981; Mohatt & Erickson, 1980; Philips, 1972).

What makes appropriation so difficult is that discourses are inherently ideological; they crucially involve a set of values and viewpoints in terms of which one speaks, acts, and thinks (Bakhtin, 1981; Gee, 1989). As a result, discourses are always in conflict with one another in their underlying assumptions and values, their ways of making sense, their viewpoints, and the objects and concepts with which they are concerned. Each gives a different shape to experience. Therefore, appropriating any one discourse will be more or less difficult depending on the various other discourses in which students (and their teachers) participate.

From this perspective, then, we do not define scientific literacy as the acquisition of specific knowledge (facts) or skills, nor even from a cognitive perspective as the refinement of a mental model. Rather we understand scientific literacy to be a socially and culturally produced way of thinking and knowing, with its own sense-making practices, its own values, norms, beliefs, and so forth. In this light, when students participate in a community of scientific practice, they begin to appropriate not scientific facts but socially mediated ways of knowing, thinking, and using language (both first and second languages) to construct scientific meanings. Our belief is that this discourse perspective is necessary if we are to understand how schools can better meet the challenge of educating bilingual students.

In this chapter we will explore the efforts of some high school students to make sense of data they collected about the quality of their community's drinking water. The focus of our analysis will be on the relationship between voice and social practice—in particular, how the students struggled to appropriate a scientific voice as they constructed scientific meanings. As part of this analysis, we will contrast the uses of language that emerged in the context of authentic scientific practice on the one hand and conventional school practice on the other. In the conclusion, we will explore more broadly the educational implications of the analysis for language minority students.

Background

Before launching into the details of the case, some background on what we mean by "communities of authentic scientific practice" is needed. First, we ground our work in the research literature. Secondly, we outline a perspective on scientific practice that draws on several sources, including the reflections of practicing scientists and ethnographic studies of laboratory life. Finally, we offer a general approach to building communities of scientific practice in the bilingual classroom.

A new conceptualization of learning is emerging in the research literature (Brown, Collins, & Duguid, 1989; Lampert, 1990; Lave, 1988, 1991; Resnick, 1989; Schoenfeld, 1992; in press). Drawing heavily on Vygotsky (1978, 1985) and on anthropological perspectives on learning and cognition (Geertz, 1973, 1983; Lave, 1988), this literature views learning as an inherently cognitive *and* social activity. The child appropriates new forms of discourse, knowledge, and reasoning through his or her participation in socially defined systems of activity. As Resnick (1989) has recently argued, education may be better thought of as a process of socialization, rather than instruction, into ways of thinking, knowing, valuing, and acting that are characteristic of a particular discipline.

Central to this view is the idea that concepts are constructed and understood in the context of a community or culture of practice; their meaning is socially constituted (Brown et al., 1989). Within this community, moreover, practitioners are bound by complex, socially constructed webs of belief that help to define and give meaning to what they do (Geertz, 1983). As Mehan (1992) has noted, members of a community "cannot make up meanings in any old way" (p. 77). Rather, they build up ways of knowing, talking, acting, and valuing, which help to constrain the construction of meaning within the discipline. Within this framework, the learner is conceptualized as one who appropriates new forms of knowledge through apprenticeship in a community of practice (Brown et al., 1989; Collins, Brown, & Newman, 1989; Lampert, 1990; Lave, 1988, 1991; Resnick, 1989; Rosebery et al., 1990, 1992; Schoenfeld, 1992, in press; Warren et al., 1989).

What, then, is the nature of scientific practice? For the Nobel laureate scientist, Sir Peter Medawar (1987), scientific sense-making is a kind of storytelling:

> Like other exploratory processes, [the scientific method] can be resolved into a dialogue between fact and fancy, the actual and the possible; between what could be true and what is in fact the case. The purpose of scientific enquiry is not to compile an inventory of factual information, nor to build up a totalitarian world picture of Natural Laws in which every event that is not compulsory is forbidden. We should think of it rather as a logically articulated structure of justifiable beliefs about a

Possible World—a story which we invent and criticize and modify as we go along, so that it ends by being, as nearly as we can make it, a story about real life. (p. 129)

Medawar's use of the story metaphor represents a bold challenge both to typical school beliefs about what it means to be scientifically literate and to the larger culture's assumptions about the nature of scientific knowledge. First, he challenges the belief that science, at bottom, is the discovery of a reality that exists "out there," pregiven but hitherto concealed (Latour & Woolgar, 1986). Secondly, he challenges the belief that scientists work according to a rigorously defined, logical method, known popularly as "the scientific method." And thirdly, through his emphasis on story building, he challenges the belief that scientific discourse, the construction of scientific meaning, is represented uniquely by forms of writing and speech that are thoroughly objective and impersonal.

Central to Medawar's vision is an idea of scientific practice in which creativity and construction, rather than discovery, predominate. His language suggests that science is projective rather than objective: Scientists build stories about a possible world; they do not discover the truth that already exists out there. Further, he insists on the dialogic quality of scientific activity: fact and fancy, invention and criticism interacting.

Contemporary sociological and anthropological studies of the nature of scientific activity in laboratory settings add an explicit social dimension to this picture (Knorr-Cetina & Mulkay, 1983; Latour, 1987; Latour & Woolgar, 1986; Longino, 1990; Lynch, 1985). These studies show that scientists construct and refine their ideas within a community in which they transform their observations into findings through argumentation and persuasion, not simply through measurement and discovery. The apparent logic of scientific papers is really the end result of the practice of a group of scientists whose goal is to eliminate as many alternative interpretations as possible in their account of the phenomena being studied. (It is hard not to hear an echo of Medawar's storytelling in this.) Through the "superimposition of inscriptions" (Latour & Woolgar, 1986) (graphs, notes, statements, drafts of papers, published papers), accounts are constructed, claims are negotiated, analogies are sought, arguments are put forward and defended against attack, and objections are anticipated. As Latour and Woolgar (1986) show, the scientists they studied claimed merely to be discovering facts, but close observation revealed that they were writers and readers in the business of being convinced and convincing others. Throughout this process, the "facticity" of statements is in constant flux as statements are evaluated and reevaluated. Rather than the orderly, logical, and coherent process that is described in science textbooks as the scientific method, actual scientific practice entails making sense out of frequently disorderly observations, and negotiating among alternative interpretations. However, once a statement or account has stabilized, all traces of its production are eliminated and, as in journal articles, it appears that reality is the cause rather than the consequence of its construction.

Through our work with bilingual teachers and students, we are attempting to elaborate an approach to science teaching and learning that supports the development of classroom communities of authentic scientific practice. This approach entails a radically different orientation to teaching and learning than that found in traditional classrooms—one in which students construct their scientific understanding through an iterative process of theory building, criticism and refinement organized around their own questions, and hypotheses and data analysis activities. Fundamentally, the idea is to place question posing, theorizing, and argumentation at the heart of students' scientific activity. Students explore the implications of the theories they hold (sometimes called "naive" theories), examine underlying assumptions, formulate and test hypotheses, develop evidence, negotiate conflicts in belief and evidence, argue alternative interpretations, provide warrants for conclusions, and the like. Conceptually, they investigate their own questions and the beliefs or theories from which they derive; epistemologically, they explore relationships among truth, evidence, and belief in science. They, in short, become authors of ideas and arguments (cf. Lampert, 1990; Warren et al., 1989). In practice, the approach is one of collaborative inquiry. The heart of the approach is for students to formulate questions about phenomena for which they have some prior belief (e.g., Is our school's water safe to drink? Is the air temperature hottest at noon? Is salt consumption related to physical fitness?). They then build and criticize theories, collect and analyze data, evaluate hypotheses through experimentation, observation, and measurement, and interpret and communicate their findings.

More than simply involving students in hands-on science, the classrooms evolve into communities in which scientific sense-making is actively practiced. Toward this end, investigations are also collaborative, just as most authentic scientific activity is. The emphasis on collaborative inquiry reflects our belief, building on Vygotsky (1978), that robust knowledge and understandings are socially constructed through talk, activity, and interaction around meaningful problems and tools. Collaborative inquiry provides direct cognitive and social support for the efforts of a group's individual members. Students share the responsibility for thinking and doing, distributing their intellectual activity so that the burden of managing the whole process does not fall to any one individual. The distribution and sharing of intellectual responsibility is particularly effective for language minority students, for whom the language demands of tasks are often overwhelming and can often mask their abilities and understanding. In addition, collaborative inquiry creates powerful contexts for constructing scientific meanings. In challenging one another's thoughts and beliefs, students must be explicit about their meanings; they must negotiate conflicts in belief or evidence; and they must share and synthesize their knowledge in order to achieve a common goal, if not a common understanding (Barnes & Todd, 1977; Brown & Palincsar, 1989; Hatano, 1981; Inagaki & Hatano, 1983).

Finally, investigations are interdisciplinary; science, mathematics, and language (speaking, reading, and writing) are intimately linked. Mathematics and language are recognized as essential tools of scientific inquiry, a recognition that stands in sharp contrast to traditional schooling in which science is separated from math, and the role of language in each is hardly acknowledged. The importance of an interdisciplinary approach cannot be overstated with regard to language minority students. It involves them directly in the kinds of purposeful, communicative interactions that promote genuine language use—interactions that arguably are the most productive contexts for language acquisition—such as talking in the context of doing science and trying to solve a meaningful problem. It also creates opportunities for students to use the languages of science and mathematics in ways that schools and the society at large require: not just to read textbooks or do computations, but to write reports, argue a theory, develop evidence, and defend conclusions.

Bacteria Study

To illustrate the approach, we offer an example taken from a bilingual basic skills class in a large urban high school. There were 22 students in the class representing six different language groups: Haitian Creole, Spanish, Portuguese, Amharic, Tigrinya, and Cape Verdean Creole. The students were for the most part recent immigrants who knew little or no English. Many could not read or write in their first languages. Most had acquired only basic mathematical skills (e.g., addition and subtraction) and had no previous experience with science.

During the spring the class studied a local pond bordering the city's water reservoir. On an earlier trip to the pond, the students had been struck by its poor condition as well as its proximity to the city's drinking water supply. An empty oil barrel and a shopping cart sat in the shallows; bottles and broken glass littered the shore; and the water was murky and slick with oil. The students wondered how the pond came to be a dumping ground and if it posed any hazard to the city's water supply.

In the context of their field study, the students analyzed some of the pond's chemical, biological, and physical characteristics. They also investigated the city's water supply, learning about its sources, how it is purified, and how it is piped throughout the city. Groups of students took responsibility for different aspects of the study.

As part of their spring investigation, the students compared the bacteria level of the pond to the bacteria level of their community's tap water. They were interested in two things: How much bacteria was in the pond? How much bacteria was in their drinking water? They collected water samples from the pond and brought them back to the classroom. They also brought in samples of their home tap water and sampled several drinking fountains in the school.

To determine the bacteria levels in these different water sources, they performed a test for fecal coliform using commercially available culture kits called Millipore samplers. A Millipore sampler consists of an absorbent, nutrient-filled pad that fits into a plastic holder. The pad is marked with a grid. To test for bacteria, the pad is immersed in a water sample, placed inside the plastic holder, and incubated for twenty-four hours. At the end of twenty-four hours, the grid on the pad is inspected for bacteria colonies, which appear as tiny black, blue, or green spots. A pamphlet accompanying the samplers allows the user to assign a water quality grade based on the number of colonies that grow. To be drinkable, water must have a count of zero.

The students grew cultures from pond water, home tap water, and school water. However, many of the cultures did not take, possibly because of inadequate incubation. (The precise reasons were never determined.) A few survived, however, and one Haitian student, Rose, used them as the basis for investigating the bacteria level in the city's tap water.

Rose's first step was to document the results from a successful home tap water culture. In her lab notebook, she drew a facsimile of the Millipore sampler and reproduced the position and size of each of the 57 bacteria colonies that had grown (see Figure 1). This entailed meticulous attention to detail. The original grid measured only 1.75" X 3", and the colonies were best seen under magnification. Working carefully from the sampler, Rose produced an accurate rendering of the culture.

Figure 1.
Rose's Reproduction of the Bacteria Sampler and Interpretation of the Data

57

I counted the bacteria in the tape water
I find fivlty seven bacteria in the tape
water. That's mine you cannot not drinking
but you can swimm on that water
Grade B for that water because whole body
contact no more than 200/100 mL

Rose's findings corroborated an estimate of the presence of 60 colonies given earlier by another student who had examined the sampler with a hand lens. While she was pleased that her results were confirmed by the earlier estimate, her contentment was quickly overshadowed by her realization of their significance. According to the standards stated in the Millipore pamphlet, the tap water, which had come from a student's home, was not fit to drink. She proceeded to document her finding in English, as shown in the figure.

Rose's report, brief as it is, utilizes different kinds of information and draws on diverse resources and voices to communicate her finding and its significance. In it, she puts the reader in contact, even if only implicitly, with other texts such as the written standards that accompany the Millipore samplers. She documents her narrative with representations (both graphical and numerical) of the culture, thereby adding to the credibility of her report and interpretation. She describes how she came to her results, emphatically marking them as the product of her own activity through use of the first person authorial voice ("I counted," "I find"). Through this use of voice, Rose marks the finding as a personal construction; it does not exist apart from her agency.

It is interesting that, when interpreting the data according to the standards, Rose switches from the first person to the more authoritative, objective voice signalled in, "That's mine (That means) you can't not drinking but you can swim on that water. Grade B for that water because whole body contact no more than 200/100 ml." Here she is appropriating the words of the Millipore pamphlet to interpret her finding and to inform others of its significance: The water used in this sample is fit for whole body contact but not for drinking. (Grade B water, which is suitable for whole body contact such as swimming, can contain a bacterial count of 1–200 colonies per 100 ml of water.) The switch in voice suggests Rose's awareness of the need for credibility; reference to the water quality standards stated in the pamphlet lend her argument a validity it would not otherwise have.

From our perspective, what stands out in this episode is the way in which Rose has taken control of the bacteria study, shaped it to her own purposes and taken a point of view, and then interpreted her activity and its significance for a larger community. The mixed levels of description and explanation, the orchestration of multiple voices, the recourse to standards and multiple representations reflect her own efforts at sense-making and belie the surface simplicity of her report. These sense-making efforts reflect her struggle to appropriate scientific ways of thinking, knowing, and writing; in short, to forge a scientific voice. She is working through for herself the relationship between the processes by which she produced her finding and the means for communicating that finding. This effort is a key aspect of scientific practice, one that is well known to anyone who has struggled to craft a "story" about one's data. That Rose does this in English, by her own choice, only adds to the complexity of her task.

Around the time of the bacteria study, the class as a whole was preparing for a field trip to the city's reservoir and water treatment facility. The students were told that at the end of the trip they would have a chance to ask questions of the city's water chemist. In preparation for the trip, many of the students read a booklet, *The Story of Water*, prepared by the city's water department. It explained in pictures and words the water cycle and water treatment process. The teacher guided the students in developing the following kinds of questions that the students then copied into their notebooks:

What machines are used to purify water?

What is chlorination?

What is filtration?

These questions are typical of those often asked of students in school. To hark back to the introduction, "it is as if they [the words] put themselves in quotation marks against the will of the speaker" (Bakhtin, 1981). The question arises: Whose questions are they? Why are they being asked? Clearly, they are not questions for which the answer is unknown or genuinely sought. Rather they seek to test comprehension of information readily available in some external authority such as a text or dictionary, or in this case, the water department's booklet. The focus is on defining technical terms, not on constructing knowledge or solving a problem. The lack of student agency and purpose is perhaps most clearly reflected in the impersonal, objective voice in which the questions are cast. There is no sense of ownership, of the students as agents in their own learning.

In contrast, Rose and another student, Marie, used the bacteria results as the basis for developing questions designed to pursue the full implications of those findings. Not surprisingly, their questions differed markedly from those of their classmates, in both substance and tone (we have not corrected the students' writing):

I went a know how come bacteria come in the water?

How come they clearn the water but it still has
bacteria in it?

I went to know how often they clean the water?

Through these questions, Rose and Marie are assuming an active,
critical stance toward language use. In a very real sense, their discourse is an action, asserting a will to know ("I went to know"). It is
also productive, literally putting into question the dilemma posed by
Rose's findings ("How come they clearn the water but it still has
bacteria in it?") and seeking to resolve it. Unlike the class's questions, these questions are openly evaluative, expressing a particular
point of view. Moreover, to construct them, Rose and Marie had to
engage the problem of communication directly, determining their
attitude toward the bacteria findings, judging their audience and,
based on these, determining their modes of expression. Their struggle
is reflected directly in their choice of pronouns. Rose and Marie
actively take on the role of interrogator through use of the first
person ("I went to know"). However, they do not then directly
address the water chemist; rather they use the adversarial, impersonal third person plural "they" ("I went a know how often they
clean the water"). The struggle evidenced here is somewhat ambigu-
ous. It is possible that they are not entirely sure who their audience
is—the water officials, the teacher, or both—and so they find themselves caught between two discourse worlds, that of the school and
that of their own scientific practice. Alternatively, it is possible that
the water chemist represents for them an anonymous authority since
they have not yet met him. The ambiguity, however, hints at an
important point. Rose and Marie's words are not entering into a
vacuum, but a "tension-filled environment" (Bakhtin, 1981, p. 276)
potentially charged with different points of view and conflicting
values: theirs and those of the water officials. Through their questions, Rose and Marie are active participants in social dialogue.

It is precisely this kind of struggle, involving various kinds and
levels of evaluation, that constitutes authentic language use and determines the expressive aspect of speech (Holquist, 1990). It is typically absent from most work in schools where language is treated as
objective and neutral, as a set of authoritative forms to be learned
and assimilated, and not as a socially constructive process that takes
place between speakers. Rose and Marie's questions are not merely

assertive in form, they are real assertions in a chain of activity and communication designed to produce real answers. It is also interesting how form can belie content. Notice that although the class's questions look factual (i.e., seeking authoritative definitions for technical terms), they are not factual in the scientific sense (based on scientific evidence). In contrast, although Rose and Marie's questions sound personal, they are grounded scientifically.

Through their scientific activity, Rose and Marie began to appropriate language to their own intention in order to resolve the dilemma raised by their inquiry and reflected in the question: "How come they clearn the water but it still has bacteria in it?" Marie's attitude toward this contradiction was a mixture of indignation and excitement. She marvelled in class that her town's water, which was supposed to be clean, could have bacteria in it. On the field trip, she looked forward to the opportunity to confront the authorities at the water treatment plant with her evidence that things were not as they should be. In short, she felt empowered by her knowledge. Unfortunately, the eagerly anticipated question-and-answer period never materialized because the plant tour went on longer than expected. So bitter was Marie's disappointment that in an interview conducted two months later, she referred to the water treatment plant as "*kote nou te—tap pose moun yo kesyon epi nou pat pose moun yo kesyon anko*," effectively, "the place we were going to ask the people questions and we didn't get to."

Ironically, Marie's frustration reveals the power of her experience. Like Rose, she had appropriated the results of the bacteria study, their meaning being most forcefully expressed in the questions the two girls prepared for the field trip. Marie's ownership, like Rose's, resulted from having thought seriously about the implications of the data for the quality of drinking water in her town and having prepared to confront the authorities about them. That Marie was still thinking about her missed opportunity at the end of the year, weeks after the investigation, suggests that she internalized what she had learned about water quality and experimental analysis on the one hand, and the inherent conflict between scientific practice and school practice on the other.

Conclusion

In this chapter we have explored the multivocal nature of literacy both in theory and in practice. In the bacteria investigation, we saw how the students began to appropriate the intentional possibilities of language in order to construct scientific meanings and resolve the dilemma posed by the evidence they had developed. We saw also how Rose's and Marie's struggle to orient themselves in a heteroglot environment contrasted markedly with the rest of the class's work, in which words were treated as if their meanings resided in dictionaries rather than in concrete sociohistorical contexts. In the former case, the language used is authoritative; it is distanced from the students' own sense-making (Emerson, 1986). In the latter case, the students are actively constructing meaning; in Bakhtin's terms, they are developing "internally persuasive" discourse. As Emerson (1986) suggests, this struggle between authoritative and internally persuasive discourse is a key to intellectual growth.

The perspective on literacy we have outlined helps reframe the problem of learning in multilingual and multicultural contexts. It recognizes the inextricable connection of literacy to social practice, emphasizing first the pluralistic nature of literacy and, secondly, the idea that all literacies or discourses are specific points of view on the world, each characterized by its own objects, meanings and values (Bakhtin, 1981):

> For any individual consciousness living in it, language is not an abstract system of normative forms but rather a concrete heteroglot conception of the world. . . . Each word tastes of the context and contexts in which it has lived its socially charged life; all words and forms are populated by intentions. (p. 293)

In this view, the learner appropriates new ways of knowing through active participation in a community of practice (Brown et al., 1989; Collins et al., 1989; Lave, 1991). These ways of knowing are not reducible to specialized vocabularies or specific forms for expressing explanations. Rather they represent whole systems of meaning permeated with specific values and accents.

This perspective on literacy, as we have tried to suggest, carries important implications for learning. It suggests a view of learning that differs in fundamental ways from traditional schooling in which lecture and textbooks are the foundation, and the preferred social unit is the individual. In bilingual contexts, this model is often more extreme when applied to subjects like science and ESL; the result is an emphasis on assimilating decontextualized vocabulary, grammar, and facts. In a community of practice, in contrast, the ways in which students do science or any other subject closely parallel those of actual practitioners. In the process, students construct their knowledge by confronting authentic dilemmas, arguing alternative interpretations, posing questions, establishing standards of evidence, and exploring modes of argumentation. We think that the example of Rose and Marie illustrates this approach to learning, one that is richer, more effective, and ultimately more empowering.

In this chapter we have tried to present a view of literacy and learning that, together with the other chapters in this book, reframes what it means to learn and to use language. Further, it directly calls into question some of the educational practices that predominate in bilingual and ESL classrooms. Rather than seeing language as a static, unitary, and abstract system, it sees language as dynamic, multivocal, and socially and historically situated. This perspective helps us to understand diversity as a fundamental aspect of human culture, a strength to be cultivated rather than a problem to be solved.

> At any given moment of its evolution, language is stratified not only into linguistic dialects in the strict sense of the word (according to formal linguistic markers, especially phonetic), but also—and for us this is the essential point—into languages that are socio-ideological: languages of social groups, "professional" and "generic" languages, languages of generations and so forth. And this stratification and heteroglossia, once realized, is not only a static invariant of linguistic life, but also what insures its dynamics: stratification and heteroglossia widen and deepen as long as language is alive and developing. (Bakhtin, 1981, pp. 271-272)

Notes

We should note that the classroom described in this chapter functioned as a bilingual community. Both first (Haitian Creole, Spanish, Cape Verdean Creole, Portuguese, Amharic, and Tigrinya) and second languages were used by the students. Language choice was usually determined by purpose. English was used predominantly when the students were communicating with an English-speaking audience (e.g., water department officials) or, as in Rose's case, when they were writing for publication. The students used their first language most of the time to "talk science" in the classroom. Sometimes, the students translated their writing from their first language to English.

The work reported in this chapter was supported under the Innovative Approaches Research Project, Contract No. 300-87-0131, from the U.S. Department of Education, Office of Bilingual Education and Minority Languages Affairs (OBEMLA). Preparation of the chapter was also supported by the National Center for Research on Cultural Diversity and Second Language Learning, under the Educational Research and Development Center Program (Cooperative Agreement No. R118G10022), administered by the Office of Educational Research and Improvement (OERI), U.S. Department of Education. The views expressed here do not necessarily reflect the positions or policies of OBEMLA or OERI.

We gratefully acknowledge the work of the teachers and students who participated in this research.

References

Au, K. (1980). Participation structures in a reading lesson with Hawaiian children: Analysis of a culturally appropriate instructional event. *Anthropology and Education Quarterly, 11*(2), 91-115.

Au, K., & Jordan, C. (1981). Teaching reading to Hawaiian children: Finding a culturally appropriate solution. In H.T. Trueba, G.P. Guthrie, & K. Au (Eds.), *Culture and the bilingual classroom: Studies in classroom ethnography* (pp. 139-152). Rowley, MA: Newbury House.

Bakhtin, M. (1981). *The dialogic imagination*. Austin: University of Texas.

Barnes, D., & Todd, F. (1977). Talk in small learning groups: Analysis of strategies. In C. Adelman (Ed.), *Uttering, muttering: Collecting, using and reporting talk for social and educational research* (pp. 69-77). London: Grant McIntyre.

Booth, W.C. (1986). Freedom of interpretation: Bakhtin and the challenge of feminist criticism. In G. Morson (Ed.), *Bakhtin: Essays and dialogues on his work* (pp. 145-176). Chicago: University of Chicago Press.

Brown, A., & Palincsar, A.M. (1989). Guided, cooperative learning and individual knowledge acquisition. In L.B. Resnick (Ed.), *Cognition and instruction: Issues and agendas* (pp. 393-451). Hillsdale, NJ: Erlbaum.

Brown, J.S., Collins, A., & Duguid, P. (1989). Situated cognition and the culture of learning. *Educational Researcher, 18*(1), 32-42.

Collins, A., Brown, J.S., & Newman, S.E. (1989). Cognitive apprenticeship: Teaching the craft of reading, writing, and mathematics. In L.B. Resnick (Ed.), *Knowing, learning, and instruction: Essays in honor of Robert Glaser* (pp. 453-494). Hillsdale, NJ: Erlbaum.

Emerson, C. (1986). The outer word and inner speech: Bakhtin, Vygotsky, and the internalization of language. In G. Morson (Ed.), *Bakhtin: Essays and dialogues on his work* (pp. 21-40). Chicago: The University of Chicago Press.

Gee, J.P. (1989). *What is literacy?* (Tech. Rep. No. 2). Cambridge, MA: Education Development Center, The Literacies Institute.

Geertz, C. (1973). *The interpretation of culture*. New York: Basic Books.

Geertz, C. (1983). *Local knowledge*. New York: Basic Books.

Hatano, G. (1981). Cognitive consequences of practice in culture specific procedural skills. *The Quarterly Newsletter of the Laboratory of Comparative Human Cognition, 4*, 15-18

Holquist, M. (1990). *Dialogism: Bakhtin and his world*. New York: Routledge.

Inagaki, K., & Hatano, G. (1983). Collective scientific discovery by young children. *The Quarterly Newsletter of the Laboratory of Comparative Human Cognition, 5*(1), 13-18.

Knorr-Cetina, K.D., & Mulkay, M. (Eds.). (1983). *Science observed: Perspectives on the social study of science*. London: Sage.

Lampert, M. (1990). When the problem is not the question and the solution is not the answer: Mathematical knowing and teaching. *American Education Research Journal, 27*(2), 29-63.

Latour, B. (1987). *Science in action*. Cambridge: Harvard University Press.

Latour, B., & Woolgar, S. (1986). *Laboratory life: The social construction of scientific facts*. Princeton: Princeton University Press.

Lave, J. (1988). *Cognition in practice*. New York: Cambridge University Press.

Lave, J. (1991). Situating learning in communities of practice. In L. Resnick, J. Levine, & S. Teasler (Eds.). *Perspectives on socially shared cognition*. Washington, DC: American Psychological Association.

Longino, H. (1990). *Science as social knowledge*. Princeton: Princeton University Press.

Lynch, M. (1985). *Art and artifact in laboratory science: A study of shop work and shop talk in a research laboratory*. London: Routledge and Kegan Paul.

Medawar, P. (1987). *Pluto's republic*. Oxford: Oxford University Press.

Mehan, H. (1992). The school's work of sorting out students. In D. Boden & D.H. Zimmerman (Eds.), *Talk and social structure* (pp. 75-100). London: Polity.

Mohatt, G., & Erickson, F. (1980). Cultural differences in teaching styles in an Odawa school: A sociolinguistic approach. In H.T. Trueba, G.P. Guthrie, & K. Au (Eds.), *Culture and the bilingual classroom: Studies in classroom ethnography* (pp. 105-119). Rowley, MA: Newbury House.

Philips, S. (1972). Participant structures and communicative competences: Warm Springs children in community and classroom. In C. Cazden, D. Hymes, & V. John (Eds.), *Functions of language in the classroom* (pp. 370-394). New York: Teachers College Press.

Resnick, L. (1989). Treating mathematics as an ill-structured discipline. In R. Charles & E. Silver (Eds.), *The teaching and assessing of mathematical problem-solving* (pp. 32-60). Reston, VA: National Council of Teachers of Mathematics.

Rosebery, A., Warren, B., & Conant, F. (1990). *Making sense of science in language minority classrooms* (Tech. Rep. No. 7306). Cambridge, MA: Bolt, Beranek, & Newman.

Rosebery, A., Warren, B., & Conant, F. (1992). Appropriating scientific discourse: Findings from language minority classrooms. *Journal of the Learning Sciences, 2*(1), 1-94.

Schoenfeld, A. (1992). Learning to think mathematically: Problem solving, metacognition, and sense-making in mathematics. In D. Grouws (Ed.), *Handbook for research on mathematics teaching and learning*. New York: MacMillan.

Schoenfeld, A. (in press). Reflections on doing and teaching mathematics. In A. Schoenfeld (Ed.), *Mathematical thinking and problem solving*. Hillsdale, NJ: Erlbaum.

Vygotsky, L.S. (1978). *Mind in society*. Cambridge, MA: Harvard University Press.

Vygotsky, L.S. (1985). *Thought and language*. Cambridge, MA: MIT Press.

Warren, B., Rosebery, A., & Conant, F. (1989). *Cheche Konnen: Science and literacy in language minority classrooms* (Tech. Rep. No. 7305). Cambridge, MA: Bolt, Beranek & Newman.

CHAPTER 10

Engaging Students in Learning: Literacy, Language, and Knowledge Production with Latino Adolescents

Catherine E. Walsh
University of Massachusetts, Boston

I want to begin by posing a series of questions that generally underlie the book's theme of biliteracy in the United States and specifically frame the substance of my chapter. The questions are not necessarily new; they are ones that theoreticians and practitioners from a variety of ideological leanings have probably asked before. My intent in raising them here is not to afford nor even to suggest definitive answers. Rather, it is to illuminate—through the discourse I use in posing and discussing them—the tentative, speculative, complex, and shifting nature of work in and about literacy for language minority populations. Reflected in the questions is my own ongoing struggle to understand, and to understand how I understand, literacy theory and practice and the bilingual students, communities, and contexts that I study, speak, and write about, work with, and learn from. These are the questions:

- What is literacy?
- What is knowledge?
- What is the relation between literacy and knowledge?
- What does this relation suggest for classroom practice?
- What are the conditions that limit, restrict, or enable access to literacy and knowledge?
- Are these conditions the same for all populations?
- Who are the students and communities that are the "subjects" of our work?
- In what ways do society, schools, and programs define and thus position them?

211

- Are the understandings of society, schools, and programs similar or different?
- How do the students and their communities perceive and describe their own realities, conditions, and subjectivities?
- How do we interpret these individuals' educational, linguistic, and literacy needs and experiences?
- What are the individuals' own interpretations?

While numerous issues, concerns, perspectives, and experiences are probably brought to mind in pondering these queries, the context for my own analysis and discussion is partially revealed by the spoken words of a 19-year-old Latino high school student from the Boston area who told me about his experience with literacy, the English language, and formal education.

> *The school, yeah, I guess that's where you could say they taught me to read. But it's on the street that I really learned English . . . . The problem is the reading and writing, it don't do me no good 'cause I say and write words but when I try and read the book in them classes I don't understand nothin'. Sometimes I think they do it to hold us back . . . . You know, to make sure los hispanos don't make it . . . .*

This student's brief statement reveals a lot about (bi)literacy, knowledge, and school instruction, about issues of access and control, and about students' awareness of and ability to speak about their lived realities and the ways schools have failed them. Although this student graduated from high school several months after he talked to me, many of his peers were retained for the second, third, or even fourth time. Some were referred for special education while others kept on in the bilingual program with the same classes and the same teachers as the year before. The dropout rate for Latinos in the community at the time was around 70%. The reasons for dropping out were not attributable to literacy levels per se. Yet, if one were to assess the literacy abilities of those retained, referred, or who had left school, chances are high that a large percentage lacked the reading, writing, and comprehension required and expected. In fact, assumptions among teachers and administrators were that high school students should already be able to read and write; if they could not, it certainly was not part of a high school teacher's job to teach them.

As in many cities throughout the country, a growing number of adolescents and young adults in this Boston-area community lack the literacy-related abilities to succeed in traditional bilingual or English-only programs. Some come from rural areas of Puerto Rico, the Dominican Republic, or Central America and have had limited access to formal schooling. Others have been in and out of schools for years, subjected to inappropriate or inconsistent instructional approaches, and/or bounced between a number of linguistic, cultural, social, and educational environments. Most probably fit the profile of adult literacy students who are unable to gain or produce meaning through print in English or in their native language. Many are over 16 and have adult responsibilities. However, because they are enrolled in a high school, the majority have until just recently been afforded minimal (if any) access to literacy learning and, as a result, to other academic content instruction. While the desire to read and write, learn English, and study are the stated reasons why many keep coming to school, instructional attitudes, policies, practices, programs, and approaches work both to limit and position this acquisition; students are not given the opportunity to develop the literacy skills required for further learning (in Spanish or in English) and, for the most part, see little relation between what they are taught and real life existence. Moreover, the natural and dynamic bilingualism that frames many of these students' identities and interactions—that is, the communicative varieties and standard and nonstandard forms of Spanish and English as well as Spanish-English codeswitching—is not only ignored but generally forbidden in formal instruction. [Editor's note: For a broader discussion of the language use of Hispanics in the United States, see Ramírez, this volume.] In other words, students are told to speak and to write in one language or the other, emphasis is on the standard dialect (which may vary greatly from the language students speak), and preference is always for English. This discordant reality seems to have a lot to do with the way literacy, knowledge, and schooling are traditionally understood in our society, with dominant and subordinate relations of power, and with the rationality that typically underlies mainstream approaches to instruction.

In this chapter, I explore these issues, from both a theoretical and a practical perspective, as they relate to instructional practice and programmatic design in a Boston-area high school, which for purposes of confidentiality will be referred to as City High. In so doing,

I will discuss the different understandings that the school's administrators, teachers, and students have of what these practices and designs offer, at the same time referring back to the theoretical questions posed earlier. I also examine the process by which I arrive at my own understandings and interpretations of what, as a researcher/practitioner, I am seeing, reading, and hearing.

Finally, the paper analyzes the pedagogical approaches I used to encourage Latino adolescents and young adults with limited school-based literacy skills to talk, to theorize, and to write about the contexts and contents of their lives in and out of school, and about how their education could be more relevant and better directed. The significance of these approaches for (bi)literacy development and knowledge production as well as for self-esteem and academic and social engagement is made clear through examples of the students' dialogues, analyses, and written products. Further made evident is the psychosocial significance of dual language (L1/L2) literacy promotion.

Literacy, Knowledge, and Schooling: Dominant Perspectives

Literacy has long been considered the basis for higher order, analytical thought and the gateway into material success in industrialized capitalist societies. While numerous authors have criticized this notion as mythical in real life (e.g., Graff, 1987; Walsh, 1991b), educational institutions generally continue to maintain and promote the literacy and success relation. Public school students are told that English reading and writing skills and a high school diploma are essential for employment, although little or no opportunity is provided for students (particularly poor students for whom standard English is a second language or dialect) to develop literacy after primary school. In fact, the acquisition and imparting of literacy, at least in the context of Western developed societies, is associated with the early school years; those who do not become literate as children are deemed deficient, backward, problematic, and less intelligent. The comments of a Boston-area school administrator make evident this understanding:

> *Those Hispanic students, the ones that can't even read and write, you know, they don't really know how to think either. Their parents are the same way. Why do you think they're on*

welfare, unemployed, always in trouble? . . . We do what we can, that is, for the majority in this school. Those kids, they don't belong here, in this building anyway.

When literacy instruction is provided for these high school students in need, it generally assumes an elementary substance and orientation. The worksheet below, from a Boston high school ESL literacy teacher's classroom, provides an example.

Some students classified as lacking literacy skills arrive in the United States with limited formal schooling, and a significant proportion of students pass through U.S. primary schools without acquiring the literacy skills supposedly taught to them. In 1988, 56% of Latino 17-year-olds and 47% of African-American 17-year-olds were classified as functionally illiterate compared with 13% of white 17-year-olds (Fueyo, 1988). Latino students are also much more likely than whites to have low academic achievement, be retained in grade, and enter high school overage (Hispanic Policy Development Project, 1988). Educators often label such students "at risk" and blame them for the crisis in education. Yet, as minority groups increasingly make up the majority of students in urban schools, school officials are faced with the fact that the at-risk categorization fits most of the student body. What does this say about the U.S. educational system in general and about equality and access in particular?

Research has demonstrated that instructional approaches, ability groupings, choice of texts, language use, contextual situations, and cultural and experiential inclusions and exclusions, among other things, work differentially to control and position literacy development (e.g., Cummins, 1986; Roth, 1984; Shannon, 1989; Walsh 1991a). But even for those who become literate, promise of economic success is still limited by race, ethnicity, class, and gender. Male dropouts from wealthy neighborhoods for example, are much more likely to find jobs than male graduates from poor neighborhoods (Fine, 1987). And (high school and college) diploma-wielding women of color, when they find jobs, continue to be the lowest paid and most underemployed segment of the workforce. Literacy, in and of itself, presents no monetary assurances nor hope for a different future. This is not to say that literacy is not essential to full societal participation or that literacy does not enhance access to information or the development of critical analysis. Rather, it is to argue that the understandings and discourses of and practices toward literacy in the United States are complexly intertwined with the social dynamics and structural inequities of this society. This relationship is further revealed in the definitional conception that guides most public school and adult literacy instruction. Within educational institutions, literacy is most often thought of as comprising the basic, specific, hierarchical, controlled, and measurable skills associated with reading and writing. It is perceived as a singular entity—literacy, not literacies—and as a have or have-not condition. To be literate means that one is both educated and educable (Cook-Gumperz, 1986), able to utilize the cognitive higher order skills associated with real (academic) learning. As Ferdman (1990) points out:

> Given broad cultural consensus on the definition of literacy, alternative constructions are either remote or invisible, and so literacy becomes a seemingly self-evident personal attribute that is either present or absent. In such an environment, literacy is experienced as a characteristic inherent in the individual. Once a person acquires the requisite skills, she also acquires the quality of mind known as literacy, together with the right to be labeled a literate person. (p.186)

Recent research has shown literacy to be complex and pluralistic, socially, culturally, and contextually bound, interactive, and process-rather than product-oriented in nature (Cook-Gumperz, 1986; Ferdman, 1990; Scribner, 1984). Yet, public schools continue to operate on the belief that literacy develops from the bottom up in small incremental steps, that it is academic, that it is school- rather than community-based or oriented, that it is monolinguistic (developed in one language at a time), and that it can be assessed through quantifiable measures. From where does this understanding derive? Is it solely pedagogical? Or is it also shaped by ideological concerns that extend beyond classrooms?

As I have pointed out elsewhere (Walsh, 1991b), the understandings of and approaches to literacy in schools appear to be tied, in large part, to "beliefs and assumptions about the nature of knowledge, of people (i.e., teachers and students), and of experience and to the relations of power and of social and cultural control which these beliefs and assumptions both construct and incorporate" (p. 9). The orientation that underlies most traditional educational programs, for instance, overwhelmingly derives from a positivist conception of knowledge, a rationality that situates both knowledge and literacy as separate from learners and from their own and their communities' actions, histories, experiences, and lived social, cultural, and linguistic realities. In this sense, knowledge is considered neutral, universal, verifiable information that must be formally acquired and taught. The acquisition or learning of knowledge is treated as deductive and deterministic; instruction breaks it down into discrete, decontextualized pieces that are systemically fed to students by transmission-oriented and task-directed instructors. As a result, the teachers and students held captive within this positivist rationality come to be seen as the objects of knowledge, unable to act with or upon it. Further, the acts of teaching and learning come to be stabilized through measurable productivity while teacher and student agency (i.e., their capacity to act in and on their environments), creativity, and difference are discounted. Ignored are the enigmatic processes involved in how one comes to know as well as how one comes to relate knowledge to practical, human purposes.

Although positivist pedagogies limit the possibilities of all students, they are particularly problematic for those whose lived experience and cultural frames of reference fall outside the boundaries of the universal image. In other words, while such instructional approaches tout knowledge as neutral, they tend to verify, legitimize, and reinforce the language and literacy-related experiences, the community "social funds" of knowledge (Moll, 1989), and the cultural capital of the white, English-speaking, middle classes. (And within this grouping, the knowledge and experiences of men are legitimized, verified, and reinforced more than those of women.) It is this prerequisite knowledge that is positioned as the desired, universal "standard" (e.g., Bloom, 1987; Hirsch, 1987).[1] Consequently, class, racial, ethnic, and gender stratifications are exacerbated; access to literacy development and knowledge production is mediated through unequal power relations. This happens even in bilingual programs. Students' native language may be intermittently used but this use is seen by teachers and students as remedial in that it is intended to provide a transition to standard English. Biliteracy is neither a goal nor an accepted medium. Furthermore, curriculum and texts (regardless of the language they are written in) corroborate a homogeneity that denies the realities of urban life for bilingual communities.

The recent interest in whole-language approaches to literacy instruction in elementary schools and problem-posing, Freirean-type approaches at the adult level have helped introduce new understandings of the ways literacy develops and students learn. Moreover, these approaches challenge the effectiveness of methodologies that derive from a positivist orientation. In high schools, however, the mainstream, traditional methods still reign; administrators and teachers generally remain stalwart in their goals and structure and are the most resistant to change and innovation.

For the past five years, I have been actively involved in trying to promote change at City High School. While I remain an outsider to City High's school district in that I am not their employee, my role as an educational expert appointed in a legal consent decree between the school system and Latino parents affords me some authority within the system. As might be expected, however, this role also engenders tension. A large part of my involvement has been focused on addressing the high dropout rate and suspension of Latino students at City High and in trying to initiate policy changes and pedagogical improvements. One aspect of this work has included a several-year effort to develop a new program within the existing bilingual program—a program that would specifically address the biliteracy needs of students and validate and build upon the experiences and knowledge that the students bring with them. While such a program began on a pilot basis during the 1989-1990 school year (the advanced basic skills classroom referred to earlier) and is being further developed this year (1990-91), administrators in the school, along with some teachers, remain opposed to its presence and to its pedagogical purpose and orientation. Their complaints range from the teacher's untraditional approach, classroom management and organization, and noise level, to the problematic nature of the student population and the negative image that they give to the school. One administrator made clear to me his intention in a conversation during fall 1990:

> *I am fed up with that class and with the teacher . . . . She has the students sitting in a circle instead of rows, that leads to disrespect, a lack of focus, and confusion . . . . The [monolingual Anglo male] teachers on either side come to me all the time about the noise, it seems like all the kids are ever doing is talking . . . . you, know, all at once. There is no teacher control, they are not learning anything . . . . I want her out . . . . The kids are the main ones that cause problems in this school. This program, I don't think it's any good. Maybe you should put it somewhere else. If it were up to me, I'd just get rid of it.*

The guidance counselor also contends that the program does not belong in an academic high school; "the kids would be better off getting their GED or in a vocational setting," she said. In contrast, the students view the program as their last chance to survive high school. As one student explained in Spanish:

We know they don't want us. They don't want us to learn. . . . Here in this class we are learning. It's different, not like the classes before. Sometimes it's hard because we don't have just one book, we don't just copy, we have to think different and more. But now I see that we're together here, like family . . . . am me . . . . we share and sometimes we don't agree . . . . For the first time, I feel like I know something, that what I think matters . . . . Now I think maybe I can stick it out and get a diploma. [Translation mine]

These administrators' and this student's words make real the tensions, conflicts, and possibilities that surround literacy development and instruction for adolescents and young adults in many public high schools, not just City High. They point to the difficulties in getting urban secondary schools to accept that (a) an increasing number of their incoming students may not speak English or be literate in any language and yet are intelligent human beings; (b) the present conditions of public schooling help place these students at further risk; and (c) the dominant understandings of and approaches to classroom organization, instructional content, pedagogy, and teacher/student and student/student relations need to be reexamined.

Critical Pedagogy, (Bi)literacy Development, and Student Engagement

The African-American feminist writer, bell hooks[2] (1989), maintains the following:

Students also suffer, as many of us who teach do, from a crisis of meaning, unsure about what has value in life, unsure even about whether it is important to stay alive. They long for a context where their subjective needs can be integrated with study, where the primary focus is a broader spectrum of ideas and modes of inquiry, in short, a dialectical context where there is serious and rigorous critical exchange. (p. 51)

It was promoting this critical exchange and encouraging a connection between lived experience and academic learning that was to be the focus of my work with the advanced basic skills students. In fact, the teacher had already begun to craft this pedagogical orientation when she and the students invited me in the spring of 1990 to work with them on a classroom project that would address the theme, "a dropout comes back to school."

The students' initial desire was to develop a sociodrama—a dramatization of a plausible (but fictional) social situation—and record it on video. Because I had worked on such a project with some of the same students two years before, the students were familiar with and aware of the effectiveness of both the method and the medium. They saw sociodrama as a nonthreatening form that enabled them to depict and recount the struggles, conflicts, and meaningful issues of their lives without having to personally reveal themselves. Many students were also intrigued with having their images and words recorded on camera. While I respected their wishes, my interest was to move beyond what had already been done and to present us all with a new challenge. I was interested in encouraging the students to make a connection between oral communication and print, a difficult task since most had very limited literacy skills and had demonstrated a resistance to any school task that required writing. My intent was to help create a purposeful, meaningful, and collaborative context for literacy development in the classroom—one that would engage students in collectively constructing text, in discussing, analyzing, and critiquing the context and language (varieties, dimensions, linguistic and grammatical forms) that would go into the text, and in assuming the role and responsibility of authorship. I wanted the students to move from thinking of themselves as objects to being subjects (since in my mind this is a key aspect of the literacy process). I also wanted the students to begin to understand the complex, tenuous, and often contradictory relationships with and among language, literacy, schooling, and lived experience. This entailed encouraging students to talk, to theorize, and to write (in any and all languages and varieties) about the contexts, contents, and meanings of their lives in and out of school, and to critically explore both their subjective positions and the existing and often conflicting discourses within these contexts.

The visual medium that I had in mind to ground the process and afford a purposeful context was that of a photonovel, a comic-book-like format with photographs rather than caricatures. I talked with students about collectively constructing a sociodrama—a story about a student who dropped out of school and decided to come back—drawing pictures to represent initially the characters, actions, and contexts that went with the words, and then eventually staging photographs to provide the real-life images for the real-life dialogue. In this talk, my focus was on the creation of the story and its visual display rather than on the task of writing per se. After considerable discussion and questions, there was consensus.

The production of the photonovel occurred over the period of approximately three months, during which I spent one or two periods a week offering feedback and technical assistance. Students and teacher continued to work on the project during other periods. While there are numerous aspects of this process of students' engagement and of their emergent biliteracy that I could analyze and discuss, I will focus here on only three.

Theme dynamics and language and literacy status

The first aspect is that of the underlying significance of students' choice of the theme in terms of their own subjective positions. This is important because it reveals much about how students individually perceive themselves, their social relations, and their language, literacy, and academic status within the school and the classroom. It also suggests how some of these perceptions are constructed and illustrates how these perceptions can structure what goes on in the classroom in terms of interactions, engagement, language use, (bi)literacy learning, knowledge production, and instruction. The initial interest in "a dropout comes back to school" was stimulated by discussions students had had both among themselves and with the teacher about two peers who had left school and were considering returning. Both of these peers had actually "illegally" shown up in school on a couple of occasions, coming to this class because of the widely held respect among Latino at-risk students for this particular teacher. Their presence engendered both dialogue and speculation about why they had left, about the tensions inherent in pondering whether or not to return, and about the disparities between the worlds of school and community. Although they never came out and actually said it, many of the students alluded to their own proximity to this reality. They had also been overtly reminded of this proximity by a letter the bilingual program administration wrote to the parents of these students earlier in the year stating that because of their low achievement they had been placed in advanced basic skill classes. The letter began: "Dear Parent of a Potential Dropout." It was handed as an open sheet of paper to each student in the class to bring home to their parents. All of the students were both angered and taken aback by this direct naming of their status. For the newly arrived students, many of whom had high aspirations for school and life success in the United States, the letter also produced confusion about their present circumstance and their future.

Because of different subjective experiences, the significance of the dropout theme varied from student to student. For example, a few of the students had critically explored the dropout theme in the production of the previously mentioned video; some also had been in the city or other U.S. schools for a number of years and were bilingual. As compared to the more recent arrivals, they demonstrated more of an awareness of the attitudes toward Latinos in general and the low-literate, at-risk Latinos in particular. They talked about feeling like they were being pushed out of school. And, because of their proficiency in English, they also understood the often derogatory comments of some Anglo teachers and the school administration. Their resistance to this oppressive reality was made evident in numerous ways (see Walsh, 1991a), as was the administration's attempts to break them. These students hovered alarmingly close to the school door; the ingrained belief that a diploma would lead to economic success (despite the fact that reading and writing abilities in either language were very limited) seemed to be the only motivation for staying. In contrast, the Spanish-dominant fairly recent arrivals tended to blame themselves and the conditions of their lives (e.g., limited formal schooling in the native country, frequent absenteeism due to job and family responsibilities) for their potential dropout status. They still had the hope of learning (a hope many of the others seemed to have lost), yet encountered teachers and curricula unwilling and unable to address appropriately the literacy development they required.

Chris Weedon (1987) maintains that the ways people make sense of their lives is a necessary starting point for understanding how power relations structure society. As she explains:

How we live our lives as conscious thinking subjects, and how we give meaning to the material social relations under which we live and which structure our everyday lives, depends on the range and social power of existing discourses, our access to them, and the political strength of the interests which they represent. (p. 26)

Because of their subjective positions in the school, classroom, and community, students in the class had differential access to the discourses that surrounded and situated dropping out, being at risk, and limited in school-based literacy. Consequently, their understandings of themselves as well as their understandings of one another differed greatly. The more recently arrived Spanish-dominant students viewed those bilingual ones who had been in the system, accustomed to urban life, and overtly resistant, as *los tigres* (the tigers)—the street-wise, tough kids who provoked problems and would be better off out of school or, at the very least, out of their classroom. In contrast, the designated *tigres* perceived those newly arrived who had come from rural areas as *los jíbaros del campo*, the backward peasants from the countryside. They chastised and taunted the *jíbaros* (oftentimes in English) for their lack of formal schooling, their passivity, their dress, their regional varieties of Spanish, and their inability to employ the strategies of codeswitching that they considered as indicative of status and group identification. The other students in the class who fell somewhere in between these two designated groups aspired toward acceptance by the *tigres* and, as a result, also actively put down the *jíbaros*. While the literacy abilities of all were limited, the members of the more recently arrived group were also perceived as the *brutos,* the dumb ones who were non-English-speaking, illiterate, and less intelligent. It seems that the discourse used by the school administration to describe the entire class had been appropriated by some to position and exert power over the others.

What is particularly interesting is the role language and literacy assumed in these group dynamics. Bilingualism, that is, the ability to switch into English at will or to insert English words and phrases at opportune moments, helped define status. In fact, status within the group seemed to be proportionately associated with English ability. Thus, while Spanish was the dominant language of the entire group, those with the greater English ability, the most bilingual, clearly had higher status and more power within the classroom. They also considered themselves to be superior. Although the more recently arrived Spanish-speaking students complained about the bilinguals' self-positioning, they frequently tried to emulate them. [Editor's note: See Hornberger, this volume, for another description of tensions regarding language use and ability in a Puerto Rican youth program in Philadelphia. Ramírez, also this volume, offers a description of the language attitudes of Hispanic adolescents enrolled in Texas and California schools.]

Biliteracy similarly assumed a significance within these power relations. Although the bilingual students displayed major difficulties in reading and writing in both languages, they contended that they could read and write; it was just that they did not want to. Because they had been in U.S. schools for a while and had learned some English, most could in fact write some English words. As with oral language, this ability served to position them differentially in relation to the more recent arrivals who could neither speak nor write English and who were more open about both their inabilities and their desire to learn.

The differential understandings of the material social relations and the subjective positionings in the classroom were further illuminated in the students' choice of a fellow student to play the main character for the photonovel. Numerous names were placed in nomination, but each student nominated refused to accept the part. Criteria were also discussed but none could be agreed upon. Finally, one of the rural, more recently arrived group put forth the name of Julian (a pseudonym), a fellow group member. Julian beamed with pride. At first, *los tigres* argued that there was no way he could assume the role because he lacked the finesse in dress, style, and identity that was required. But when no one else was willing to take the lead, they and their allies began to joke about letting Julian make a fool of himself; by their talk it became clear that none wanted to assume the dropout identity for fear of exposing (either to their peers or to themselves) their own proximity. However, there was still an uneasiness in permitting Julian to do so. One student's words (rendered in Spanish) serve as an example:

> *Let him play the jerk, what do we care. He's dumb enough that he doesn't know better. I don't want everybody to think that's me. You know I'd look good . . . . but that isn't me . . . . But nobody is going to believe the story with him in it either.*
> [Translation mine]

The significance underlying the theme and students' struggle over its meaning and physical depiction is illustrative in that it provides a window into the competing social realities and complex power relations that are too often ignored or glossed over in discussions of literacy, language, and pedagogy. Thus, while bilingualism and biliteracy may be our ultimate goal for the students with whom we work, we must be cognizant of the divergent and often conflicting meanings, interpretations, experiences, identities, and subjective positions that shape and situate students' linguistic, cultural, and social relationships, alliances, status, and groupings within schools, classrooms, and communities as well as the ways these environments impact language, literacy, and pedagogical possibilities.

The tensions of lived experience and the power of collaboration

A second aspect of the photonovel process that I want to discuss is how, through theme-related dialogue and collaborative writing, students began to explore their understandings of the at-risk/dropout condition. As they began to uncover the power relations at work in the school and how they were differentially affected, the role and function of literacy began to take on new meaning.

The initial context of the photonovel dialogue that the students collectively developed and collaboratively wrote focused on the character of Julian—specifically, his decision to leave school, his economic and familial responsibilities, his search for employment, and the low wages and heavy physical labor that went with the job he found and that led to a reconsideration of his dropout decision.[3] (Since Spanish was the dominant language of the class, this dialogue was conducted primarily in Spanish.) It was in discussing how to document and portray Julian's thought about returning that the tone and substance of students' dialogue and discussion about Julian's lived reality shifted. As a group, the students began to explore critically the reasons Julian left school to begin with and what might have to change in terms of both him and the school if he were to return.

In students' brainstorming at the outset of the project, they identified two major reasons for Julian's leaving: the treatment inside school and the need for money. The issue of treatment led to discussions about and elaborations on Julian's inappropriate behavior, his problems with teachers, and the suspensions and disciplinary actions that were the result.[4] There was consensus that Julian was individually at fault; mention of the school standards, policies, and practices that determine what is appropriate behavior and what is not was absent. Similarly, when we began to discuss Julian's possible return to school, most of the students argued that he would have to change. In their cooperative working teams, some began to write about what this change meant. Here are two examples:

bueno el Tiene que
cambiar portarse
bien en la escuela
y no faltar el Repeto
a lo profesore yno
equipiar la clase
asitir a todo la clase
y no irna dile congo
Tra a la escuela

(well he has to change behave good in the school and not be disrespectful to the teacher and not skip class attend all class and not to go nobody with hat to the school)

(I did this before but when I return to school I am not going to do it.)

As someone with no formal administrative, instructional, or student status in the school, I began to question students as to the rules they were required to follow, asking what these rules were, where they were documented, who had made them, how they were instituted and maintained, and who controlled them. These questions promoted a dialogue that went on for weeks and that led to students eventually studying the code of discipline, discussing why rules were necessary, which rules were fair and which were unfair, and actually rewriting it. However, before reading and working on the actual code, the students began to raise questions about the ways some students were treated as compared to others and to critically examine the differential ways the school rules were carried out. One working team decided to document their thoughts and discussion for possible use later:

> NO TODAS LASLeLLes son jUSTAS LA de -
> La school.
> becose is De MaCiADO estrictas.
> sifueran mas mo de rada los muchachos
> no se pu si e ran de revelde.
> con los maes tros y los prinsiPALes,
> ni LOS CON sejeros.
> las lelles que ellos tienen SON mui fuerts
> solo con los is pano.
> Ricky piens A que si las lelles son
> cun p lidas los muchachos Ispanos
> las cunpliRAN. LLA que
> quieren ponel Las Lelles A LOS
> ispano SOLAMENTES
> y LAR gunos gringo ((NO))

(Not all the school laws are just
because is overly strict.
if [they were] more moderate the students
    wouldn't be rebellious.
with the teachers and the principals,
    nor with the counselors.
the laws that they have are very strong
    only with the Hispanics.

Ricky thinks that if the laws were
carried out [with everybody] the Hispanic kids
would fulfill them. It's that
they want to put the laws just to the Hispanics
and to the gringos <<NO>>)
[Translation mine]

There is much that could be analyzed in these students' composition. Certainly issues of syntax, morphology, semantics, and textual organization could be examined as could the students' strategies for word and syllable emphasis, their regional variety of spoken Spanish, their association of oral language and script, and their occasional use of English. Instead, I would like to focus briefly here on why this text is significant in terms of students' collaboration, their (bi)literacy development, knowledge production, and their understanding of the subjectivities, conflicting discourses, and power relations that surrounded them.

The student who actually wrote the text was one of the more recently arrived rural Dominican students. His (mutually chosen) team member who was Puerto Rican had spent more time in the United States and had more experience with the English language. However, as the only Puerto Rican actively involved in the project, his identity in the class was fragile. Both students had told me at the start of the project that they could not write. Indeed, their participation in the actual writing of the dialogue of the photonovel had, up until this time, been very limited. They also had not been particularly vocal about their own opinions with regard to school rules during dialogues in class. Both their production of this piece, its impassioned tone, and their explicit collaboration therefore surprised me.

The purpose of the text was, as these two students explained, *para recordar* (to remember) what they as well as a lot of the students in the class thought about the fact that Latinos were always being suspended. (Sixty-four percent of the bilingual program Latinos in this school were suspended the previous year.) They said that it might be of possible use at some later point in the project. For them, the text represented oral speech written down; capitalization offered a way to remember the emphasis they put on particular words when they said it aloud, and the intermix of English is as it was spoken.

Writing gave these students a voice; it came to afford a function that, at least in the context of something truly meaningful to them, the students had probably not had the opportunity to consider previously. Furthermore, it offered an outlet to express their awareness and understanding of and anger about the unequal power relations and conflicting discourses in the school and, in so doing, gave the photonovel more authentic and personal significance. It also helped explain and give meaning to some of their peers' disruptive and resistant behavior. When they read what they had written back to the entire class, the other students affirmed the two students' literary as well as subjective positions both by agreeing with what they had written and by reacting with further discussion and personal applications. In the next class, the students embarked on an active, emotional dialogue about if and how they could change the reality and conditions. They endeavored to tackle, in a sense, the fundamental poststructural question of "how and where knowledge is produced and by whom, and of what counts as knowledge" (Weedon, 1987, p. 7). It was at this point that they expressed a desire to read the code of discipline, examine the rules that they were most often suspended for, and possibly rework those that seemed inappropriate or irrelevant. They talked to me and to the teacher about if and how their suggestions could be given to the administration. They also conversed among themselves about whether the adults in the building should not also have to abide by the rules and discussed how student review boards might be a way to intervene before sending students to the vice principal. This process demonstrated alternative forms of knowledge production that led to a realization for many that the established discourses, meanings, relations, and conditions for Latinos in the school did not necessarily have to be taken for granted. Reading and writing became the tools that assisted them in their work and analysis. While they occasionally needed technical assistance from adults in the class, they had clearly determined the project and taken ownership. Its significance was recognized when, at the end of the school year, they presented the new code along with the photonovel to the superintendent, his assistant, and to one of the school vice-principals.

Although some of the students could have made the presentation in English, the group decided that it was their context to control; Spanish was the language of the meeting and non-Spanish-speaking guests were required to communicate through the designated translator (the teacher). The administrators listened to the students give an overview of both the new code and the photonovel in Spanish, and to the teacher's translation. They asked numerous questions about students' opinions of their schooling and respectfully waited for the Spanish transmission and the translation into English of students' responses. This was the first time the students had had such control (linguistically, socially, and intellectually); it was also the first time these administrators had shown an intense interest in what these students were saying. The administrators voiced a commitment to consider the suggestions presented, and in September some were actually implemented.

Coming to authorship

The third aspect of the photonovel process that I briefly want to mention is the students' coming to and assumption of authorship. As I mentioned earlier, none of the students at the outset of the project enjoyed, felt competent in, or saw the purpose of writing. Reading was also perceived as a teacher-directed task that seemed alien in purpose and, because of their (actual and perceived) abilities, labor intensive and devoid of meaning. The context and content of the returning dropout theme, the medium of the photonovel, and the participatory and critical nature of the pedagogy seemed to afford a space, a reason, and a place (a) for students' perspectives, experiences, and understandings to emerge; (b) for further investigation and interrogation to occur; and (c) for this all to be documented so that others could read it and so that it would be remembered.[5] The teacher, who is a recognized adult biliteracy specialist, saw this assumption of the role of authors as tied to an increase in students' control over and understanding of the writing process. In contrast to the remedial, skills-type approaches these students had been exposed to in other classrooms, she viewed the photonovel methodology, particularly its use of visual images, as enabling students to become writers. As she explained:

> It helped students not just write words but use the skills of more critical analysis; the use of visual images provides a context that helps students detect where details are lacking in the story and to elaborate. It provides contextual cues that enable them to reflect, judge, and to assess their writing.

The students' collective assumption of the author role became particularly evident in the final stages of the project. As the end of the school year neared, there were three things that still had to be done before we could send the books to be printed: a clear display of the text (handprinted or typed), editing, and layout. The teacher and I discussed these needs and the short amount of time left with the students and asked them how they thought we should proceed and whether they wanted us to assume any or all of the responsibilities. They felt these tasks were theirs to do and requested that we only provide technical assistance. They divided themselves into three groups: the computer word-processing team (some of whose members had never before used computers), an editorial board, and a layout crew. The teacher was asked to provide technical help to the first team while I was asked to offer assistance to the latter two. We worked collectively for seven hours nonstop on two consecutive days to complete the project. Students who I had been told by others in the building had an attention span of about 15 minutes did not even want to break for a lunch period.

While both the teacher and I were pleased that the students themselves had taken control of the photonovel's completion, we were hesitant about letting them assume the editorial function. We wondered, as teachers often do, whether we should correct spelling and grammar. What would it mean (for us, for the student-authors, and for potential readers) if the text was not standard? After much deliberation, we shared this concern with the students. They reminded us the text was theirs, that they appreciated our concern, but that the decision, responsibility, and authority was with the editorial board they had designated. As adults and as educators, we had to let go; the students themselves had taken literacy, knowledge, and pedagogy and run with it.[6]

On the last day of school, we organized a book party for the students in the class and for their invited friends. (The above-mentioned administrators, the bilingual guidance counselor, and the bilingual director were also invited after the students were each formally presented with their copies.) The students, all dressed up for the occasion, gave speeches about what the project and the final publication of the book meant. Pride was evident in their bodily stance, in their words, tears, and in their friends' respect and admiration. While each testimony was equally poignant, I especially recall the whispered words to me of the lone Salvadoran student in the class whose engagement in the project was quiet but constant.

Soy autor. I am an author! You know, my family, they laughed when I told them I was writing a book. They said I was making it up. You know, I only went to the first and part of the second grade in El Salvador. Now I can show them that it is true, my name is here, soy autor. I even want to send a copy to my relatives back home, they'll be surprised . . . . they'll see, I'm an author, I still have a lot to learn but I've made it. [Translation mine]

Conclusion

This chapter offers a glimpse into the dynamics, tensions, and possibilities that surround biliteracy development and knowledge production for linguistic minority adolescents and young adults in U.S. public schools. In contrast to many adult education contexts, these students are surrounded by the conceptions, orientations, and relations of an academic setting that has little or no use for lived experience, linguistic and cultural difference, or for students who do not measure up to the age-specific standards of literate and intellectual performance. Within this context, knowledge is wielded as distinct from and outside the realm of the real world and the community; instruction only serves to emphasize what students do not know. Literacy learning, if it occurs at all, is most often dependent upon individual will and/or a singular teacher's interest and dedication rather than on a focused program and pedagogy for action.

My discussion of the photonovel project and the students' construction of popular text affords one example of the learning and engagement that can occur when the traditional pedagogy and curriculum that place students with limited formal schooling at risk are challenged. It points to the need to build upon the experiences, concerns, and perspectives of students and to make these the base from which literacy learning and knowledge production can emerge. It also demonstrates the potential that a more critical pedagogy can offer in terms of repositioning marginalized students as knowers and as teachers, rethinking the content, context, and social character of classroom instruction, and encouraging critique, engagement, responsibility, community, and a questioning of the status quo.

Finally, the chapter helps make evident the complex significance of language and literacy, and the conditions, relationships, and practices that surround their use and development. In so doing, it demonstrates that bilingualism and biliteracy are more than just taught and learned communicative forms: They are dynamic, complicated, political relations. As a result of the contexts, intentionalities, and competing tensions that surround one's place within both the immediate and the broader social order, these relations are in a constant state of shift, conflict, growth, and change.

Notes

[1] I recently witnessed this in action in a classroom of what were referred to as "advanced basic skill" (i.e., limited-literacy, at-risk) students. A (white) school administrator had voluntarily assumed a mentor role with the group of mostly males because of their high-risk status in the building. While this involvement initially consisted of focused discussion, group counseling, and an effort to establish alliances based on his own non-English upbringing, it shifted at one point to what he thought the students should know, based on E.D. Hirsch's (1987) standards for "cultural literacy." The students' lack of knowledge and disinterest in the majority of items on Hirsch's list were met by the administrator with alarm and dismay. He could not understand how students had reached high school without this knowledge; certainly success in the United States required, at least from his perspective, that this knowledge be taught and learned, in the school if not at home, and its inherent values internalized.

[2] In accordance with this writer's practice in signing her own name, I have used initial lowercase letters.

[3] This development and writing were done in small working groups of two or three, thus encouraging students to talk about meaning and word use, and to alleviate the individual burden of syntactical and morphological form and composition. The products of these groups were then shared with the entire class. While suggestions and recommendations were elicited, the final decision on content and form was left up to the original authors.

[4] The purpose of this initial brainstorming was to encourage a dialogue about the conditions of Julian's (and their) life that could eventually lead to the development of a story. Because students

were wary about having to write, the first couple of weeks were spent with them talking and me informally recording their comments so that we would remember. The visual format that I used to do this recording on the blackboard was a problem-posing tree; at the base of the tree trunk were the two identified reasons for his leaving and below we identified the "roots"—the problems, concerns, issues, and situations that prompted his leaving. The branches of the tree became the problems, issues, and circumstances that were created because of the leaving. The tree strategy provided a visual, graphic, and contextual way to represent the class discussions that made sense even to those students who had difficulty reading the actual words the tree included. In some instances, to make the tree even more comprehensible, I made a small drawing to represent the thought and to accompany the word or words that I wrote.

[5] This documentation was done first in Spanish since this was the dominant language of most in the class (including the teacher). A small group of bilingual students worked on the English version at the same time, drawing from the Spanish text but adding their own understandings and interpretations.

[6] The students' decision to edit the photonovel reflected neither an unawareness about their own limited abilities nor of the role of importance of the standard, grammatically correct form. In the final composition of the new code of discipline, for instance, students requested that the teacher do the final editing. They knew that because it was to be given to administrators, it should be in the standard and appropriate form. The photonovel, in contrast, had a very different audience and purpose.

References

Bloom, A. (1987). *The closing of the American mind: How higher education has failed democracy and impoverished the souls of today's students*. New York: Simon and Schuster.

Cook-Gumperz, J. (1986). Literacy and schooling: An unchanging equation. In J. Cook-Gumperz (Ed.), *The social construction of literacy* (pp. 16-44). New York: Cambridge University Press.

Cummins, J. (1986). Empowering minority students: A framework for intervention. *Harvard Educational Review, 56,* 18-36.

Ferdman, B. (1990, May). Literacy and cultural identity. *Harvard Educational Review, 60,* 181-204.

Fine, M. (1987, February). Silencing in public schools. *Language Arts, 64*(2), 157-174.

Fueyo, J.M. (1988). Technical literacy vs. critical literacy in adult basic education. *Journal of Education, 170*(1), 107-118.

Graff, H. (1987). *The legacies of literacy: Continuities and contradictions in western culture and society.* Bloomington: Indiana University Press.

Hirsch, E.D. (1987). *Cultural literacy: What every American needs to know.* Boston: Houghton Mifflin.

Hispanic Policy Development Project (HPDP). (1988). *Closing the gap for U.S. Hispanic youth.* Washington, DC: Author.

hooks, b. (1989). *Talking back: Thinking feminist, thinking black.* Boston: South End.

Moll, L. (1989). *Community knowledge and classroom practice: Combining resources for literacy instruction* (Year one progress report to Development Associates/U.S. Dept. of Education). Washington, DC: U.S. Department of Education.

Roth, R. (1984). Schooling, literacy acquisition, and cultural transmission. *Journal of Education, 166*(3), 291-308.

Scribner, S. (1984). Literacy in three metaphors. *American Journal of Education, 93*(1), 6-21.

Shannon, P. (1989). *Broken promises: Reading instruction in twentieth-century America.* South Hadley, MA: Bergin and Garvey.

Walsh, C.E. (1991a). *Pedagogy and the struggle for voice: Issues of language, power, and schooling for Puerto Ricans.* NY: Bergin and Garvey.

Walsh, C.E. (1991b). Literacy as praxis: A framework and introduction. In C.E. Walsh (Ed.), *Literacy as praxis: Culture, language, and pedagogy* (pp. 1-22). Norwood, NJ: Ablex.

Weedon, C. (1987). *Feminist practice and poststructuralist theory.* New York: Basil Blackwell.

Language in Education: Theory and Practice

The Educational Resources Information Center (ERIC), which is supported by the Office of Educational Research and Improvement of the U.S. Department of Education, is a nationwide system of information centers, each responsible for a given educational level or field of study. ERIC's basic objective is to make developments in educational research, instruction, and teacher training readily accessible to educators and members of related professions.

The ERIC Clearinghouse on Languages and Linguistics (ERIC/CLL), one of the specialized information centers in the ERIC system, is operated by the Center for Applied Linguistics (CAL) and is specifically responsible for the collection and dissemination of information on research in languages and linguistics and on the application of research to language teaching and learning.

In 1989, CAL was awarded a contract to expand the activities of ERIC/CLL through the establishment of an adjunct ERIC clearinghouse, the National Clearinghouse for ESL Literacy Education (NCLE). NCLE's specific focus is literacy education for language minority adults and out-of-school youth.

ERIC/CLL and NCLE commission recognized authorities in languages, linguistics, adult literacy education, and English as a second language (ESL) to write about current issues in these fields. Monographs, intended for educators, researchers, and others interested in language education, are published under the series title, *Language in Education: Theory and Practice (LIE)*. The *LIE* series includes practical guides for teachers, state-of-the-art papers, research reviews, and collected reports.

For further information on the ERIC system, ERIC/CLL, or NCLE, contact either clearinghouse at the Center for Applied Linguistics, 1118 22nd Street, NW, Washington, DC 20037.

Vickie Lewelling, ERIC/CLL Publications Coordinator
Joy Kreeft Peyton, NCLE Publications Coordinator

Other *LIE* Titles Available from Delta Systems Co., Inc.

The following are other titles in the *Language in Education* series published by the Center for Applied Linguistics and Delta Systems Co., Inc.:

Making Meaning, Making Change: Participatory Curriculum Development for Adult ESL Literacy (ISBN 0-937354-79-1)
by Elsa Roberts Auerbach

Talking Shop: A Curriculum Sourcebook for Participatory Adult ESL (ISBN 0-937354-78-3)
by Andrea Nash, Ann Cason, Madeline Rhum, Loren McGrail, and Rosario Gomez-Sanford

Speaking of Language: An International Guide to Language Service Organizations (ISBN 0-937354-80-5)
edited by Paula Conru, Vickie Lewelling, and Whitney Stewart

Cooperative Learning: A Response to Linguistic and Cultural Diversity (ISBN 0-937354-81-3)
edited by Daniel D. Holt

Approaches to Adult ESL Literacy Instruction (ISBN 0-937354-82-1)
edited by JoAnn Crandall and Joy Kreeft Peyton

To order any of these titles, call Delta Systems, Co., Inc. at (800) 323-8270 or (815) 363-3582 (9-5 EST) or write them at 1400 Miller Pkwy., McHenry, IL 60050.

Varieties of Cultural History

PETER BURKE

Cornell University Press
Ithaca, New York

First published in 1997 by Cornell University Press in association with Polity
Press (UK), the originating publisher.

A CIP catalogue record is available from the Library of Congress.

ISBN 0-8014-3491-2 (cloth)
ISBN 0-8014-8492-8 (paperback)

This book is printed on acid-free paper.

Printed in Great Britain.

Contents

Preface   vii

Acknowledgements   ix

1 Origins of Cultural History   1
2 The Cultural History of Dreams   23
3 History as Social Memory   43
4 The Language of Gesture in Early Modern Italy   60
5 Frontiers of the Comic in Early Modern Italy   77
6 The Discreet Charm of Milan: English Travellers in the Seventeenth Century   94
7 Public and Private Spheres in Late Renaissance Genoa   111
8 Learned Culture and Popular Culture in Renaissance Italy   124
9 Chivalry in the New World   136
10 The Translation of Culture: Carnival in Two or Three Worlds   148
11 Strengths and Weaknesses of the History of Mentalities   162
12 Unity and Variety in Cultural History   183

Bibliography   213

Index   241

Preface

T he aim of this collection of twelve essays is to discuss and
illustrate some of the main varieties of cultural history
which have emerged since the questioning of what might
be called its 'classic' form, exemplified in the work of Jacob
Burckhardt and Johan Huizinga. This classic model has not been
replaced by any new orthodoxy, despite the importance of
approaches inspired by social and cultural anthropology.

The collection opens with a chapter on the origins of cultural
history which raises general questions about the identity of the
subject. The chapters on dreams and memory are substantive but
they are also comparative and they too attempt to engage with
general problems in the practice of cultural history.

There follow five case-studies of early modern Italy, which was
the main area of my research from the mid-1960s to the mid-1980s.
All these studies are located on the frontiers of cultural history (in
the sense of areas only recently explored) and also on cultural frontiers – between learned and popular culture, between the public and
the private spheres, between the serious and the comic.

Then come two essays on the New World, especially Brazil (a
new world I discovered only a decade ago). They focus on
romances of chivalry and on carnival but their essential concern
is with cultural 'translation' in the etymological, literal and
metaphorical senses of that term. Particular emphasis is placed
on the consequences of cultural encounters, whether they should
be described in terms of mixing, syncretism or synthesis.

The volume ends with two theoretical pieces, an essay on men-talities which offers both a criticism of that concept and a defence of the approach associated with it against recent critics, and a general discussion of varieties of cultural history, compar-ing and contrasting the classic style with the 'new' or 'anthropo-logical' one and attempting to answer the question whether the so-called 'new' cultural history is condemned to fragmentation.

The ideas presented here have developed out of a kind of dia-logue between sixteenth- and seventeenth-century sources, earlier historians (Jacob Burckhardt, Aby Warburg, Marc Bloch, Johan Huizinga), and modern cultural theorists, from Sigmund Freud, Norbert Elias and Mikhail Bakhtin to Michel Foucault, Michel de Certeau, and Pierre Bourdieu. In the essays which follow, I shall be trying to avoid the opposite dangers of new-fangled 'con-structivism' (the idea of the cultural or discursive construction of reality), and old-fashioned 'positivism' (in the sense of an empiri-cism confident that 'the documents' will reveal 'the facts').

I dedicate this book to my beloved wife and fellow-historian, Maria Lúcia Garcia Pallares-Burke.

Acknowledgements

In the course of elaborating these essays I have learned much
from dialogues over the years with Jim Amelang, Anton Blok,
Jan Bremmer, Maria Lúcia Pallares-Burke, Roger Chartier,
Bob Darnton, Natalie Davis, Rudolf Dekker, Florike Egmond,
Carlo Ginzburg, Eric Hobsbawm, Gábor Klaniczay, Reinhart
Koselleck, Giovanni Levi, Eva Österberg, Krzysztof Pomian,
Jacques Revel, Peter Rietbergen, Herman Roodenburg, Joan Pau
Rubies i Mirabet, Bob Scribner, and Keith Thomas. In the study
of dreams I was helped by Alan Macfarlane, Norman Mackenzie,
Anthony Ryle, and Riccardo Steiner. Gwyn Prins and Vincent
Viaene eased my way into African history. For the title of chapter
6 I am grateful to Aldo da Maddalena.

Chapter 1 is a revised version of 'Reflections on the Origins of
Cultural History', in *Interpretation in Cultural History*, ed. Joan
Pittock and Andrew Wear (1991), pp. 5–24, by permission of
Macmillan Press.

Chapter 2 has been revised from the original English version of
'L'histoire sociale des rêves', *Annales: Économies, Sociétés,
Civilisations* 28 (1973) pp. 329–42. It is published in English for
the first time.

Chapter 3 is a revised version of 'History as Social Memory',
in *Memory*, ed. Thomas Butler (1989); pp. 97–113 by permission
of Blackwell Publishers.

Chapter 4 is a revised version of 'The Language of Gesture in
Early Modern Italy', in *A Cultural History of Gesture*, ed. Jan

Bremmer and Herman Roodenburg (1991), pp. 71–83. Copyright
© Peter Burke 1991, by permission of Polity Press and Cornell
University Press.

Chapter 5 is a revised version of 'Frontiers of the Comic in
Early Modern Italy', in *A Cultural History of Humour*, ed. Jan
Bremmer and Herman Roodenburg (1997) pp. 61–75, by permis-
sion of Polity Press.

Chapter 9 is a revised version of 'Chivalry in the New World',
in *Chivalry in the Renaissance*, ed. Sydney Anglo (1990),
pp. 253–62, by permission of Boydell and Brewer Ltd.

Chapter 11 is a revised version of 'Strengths and Weaknesses
of the History of Mentalities', *History of European Ideas* 7
(1986), 439–51, by permission of Elsevier Science Ltd.

I

Origins of Cultural History

There is no agreement over what constitutes cultural history, any more than agreement over what constitutes culture. Over forty years ago, two American scholars set out to chart the variations in the use of the term in English, and collected more than two hundred rival definitions.[1] Taking other languages and the last four decades into account, it would be easy to collect many more. In the search for our subject it may therefore be appropriate to adapt the existentialists' definition of man and to say that cultural history has no essence. It can only be defined in terms of its own history.

How can anyone write a history of something which lacks a fixed identity? It is rather like trying to catch a cloud in a butterfly net. However, in their very different ways, Herbert Butterfield and Michel Foucault both demonstrated that all historians face this problem. Butterfield criticized what he called the 'Whig interpretation of history', in other words the use of the past to justify the present, while Foucault emphasized epistemological 'ruptures'. If we wish to avoid the anachronistic attribution of our own intentions, interests and values to the dead, we cannot write the continuous history of anything.[2] On one side we face the danger of 'present-mindedness', but on the other the risk of being unable to write at all.

---

[1] Kroeber and Kluckhohn (1952).
[2] Butterfield (1931); Foucault (1966).

Perhaps there is a middle way, an approach to the past which asks present-minded questions but refuses to give present-minded answers; which concerns itself with traditions but allows for their continual reinterpretation; and which notes the importance of unintended consequences in the history of historical writing as well as in the history of political events. To follow such a route is the aim of this chapter, which is concerned with the history of culture before the 'classic' period discussed in the concluding chapter, in other words before the term 'culture' came into general use.[3]

In this case the present-minded questions are the following: how old is cultural history, and how have conceptions of cultural history changed over time? The difficulty to be avoided is that of giving these questions equally present-minded answers. The problem is a slippery one. We are not the first people in the world to realize that culture, as we now call it, has a history. The term 'cultural history' goes back to the late eighteenth century, at least in German. Johan Christoph Adelung published an 'Essay in a history of the culture of the human race', *Versuch einer Geschichte der Kultur des menschlichen Geschlechts* (1782), while Johan Gottfried Eichhorn published a 'General history of culture', *Allgemeine Geschichte der Kultur* (1796–9), presented as an introduction to the 'special histories' (*Spezialgeschichte*) of the different arts and sciences.

The idea that literature and philosophy and the arts have histories is much older. This tradition deserves to be remembered. The difficulty is to do this without falling into the error of imagining that what we have defined (and indeed in some places, institutionalized), as a 'subject' or 'subdiscipline' existed in the past in this form.

In some respects the most historically minded manner of approaching the problem would be to tell the story backwards from today, showing how Huizinga's conception of cultural history differs from that of the 1990s, how Burckhardt's differed from Huizinga's, and so on. In liberating us from assumptions of continuity, however, this backward narrative would obscure the ways in which practical, partial and short-term aims and motives (such as civic pride and the search for precedent) contributed to the development over the long term of a more general study often

[3] Bruford (1962), ch. 4.

pursued for its own sake. The best thing to do is perhaps for the author to share the difficulties with the reader in the course of the narrative. In other words, like some contemporary novelists and critics, I shall try to tell a story and at the same time to reflect on it and even, perhaps, to undermine it.

Whenever one begins the story, it can be argued that it would have been better to have started earlier. This chapter begins with the humanists of Renaissance Italy, from Petrarch onwards, whose attempts to undo the work of what they were the first to call the 'Middle Ages' and to revive the literature and learning of classical antiquity implied a view of three ages of culture: ancient, medieval and modern. In fact, as the humanists well knew, some ancient Greeks and Romans had already claimed that language has a history, that philosophy has a history, that literary genres have a history, and that human life has been changed by a succession of inventions. Ideas of this kind can be found in Aristotle's *Poetics*, for example, in Varro's treatise on language, in Cicero's discussion of the rise and fall of oratory, and in the account of the early history of man given in the poem of Lucretius on the nature of things (so important for Vico, and others in the seventeenth and eighteenth centuries).[4]

History of Language and Literature

However, the humanists had a more dramatic story to tell about language and literature than their ancient models. A story of barbarian invasions and of the consequent decline and destruction of classical Latin, followed by an account of revival, the work (of course) of the humanists themselves. In other words, an age of light was followed by the 'Dark Ages', followed in turn by the dawn of another age of light. This is the story which emerges from some Italian texts of the early fifteenth century, Leonardo Bruni's lives of Dante and Petrarch, for example, the history of Latin literature written by Sicco Polenton, or the historical introduction to Lorenzo Valla's Latin grammar, the *Elegantiae*.[5] This interpretation of the history of literature formed part of the justification of the humanist movement.

[4] Edelstein (1967).
[5] Ferguson (1948), 20ff.; McLaughlin (1988).

In the fifteenth and sixteenth centuries, debates about the relative merits of Latin and Italian as a literary language and the best form of Italian to use generated research into the history of language by Leonardo Bruni, Flavio Biondo, and others. They discussed, for example, what language the ancient Romans had actually spoken, Latin or Italian.[6] In the early sixteenth century, the humanist cardinal Adriano Castellesi produced a history of Latin, *De sermone latino* (1516), divided into four periods – 'very old', 'old', 'perfect' (the age of Cicero), and 'imperfect' (ever since). Another humanist and critic, Pietro Bembo, who did as much as anyone to freeze Italian at a particular point in its development, allowed one of the characters in his famous dialogue on the vernacular, the *Prose della volgar lingua* (1525), to point out that language changes 'like fashions in clothes, modes of warfare, and all other manners and customs' (book 1, chapter 17).

Northern humanists, at once imitators and rivals of their Italian predecessors, amplified the story by drawing attention to literary and linguistic developments in their own countries. In France, for instance, two humanist lawyers, Étienne Pasquier in his *Recherches de la France* (1566) and Claude Fauchet in his *Origine de la langue et poésie françoises* (1581), chronicled and celebrated the achievements of French writers from the thirteenth century to the age of François I and the Pléiade.[7] In England, a discussion of English poetry from Chaucer onwards can be found in the treatise called *The Arte of English Poesie* published in 1589 and attributed to George Puttenham. A history of Spanish, *Del origen y principio de la lengua castellana*, was published by Bernardo Aldrete in 1606, in the same year as a similar study of Portuguese, *Origem da língua portuguesa*, by the lawyer Duarte Nunes de Leão. The Germans had to wait until the later seventeenth century for an equivalent history, just as they had to wait until the seventeenth century for an equivalent of the poets of the Pléiade, but the history, when it arrived, was more elaborate and comparative. The polymath Daniel Morhof placed the history of the German language and German poetry in a comparative European framework in his *Unterricht von der Teutschen Sprache und Poesie* (1682).[8]

Building on these foundations, a number of eighteenth-century

[6] Grayson (1959).
[7] Huppert (1970).
[8] Batts (1987).

scholars produced multivolume histories of national literatures, notably those of France (by a research team of Benedictine monks headed by Rivet de la Grange), and of Italy (compiled single-handed by Girolamo Tiraboschi). The breadth of Tiraboschi's notion of 'literature' is worth noting.[9] In Britain there were similar plans afoot. Alexander Pope put forward a 'scheme of the history of English poetry'; Thomas Gray amended it. Meanwhile, the history had been undertaken by Thomas Warton. Warton never went beyond the early seventeenth century, but his unfinished *History of English Poetry* (4 vols, 1774–8) remains impressive.[10]

Monographs were also written on the history of particular literary genres. The French Protestant scholar Isaac Casaubon published a study of Greek satire in 1605, and John Dryden, following his example, wrote a *Discourse concerning the Original and Progress of Satire* (1693) discussing its development from what he called the 'rough-cast, unhewn' extempore satire of ancient Rome to the polished productions of a period when the Romans 'began to be somewhat better bred, and were entering, as I may say, into the rudiments of civil conversation'. Again, the rise of the novel in the seventeenth and eighteenth centuries was accompanied by investigations of its oriental and medieval origins by the polymath bishop Pierre-Daniel Huet, in his *Lettre sur l'origine des romans* (1669), and following him by Thomas Warton, who inserted into his history of poetry a digression 'On the Origin of Romantic Fiction in Europe'.

History of Artists, Art and Music

It is hardly surprising to find men of letters devoting attention to the history of literature. Art was a less obvious object for a historian's attention, even in the Renaissance. Learned men did not always take artists seriously, while artists generally lacked the kind of preparation necessary for historical research. When, in fifteenth-century Florence, the sculptor Lorenzo Ghiberti produced a literary sketch of the history of art in his autobiographical *Commentaries*, he was doing something rather unusual.[11]

---

[9] Escarpit (1958); Goulemot (1986); Sapegno (1993).
[10] Wellek (1941); Lipking (1970), 352f.; Pittock (1973), ch. 5.
[11] Grinten (1952); Tanturli (1976).

We ought not to take Vasari for granted either. He was remarkable in his own day because he had a double education, not only a training in an artist's workshop but a humanist education sponsored by Cardinal Passerini.[12] His *Lives of the Painters, Sculptors and Architects*, first published in 1550, was written, so the author tells us, in order that young artists might learn from the example of their great predecessors, and also (one may reasonably suspect) for the greater glory of his adopted city Florence, and his patrons the Medici (it was in fact published by the Grand Duke's press).[13]

However, Vasari's book is much more than a work of propaganda. It is also, of course, a good deal more than a biographical collection. The prefaces to the three parts into which the work is divided include an account of the rise of art in antiquity, its decline in the Middle Ages, and its revival in Italy in three stages, culminating in Vasari's master Michelangelo. It has been shown by Ernst Gombrich that Vasari's developmental scheme was adapted from Cicero's account of the history of rhetoric. Without Vasari's double education, such an adaptation would have been virtually inconceivable, even if we allow for the fact that Vasari was helped by a circle of scholars including Gianbattista Adriani, Cosimo Bartoli, Vincenzo Borghini, and Paolo Giovio.[14] Vasari's concern with art rather than artists was given still more emphasis in the second edition (1568).

Vasari's book was treated as a challenge. Artists and scholars from other parts of Italy compiled lives of local artists in order to show that Rome, Venice, Genoa, and Bologna were worthy rivals to Florence. However, they paid much less attention than Vasari had done to general trends in art. The same goes for responses to Vasari outside Italy, in the Netherlands, by Karel van Mander in *Het Schilderboek* (1604), and in Germany, by Joachim von Sandrart in his *Deutsche Akademie* (1675–9), who argued that the age of Albrecht Dürer marked the shift of cultural leadership from southern Europe to the north. It was only in the mid-eighteenth century that Horace Walpole's *Anecdotes of Painting*, intended as a Vasari for England (Walpole joked about his 'Vasarihood'), found room not only for biographies but also for chapters on the 'state of painting' at different periods, the equiva-

---

[12] Rubin (1995).
[13] Cf. Chastel (1961), 21ff.
[14] Gombrich (1960a).

lent of the chapters on economic, social and literary history to be found in the contemporary *History of England* by David Hume.[15]

The rise of what it is retrospectively convenient to call the history of art as opposed to the biographies of artists took place earlier in studies of classical antiquity, for a sufficiently obvious reason. Despite the famous anecdotes of Greek artists told by Pliny (and adapted by Vasari), little was known about Apelles, Phidias and the rest, making it difficult to organize a study of ancient art as a series of biographies. The Florentine scholar Gianbattista Adriani, who composed a brief history of ancient art in the form of a letter to Vasari (1567), to help him in his second edition of the *Lives*, chose to arrange it around the idea of artistic progress. Other studies of ancient art were made by the Dutch humanist Franciscus Junius in his *De pictura veterum* (1637), and by André Félibien (historian of buildings to Louis XIV, apparently the first post in art history ever to be created), in his *Origine de la peinture* (1660).[16]

Félibien's essay on the origin of painting and Huet's on the origin of romances were written in France in the same decade, the 1660s, as if expressing a more general change in historiographical taste. In the tradition of Félibien was the work of the court painter Monier, *Histoire des arts* (1698), originally lectures for students of the Royal Academy of Painting. Monier's cyclical interpretation began with the rise of art in antiquity and proceeded to its decline in the Dark Ages and its revival between 1000 and 1600. The relatively early dating of the revival allowed Monier to give an important role to the French, like Pasquier and Fauchet in the domain of literature.

The outstanding achievement in this area, Johan Joachim Winckelmann's great *History of Ancient Art* (1764), should be considered not as a radically new departure but as the culmination of a trend, a trend which was encouraged not only by the example of histories of literature but also by several new cultural practices, among them the rise of art collecting, the art market and connoisseurship.[17]

The history of music, on the other hand, was virtually an eighteenth-century invention. Some sixteenth- and seventeenth-century scholars, such as Vincenzo Galilei (father of the scientist)

[15] Lipking (1970), 127f.
[16] Lipking (1970), 23ff.; Grinten (1952).
[17] Grinten (1952); Alsop (1982).

and Girolamo Mei, had been well aware of changes in style over the long term and indeed discussed them in their comparisons of ancient and modern music published in 1581 and 1602 respectively, but their aim was simply to attack or defend particular styles. In the eighteenth century, on the other hand, there was an explosion of interest in music history. In France, one major study, *Histoire de la musique*, was published in 1715 by the Bonnet-Bourdelot family, and another was written, but not published, by P. J. Caffiaux, a learned Benedictine who was, appropriately, doing for music something like what his colleague Rivet was doing for literature. In Italy, Gianbattista Martini published an important study of the music of antiquity, *Storia della musica* (1757). In Switzerland another Benedictine, Martin Gerbert, made an important contribution to the history of church music in his *De cantu et musica sacra* (1774). In England, Charles Burney and John Hawkins were contemporaries and rivals, Hawkins with his *General History of the Science and Practice of Music* (1766) and Burney with *A General History of Music* (1776–89). In Germany, J. N. Forkel of the University of Göttingen summed up the work of the century in his *Allgemeine Geschichte der Musik* (1788–1801).[18]

The History of Doctrine

The histories of language, literature and the arts seem to have begun as side-effects of the Renaissance. The Reformation also had its historical by-products. As the humanists defined their place in history by dividing the past into ancient, medieval and modern, so did the reformers, who saw themselves as going back behind the Middle Ages and reviving Christian antiquity or the 'primitive church', as they called it. Histories of the Reformation begin with the Reformation itself. Among the most famous were the *Commentaries* of Johann Sleidan (1555) and the *Acts and Monuments* of John Foxe (1563). They tended to be histories of events or histories of institutions, but some of them – like their

---

[18] *Grove's* (1980), article 'Caffiaux'; Heger (1932); Lipking (1970), 229ff., 269ff.

model the *Ecclesiastical History* by the early Christian, Eusebius of Caesarea – found a place for the history of doctrines.[19]

The concern with changes in doctrine can be seen with still greater clarity in the seventeenth century. On the Protestant side, Heinrich Alting's *Theologia historica* (1664) argued for a 'historical theology' on the grounds that church history was not only the story of events but also of dogmas (*dogmatum narratio*), their corruption (*depravatio*) and their reform (*reparatio, restitutio, reformatio*). On the Catholic side, the idea of change in the doctrines of the church was more difficult to accept, despite the example of the Spanish Jesuit Rodriguez de Arriaga (d. 1667), who presented what has been called 'one of the most extreme theories of development ever put forward by a reputable Catholic thinker'. Arriaga, a professor in Prague, taught that the proclamation of doctrine by the church 'is the making explicit what was not explicit, and need not have been implicit, earlier'.[20]

It was easier to accept change in the history of heresy, as some seventeenth-century Catholic histories of the Reformation did: Florimond de Raemond, for example, in his *Histoire de la naissance, progrès et décadence de l'hérésie de ce siècle* (1623); Louis Maimbourg, in his *Histoire du Calvinisme* (1682); and, most famous of all, Jacques-Bénigne Bossuet in his *Histoire des variations des églises protestantes* (1688).[21]

These three works were not exactly examples of the study of the past for its own sake; they were highly polemical. The books of Maimbourg and Bossuet were written for a political purpose, to support Louis XIV's anti-Protestant policies at the time of the Revocation of the Edict of Nantes. However, their central idea that doctrines (at least false doctrines) have a history, an idea expounded most fully, brilliantly and destructively by Bossuet, was to have a considerable appeal outside the polemical context in which it was originally developed. It was deployed, for instance, by an apologist for unorthodoxy, Gottfried Arnold, in his *Unpartheyische Kirche- und Ketzer-Historie* (1699–1700). For Arnold, church history was little more than the history of

---

[19] Headley (1963); Dickens and Tonkin (1985). On Eusebius, Momigliano (1963).
[20] Chadwick (1957), 20, 45–7.
[21] Chadwick (1957), 6–10.

heresies, some of which hardened into official doctrine (as Luther's had done), only to be challenged by later generations.[22]

From the history of religious doctrine it seems no great step to its secular equivalents. Yet in this area (unlike art history or the history of literature and language), there seem to have been few significant developments before the year 1600. Perhaps the need to assess past achievements was a by-product of the scientific revolution of the seventeenth century, in which the 'new' mechanical philosophy, as it was often called, became a matter for debate. In any case, the seventeenth century saw a number of histories of philosophy, including Georg Horn's *Historia philosophiae* (1655) and Thomas Stanley's *History of Philosophy* (1655). In the eighteenth century the trend continued with A. F. Boureau-Deslande's *Histoire critique de la philosophie* (1735), and Jacob Brucker's *Historia critica philosophiae* (1767).[23] A certain Johannes Jonsonius even produced a history of the history of philosophy, published in 1716.

The classical exemplar for the history of philosophy was the *Lives of the Philosophers* written in the third century AD by Diogenes Laertius, a model which Eusebius adapted in the following century for his account of early Christian sects and which Vasari reshaped still more radically for his lives of artists.[24] This biographical model remained a tempting one. However, attempts were also made to tell a story as well as to collect biographies, to practise what Thomas Burnet (nearly three centuries before Foucault) called 'philosophical archaeology', and to write the intellectual history not only of the Greeks and Romans but also of the 'barbarians', as in the case of Otto Heurn's *Barbarica philosophia* (1600) and Christian Kortholt's *Philosophia barbarica* (1660). Scholars studied the ideas of the Chaldeans, the Egyptians, the Persians, the Carthaginians, the Scythians, the Indians, the Japanese and the Chinese (Jacob Friedrich Reimann's history of Chinese philosophy was published in 1727).

Some of these histories were written for their own sake, others with polemical intent, for example to encourage scepticism by emphasizing the contradictions between one philosopher and another. They modified the traditional biographical framework by discussing the development of philosophical schools or 'sects', as in the *De philosophorum sectis* (1657) of the Dutch scholar

---

[22] Seeberg (1923); Meinhold (1967).
[23] Rak (1971); Braun (1973); Del Torre (1976).
[24] Momigliano (1963).

Gerard Voss, or by distinguishing periods, as Horn did, contrasting the 'heroic', 'theological or mythical' and the 'philosophical' ages of Greek thought.

The phrase 'history of ideas' is generally believed to have been launched by the American philosopher Arthur Lovejoy when he founded the History of Ideas Club at Johns Hopkins University in the 1920s. It had actually been employed two hundred years earlier, by Jacob Brucker, who referred to the *historia de ideis*, and by Gianbattista Vico, who called in his *New Science* for 'una storia dell'umane idee'.

The History of Disciplines

Out of the history-of-philosophy tradition branched a number of studies of specific disciplines.[25]

On the arts side, the history of rhetoric and the history of history itself deserve to be mentioned. A French Jesuit, Louis de Cresolles, produced a remarkable history of the rhetoric of the ancient sophists, the *Theatrum veterum rhetorum* (1620), in which he discussed, among other topics, the training of the sophists, the competition between them, their income, and the honours they received.[26] The first history of historical writing was produced by the seigneur de La Popelinière in his *L'Histoire des histoires* (1599), arguing that historiography went through four stages – poetry, myth, annals and finally a 'perfect history' (*histoire accomplie*), which was philosophical as well as accurate.[27]

The history of the graduate discipline of law also attracted considerable interest. Fifteenth-century humanists such as Lorenzo Valla and Angelo Poliziano concerned themselves with the history of Roman law as part of the ancient Roman world which they were trying to revive, criticizing the professional lawyers of their own day for misinterpreting the texts. Valla and Poliziano were amateurs in this field but they were followed in the sixteenth century by scholars such as Andrea Alciato and Guillaume Budé who were trained in both law and the humanities. One of these humanist lawyers, François Baudouin, went so far as to suggest that 'historians would do better to study the

[25] Graham et al. (1983); Kelley and Popkin (1991).
[26] Fumaroli (1980), 299–326.
[27] Butterfield (1955), 205–6; Kelley (1970), 140–1; Huppert (1970), 137–8.

development of laws and institutions than devote themselves to
the investigation of armies, the description of camps of war, the
tale of battles and the counting of dead bodies', a critique of
'drum-and-trumpet history' of a kind which would become commonplace by the eighteenth century.[28]

In the case of medicine, some sixteenth-century physicians
(notably Vesalius and Fernel), took sufficient interest in history to
place their own work in the context of the intellectual revival or
Renaissance through which they were living. The first substantial
study of medical history, however, was published considerably
later, at the end of the seventeenth century. This history of medicine by Daniel Leclerc (the brother of the critic Jean Leclerc)
begins by surveying earlier studies and dismisses them for
concentrating on biography. 'There is a big difference between
writing the history or biographies of physicians', he remarks in
his preface, '... and writing the history of medicine, studying the
origin of that art, and looking at its progress from century to
century and the changes in its systems and methods ... which is
what I have undertaken.' Leclerc's title page also emphasizes his
concern with medical 'sects' along the lines of the interest in sects
of the history of philosophy, which he seems to have taken as his
model.

Unfortunately, Leclerc's account (like Martini's history of
music) never got beyond classical antiquity. For the modern part
of the story it was necessary to wait until 1725 and the second
volume of Freind's *History of Physick*, which took the story from
the Arabs to Linacre (deliberately stopping short of Paracelsus).
As his title page boasted, Freind differed from Leclerc in concentrating on 'practice'. His second volume is as much a history of
illness (notably the sweating sickness, venereal disease, and
scurvy) as it is a history of medicine. It is almost a history of the
body.

In the historiography of most other disciplines, the eighteenth
century marks a turning point. For example, although a short
account of the development of astronomy was given by Johan
Kepler, this history was much amplified by Johann Friedrich
Weidler (1740) and by Pierre Estève (1755).[29] Estève criticized
his predecessors for being too narrow and tried to produce what

[28] Kelley (1970).
[29] Jardine (1984).

he called a 'general history' of astronomy, linked to other intellectual changes, as well as a 'particular' history focused on detail. In Voltairean style he declared that 'the history of the sciences is much more useful than that of the revolutions of empires.'

In the history of mathematics, studies of the lives of mathematicians on the model of Diogenes Laertius were followed in the eighteenth century by more ambitious enterprises. Pierre Rémond de Montmort intended to write a history of geometry on the model of the existing histories of painting, music and so on, but died in 1719 before he could carry out his plans. The *Histoire des mathématiques* (1758) by Jean Étienne Montucla, a member of Diderot's circle, criticized the biographical approach, just as Leclerc (discussed below) had already done for medicine. Montucla aimed instead at making a contribution to the history of the development of the human mind.

So did the author of *Geschichte der Chemie* (1797–9), a history of chemistry which made a considerable effort to place the development of the subject in its social, political and cultural context. This monograph was presented by its author, J. F. Gmelin, a Göttingen man, as a contribution to a series of histories of arts and sciences from the time of their 'Renaissance' (*Wiederherstellung*) onwards, a project on which a society of learned men was currently at work. The milieu of the new University of Göttingen seems to have been particularly favourable to cultural history. Forkel was writing his history of music there at much the same time as Gmelin was working on the history of chemistry.[30]

With the history of disciplines we may group the history of inventions, which goes back to the Italian humanist Polydore Vergil at the beginning of the sixteenth century and his *De inventoribus* (1500). Polydore's concept of 'invention' was a wide one by modern standards. For instance, according to him, the English parliament was invented by King Henry III.[31] Two inventions dear to scholars, writing and printing, had monographs devoted to them in the seventeenth and eighteenth centuries. Writing was studied by Herman Hugo (1617) and Bernard Malinckrott (1638), and their works were used by Vico for his now famous

---

[30] Butterfield (1955), 39–50; Iggers (1982).
[31] Hay (1952); Copenhaver (1978).

reflections on orality and literacy. Samuel Palmer's *General History of Printing* (1732) was the work of a scholar-printer.

The History of Modes of Thought

Another development from the history of disciplines was the history of modes of thought.[32] This development bears a striking and not altogether illusory resemblance to some of the 'new directions' preached and practised today. It is necessary to walk an intellectual tightrope at this point in order to give the eighteenth-century historians of mentalities the credit that is due to them without turning them into clones of the French historians associated with the journal *Annales*.

In the seventeenth century, John Selden had already recommended to the listeners to his Table-Talk the study of 'what was generally believed in all ages', adding that in order to discover this, 'the way is to consult the liturgies, not any private man's writings.' In other words, rituals reveal mentalities. John Locke was acutely aware of differences between modes of thought in different parts of the world. 'Had you or I' (he wrote in *Concerning Human Understanding*), 'been born at the Bay of Saldanha, possibly our thoughts and notions had not exceeded those brutish ones of the Hottentots that inhabit there.' This relativist argument, nourished by recent accounts of Africa, gives obvious support to Locke's polemic against innate ideas.

It is not such a long step from a concern with variations in thinking in different places to a concern with different periods. It may well have been the revolution in thought associated with the rise of the 'mechanical philosophy' which made some Europeans aware of the intellectual 'world they had lost'. Curiously enough, the eighteenth-century scholar Richard Hurd employs a similar phrase when discussing the rise of reason since Spenser's day. 'What we have gotten by this revolution, you will say, is a great deal of good sense. What we have lost is a world of fine fabling.'[33] At all events, one finds this awareness in Fontenelle, in Vico, in Montesquieu and elsewhere in the eighteenth century, especially in the context of attempts to understand alien features of early literature and law.

[32] Crombie (1994), 1587–633.
[33] Quoted in Pittock (1973), 85.

Fontenelle's essay *De l'origine des fables* (or, as we would say, the origin of 'myths'), published in 1724 but written in the 1690s, argued that in less polished ages (*siècles grossiers*), systems of philosophy were necessarily anthropomorphic and magical. Vico arrived independently at similar conclusions, expressed with rather more sympathy for what he called the 'poetic logic' of early man. A Danish scholar called Jens Kraft published in 1760 a general description of the 'savage mind', or more exactly of savage peoples (*de Vilde Folk*) and their 'mode of thought' (*Taenke-Maade*). A similar phrase had been used by Montesquieu in his *De l'esprit des lois* (1744), when he was trying to reconstruct the logic of the medieval ordeal, in other words establishing one's innocence by carrying a hot iron without being burned, and so on (book 28, chapter 17). Montesquieu explained this custom by what he called 'the mode of thought of our ancestors' ('la manière de penser de nos pères').

The same kind of concern with an exotic mentality underlay the increasing interest in the history of chivalry, studied by the French scholar Jean-Baptiste de La Curne de Sainte-Palaye on the basis of medieval romances and other sources.[34] Sainte-Palaye's *Mémoires sur l'ancienne chevalerie* (1746–50) was studied by a number of the thinkers cited in this essay, including Voltaire, Herder, Horace Walpole and William Robertson. In the famous 'view of the progress of society' prefixed to his *History of Charles V* (1769), Robertson argued that 'chivalry ... though considered commonly as a wild institution, the effect of caprice, and the source of extravagance, arose naturally from the state of society at that period, and had a very serious influence in refining the manners of the European nations.' In his *Letters on Chivalry* (1762), Richard Hurd had already discussed medieval romances (and even the *Faerie Queene*) as expressions of what he called the 'Gothic system' of 'heroic manners'.

Hurd's friend Thomas Warton had similar interests. He too read Sainte-Palaye. His essay on the rise of 'romantic fiction' argued that it originated 'at a time when a new and unnatural mode of thinking took place in Europe, introduced by our communication with the East', in other words the Crusades. His *Observations on the Faerie Queene* (1754) showed rather more sympathy for alien mentalities,

---

[34] Gossman (1968).

indeed empathy with them, and his observations on method have lost none of their relevance today.

> In reading the works of an author, who lived in a remote age, it is necessary that ... we should place ourselves in his situation and circumstances; that we may be the better enabled to judge and discern how his turn of thinking, and manner of composing, were biass'd, influenc'd and as it were tinctur'd, by very familiar and reigning appearances, which were utterly different from those with which we are at present surrounded.

The history of unspoken assumptions and of representations remains central to the enterprise of cultural history, as the following chapter will argue.

Some men of letters took an interest in the history of what J. C. Adelung and J. G. Herder, both writing at the end of the eighteenth century, seem to have been the first to call 'popular culture' (*Kultur des Volkes*). A group of learned Jesuits writing the lives of the saints had already (in 1757) coined the phrase 'little traditions of the people' (*populares traditiunculae*), much like the 'Little Tradition' to which the American anthropologist Robert Redfield drew attention in the 1930s. By the year 1800 there was so much interest in folksongs and folktales that it seems reasonable to speak of the 'discovery' of popular culture on the part of European intellectuals.[35]

The History of Culture

Given the increasing number of histories of arts and sciences in the early modern period, it is scarcely surprising to find that some people attempted to fit them together. For example, in his polemical treatise *On the Causes of the Corruption of the Arts* (1531), the Spanish humanist Juan Luis Vives pressed the history of learning, conceived more or less along the lines of Valla's history of language, into the service of a campaign for the reform of universities. Among the causes of corruption listed by this disciple of Erasmus were 'arrogance' and 'wars'.

However, the principal model of general cultural history in the early modern period might be described as that of the *translatio*

[35] Burke (1978), ch. 1.

studii, in other words the successive dominance either of different regions of the world or of different disciplines. In his remarkable essay in comparative history, the *Vicissitudes* (1575), the French humanist Louis Le Roy argued that that 'all liberal and mechanical arts have flourished and declined together' ('tous arts liberaux et mecaniques ont fleuri ensemble, puis decheu'), so that different civilizations, Greek, Arab, Chinese and so on, have their different peaks and troughs. A minor German humanist, Rainer Reineck, in his *Method for Reading History* (1583), modelled on Jean Bodin's famous study of the same name, discussed what he called *historia scholastica*, in other words the history of literature, the arts and intellectual disciplines.

Francis Bacon was acquainted with the work of Le Roy, as he was with the treatise by Vives, but he went further, at least in intention, in his famous call in the second book of his *Advancement of Learning* (1605) for 'a just story of learning, containing the antiquities and original of knowledge and their sects, their inventions, their traditions, their diverse administrations and managings, their flourishings, their oppositions, decays, depressions, oblivions, removes, with the causes and occasions of them'. The reference, unusual for its time, to the 'administrations and managings' of learning surely betrays the man of affairs. These affairs prevented Bacon from producing such a history of learning but his programme inspired some writers of the following century.

Voltaire's *Essay on Manners* (1751) and his *Age of Louis XIV* (1756) were manifestos for a new kind of history which would give less space to war and politics and more to 'the progress of the human mind'. In practice, Voltaire gave more space to the wars of Louis XIV than to his patronage of the arts and sciences, but his histories do have a good deal to say on the revival of letters and the refinement of manners. D'Alembert gave a similar account of intellectual progress in his preliminary discourse to the *Encyclopédie* (1751), drawing on some of the histories of disciplines (such as Montucla on mathematics), and arguing that history should be concerned with culture as well as with politics, with 'great geniuses' as well as 'great nations', with men of letters as well as kings, with philosophers as well as conquerors.

Decline attracted attention as well as progress and there was considerable debate about the reasons for cultural peaks and troughs. Some scholars suggested that despotism leads to cultural decline – this was the opinion of the humanist Leonardo Bruni in the early fifteenth century, as it was the view of the Earl of Shaftesbury three hundred years later. Others searched for physical rather than moral causes, notably the climate, which Vasari had invoked as an explanation for Florentine artistic achievements, and which was discussed in a more systematic manner – together with patronage, wealth, manners, and other factors – in the *Réflexions critiques sur la poésie et la peinture* (1719) of the Abbé Jean-Baptiste Dubos. Winckelmann too was interested in the influence of climate on art.

In short, there was an interest in the links between what we call 'culture' and 'society'. Voltaire's famous *Essay on Manners* was far from alone in this respect. It was commonly assumed by eighteenth-century intellectuals that differences between 'rough' and 'polished' manners were associated with different modes of thought. More precise studies of the topic were also produced at this time.

In Germany, for instance, Adelung's essay, discussed at the beginning of this chapter, attempted to relate 'spiritual culture' to 'social life' and the 'refinement of manners', and suggested that every state had the level of culture it deserved.[36] In Britain, Horace Walpole's *Anecdotes of Painting* (1761) suggested various connections between the 'state of English painting' at particular moments and the state of society. In the second chapter on the late Middle Ages, for instance, the dominance of 'a proud, a warlike and ignorant nobility' was responsible for work which was 'magnificent without luxury and pompous without elegance'. David Hume's essay 'of refinement in the arts' discussed the relation between art, liberty, and luxury. It is likely that the history of literature and philosophy planned by Adam Smith at the end of his life would have adopted a similar approach.

A concern for the relation between what he calls *le cose d'ingegno* (matters of intelligence) and *umani costumi* (human customs) can also be found in a remarkable essay published in 1775 by the Italian Jesuit Saverio Bettinelli, dealing with the *risorgimento* or 'revival' of Italy after the year 1000. Bettinelli ranged from art, literature and music to chivalry, commerce, luxury and festivals. Robert Henry's six-volume *History of Great Britain* (1771–93) was still more ambitious, attempting what

[36] Garber (1983), 76–97.

would later be called a 'total' history of Britain from the arrival
of the Romans to the death of Henry VIII, drawing on the work
of Warton, Brucker and Sainte-Palaye (among others) and paying
attention to religion, learning and the arts as well as to politics,
commerce and 'manners'. Connections between changes in society and changes in the arts were also emphasized in the *Life of
Lorenzo de' Medici* (1795) by the Liverpool banker William
Roscoe, and in the Swiss historian J. C. L. S. de Sismondi's
Histoire des républiques italiennes (1807–18), in which the central theme was the rise and fall of liberty.[37]

The idea that a culture is a totality, or at least that the
connections between different arts and disciplines are extremely
important, also underlay one of the major achievements of early
modern scholars, their development of techniques for detecting
forgeries. These techniques of detection depended on an increasingly sharp awareness of anachronism. From Lorenzo Valla's
exposure of the so-called *Donation of Constantine* in the middle
of the fifteenth century to the rejection of the poems of 'Ossian'
at the end of the eighteenth century, there was a long series of
debates on the authenticity of particular texts, or more rarely,
artefacts such as medals or 'Doctor Woodward's Shield'.[38] In
these debates the protagonists were forced to formulate their
criteria more and more precisely.

Valla, for example, noted anachronisms in the *Donation*'s
style or mode of expression (*stilus, modus loquendi*). Richard
Bentley, in his *Dissertation upon the Epistles of Phalaris* (1697),
that famous exposure of a forged classical text, went into rather
more detail on the history of Greek, noting that the 'idiom and
style' of the letters 'by the whole thread and colour of it betrays
itself to be a thousand years younger' than the ruler to whom
they had been attributed. Thomas Warton discusses his criteria
still more fully in his exposure of the 'medieval' poems
Chatterton sent to Horace Walpole, *An Enquiry into the
Authenticity of the Poems attributed to Thomas Rowley* (1782).
Warton used his knowledge of what he called 'the progression of
poetical composition' to show up the forgery, noting anachronisms both in the language ('optics', for example) and in the style

---

[37] Haskell (1993).
[38] Levine (1977).

(full of abstractions and 'sophistications' impossible in the fifteenth century).

The view that a culture forms a whole, a view implicit in
demonstrations such as these, was gradually formulated more
and more clearly. The French scholar Étienne Pasquier was one
of the first to make the point explicit when he remarked in his
Recherches de la France (1566, book 4, chapter 1), that 'any
intelligent man' would 'virtually be able to imagine the humour
of a people by reading its ancient statutes and ordinances', and
conversely, to predict the laws of a people on the basis of its
'style of life' (*manière de vivre*).

The spread of the idea can be documented from the increasingly common use of such terms as the 'genius', 'humour' or
'spirit' of an age or people. In later seventeenth-century English
texts, for example, we find phrases such as 'the temper and
geniuses of times' (Stillingfleet); 'the genius of every age'
(Dryden); 'the general vein and humour of ages' (Temple). In
France in the age of Montesquieu and Voltaire, references to
changes in the *esprit général*, or *esprit humain*, or *génie*, are frequent. The same goes for the Scots in the age of Hume and
Robertson: 'the spirit of the nation', 'the spirit of enquiry', 'the
humour of the nation', 'the reigning genius', 'the genius of
government', and so on.

When the term *Kultur* came into general use in Germany in the
1780s, it may, like the term *Geist*, have marked a sharper awareness of the links between changes in language, law, religion, the
arts and sciences on the part of Johann Gottfried Herder and
other writers (such as Adelung and Eichhorn) who used these
expressions. All the same, this awareness was not something
completely new. After all, Herder's famous *Ideas on the
Philosophy of the History of Mankind* (1784–91) made considerable use of the work of such earlier historians of ideas and of the
arts as Sainte-Palaye and Goguet.[39]

Where the Germans spoke of culture, the French preferred the
phrase, *les progrès de l'esprit humain*. Employed by Fontenelle,
the phrase was taken up in the 1750s by Voltaire, by Estève in
his history of astronomy and by Montucla in his history of mathematics. At the end of the century it became the organizing concept for a history of the world, Condorcet's *Esquisse d'un*

[39] Bruford (1962), ch. 4.

tableau historique des progrès de l'esprit humain (1793), a history of the world divided into periods according to cultural as well as economic criteria, with writing, printing and the philosophy of Descartes marking epochs.

In other words, it is not quite accurate to assert – as Sir Ernst Gombrich did in a famous lecture – that cultural history was built on 'Hegelian foundations', however influential Hegel's concept of the *Zeitgeist* was to be in the nineteenth and twentieth centuries.[40] Hegel built his own structure on the foundations of work of the previous generation of German intellectuals, notably Johann Gottfried Herder, while they built on that of the French, and so on. This regress leads us back to Aristotle, who discussed the internal development of literary genres such as tragedy in his *Poetics*, while his teleological views might entitle him to be called the first recorded Whig historian.

All the same, it is appropriate to end this essay on the origins of cultural history around the year 1800. By this time the idea of a general history of culture and society had established itself in some intellectual circles at least from Edinburgh to Florence, from Paris to Göttingen. In the next generation, this style of history would be marginalized by the rise of Leopold von Ranke in the early nineteenth century and of the document-based narrative political history associated with him and his school.

This is not to say that cultural history completely disappeared in the nineteenth century. Jules Michelet's conception of history was broad enough to include culture (notably in his volume on the French Renaissance). So indeed was Ranke's. His *History of England* (1859–68), which concentrated on the seventeenth century, found space for an account of the literature of the time. Studies concentrating on culture include François Guizot's lectures on the *General History of Civilisation in Europe* (1828) and the *History of Civilisation in France* (1829–32), which went through many editions in French and other languages. Jacob Burckhardt's classic study of *The Civilization of the Renaissance in Italy* (1860) was much appreciated in the later nineteenth century, although it attracted relatively little notice at the time of publication. In the German-speaking world, the importance of cultural history and the way in which cultural history should be written remained topics for debate. It has been argued that in the

[40] Gombrich (1969).

later nineteenth century the reaffirmation of allegiance to tradition of cultural history was a way of expressing opposition to the post-1871 regime.[41]

All the same, the nineteenth century witnessed a widening gap between cultural history, virtually abandoned to the amateur, and professional or 'positivist' history, increasingly concerned with politics, documents and 'hard facts'. Despite the changes which have taken place in the last generation, among them the rise to academic respectability of 'cultural studies', it may still be too soon to assert that this gap has been bridged. To contribute to the construction of such a bridge is one of the aims of the essays which follow.

[41] Gothein (1889); Schäfer (1891); cf Elias (1989), 118, 127, 129.

2

The Cultural History of Dreams

In the last generation or so, many areas of human life which were once thought to be unchanging have been claimed as territories of the historian. Madness, for instance, thanks to Michel Foucault; childhood, thanks to Philippe Ariès; gestures (below, chapter 4); humour (chapter 5); and even smells, studied by Alain Corbin and others, have been incorporated into history.[1] In this movement of colonization, historians – with distinguished exceptions such as Reinhart Koselleck and Jacques Le Goff – have paid relatively little attention to dreams.[2] This essay presents a historical reconnaissance of this territory. The evidence is drawn almost entirely from the English-speaking world in the seventeenth century, but the real point of the essay is to argue for the possibility of a cultural history of dreaming. Not a history of interpretations of dreams, interesting as this may be.[3] A history of the dreams themselves.

Theories of Dreams

The idea that dreams have a history is denied, at least implicitly, by what might be called the 'classical' theory of dreams put

---

[1] Foucault (1961); Ariès (1960); Corbin (1982).
[2] Koselleck (1979); Le Goff (1971, 1983, 1984).
[3] Price (1986); Kagan (1990), 36–43.

forward by Freud and Jung.[4] According to them, dreams have two levels of meaning, the individual and the universal. At the individual level, Freud viewed dreams as expressions of the unconscious wishes of the dreamer (a view he later modified to account for the traumatic dreams of the shell-shocked). For his part, Jung argued that dreams performed a variety of functions, such as warning the dreamer about the dangers of his way of life or compensating for his conscious attitudes. At the universal level, Freud was especially concerned to pierce beneath the manifest content of the dream to its latent content. He suggested, for example, that in dreams 'all elongated objects ... may stand for the male organ,' and all boxes for the uterus; that kings and queens usually represent the parents of the dreamer; and so on. He accounted for manifest content in terms of day residues, but this point was marginal to his main concern.

Jung was more interested than Freud in the manifest content of dreams, but he too treated some dream symbols as universals; the Wise Old Man, for example, and the Great Mother were in his view 'archetypes of the collective unconscious'. Both men drew attention to the analogy between dream and myth, but Freud tended to interpret myths in terms of dream, whereas Jung normally interpreted dreams in terms of myth. Neither Freud nor Jung treated dream symbols as fixed, although they have often been criticized for so doing. They were too much concerned with the individual level to freeze meanings in this way. Where the classical theory is more vulnerable to criticism is in its neglect of a third level of meaning, intermediate between the individual and the universal: the cultural or social level.

The case for ascribing social or cultural meanings to dreams was first made by anthropologists, in particular by psychological anthropologists, trained in two disciplines as well as working in two cultures. In a pioneering study, Jackson S. Lincoln suggested that two kinds of dream could be found in primitive cultures, both with social meanings. The first kind was the spontaneous or 'individual' dream, the manifest content of which reflected the culture while the latent content was universal. The second kind he called the 'culture pattern' dream, which in each tribe conformed to a stereotype laid down by the culture. In these cases even the latent content of the dream was influenced by the

[4] Freud (1899); Jung (1928, 1930, 1945).

culture. In short, in a given culture people tend to dream particular kinds of dream.[5]

These are strong claims, but the evidence in their support is also strong. The best-known examples of the culture pattern dream come from the Indians of North America, and in particular from the Ojibwa, who lived in what is now Michigan and Ontario. Dreams played an important part in their culture, at least before 1900 or so. Boys could not come of age without taking part in what was called a 'dream fast'. They would be sent into the wilderness for a week or ten days in order to wait for dreams. The Ojibwa believed that supernatural beings would take pity on the boys when they saw them fasting and come to their aid, give them advice and become their guardian spirits for life. These supernatural beings would appear in the form of an animal or bird. The remarkable thing is that the appropriate dreams seem to have come when required, at least after a few days of hunger, a state apparently conducive to visions. To take an example recorded by the American anthropologist Paul Radin:

> I dreamt that I was alongside a lake and had not had anything to eat for some time. I was wandering in search of food for quite a time when I saw a big bird. This bird came over where I was staying and spoke to me, telling me that I was lost and that a party was out searching for me and that they really intended to shoot me instead of rescuing me. Then the bird flew out into the lake and brought me a fish to eat and told me that I would have good luck in hunting and fishing; that I would live to a good old age; and that I would never be wounded by shot-gun or rifle. This bird who had blessed me was the kind that one rarely has the chance of shooting. From that time on the loon was my guardian spirit.

In this case the informant was not a boy but an old man remembering his boyhood, and perhaps hindsight made the dream clearer than it originally had been. The wish-fulfilment element in the dream will be obvious. The statement that 'they really intended to shoot me' is interesting as an expression of aggressive feelings towards the adults who had made him fast in the wilderness.

Assuming that this first-hand account of a dream-fast is fairly accurate and reasonably typical, the problem remains of

[5] Lincoln (1935); cf. D'Andrade (1961).

explaining why the culture pattern dream actually occurred. No doubt the fasting helped, and also the expectation that a dream of this kind was going to make its appearance. A vague dream might well be assimilated to the stereotype and both recounted and remembered in a culturally appropriate way. Boys unlucky enough to have no dreams of the right kind presumably resorted to fabrication, though it is not clear in the ethnographies whether or not they would have been able to find out in advance what kind of dream the adults wanted to hear. The wrong kind of dream sometimes occurred, and it would be rejected. In another story retailed to Radin, 'The boy's father came and asked him of what he had dreamt. The boy told him, but it was not what the father wanted him to get, so he told him to go right on fasting.'[6] Sooner or later the right kind of dream made its appearance, which is not too surprising, since what the fathers wanted to hear was a dream about the central symbols of the culture.

Only a few peoples have the dream-fast among their cultural practices, but elsewhere too dreams follow the stereotypes of the local culture. A water serpent played an important part in the dreams of the Hopi Indians, as studied by the anthropologist Dorothy Eggan. For example, 'I come toward my home village. People are frightened. Children run toward where I am and tell me there is a big Water Serpent in the pond standing out of it four feet high, making an awful noise.'

Dreams of snakes and serpents are not uncommon in other cultures, and Freud interpreted them as symbols of the male genitals. However, the Water Serpent plays an important part in Hopi myths, where it represents authority. Hopi children were taught these myths, which were made easy to visualize by means of dramatic rituals. Hence it is hardly surprising to find that this imagery recurs in Hopi dreams, although no one was required to dream dreams of a particular kind. It is plausible to suggest that the Water Serpent has the same meaning in Hopi dreams as in Hopi myths: authority.[7]

The hypothesis that dreams have a cultural meaning has been confirmed by studies of the Zulu, of the villagers of Rajastan, of blacks in São Paulo, and of students in Tokyo and Kentucky.[8]

---

[6] Radin (1936); cf. Hallowell (1966).
[7] Eggan (1966).
[8] Carstairs (1957), 89ff.; Bastide (1966); Griffith et al. (1958).

Taken together, these studies suggest, as J. S. Lincoln's work does, that dreams are shaped in two ways by the dreamer's culture.

In the first place, dream symbols may have particular meanings in a given culture, as in the example of the Water Serpent among the Hopi. When a dreamer dreams a myth, we should not take it for granted, as Jung and his followers appear to do, that this is a spontaneous re-creation of the myth, an 'archetype of the collective unconscious'. We should begin by asking whether or not the dreamer is in fact aware of the myth. It may be objected that variations in the manifest content of dreams are not important; the sociology of dreams is a superficial one if it leads only to the conclusion that the same basic themes or problems are symbolized in different ways in different societies. This question of the relative importance of the manifest content of dreams is a controversial one among psychologists, in which historians should not meddle. However, they may be allowed to point out that if people in a given culture dream the myths of that culture, then their dreaming in turn supports belief in the myths, particularly in cultures in which dreaming is interpreted as 'seeing' another world. Myths shape dreams, but dreams in turn authenticate myths, in a circle which facilitates cultural reproduction or continuity.

In the second place, it may be argued that the latent content too is shaped in part by the dreamer's culture. A brief justification for this hypothesis, which is at once more fundamental and more controversial than the previous one, might run as follows. Dreams are concerned with the stresses, anxieties and conflicts of the dreamer. Typical or recurrent stresses, anxieties and conflicts vary from one culture to another. One cross-cultural study of 'typical dreams' showed that the relative frequency of different anxiety dreams varied considerably. Americans, for example, dreamed more often of arriving late for appointments and of being discovered naked, while Japanese dreamed of being attacked. The contrast suggests what other evidence confirms, that Americans are more concerned with punctuality and with 'body shame', while Japanese are more anxious about aggression.[9]

[9] Griffith et al. (1958).

Dreams in History

What have these findings to do with cultural history? The fact that people have dreamed in the past and have sometimes recorded their dreams is a necessary but not a sufficient condition for historians to take an interest in them. If dreams are meaningless, they need not concern themselves any further. If the universal meaning of dreams were the only meaning, historians could confine themselves to noting the recurrence in their period of dreams of flying, pursuit, or loss of teeth, and they could immediately pass on to other topics.

If, however, dreams tell us something about the individual dreamer, then historians need to pay them more attention. They become a potential source, to be approached, like other sources, with caution, as Freud himself noted on occasion.[10] Historians need to bear constantly in mind the fact that they do not have access to the dream itself but at best to a written record, modified by the preconscious or conscious mind in the course of recollection and writing (for the problem of 'memory', see chapter 3 below). However, such 'secondary elaboration' probably reveals the character and problems of the dreamer as clearly as the dream itself does.

Historians also need to remember that unlike psychoanalysts they do not have access to the associations of the dreamer to the incidents of the dream, associations which enable analysts to avoid a mechanical decoding and help them discover what dream symbols mean to the dreamers themselves. The best that historians can do is to work with a series of dreams by the same individual and to interpret each one in terms of the others. For example, the Swedish theologian Emmanuel Swedenborg recorded over 150 dreams in a single year, 1744.[11] In favourable cases like these, dreams provide biographers with evidence which cannot be obtained by any other means.

If, as we have argued above, dreams have a cultural layer of meaning as well as a personal and a universal layer, still more exciting possibilities open up for historians. In the first place, the study of changes in the manifest content of dreams should reveal changes in the myths and images which were psychologically

[10] Freud (1929).
[11] Freud (1929).

effective at the time (as opposed to the myths which were merely in circulation). In the second place, dreams, like jokes (below, chapter 5), deal obliquely with what is inhibited or repressed, and this varies from period to period. Repressed wishes, anxieties and conflicts are likely to find expression in the latent content of dreams, which must therefore change over time, and may help historians reconstruct the history of repression.

All the same, until quite recently it was a rare historian who was prepared to take dreams seriously as evidence. Take the case of Archbishop William Laud, for example, who recorded some thirty dreams in his diary between 1623 and 1643. One of his biographers, W. H. Hutton, referred in 1895 to the 'quaint humour' which made Laud record 'the curious visions which came to him as he slept', visions which 'do not read seriously'. In her *Strafford* (1935), C. V. Wedgwood was even more dismissive, writing that Laud 'set down in his diary the silliest dreams as though they had some profound significance'. The most recent biographer of Laud, on the other hand, uses dreams as evidence of the Archbishop's state of mind.[12]

A pioneering historian in this field, as in others, was the classical scholar E. R. Dodds, who wrote about the dreams of ancient Greeks.[13] He was more concerned with Greek dream interpretation (Artemidorus, for example) than with the dreams themselves, but he discussed culturally stereotyped dreams and also the cultural practice of 'incubation', in other words sleeping in a holy place in order to obtain an oracle dream advising the dreamer what to do, a practice not unlike the Ojibwa dream-fast. Among historians of the Middle Ages, Jacques Le Goff has paid particular attention to dreaming.[14] Early modern historians are moving in the same direction.[15] So are historians of the nineteenth and twentieth centuries. Alain Besançon, for example, has argued that the dreams of a culture can and should be interpreted like the dreams of an individual and he has offered analyses of dreams in Russian literature, such as Grinev's in Pushkin's *The Captain's Daughter* and Raskolnikov's in *Crime and Punishment*.[16]

[12] Carlton (1987), 56, 144–5, 148–53.
[13] Dodds (1951); cf. Dodds (1965) and Miller (1994).
[14] Le Goff (1983, 1984); cf. Dutton (1994).
[15] Macfarlane (1970); Kagan (1990).
[16] Besançon (1971); Koselleck (1979); Theweleit (1977).

Let us now examine some early modern examples. In Europe in the sixteenth and seventeenth centuries, as in antiquity and the Middle Ages, dreams were taken seriously for what they revealed about the future. Manuals of dream interpretation abounded and there were practices equivalent to incubation, notably sleeping in cemeteries and sleeping with the Bible under the pillow.[17] The examples which follow are divided into two groups, following Lincoln's classification. In the first place, the 'individual' dreams, and then the 'culture pattern' dreams.

Individual Dreams

On 11 November 1689, the Paris *Gazette* offered 20,000 louis reward for the interpretation of a dream of Louis XIV's (it is not known whether any successful Joseph appeared before Pharaoh). It is a pity to evade this challenge, but the danger of misinterpreting isolated dreams is an obvious one. It is better to concentrate on dream series.

In the seventeenth century, series of dreams were recorded by at least three Englishmen (Elias Ashmole, Ralph Josselin and William Laud) and, across the Atlantic, by the New Englander Samuel Sewall.[18] Between them these four men recorded 120 dreams (42 for Ashmole, 31 each for Josselin and Laud, and 16 for Sewall). This sample is of course a ridiculously small one for the analysis of the dreams of a whole culture (or rather, two related cultures), but it may at least be sufficient to illuminate the principal problems of method. In a study of the cultural meanings of dreams it remains necessary to bear in mind that there are other levels of analysis and that the dreams of all four men were related to their private lives and problems. A few biographical details are therefore in order. The eldest of the group, William Laud (1573–1645), Archbishop of Canterbury, recorded most of his dreams in the years 1623–8, when he was in his fifties. Contemporaries remarked on his 'arrogant pride' when he was in power, his insistence on authority, obedience and discipline in church and state. Since Laud was a man of low birth and low stature, he looks like a classic case of an inferiority complex. He

---

[17] Cardano (1557), ch. 44.
[18] Ashmole (1966); Josselin (1976); Laud (1847–60); Sewall (1878).

was the son of a prosperous Reading cloth merchant, but in the circles in which he came to move this origin was a humble one, often mocked by his political opponents. That Laud felt insecure even when in power is suggested by some of his dreams. His enemies thought him close to King Charles I, but 'I dreamed marvellously, that the King was offended with me, and would cast me off, and tell me no cause why.' Or more vividly, 'I brought him drink, but it pleased him not. I brought him more, but in a silver cup. Thereupon His Majesty said: you know that I always drink out of glass.' Elias Ashmole (1617–92), a professional astrologer, recorded dreams between 1645 and 1650, when he was in his late twenties and early thirties. From 1647 onwards he was courting the woman who became his second wife in 1649, and several dreams were concerned with this relationship. Ralph Josselin (1617–83), an Essex parson, was the only one of the four not to have a distinguished career. He recorded most dreams in the 1650s, when he was in his thirties and early forties. Samuel Sewall (1652–1730), the youngest of the group, as well as the only American, was a judge. The sixteen dreams he recorded are thinly spread over a long period, 1675–1719, beginning just before his first marriage.

In order to analyse the manifest content of these 120 dreams, it is necessary to distinguish categories or themes. Ideally, these categories would not only be appropriate to the dreams analysed, but also allow comparisons with the dreams of other cultures. Such categories are not easy to devise. A content analysis of 10,000 American dreams made by Calvin Hall in the late 1940s grouped the dreams by (1) settings, (2) characters, (3) action, (4) the interaction of the characters, and (5) the emotion felt by the dreamer. This is excellent if the analyst can make use of a questionnaire, but our four dreamers do not often provide information under all five heads.[19]

By contrast Dorothy Eggan's analysis of Hopi dreams employed seven more concrete categories as follows: (1) security, (2) persecution and conflict, (3) physical hazard, (4) heterosexual elements, (5) crops and stock, (6) water, and (7) religion.[20] These categories may well be the most useful for the study of Hopi dreams, but 'water' and 'crops' are not recurrent themes in the

[19] Hall (1951).
[20] Eggan (1952).

dreams to be considered here. Until a set of cross-cultural categories is worked out, it seems best to work with categories
which will (like Eggan's) apply at least to the culture being studied, paying the price of making comparison more difficult.

In our seventeenth-century cases, the most important recurrent
themes are those of (1) death and burial, (2) the church, (3)
kings, (4) wars, (5) politics, and (6) injury to the dreamer or to
something associated with the dreamer. These themes are in
strong contrast to the central themes found by Hall in twentieth-
century American dreams.

There are nineteen death and burial dreams among the 120 in
our sample, although nine of them come from one dreamer, Elias
Ashmole. In three cases the dream refers to the death of the
dreamer's wife; in three cases to the death of another close relative (mother, father or children); and in four cases the death is
that of the dreamer himself. Josselin and Sewall both dreamed of
their trial and condemnation to death, while Ashmole dreamed
that he was actually beheaded (and on another occasion, that he
was poisoned). Curiously enough, the only one of the four who
did not have a dream of this kind, William Laud, was also the
only one to be condemned and executed in real life.

There are also five cases of references to a grave, a tomb or
monument or a burial. In contrast to this preoccupation, the
theme of death and burial was not important enough in the
1940s to be mentioned in Hall's analysis. It looks as if seventeenth-century Englishmen were more anxious about death than
twentieth-century Americans, an anxiety which reflected their
lower expectation of life. If seventeenth-century people dreamed
more of burials and tombs than we do, this is surely related to
the greater emphasis placed in their waking lives on the public
and ceremonial aspects of death.

Turning to our second category (in order of frequency), there
are fourteen dreams of the church in the sample; six dreams
located in a church or churchyard, and eight dreams of clergy-
men and ecclesiastical affairs. In Hall's analysis of twentieth-
century dreams, the church setting is so rare that it is placed
(together with bars) in a 'miscellaneous' category. This makes
another obvious contrast between the two centuries. It is necessary to bear in mind that thirteen out of the fourteen dreams of
the church come from our two clerical dreamers – the exception
being Ashmole dreaming that he was in Litchfield Minster – and

so to be cautious in drawing conclusions about general attitudes to the church. One might indeed regard churches as the clergy's place of work – but in the United States in the 1940s, to dream of one's place of work was itself unusual, so that contrasts between the centuries remain.

As for the eight dreams of the church as an institution, it is worth noting that both the Anglican clerics were attracted to Rome in their sleep. Laud dreamed that he was 'reconciled to the church of Rome', and feeling guilty about this in the dream itself, went to beg pardon of the church of England. As for Josselin, he dreamed that he was 'familiar with the pope'. There are of course all too many ways to interpret these dreams, from simple wish-fulfilment, not so implausible in Laud's case, to compensation for hostility to Rome in waking hours. It is intriguing to discover that both Laud and Josselin recorded versions of what might be called the 'classic' clerical dream. Laud dreamed that when he was officiating at a wedding 'I could not find the order for mar-riage' in his book, while Josselin dreamed that when he was con-ducting a service, he 'could not read the psalms, or sing', or find his Bible. Again, Laud dreamed 'that I put off my rochet [sur-plice] all save one sleeve; and when I would have put it on again, I could not find it.' It might be interesting to attempt a sociology of anxiety dreams of this kind among people of different occupa-tions. Besides the fourteen dreams of the church, there were three more concerned with the supernatural. Laud and Sewall dreamed of Jesus Christ, and Sewall of going up to heaven.

Turning to the third category, we find eight dreams of kings (one of James I, six of Charles I, and one of Charles II). It is of course common for psychoanalysts to claim, following Freud, that a king in a dream symbolizes the father of the dreamer. However, like a literal-minded historian, I am convinced that in the sample, at least on one level and on some occasions, 'the king' meant the king. After all, Laud, who dreamed of the king most (four times) frequently saw and spoke to Charles I. Ashmole dreamed of the king three times in 1645–6, in other words at the height of the Civil War. Josselin dreamed of the deposition of Charles II. On the other hand Sewall, far away in America, was the only one of the four not to dream of a king at all.

This point about kings is a special case of a more general con-trast between the seventeenth century and the twentieth. Calvin

Hall found that only 1 per cent of the dreams he collected were of what he called 'famous or prominent public figures', while seventeen of the dreams studied here (about 14 per cent) fall into this category. Once again, distinctions between our four dreamers are in order. Laud, who is responsible for nine out of the seventeen dreams of public figures, knew some of them very well. The Duke of Buckingham, for example, was a personal friend, and the Bishop of Lincoln a personal enemy. However, Josselin, who had no celebrated friends or acquaintances, dreamed not only of Charles II but also of the Pope, Oliver Cromwell and Mr Secretary Thurlow. In similar fashion, Swedenborg dreamed of King Charles XII, the King of Prussia, the King of France, the King of Poland and the Tsar.[21] A similar contrast between the seventeenth century and the twentieth emerges from the eight dreams in the fourth category, wars. Laud did not record any dreams of this kind, but Ashmole dreamed of Charles I marching out of Oxford and of the king besieged; Josselin, of the defeat of the Scots, of an English army in France, and of civil war; Sewall of the French (twice) and once of what he called 'a military flame'.

Another eight dreams were concerned with politics. Laud dreamed once of parliament, for example, while Josselin (who was not a member of parliament) dreamed of it twice. Ashmole dreamed of taking the Negative Oath, and Sewall that he was chosen Lord Mayor. In contrast to this, Hall found that in his sample, dreams had 'little or nothing to say about current events', though a study of German dreams during the Nazi period came to opposite conclusions.[22] How can this contrast be explained? Eleven of the sixteen dreams concerned with war and politics in the seventeenth century dated from 1642–55, a period of civil war and other conflicts when people might be expected to have been more anxious than usual about political affairs. Yet Hall collected his sample from Americans at the very time when the atom bomb was dropped on Japan, without it making much impact on their dreams. His conclusion was that political concern 'does not go very deep nor is it emotionally relevant for us'. For the seventeenth century, exactly the opposite conclusion seems in

[21] Swedenborg (1744), 1–2 Apr., 19–20 Apr., 24–25 Apr., 28–29 Apr., 16–17 Sept., 17–18 Sept., 6–7 Oct., 20–21 Oct.
[22] Beradt (1966).

order. The relative frequency of political dreams suggests that political concern did go deep and also – to employ Hall's useful term – that it was emotionally relevant.

Exactly how deep and how relevant it is of course impossible to say. It may be that these seventeenth-century dreamers were making use of political events and figures to symbolize private anxieties. We have returned to the problem of distinguishing manifest from latent content, the problem whether 'the king' in Laud's dreams really meant Charles I or not. However, if seventeenth-century dreamers were more likely to symbolize their private anxieties by political images than twentieth-century dreamers are, that fact already tells us something about the emotional relevance of politics in the seventeenth century. A similar point might be made about religion. Even if a dream of the church or of Christ had a latent private meaning, it remains evidence of the emotional relevance of Christianity.

The last of our six categories, overlapping with the first, is that of injury to the dreamer, which occurs in eight dreams in the sample. Laud dreamed twice of his teeth falling out. Dreams of the loss of teeth are common to many cultures, as anthropologists testify and as an inspection of dream-books from Artemidorus onwards will confirm. The dream-books usually say that this dream portends the loss of a relative. Freud, on the other hand, treated teeth as a symbol for the genitals, while some more recent psychoanalysts interpret this dream as an expression of defencelessness against aggression. In both cases, a loss of power or potency is involved.

As for other dreams of injury, Ashmole dreamed that he was going bald, that his hand had rotted off, and that his head was cut off, while Josselin and Sewall dreamed, as already noted, that they were condemned to death. Laud also dreamed of damage to St John's College, Oxford, his old college and one which he had partly rebuilt. The category of injury does not ocur at all in Hall's analysis, so the only comparison which can be made is an extremely vague one, the proportion of pleasant and unpleasant dreams in the two samples. Hall claimed that 64 per cent of dream emotions in his sample were unpleasant: apprehension, anger and sadness were the dominant emotions. In the case of the seventeenth-century sample, it was difficult to place half the dreams in either the 'pleasant' or the 'unpleasant' category. Of those which remained, about 70 per cent were unpleasant. Given the small size of the sample, the difference between 70 per cent and 64 per cent should not be taken too seriously. In other words, the evidence of these dreams cannot be used to show that seventeenth-century people were either more or less anxious than moderns, although the objects of their anxiety may well have differed.

Culture-Pattern Dreams

The 120 dreams discussed above belong to Lincoln's category of 'individual' dreams which draw elements from the dreamer's culture. It may also be possible to identify in early modern Europe what Lincoln called 'culture-pattern' dreams, as stereotyped as the dreams of Ojibwa boys. A number of recorded dreams lend themselves to interpretations in these terms. For example:

> In the year 1525, after Whitsuntide, in the night between Wednesday and Thursday, I saw this vision in my sleep, how many big waters fell from the firmament. And the first hit the earth about four miles from myself with great violence and with enormous noise, and drowned the whole land. So frightened was I that I woke before the other waters fell.

Albrecht Dürer, for it was he, drew a picture of the 'big waters' beside his text. It is hardly surprising to find a dream of destruction occurring at the time of the German Peasants' War, nor, given the Christian tradition, is it odd to find the dreamer symbolizing destruction by a flood, especially at a time of heavy rains. In Germany at this time there were a number of texts in circulation predicting disasters of this kind and at this time.[23]

A second vivid example of a culturally stereotyped dream is provided by another sixteenth-century artist, Benvenuto Cellini. According to his autobiography (part 1, section 89), when Cellini was seriously ill he dreamed that 'a terrifying old man appeared at my bedside and tried to drag me by force into his enormous boat.' Cellini resisted, and he recovered from his illness. A curious feature of the story is that the teller does not name the old man – yet who else could he be but Charon? We need have no

---

[23] Dürer (1956), 214.

recourse to a theory of archetypes to explain the appearance of Charon to an Italian Renaissance artist, familiar with Dante (if not with Lucian and his recent imitators) and with the figure of Charon in Michelangelo's *Last Judgement* (which existed in 1550, when he was writing, though not at the time of the illness he wrote about).

It may also be argued that two phenomena which are well documented for the early modern period but have often puzzled historians may be explained in terms of culturally stereotyped dreams; religious visions and the witches' sabbath.

Historians have carried out some fascinating research on visions since this essay was first published.[24] Of these the most relevant to the present chapter is that of David Blackbourn. His book concentrates on a single story, that of the apparition of the Virgin Mary to some children in the village of Marpingen in the age of Bismarck and the pilgrimages to the 'German Lourdes' which followed. However, the author places this story in a much wider context, that of a 'great wave of visions' of the Virgin Mary which took place after 1789. Blackbourn explains this wave not only in religious terms (the 'Marianization' of popular Catholicism), but also by war and political upheaval, including Bismarck's campaign against the Catholic church.

Blackbourn's point about the link between visions and political upheaval is confirmed by what might be called an 'epidemic' of visions in Silesia (at that time part of the Kingdom of Bohemia) in the early to middle seventeenth century, a time when the Thirty Years' War was raging in the region and the belief in the imminent end of the world was unusually widespread.[25] The visionaries included Mikulas Drabic, Christoph Kotter, Christiana Poniatowska and Stephan Melisch.[26] The texts of these 'revelations' appeared in several languages but probably achieved their widest currency as a result of the Latin translations of the visions of Drabic and Kotter by the famous Czech scholar Jan Amos Comenius. What follows will concentrate on Melisch.

An example from his revelations runs as follows:

---

[24] Christian (1981); Dinzelbacher (1981); Gurevich (1984); Kagan (1990); Sallmann (1992); Blackbourn (1993).
[25] Haase (1933).
[26] Benz (1969), 300ff., 460ff., 501ff. on Kotter, and 113ff., 145ff., 171ff., 300ff., 599ff. on Poniatowska.

I saw red foxes come from the east, every one having a great tooth. And a gold yellowish lion stood upon a green place, about whom the foxes were leaping. Instantly after came a fiery man like a flame, with a black sword of iron; and against him a bright shining man, like the sun, with such a sword like a flash of lightning. Betwixt these there was such a fight, that many thousands did fall in the place, and none was left remaining but very few. Between them stood a white eagle ... I saw that the bright sun-shining man had cut off the head of the white eagle, and that head was given with the crown to the North; but the body of the eagle was given to a red eagle, and the wings to the East.[27]

This vision dates from 1656, and it is not difficult to identify the theme, even without the glosses provided, as the invasion and division of Poland by Russian, Swedish and Prussian forces from 1654 onwards, an episode which the Poles still describe as the 'Deluge'. The vision might be described as 'apocalyptic' in tone, and many of Melisch's visions do indeed echo the Apocalypse. There are references to the 'Babylonish beast'; to the Lamb, the book, the seals; and to a time, times, and half of half a time. The images which do not come from Revelation are often heraldic beasts like the Polish eagle and the Swedish lion. In other words, Melisch's visions have literary and visual sources, and the same is true of the other visionaries mentioned above. What might be called the 'iconography' of visions deserves further study.[28]

It may seem natural to conclude that the visions are all conscious fabrications, to be classified with a well-known literary genre, of which Francisco de Quevedo's *Sueños* and Johan Kepler's *Somnium* are famous seventeenth-century examples. In favour of this conclusion is the fact that the visions, when read one after another, do not give the impression of dreams. They are too coherent. They do not keep changing the subject or the scene as dreams so often do, and their political or religious meaning is consistent and clear. They read like allegories, and some of them even use the literary device of the dreamer asking someone what the vision means, and having it all explained.

Implicit in this argument, however, is a dichotomy which is open to criticism. The assumption is that a given text must be either an accurate transcript of a dream or a literary effusion

---

[27] Melisch (1659), no. xv; the translation in his *Twelve Visions* (1663), no. 4.
[28] Cf. Benz (1969), 311–410.

couched in the form of a dream. However, the discovery of the culture-pattern dream suggests that this dichotomy is a false one. Melisch and the other visionaries clearly studied Revelation with care, and it meant a great deal to them. The French Calvinist pastor Moïse Amyraut used their studies against them, arguing that the images from biblical prophecies were 'painted in their minds' (*peintes dans l'esprit*), persuading them that they had genuine visions when they did not.[29] The comment is an acute one, but a sharp distinction between a 'genuine' vision and a false one can only be justified on theological grounds.

It is likely that reading the Apocalypse of St John produces apocalyptic dreams in some people. Ralph Josselin and Emmanuel Swedenborg both recorded dreams of this kind in their diaries. Josselin, for example, dreamed of a black cloud in the shape of a stag, with a man riding it. His wife dreamed of lights blazing in the sky, 'flames exceeding terrible', and 'three smokes like pillars out of the earth'. On waking, she thought of Revelation 19: 3.[30] In similar fashion, Swedenborg once dreamed of thrusting a sword into the jaws of a great beast, and recorded that he had been 'thinking during the day about the woman and the dragon in the Apocalypse'.[31] A Freudian would doubtless interpret Swedenborg's dream in a quite different way, and might well be right in doing so, but this should not stop us from seeing the dream's cultural component. Like the Hopi and the Ojibwa, Swedenborg was dreaming one of the central myths of his culture.

These analogies suggest what cannot of course be verified or falsified, that the 'revelations' of Melisch and the others were dream experiences, stimulated by literary sources, interpreted in terms of literary models, and finally elaborated and made more coherent for publication. Drawing a parallel with some seventeenth-century autobiographies, for example John Bunyan's *Grace Abounding*, may be illuminating. It has been shown that this work has literary sources, St Paul for example, and that it follows a pattern of development from sinfulness to conversion which can be found in many spiritual autobiographies of the period. It would therefore be unwise to accept it as a completely accurate account of Bunyan's life. However, it would be equally

[29] Amyraut (1665).
[30] Josselin (1976).
[31] Swedenborg (1744).

unwise to dismiss the text as nothing but fiction. It is more likely to be an account of genuine experiences perceived and ordered in terms of cultural schemata or stereotypes (cf. p. 50 below).[32]

A similar approach may help us understand a well-known series of less orthodox visions, visions of the 'witches' sabbath'. As is well known, there were many trials in early modern Europe in which the accused confessed to flying to nocturnal feasts and dances at which the devil presided. The interpretation of these confessions was and remains controversial.[33] Writers of treatises on witchcraft discussed in learned detail whether the witches went to their sabbaths 'in the body' or 'in the spirit'. One suggestion was that the witches dreamed that they went. The problem with this suggestion, as the Italian physician Girolamo Cardano pointed out, was the implication that different people dreamed the same dream, which seemed contrary to experience.[34] The anthropologists have answered Cardano's objection. The sabbath dream, if it is a dream, is no more stereotyped than the Ojibwa puberty dream. If the notorious ointment which witches were supposed to use contained narcotics, as has been suggested more than once, this would explain how the so-called witches dreamed of flying.[35]

It is of course perfectly possible, and even likely, that the accused elaborated their dreams during interrogation, or interpreted them in the way they thought the interrogators wanted. It is less likely that they manufactured the whole story of the sabbath in order to satisfy the inquisitors, because in some cases at least their story ran counter to the expectations of their interrogators. The best-known examples of confessions which disconcerted the inquisitors are those discussed in Carlo Ginzburg's well-known study of the so-called 'good walkers' or *benandanti* of Friuli.[36] When Piero Gasparutto was interrogated on suspicion of witchcraft at Cividale in Friuli in 1580, he burst out laughing. How could he be a witch? He was, he explained, a *benandante*, and that meant that he fought witches. He and others went out to fight on certain nights of the year armed with sticks of fennel, while their enemies, the witches, carried sticks of sorghum. 'And

[32] Tindall (1934).
[33] Ginzburg (1990); Muchembled (1990).
[34] Cardano (1557).
[35] Clark (1921); cf. Castaneda (1968), 43ff.
[36] Ginzburg (1966).

if we are the victors,' another *benandante* declared, 'that year is abundance, but if we lose there is famine.'

These imagined night battles were more than a local custom. Ginzburg himself drew a parallel with the phenomenon of the good werewolf in seventeenth-century Livonia, while a Hungarian historian has compared the *benandante* to the Hungarian *táltos* or shaman.[37] The reference to shamans suggests comparisons with much of Asia and the Americas. In East Africa too there is a parallel to the *benandanti*. Among the Nyakyusa of Tanganyika (as it then was) in 1951, it was 'thought that in every village there were defenders [*abamanga*] who see the witches in dreams and fight them and drive them off'.[38]

Ginzburg's book has attracted much attention as a contribution to witchcraft studies. However, it also deserves attention as a contribution to the study of dreams and visions. Indeed, the history of witchcraft itself needs to be viewed, as it has been in recent years, from the perspective of the history of the collective imagination. The activities of the *benandanti* make fine examples of culturally stereotyped dreams. It is in this context that we should consider two points made by the *benandanti* in the course of explaining their activities to the inquisitors. The first point is that they went out not in the body but 'in the spirit', so that

> if by chance while we were out someone should come with a light and look for a long time at the body, the spirit would never re-enter it until there was no one around to see it that night; and if the body, seeming to be dead, should be buried, the spirit would have to wander around the world until the hour fixed for that body to die.[39]

The second point is that of the suggestibility of the new recruits, who testified that they were 'summoned' to the night battles and had no choice but to go. Bastiano Menos, for example, declared that one night a certain Michele 'called me by name and said, "Bastiano, you must come with me," ' and he did.[40] The parallel with the more indirect suggestions made to the Ojibwa boys enduring the dream-fast discussed above is clear enough.

This essay has emphasized analogies between seventeenth-

[37] Klaniczay (1984).
[38] Wilson (1951).
[39] Ginzburg (1966), ch. 1, section 11.
[40] Ginzburg (1966), ch. 4, section 13.

century dreams and the dreams of some tribal societies. Among
the Ojibwa and the Hopi, as in early modern Europe, dreams,
like myths, were often concerned with religion and dreamers
often made contact with supernatural beings. In twentieth-century American dreams, by contrast, supernatural elements are
almost entirely lacking. In his study of Ojibwa puberty dreams,
the anthropologist Paul Radin pointed out that as long as traditional culture remained strong, the dreams were concerned with
the myths. When the traditional culture disintegrated, around
1900, Ojibwa dreams became personal in theme.[41] The same
process of transition from public symbols to private ones seems
to have taken place in the West between the seventeenth century
and the present, as is shown not only by dreams but also by the
changing subjects of plays and stories.

At the level of manifest content, then, a cultural interpretation
of dreams does seem possible. At the more interesting level of
latent content it is obviously more difficult to give a confident
answer. An attractive hypothesis, impossible to verify, is that in
the early modern period repression was more concerned with
political and religious temptations and less with sexual ones than
is the case today. This is not to say that sex was unimportant in
the period or even that it was unimportant in the dreams of the
period. Sexual problems are explicit in two dreams of Ashmole's
(wanting to make love to two ladies, and being frustrated). Laud
dreamed that the Duke of Buckingham got into his bed. Other
dreams discussed here for their manifest content could be given
sexual interpretations, like the dream of Swedenborg's mentioned
above.

However, many other dreams refer to public problems, such as
the unconscious attraction of Catholicism for some Protestants.
The high proportion of public themes, whether religious or political, in the dreams discussed here ought to give historians food for
thought. It seems plausible to suggest that seventeenth-century
Englishmen, at least, were more anxious about public issues than
seems to be the case with twentieth-century Americans. The
German classical scholar Werner Jaeger once remarked on the
'public conscience' of the ancient Greeks.[42] His point seems valid
for seventeenth-century England as well.

[41] Radin (1936).
[42] Jaeger (1933).

3

History as Social Memory

The traditional view of the relation between history and memory is a relatively simple one. The historian's function is to be the custodian of the memory of public events which are put down in writing for the benefit of the actors, to give them fame, and also for the benefit of posterity, to learn from their example. History, as Cicero wrote in a passage which has been quoted ever since (*De oratore*, ii. 36), is 'the life of memory' (*vita memoriae*). Historians as diverse as Herodotus, Froissart and Lord Clarendon all claimed to write in order to keep alive the memory of great deeds and great events.

Two Byzantine historians made the point particularly fully in their prologues, utilizing the traditional metaphors of time as a river and of actions as texts which may be obliterated. The Princess Anna Comnena described history as a 'bulwark' against the 'stream of time' which carries everything away into 'the depths of oblivion', while Procopius declared that he wrote his history of the Gothic, Persian and other wars 'to the end that the long course of time may not overwhelm deeds of singular importance through lack of a record, and thus abandon them to oblivion and utterly obliterate them'. The idea of actions as texts can also be seen in the notion of the 'book of memory', employed by Dante and Shakespeare, who wrote of 'blotting your name from books of memory' (*Henry VI, Part 2*, Act 1, Scene 1).

This traditional account of the relation between memory and written history, in which memory reflects what actually happened

and history reflects memory, now seems much too simple. Both
history and memory have come to appear increasingly problematic. Remembering the past and writing about it no longer seem
the innocent activities they were once taken to be. Neither memories nor histories seem objective any longer. In both cases historians are learning to take account of conscious or unconscious
selection, interpretation and distortion. In both cases they are
coming to see the process of selection, interpretation and distortion as conditioned, or at least influenced, by social groups. It is
not the work of individuals alone.

The first serious explorer of the 'social framework of memory',
as he called it, was of course the French sociologist or anthropologist Maurice Halbwachs, in the 1920s.[1] Halbwachs argued
that memories are constructed by social groups. It is individuals
who remember, in the literal, physical sense, but it is social
groups who determine what is 'memorable' and also how it will
be remembered. Individuals identify with public events of importance to their group. They 'remember' a great deal that they have
not experienced directly. A news item, for example, can become
part of one's life. Hence memory may be described as a group
reconstruction of the past.

Like a faithful pupil of Émile Durkheim, Halbwachs couched
his arguments about the sociology of memory in a strong if not
an extreme form. Halbwachs did not assert (as the Cambridge
psychologist Frederick Bartlett once accused him of asserting)
that social groups remember in the same literal sense that individuals remember.[2] As we shall see (below, p. 170), a similar misunderstanding of Durkheim's position was shown by those British
historians who claimed that the 'collective mentalities' studied by
their French colleagues stand outside individuals rather than
being shared by them.

However, Halbwachs was more vulnerable to the more precise
criticisms of the great French historian Marc Bloch. It was Bloch
who pointed out the danger of borrowing terms from individual
psychology and simply adding the adjective 'collective' (as in the
cases of *représentations collectives, mentalités collectives, conscience collective*, as well as *mémoire collective*).[3] Despite this

---

[1] Halbwachs (1925); cf. Halbwachs (1941, 1950); Lowenthal (1985), 192ff.;
   Hutton (1993), 73–90.
[2] Bartlett (1932), 296ff.; Douglas (1980), 268.
[3] Bloch (1925); cf. Connerton (1989), 38.

critique, Bloch was prepared to adopt the phrase *mémoire collective* and to analyse peasant customs in these interdisciplinary terms, noting for example the importance of grandparents in the transmission of traditions (a later historian of the *Annales* school has criticized this 'grandfather law', in the seventeenth century at least, on the grounds that grandparents rarely survived long enough to teach their grandchildren, but he does not cast doubt on the importance of the social transmission of tradition).[4]

Halbwachs made a sharp distinction between collective memory, which was a social construct, and written history, which he considered – in the traditional manner – to be objective. However, many recent studies of the history of historical writing treat it much as Halbwachs treated memory, as the product of social groups such as Roman senators, Chinese mandarins, Benedictine monks, university professors and so on. It has become commonplace to point out that in different places and times, historians have considered different aspects of the past to be memorable (battles, politics, religion, the economy and so on) and that they have presented the past in very different ways, concentrating on events or structures, on great men or ordinary people, according to their group's point of view.

It is because I share this view of the history of history that this chapter is entitled 'History as social memory'. The term 'social memory', which has established itself in the last decade, has been chosen as a useful piece of shorthand which sums up the complex process of selection and interpretation in a simple formula and stresses the homology between the ways in which the past is recorded and remembered.[5] The phrase raises problems which need to be addressed at the start. The analogies between individual and group thought are as elusive as they are fascinating. If we use terms like 'social memory' we do risk reifying concepts. On the other hand, if we refuse to use such terms, we are in danger of failing to notice the different ways in which the ideas of individuals are influenced by the groups to which they belong.

Another serious problem is raised by the historical relativism implicit in this enterprise. The argument is not that any account of the past is just as good (reliable, plausible, perceptive, and so on) as any other. Some investigators can be shown to be better informed or more judicious than others. The point is that all of

[4] Goubert (1982), 77.
[5] Connerton (1989); Fentress and Wickham (1992).

us have access to the past (like the present) only via the categories and schemata – or as Durkheim would say, the 'collective representations' – of our own culture (discussed in chapter 11).

Historians are concerned, or at any rate need to be concerned, with memory from two different points of view. In the first place, they need to study memory as a historical source, to produce a critique of the reliability of reminiscence on the lines of the traditional critique of historical documents. This enterprise has in fact been under way since the 1960s, when historians of the twentieth century came to realize the importance of 'oral history'.[6] Even historians who work on earlier periods have something to learn from the oral history movement, since they need to be aware of the oral testimonies and traditions embedded in many written records.[7]

In the second place, historians are concerned with memory as a historical phenomenon; with what might be called the social history of remembering. Given the fact that the social memory, like the individual memory, is selective, we need to identify the principles of selection and to note how they vary from place to place or from one group to another and how they change over time. Memories are malleable, and we need to understand how they are shaped and by whom, as well as the limits to this malleability.

These are topics which for some reason attracted the attention of historians only in the late 1970s. Since that time, books and articles and conferences about them have multiplied, including the multivolume survey of 'realms of memory' edited by Pierre Nora, developing the insights of Halbwachs into the relation between memory and its spatial framework and offering a survey of French history from this point of view.[8]

The social history of remembering is an attempt to answer three main questions. What are the modes of transmission of public memories and how have these modes changed over time? What are the uses of these memories, the uses of the past, and how have these uses changed? Conversely, what are the uses of oblivion? These broad questions will be examined here only from

[6] Thompson (1978).
[7] Davis (1987).
[8] Nora (1984–92); cf. Le Goff (1988); Hutton (1993), esp. 1–26; Samuel (1994).

the relatively narrow point of view of a historian of early modern Europe.

Transmission of the Social Memory

Memories are affected by the social organization of transmission and the different media employed. Let us consider for a moment the sheer variety of these media, five in particular.

(1) Oral traditions, discussed from a historian's point of view in a famous study by Jan Vansina. The transformations of this study between its original publication in French in 1961 and the much revised English version of 1985 make useful indicators of the changes which have taken place in the discipline of history in the last generation, notably the decline of the hope of establishing the objective 'facts' and the rise of interest in symbolic aspects of narrative.[9]

(2) The traditional province of the historian, memoirs and other written 'records' (another term related to remembering, *ricordare* in Italian). We need of course to remind ourselves that these records are not innocent acts of memory, but rather attempts to persuade, to shape the memory of others. We also need to keep in mind, as historians have not always done, the warning of a perceptive literary critic: 'As we read the writings of memory, it is easy to forget that we do not read memory itself but its transformation through writing.'[10] However, a similar point could be made about oral tradition, which has its own forms of stylization. Hence it is difficult to justify a sharp contrast like Pierre Nora's between the spontaneous 'memory' of traditional societies and the self-conscious 'representation' of modern ones.[11]

(3) Images, whether pictorial or photographic, still or moving. Practitioners of the so-called 'art of memory' from classical antiquity to the Renaissance emphasized the value of associating whatever one wanted to remember with striking images.[12] These were

---

[9] Vansina (1961).
[10] Owen (1986), 114; cf. Fussell (1975).
[11] Nora (1984–92), vol. 1, xvii–xlii.
[12] Yates (1966); cf. Bartlett (1932), ch. 11.

immaterial, indeed 'imaginary' images. However, material images have long been constructed in order to assist the retention and transmission of memories – 'memorials' such as tombstones, statues and medals, and 'souvenirs' of various kinds. Historians of the nineteenth and twentieth centuries in particular have been taking an increasing interest in public monuments in the last few years, precisely because these monuments both expressed and shaped the national memory.[13]

(4) Actions transmit memories as they transmit skills, from master to apprentice for example. Many of them leave no traces for later historians to study, but ritual actions at least are often recorded, including rituals of 'commemoration': Remembrance Sunday in Britain, Memorial Day in the USA, 14 July in France, 12 July in Northern Ireland, 7 September in Brazil, and so on.[14] These rituals are re-enactments of the past, acts of memory, but they are also attempts to impose interpretations of the past, to shape memory and thus to construct social identity. They are in every sense collective re-presentations.

(5) One of the most interesting observations in Halbwachs's study of the social framework of memory concerned the importance of a fifth medium in the transmission of memories: space.[15] He made explicit a point which had been implicit in the classical and Renaissance art of memory, the value of 'placing' images that one wishes to remember in impressive imaginary locations, such as memory palaces or memory theatres, thus exploiting the association of ideas. One group of Catholic missionaries in Brazil, the Salesian fathers, were apparently aware of the link between spaces and memories. One of their strategies for the conversion of the Bororo Indians, as Claude Lévi-Strauss has reminded us, was to move them from their traditional villages, in which houses were arranged in a circle, to new ones in which the houses were arranged in rows, thus wiping the slate clean and making the Indians ready to receive the Christian message.[16] We might ask ourselves whether the European enclosure movement may not have had similar effects (however unintentional) in wip-

[13] Nipperdey (1981); Ozouf (1984).
[14] Warner (1959); Amalvi (1984); Larsen (1982).
[15] Hutton (1993), 75–84.
[16] Lévi-Strauss (1955), 220–1.

ing the slate clean for industrialization, especially in Sweden, where the enclosure decree of 1803 was followed by the destruction of traditional villages and the dispersal of their inhabitants.[17]

Yet in certain circumstances, a social group and some of its memories may resist the destruction of its home. An extreme example of uprooting and transplantation is the case of the black slaves transported to the New World. Despite this uprooting, the slaves were able to cling to some of their culture, some of their memories, and to reconstruct them on American soil. According to the French sociologist Roger Bastide, the Afro-American rituals of *candomblé*, still widely practised in Brazil, involve a symbolic reconstruction of African space, a kind of psychological compensation for the loss of a homeland. Bastide thus uses evidence from Afro-American religious practices to criticize and refine the ideas of Halbwachs. The loss of local roots was compensated, to some degree at least, by a more general African consciousness.[18]

From the point of view of the transmission of memories, each medium has its own strengths and weaknesses. I should like to place most emphasis on an element common to several media which has been analysed by investigators as different as the social psychologist Frederick Bartlett, the cultural historian Aby Warburg, the art historian Ernst Gombrich, and the Slavist Albert Lord, who studied oral poetry in Bosnia.[19] This common feature is the 'schema'. The schema is associated with the tendency to represent – and sometimes to remember – a given event or person in terms of another.

Schemata of this kind are not confined to oral traditions, as the following chain of written examples may suggest. In his fine study of *The Great War and Modern Memory*, the American critic Paul Fussell noted what he calls 'the domination of the Second War by the First', not only at the level of the generals, who are supposed always to be fighting the previous war, but at the level of ordinary participants as well.[20] The First World War in its turn was perceived in terms of schemata, and Fussell notes

[17] Pred (1986).
[18] Bastide (1970).
[19] Bartlett (1932), 204ff., 299; Warburg (1932); Gombrich (1960b); Lord (1960).
[20] Fussell (1975), 317ff.

the recurrence of imagery from Bunyan's *Pilgrim's Progress*, especially the Slough of Despond and the Valley of the Shadow of Death, in descriptions of life in the trenches in memoirs and newspapers.[21] To go back a little further, Bunyan's own writing – including his autobiography, *Grace Abounding* – also made use of schemata (cf. p. 140 above). For instance, Bunyan's account of his conversion is clearly modelled, consciously or unconsciously – it is difficult to say which – on the conversion of St Paul as described in the Acts of the Apostles.[22]

In early modern Europe, many people had read the Bible so often that it had become part of them and its stories organized their perceptions, their memories and even their dreams (above, chapter 2). It would not be difficult to cite scores of examples of this process. For example, the French Protestant community viewed the sixteenth-century wars of religion through biblical spectacles, including the Massacre of the Innocents. In the nineteenth and twentieth centuries they 'remembered' the houses of Protestants as having been marked for the slaughter by the Catholics at the time of the Massacre of St Bartholomew in 1572.[23] To go back still further, Johan Kessler was a Swiss Protestant pastor of the first generation. In his memoirs, he tells the story of how, as he puts it, 'Martin Luther met me on the road to Wittenberg.' When he was a student, he and a companion stayed the night in the Black Bear at Jena, where they shared a table with a man who was dressed as a knight but was reading a book – which turned out to be a Hebrew psalter – and was eager to talk about theology. 'We asked, "Sir, can you tell us whether Dr Martin Luther is in Wittenberg just now, or where else he may be?" He replied, "I know for certain that he is not at Wittenberg at this moment" ... "My boys," he asked, "what do they think about this Luther in Switzerland?"' The students still don't get the point until the landlord drops a hint.[24] My own point, however, is that consciously or unconsciously, Kessler has structured his story on a biblical prototype, in this case that of the disciples who met Christ at Emmaus.

The chain of examples could be stretched still further back, since the Bible itself is full of schemata, and some of the events

[21] Fussell (1975), 137ff.
[22] Tindall (1934), 22ff.
[23] Joutard (1976).
[24] Kessler (1540), 23ff.

narrated in it are presented as re-enactments of earlier ones.[25] However, the examples already given are perhaps sufficient to suggest some features of the process by which the remembered past turns into myth. It should be emphasized that the slippery term 'myth' is being used here not in the positivist sense of 'inaccurate history' but in the richer, more positive sense of a story with a symbolic meaning involving characters who are larger than life, whether they are heroes or villains.[26] These stories are generally made up of a sequence of stereotyped incidents, sometimes known as 'themes'.[27]

There is an obvious question for a historian to ask at this point. Why do myths attach themselves to some individuals (living or dead) and not to others? Only a few European rulers have become heroes in popular memory, or at least remained heroes over the long term: Henri IV in France, for example, Frederick the Great in Prussia, Sebastian in Portugal, William III in Britain (especially Northern Ireland), and Matthias Corvinus in Hungary, of whom it was said that 'Matthias died, justice perished.' Again, it is not every holy man or woman who becomes a saint, official or unofficial. What is it that determines success?

The existence of schemata does not explain why they become attached to particular individuals, why some people are, shall we say, more 'mythogenic' than others. Nor is it an adequate answer to do what literal-minded historians generally do and describe the actual achievements of the successful rulers or saints, considerable as these may be, since the myth often attributes qualities to them which there is no evidence that they ever possessed.[28] The transformation of the cold and colourless William III into the popular Protestant idol 'King Billy' can hardly be explained in terms of his own personality alone.

In my view, the central element in the explanation of this mythogenesis is the perception (conscious or unconscious) of a 'fit' in some respect or respects between a particular individual and a current stereotype of a hero or villain – ruler, saint, bandit, witch, or whatever. This 'fit' strikes people's imagination, and stories about that individual begin to circulate, orally in the first instance. In the course of this oral circulation, the ordinary

[25] Trompf (1979).
[26] Burke (1996).
[27] Lord (1960).
[28] Burke (1982, 1984).

mechanisms of distortion studied by social psychologists, such as 'levelling' and 'sharpening', come into play.[29] More speculatively, one might suggest that processes like condensation and displacement, described by Freud in his *Interpretation of Dreams*, are also to be found in these collective dreams or quasi-dreams. These processes assist the assimilation of the life of the particular individual to a particular stereotype from the repertoire present in the social memory in a given culture.[30] A process of what might be called 'crystallization' occurs in which traditional free-floating stories are attached to the new hero.

Thus bandits (Jesse James, for instance) turn into Robin Hoods, robbing the rich to give to the poor. Rulers (Harun al-Rashid, Henri IV of France, Henry V of England, and so on) are perceived as travelling their kingdom in disguise to learn about the condition of their subjects. The life of a modern saint may be remembered as a re-enactment of the life of an earlier one: St Carlo Borromeo was perceived as a second Ambrose, and St Rose of Lima as a second Catherine of Siena. In similar fashion the emperor Charles V was perceived as a second Charlemagne (his name helping in the process), while William III of England was perceived as a second William the Conqueror, and Frederick the Great as a new 'Emperor Frederick'.

Explanations of the process of hero-making in terms of the media are of course insufficient in themselves. To present them in this way would be politically naive. It is equally necessary to consider the functions or uses of the social memory.

Uses of the Social Memory

What are the functions of the social memory? It is hard to get a purchase on such a large question. A lawyer might well discuss the importance of custom and precedent, the justification or legitimation of actions in the present with reference to the past, the place of the memories of witnesses in trials, the concept of 'time immemorial', in other words time 'whereof the memory of man ... runneth not to the contrary', and the change in attitudes to the evidence of memory consequent on the spread of literacy

---

[29] Allport and Postman (1945).
[30] Freud (1899); cf. Allport and Postman (1945).

and written records. Custom was indeed discussed in the article on *mémoire collective* by Bloch, cited above, and a few medievalists have pursued these questions further.[31]

The examples of rulers as popular heroes, discussed above, also illustrate the social uses of collective memories. In the stories, disasters follow the death or disappearance of the hero. However, there is a case for turning this point around and arguing that a ruler whose reign is followed by disasters, from foreign invasion to steep rises in taxation, stands a good chance of turning into a hero, since the people will look back with nostalgia to the good old days under his rule.

For example, the Ottoman invasion of Hungary in 1526, a generation after the death of Matthias, and the Spanish takeover of Portugal soon after the death of Sebastian were good for the posthumous reputation of these two kings. In similar fashion, Henri IV may well have seemed a hero to the French people not only because he followed the disorder of the wars of religion but also because the reign of his son and successor Louis XIII was marked by a sharp rise in taxes. The appeal to memories of this kind is one of the main ideological resources of rebels, at any rate in traditional societies. Thus the Spanish rebels of the 1520s, the *comuneros*, appealed to the memory of the late King Ferdinand, while the Normans who rose against Louis XIII in 1639 expressed their desire to return to the 'golden age' of Louis XII, who was said to have wept whenever he had to tax the people.[32]

Another approach to the uses of social memory is to ask why some cultures seem to be more concerned with recalling their past than others. It is commonplace to contrast the traditional Chinese concern for their past with the traditional Indian indifference to theirs. Within Europe, contrasts of this kind are also apparent. Despite their reverence for tradition and concern for 'the national heritage', the social memory of the English is relatively short. The same point has been made about the Americans, notably by a penetrating French observer, Alexis de Tocqueville.[33]

The Irish and the Poles, on the other hand, have social memories which are relatively long. In Northern Ireland, it is possible

---

[31] Guénée (1976–7); Clanchy (1979); Wickham (1985).
[32] Foisil (1970), 188–94; cf. Fentress and Wickham (1992), 109.
[33] Schudson (1992), 60.

to see portraits of William III on horseback, chalked on a wall, with the inscription, 'Remember 1690'.[34] In the south of Ireland, people still resent what the English did to them in Cromwell's time as if it were yesterday.[35] As the American bishop Fulton Sheen once put it, 'The British never remember it: the Irish never forget it.'[36] In Poland, Andrzej Wajda's film *Ashes* (1965), translating into cinematic terms a classic novel of 1904 about the Polish Legion in the army of Napoleon, provoked national controversy about what Wajda presented as the Legion's futile heroism.[37] In England, on the other hand, at much the same time, Tony Richardson's film *The Charge of the Light Brigade* (1968) was viewed as little more than a costume picture. The English seem to prefer to forget. They suffer from, or rejoice in, what has been called 'structural amnesia'.[38] Since structural amnesia is the complementary opposite to the concept 'social memory', I shall refer to it henceforth as 'social amnesia'.

Why should there be such a sharp contrast in attitudes to the past in different cultures? It is often said that history is written by the victors. It might also be said that history is forgotten by the victors. They can afford to forget, while the losers are unable to accept what happened and are condemned to brood over it, relive it, and reflect how different it might have been. Another explanation might be given in terms of cultural roots. When you have these roots you can afford to take them for granted, but when you lose them you feel the need to search for them. The Irish and the Poles have been uprooted, their countries partitioned. It is no wonder that they seem obsessed by their past. We have returned to that favourite theme of Halbwachs, the relation between place and memory.

The Irish and the Poles offer particularly clear examples of the use of the past, the use of the social memory and the use of myth in order to define identity. The point of remembering 1690 (in a particular way), or re-enacting the 12th of July, or of blowing up Nelson's Pillar in Dublin – as the IRA did in 1966 – or of reconstructing the old centre of Warsaw, after the Germans had blown it up – as the Poles did after 1945 – the point of all this is surely

[34] Cf. Larsen (1982), 280.
[35] Macdonagh (1983), ch. 1.
[36] Quoted Levinson (1972), 129; cf. Buckley (1989).
[37] Michalek (1973), ch. 11.
[38] Barnes (1947), 52; Watt and Goody (1962–3).

to say who 'we' are, and to distinguish 'us' from them. Such examples could be multiplied. In the case of Europe, they are particularly easy to find in the nineteenth century.

The later nineteenth century has been provocatively described by Eric Hobsbawm as the age of the 'invention of tradition'.[39] It was certainly an age of a search for national traditions, in which national monuments were constructed and national rituals (like Bastille Day) devised, while national history was given a more important place in European schools than ever before or since. The aim of all this was essentially to justify or 'legitimate' the existence of the nation-state; whether in the case of new nations like Italy and Germany, or of older ones like France, in which national loyalty still had to be created, and peasants turned into Frenchmen.[40]

The sociology of Émile Durkheim, with its emphasis on community, consensus and cohesion, itself bears the stamp of this period. It would be unwise to follow Durkheim and his pupil Halbwachs too closely in this respect, and to discuss the social function of the social memory as if conflict and dissent did not exist. Northern Ireland has made its appearance several times already and the region offers a classic example, though far from the only one, of both memories of conflict and conflicts of memory. The seventeenth-century siege of Londonderry ('Derry') and the battle of the Boyne are re-enacted every year by the Protestants who identify with the victors and apply the phrases of the past ('No Surrender', for example) to the events of the present.[41] In the south of Ireland, the memory of the rising of 1798 against the British is still very much alive. For a French parallel, one might turn to western France, especially Anjou, where the memory of the Vendée, the peasant rising of the 1790s, remains alive and controversial, so much so that a recent historian has described the situation as a 'war over memory'.[42]

Given the multiplicity of social identities, and the coexistence of rival memories, alternative memories (family memories, local memories, class memories, national memories, and so on), it is fruitful to think in pluralistic terms about the uses of memories to different social groups, who may well have different views about

[39] Hobsbawm and Ranger (1983).
[40] Weber (1976), esp. 336ff.
[41] Larsen (1982); Bell (1986); Buckley (1989).
[42] Martin (1987), ch. 9.

what is significant or 'worthy of memory'.[43] The American literary critic Stanley Fish has coined the phrase 'interpretative communities' in order to analyse conflicts over the interpretation of texts. In a similar way, it might be useful to think in terms of different 'memory communities' within a given society. It is important to ask the question, who wants whom to remember what, and why? Whose version of the past is recorded and preserved?

Disputes between historians presenting rival accounts of the past sometimes reflect wider and deeper social conflicts. An obvious example is the current debate about the importance of history from below, a debate which goes back at least as far as Aleksandr Pushkin, a historian as well as a poet, who once told the Tsar that he wanted to write about the eighteenth-century peasant leader Pugachev. The Tsar's reply was brutally simple: 'Such a man has no history.'

Official and unofficial memories of the past may differ sharply and the unofficial memories, which have been relatively little studied, are sometimes historical forces in their own right; the 'Good Old Law' in the German Peasant War of 1525, the 'Norman Yoke' in the English Revolution, and so on. Without invoking social memories of this kind, it would be hard to explain the geography of dissent and protest, the fact that some Calabrian villages, for example, take part in different protest movements century after century, while their neighbours do not.

The systematic destruction of documents which is such a common feature of revolts – think of the English peasants in 1381, the German peasants in 1525, the French peasants in 1789, and so on – may be interpreted as the expression of the belief that the records had falsified the situation, that they were biased in favour of the ruling class, while ordinary people remembered what had really happened. These acts of destruction broach the last theme of this chapter, the uses of oblivion or social amnesia.

The Uses of Social Amnesia

It is often illuminating to approach problems from behind, to turn them inside out. To understand the workings of the social memory it may be worth investigating the social organization of

[43] Wickham (1985); cf. Fentress and Wickham (1992), 87–143.

forgetting, the rules of exclusion, suppression or repression, and the question of who wants whom to forget what, and why. In a phrase, social amnesia. Amnesia is related to 'amnesty', to what used to be called 'acts of oblivion', the official erasure of memories of conflict in the interests of social cohesion.

Official censorship of the past is all too well known, and there is little need to talk about the various revisions of the Soviet Encyclopaedia, with and without the entry on Trotsky. Many revolutionary and counter-revolutionary regimes like to symbolize their break with the past by changing the names of streets, especially when these names refer to the dates of significant events. When I visited Bulgaria in the mid-1960s, the only guide-book I had with me was a Guide Bleu of 1938. Despite the useful street-maps it provided I sometimes lost my way, and so I had to ask passers-by how to find 12 November Street, or whatever it was. No one looked surprised, no one smiled, they simply directed me, but when I arrived, 12 November Street turned out to be 1 May Street, and so on. In other words, I had been quoting dates associated with the fascist regime without knowing it. This incident may be taken as a reminder of the strength of unofficial memories and the difficulty of erasing them, even under the so-called 'totalitarian' regimes of our own day.

As it happens, what might be called the 'Soviet Encyclopaedia syndrome' was not the invention of the Communist Party of the Soviet Union. In early modern Europe too, events could become non-events, officially at least. King Louis XIV and his advisers were very much concerned with what we would call his 'public image'. Medals were struck to commemorate the major events of the reign. These medals included one of the destruction of the city of Heidelberg in 1693, complete with inscription HEIDELBERGA DELETA. However, when the medals were collected together to form a 'metallic history' of the reign, this particular medal disappeared from the catalogue. It seems that Louis had come to realize that the destruction of Heidelberg had not added to his reputation, his glory, and so the event was officially suppressed, erased from the book of memory.[44]

The official censorship of embarrassing memories, 'organized oblivion' as it has been called, is well known.[45] What is in greater

---

[44] Burke (1992), 110–1.
[45] Connerton (1989), 14.

need of investigation is their unofficial suppression or repression in post-Nazi Germany, post-Vichy France, Franco's Spain and so on.[46] This topic raises once more the awkward question of the analogy between individual and collective memory. Freud's famous metaphor of the 'censor' inside each individual was of course derived from the official censorship of the Habsburg Empire. In a similar manner, a social psychologist, Peter Berger, has suggested that we all rewrite our biographies all the time in the manner of the Soviet Encyclopaedia.[47] But between these two censors, public and private, there is space for a third, collective but unofficial. Can groups, like individuals, suppress what it is inconvenient to remember? If so, how do they do it?[48]

Consider the following story, recorded by the anthropologist Jack Goody. The origin of the territorial divisions of Gonja, in northern Ghana, was said to have been the act of the founder, Jakpa, who divided the kingdom among his sons.

> When the details of this story were first recorded at the turn of the present century, at the time that the British were extending their control over the area, Jakpa was said to have begotten seven sons, this corresponding to the number of divisions ... But at the same time as the British had arrived, two of the seven divisions disappeared ... sixty years later, when the myths of state were again recorded, Jakpa was credited with only five sons.[49]

This is a classic case of the past being used to legitimate the present, of what the anthropologist Bronislaw Malinowski described as myth functioning as the 'charter' of institutions (borrowing the term 'charter' from the historians of the Middle Ages).

I would not care to assert that this adjustment of the past to the present is to be found only in societies without writing. Indeed, it is often quite easy to show major discrepancies between the image of the past shared by members of a particular social group, and the surviving records of that past. A recurrent myth (to be found in many forms in our own society, today) is that of the 'founding fathers'; the story of Martin Luther founding the Protestant church, of Émile Durkheim (or Max Weber)

[46] Rousso (1987).
[47] Cf. Erikson (1968), esp. 701ff.
[48] Reik (1920).
[49] Watt and Goody (1962–3), 310.

founding sociology, and so on. Generally speaking, what happens in the case of these myths is that differences between past and present are elided, and unintended consequences are turned into conscious aims, as if the main purpose of these past heroes had been to bring about the present – our present.

Writing and print are not powerful enough to stop the spread of myths of this kind. What they can do, however, is to preserve records of the past which are inconsistent with the myths, which undermine them – records of a past which has become awkward and embarrassing, a past which people for one reason or another do not wish to know about, though it might be better for them if they did. It might, for example, free them from the dangerous illusion that the past may be seen as a simple struggle between heroes and villains, good and evil, right and wrong. Myths are not to be despised, but reading them literally is not to be recommended. Writing and print thus assist the resistance of memory to manipulation.[50]

Historians also have a role to play in this process of resistance. Herodotus thought of historians as the guardians of memory, the memory of glorious deeds. I prefer to see historians as the guardians of the skeletons in the cupboard of the social memory, the 'anomalies', as the historian of science Thomas Kuhn calls them, which reveal weaknesses in grand and not-so-grand theories.[51] There used to be an official called the 'Remembrancer'. The title was actually a euphemism for debt collector. The official's job was to remind people of what they would have liked to forget. One of the most important functions of the historian is to be a remembrancer.

[50] Schudson (1992), 206.
[51] Kuhn (1962), 52–3.

4

The Language of Gesture in Early Modern Italy

> The knowledge of gestures is necessary to the historian.
> Bonifacio, *L'arte dei cenni* (1616)

This chapter will discuss, with special reference to Italy, the problems involved in writing the history of gesture, or better, in integrating gesture into history. It will be concerned with the problem of conceptualization, distinguishing conscious and unconscious, ritualized and spontaneous gestures, with the sources (visual as well as literary), with regional and social variations, and above all with changes over time, notably the increasing emphasis on bodily discipline or self-control, recommended in treatises by authors as different as Baldassare Castiglione and Carlo Borromeo. What was the significance of this new emphasis? What difference did it make to everyday life? Who was supposed to show this control, and in what situations? What forms did this discipline take? What possible relation can it have to the foreign travellers' stereotype of the wildly gesticulating Italian?

In the last generation, as was noted in chapter 2 above, the territory of the historian has expanded to include many new topics, such as the history of the body, including gesture.[1] Here as elsewhere Jacques Le Goff has been among the pioneers.[2] Opponents of this 'new history', as it is often called, assert that historians of this school trivialize the past. Three responses to this charge seem

---

[1] Barasch (1987); Schmitt (1981, 1990); Bremmer and Roodenburg (1991).
[2] Le Goff (1982, 1985).

appropriate. The first is to recognize the very real danger of trivialization whenever one of these topics is pursued for its own sake without any attempt to connect it with the surrounding culture. For an example of this approach one might cite Câmara Cascudo's historical dictionary of Brazilian gestures, a scholarly and fascinating book (and a good basis for future work), but a study which collects information without raising questions.[3]

A second response might be to argue that the notion of the 'trivial' needs to be problematized and relativized and more specifically that gestures were not taken lightly in early modern Europe. In England, the Quakers refused to observe what they called 'hat honour', in other words the custom of raising the hat to social superiors. In Russia, the question whether the act of blessing should be performed with two fingers or three was one of the issues leading to the schism in the Orthodox Church in the middle of the seventeenth century. Early modern Italy may lack spectacular debates over gesture of this kind. All the same, a Genoese patrician, Andrea Spinola, a crusader for the vanishing ideal of republican equality (below, p. 120), claimed that he had been imprisoned unjustly on account of his *gesti del corpo*, such as his proud way of walking into the room and his failure to stand up straight before the chancellor.[4] These gestures were regarded by the Genoese government as a form of 'dumb insolence', a phrase still current in the British army and a reminder that in some quarters at least, the rules of gesture continue to be taken seriously.

The third response might be to follow Sherlock Holmes, Sigmund Freud and Giovanni Morelli – not to mention Carlo Ginzburg, who first linked the three of them – and to assert the importance of the trivial, on the grounds that it so often provides clues to what is more significant.[5] Historians, like anthropologists and psychologists, can study gesture as a subsystem within the larger system of communication which we call 'culture'. This assumption is currently shared by many social and cultural historians. It may even seem obvious. So it may be useful to remind the reader at this point of the existence of a 'universalist' approach to gesture, reincarnated in the well-known books by

[3] Câmara Cascudo (*c.*1974).
[4] Spinola (1981), 126.
[5] Ginzburg (1990), 96–125.

Desmond Morris – despite the unresolved tension in his work between universalizing zoological explanations of the gestures of the 'naked ape' and attempts to map their cultural geography.[6]

As an example of more rigorous analysis pointing in the opposite direction, we may cite Ray Birdwhistell's famous demonstration that even unconscious gestures, such as modes of walking, are not natural but learned, and so vary from one culture to another. The same point had been made in the 1930s in a famous essay by the anthropologist Marcel Mauss, who claimed to be able to detect which Frenchwomen had been educated at convent schools by observing the position of their hands when they were walking.[7] It is this 'culturalist' approach which will be pursued here, in the case of a society in which – according to its northern visitors, at least – the language of gesture was and is particularly eloquent: Italy.

To follow this road to the end it would first be necessary to reconstruct the complete repertoire of gestures available in Italian culture, the 'langue' from which individuals choose their individual 'paroles' according to their personalities or social roles. The way would then be clear for a general discussion of the relation between that repertoire and other aspects of the culture, including the local contrasts between public and private, sacred and profane, decent and indecent, spontaneous and controlled behaviour, male and female decorum, and so on.

The surviving sources are inevitably inadequate for these tasks, although they are quite as rich as any early modern historian has a right to hope. They include contemporary encyclopaedias of gestures such as *The Art of Gesture* (1616) by the lawyer Giovanni Bonifacio and, at the end of the period, Andrea di Jorio's *The Imitation of the Ancients Investigated in the Gestures of the Neapolitans* (1832), which compares the evidence of classical vases and statues with what could be seen in the streets of Naples in his own day.[8] More ambitious still, a book by Scipione Chiaramonti, published in 1625, discussed gesture as part of a general study of signs or 'semiotics', as he already called it. Chiaramonti also devoted a few pages to the peculiarities of the Italians.[9]

---

[6] Morris (1977, 1979).
[7] Birdwhistell (1970); cf. Mauss (1935).
[8] Bonifacio (1616); Jorio (1832); cf. Knowlson (1965); Chastel (1986).
[9] Chiaramonti (1625), 70ff.

To these systematic compilations may be added a number of observations by foreign travellers, casual but vivid and direct. The Catholic Montaigne, passing through Verona, and the Protestant Philip Skippon, passing through Padua, were both impressed by the lack of reverence shown by Italians in church, chatting during Mass, standing with their hats on and their backs to the altar or 'discoursing and laughing with one another'.[10] In Venice, John Evelyn recorded at least one insulting gesture which the two lexicographers mentioned above seem to have missed, biting one's own finger (presumably as a symbol of the adversary's penis). Shakespeare was already familiar with this insult, to which he gave an Italian context: 'I will bite my thumb at them; which is a disgrace to them if they bear it' (*Romeo and Juliet*, Act 1, scene 1).

Italian judicial archives are another important source. Courts often note the gestures leading to cases of assault and battery, including staring at one's adversary, *bravando* (strutting in a provocative manner) and of course offering insults such as 'making horns', publicly displaying one's private parts, and so on. Among other things, the archives confirm the existence of the finger-biting gesture mentioned by Evelyn, *mittendosi la dita in bocca*.[11] The Inquisition archives are of particular value because interrogators and clerks were instructed to observe and record with care the gestures of the accused.[12] It was for instance the Inquisition which recorded another gesture absent from both Bonifacio and Jorio, the denial of Christianity by pointing the index figure of the right hand heavenwards.[13] The art of the period can also be utilized as a source, despite the difficulty of measuring the distance between painted gestures and their equivalents in everyday life. A few art historians have commented on the representation of gestures of respect, submission, greeting, prayer, silence, admonition, despair, pride, aggression, and so on.[14]

The task of reconstructing the complete repertoire of Italian gestures is clearly too ambitious for a short chapter. All that can

[10] Montaigne (1992), 64; Skippon (1732), 534.
[11] Evelyn (1955), vol. 2, 173; Rome, Archivio di Stato, Tribunale del Governatore, Processi Criminali, '600, busta 50.
[12] Masini (1621), 157.
[13] Bennassar and Bennassar (1989), 313.
[14] Baxandall (1972), 56ff.; Heinz (1972); Chastel (1986); Barasch (1987); Spicer (1991); Fermor (1993).

reasonably be done is to discuss what appear to be the major changes in the system between 1500 and 1800. Unlike earlier work on the topic, this chapter will focus on everyday life rather than the ritualized gestures of kissing the Pope's foot, walking in procession, and so on.[15] Following the bias of the sources, it will be difficult to avoid devoting disproportionate attention to the upper classes and also to males, since one of the rules of the culture was that respectable women did not gesture, or at least not very much.

The changes to be emphasized here may be summed up in three hypotheses. The first is that of an increasing interest in gestures in this period, not only in Italy but in Europe more generally. The second hypothesis is that this self-consciousness was encouraged by a movement for the 'reform' of gesture which occurred in both Catholic and Protestant Europe in the age of the Reformations. The third and last hypothesis attempts to link this reform to the rise of the northern stereotype of the gesticulating Italian.

A New Interest in Gestures

The French historian Jean-Claude Schmitt has noted a new interest in gestures in the twelfth century. A similar point might be made about Western Europe in the early modern period, especially in the seventeenth century, as Schmitt himself admits.[16] In the case of England, for example, this interest can be seen in the writings of Francis Bacon; in John Bulwer's guide to hand gestures, the *Chirologia* (1644), which argued that these gestures 'disclose the present humour and state of the mind and will'; and in the observations of travellers abroad, including John Evelyn, Thomas Coryate and Philip Skippon.

In the case of France, penetrating analyses of gesture can be found in the writings of Montaigne, Pascal, La Bruyère, La Rochefoucauld, and Saint-Simon, as well as in the art theory of Charles Lebrun. The history of gesture and posture attracted the attention of scholars and of artists such as Nicolas Poussin, whose *Last Supper* reveals his awareness of the ancient Roman

---

[15] Trexler (1980), 87–94, 99–111, etc.; Muir (1981).
[16] Schmitt (1990), 362–3.

custom of reclining to eat. More practical advice was offered in Antoine Courtin's *Nouveau traité de la civilité* (1671), which told readers not to cross their legs or to make 'grand gestures with the hands' when speaking. Crossed legs, incidentally, had a variety of meanings. In some contexts they signified power, but in others lack of dignity. The posture was forbidden to women, but it was not always permitted to men either.[17]

The contrast between Spanish gravity and French vivacity made by Baldassare Castiglione in his *Courtier* (book 2, chapter 37) became a commonplace in the seventeenth century. For example, Carlos García's treatise of 1617 on the 'antipathy' between the French and the Spaniards drew attention to the different ways in which they walked, ate, or used their hands. According to García, the Frenchman walks with his hand on the pommel of his sword and his cloak on one shoulder, while the Spaniard throws out his legs like a cock and pulls at his moustache. 'When Frenchmen walk the streets in a group they laugh, jump, talk and make such a noise that they can be heard a league away; the Spaniards on the contrary walk straight ahead, gravely and coolly, without speaking or engaging in any immodest or extravagant action.'[18]

García's work is not without relevance to Italy. Indeed, it went through thirteen Italian editions between 1636 and 1702, besides being translated into English and German. At a time when France and Spain were the leading European powers, the book had political relevance. García's influence, or at least that of the commonplaces which he articulated with unusual vivacity and detail, can be seen in an anonymous manuscript account of the Venetian Republic written in the late seventeenth century, the *Historical-Political Examination*, which divided a hundred leading politicians into those with the grave 'Spanish genius' (*genio spagnuolo*), and those with a livelier *genio francese*.[19] There was a similar conflict between the French and Spanish styles in mid seventeenth-century Rome. The architect Francesco Borromini, for example, wore Spanish dress (unfortunately his gestures are not recorded).[20] No wonder then that the Englishman Richard Lassels described 'the Italian humour' as 'a middling humour

[17] Barasch (1987), 180–1.
[18] García (1617), ch. 14.
[19] Venice, Biblioteca Marciana, MS Gradenigo 15.
[20] Wittkower (1967).

between the too much of the French and the too little of the Spaniard'.[21]

Linguistic evidence points in the same directions. In the first place, towards an increasing interest in gesture, revealed by the development of an increasingly rich and subtle language to describe it. In the second place, towards the Spanish model, for the language of gesture developed in early modern Italy by borrowing from Spanish such terms as *etichetta*, *complimento*, *crianza* (good manners), *disinvoltura* (negligence) and *sussiego* (gravity or calm).[22]

The multiplication of Italian texts discussing gesture from the Renaissance onwards (a century or so earlier than in other countries) confirms the impression of increasing interest in the topic. The literature of morals and manners contains many relevant observations on appropriate gestures for women as well as for men. For example, the anonymous *Decor puellarum* (1471), a vernacular text despite its Latin title, tells girls to keep their eyes on the ground, to eat and speak with gravity, to walk and stand with the right hand over the left, and to keep their feet together, so as not to look like the prostitutes of Venice. The gesture of one hand clasping the other was a 'formula of submission' to be found for example in some of Giotto's female figures.[23] Castiglione's *Courtier* (1528) also comments on the appropriate posture (*lo stare*) and gestures (*i movimenti*) for both women and men, emphasizing the need for 'supreme grace' in women, and also a kind of timidity which reveals their modesty.[24]

Alessandro Piccolomini's dialogue *La Rafaella* (1539) follows in the footsteps of Castiglione but is concerned exclusively with the education of women, including their movements and 'carriage' (*portatura*). Ladies are told to walk slowly, but also 'to flee affectation' and 'to show a certain negligence and a certain don't think much about it' [*mostrar un certo disprezzo e un certo non molto pensare*], a close relative of Castiglione's famous *sprezzatura*.[25] Angelo Firenzuola's dialogue *Delle bellezze delle donne* (1541) is concerned with grace as well as beauty. The speakers

[21] Lassels (1654), 150.
[22] Beccaria (1968), 161–207.
[23] Barasch (1987), 42, 46.
[24] Burke (1995), 29–30.
[25] Piccolomini (1539), 56–7.

recommend 'elegance' (*leggiadria*) defined in terms of grace, modesty, nobility, measure and good manners. They also praise the 'air' of a beautiful woman and the 'majesty' of a woman who 'sits with a certain grandeur, speaks with gravity, smiles with modesty and behaves like a queen'. Giovanni Della Casa's *Galateo* (1558) and Stefano Guazzo's *Civile conversatione* (1574) also make a number of points about appropriate gesture and the eloquence of the body. So does the literature of the dance, notably the treatise *Il ballarino* (1581) by Fabrizio Caroso, which discusses not only the various kinds of step but also tells gentlemen how to deal with their cloak and sword, how to make a proper bow, how to take a lady's hand, and so on.

In the seventeenth century, as we have seen, a lawyer from Verona, Giovanni Bonifacio, produced the first encyclopaedia of gesture. Bonifacio based himself mainly on the Bible and on classical authors, which makes him less useful than he might have been as a source for Italian social history. All the same, his book bears eloquent witness to contemporary interest in the topic. So do the books about the theatre which begin to appear at this period. G. D. Ottonelli's *The Christian Moderation of the Theatre* (1652) and A. Perrucci's *Art of Representation* (1699) were both concerned with what they call the 'art' or 'rules' of gesture. The relation between happenings on and off the stage is not a simple one, but to foreign visitors at least actors appear to stylize and perhaps to exaggerate the gestures current in their culture.

In their different ways, the texts cited above reveal considerable interest not only in the psychology of gestures, as the outward signs of hidden emotions, but also – and this is the innovation – in what we might call their 'sociology'. It was frequently asserted that gestures formed a universal language, but this 'universalist' position was opposed by a 'culturalist' one. A number of authors were concerned with the way in which gestures vary, or ought to vary, according to what might be called the various 'domains' of gesture (the family, the court, the church and so on), and also to the actors – young or old, male or female, respectable or shameless, noble or common, lay or clerical. One might say therefore that early modern texts bear witness to an increasing interest not only in the vocabulary of gesture, exemplified by Bonifacio's dictionary, but also in its 'grammar', in the sense of the rules for correct expression, and finally in its various 'dialects' (to use di Jorio's term) or 'sociolects' as modern linguists would put it.[26]

It is worth emphasizing the connections between this interest in gesture and contemporary concerns with social variations in language and costume, and more generally with the study of men and animals in the so-called 'age of observation'. For an example of the practical value of this knowledge, we may turn to an English visitor to Italy, Fynes Morison. Morison wanted to see Cardinal Bellarmine in Rome and paid him a visit, 'being attired like an Italian and careful not to use any strange gesture' which might have given him away as an English Protestant.[27]

The Reform of Gesture

The increasing consciousness of gesture was linked to attempts by some people to change the gestures of others. Protestants were concerned with behaviour as well as belief, while in Catholic countries a reform of gesture formed part of the moral discipline of the Counter-Reformation.[28] For example, in the *Constitutions* which he issued for his diocese of Verona around the year 1527, Gianmatteo Giberti, who came to be regarded as a model bishop, ordered his clergy to show gravity 'in their gestures, their walk and their bodily style' ('in gestu, incessu et habitu corporis'). The term 'habitus' was of course well known in this period thanks to Latin translations of Aristotle, long before Marcel Mauss and Pierre Bourdieu made it their own. San Carlo Borromeo, another model bishop, also recommended *gravitas* and decorum to the clergy of his diocese, 'in their walking, standing, sitting' and in 'the lowering of their eyes'. He told preachers to avoid 'histrionic' gestures, such as throwing out their arms like a 'gladiator' or making indecorous movements of the fingers.[29] San Carlo would not have approved of the preachers described by Giraldi in his discourse on comedies, whose gestures resembled those of actors or charlatans.

San Carlo, however, concerned himself with the laity as well, recommending decorum, dignity and 'moderation' (*misura*) and

[26] Jorio (1832), xxii; cf. Bremmer and Roodenburg (1991), 3, 36.
[27] Quoted in Mączak (1978), 191.
[28] Knox (1990), 113–14.
[29] Borromeo (1758), 23, 87, 90.

warning them against laughing, shouting, dancing and tumul-
tuous behaviour.[30] At much the same time, his episcopal colleague at Tortona concerned himself with behaviour in church.
'Let no one dare to stroll through the church . . . or lean on the
altars, holy water stoup or font. Or sit irreverently with their
backs turned to the Blessed Sacrament,' make 'dishonourable
signs' to a woman, or talk of secular business.[31] A little later, the
anonymous *Discourse against Carnival* discussed the need for
order, restraint, prudence and sobriety and underlined the dangers of *pazzia*, a term which might in this context be translated
not as 'madness' but as 'loss of self-control'.[32]

The reform of Italian gesture should not be tied too closely to
the Counter-Reformation. Cicero had already discouraged what
he called 'theatrical' movements or walking too quickly (or too
slowly), and from the Renaissance onwards his authority was
taken as seriously in the domain of gesture as in that of speech.[33]
In the case of women, there is a long tradition of texts advising
restraint. In the fourteenth century, young women were recommended to show timidity and modesty in their gestures. They
were to take small steps when they walked. They were not to
support their head with their hands, not to show their teeth when
they smiled and not to weep loudly.[34] The humanist Francesco
Barbaro's treatise *On Marriage* (1416) told wives to show
restraint 'in the movements of the eyes, in their walking, and in
the movement of their bodies; for the wandering of the eyes, a
hasty gait, and excessive movement of the hands and other parts
of the body cannot be done without loss of dignity, and such
actions are always joined to vanity and are signs of frivolity.'[35]
Similar recommendations for unmarried girls were made in the
fifteenth-century treatise *Decor puellarum*, discussed above.

On the other hand, it was relatively rare before 1500 to advise
boys or men to restrain their behaviour in this way. The fifteenth-
century humanist Matteo Vegio was unusual in warning boys (in
a treatise on education, *De liberorum educatione*, book 5,
chapter 3) to concern themselves with the modesty of their

---

[30] Taviani (1969), 5–43; San Carlo (1986), 911, 926–7.
[31] Quoted Tacchella (1966), 75–6.
[32] Taviani (1969), 67–81.
[33] Bremmer and Roodenburg (1991), 28–9.
[34] Lazard (1993).
[35] Kohl and Witt (1978), 202.

gestures ('verecundia motuum gestuumque corporis'). It was the sixteenth-century reform of gesture which extended to males, first the clergy and then the upper-class laity, ideals of restraint which had earlier been formulated with women in mind.

In his treatise *On the Position of Cardinal* (1510), the clerical humanist Paolo Cortese warned against ugly movements of the lips, frequent hand movements and walking quickly, recommending what he called a senatorial gravity. Again, Baldassare Castiglione warned his readers against affected gestures and recommended the courtier to be 'restrained' (*ritenuto, rimesso*). Although Castiglione's dialogue deals with men and women separately and might thus be taken as a guide to the construction (or reconstruction) of masculinity and femininity, his stress on restraint may be viewed as an example of the feminization of polite behaviour at a time when the nobility was losing its military role.

The most detailed as well as the best-known Italian recommendations for the reform of gesture are those to be found in Giovanni Della Casa's *Galateo*. The ideal of this Counter-Reformation prelate is almost as secular as that of Castiglione or Firenzuola. It is to be 'elegant' and 'well bred' (*leggiadro, costumato*) 'in walking, in standing, in sitting, in movements, in carriage and in clothing' (chapter 28). To achieve elegance, it is necessary to be aware of one's gestures in order to control them. The hands and legs in particular need discipline. For example, in chapter 6 of the treatise noblemen are advised, in the author's version of the classical topos, not to walk too quickly (like a servant), or too slowly (like a woman), but to aim at the golden mean.

A number of Italian writers of this period contributed to the chorus urging restraint. For example, Giovanni Battista Della Porta, whose activities as scientist and dramatist should have given him a double interest in the subject, recommended the readers of his *On Human Physiognomy* (1586) not to make hand gestures while speaking (in Italy!). Stefano Guazzo, whose book on conversation and deportment was cited above, discussed the need to find the golden mean, as he put it, between 'the immobility of statues' and the exaggerated movements of monkeys ('l'instabilità delle simie'). As for Caroso's treatise on dancing, it has been argued that it expresses a more restrained ideal than its predecessors, suggesting that the court dance was diverging more and more from the peasant dance in this period.[36] After one reads this corpus of texts, not to mention the observations on movement made by contemporary art critics such as Giorgio Vasari and Ludovico Dolce, many Italian portraits of this period begin to look like translations into visual terms of the recommendations of the treatises. Whether a given portrait expresses the ideals of the artist, the self-image of the sitter or the artist's image of the sitter's self-image, the gestures portrayed – which to post-romantic eyes often seem intolerably artificial – may be read as evidence of attempts to create new habits, a second nature.

Movement was represented as gender-specific, with female delicacy complementing male vivacity.[37] It should be added that the range of female gestures in Renaissance portraits (one hand holding a fan or a book, or one hand on the breast, or the hands clasped in the submissive gesture already discussed) is much narrower than that available to males. The gestures portrayed in portraits of men in this period include the hand on the hip or sword, the hand supporting the cheek (a sign of melancholy), the hand pressed to the heart, and the hand extended in the orator's pose recommended by Cicero and Quintilian, while full-length portraits of standing figures began to show them with crossed legs, now a sign of ease rather than of lack of dignity.[38] However, the rejection by the priests who had commissioned it of Caravaggio's painting of St Matthew because it showed the saint sitting with his legs crossed (*le gambe incavalcate*) reminds us that the clergy had to be almost as sensitive to decorum as women.[39] In eighteenth-century Venice, anonymous verses about the fashionable ladies of the time were still mocking *el sentar a la sultana*, in other words crossing the legs when seated.[40] The verses may express a reaction against the relaxation of manners characteristic of the European nobility in the age of Rousseau, but the values they express are traditional.

Della Casa's points are mainly negative. One suspects that this inquisitor kept in mind, if not in his study, an index of forbidden gestures (including the hand on the hip, which he interpreted as a

---

[36] *Dizionario Biografico degli Italiani* (43 vols, in progress, Rome 1960–), s.v. 'Caroso'.
[37] Fermor (1993).
[38] Heinz (1972); Burke (1987); Spicer (1991).
[39] Bellori (1672), 219.
[40] Molmenti (1879), 3, 311–12.

sign of pride). Yet it would be a mistake to discuss the reform of gesture in purely negative terms, as part of the history of repression. It can also be viewed more positively as an art, or a contribution to the art of living. This is the way in which Castiglione saw it, not to mention the dancing-masters – and in the seventeenth century, if not earlier, dancing formed part of the curriculum of some Italian colleges for nobles. It was a festive mode of inculcating discipline.[41]

If the reformers of gesture had a positive ideal in mind, what was it? The ideal might be (and sometimes was, as we have seen) described as a Spanish model, influential in central Europe as well as Italy and including language and clothes as well as gesture. If this ideal had to be summed up in a single word, that word might well be 'gravity'. The German humanist Heinrich Agrippa testified in 1530 that the Italians 'walk rather slowly, are dignified in their gestures'.[42] Another German, Hieronymus Turler, made the same point (whether from observation or copying Agrippa) in the 1570s; 'the Italian has a slow gait, a grave gesture' ('incessum tardiusculum, gestum gravem').[43] Joseph Addison, arriving in Milan (still part of the Spanish Empire) from France, found the Italians 'stiff, ceremonious and reserved' by contrast to the French.[44]

The Italians were or had been closer to the French style of vicacity, so much so that they sometimes perceived Spanish gesture as an absence. Thus Pedro de Toledo, Viceroy of Naples in the middle of the sixteenth century, surprised the local nobility by the fact that when he gave audience he remained immobile, like a 'marble statue'.[45] The phrase was, or became, a topos. One of Toledo's successors was described by the political theorist Traiano Boccalini, who viewed him in Naples in 1591, as so grave and motionless 'that I should never have known whether he was a man or a figure of wood'. According to Boccalini, the viceroy did not even blink. The Venetian ambassador to Turin in 1588 described the prince's wife, a Spanish Infanta, as 'brought up in the Spanish style ... she stands with great tranquillity [sussiego], she seems immobile.' Guazzo's remark about the need

[41] Brizzi (1976), 254–5; cf. Lippe (1974); Braun and Gugerli (1993).
[42] Quoted Knox (1995), 33–4.
[43] Turler (1574), book 1, ch. 4.
[44] Addison (1705), 373.
[45] Caraffa (1880).

to avoid the immobility of statues, quoted above, must have had a topical ring to it.[46]

The employment of the term 'model' is not intended to imply that the Italians of the period always idealized the Spaniards. On the contrary, they were much hated and frequently mocked, the mockery extending on occasion to their gestures. Their gravity was sometimes interpreted as the stiffness of arrogance. The charge of arrogance was incarnated in the figure of 'Capitano' on the Italian stage. This figure from the Commedia dell'Arte was often given a Spanish name such as 'Matamoros', together with stylized *bravure*, in other words aggressive, macho gestures intended to challenge or provoke his neighbours. An eighteenth-century description of Naples under Spanish hegemony, the *Massime del governo spagnolo* written by the nobleman Paolo Matteo Doria (a friend of Vico's), gave a highly critical account of the hispanized gestures of the upper nobility, notably an 'affected negligence' (*affettata disinvoltura*) and 'determined, arrogant movements' (*movimenti risoluti e disprezzanti*), displaying superiority over others.

This discussion of Italian perceptions of Spain makes no claim that Spaniards of this period always followed the model just described. It was probably restricted to upper-class males, or to some of them, and it may also have been limited to particular situations, notably rituals – although, curiously enough, the notoriously rigid rituals of the court seem to have reached Spain from Burgundy only in the mid-sixteenth century.[47] As for the explanation of change in Italy, it would be facile and superficial to attribute it to Spanish 'influence'. The appeal of the Spanish model in the sixteenth and seventeenth centuries was surely that it met a pre-existing demand for stricter bodily control, the reform of gesture discussed in this section.

The history of that demand has been written by the sociologist Norbert Elias in his famous study of the 'process of civilization' (by which he generally means self-control, more especially table manners), concentrating on northern Europe but including a few observations on the Italians, who were, after all, pioneers in the use of the fork.[48] More recently, Michel Foucault offered an alternative history of the body, examining the negative aspects in

---

[46] Burke (1987); cf. Knox (1989).
[47] Hofmann (1985).
[48] Elias (1939).

his *Discipline and Punish*, the more positive ones in his *History of Sexuality*, and emphasizing control over the bodies of others as well as over the self. Elias and Foucault were concerned with the practice as well as the theory of gesture and bodily control. It is time to ask whether the Italian reformers of gesture succeeded in their aims.

The Gesticulating Italian

The reform discussed in the previous section was not peculiarly Italian, but part of a general Western 'process of civilization' (there are parallels in other parts of the world, such as China and Japan, but their history remains to be written). The hypothesis to be presented here is that the reform of gesture, if not more rigorous, was at least more successful in the northern Protestant parts of Europe, such as Britain, the Netherlands and the German-speaking regions, than in the Catholic south. The result was to increase the gap between northern and southern behaviour and in particular to make northerners more critical of Italians. The stereotype of the gesticulating Italian seems to have come into existence in the early modern period, reflecting the contrast between two gestural cultures, associated with two styles of rhetoric (laconic versus copious) and other differences as well.

The contrast is not one between the presence and the absence of gesture, though it was sometimes perceived as such. Nor is it an opposition between a natural and an artificial style, for all body languages are artificial in the sense that they have to be learned.[49] What we observe in this period – at second hand – is rather the increasing distance between two body languages, which might be described as the flamboyant and the disciplined. If the Italians perceived the Spaniards as gesturing too little, the northerners came increasingly to perceive the southerners as gesturing too much. Their criticisms echoed and perhaps exaggerated the criticisms of the Italian reformers, some of which have been quoted above.

In the Netherlands, the critique of gesticulation goes back at least as far as Erasmus and his textbook of good manners for boys, *De civilitate morum puerilium*. An eighteenth-century

[49] Birdwhistell (1970).

Dutch manual of etiquette condemned the Italians 'who speak with their head, arms, feet and the whole body', and claimed that the French, the English and the Dutch had all abandoned such gesticulations.[50] It might be more accurate to say that France was divided between the northern and the southern styles, just as it was split between Catholics and Protestants. In this context it is interesting to find a French Calvinist, the printer Henri Estienne, criticizing the exaggerated gestures of the Italians in a dialogue he published in 1578, and claiming that the French 'n'aiment les gesticulations'.[51] In the nineteenth century, a French book on etiquette warned its readers, 'Gardez-vous de gesticuler comme un Gascon.'[52]

In English, the pejorative term to 'gesticulate', defined by the *Oxford English Dictionary* as the use of 'much' or 'foolish' gestures, is documented from 1613 onwards.[53] From about this time onwards, we find British observers commenting with surprise or disdain on what they regard as the excessive gesticulations of the Italians – or the Greeks, or the French, mocked by *The English Spy* in 1691 for their 'Apish Gestures' and their 'Finger-Talk as if they were conversing with the Deaf'. For example, Thomas Coryat, in Venice in 1608, noted what he called the 'extraordinary' greeting customs of the natives, striking the breast or kissing one another. In the church of San Giorgio, he noted 'one kind of gesture which seemeth to me both very unseemly and ridiculous', that of people who 'wag their hands up and down very often'.[54]

The gestures of preachers attracted particularly unfavourable attention from Protestant observers. William Bedell, in Venice at the same time as Coryat, condemned the friars for 'the antics of their gesture more than player- or fencer-like'. Philip Skippon, in Rome in 1663, described a Jesuit preaching on Piazza Navona 'with much action and postures of his body', while Gilbert Burnet, who visited Italy in the 1680s, complained of the 'many comical expressions and gestures' of a Capuchin preacher in Milan.[55] Burnet would not have appreciated being told that he

[50] Bremmer and Roodenburg (1991), 160.
[51] Quoted Knox (1990), 103.
[52] Montandon (1995), 62.
[53] Cf. Schmitt (1981).
[54] Coryat (1611), 399, 369.
[55] Bedell quoted in Chambers and Pullan (1992), 195; Skippon (1732), 665; Burnet (1686), 110, cf. 197.

was echoing the recommendations of San Carlo Borromeo, just as Borromeo would not have appreciated learning that resistance to his decrees had lasted more than a century.

In Naples, the language of the body was even more visible than it was elsewhere, at least to the British visitor: to John Moore in 1781, for example, noting the 'great gesticulation' of a storyteller, or to J. J. Blunt in the 1820s, observing 'infinite gesticulation' during a reading of Ariosto.[56] In the early nineteenth century, an American writer, Washington Irving, was still more explicit in his diagnosis of the symptoms of the Italian national character, as he viewed from his café table on Piazza San Marco a conversation conducted 'with Italian vivacity and gesticulation'.[57] Stendhal too commented on the southern love of 'pantomime' and the preference for gesturing over speaking.[58]

The texts quoted here remain insufficient to support any grand hypotheses, but at least they may give a fascinating problem more visibility. The simple contrast between north and south, Protestant and Catholic, will of course have to be refined. Where, for example, should one place Poland? In what ways did Spanish gravity differ from British self-control? To what extent were these stereotypes of national character generalizations about a single social group, the noblemen?

---

[56] Moore (1781), letter 60; Blunt (1823), 290.
[57] Irving (1824), vol. 1, 103.
[58] Crouzet (1982), 90, 106.

5

Frontiers of the Comic in Early Modern Italy

Like gestures, discussed in the previous chapter, joking – or laughter – has its place among the objects of the new socio-cultural history. In the 1960s, Mikhail Bakhtin made the topic central to his study of Rabelais, emphasizing what he described as the liberating function of 'folk laughter'. In the 1970s, Keith Thomas devoted a lecture to 'the place of laughter' in early modern England. In the 1980s, Robert Darnton retold the story of 'the great cat massacre', a grisly practical joke played by some eighteenth-century Paris apprentices on their master and mistress.[1]

What is the point of the history of jokes? There are actually two points to make about change. In the first place, attitudes to joking have changed over time. Bakhtin, for example, suggested that the subversive laughter institutionalized in carnival was tolerated by the authorities in church and state in the Middle Ages and the Renaissance, but repressed thereafter. Another cultural theorist, Norbert Elias, might also be invoked here (although he had little explicit to say about laughter), because his idea of the rise of self-control and the raising of the 'threshold of embarrassment' is as applicable to joking as it is to table manners. In early modern Europe, jokes which had once been acceptable in dignified public places such as churches and courts were officially banished from them.

[1] Bakhtin (1965); Thomas (1977); Darnton (1984).

In the second place, the jokes themselves change over the centuries. They are difficult to translate from one period to another just as they are difficult to translate from one culture to another. What makes one generation laugh has little effect on the next. Hence there is a place for the history of laughter as there is for the sociology or anthropology of laughter.[2] Freud, of course, believed that jokes reveal underlying unconscious wishes or anxieties, which he viewed as unchanging.[3] His view of jokes was similar to his view of dreams, discussed in chapter 2 above. His emphasis on humour as an expression of anxiety offers us an important alternative to Bakhtin's view of liberating laughter (which had actually been put forward as an alternative to Freud).

The challenge to the cultural historian is to historicize Freud's theory. At the deepest psychological level he may well be right. All the same, changes in jokes over the long term suggest that a case can be made for the existence of a level intermediate between the worlds of consciousness and unconsciousness. At this level jokes change over time because the objects of anxiety change over time. For example, jokes about cuckoldry fall flat today, as revivals of Elizabethan or Restoration comedy demonstrate, although they seem to have made the contemporaries of Shakespeare and Wycherley dissolve into laughter. Joking may also be analysed in terms of displaced or sublimated aggression: class war, ethnic war or the war between the sexes conducted by other means. An anthropologist once described accusations of witchcraft as a social 'strain-gauge' which revealed the tensions specific to particular cultures.[4] Jokes are another such gauge.

Hence the need for cultural historians to ask: When is a joke not a joke? When, where, for whom is a given joke funny or unfunny? What are the limits, the boundaries, the frontiers of the comic? How different do jokes appear from different viewpoints and how do their meanings shift in the course of time? The aim of this chapter is to address such problems by focusing on a single comic genre, the practical joke or *beffa*, reinserting it into what might be called the contemporary 'system of the comic', in other words the varieties of humour recorded in Italy in the late medieval and early modern period, their definitions, their functions, their genres and so on.

[2] Propp (1976); Apte (1985); Mulkay (1988).
[3] Freud (1905).
[4] Marwick (1964).

The approach adopted here will be an anthropological one, in the sense of keeping close to indigenous categories and distinctions between jest and earnest. This is the justification for the many Italian words which will appear below. An attempt will be made to follow Darnton's advice to 'capture otherness', in other words to concentrate on what is most alien to us in the past and to try to make it intelligible.[5] Hence the emphasis here will fall on what is funny no longer, rather than on cultural continuities, important as they are.

The System of the Comic in Italy, 1350–1550

To begin with a sketch of this 'system' from Boccaccio to Bandello, or more generally from the Black Death to the Counter-Reformation. Despite the fact that Jacob Burckhardt, in his famous essay on the Renaissance, devoted some perceptive pages to what he called 'modern mockery and humour' ('der moderne Spott und Witz'), the subject has not attracted many historians.[6] Yet it certainly interested contemporaries, as the language of the period quickly reveals.

In the Italian of this time, there was a rich variety of terms available to distinguish varieties of play and humour. Words for the joke itself included *baia, beffa, burla, facezia, giuoco, leggerezza, pazzia, piacevolezza* and *scherzo*, while the joker was known as a *beffardo, beffatore, buffone, burlona, giuocatore* or *scherzatore*. Verbs included *burlare, giocare, uccellare*, while a distinction was made between *beffare* and the milder but more continuous *beffeggiare*, which we might translate as 'to tease'. Adjectives were richest of all: *beffabile, beffevole, burlesco, faceto, festevole, giocoso, grottesco, mottevole, scherzoso, sciocco*, and so on. The richness of vocabulary suggests that Italians were indeed connoisseurs in this domain.

The variety of comic genres deserves to be emphasized. They included comedy itself, whether 'learned' or popular, including the original 'slapstick' comedy of Harlequin in the Commedia dell'Arte. Stories (*novelle*) were often comic, while jokes often took the form of stories, *facezie*, which were collected and

---

[5] Darnton (1984), 4.
[6] Burckhardt (1860), ch. 2, section 4.

printed. Famous collections include the stories attributed to the Tuscan priest Arlotto Mainardi and those collected by the humanists Poggio Bracciolini and Angelo Poliziano, the latter published in 1548 under the name of the editor, Ludovico Domenichi.[7] Sermons often contained funny stories of this kind, thus combining the serious with the comic.

Paradox was much appreciated, as in the mock eulogies by Francesco Berni and Ortensio Lando.[8] So was nonsense-verse. The Florentine barber-poet Burchiello's contributions to this genre were immortalized by a new verb, *burchielleggare*. Parody was another favoured genre. Pulci's *Morgante*, for instance, mocked romances of chivalry. Aretino's *Ragionamenti* mocked courtesy books. The *Aeneid* and the epitaph were parodied in now-forgotten works of the seventeenth century such as Gianbattista Lalli's *L'Eneide travestite* (1618) or the Venetian patrician Gianfrancesco Loredan's *Il cimiterio* (1680) or A. M. del Priuli's *Epitafi giocosi* (1680).[9]

There were also a number of comic forms in the visual arts. In the Palazzo del Te in Mantua, designed by Giulio Romano, there are visual shocks like the frieze in which some pieces seem to be slipping and the frescoed ceilings which appear to be crashing down on the visitor.[10] They should perhaps be understood as a kind of practical joke. The portraits of the Milanese painter Arcimboldo, who made faces out of fruit, or fish, or books, were demonstrations of his wit. The imitation of the recently rediscovered classical 'grotesques' included statues for gardens, like Grand Duke Cosimo de' Medici's court dwarf Morgante (named after a famous giant) in the Boboli Gardens in Florence, represented naked, paunchy and sitting astride a turtle with his penis hanging down onto the shell.[11] Gardens were a place for play, for liberation from social conventions. In what we might describe as the private 'theme park' of Bomarzo, constructed a few miles from Viterbo for one of the Orsini family in the late sixteenth century, there was, for instance, a gigantic stone hell mouth which apparently functioned as a cool site for picnics. That this part of the 'Sacred Wood' was a joke, even if a joke on the edge

---

[7] Luck (1958); Fontes (1987).
[8] Grendler (1969); Borsellino (1973), 41–65.
[9] Rochon (1975), 83–102; Larivaille (1980).
[10] Gombrich (1984).
[11] Battisti (1962), 278ff.; Barolsky (1978), 153ff.

of blasphemy, is suggested by the inscription, 'lasciate ogni pen-
siero' ('leave behind every thought'), parodying Dante, and confirmed by the remarks in a contemporary discussion of grottos
that they should be furnished with 'frightful or ridiculous
masks'.[12]

No discussion of medieval or early modern humour would be
complete without reference to the professional fools who could
be found at court and elsewhere. A number of Italians of the time
achieved inter-regional if not international fame in this profession, among them Dolcibene, the two Gonellas, Borso d'Este's
Scocola at Ferrara (immortalized in the frescoes at Schifanoia),
Beatrice d'Este's Diodato at Milan, and Isabella d'Este's Fritella
at Mantua.[13]

The idea of the comic or the playful was not sharply defined in
this period but shaded into entertainment, or diversion – *spasso,
diporto, trattenimento, trastullo* – at one end of the spectrum,
and at the other into tricks and insults – *inganni, truffe, affronti,
diffamazioni, offese, scherni.* Two sixteenth-century informants
bear witness to the difficulty of marking the boundary. In his dialogue *The Courtier* (1528)', Baldassare Castiglione defined the
burla as a 'friendly deceit' which 'does not give offence, or at
least not very much' (book 2, section 85). Again, in his conduct
book the *Galateo* (1558), Giovanni Della Casa distinguished
beffe from insults only in terms of the intention of the perpetra-
tor, since the effects on the victim were more or less the same
(chapter 19). This ambiguity, or ambivalence, raises the question
of the limits of the permissible. How far could one go without
going too far, in what direction, with whom, about what?
Although the idea of transgression is central to the comic, the
limits or boundaries transgressed are always unstable, varying
with the locale, region, moment, period, and the social groups
involved.

Looking back at Renaissance Italy from our own time, or even
from the seventeenth century, what appears most striking, or
strange, is the generosity or permeability of the limits. Religious
matters might be the object of jokes without causing offence, at
least on occasion. Mattello, a court fool at Mantua, dressed as a

---

[12] Battisti (1962), 125ff.; Barolsky (1978); Bredecamp (1985); Lazzaro (1990),
137, 142, 306.
[13] Luzio and Renier (1891); Malaguzzi Valeri (1913–23), vol. 1, 563–4;
Welsford (1935), 8–19, 128–37.

friar and parodied ecclesiastical rituals.[14] In the introduction to the stories of Antonfrancesco Grazzini, set at carnival, a lady says that even friars and nuns are allowed to enjoy themselves at this time and to dress as members of the opposite sex. Priests might be jesters, like Fra Mariano at the court of Leo X.[15] Boundaries existed all the same. In Castiglione's *Courtier* (book 2, section 93), for instance, Bernardo Bibbiena criticizes Boccaccio for a joke which 'goes beyond the limits' (*passa il termine*).

Ambiguity also leads to the question of function. Was laughter always an end in itself, or might it be a means to another end? One possibility to be taken seriously is the Russian folklorist Vladimir Propp's idea of laughter on certain occasions as a kind of ritual. Easter laughter in particular may be interpreted as ritual laughter. A case has been made for the presence of ritual elements in the humour of a sixteenth-century comic figure, Bertoldo.[16] We shall soon see examples of laughter as an instrument of vengeance.

The *Beffa*

The practical joke, trick or *beffa*, otherwise known as the *burla*, *giarda* or *natta* and frequently described in Italian jest-books, stories and other sources, was not of course unique to the peninsula or to the period under discussion. Whether or not practical jokes are a cultural universal, the recurrent figure of the trickster in world folklore (including that of China, West Africa, and the Indians of North America) suggests that they are at the very least extremely widespread. Such figures as Panurge and Till Eulenspiegel (not to mention medieval *fabliaux*) bear witness to the love of *beffe* in northern and central Europe, while in parts of the Mediterranean world, from Andalusia to Crete, anthropologists find the custom very much alive among young adult males.[17]

All the same, there was apparently an unusual emphasis on this kind of humour in Italy, especially in Florence, 'la capitale de la *beffa*'.[18] Boccaccio's *Decameron* makes an obvious starting-

---

[14] Malaguzzi Valeri (1913–23), vol. 1, 563.
[15] Graf (1916).
[16] Propp (1976), ch. 9; Bernardi (1990), 153; Camporesi (1976), 92.
[17] Brandes (1980); Herzfeld (1985).
[18] Rochon (1972), 28.

point for the study of the genre. The tricks occur in twenty-seven stories altogether, and the terms *beffa*, *beffare*, and *beffatore* are used eighty times.[19] Later in the century, *beffe* recur in the stories of Francesco Sacchetti. In the fifteenth century, they can be found in the tales of Masuccio Salernitano and Sabadino degli Arienti.[20] There is also the anonymous fifteenth-century story of a joke played on a fat carpenter by the architect Filippo Brunelleschi. This example is all the more interesting because it plays with the idea of identity in a period which Burckhardt has described as an age of individualism.[21]

As for *beffe* in the sixteenth-century *novella*, one finds them everywhere. In the stories of Antonfrancesco Grazzini (died 1584), 'the *beffa* is the key,' as a French critic puts it, occurring in eighteen stories.[22] They are even more important in Matteo Bandello, seventy *beffe* in 214 *novelle*.[23] The sixteenth-century material also includes plays, such as Machiavelli's *Mandragola* and Pietro Aretino's *Il Marescalco*, a carnival entertainment in which the Master of the Horse at the court of the Duke of Mantua is informed that the duke wishes him to marry. Bad news for him, since his tastes were not for the opposite sex, but he goes through the ceremony only to discover that his 'bride' is a page. The incident is described in the play as a '*burla*' (Act 5, Scene 11).[24]

To sum up this evidence and place it in comparative perspective, we might compare the American folklorist Stith Thompson's world survey of folktales with a specialized motif-index of the Italian *novella* by D. P. Rotunda. For category X 0–99, 'Humor of Discomfiture', for instance, Thompson gives four examples, Rotunda twenty. In the case of category K 1200–99, 'Deception into a Humiliating Position', Thompson gives twenty-seven examples (including eight from Boccaccio), while Rotunda offers no fewer than seventy-two.[25] The Italians, more exactly the Tuscans, appear to have been obsessed by this theme.

Needless to say there are problems for a cultural historian in handling such literary evidence. The stories are stylized, indeed

---

[19] Cf. Mazzotti (1986).
[20] Rochon (1975), 65–170.
[21] Varese (1955), 767–802; Rochon (1972), 211–376.
[22] Rochon (1972), 45–98; cf. Rodini (1970), 153–6.
[23] Rochon (1972), 121–66.
[24] Rochon (1972), 99–110.
[25] Thompson (1955–8); Rotunda (1942).

they were subject to a double stylization as they circulated through two media, oral and printed. They are full of *topoi*. The same stories have different heroes. Fiction is of course good evidence of fantasy, of the collective imagination. But can we draw conclusions about social life from this evidence? Was the *beffa* a social custom or just a literary game? Practical jokes are known to have been played in some courts in Renaissance Italy, for example in Milan under the Sforza or in Ferrara under the Este.[26] Other evidence comes from judicial records regarding joking which gave offence and so led to legal proceedings. These records suggest that taverns were a favourite locale for *beffe*, as in the case of the trick played on a certain Furlinfan in the village of Lio Maggiore in 1315, for instance.[27] They also suggest that carnival was a favourite time for *beffe*, witness the case of a mysterious coil of rope, from Rome in 1551, when seven Jews pretended to arrest a Neapolitan, at the time of their carnival (Purim), not the carnival of the Christians. This 'case' could have been made into a *novella*.[28]

Material culture also provides evidence of joking. Let us return for a moment to the Renaissance garden, where there might be hidden fountains activated at a sign from the host, taking the guests by surprise and soaking them to the skin. This mild form of *beffa* was current in aristocratic circles, and can be documented at Caprarola, for instance, designed by Vignola for the Farnese, as well as at Pratolino, designed by Buontalenti for Francesco I de' Medici, where Montaigne was among the victims.[29] It was not very different from the common Italian practice of throwing water at carnival.

Some of the examples cited above raise the problem of the limits of joking, the frontier between relatively harmless or disinterested deception and more serious trickery or aggression. In northern Italy in the sixteenth century, *dare la burla* was a standard phrase employed to describe false promises of marriage.[30] Again, in an age when jokes were often insulting and insults sometimes took playful forms, it was inevitable that someone would overstep the customary limits and that some cases would

[26] Malaguzzi Valeri (1913–23), vol. 1, 560ff.; Prandi (1990), 78.
[27] Ortalli (1993), 67.
[28] Cohen (1988).
[29] Robertson (1992), 128; Lazzaro (1990), 65–8.
[30] Muir and Ruggiero (1990), 351.

end up in court. The difficulty of defining the frontiers of the comic is apparent in these records. In sixteenth-century Bologna, one victim of a verbal assault (by means of a sonnet) complained to the tribunal, but they considered the letter not to be defamatory but only 'a joke, containing something laughable'.[31] On the other hand, the painter Michelangelo di Caravaggio, who had a gift for getting himself into trouble, was called before the Tribunal of the Governor of Rome in 1603 (in company with other painters), charged with what their colleague Baglioni called 'verses in my dishonour'.[32]

Turning to the world of politics, think of Cesare Borgia and the famous trick he played on his enemies at Sinigaglia, a 'torpedo' (as Italo-American gangsters would have called it in the age of Al Capone). The story is told by Machiavelli in his famous 'Description of the way in which Duke Valentino (Cesare) assassinated Vitelozzo Vitelli', inviting Vitelozzo and his companions to enter his lodgings unarmed and having them strangled there. Machiavelli wrote in a cool deadpan manner, but elsewhere he expresses his enormous admiration for Cesare. It may not be too far from the point to suggest a link between his politics and his dramatic interest in *beffe*. His play *Mandragola* is 'Machiavellian' in its interest in stratagems, while his history of Florence is presented in dramatic terms.

Five further comments may place the *beffa* more firmly in its cultural context.

(1) The *beffa* was often presented as a 'work of art', to adapt Burckhardt's view of the Renaissance in general. It was supposed to give aesthetic pleasure, as well as the more obvious *Schadenfreude*, and it was sometimes described as *bella*. The titles of stories, Bandello's for instance, refer to a 'giocosa astuzia' (book 2, no. 45), or a 'piacevole e ridicolo inganno' (book 2, no. 47). Pleasant, that is, from the point of view of the joker or the bystanders, which is the point of view the reader is generally encouraged to take. Unless of course the victim turns the tables on the aggressor, for special pleasure is taken in what is called 'il contracambio', in other words the theme of *beffatore beffato*, the biter bit (Bandello, book 1, no. 3, for instance).

---

[31] Evangelisti (1992), 221.
[32] Friedlaender (1955), 271–2.

(2) The *beffa* was an appropriate form of joking in a competitive culture which was also what might be called a 'culture of trickery', in which the rulers were often civilians rather than soldiers, or in Machiavellian language foxes rather than lions. Even today, Italians explicitly approve of people who are cunning (*furbo*), witness the account of daily life in a small town in southern Italy in the 1970s by a British anthropologist who describes a father repeatedly asking his small son, 'Sei furbo?' The answer he wanted, expected and rewarded was of course 'yes'.[33]

(3) The *beffa* was often not 'pure' amusement but a means of humiliating, shaming, and indeed of socially annihilating rivals and enemies. This was a culture in which honour and shame were leading values. The titles of some stories reinforce this perception, as in the case of Sabadino degli Arienti, for instance, in which a recurrent phrase is 'se trova vergognato' (no. 1), 'remase vergognato' (no. 16), or 'resta vergognato' (nos 31, 35). The culture of Renaissance Italy was an agonistic one, most vividly exemplified in Florence.[34] Revenge (*bella vendetta*, as it is sometimes called) is another recurrent motif in the *novelle* (Bandello, book 4, no. 6; Grazzini, book 2, no. 9, etc.). So is cuckoldry. Aggression and sadism also recur, for instance in two famous stories in which what is supposed to be so funny is the castration of the victim (Bandello, book 2, no. 20; Grazzini, book 1, no. 2). These examples underline a point which Bakhtin's famous discussion of festive aggression seems to forget, that jokes were not amusing for everyone, that there were victims as well as spectators or listeners.

(4) That brings us to what Bakhtin called the 'lower bodily stratum'. In a story told by Sabadino (no. 16), a craftsman goes to the barber to be shaved and sees that the barber's shoes are very large. 'He felt an urge to piss in them,' and he did so. In a story by Bandello (book 1, no. 35), Madonna Cassandra has an affair with a friar, the husband discovers, dresses as the friar, takes laxative pills and shits all over her in the bed. Readers will probably find the story quite revolting. That is precisely why it is quoted here, at the price of transgressing the boundaries of the

---

[33] Davis (1973), 23; cf. Brandes (1980), 115ff.; Herzfeld (1985), 148.
[34] Burckhardt (1860), part 2.

acceptable in our own culture, in order to remind us of the 'otherness' of sixteenth-century Italy.

(5) The sense of cultural distance becomes still greater if we call to mind the fact that the last story was not only told about a lady but also dedicated to another lady, Paola Gonzaga, by a priest, at the time of the Council of Trent. Today, we tend to think of priests as serious or even as solemn people, at least in public. However, fifteenth-century Tuscans enjoyed the jests they attributed to a rural parish priest of the region, Arlotto Mainardi, and as we have seen Fra Mariano played the fool at the court of Pope Leo X. Again, we tend to think of Renaissance rulers such as Isabella d'Este of Mantua and Cosimo I of Tuscany as if they were always serious, although they are known to have enjoyed the wit and the antics of dwarves and fools.[35] The point to underline, at least for the period 1350–1550, is the widespread participation – both as jokers and victims – of princes and peasants, men and women, clergy and laity, young and old. Archive evidence confirms the testimony of fiction in this respect. At the court of Milan in 1492, for instance, Princess Beatrice d'Este played a trick on the ambassador of Ferrara, causing his garden to be invaded by wild animals, which killed his chickens, to the amusement of Beatrice's husband, Lodovico Sforza, the ruler of the state.[36] However, this situation would not last. It is time to turn to change.

Changes in the System

What then were the major changes in the system, in attitudes to jokes among Italians? Although a shift is perceptible by the 1520s, if not before, it is more obvious in the period 1550–1650, supporting Enid Welsford's point about 'the decline of the court-fool' in the seventeenth century, and Bakhtin's assertion about the 'disintegration of folk laughter' in the same period.[37] In reflecting on the reasons for these changes, it may be useful to distinguish between the religious and the secular aspects of what Norbert Elias called the 'process of civilization', a European

[35] Luzio and Renier (1891).
[36] Malaguzzi Valeri (1913–23), vol. 1, 560–1.
[37] Welsford (1935), 182–96; Bakhtin (1965).

movement of self-control (more precisely, 'the social constraint towards self-constraint'), considered here in its Italian Counter-Reformation version.

Some traditional forms of joking which had already been criticized by foreign clergy, from Erasmus on carnival to the Swiss reformer Oecolampadius on Easter laughter, were now condemned by Italians on religious or moral grounds. Aretino joined Luther and Calvin on the Index of Prohibited Books (compiled in Italy though binding on the whole church). The stories of the jester-priest Arlotto, first published in 1516 or thereabouts, were expurgated from 1565 onwards, with an introductory note explaining the need to remove the jokes 'which seemed to the inquisitor to be too free'. Bandello published his stories only just in time, in 1554, while the stories of the Florentine writer Antonfrancesco Grazzini, written around 1580, remained unpublished till the eighteenth century. Oral tales could not easily be censored, but all the same the storyteller Straparola was once summoned before the Venetian Inquisition.

Printed *beffe* were increasingly edited in order to point a moral, underlined by means of metaphors such as 'cures', 'lessons' and 'punishments'. Arlotto had already been described as curing someone of his bad habit of spitting near the altar, and teaching a lesson to the young men who want a quick 'hunter's Mass' (nos 5, 6). Bandello drew attention to the ethical implications of his stories (in book 1, nos 3, 35, etc.), although readers may not find this moral packaging altogether convincing. The editor Ludovico Domenichi made cuts in the 1548 edition of the *facezie* compiled by the humanist Angelo Poliziano, and revised them still further for the 1562 edition, changing the title to the more serious *Detti e fatti*, removing blasphemies and anticlerical remarks, and adding morals to each joke.[38] A collection of jokes by Luigi Guicciardini were also described on the title page as 'moralized' ('ridotti a moralità').

The changing reception of the *Decameron* makes an illuminating case-study in changing attitudes. Boccaccio's stories might have been prohibited altogether by the Council of Trent if the Duke of Florence, Cosimo de' Medici, had not sent an ambassador to the Council to beg for a reprieve. The stories reappeared in expurgated form in 1582. One story, concerning the hypocrisy

---

[38] Richardson (1994), 135.

of an inquisitor, had disappeared entirely from the collection, while other stories which mocked the clergy suffered drastic revision. Terms like 'friar' and 'archangel' were removed, at the price of making one story completely meaningless – that of Friar Alberto, who pretended to be the archangel Gabriel in order to seduce a pious Venetian lady.[39] The jokes in book 2 of Castiglione's *Courtier* were subjected to similar treatment in the expurgated edition of 1584.[40]

The Counter-Reformation clergy had embarked upon a 'cultural offensive', not to ban joking altogether but to reduce its domain. Jokes were increasingly considered indecorous if told by the clergy, whose behaviour should be marked by *gravitas*, or in church, because it was a holy place, or on sacred subjects. The careers of the jester-priests Arlotto and Fra Mariano began to seem indecorous – and later, almost unimaginable.

In his provincial council of 1565, San Carlo Borromeo denounced Easter plays for provoking laughter. He would not have agreed with Vladimir Propp about ritual laughter. As Borromeo saw it, the pious custom of representing the lives of Christ and the saints had been corrupted by human perversity, resulting in scandal, laughter, and contempt. He also instructed preachers not to tell funny stories.[41] Pope Pius V issued a decree against 'immoderate' laughter in church.[42] The Index of Sixtus V (1590), stricter than its predecessors, included the collections of *facezie* edited by Domenichi and Guicciardini, despite their claims to be moralists.[43] In a letter of 1608, Robert Bellarmine, another leading figure of the Counter-Reformation, expressed his opposition to revealing details about the lives of saints which might encourage laughter rather than edification ('quae risum potius quam aedificationem pariant'). Perhaps he was thinking of the traditional image of St Joseph, cuckolded by the Holy Ghost.

This clerical offensive needs to be seen as part of a wider movement, or at least of a wider shift in attitudes (among the upper classes at any rate), extending from the rise of classicism in the arts to the withdrawal from participation in popular culture, a shift which Elias described in terms of increasing self-control or

[39] Sorrentino (1935); Brown (1967).
[40] Cian (1887).
[41] Bernardi (1990), 256, 259; Taviani (1969); Borromeo (1758), 44.
[42] Azpilcueta (1582), 42–3.
[43] Reusch (1886), 481.

'civilization'.[44] For example, the *Discourses on What is Appropriate for a Young Noble who Serves a Great Prince* (1565) by Gianbattista Giraldi Cinthio (better known as a playwright) told its readers not to be the first to joke, since this might be construed as disrespect for the prince. The Genoese patrician Ansaldo Cebà emphasized the need for moderation in jokes, which should be adapted to places, times and persons and should not be unworthy of a gentleman ('che non disdicano ad huom libero e costumato').[45]

Changes in the *Beffa*

To return to the *beffa*. From the 'civilization' point of view, it is surely significant that among the critics of the *beffa*, as we have seen, are two authors whose conduct books became famous: the *Cortegiano* of Baldassare Castiglione and the *Galateo* of Giovanni Della Casa. Castiglione's speakers criticize *beffe* on moral grounds, preferring verbal jokes to practical ones, while the author censored some of his own jokes in the third manuscript version of his treatise. The criticisms may seem anodyne today, but in the context of the early sixteenth century they look almost puritanical, or revolutionary.[46] As for the Counter-Reformation moralist Della Casa, he admitted the need for people to play tricks on one another because life in this vale of tears needed some kind of solace (*sollazzo*), but he also criticized some kinds of *beffa*.[47]

Other evidence also points in the direction of the sharper definition of standards and a shrinking in the area of the publicly permissible. A noble dramatic society of Siena, the Intronati, now took care not to offend the modesty of ladies by their *burle*. In the case of the *beffe* recounted by Grazzini, probably in the 1580s, it has been claimed by a recent critic that there was a change of perspective from joker to victim.[48] Another recent writer on Italian literature has remarked on the seventeenth-

---

[44] Elias (1939); Burke (1978), 270–80.
[45] Cebà (1617), ch. 43.
[46] Grudin (1974); Rochon (1975), 171–210.
[47] Della Casa (1554), chs 11, 19.
[48] Plaisance (1972), 46.

century 'crisis' and decline of the *beffa*.[49] At the very least, it was purified.

What replaced the traditional *beffa*? Typical of the new regime of humour is Girolamo Parabosco's relatively mild *beffa* in which 'a large jar of water and hot ash' falls on the head of a lover as he arrives at the house of his lady. The tricks played by Bertoldo, the hero of a late sixteenth-century cycle of jests written by Giulio Cesare Croce, include violence but no scatology. There also seems to have been a shift among the upper classes in the direction of wit and verbal humour. This shift may be illustrated from the life of the academies, an increasingly important form of upper-class sociability in Italian cities of the sixteenth and seventeenth centuries. These discussion groups, which went back to the early Renaissance, now became at once increasingly formal and increasingly playful, in a respectable way. The change may be illustrated from the humorous names which became virtually *de rigueur* for members and for the academies themselves – the 'Sleepyheads' (Addormentati); the 'Confused' (Confusi); the 'Frozen' (Gelati); the 'Immature' (Immaturi); the 'Thoughtless' (Spensierati); the 'Uncivilized' (Incolti); and so on – as well as from mock lectures and parodies which figured largely on their programmes, some of which are reproduced in Gianfrancesco Loredan's *Bizarrie academiche* (1638).[50]

The seventeenth-century rhetorician Emmanuele Tesauro (who might be described in the language of today as a literary theorist), expressed a new ideal of elegance, dismissing 'popular jokes' (*facetie popolari*). He did not reject the *beffa* altogether, but he was much more concerned with verbal than practical jokes.[51] In this respect he was a typical representative of the cultural movement we now call 'baroque'. It does not seem unreasonable to suggest that the baroque obsession with word-play was a form of psychological compensation, a reaction to the shrinking of the domain of the comic. Another form of compensation was the rise of the caricature, which was invented in the circles of the Carracci and Bernini in the early to mid-seventeenth century. In other words, it was the work of artists famous for their classicism, suggesting that they needed some respite from

[49] Rochon (1972), 179–202.
[50] Quondam (1982), 823–98.
[51] Tesauro (1654), 38, 223, 583ff., 682.

idealization, while earlier forms of comic relief were now denied them.[52]

Of course the Elias thesis of the rise of self-control or 'civilization' should not be enunciated in too simple a manner. The trend was gradual not sudden, it provoked resistance, and it was successful only to varying extents and at different moments in different places, among different groups, or even in different kinds of situation. For example, Adriano Banchieri, a Benedictine monk, published comic works in the seventeenth century, although he did so under a pseudonym, thus revealing as well as breaking the Counter-Reformation taboo. The Florentine patrician Niccolò Strozzi in the mid-seventeenth century told the story of a *beffa* in which the victim was left on Piazza della Signoria all night.[53] At Pratolino, the fountains were still at work in the seventeenth century or even later, as two English travellers (among others) testify. John Evelyn, visiting in 1645, says that he and his companions were 'well washed for our curiosity'.[54] Richard Lassels recorded visiting 'the Grotto of Cupid with the wetting-stools upon which, sitting down, a great Spout of Water comes full in your face'.[55]

In the eighteenth century we find a return to the Renaissance, but with a difference. Several sixteenth-century comic texts reappeared at this time, but in revised forms. *Bertoldo*, for instance, was republished in 1736, rewritten by twenty men of letters, in verse, with allegories. G. C. Becelli rewrote the exploits of the famous medieval jester as *Il Gonnella* (1739). Grazzini's *beffe*, written about 1580, were published for the first time in 1756. A life of the celebrated jester-priest Arlotto Mainardi was published in Venice in 1763. Thus the eighteenth-century revival of the Renaissance was accompanied by – and perhaps depended on – a kind of cultural distanciation.

To pursue this theme of distanciation, we may turn to a mid twentieth-century story told by the novelist Vasco Pratolini in his novel *The Girls of San Frediano* (1949), an evocation of traditional working-class culture in the years following the Second World War. The punishment of 'Bob', the local Don Giovanni, by a gang of six girls whom he has tried to seduce individually,

---

[52] Kris (1953), chs 6–7; Lavin (1983).
[53] Woodhouse (1982).
[54] Evelyn (1955), vol. 2, 418.
[55] Lassels (1670), 134.

takes the form of a *beffa* in the Florentine tradition, in which he is tied up and paraded through the streets with his genitals exposed. Pratolini is not only placing himself in a high literary tradition, but also in a popular tradition, that of Florentine working-class culture, out of which he came and which he celebrates throughout his work. We do not seem to have moved very far in the 400 years separating Pratolini from Pratolino, or even the 600 years separating him from Boccaccio. The 'gang', or *brigata*, is central in both instances. However, the social frontiers of the comic have changed. What was represented in the fourteenth century as a general social custom is now associated with young adults of the working class.

At this point it may be useful to go back to Darnton's comments about otherness. Are we less cruel and more civilized, as he suggests? Is a cat massacre impossible today? In the *Cambridge Evening News* in the early 1990s, an incident was reported in which a young man who had quarrelled with his girlfriend revenged himself on her by putting her cat in the microwave. The example suggests that it might be prudent to speak not so much of a deep change in human psychology as of changes in social conventions, in the rules of the game, in the frontiers of the comic. Like sex, laughter is impossible to repress altogether. Rather than speaking of the 'decline' of traditional forms of humour from the later sixteenth century onwards, we might employ Bakhtin's more precise term 'distintegration'. What we find in the period 1550–1650 in particular are increasing restrictions on the public participation of clergy, women, or gentlemen in certain kinds of joke, a reduction of comic domains, occasions, and locales; a raising of the threshold; an increase in the policing of the frontiers.

6

The Discreet Charm of Milan: English Travellers in the Seventeenth Century

If we can only learn how to use them, travelogues will be among the most eloquent sources for cultural history. By a 'travelogue' I mean a journal or diary kept by a traveller, usually in a foreign country, or a series of letters describing his or her impressions. The temptation to historians as to other readers is to imagine ourselves looking through the writers' eyes and listening through their ears and so perceiving a now remote culture as it really was.

The reason we should not succumb to this temptation is not that travellers differ, since it is relatively easy to check one account against another. The point to emphasize is the rhetorical aspect of their descriptions, notably the importance of commonplaces and schemata. The texts are no more completely spontaneous and objective descriptions of new experiences than autobiographies are completely spontaneous and objective records of an individual life (above, p. 39). Some of these descriptions at least were written with publication in mind, and all follow certain literary conventions. Others simply reflect prejudices, in the literal sense of opinions formed before the travellers left their own country, whether these opinions were the result of conversation or reading.

An anthropological study of the 'man-eating myth' notes how common it is for travellers to perceive the inhabitants of a culturally distant society as cannibals. 'The cannibal epithet at one time or another has been applied by someone to every human group.' Another well-known example of prejudice, most carefully studied in the case of Europeans in the Far East, has been christened 'the myth of the lazy native'. Time and time again Europeans comment on the 'idleness', 'indolence', or 'disinclination to work' of the Malays, Filipinos, Javanese and so on.[1] Again, from the days of Herodotos onwards, the schema of the world turned upside down has appealed to travellers in what they regard as exotic places as a way of oganizing their observations. More than one of the characters in the novels of E. M. Forster see foreign parts as the reverse of their own country. In both *A Room with a View* (1908), set in Italy, and *A Passage to India* (1924), someone complains about the terrible lack of privacy.

How to Travel

It also turns out that a number of travelogues follow the recipes given in books on the 'art of travel'. Instructions 'how to travel' were an established literary genre by the seventeenth century. Contributions to what was sometimes called the 'apodemic art', in other words methodical travel, include Hieronymus Turler's *De peregrinatione* (1574), Hilarius Pyrckmair's *De arte apodemica* (1577), Theodor Zwinger's *Methodus apodemica* (1577), Justus Lipsius's *De ratione peregrinandi* (1578), Albert Meier's *Methodus* (1587), Salomon Neugebauer's *De peregrinatione* (1605), and Henrik Rantzau's *Methodus peregrinandi* (1608).[2]

In texts like these, intending travellers were advised to observe in each place they visited the funeral monuments; the paintings; the buildings, public and private, religious and secular; the fortifications; the fountains; the political system; and the manners and customs of the inhabitants. They were also advised to carry a guidebook and to take careful notes on what they saw. Englishmen who could not read Latin still had access to the texts by Turler (translated into English in 1575), Meier (translated 1589) and Lipsius (translated 1592), as well as to Francis Bacon's essay 'Of Travel', first published in 1612. Although some

---

[1] Arens (1979), 13; Alatas (1977).
[2] Stagl (1980, 1990); Rubiès (1995).

travellers, notably Michel de Montaigne, used their eyes and ears
to produce original accounts, the writers of many travel journals
followed the advice given in these 'apodemic' texts, simply privileging one category rather than another according to taste. Thus
the Englishman Thomas Coryat anticipated the criticism that he
was 'a tombstone traveller' who copied too many epitaphs and
said too little about forms of government, his defence being that
he was 'a private man and no statist'.[3]

Despite occasional expressions of scepticism, travellers also
followed the assertions made in books published by earlier travellers, including the guidebooks to foreign countries which were
being published in increasing numbers in the seventeenth century.
As a result, many of their descriptions have a formulaic quality.
In their relatively brief notes on Genoa, for example, one
Englishman comments on the 'kingly magnificence' of the city
and another on the 'kingly luxury' (cf. chapter 7 below).[4]
'Magnificence' was an overworked word in these descriptions.

Not only brief formulae but also topics or themes occur again
and again.[5] They include processions (especially of flagellants)
and ex-votos, signs of Catholic 'superstition' which fascinated the
Protestant visitors. They also include violence, vengeance, the
guarding of women by their menfolk, and *lazzaroni*. Accounts of
Italy written by English, French and German travellers in the
seventeenth, eighteenth and nineteenth centuries offer a European
version of the myth of the lazy native in their recurrent descriptions of the *lazzaroni* of Naples, able-bodied men lying in the sun
and doing nothing, the *dolce far niente* being an indispensable
part of the Italian *dolce vita* as northerners saw it.[6] The
Englishman Samuel Sharp wrote of 6,000 *lazzaroni* who sleep in
the streets and 'are suffered to sun themselves a great part of the
day under the palace walls'. A fellow-countryman of his extended
the idea, claiming that 'the wants of nature are so easily satisfied
here that the lower class of people work but little: their great
pleasure is, to bask in the sun and do nothing.'[7] French and
German writers made the same point – apart from Goethe, who

[3] Coryat (1611), 11–12.
[4] Moryson (1617), 167; Raymond (1648), 13.
[5] Lord (1960).
[6] Crouzet (1982), 112, 114; Burke (1987), 15–19; cf. Comparato (1979); De'
Seta (1981).
[7] Sharp (1766), letter 24; Martyn (1787), 264; cf. Croce (1895); Michéa
(1939).

dismissed the idea as an example of the northern stereotype of the south.[8]

These descriptions are not necessarily pure plagiarism. It is likely that the travellers actually saw men lying in the sun, whether or not resting after work, interpreting them as *lazzaroni* because they fulfilled expectations created either by books or by oral tradition. By the eighteenth century (if not before) the travellers were looking for the 'picturesque', a new and fashionable word which reveals the habit of viewing everyday life through the spectacles of the old masters. A little later, in 1814, the English poet Samuel Rogers described the balconies in Milan 'from which a female figure is always looking as in P. Veronese and Tintoret'.[9] It is not only in the case of visionaries, discussed in chapter 2 above, that paintings have the power to modify perceptions of reality. In any case, entering an alien or semi-alien culture turns the traveller into a spectator, a viewer if not a voyeur. As Henry James put it in his *Italian Hours* (1877), 'To travel is, as it were, to go to the play.'

After so many critical observations, the reader may be expecting me to throw these travel narratives into the wastebasket, or to describe the Italy of their authors as pure 'invention'. As elsewhere in this volume, however, I shall try to avoid the opposite dangers of positivism and constructivism. The narratives will be analysed here as sources for the history of attitudes or mentalities.[10] They are precious documents of cultural encounters, revealing both the perception of cultural distance and the attempt to come to terms with or 'translate' it into something more familiar.

Views of Italy

For concrete examples of such perception of distance, we may turn to the case of northern European and more especially British travellers in early modern Italy.[11] In the early modern period northerners already tended to see Italy as the Other. It is tempting but too facile to explain this cultural distance in religious

[8] Goethe (1951), 28 May 1787.
[9] Rogers (1956), 165.
[10] Harbsmeier (1982).
[11] Stoye (1952); Sells (1964); Comparato (1979); De' Seta (1981).

terms as the result of the Reformation. Too facile, because a case could be made for explaining the Reformation in terms of this very cultural distance. Two leading reformers, Erasmus and Luther, visited Italy and recorded their dislike of some Italian customs, such as the carnival in Siena which Erasmus witnessed in 1509. All the same, the rejection of images, rituals, saints and so on at the Reformation can only have increased the distance from Italian culture experienced by northern Protestant travellers.

Despite their contempt for, or fear of, Catholicism (or 'Popery' as they put it), a considerable number of the British upper classes took a lively interest in Italian culture. Philip Sidney, William Harvey, John Milton, John Evelyn, Joseph Addison and Tobias Smollett are among the most famous of the many Englishmen who spent time in Italy in the early modern period. Italian art and architecture was quite well known in Britain, not only that of the Renaissance but also the work of seventeenth-century artists such as the Caracci, Guido Reni, Guercino and Salvator Rosa.[12] Sir Henry Wotton, who spent many years as ambassador in Venice, was an important mediator between his fellow-countrymen and Italian culture. So was the famous connoisseur Thomas Howard, Earl of Arundel, who took Inigo Jones with him on a visit to Italy in 1613. More than thirty years later, in 1646, the Earl gave Evelyn 'remembrances' of what to see in Italy.[13]

Italian was probably the best-known foreign language of the English at this time, overtaken by French only in the course of the eighteenth century. Italian literature was much admired, notably the poetry of Petrarch, Ariosto and Tasso (whose *Jerusalem Delivered* was published in an English translation by Edward Fairfax in 1600). A number of works by seventeenth-century Italian writers were translated into English without delay, including Paolo Sarpi's *History of the Council of Trent* (1620), Virgilio Malvezzi's *Romulus and Tarquin* and *David Persecuted* (both 1637), Enrico Davila's *History of the Civil Wars in France* (1647), Traiano Boccalini's *Advertisements from Parnassus* (1656), and Galileo's *System of the World* (1661).

It is not surprising, then, that there was a substantial number

[12] Hale (1954), 65–75
[13] Hervey (1921); White (1995).

of British travellers to Italy in the early modern period. As Addison put it, 'There is certainly no place in the world where a man may travel with greater pleasure and advantage than Italy.'[14] The arts of travel described above, notably the works by Pyrckmair, Turler and Lipsius, had referred to Italy in particular detail. Italy was the principal goal of the 'Grand Tour', a phrase just coming into use to describe a sojourn abroad by one or more young noblemen, often accompanied by a tutor.[15] One of our informants, John Ray, wrote in his preface of his plan of 'making Grand Tour (as they there call it)' in France. The tour, which was an important European cultural institution between the late sixteenth and late eighteenth centuries, often lasted for years. A considerable proportion of the time was spent in Italy, not only by British 'grand tourists' but also by Dutchmen, Danes and Poles.[16] The demand was sufficient to generate a number of guidebooks, whether to Italy in general or to major cities such as Venice or Rome.

Differences in religion, language, climate and customs gave the travellers an acute sense of cultural distance. John Ray, who devoted more than ten pages to Italian manners and morals, emphasized revenge, lust and jealousy. Elias Veryard came to similar conclusions (or copied those of Ray): 'The Italians are generally ... lascivious, jealous and revengeful.'[17] Richard Lassels, a Catholic priest who spent a long time in Italy, presented Italian manners as 'most commendable', but even he noted that Italians were vengeful, as well as 'sensible of their honour' and 'strict to their wives even to jealousy'.[18]

Another aspect of Italy which impressed the foreign visitors was the concern with display. Lassels made the point more sympathetically when he described Italians as 'sparing in diet that they may both love and live handsomely; spending upon the back what we spend on our bellies'. Ray thought the houses 'rather great and stately than commodious for habitation', and noted that 'the inferior gentry affect to appear in public with as much splendour as they can, and will deny themselves many satisfactions at home that they may be able to keep a coach and therein

[14] Addison (1705), 357.
[15] Black (1985); Chaney (1985).
[16] Mączak (1978); Frank-van Westrienen (1983).
[17] Veryard (1701), 263.
[18] Ray (1673), 150–1.

make the tour à la mode about the streets of their city every eve.' In similar fashion, Veryard asserted that the nobles 'spend their estates ... in making the greatest figure their degree and dignity will permit'. Italy was already perceived as the land of appearances and façades. Given the similarity of the last phrase to the consecrated Italian expression *fare bella figura*, we may hazard the guess that Veryard and other foreign visitors often recorded observations which they had originally heard from the Italians themselves. Travelogues include what Bakhtin would call a 'heteroglossic' dimension, recording not pure observation but the interaction between travellers and 'travelees', as a recent critic calls them.[19] The relation between the stereotypes of national character current inside and outside a given country is a topic deserving systematic investigation.

The sense of distance was sometimes acute enough for visitors to employ the topos of the world turned upside down. Thus Gilbert Burnet, Bishop of Salisbury, a Scottish Calvinist, viewed the Italy through which he travelled in the 1680s as the converse of the enlightenment, freedom and industriousness which he attributed to his own country. He too contributed to the myth of the lazy native with his reference to 'the sloth and laziness of this people'.[20] Addison did the same, blaming 'idleness' on the number of monasteries and hospitals to be found in Italy and operating with a similar system of binary oppositions to Burnet (whose analysis he praised), contrasting Catholics and Protestants, tyranny and liberty, idleness and industry, Self and Other.[21]

These writers were influenced by and also contributed to what has been called the 'myth' of Italy, part of a stereotyped contrast between north and south (culture and nature, civilization and savagery), which became even sharper in the nineteenth century.[22] Italy had formerly been viewed as the centre of civilization, but in the eighteenth century it was turning into an Arcadia. In both cases we find a myth of place not so unlike the myths of time discussed in chapter 3 above, a vision in which everything was larger (or sharper) than life. If the northerners found the south of Europe exotic, the reverse was also the case. It was at this time, for example, that count Maiolino Bisaccioni, a prolific

[19] Pratt (1992), 135–6.
[20] Burnet (1686), 108.
[21] Addison (1705), 420–1.
[22] Crouzet (1982), 2, 38–49, 75, 79, 120, 242.

writer of history and fiction, published books on *Demetrius the Muscovite* (1639) and *Historical Memoirs of Gustavus Adolphus* (1642) as well as locating one of the stories in his collection *The Ship* (1643) in Norway and another in Russia.

The myth of Italy did not prevent some visitors from carefully observing the local customs, as the guides to travel advised. As we saw in chapter 4, northern visitors became increasingly conscious of the theatricality of Italian gestures (whether or not assisted in this process by the criticisms of Italian reformers). Fynes Morison, in Venice in the 1590s, was impressed by the 'variety of apparel, languages and manners'.[23] Thomas Coryat observed the uses of fans, forks and umbrellas, all alien objects in England at the time he was writing. Philip Skippon, who was in Italy in the 1660s, made careful notes on food ('they strew scraped cheese on most of their dishes'), clothes (with a sketch of a doge's cap), flagellants ('whippers'), funerals, blasphemies, silk production, the guillotine used in Milan, the voting system in Venice (complete with a diagram of a ballot box), the way in which the washing was hung out to dry on iron bars across the streets, and much else. Skippon is an unjustly neglected travel writer, with eyes and ears perhaps sharpened by his scientific training at Cambridge, where he studied with the famous botanist John Ray. It is a pity that his account of his journey to Italy has not been reprinted since 1732, while one of the few studies devoted to English travellers in Italy in the seventeenth century omits him altogether.[24]

Views of Milan

For a more precise case-study of the interaction between cultural stereotype and personal observation we may turn to the views of Milan recorded by British travellers in the course of a long seventeenth century, from the 1590s to the early 1700s. By this time, the British had a fairly clear impression of at least four Italian cities. Rome was of course associated both with the ruins of antiquity and with the papacy. Venice was known for its carnival as well as for its long-lived 'mixed constitution'.[25]

[23] Moryson (1617), 90.
[24] Skippon (1732); Sells (1964).
[25] Gaeta (1961); Bouwsma (1990); Haitsma Mulier (1980).

Florence was famous for its works of art, and Naples for its natural beauty.

By contrast, the British view of Milan was rather vague. According to the common saying, Rome was the Holy, Venice the Rich, Naples the Gentle (in the sense of noble), Florence the Fair, Genoa the Superb (in the sense of 'proud'), Bologna the Fat, Padua the Learned, and Milan the Great – in other words, large. For anyone interested in reading something in English about the city or state of Milan, there was little material available, especially in the first half of the century. Two plays performed on the London stage at this time provided a little information on the history of the city. Philip Massinger's *The Duke of Milan* (1621) and Robert Gomersall's *The Tragedie of Lodovick Sforza Duke of Milan* (1628) were both set in the late fifteenth century and based on the English translation of Francesco Guicciardini's *History of Italy*. The only concrete reference to contemporary Milan occurs in Thomas Dekker's *Honest Whore*, in which a scene takes place in a shop selling fine cloth.[26] The seventeenth century was the age of the first newspapers, but it was rare for them to report events from the region, apart from the plague of 1630 and the earthquake of 1680. At the beginning of our period, travellers are unlikely to have associated Milan with much more than St Ambrose and San Carlo Borromeo. Later, they could read the descriptions by earlier travellers such as Thomas Coryat (published in 1611), Fynes Morison (published in 1617), Raymond (1648), and so on.

Then as now, the British generally visited Milan on the way to somewhere else, if they did not omit it from their itineraries altogether. Milton, for example, spent a good deal of time in Florence, Rome, Naples and Venice in the years 1638–9, but there is no evidence of his having set foot in Milan (he approached Florence via Genoa and Livorno).[27] As for Edward Lord Herbert of Cherbury, who was there in 1615, all he could find to say about the city in his autobiography was that he had heard a famous nun sing there to the accompaniment of an organ.

The British travellers whose testimonies will be used below deserve to be introduced to the reader. They were virtually all members of the upper classes. In chronological order, they are

[26] Cf. Rebora (1936).
[27] Arthos (1968).

the gentleman Fynes Morison, who was in Milan in 1594; Thomas Coryat, who visited the city in 1608; Sir Thomas Berkeley (1610); the Earl of Arundel, who was there in 1613 and 1622; Peter Mundy, who visited in 1620 and recorded his impressions in sketches as well as texts; John Raymond, who was there in the 1640s; John Evelyn, gentleman and virtuoso (1646); Richard Symonds, another art-loving gentleman (*c*.1650); the Catholic priest Richard Lassels, who spent many years in the peninsula, and wrote a description of Milan in 1654; the Cambridge don John Ray and his pupil Philip Skippon, who were there together in 1663; the extremely Protestant Gilbert Burnet (1686); William Bromley, later a secretary of state (the 1680s); William Acton, a tutor who accompanied a young nobleman on the Grand Tour (*c*.1690); the physician Elias Veryard, who was in Italy at the end of the century; and Joseph Addison, who was there from 1701 to 1703. Of these sixteen visitors, nine published accounts of their travels in their lifetimes. Two different accounts have, somewhat implausibly, been attributed to Bromley. For convenience I will call the account of 1692 'Bromley' and the account of 1702 'pseudo-Bromley', without prejudice to what future research may reveal.

In general, British visitors tended to spend only a few days in Milan, compared to weeks or months in Venice or Rome. John Raymond spent four days and Richard Lassels, six. There was no ambassador in Milan as there was in Venice and official contacts were rare, although British diplomats and other important people might be received by the Spanish governor. For information about Milan the British relied on unofficial agents, or not to put too fine a point on it, spies. The importance of the information provided by these underground agents is revealed by the fact that in order to discover the plans of the governor of Milan, the doge once consulted the British ambassador in Venice.[28]

What follows is a collective portrait of Milan as seen by the British travellers. The method is to juxtapose or superimpose different images. The object of the exercise is to describe not the city itself so much as the impression it made on visitors – the sense of cultural distance, the mixture of attraction and repulsion. These visitors were all individuals with their own particular interests – Addison and Burnet in the Italian economy, Evelyn in the arts,

---

[28] Wotton (1907), 359, 399, 404; Brown (1864), vol. 10, nos 658, 673.

Lassels and Burnet in religion, Ray in science, Skippon in everyday life. On the other hand, they were often aware of their predecessors, if only to claim their unwillingness to 'transcribe the
travels of others'.[29] Both commonplaces and individualized observations will be studied not so much for what they tell us about
Milan as for what they tell us about the attitudes of the travellers
themselves. Particular attention will be given to what they found
surprising or disconcerting.

The first point to make is that the British regarded Milan, at
least in the early part of the century, as a sinister, dangerous
place, much as their descendants viewed Eastern Europe in the
1950s, with the Inquisition in the place of the KGB. There was
indeed a kind of 'cold war' in progress at this time. The rebel
Earl of Tyrone received a warm welcome from the governor of
Milan after he fled from Ireland in 1608. The man who
attempted to assassinate King James I in 1613 came from Milan.
In 1617, a possible attack on Milan by the joint British, Venetian
and Savoyard forces was seriously discussed.[30]

Unpleasant events occurred often enough to justify the anxiety
of travellers, or to give them a thrilling sense of adventure. In
1592, Wotton wrote that he had planned to visit Milan, but
found it too dangerous. Fynes Morison, normally an intrepid
traveller, spent only a little time there in 1594 'for the danger of
my abode there'.[31] One of Wotton's spies in Milan, Roland
Woodward, was arrested by the Inquisition in 1606, and
another, Charles Bushy, in 1607.[32] In 1608, Coryat had an
unpleasant experience when he was visiting the Castello and was
mistaken for a Dutchman.[33] In 1610, when Viscount Cranborne,
the son of the Earl of Salisbury, was passing through Milan, a
member of his entourage was arrested for carrying a pistol.[34] In
1613, the Earl of Arundel left the city in a hurry because the governor of Milan had not treated him with the courtesy customary
to someone of his rank.[35]

After 1640, a political thaw was in progress, and the state

[29] Bromley (1692), 52.
[30] Brown (1864), vol. 11, no. 213; vol. 12, no. 786; vol. 14, no. 665.
[31] Moryson (1617), 171.
[32] Wotton (1907), 327, 399.
[33] Coryat (1611), 102.
[34] Brown (1864), vol. 12, no. 125.
[35] Hervey (1921), 76.

papers refer much less to Milan. All the same, it took time for travellers to adapt themselves to the new climate, and in any case the Inquisition remained a presence in the city. In 1646, Evelyn noted that the English were known to visit Milan but rarely, 'for fear of the Inquisition', while some of his fellow-travellers '(in dread of the Inquisition, severer here than in any place of all Spain) thought of throwing away some Protestant (by them called Heretical) books and papers'. Evelyn himself was bold enough to enter the palace of the governor, 'tempted by the glorious tapestries and pictures', but left hurriedly when he was taken for a spy.[36]

Despite the dangers, Milan made a positive impression on most of our travellers, and the reasons for this tell us something about English cities as well as about the manner in which cities were perceived at this time. Morison, for example, noted that 'the streets are broad.' Coryat mentioned the population (300,000, certainly an exaggeration) and the importance of handicrafts (a point also made by Veryard nearly a century later).[37] Ray also recorded the figure of 300,000, 'but I believe they who report it, speak by guess and at random.' What impressed him was the cheapness of 'all provisions for the belly'. Veryard too noted the plenty of provisions, while Raymond thought it 'worth a day's journey only to see the market of Milan'. Bromley also noted the population ('300,000 souls') and also the 'many gardens'.[38] Evelyn thought it 'one of the princeliest cities in Europe' and was impressed by the 'stately wall' and the number of 'rich coaches' in the streets. Raymond noted the 'more than common breadth' of those streets, and Burnet 'the surprising riches of the churches and convents'. Berkeley commented on the size of the city ('above 500 thousand', a wild overestimate), and on the fact that 'there is no man can go armed with as much as a poiniard or knife in this town.'[39] Raymond and Addison were impressed by the 'Colonna infame' (later made famous by the novelist Alessandro Manzoni), the pillar erected in dishonourable memory of a barber accused of spreading the plague of 1630.

As recommended in the treatises on the art of travel, including

---

[36] Evelyn (1955), vol. 2, 491, 494, 507.
[37] Veryard (1701), 116.
[38] Bromley (1692), 64.
[39] Sloane 682, f. 11 verso (British Library, Dept of MSS).

Bacon's essay on the subject, churches, fortifications, hospitals
and libraries occupy most of the space in British accounts of
Milan.

The sheer number of churches in the city impressed more than
one visitor, 'near 100' according to Evelyn, '200' according to
Bromley, and '238' according to Ray, while Raymond asserted
that 'the great number of churches' was one reason for the nickname 'Milan the Great'. Almost everyone who visited Milan had
something to say about the cathedral or Duomo, a medieval
structure to which important additions were made in the early
seventeenth century. What is interesting to note is the variety of
reactions to the Gothic architecture, which was not condemned
as universally as one might have imagined. Coryat, for instance,
found the cathedral 'exceedingly glorious and beautiful'.
Raymond called it 'the most like ours' of the churches he saw in
Italy, possibly expressing homesickness but also giving us a valuable hint of the cultural distance between some British observers
and the architecture of the baroque. In similar fashion, Lassels
described the Duomo as built 'like our old cathedrals with aisles
and huge pillars'.[40] Evelyn praised the marble portico and the
exterior of the Duomo with '4000 statues all of white marble',
while he found the cupola 'unfortunate in nothing but the Gothic
design' (he was, incidentally, the first recorded Englishman to use
the term 'Gothic' to refer to architecture).[41] Ray considered the
cathedral, next to St Peter's, 'the greatest, most sumptuous and
stately pile of building in Italy'.[42] Pseudo-Bromley thought it 'one
of the handsomest and largest churches I had seen'. Acton was
still more enthusiastic. 'The Duomo or cathedral church is the
finest fabric in Milan, and if one had a month to spend there, one
might see it every day and yet find something to please one's
curiosity, that one had not seen or at least taken notice of
before.'[43] Veryard thought it 'a stately pile of old Gothish work'.
The only dissentient voices were those of Burnet and Addison.
For Burnet, 'The Dome hath nothing to commend it of architecture, it being built in the rude Gothic manner.' As for Addison,
he records his disappointment on entering 'the great church that I

---

[40] Lassels (1654), 164.
[41] Evelyn (1955), vol. 2, 493; cf. Frankl (1960), 356ff.
[42] Ray (1673), 243.
[43] Acton (1691), 73.

had heard so much of', a 'vast Gothic pile' of marble, but the interior 'smutted with dust and the smoke of lamps'.[44]

After the churches, the fortifications. Not the city walls, though they too were considered impressive, but the Castello Sforzesco, not (as for tourists today) as a monument of the Renaissance, but as a functioning fortress and a reminder of Spanish power. Some visitors did not try to enter. Morison decided not to visit the Castello 'lest I should rashly expose myself to great danger'. Mundy 'passed by the Castle, accounted one of the strongest in Christendom'. Ray used a similar formula, 'esteemed one of the principal fortresses of Europe'. So did Evelyn, who commented that 'for its strength, works, and munition of all kinds, the whole world shows none like it.' Coryat called it 'the fairest without any comparison that ever I saw'; 'it seemeth rather a town than a citadel.' For Lassels it was 'one of the best in Europe'. Raymond called it 'the fairest, the strongest fortification or citadel in Europe', adding that 'they are very cautelous in letting strangers to see it.' Bromley managed with 'some difficulty' to enter the Castello, although his party was 'strictly examined' because they were suspected of being French in the age of Louis XIV's conflicts with Spain. Acton described the Castello in loving technical detail. 'It is a very regular Hexagon with half moons; it is esteemed one of the completest pieces of fortification in all Italy, and of great strength, upon every one of the bastions is planted twelve pieces of cannon.' Addison, on the other hand, dismissed it in a sentence. 'The citadel of Milan is thought a strong fort in Italy.'

After the fortifications, the hospital. Coryat called it 'very magnificent' and noted that it could relieve four thousand people. Evelyn thought it 'of a vast compass' and 'in earnest a royal fabric', a formula which was echoed again and again, making one suspect that it was used by professional guides. For Raymond, it was 'fitter to be the court of some kings than to keep almsmen in'. Lassels called it 'the rare hospital surpassing in beauty the best king's house I have yet seen', adding with his usual humour that 'it would almost make a man wish to be sick a while therein.' For Ray, it was 'more like a stately cloister or Prince's Palace than a hospital'. For Burnet, it was 'a royal building', for Bromley 'very stately', its apartments 'very commodious'.

---

[44] Addison (1705), 367.

Pseudo-Bromley found it 'so large that . . . I concluded at my first entrance I was in the palace of some prince.' Acton considered it 'well worth taking notice of', though Addison did not notice it at all.

Views of the Ambrosiana

Cabinets of curiosities were among the sights recommended to intending travellers. Milan was the site of one of the most famous of such cabinets, the museum of Canon Manfredo Settala.[45] It attracted the attention of Evelyn, Acton (who most admired what he called 'three large Unicorns horns'), and especially Ray, who was also impressed by the 'rhinoceros horns' as well as the flies in amber, 'pictures made of feathers by the Indians', and machines 'counterfeiting a perpetual motion'.

However, Settala's museum was overshadowed by the great new library of Milan, founded by Federigo Borromeo and named in honour of Carlo Borromeo's hero, St Ambrose. It already attracted the attention of Coryat in 1608, when it was 'not fully finished, so that there is not one book in it'. As in the case of the rest of the city, or indeed the rest of Italy, travellers tended to make the same kind of comment about the library, whether or not they had consulted the description published by Pietro Paolo Boscha, *De origine et statu bibliothecae ambrosianae* (1672). For this reason it is convenient to summarize their remarks topic by topic.

In the first place – and for the majority of visitors this was indeed the most important aspect of the Ambrosiana – the building and the decoration. Evelyn noted that a 'vast sum' had been spent on the construction. Ray and Skippon called it 'a handsome building' and 'a fair building' respectively. Burnet thought it 'a very noble room'. Almost equally impressive were the 'curiosities' (Evelyn), 'curious pictures' (Skippon) or 'many choice pieces' (Veryard) in the picture gallery attached to the library. The 'portraits of divers learned men' in the reading room also attracted attention, though not always favourably. Lassels, for instance, described the series as 'a thing of more cost than profit, seeing with that cost many more books might have been bought' (a few

---

[45] Impey and Macgregor (1985).

years earlier he had been more complimentary).[46] Burnet jumped to the conclusion that 'their libraries ... all Italy over are scandalous things, the room is often fine and richly adorned, but the books are few, ill bound and worse chosen.' Bromley, more empirically, complained of the lack of books in the libraries of Venice, Mantua and Naples. Whether or not he had been reading his predecessors, Addison made a similar comment, which he turned into a general critique of Italian culture, 'the Italian Genius' as he called it. 'I saw the Ambrosiana Library, where, to show the Italian Genius, they have spent more money on Pictures than on Books ... Books are indeed the least part of the Furniture that one ordinarily goes to see in an Italian Library, which they generally set off with Pictures, Statues and other ornaments.' The comment (like Ray's thirty years earlier, quoted above) is a relatively early example of the northern European propensity to see Italy, and the south in general, as a land of façades.

We come at last to impressions of the books and manuscripts. The figure of 40,000 items, mentioned in a guidebook of 1628, was echoed by visitors for the rest of the century (despite more than seventy years of new accessions), until pseudo-Bromley updated it to 50,500. Travellers were equally fond of repeating the story that a king of England, sometimes identified as James I, had offered a vast sum for the Leonardo manuscript, a story which can be traced back to a notice on the library wall.

The collection was condemned by Burnet because it 'is too full of School-men and Canonists, which are the chief studies of Italy, and it hath too few books of a more solid and useful learning.' Skippon noted the detail of the 'wire lattices' in front of the books, 'which the library-keeper opens as there is occasion'. As a Protestant, he found two Catholic features of the library exotic enough to be worthy of note. In the first place, the notice excommunicating anyone who removed books from the library, a document he found so remarkable that he transcribed it in his text. In the second place, ecclesiastical censorship. 'We looked into Gesnerus his works, printed at Frankfurt, and observed on the top of the title page, *Damnati Authoris, etc*, was written; and all those notes which Gesner calls superstitious and magical were blotted out.'

[46] Lassels (1670); Lassels (1654), 164; Veryard (1701), 115.

A more positive feature of the Ambrosiana also surprised British and other foreign visitors. Ray noted that the library was 'free for all persons, as well strangers as citizens, to enter into and make use of'. Skippon added the vivid detail that books will be delivered to 'any one that will study here, who must then sit down in a chair on one side of the room'. Lassels waxed enthusiastic. 'The Bibliotheca Ambrosiana is one of the best libraries in Italy, because it is not so coy as the others, which scarce let themselves be seen; whereas this opens its doors publicly to all comers and goers, and suffers them to read what book they please.' Even the grudging Burnet produced a sentence of pure praise. 'One part of the disposition of the room was pleasant, there is a great number of chairs placed all round it at a competent distance from one another, and to every chair there belongs a desk with an escritoire that hath pen, inks and paper in it, so that every man finds tools here for such extracts as he would make.' It is clear that our travellers did not expect a major library to be truly accessible. In Oxford, foreigners could not take notes on books in the Bodleian Library unless they were supervised by a graduate of the university. In London, the famous Reading Room of the British Museum, complete with desks and pens, did not open until the middle of the nineteenth century. For once, the upside-down world proved to have its advantages.

7

Public and Private Spheres in Late Renaissance Genoa

Urban historians and urban sociologists used to concentrate their attention on the economy of cities, their social structure and their politics, but in the last generation they have become increasingly concerned with what has been termed 'the city as artefact', including the history of urban space. What he calls 'the fall of public man', and its complementary opposite, the increasing value attributed to private life, have been studied by the American sociologist Richard Sennett in spatial terms. Sennett describes the social and political 'theatre' of Paris and London and its setting, the public squares, from which trading and popular entertainment were banned from the late seventeenth to the early eighteenth century, and other places, from theatres to parks, where strangers might meet. In the nineteenth century, he argues, the rise of the bourgeoisie led to a withdrawal into domestic space and private affairs.[1] His book is a fascinating one, but its central argument can be challenged. How, for example, is it related to the famous thesis of Jürgen Habermas about the rise of the 'public sphere' in the same cities and the same period? Habermas too looks at spaces, the public spaces of coffee-houses and the semi-public spaces of clubs.[2] Again, if the argument is supposed to apply to Western society in general, Sennett's chronology is somewhat problematic, as the example of Renaissance serves to demonstrate. Studies of Florence and

[1] Sennett (1977).
[2] Habermas (1962); cf. Brewer (1995), 341–5.

Venice have linked the history of public life to that of public space, especially the space of the piazza. In Florence, government buildings were supposed to be treated as 'sacred places', and gambling, drinking and whoring in the vicinity was forbidden. In this way the Florentines constructed what has been called 'worshipful space'.[3]

In Venice, Piazza San Marco was at once the sacred centre and the civic centre. The church was the Doge's chapel, while his palace was the setting for meetings of the senate and the great council. The theatrical appearance of Piazza San Marco and the adjoining piazzetta has often been noted, especially as viewed from the balcony of the Doge's Palace, with the Doge himself in his 'box' overlooking events. The piazza was redesigned in the early sixteenth century, by a leading architect, Jacopo Sansovino, at the initiative of Doge Andrea Gritti. Shops and stalls were cleared away from Piazza San Marco, a library built and a loggetta added to the base of the Campanile. As important as the buildings themselves was the reconstruction of the public space which they enclosed. One of the purposes of this reconstruction was to create a more appropriate setting for public rituals, rituals which were of particular importance in what has been called the 'republic of processions'.[4]

The implication of these studies of Florence and Venice is that the heyday of 'public man' was the fifteenth century in the first case and the sixteenth century in the second, the 'fall' occurring with the end of the Florentine republic in 1530 and with the less dramatic, more gradual decline of Venice in the seventeenth century. The case of Genoa is rather different. Here it might be suggested that public man did not fall because he never rose; or to use the language current in Renaissance studies, because the 'civic humanism' so important in the history of Florence and Venice was lacking.[5] The point of this chapter is to argue that there was a civic humanist movement in Genoa, although it arrived relatively late and was never very strong. The writings of these civic humanists have something important to tell us about perceptions of the public sphere and of public space in the late Renaissance.

Genoa is the Cinderella of Italian Renaissance studies, gener-

[3] Trexler (1980), 47–54.
[4] Tafuri (1969); Howard (1975), 13ff.; Muir (1981), ch. 5.
[5] On the idea of civic humanism, Baron (1955).

ally neglected. Up to a point this neglect is almost justified, in the sense that in the early Renaissance and even in the High Renaissance, the Genoese did not make the contribution one might have expected from a northern Italian city of this size (about 85,000 people).[6] In a study of Italy in the fifteenth and early sixteenth centuries I have discussed the local origins of 600 Italian artists, writers and scholars. Tuscany, with 10 per cent of the total population, provided 26 per cent of this 'creative elite', but Liguria, with 5 per cent of the population, provided only 1 per cent. The only Genoese humanist of this period reasonably well known today is Bartolommeo Fazio. We remember Federico and Ottaviano Fregoso only because Castiglione gave them speaking parts in his *Courtier*. Even the patronage of art and humanism seems to have lacked the importance it possessed in Milan, let alone Venice or Florence.

Historians, notably Roberto Lopez, himself Genoese by birth, have offered various explanations for the lack of Genoese participation in the Renaissance.[7] To my mind one of the most convincing is the lack of civic patronage, linked in turn to lack of civic or public spirit. Compared with Florence and Venice the Genoese state was weak, unable to tame the magnates. Genoa was a classic case of 'private affluence and public squalor', to quote John Kenneth Galbraith's famous phrase describing the United States in the 1950s – still more true today.[8] As Galbraith was doubtless aware, he was repeating the ancient historian Sallust's verdict on Rome. Sallust's words were *publice egestas, privatim opulentia*. An anonymous sixteenth-century dialogue on Genoese affairs made a similar point in its discussion of the physical spaces of the city, the foreigner admiring the 'superb palaces' and the 'charming gardens', while the native points out that the streets by contrast are 'narrow and twisted'.[9]

The point was that in Renaissance Genoa the magnates still ruled. The great families or clans (*alberghi*) had private armies and private prisons.[10] As in Florence, the members of a particular family tended to live in the same quarter of the city, and they sometimes 'privatized' some of its public spaces. Piazza San

[6] Heers (1961).
[7] Lopez (1952).
[8] Galbraith (1958), 211.
[9] 'Genovese e Romano' (attributed to Leonardo Lomellini, Paris, Bibliothèque Nationale, MSS ital. 751, f. 2).
[10] Heers (1961).

Matteo, for example, was effectively the territory of the Doria clan. As late as 1565 Piazza San Luca was in dispute between the Spinola and the Grimaldi, each clan claiming the right to celebrate St John's Eve with a bonfire in the square.[11]

The patricians' sense that public spaces were really their territory is vividly illustrated in the journal kept by one of them, Giulio Pallavicino, between 1583 and 1589. At one point he describes how an aristocratic youth club of which he was a member, the Giovani di San Siro, commandeered the Strada Nuova and organized tournaments in fancy dress. On a more everyday occasion, Pallavicino records the reaction of a patrician who was bumped by a man with a mule passing in the street. 'You didn't notice me [Tu non mi vedi],' he complained (one can imagine his tone). 'Neither did you [E voi non vi vedete],' came the cheeky answer. The patrician ordered his servant to beat up the muleteer (*dargli delle bastonate*). In similar fashion, Pallavicino himself felt on another occasion that his personal space had been invaded by a commoner (*un certo forfante*). His reaction too was the apparently formulaic complaint *non mi vedi*. When the other did not reply or at least not audibly, Pallavicino gave him *un buon schiaffo*. When the man responded, he received a stab in the back, *una pugnalata nelli schiene*.[12] One is reminded of colonial cities in which whites expected blacks to step into the road to let them pass. The point is not that this virtual claim to own the city was unique to the patricians of Genoa, for there are parallels in Venice, Rome and elsewhere. However, this territorial imperative was even stronger or at least better documented in Genoa.

The grasp on the city of the patricians, or more exactly of a minority of patricians, tightened in the course of the sixteenth century. The crucial date is 1528, when Andrea Doria, who had served François I, changed sides and made a pact with Charles V. As his supporters put it, Doria 'liberated' Genoa, to rule it for more than thirty years. The century following 1528 was the century of what might be called the 'Spanish connection', in which Genoese patricians established themselves in Seville, supplied galleys to the Spanish navy, and above all lent money to the Spanish Habsburgs. Genoa had been a satellite of Milan and of France. Now it had become a satellite of Spain. One might speak of the

---

[11] Grendi (1987), 85.
[12] Pallavicino (1975), 6, 73.

Genoese 'military-financial complex' in the sense that the same families (Grimaldi, Pallavicino, Spinola, etc.) were involved in both the military and the financial operations. The military success of Ambrogio Spinola, who commanded the Spanish army in the Low Countries in the early seventeenth century, was due in part to the fact that he paid his troops regularly, and he was able to do so by spending his own money.

The years after 1528 ('28', as the Genoese called it) were marked by cultural changes as well as economic and political ones. The Venetian Renaissance is sometimes described as 'retarded', but the Genoese entered the field still later. Conspicuous consumption on art and architecture began in the age of the Spanish connection. The commune built a palace for Andrea Doria on Piazza San Matteo, while Andrea built himself a magnificent villa at Fassolo.[13] The decoration of the Palazzo Doria by Raphael's pupil Perino del Vaga was praised by no less a critic than Michelangelo.

However, the true turning-point came in the 1550s, with the construction of Strada Nuova, a street of palaces belonging to the great financial dynasties.[14] According to the Englishman Richard Lassels, the Strada Nuova 'surpasseth in beauty and building all the streets of Europe that ever I saw anywhere, and if it did but hold out at the same rate a little longer it might be called the queen street of the world.'[15] The street is now known as Via Garibaldi but the palaces still exist, appropriately enough owned by financial organizations like the Banca d'America e d'Italia. The same families built splendid villas for themselves outside the city.[16] As for painting, it was in the 1550s that the first important Renaissance artist who was Genoese by birth began his work: Luca Cambiaso, a follower of Giulio Romano. A concern was shown for vernacular literature. The poet Torquato Tasso was invited to lecture in Genoa, and local patricians published poems, particularly in the circle of the academy of the Addormentati, first recorded around 1563.

There was also a rise of political literature (in print and manuscript), from 1559, when the humanist lawyer Oberto Foglietta published his *Repubblica di Genova*, to the early 1620s, when

[13] Grendi (1987), 139–72.
[14] Poleggi (1968).
[15] Lassels (1654), 156.
[16] Poleggi (1969).

Ansaldo Cebà published his plays. This literature deserves a larger place in the history of political thought than it has so far been given outside Genoa.[17] Political thought is too often identified with political 'theory' in the strict sense of the term. For a 'total history' of political thought historians need to spread their nets more widely.

Generally speaking, what is published is the most important, but it might be argued that in late Renaissance Genoa things were the other way round. What was published was usually (though not always) anodyne. On the other hand, criticisms of the government circulated in manuscript, sometimes in multiple copies, a kind of *samizdat*. The works were usually anonymous. Some took the form of humanist dialogues in the manner of Lucian, with titles such as 'The Dream' or the 'Dialogues of Charon'.[18] Others took the form of *Relationi*, the genre pioneered by the Venetian ambassadors but widely imitated elsewhere, sometimes by satirists describing their own cities as if from outside.[19] One, the *Discordie*, is a work of history reminiscent of Sallust's *Conspiracy of Catiline*, stressing the evils of faction and offering a sophisticated analysis in terms of *interessi* and *contrapeso*.[20]

The language of more than one text is reminiscent of Machiavelli, applying his ideas to the analysis of Genoa and its factions, and one dialogue mentions him by name.[21] One of the few printed texts is in verse, a series of sonnets in dialect, describing the Roman Republic, 'Quell' antiga Repubrica Romanna', but obviously thinking of the present. Some of these texts were printed in the nineteenth and twentieth centuries, but others remain in manuscript in Genoese archives and libraries. They deserve a more detailed analysis from the point of view of historians of political thought than they have received so far. In any case, they form the basis for this chapter.

---

[17] Costantini (1978), ch. 7; cf. Savelli (1981), 40ff., on the *Sogno*.

[18] 'Dialoghi di Caronte', Archivo Storico del Comune di Genova (henceforward ASCG), MS 164; 'Sogno', ASCG, fondo Brignole Sale, 104 A21.

[19] Goffredo Lomellino, 'Relatione della repubblica di Genova' (1575), ASCG, MS 120; 'Relazione dello stato politico ed economico della serenissima repubblica di Genova' (1597), Genoa, University Library, MS B. VI. 23; [Giacomo Mancini], 'Relazione di Genova' (1626), Florence, Biblioteca Nazionale, fondo G. Capponi, vol. 81, no. 4.

[20] Lercari (1579).

[21] Lercari (1579); [Mancini], 'Relazione di Genova'; 'Dialoghi di Caronte', f. 9 verso.

This political literature contrasts with what was produced in the sister republic of Venice, a series of eulogies of the system which historians now describe as 'the myth of Venice'.[22] There was no 'myth of Genoa', but the opposite, an anti-myth. The Genoese patricians were constantly criticizing their political system. In this political literature there were three main themes.

The first theme was the conflict between the 'old' noble families and the new, the *vecchi* and the *nuovi*. It was the *vecchi* who were becoming rich from banking and who were building palaces in the Strada Nuova. But there were only about 700 male *vecchi* by the middle of the century, compared to some 1,400 *nuovi*. The *vecchi* believed that there should be parity between the two groups, as was decreed in 1547. The *nuovi* continued to argue that there should be equal access to office on an individual basis. Two rival concepts of equality, one might say. The conflict was aggravated by the fact that the old nobles, female as well as male, excluded the new from social intercourse (*conversazioni famigliari*). As in Naples, the nobles had the custom of meeting regularly in certain loggias or porticos to discuss politics and other subjects. The action of the *vecchi* forced the *nuovi* to create their own meeting place in another part of the city.[23]

The conflict between old and new boiled up in 1575, when the young men of the *nuovi* organized a carnival tournament in Piazza Ponticello, a 'popular' quarter, thus expressing in one dramatic gesture their claim to parity with the *vecchi* and their link to the *popolari*. The *vecchi* reacted with scorn and satire, referring to the recent trading origins of their rivals. This acting out of social hostilities in the piazza is reminiscent of the urban carnival staged five years later, in Romans (a small town in Dauphiné), and made famous a few years ago by Emmanuel Le Roy Ladurie.[24]

In the case of Genoa, there was nearly a civil war. Barricades were erected in the streets and the *vecchi* called their rural vassals to arms. All the same, they were forced to concede the official abolition of the distinction between old and new.[25] The humanist Oberto Foglietta, who had been exiled for criticizing the *vecchi* in

[22] Gaeta (1961); Haitsma Mulier (1980).
[23] Lercari (1579), 16; cf. Lomellino, 'Relatione', 130–1; 'Relazione dello stato politico'.
[24] Le Roy Ladurie (1979).
[25] Costantini (1978), 101–22; Savelli (1981), ch. 1.

print (in a book published in Rome in 1559), and for daring to suggest that more *popolari* should be allowed into the patriciate, was not only allowed to return but also appointed official historian of the city.[26]

The second major political theme was the fear of Spain, connected to the first theme because the *vecchi* were more involved with Spain than the *nuovi*. Indeed, in '75 (as the Genoese called it) there was a rumour that the *vecchi* wanted to hand the city over to Spain.[27] The Spaniards hated the economic dominance of the Genoese, commemorated in Quevedo's bitter poem *Don Dinero*.

> Nace en las Indias honrada
> Donde el mundo le acompaña,
> Vien a morir en España
> Y es en Génoa enterrada.

For their part, the Genoese, or some of them, feared the political dominance of the Spaniards. They were afraid that the Spanish Empire might swallow them up. The threat gave some of them what has been described as a 'siege mentality'.[28] A dialogue of *c*.1574 presents the Duke of Alba in conversation with Philip II about the possibility of taking over Genoa. Alba warns the king of the difficulties, and suggests that it would be cheaper to make use of Genoa while allowing it independence. Philip on the other hand argues that a takeover would be easy because the Genoese are more concerned with private than with public affairs, loving *il ben proprio* more than *libertà*.[29] Spanish mediation was important in the peace of 1576. In the 1580s there was another dispute with Spain because the Spaniards refused to give the republic the title of Serenissima. The opponents of Spain saw themselves as 'lovers of liberty'.[30]

The third major theme in this literature, and the one at the centre of this contribution, is that of civic spirit. I want to suggest that the threat from Spain (present from 1528 but apparently most acute from the 1570s to the 1620s) awakened the civic

---

[26] Foglietta (1559); cf. Costantini (1978), 66ff.
[27] [Mancini], 'Relazione di Genova', ch. 10.
[28] Spinola (1981), 43; cf. ibid., 87, 98, 100, 114, 189.
[29] 'Dialogo', Florence, Biblioteca Nazionale, fondo Capponi, 109.c.6.
[30] Pallavicino (1975), 158, 192.

consciousness or civic patriotism of some Genoese patricians in much the same way that, according to Hans Baron, the threat from Milan had encouraged the rise of Florentine 'civic humanism' nearly 200 years earlier. Indeed, the phrase 'civic humanism' itself seems appropriate in at least two cases, since the thought of Ansaldo Cebà and his friend Andrea Spinola was nourished by the classics, notably (as one might expect by the early seventeenth century) Seneca and Tacitus.[31]

Unlike Florence according to Baron, however, the rise of civic patriotism appears to have been a reaction not only to a political threat but also to an economic one, the rise of luxury. What was perceived as the rise of *fasto, splendore, grandezza, lusso* – or as we might say, following Veblen, 'conspicuous consumption' – became a serious preoccupation in Genoa from the middle of the sixteenth century onwards (in Florence, Guicciardini had already shown a similar preoccupation in his *Discorso di Logrogno* early in the century).[32] The magnificence of certain individuals was criticized as a threat to civic liberty, notably in the play by Paolo Foglietta (Oberto's brother), *Il Barro*. Among the individuals criticized by name at this time was Doge Gianbattista Lercari, for instance, whose quasi-regal manner gave offence, and the Prince of Salerno, who was nicknamed *il monarca*. A text of 1575 (attributed to Gioffredo Lomellino, a noble who made an epitome of one of the moral works of Seneca) notes that 'splendour has increased, and expensive buildings, clothes and luxurious foods have been introduced into Genoa,' and relates this to a withdrawal from public affairs by the *vecchi*, who preferred *la grandezza privata* to the public good.[33] A text of 1579 claims that the *vecchi*, richer than ever before, had been abandoning their civic lifestyle (*modi civili*), 'building sumptuous palaces with royal ornaments and living in the houses with unprecedented splendour and grandeur, much in excess of civic moderation [*la modestia civile*]'. A dialogue of 1583 refers to the 'proud palaces, that look more like the habitations of princes than of private individuals'.[34]

There is a hint that this trend exemplified not only the moral corruption which follows enrichment but was an attempt on the

[31] Burke (1991).
[32] Pocock (1975), 135–6.
[33] Lomellino, 'Relatione', 173–6.
[34] Lercari (1579), 17; Paschetti (1583), 6.

part of the old families to differentiate themselves from the new nobles. In similar fashion, it was said that the old families called themselves *vecchi* and used double-barrelled names 'to reveal the difference' (*far palese la differenza*) between themselves and the *nuovi*. These people seem to have known their Bourdieu as well as their Veblen.[35]

The most elaborate and thoughtful expressions of civic values in this period of crisis came in the early seventeenth century. They were the work of two friends, both minor patricians and both members of the academy of the Addormentati. Ansaldo Cebà (*c.*1565–1623) has a secure though small place in histories of Italian literature. He studied with Sperone Speroni in Padua, was a friend of the poet Gabriele Chiabrera, and himself wrote an epic, *La reina Esther* (1615), and a number of plays. *Esther* concentrates on the theme of liberation, and its aim (according to the preface) was to kindle the love of great enterprises in the hearts of readers. The tragedy *Alcippo* (1622) is equally political, concerned as it is with a noble Spartan who is accused of 'royal pride' (like Doge Lercari) and of hostility to the free city, though his defenders describe him as a man of modest habits. In a letter to his friend Gioffredo Lomellino, Cebà argues that the family of a senator should live with more modesty than a lesser noble, and that the senator himself should be a champion of liberty and strive for constancy of mind in times of adversity.[36] Even more important for the purposes of this chapter is Cebà's treatise *Il cittadino di repubblica* (1617).[37] Much of this treatise is conventional or anodyne enough, but not all of it. Written for young men in a free city, and making regular reference to Plutarch, Sallust and Seneca, *Il cittadino* recommends its readers to study Tacitus, and to be suspicious of both authority and luxury.[38] What is needed, according to Cebà, is 'civic discipline' (*disciplina civile*), to be encouraged by meditating on the continence of Scipio (who figures in the same author's *Silandra*) and the self-denial of Cato the Censor.[39] Similar attitudes to the control of the passions are expressed in his *Esther*.

Andrea Spinola (1562–1631), on the other hand, did not

---

[35] Lercari (1579), 17; [Mancini], 'Relazione di Genova', ch. 8.
[36] Cebà (1623), 49ff.
[37] Cebà (1617). On him, Costantini et al. (1976), 75–114.
[38] Cebà (1617), 35.
[39] Cebà (1617), 69.

publish his reflections and was virtually forgotten even in Genoa until a few years ago. Although a Spinola, he was comfortably off rather than rich.[40] He made himself a spokesman for the interests of the second-class patricians, and was once reprimanded, in 1616, for speaking too freely, and once imprisoned, three years later, for criticizing his colleagues in office. Spinola's nickname was *il filosofo*. He wrote down his thoughts in a text variously known as his *Capricci*, his *Dizionario*, or his *Ricordi politici*, consisting of thoughts arranged in alphabetical order on such themes as 'Corruption', 'Discipline' and 'Equality'. The text was a kind of political commonplace book.[41]

This text shows that Spinola was a civic humanist whose points of reference included Juvenal, Sallust, Seneca and Tacitus.[42] What Spinola opposed was corruption, luxury and tyranny. For example, he criticized the 'ridiculous ceremonial' associated with 'despots' such as the King of Spain, and now appropriated by Genoese doges and even ordinary citizens.[43] He was also against the acceptance of places in Spanish military orders (*habiti e croci*), which made free citizens into slaves. Spinola also criticized the magnificence of recent funerals (if they were really necessary, he remarks, the poor could not afford to die).[44] He rejected the word 'palace' and the habit of living in grand houses on the grounds that this lifestyle gave children over-ambitious ideas (*opinioni vane*).[45] He regarded the new fashion for carriages as a 'mad' form of luxury.[46] Just as he criticized private luxury, he condemned 'public poverty'.[47]

What Spinola passionately supported was republican liberty and equality ('l'egualità civile') and the tradition of a simple, thrifty life ('l'antico severità del vivere parco'). 'Equality' is a term which echoes through his writings.[48] The models he held up

[40] Bitossi, (1976) 158n.
[41] The MSS quoted here are ASCG, fondo Brignole Sale, 106 B3 and 106 B11–12 (henceforth B3 and B11–12). On the author, Fenzi (1966); Bitossi (1976).
[42] On Juvenal, B11–12, s.v. 'Educatione'; on Sallust, Spinola (1981), 102, 187; on Seneca, ibid., 102, 201, 204, 248, 256, 265, 292; on Tacitus, ibid., 79, 84–6, 101–2, 121, 139, 165, 167, 195, 204, 259, 260.
[43] B11–12, s.v. 'Cerimoniale'.
[44] B11–12, s.v. 'Essequie private'.
[45] B11–12, s.v. 'Palazzi di cittadini'.
[46] B11–12, s.v. 'Carrozze'.
[47] On luxury, Spinola (1981), 97, 100, 187, 252ff.; on public poverty, 97.
[48] Bitossi (1976), 98–9, 102, 187; B11–12, s.v. 'Egualità civile'.

to his fellow Genoese were ancient Rome, ancient Sparta and modern Switzerland, which might be rough but which preserved the customs of free men ('con qual vivere loro rozzo e parco hanno costumi proprii d'uomini liberi').[49] He even left money to the Swiss cantons.[50] In order to keep republican values alive, he recommended public lectures on ethics and politics.[51] Like Foglietta sixty years before, Spinola wanted more commoners admitted into the nobility. Unlike Pallavicino (above, p. 114), he considered that the nobles should show courtesy to commoners, returning their greetings for example.[52]

Metaphorically speaking, one might say that Spinola wanted to enlarge public space (or if you prefer, the public sphere) at the expense of the private. However, he also expressed views on public space in the literal sense of the term. For example, he complained about the lack of respect for public buildings. He suggested that the watchmen should police the Loggia di Banchi (the building where the merchants met, restructured in the late sixteenth century), in order to prevent youths sleeping there or playing football there. In other words Spinola had a sense of the sacrality of public buildings of the kind which the American historian Richard Trexler has noted in the case of Florence.[53]

More positively, Spinola suggested spending money on street cleaning, since it was indecorous as well as insanitary to allow pigs to search for food in the centre of the city.[54] Money should also be spent on the Palazzo publico, which Spinola refused to call the Doge's Palace, gilding the ceiling, laying a marble pavement and decorating the walls with pictures. This magnificence, he explained, is not vanity. 'Such decorations serve to maintain the *maestà publica*.'[55] He also recommended the erection of a marble statue in the Piazza della Signoria in honour of the local hero, Christopher Columbus.[56] Spinola was an admirer of Venice, 'the most prudent regime there has ever been in the world.'[57] There was of course a similar trend in Venice at much

[49] On Sparta, Spinola (1981), 79, 111, 232; on the Swiss, 83, 149
[50] Bitossi (1976), 151.
[51] B11–12, s.v. 'Scuole pubbliche'.
[52] B3, f. 63 verso: B11–12, s.v. 'Cavarsi di beretta'.
[53] Trexler (1980), 51–2.
[54] B11–12, s.v. 'Strade pubbliche'.
[55] B11–12, s.v. 'Palazzo pubblico'.
[56] B11–12, s.v. 'Statue'.
[57] Spinola (1981), 81, 83, 111, 122, 129, 165, 214; B11–12, s.v. 'Venetia'.

the same time, which came to a head in the movement of Renier Zen, a leading noble who became the spokesman of the poor nobles.[58] A movement which did not last.

In similar fashion, the appeal of Cebà and Spinola to traditional republican values went unheeded in Genoa. It is impossible to say how many people shared their opinions. The sixteenth-century texts quoted above show that they did not stand completely alone, and the circulation of Spinola's reflections in manuscript suggests sympathy for his ideas, but on the other hand the two friends were unable to make much impression on the system. In the next generation the greatest literary and intellectual figure was a patrician of quite another stamp, Anton Giulio Brignole Sale, yet another member of the Addormentati, who wrote against Tacitus, built a magnificent palace and had himself painted on horseback by Van Dyck before joining the Jesuits. English visitors were impressed by the 'Kingly magnificence' of the Strada Nuova and the 'Kingly luxury' of the Genoese.[59] This luxury led Joseph Addison, who visited the city at the beginning of the eighteenth century, to the Sallustian conclusion that 'as the state of Genoa is very poor, though several of its members are extremely rich, so one may observe infinitely more splendour and magnificence in particular persons' houses, than in those that belong to the public.'[60]

The traditional dominance of the private sphere – *publice egestas*, *privatim opulentia* – was too strong to break. Indeed, a seventeenth-century Genoese writer, inverting Spinola and anticipating Bernard Mandeville, argued that private vices were public benefits: 'che è danno e vizio del privato risulta in qualche maniera in grandezza e gloria del pubblico.'[61] It is no surprise to find that the mid seventeenth-century Dutch businessman and political writer Pieter de la Court, in his *Politike Weegschaal* (1661), described Genoa as 'marvellous and noteworthy' ('verwonderens en aanmerkenswaardig'), an even better model for the Dutch Republic than Venice.[62]

---

[58] Cozzi (1958), 243–88.
[59] Moryson (1617), 167; Raymond (1648), 13.
[60] Addison (1705), 363.
[61] Casoni, 'Costumi', ASCG fondo Brignole Sale, 110 E14, f. 2 recto.
[62] Quoted in Haitsma Mulier (1980), 153.

8

Learned Culture and Popular Culture in Renaissance Italy

The study of the Italian Renaissance continues to flourish. The history of popular culture continues to expand. Recent studies of popular culture have argued, reasonably enough, that it is more fruitful to study interactions between learned culture and popular culture than to attempt to define what separates them.[1] All the same, studies of the Italian Renaissance have little to say about popular culture, and studies of Italian popular culture even less to say about the Renaissance.[2] To consider whether the gap should be filled and how it might be filled is the purpose of this chapter.

It is understandable that the two cultures should have been studied separately, since a number of barriers excluded ordinary people from the world of Renaissance art and literature. In the first place, there was the barrier of language. Much of high culture was Latin culture, but the vast majority of the population did not study Latin. Ordinary people spoke their regional dialect, and outside Tuscany only the upper classes knew the reformed Tuscan which was on its way to becoming standard literary Italian. In the second place, there was the barrier of literacy. Reading and writing were skills possessed by only a minority of the population, even if that minority was a large one in the case

[1] Kaplan (1984); Chartier (1987).
[2] Burke (1972), 29–31, and Burke (1978), 271–2; cf. Cohn (1988).

of urban males. In the third place, there was the economic barrier preventing ordinary people from buying books or paintings.

However, all these obstacles could be surmounted. According to a recent history of Italian education in this period, 'almost all the vernacular schools taught the rudiments of Latin grammar.'[3] The dialect of Tuscans, especially Florentines, gave them access to the literary language. Inhabitants of large towns such as Venice, Florence, Rome and Milan had relatively easy access to schools, and also to works of art displayed in public places – frescoes in churches, statues on the piazza, and so on.

Historians of Italian culture of this period have therefore to deal with a two-way process. On one side, there is the spread of the forms and ideas of the Renaissance from the elites to the people, their social as well as their geographical diffusion. For convenience – using a simple spatial metaphor – we may call this a movement 'downward'. On the other side, there is movement 'upward', in which Italian artists and writers drew on the heritage of popular culture.

This essay will therefore be divided into two parts. All the same, it has a common theme. On both sides of the interaction, we must look not only for appropriation but also for reception and assimilation. Ariosto, for example, transformed the traditional romances of chivalry he read into something very different in tone and spirit. On the other side, Menocchio the miller, a long-forgotten figure restored to history by Carlo Ginzburg, read the *Golden Legend*, the *Travels* attributed to Sir John Mandeville, Boccaccio's *Decameron* and so on, but what he found in these texts was rather different from what was seen by the inquisitors who interrogated him.[4]

The Popularization of the Renaissance

In Italy in the sixteenth and seventeenth centuries, some ordinary people were familiar with a part of the classical tradition. For example, works by Cicero, Ovid and Virgil were translated into the vernacular at this time. The story about the Roman matron Lucretia and her suicide following her rape by King Tarquin appears to have been quite well known. A version quoting 'Livy

[3] Grendler (1988), 50.
[4] Ginzburg (1976), sections 12–14.

of Padua' as its source (though it probably drew more directly on Boccaccio) was turned into an Italian ballad which was printed in Venice by Agostino Bindoni, whose family of printers specialized in cheap popular texts.

A relatively clear-cut example of movement downwards is that of the popularization of Ariosto's *Orlando Furioso*. The poem was of course written by a noble for nobles, and in its published form it was quite expensive. However, the 'laments' of characters from the poem such as Bradamante, Isabella, Rodomonte, Ruggiero and so on, as well as other verse paraphrases, supplements and summaries, were available in chap-book form in the sixteenth century. Some of these texts were anonymous, but one – an attempt to compress the 'beauties' of the poem into sixteen pages – was the work of the Bolognese poet Giulio Cesare Croce, a well-known mediator between learned and popular culture.[5]

It cannot be assumed that these paraphrases and summaries were intended for ordinary people alone. The library of Henri III of France contained a book entitled *Bellezze del Furioso*, almost certainly selections from Ariosto. However, Ariosto's popular appeal was noted by some contemporary observers. According to the poet Bernardo Tasso, the *Furioso* was read by craftsmen and children. According to the Venetian publisher Comin dal Trino, it appealed to common people (*il volgo*).[6] Unusually for the sixteenth century, this modern text was taught in some schools alongside the Latin classics.[7] There is also evidence from the archives, mainly from heresy trials, for interest in Ariosto on the part of ordinary people. In Venice a swordsmith's apprentice, a silk merchant and a prostitute all confessed to reading *Orlando Furioso*. In Calvin's Geneva an Italian once found himself in trouble because he had described the book as his 'Bible'.[8]

Montaigne's journal of his visit to Italy offers us further evidence of Ariosto's penetration of popular culture. At a spa near Lucca, for example, he met a poor peasant woman named Divizia, who could not read or write but had often heard Ariosto read aloud in her father's house, thanks to which she had become a poet herself. Near Florence, and elsewhere in Italy, Montaigne

[5] Camporesi (1976).
[6] Quoted Javitch (1991).
[7] Grendler (1988), 298.
[8] Mackenney (1987), 184; Martin (1987); Ruggiero (1993); Monter (1969), 66.

tells us that he was surprised to meet peasants and shepherdesses who knew Ariosto by heart. In the eighteenth century, visitors to Naples sometimes described the professional storytellers who read, or more exactly performed Ariosto's poem in the streets and squares of the city, with the text at hand to assist their memory if it failed.[9]

The poems of Torquato Tasso also seem to have entered popular culture. His epic *Gerusalemme liberata* was translated into a number of dialects – Bolognese in 1628, Bergamask in 1670, Neapolitan in 1689, Venetian in 1693, and so on. Joseph Addison's *Remarks on Several Parts of Italy* (1705) noted the custom 'of the common people of this country, of singing stanzas out of Tasso', a point which would be repeated by Rousseau and Goethe in the case of the Venetian gondoliers.

One would of course like to know much more about these incidents – how faithfully the peasants, storytellers and gondoliers remembered the texts, and, still more important, what the epics of Ariosto and Tasso meant to them. My own hypothesis would be that ordinary people read or heard *Orlando Furioso* and *Gerusalemme liberata* as examples of romances of chivalry – or as they called them, 'books of battles' (*libri di battagie*) – which were widely available in chap-book form in sixteenth-century Italy and were sometimes used in elementary schools to encourage boys to learn to read. Menocchio the miller also enjoyed this kind of literature.[10]

In the case of the visual arts, the relation between learned and popular is considerably more complicated, because the 'high' art of the Italian Renaissance was generally produced by men with the training and status of craftsmen. They produced religious paintings without the opportunity to study theology, and scenes from classical mythology without being able to read Latin, let alone Greek. It follows that works like Botticelli's *Primavera*, or Titian's *Sacred and Profane Love*, which appear to refer to Neoplatonic ideas, must have been the outcome of a complex process of mediation between learned and popular culture, in which the participants included not only artists and patrons but also humanists, such as Angelo Poliziano and Marsilio Ficino, and popularizers, such as the Venetian professional writers or *poligrafi*.[11]

[9] Moore (1781), letter 60; Blunt (1823), 290.
[10] Grendler (1988); cf. Lucchi (1982); Ginzburg (1976), section 14.
[11] Panofsky (1939), 129–69; Ginzburg (1978).

Paintings of this kind, secular in subject-matter, were not widely seen during the Renaissance. They belonged to the 'private' rather than the 'public' circuit.[12] It was, however, possible for a wider public to see graphic versions of some of them, notably the engravings after Raphael by Marcantonio Raimondi. The work of art had already entered the age of mechanical reproduction. Like printing, engraving was a great popularizer, at least in the sense that it allowed many more people to see images, and probably more kinds of people as well.

Ceramics offered another means of diffusing images more widely, since the raw material was cheap. The majolica plates and jugs produced in Faenza, Urbino, Deruta and elsewhere were frequently decorated with scenes from classical mythology and ancient history. Some were based on the Raimondi engravings after Raphael. Some of these ceramics were made for wealthy patrons, but others were simple drug-pots for the shops of apothecaries.[13] The painted terracotta images produced by the Della Robbia family workshop in Florence might be regarded as the poor man's sculptures. The workshop produced some large expensive altarpieces for churches, but also small images for wayside shrines or private individuals. It would be an exaggeration to speak of 'mass-production' but signs of hasty work can be found and it is not uncommon for a particular image (an Adoration, say, or a Madonna and Child) to survive in eight, nine, ten, or even twenty almost identical copies.[14]

The problem is of course to discover how people who were not members of a cultural elite perceived these objects, and especially whether or not they were interested in the styles as well as the stories. In the case of Florence, at least, there is evidence of a sophisticated popular visual culture. Some ordinary people, craftsmen and shopkeepers, were not only familiar with the names of the leading artists of their city, past and present, but they were not afraid to offer opinions – often critical opinions – about the value of particular works. Some of the evidence for this statement comes from Vasari's *Lives of the Artists* (1550), which from time to time discusses popular reactions to particular works of art or artists. Particularly interesting in this respect is Vasari's discussion of Florentine responses to Perugino, beginning with

[12] Ginzburg (1978) 79, adapting Burke (1972), 144, 158.
[13] Rackham (1952).
[14] Marquand (1922), nos 122–42, 157–67, 302–9, 312–20.

enthusiasm and ending with satire. Vasari's testimony to popular interest in aesthetics may be supplemented by that of Antonfrancesco Grazzini, a man of the shopkeeper class (probably an apothecary), whose poems, or more exactly songs (*madrigalesse*), sometimes mention works of art. Two of these songs comment critically on Vasari's decision to paint the cupola of the cathedral of Florence, declaring 'the fault was George's' ('Giorgin fece il peccato') and that it showed 'little sense and less judgement' ('poco senno e men giudizio').

Popular Inspiration in the Renaissance

It is time to turn from the popularization of the Renaissance to the importance of 'low' elements in 'high' culture. The presiding genius over this section of the chapter is of course Mikhail Bakhtin, whose *World of Rabelais* (written in the 1930s, but not published until 1965) argued that the author of *Gargantua and Pantagruel* drew heavily on the 'culture of folk humour', in particular the grotesque and the carnivalesque.[15] This work, which is a *tour de force* of the historical imagination, has been taken as a model for recent studies of Breughel, Shakespeare and other artists and writers of the Renaissance.

The World of Rabelais has also been criticized by Renaissance specialists. On the assumption that Bakhtin claims that *Gargantua and Pantagruel* belongs wholly to popular culture, critics have pointed out that Rabelais was a learned man and that his work would not have been fully comprehensible to ordinary people.[16] Unfortunately, Bakhtin's account of the relation between 'high' and 'low' culture was neither precise nor explicit. At times the contrast or opposition with which he is concerned seems to be that between the culture of two social groups, the elite and the people. At other times the two opposed cultures are defined in functional terms as the 'official' and the 'unofficial'. These distinctions may overlap but they do not coincide. The students of Montpellier, for example, whose festivities Bakhtin describes, belonged to a social elite, but participated in unofficial culture.

Another important distinction which remains blurred in

[15] Bakhtin (1965).
[16] Screech (1979).

Bakhtin's work is that between appropriating (and transforming) elements from popular culture (which Rabelais certainly does) and participating fully in that culture. I have argued elsewhere that sixteenth-century European elites were 'bicultural'. They had a learned culture from which ordinary people were excluded, but they also participated in what we now call 'popular' culture.[17] Would these elites have participated in the same way as people for whom popular culture was all the culture they had? Or did they associate popular culture with particular times and places of relaxation? The concept of 'participation' is itself somewhat elusive. Despite these ambiguities, and the need to draw more careful distinctions, Bakhtin's study both could and should inspire future research on the various cultures and subcultures of Renaissance Italy, encouraging us to ask exactly what artists and writers took from popular traditions, as well as what they did with what they appropriated.

There have been relatively few studies of this kind. Before Bakhtin, Domenico Guerri had already examined what he called 'the popular current in the Renaissance', but he virtually limited himself to the subject of jokes and comic verses in Florence.[18] The art historian Eugenio Battisti published a wide-ranging study of what he called the 'Anti-Renaissance', a fascinating collection of essays on medieval, mannerist, grotesque, occult and other themes in art and literature. However, Battisti tried to pack too much into his category of 'anti-Renaissance'. His chapters range from self-conscious rejections of classicism to medieval survivals which might be better described as 'non-Renaissance'.[19]

In the case of art, one might begin the study of the interaction between high and low with certain grotesque or comic sculptures, already mentioned in the chapter on humour. It might be unwise to assume that whatever is comic is necessarily popular, but it is worth remembering that Aristotle – as interpreted by Italian humanists – argued that comedy was concerned with 'low' people. Take for example the statue by the sculptor Valerio Cioli representing Grand Duke Cosimo de' Medici's favourite dwarf, nicknamed 'Morgante' after the giant in Pulci's poem of that name. The statue was placed in the Boboli gardens, a place of

[17] Burke (1978), 24–9.
[18] Guerri (1931).
[19] Battisti (1962).

relaxation which has been described as a kind of sixteenth-century 'fun house'.[20] In similar fashion the famous gardens of Bomarzo, created for the Roman aristocrat Vicino Orsini, might be described as a kind of sixteenth-century Disneyland. The huge stone monsters, the leaning tower, and the hell mouth all play on a popular taste for the grotesque, whatever layers of learned meaning have been superimposed on it.[21]

The Commedia dell'Arte also deserves study from the point of view of this essay, with special reference to the fascinating and perplexing problem of the relation between the characters or masks of this apparently popular art form – the boastful soldier, the foolish old man, the cunning servant – and those of ancient Greek and Roman drama. Did the extemporizers owe their knowledge of these masks to the humanists? Or did the classical masks survive 'underground' in popular culture, to emerge in the sixteenth century, and inspire 'high' Renaissance drama?

The paragraphs which follow concentrate on literature, and especially on four writers: Boccaccio, Folengo, Ariosto and Aretino (at the expense of Burchiello, Berni, Pulci, Ruzante, Calmo and other examples of mediators between the two cultures). These four writers will be discussed in chronological order, which also happens to be a logical order, an order of increasing complexity in the relation between learned and popular culture. The increase in complexity over time is probably no accident, but the result of a process which may be described as the 'withdrawal' of elites from participation in popular culture.[22]

The obvious place to start is of course Boccaccio's *Decameron*. As in the case of Rabelais, Boccaccio is remembered today for his 'vulgarity', so that it needs to be emphasized that he too was a learned man, a university teacher who wrote treatises in Latin and lectured on Dante. His Tuscan was 'canonized' in the sixteenth century (along with Dante's and Petrarch's) as a model of pure Italian. All the same, it is clear that many of the stories in the *Decameron* were taken from popular oral tradition, from what nineteenth-century scholars called 'folktales', and also that they illustrate some of Bakhtin's favourite themes.

The place of the carnivalesque in Boccaccio's work is clear

---

[20] Barolsky (1978), 153ff.; Heikamp (1969).
[21] Battisti (1962), 125ff.; Bredekamp (1985); Lazzaro (1990).
[22] Burke (1978), 270–81.

enough, above all in the story of Frate Alberto (day 4, story 2), which ends with a ritualized hunt of the 'wild man' on Piazza San Marco in Venice.[23] A number of the stories include episodes of what Bakhtin calls 'grotesque realism' or 'degradation'. This would, for example, be a plausible way of reading the first story in the collection, the tale of the wicked notary who managed to trick posterity into venerating him as a saint. Tricks recur in Boccaccio's *novelle*, as they do in those of other storytellers of the Renaissance (such as Sacchetti, Masuccio Salernitano, Bandello, and Grazzini), who draw on the popular tradition of the *beffa* described above (chapter 5). For example, Bruno and Buffalmaco persuade the painter Calandrino, who is portrayed as a simpleton, to look for a magic stone which is supposed to make whoever carries it invisible, or they steal his pig and then 'prove' to him that he stole it himself.

The Benedictine monk Teofilo Folengo also drew on the tradition of the *beffa* in the twelfth section of his poem *Baldus*, describing a sea voyage with the owner of a flock of sheep, in which the trickster buys the ram and immediately throws it into the sea, where it is inevitably followed by the rest of the flock. Rabelais later appropriated this episode for his own purposes (in his *Fourth Book*, chapter 6). However, *Baldus*, published in 1517 under the pseudonym 'Merlin Cocaio', is essentially an example of the grotesque, a mock romance of chivalry narrated in a mock epic style. The poem tells the story of a young nobleman, a descendant of the paladin Rinaldo, who is raised among peasants but has his head as full of romances as Don Quixote's would be later in the century. Baldus, together with two companions, a giant called Fracassus and a trickster called Cingar, becomes involved in a series of comic adventures which draw on popular traditions. Bakhtin himself drew attention to the episode in which someone is resurrected from the dead by a drenching in urine.[24]

The subject of Folengo's poem is a hybrid, at once bucolic and chivalric, and the style, appropriately enough, is also hybrid. The language is a form of Latin which often behaves as if it were Italian or dialect – a mixture of two or three codes, or better, a product of their interaction.[25] In a battle scene, for example, the

[23] Mazzotti (1986).
[24] Bakhtin (1965), 150; cf. Bonora and Chiesa (1979).
[25] Cf. Borsellino (1973), 89.

rhetoric of the 'high' style, appropriate for epic encounters, is constantly pulled down to earth by the use of crudely Latinized technical terms such as *alebardae* (halberds), *banderae* (banners), *lanzae* (lances), *partesanae* (partisans), *picchiae* (pikes), *stendardi* (standards) and so on, or by words imitating the sound of drums and trumpets:

> Stendardique volant, banderae; timpana pon pon
> continuo chioccant; sonitantque tarantara trombae.

The epic begins with an invocation not to the muses, but to plump country girls, fattened on polenta and macaroni (or gnocchi). Hence the style is now known as 'macaronic' Latin. Folengo was the greatest master of this language but he was not its inventor. It was a literary elaboration of the language of notaries, who wrote it for convenience, and of students, who spoke it for fun.[26]

The first example, that of Boccaccio, shows a learned man drawing on a popular tradition in which he participated. The second, that of Folengo, is more complex, since it shows a learned man making a self-conscious synthesis of learned and popular traditions, or at least playing with the tensions between them.

The example of Ariosto is still more complicated. Like the *Baldus*, *Orlando Furioso* is a romance of chivalry, or a mock romance of chivalry – it is difficult to choose between these alternatives because Ariosto deliberately hovers on the edge of parody. The romance of chivalry was originally a high-status genre: stories about nobles, written for nobles, and in some cases (including that of Ariosto himself) written by nobles. However, as we have seen, this genre was also part of Italian popular culture in the sixteenth century. It took the form of printed chapbooks and also of oral performances by wandering singers of tales, or *cantimbanchi*, who sang or recited the stories on the piazza, asking for money at the end of each instalment, thus leaving the audience in suspense till they had made their contribution. The printed versions and the oral versions influenced each other.

Like other men of letters, Ariosto enjoyed these oral performances and his poem owes something to them.[27] For example, although he wrote to be read, the author took over some of the

[26] Paoli (1959).
[27] Bronzini (1966).

popular formulas telling the audience to listen – 'as I shall continue the story in the next canto' ('come io vi seguirò ne l'altro canto'), and so on. Ariosto thus exemplifies a complex process of reappropriation, that of an educated man borrowing and transforming popular themes which had earlier been borrowed from high culture. When the *Furioso* was itself popularized, as we have seen it was, we are confronted with a case of double reappropriation. Circularities of this kind are not unknown today. For example, a novel by the Brazilian writer Jorge Amado, *Tereza Batista* (1972), draws on a chap-book by Rodolfo Coelho Cavalcanti (these booklets were and perhaps still are circulating in the northeast of Brazil, at least in the areas most remote from towns and television). Cavalcanti drew in turn on the traditional theme of the *donzela guerreira* or warrior maiden which goes back to the romances of chivalry – and of course to Ariosto's heroine Bradamante (cf. chapter 9 below).[28]

The last example to be discussed here is that of Pietro Aretino. Aretino made his reputation in Rome as a composer of biting pasquinades.[29] The *pasquinata* was a genre on the frontier between learned and popular culture. The practice of attaching satiric verses to the mutilated classical statue on Piazza del Pasquino in Rome goes back to the later fifteenth century, and at that time the verses were in humanist Latin. In the early sixteenth century, it became common to write the verses in a vernacular which everyone could understand. Aretino went on to write *Il Marescalco*, the carnival comedy built around a *beffa* described in chapter 5 (above, p. 83).

However, the best example of the mixture or interaction of learned and popular elements in Aretino's work is surely his *Ragionamenti*, dialogues in which an old prostitute instructs a young one in the skills of the profession. The dialogues offer a series of scenes from low life in early sixteenth-century Rome, apparently faithful to the colloquial language and the slang of that social milieu. At the same time, humanist readers would have been aware that the dialogues borrow from and allude to a classical Greek text, Lucian's *Dialogues of the Courtesans*. The dialogues also may be read as a parody of Renaissance treatises on good manners, and especially of Castiglione's famous *Book of the Courtier*.

[28] Slater (1982), 146.
[29] Larivaille (1980), 47ff.

Here as elsewhere Aretino exploits the similarities between the terms *cortegiano*, 'courtier', and *cortegiana*, 'courtesan'.

Aretino was the son of a craftsman, he grew up in the world of popular culture, and to the end of his life he appreciated street singers. He was a friend of Andrea, one of the court fools to Pope Leo X. Like the painters already discussed, he lacked the opportunity for a conventional humanist education in Latin and Greek (it was presumably a more learned friend who drew Lucian to his attention). He came to high culture as an outsider and he rejected some of it as artificial and affected, notably the conventions for the Petrarchan love sonnet and the rules for spoken Italian laid down by Castiglione's friend Pietro Bembo (rules which are mocked in the *Ragionamenti*). Like his friend the artist Giulio Romano, Aretino liked to break rules. In this sense he was a self-conscious 'mannerist' or 'anti-classicist'.[30] Low culture, the culture in which he grew up, was his instrument to subvert high culture, or at least those parts of it which he disliked. One might say that he drew on the non-Renaissance for the purposes of an anti-Renaissance.

Cultural historians are surely right to shift, as they have been doing, from concern with popular culture in itself to a study of the long process of interaction between learned and popular elements. If we focus on the interaction between high and low, however, we need to recognize the variety or polymorphism of this process. The examples cited in this chapter do not exhaust the range of possibilities, but they may at least be sufficient to suggest the remarkable range of possible relationships between high and low, the uses of popular culture for Renaissance writers, the uses of the Renaissance for ordinary people, and finally, the importance of the 'circular tour' of images and themes, a circular tour in which what returns is never the same as what set out.

[30] Larivaille (1980); Borsellino (1973), 16–40.

9

Chivalry in the New World

The message of this chapter can be summed up in a sentence, almost a headline. Charlemagne is not dead: he is living in Latin America, or he was until comparatively recently. The New World came late to chivalry, since it was obviously impossible for its inhabitants to learn about this European value system and the romances which expressed it until 1492, and it may be thought that the behaviour of Cortés and Pizarro in Mexico and Peru did nothing to make the value system more intelligible to the Aztecs or the Incas. On the other hand, once the tradition had been transplanted, it was in the New World, or parts of it, that the romances of chivalry retained their appeal longest, notably in the north-east of Brazil.

At the time of the discovery of America, or to use a somewhat less ethnocentric expression, at the beginning of a series of encounters between the cultures of Europe and the cultures of America, the Renaissance movement had long been under way. However, as we have seen (above, chapter 8), the enthusiasm for classical antiquity did not drive out the love of romances of chivalry. In both the literal and the metaphorical sense these romances formed an important part of the baggage of the *conquistadores*.

In Spain in the Middle Ages, romances of chivalry were a popular oral and literary genre. Muslims as well as Christians composed, recited and read them, and a considerable number of these stories, including the usual giants, enchanted palaces,

swords with names and female warriors, survive in Spanish written in the Arabic script.[1] As in other parts of Renaissance Europe,
a number of Spanish humanists rejected the romances of chivalry
as 'foolish' or 'silly books', generations before the more affection-
ate mockery of Cervantes. In 1524, Juan Luis Vives condemned
Amadís, Lancelot and *Pierre de Provence*, and five years later,
Antonio de Guevara condemned *Amadís*.[2] Similar criticisms were
made later in the century by the humanists Pedro Mexia and
Benito Arias Montano and the preacher Luis de Granada.
Whatever Don Quixote may have been doing, Cervantes himself
was not tilting at windmills. In Spain in the first half of the sixteenth century, new romances of chivalry were published 'at an
average rate of almost one a year', while the total number of editions of such romances totalled over 150.[3] The authors included
at least one woman, the noble lady Beatriz Bernal of Valladolid,
who published two romances in 1545, *Don Cristalion* and
Lepomene.[4]

One at least of these romances is still taken seriously by literary critics, and was recently translated into English: the fifteenth-
century Catalan romance *Tirant lo Blanc*. Even the book-burners
in *Don Quixote* agreed to save it because it was, as the priest
said, 'the best book of its kind in the world', a judgement shared
by one of today's leading Latin American writers, Mário Vargas
Llosa. Even more successful in the sixteenth century were two
cycles of romances in Castilian. There was *Palmerín de Oliva*,
which began publication in 1511, and there was *Amadís de
Gaula*, first published about the year 1508. *Amadís* was not only
much reprinted but followed by a series of continuations by some
half-a-dozen authors, dealing with the adventures of the son of
Amadís, the grandson of Amadís, and so on, heroes with names
like Esplandián, Lisuarte and Amadís of Greece. By 1546 the
cycle had been extended to twelve books. These adventure stories
had a wide appeal in Renaissance Italy, in France, in England and
elsewhere.

In Spain the *aficionados* of these romances included Emperor
Charles V, the diplomat Diego Hurtado de Mendoza, and the

---

[1] Galmés de Fuentes (1967).
[2] Leonard (1949), 68–9; cf. Ife (1985).
[3] Thomas (1920), 147; Chevalier (1976), 67.
[4] Bennassar (1967), 519.

reformer Juan de Valdés.[5] Among the more famous examples of documented reader response are the testimonies of two Counter-Reformation saints who happen to have left us accounts of their lives. In his autobiography, Ignatius Loyola tells us that he was 'much given to reading the worldly and false books known as romances of chivalry' ('muy dado a leer libros mundanos y falsos que suelen llamar de cabellerías') and that before he was ordained priest, he kept vigil before the altar of Our Lady of Monsarrat because 'his head was full of ... Amadís of Gaul and similar books' ('tenía todo el entendimiento lleno de ... Amadís de Gaula y de semejantes libros').

Similarly, Teresa of Avila remarks in her memoirs that her mother was 'a fan of romances of chivalry' ('aficionada a libros de caballerías') and that she shared this enthusiasm in her youth, information which makes Beatriz Bernal's decision to write in this apparently male genre easier to understand. Research on the history of reading based on the study of library inventories confirms the impression of widespread enthusiasm for these books on the part of sixteenth-century Spaniards, merchants as well as nobles.[6] The romances were shortened and published in the form of verse chap-books or *pliegos sueltos*, which suggests that they had become part of popular culture.[7]

Like the Spaniards, Portuguese readers of the sixteenth century loved romances of chivalry, including the famous *Amadís*, which may have been originally composed in Portugal around the year 1350. Books 7, 9 and 10 of the continuation were printed in Lisbon in the sixteenth century.[8] The humanist João de Barros was not only a famous historian of the exploits of the Portuguese in Asia, but also the author of a romance, *Clarimundo* (1520), which enjoyed considerable success. The Palmerín cycle was continued by Portuguese writers such as Francisco de Morães and Diogo Fernández. When the poet Luis de Camões introduced his epic *The Lusiads* (1572) by contrasting his narrative with the 'fantastic' or 'fabulous' deeds of Roland and Roger, he could assume that his readers were familiar with these romances. One publisher of the Amadís and Palmerín cycles was Marcos Borges, who had been appointed royal printer in 1566. The king on the

[5] Leonard (1949), 19–21.
[6] Bennassar (1967), 511–19; cf. Chevalier (1976), ch. 1; Berger (1987).
[7] Norton and Wilson (1969).
[8] Anselmo (1926), nos 789, 815, 364.

throne at the time was Sebastian, who was killed at the battle of Alcazarkebir in 1578 after invading North Africa to conquer and convert the 'Moors'. Whether or not the king was a particular enthusiast for romances of chivalry, Sebastian certainly tried to behave like one of the heroes of these romances, while after his death he would be assimilated to these heroes, as we shall see.

Given this continuing interest in the genre in Spain and Portugal, it is scarcely surprising to find references to romances of chivalry early in the history of the conquest and settlement of the New World. Whether Columbus read them or not we cannot be sure, but a number of these romances could be found in the library of his son Fernando.[9] References in the letters of Cortés imply that he too was familiar with this literature.[10] By 1531 the government was worried enough by the spread of this enthusiasm to order the House of Trade at Seville to prohibit the export to the Indies of 'vain' romances such as *Amadís*.[11]

One of the most interesting pieces of evidence comes from the history of the conquest of Mexico written by Bernal Díaz del Castillo. When Díaz is describing the first sight of the Aztec capital, the city in the lake, he writes that 'we said that it was like the enchanted things related in the book of Amadís because of the huge towers, temples, and buildings rising from the water.' As in the case of the travellers discussed in chapter 6, we find life imitating art, or more exactly experience influenced by fiction. Díaz also made the revealing assumption that a reference to *Amadís* would make this exotic land seem more familiar to his readers. His aim was 'to translate ... the utterly strange into what we might call the familiarly strange'.[12]

Another interesting early piece of evidence about chivalry in the New World is a name: California. By the middle of the sixteenth century, it was already being used about the Pacific Coast of North America. However, the name was first used of a fictional island. In the romance *Esplandián*, a continuation of the Amadís story first published in 1510, we learn of a group of warlike women ruled by a certain Queen Calafia, 'mistress of the great island of California, celebrated for its great abundance of gold and jewels', an island on which men are forbidden to set

[9] Huntington (1905).
[10] Leonard (1949), 50.
[11] Sánchez (1958), 246–7.
[12] Sánchez (1958); Gilman (1960–3); Hulme (1994), 170.

foot. The queen challenges both Amadís and his son Esplandián to single combat, is vanquished, and becomes a Christian. The application of the name California to part of America suggests that other people besides Bernal Díaz and his comrades perceived the New World through spectacles coloured by romances of chivalry.

A similar point could be made about the vast region of Amazonia, which began to be explored by the Spaniards in the early 1540s. The expedition led by Francisco de Orellana is said to have given the River Amazon its present name after a fight with the local Indians in which women took active part. According to the Dominican friar Gaspar de Carvajal, who took part in this expedition, the women warriors were tall and pale, they were armed with bows and arrows, and they lived in villages of their own, subject to a female ruler called Coroni.[13]

Traditional myths or stereotypes of the so-called 'monstrous races' were thus revitalized and projected onto the New World.[14] Although the myth of the Amazons went back to classical times, as humanists well knew, it had been revived in fifteenth-century Italy. It was at this time that viragos begin to play an important role in Italian romances and that we find the topos of the maiden who will only accept as a husband a man who vanquishes her in battle, like Galiziella in the Aspramonte of Andrea da Barberino, an Amazon from the 'kingdom of women' (*regno feminino*). The figure of Marfisa in Matteo Boiardo's *Orlando Innamorato* (1483), of Bradamante in Ludovico Ariosto's still more famous *Orlando Furioso* (1516) and of Clorinda in Tasso's *Gerusalemme liberata* (1581) are the most memorable examples of this tradition.[15] It may at least be suggested – and it has indeed been suggested – that the Renaissance revival of interest in the classical tradition of the Amazons was encouraged by Columbus's report of Amazons in the Indies.[16] For Carvajal and Díaz alike, the New World seemed to be the place where European romances of chivalry came true.

The emigrants from Spain to Mexico and Peru took these romances of chivalry with them, or had them supplied by book-sellers, as has been shown by the American scholar Irving

[13] Carvajal (1955), 97, 105; cf. Sánchez (1958), 250–4.
[14] Friedman (1981), 9, 170–1, 197–207.
[15] Rajna (1872), 49–52; Tomalin (1982), 82ff.
[16] Leonard (1949), 53.

Leonard, who studied records of book shipments preserved in the archives of the House of Trade at Seville.[17] Thanks to his research, it is now known that in Mexico City in 1540, the printer Juan Cromberger had no fewer than 446 copies of *Amadís* in stock in his shop.[18] In Lima in 1583, Amadís was 'still among the favourites'.[19] In Tucumán in 1597, a provincial synod condemned the spread of 'immoral books and romances of chivalry'.[20] In 1600, 10,000 copies of the romance *Pierres y Magalona* entered Mexico.[21] Among the New World enthusiasts for these romances was the 'Inca Garcilaso', a Peruvian nobleman and historian who emigrated to Spain.[22]

At this point we are faced with a gap in the evidence. In the case of Brazil, there appear to be no sixteenth-century references to romances of chivalry. Indeed, a history of the press in Brazil remarks on the absence of books of any kind from inventories as late as the seventeenth century, in striking contrast with the Spanish viceroyalties of Mexico and Peru.[23] Books might be imported, but they were not allowed to be printed in Brazil until the early nineteenth century. All the same, it is in Brazil that we find the richest documentation for chivalry in the New World in the late nineteenth and early twentieth centuries. Charlemagne and his paladins occupied a significant place in the popular imagination.

About the year 1840, an American Protestant missionary, the Reverend Daniel Kidder, was visiting the small town of Maceió, in the north-east of Brazil, on the coast between Salvador and Recife. He entered a shop and found the shop assistant reading at the counter. 'His book', Kidder remarked, apparently with some astonishment, 'was a life of Carlos Magno.'[24] The missionary should not have been surprised, for the interest in stories about Charlemagne was in no way unusual for the region and the period.

The *História de Carlos Magno* which the shop assistant was reading is the key text in the Brazilian reception of the romances

[17] Leonard (1933).
[18] Leonard (1949), 98.
[19] Leonard (1949), 223.
[20] Leonard (1949), 88.
[21] Marín (1911), 36.
[22] Durand (1948), 263.
[23] Sodré (1966), 12.
[24] Kidder (1845), vol. 2, 96.

of chivalry. It was still being read in the twentieth century, when
the avant-garde writer Oswald de Andrade recorded his enthusiasm for the book, an enthusiasm which he shared with anarchists
and labour leaders.[25] Research on the history of this text goes
some way towards filling the gap mentioned above. In the
National Library of Lisbon there is a chap-book of 1794 with a
similar title, *Historia nova do imperador Carlos Magno e dos
doze pares de França*. It has been shown that this text was
derived from a Spanish romance of 1525, which drew in turn on
a French romance of 1486. The gap between Portugal in 1794
and Brazil in the 1870s has to be filled by conjecture, but it is
plausible enough to suggest that the Portuguese chap-book was
exported to Brazil, which as noted above relied more heavily on
Europe for books than the Spanish American colonies did.

In Brazil itself, chap-books, which used to be called *folhetos*
and are now best known as 'stories on a string', *literatura de
cordel*, began to be printed only in the later nineteenth century.
These texts are still produced in considerable numbers today. As
in the case of early modern European chap-books, they were and
are well adapted to a situation of restricted literacy. They are
generally in verse, normally what are known as *sextilhas* (six-line
stanzas with seven syllables to the line). They were (and are)
generally printed on small presses and distributed in the first
instance by the composers or *cantadores* themselves, who gave
oral performances accompanied by music in marketplaces on
market days and then sold the texts to the listeners. The text may
be regarded as a kind of souvenir of the performance, or the performance as a kind of commercial for the text. It does not matter
too much whether the buyers can read or not, for it is generally
possible for them to find someone else who will read or chant the
text to them.[26]

The repertoire of these *cantadores* was and remains varied, but
an important group of late nineteenth- and early twentieth-
century *folhetos* was derived from the romances of chivalry and
dealt with the exploits of Roland, the treason of Ganelon, and so
on.[27] For example, the first major writer of *folhetos*, Leandro
Gomes de Barros, who died in 1918, was well known for his

[25] Meyer (1993), 147–59.
[26] Arantes (1982); Slater (1982).
[27] Ferreira (1979); Peloso (1984), 62ff.

Batalha de Oliveiros com Ferrabrás. The story of Fierabras is a medieval French verse epic which was adapted into other languages such as Provençal, Spanish, English, German and Italian. Like the Spanish *conquistadores*, the poets of north-eastern Brazil appear at times to see the world through the spectacles of romances of chivalry. The famous bandit Lampião, for example, who was finally killed by the police in 1938, was described in contemporary ballads as 'worse than Robert the Devil' ('pior do que Roberto do Diabo'), a reference to a medieval French romance which was still circulating in Brazil at that point in time.[28]

Even today, a few *folhetos* dealing with subjects from romances of chivalry can still be found, as well as modern works which exploit this tradition. Jorge Amado, whose novels were sometimes inspired by the *cordel*, has created several modern Amazons with knives in their skirts, such as Rosa Palmeirão and Tereza Batista. The great classic of modern Brazilian literature, *Grande Sertão* (1956), by João Guimarães Rosa, may also be interpreted as a New World transformation of the romance of chivalry, by an author familiar from childhood with the *História de Carlos Magno*.[29] *Grande Sertão* deals with the adventures of Riobaldo and Diadorim, a pair of *jagunços*, that is, honourable men of violence who live in the backlands. The two comrades are as close as Roland and Oliver, or perhaps closer, but it is only at the end of the story, when Diadorim is killed in a shoot-out, that we learn that she was a beautiful woman in disguise, a warrior maiden (like Bradamante in Ariosto's *Orlando Furioso*), who had taken to the backlands to avenge the death of her father. An Amazon not so far from Amazonia.[30] The relation of Guimarães Rosa to popular culture was not unlike that of Ariosto. A diplomat, polymath and polyglot who was well acquainted with European literature, he had earlier practised as a doctor in the backlands of Minas Gerais. It is said that when his patients could not afford to pay him, he asked them to tell him a story instead. He was certainly an assiduous student of the local folklore, which appears in his own stories, coexisting and interacting, as in the case of Diadorim, with themes from European high culture.

[28] Peloso (1984), 75.
[29] Meyer (1993), 147–59.
[30] Rosa (1956); Meyer (1993), 147–59.

This classic novel was recently made into a film. Hence the remark at the beginning of the chapter that Charlemagne is still living in Latin America, and the decision of a recent Italian student of the *cordel* to call his book 'The Middle Ages in the Backlands'.[31]

Why have the Middle Ages survived so long in this region? There is of course a sense in which we can say that the romance of chivalry still forms part of Western culture. Children and adults still read adventure stories of different kinds, and some of these genres owe a good deal to the traditions of the medieval romance. It is commonplace to say that stories and films about cowboys are transformations of stories about knights, armed struggles between good and evil with the heroes using six-shooters in the place of swords and the villains wearing sombreros (or in Mexican films, stetsons) instead of turbans. The Amazon or virago has also survived as in the case of Annie in *Annie Get your Gun* (1946) or her lesser-known American predecessors such as Hurricane Nell. Science-fiction offers another type of transformation, drawing some of its material (not to mention plot structures such as the quest) from the magical world of medieval romance.

How do we account for the persistence of these themes? The answers which have been given to this question are very different. On one side we have the ideas of the Canadian critic Northrop Frye about the universal appeal of the basic plot of the romance, the importance of the quest and so on, a brilliantly developed literary analysis which assumes what it ought to prove, the universality of the appeal of this type of adventure story.[32] It may be worth remarking in passing that Frye does not discuss the adventure stories of China or Japan, from the *Water Margin* to *The Forty-Seven Ronin*, and it may be doubted whether these stories, despite their superficial similarities to 'eastern westerns' would altogether fit his categories. For example, the collective heroes of the two stories just cited are very different from the 'Lone Ranger' tradition of Western individualism.

This contrast between East and West supports explanations of the persistence of motifs which are framed in terms of cultural traditions and of social conditions which favour the persistence

[31] Peloso (1984).
[32] Frye (1959), 186ff.

of these traditions. Let us investigate this possibility in the case of the romance of chivalry.

The case of Brazil is not a unique one. In Sicily, a popular puppet theatre featuring Rinaldo and other heroes from romances of chivalry was still flourishing in the early twentieth century, even if it is the tourist industry which keeps it alive today.[33] The tales of Charlemagne and his paladins were the favourite boyhood reading of the famous bandit Salvatore Giuliano, who was killed in 1950.[34] In France, the stories were still being reprinted in cheap format in the middle of the nineteenth century, and it is said that during the First World War, some Breton soldiers passed their time in the trenches reading the medieval romance *The Four Sons of Aymon*. Vargas Llosa's admiration for *Tirant lo Blanc* has already been mentioned.[35] All the same, the continuing importance of the romance of chivalry in the culture of rural Brazil, at least in the north-east, still cries out for explanation.

In parts of Brazil, such as Minas Gerais, Bahia, Pernambuco and Ceará, certain features of the popular culture of early modern Europe remain very much alive. The most obvious example is carnival – not just the big commercialized carnival of Rio, as much for the tourists and the television cameras as for the locals, but the smaller, more traditional, participatory, violent carnivals of Olinda, Salvador, Maranhão and elsewhere (below, chapter 10). Again, *Irmandades* or religious confraternities together with their church-ales or *quermesses* still flourish in the small towns of Minas Gerais. The survival of the chap-books, and in particular of the romances of chivalry, is not an isolated phenomenon.

But how does one explain these survivals? To speak of 'archaism' is to describe, not to explain. To note other cases (such as the Appalachia studied by the musicologist Cecil Sharp) in which colonies or ex-colonies are more faithful to the cultural traditions of the mother country than the metropolis itself is helpful but not sufficiently precise.[36] If we accept the suggestion that a culture's heroes tell something about its basic values, a suggestion which has been developed in an interesting way in the case of Brazil by the anthropologist Roberto Da Matta, the

---

[33] Lanza (1931).
[34] Maxwell (1956), 34.
[35] Llosa (1969).
[36] Sharp (1907).

problem appears even more central, without of course coming any nearer to a solution.[37]

If we are trying to explain the survival of the romance of chivalry in Brazil, it is of course crucial to establish – if we can – what these stories mean to the participants. We need to take into account the responses of the readers. As it may well be imagined, this task is not an easy one.[38] It is at least possible, however, to focus on one relatively well-documented episode in twentieth-century Brazilian history in which the reading of romances of chivalry played a part. This is the popular revolt of 1912–15, the so-called 'war of Contestado'. It was a revolt of the periphery against the centralizing state, similar in this respect to the more famous revolt of the holy man Antonio Conselheiro in 1896–7, who founded the holy city of Canudos in the backlands of Bahia, in north-eastern Brazil. This revolt has inspired a classic of Brazilian literature, Euclides da Cunha's 'The backlands' (*Os Sertões*, 1902), and, more recently, a novel by Mário Vargas Llosa, *The War of the End of the World* (1980).[39] The Contestado rebellion, in the backlands of Paraná and Santa Caterina, in southern Brazil was also led by holy men, including the monk José Maria, who read to his followers from the *História de Carlos Magno*, the same text which the American missionary Kidder found in the shop in Maceió. The rebels included a small group of skilled fighters who were known as 'the twelve peers of France'.[40]

This rebellion gives us some kind of context in which to place Charlemagne. This is a context of what Eric Hobsbawm has called 'primitive' rebellions against the modern secular state, with its taxes, its censuses and so on.[41] The Brazilian rebellions were viewed by participants as a holy war against this infidel, diabolical state centred in distant Rio de Janeiro. The rebels appealed to 'Dom Sebastião', the sixteenth-century king of Portugal already mentioned, a figure who seems to have been amalgamated with St Sebastian and was expected to return, like King Arthur, in this case to free Brazil from the yoke of the Republic. The

[37] Da Matta (1978).
[38] Meyer (1993), 147–59.
[39] Cunha (1902); Levine (1992).
[40] Monteiro (1974); Diacon (1991), 2, 116, 137, 152.
[41] Hobsbawm (1959).

disobedience of Roland, who ignored the orders of Charlemagne to retreat and lost his life fighting the Moors, seems to have legitimated a revolt against a modern state.[42]

This political interpretation is a plausible one, but it needs to be placed in a wider cultural context. Like the North American cowboy and the South American *gaucho*, the Brazilian *jagunço* may be viewed as a descendant of the medieval knight, especially the knight-errant, thanks to his nomadic way of life, to his concern with honour and not least to his horsemanship, a skill displayed in dramatic form in the rodeos which still take place in Brazil as well as in the USA. As an English medievalist once remarked, 'it is impossible to be chivalrous without a horse.'[43] Like medieval La Mancha, Don Quixote's stamping-ground, and Extremadura, the native region of so many *conquistadores*, north-eastern Brazil was a frontier area, a relatively empty territory of cattle-raising and violence, out of reach of the short arm of the law.[44] In such a region, stories of individualized heroic deeds would find a public ready to listen to them.

In other words, the frontier environment is important to the romance of chivalry as well as to related literary genres such as the ballad and the oral epic.[45] The backlands of north-east Brazil were a frontier society. The New World of the sixteenth century was a frontier society. Come to that, the Iberian peninsula of the late Middle Ages was a frontier society, lacking a central authority and engaged in a constant struggle of Christians against Muslims.[46] In all these places, the ethic of independence prevailed and defiance of a distant authority made good sense. In each region the romance tradition was adapted to local circumstances, but it was because there was already some degree of 'fit' between the tradition and the circumstances that chivalry appealed to local writers, singers, listeners and readers. Transplanting is only possible in the right soil.

[42] Cunha (1902), 136, 164; Monteiro (1974), 109ff.
[43] Denholm-Young, quoted White (1962), 38.
[44] Bishko (1963).
[45] Entwistle (1939); Lord (1960).
[46] Bishko (1963); cf. MacKay (1977), 36ff.

10

The Translation of Culture: Carnival in Two or Three Worlds

For anyone living in Brazil today it is difficult to avoid hearing carnival songs or seeing carnival images all year long, especially from New Year onwards. As Shrove Tuesday approaches the newspapers carry more carnival news, and there is more and more speculation on the relative chances of different 'samba schools' winning the competition, long before the spectators enter the Passarela do Samba in Rio or in São Paulo and the great show begins. Carnival is presented as a Brazilian speciality and is viewed as such not only by Riotur, the tourist board of Rio da Janeiro, but also by many ordinary Brazilians.

Carnival is not only a theme of novels and of films about Brazil such as Marcel Carné's *Orfeu Negro* (1958), but also a recurrent theme in Brazilian culture itself. The screenplay of *Orfeu Negro* was the work of the poet Vinicius de Morães, adapting his play *Orfeu da Conceição*, while the music for the film was written by Luis Bonfa and Antonio Carlos Jobim, better known as 'Tom'. Other literary examples include Manuel Bandeira's *Carnaval* (1919), Mario da Andrade's *Carnaval Carioca* (1923), and Jorge Amado's first novel *O Pais do Carnaval* (1932). Some of the best songs by Chico Buarque, Gilberto Gil and other leading composers were originally written for particular carnivals. For representations of Carnival in popular culture one has only to look at series such as *Carnaval Duchen* (Rádio e TV Record); *Meu Carnaval não era assim* (TV Tupi); or *Carnaval do passado* (TV Rio).

Carnival is also the theme of a number of recent studies in Brazilian anthropology, sociology and history, most of them by Brazilians themselves. Of these the most famous is Roberto Da Matta's *Carnavais, malandros e heróis* (1978), not so much a study of Carnival for itself as a study of Brazil and of what the author calls 'the Brazilian dilemma'. Da Matta uses Carnival as a means to analyse the conflict between equality and hierarchy in Brazil, along the lines of Clifford Geertz's famous study of the Balinese cock-fight.[1]

Da Matta's study is a brilliant and original one, but (like that of Geertz) it may be criticized as too Durkheimian in the sense that it assumes the unity of the phenomenon, ignoring regional variation and the different meanings of the event for different social groups. Carnival may be a moment of emotional union or *communitas*, and even a truce in the class war. All the same, it does not necessarily have the same meaning for all participants – young working-class men with a need for 'release' (*desabafo*), middle-class middle-aged women who want to join the 'people', tourists who see the festival as a symbol of Brazil, and so on.[2]

Da Matta's interpretation has been supplemented by a number of in-depth studies of the Rio Escolas de Samba by his pupils, notably Maria Julia Goldwasser (1975) on the famous Estação Primeira de Mangueira.[3] One of Brazil's leading sociologists, Maria Isaura Pereira de Queiroz, recently published a history of the Brazilian carnival from colonial times to the present. Maria Isaura's conclusions, and more especially her views of nineteenth-century Rio, have recently been criticized (like Da Matta's) as too unitary.[4] This chapter is not constructed on the assumption that Carnival has a single shared meaning, but it will be limited to a single main theme, the inverse of Da Matta's. The theme, discussed in general terms in chapter 12 below, is that of cultural interaction between different groups – elites and subordinate classes, blacks and whites, men and women. Other aspects of

[1] Geertz (1973), 412–53.
[2] Cf. Turner (1983).
[3] Goldwasser (1975); Leopoldi (1978); Cavalcanti (1994).
[4] Queiroz (1992); Soihet (1993); Pereira (1994).

Carnival, notably its relation to sex and violence, will not be pursued here.[5]

The View from Europe

A European visiting Brazil in February or March may well feel that the Brazilians have annexed Carnival. After all, they did not invent it. Like other European institutions, the carnival, with all its ambiguities and ambivalence, was transported or 'translated' (in the original sense of that term) to the New World. At least to that part of it which was colonized by Catholics from the Mediterranean. It is thanks to French, Spanish and Portuguese immigrants that Carnival became important in the life of New Orleans, Port of Spain and Havana as well as in Rio, Salvador and Olinda.

Anyone familiar with European carnivals will feel at home in many ways when observing or indeed participating in carnivals in the New World. The parallels are impressive. The throwing of eggshells or wax balls full of water, much practised in nineteenth-century Rio, for example, derived from the tradition of the Portuguese *entrudo*, a tradition with many parallels in France, Spain and Italy, whether the missiles were eggs or oranges.[6] The wearing of fancy dress and masks was a traditional European custom, and even some of the favourite American costumes, such as the hussars and harlequins of Rio and the Pierrots and Punchinellos of Trinidad, followed European models. The *desfile* of the Escolas de Samba in Rio today is reminiscent of the parades and allegorical floats which could already be seen in fifteenth-century Florence and Nuremberg.

Again, the Escolas de Samba and their middle-class predecessors, such as the 'Democratics', 'Lieutenants of the Devil' and 'Fenians' in nineteenth-century Rio, are reminiscent of the Abbeys of Youth and other European festive societies. What the Fenians (founded in 1858) meant in Rio a few years later is a fascinating but elusive question. Apart from adding an exotic Irish touch to the festivities, they were probably chosen for their republicanism. This political ideal appealed to a substantial

---

[5] Parker (1991), ch. 6; Linger (1992).
[6] Graham (1988), 68; Baroja (1965), 57ff.

number of Brazilians before the Republic was founded in 1889, and political references are traditional in Brazilian carnivals. In Rio in 1903, for instance, there were criticisms of the stamp duty. In 1964, after the generals had taken power, the successful samba 'Tristeza' began 'Please go away' ('por favor vá embora'). In this case too there are European parallels, similar political themes ranging from protests against the stamp duty in Madrid in 1637 to the recent Italian carnivals mocking the corruption of the former prime minister, Benito Craxi.

In the case of Brazil's relation to Europe, we need to consider not only unconscious tradition but also conscious imitation. Brazilians of the middle classes in particular were and indeed still are much attracted by foreign cultural models. The carnivals of Venice, Rome and Nice in particular were exemplary in nineteenth-century Brazil. They were quoted in the press as models of 'civilized' Carnival in attempts to suppress the *entrudo* and to replace it with something more rational, hygienic, moral, and 'European'. To a European historian, the situation is likely to seem somewhat ironic. The Brazilian elite viewed the European carnival as non-violent, a 'good' or civilized carnival in contrast to the 'bad' or uncivilized Brazilian carnival. The European carnival may have become relatively restrained by this time, but in the early modern period violence had been commonplace. An English visitor to Venice at the end of the sixteenth century recorded that 'there were on Shrove-Sunday at night seventeen slain, and very many wounded.'[7]

The Peculiarities of the Americans

This New World carnival is much more than a European import. Like so many items of European culture, it has been transformed in the course of its sojourn in the Americas, transposed or 'translated' in the sense of being adapted to the local conditions. These transformations are most important or at least most easily noticeable in three domains – the place of women, of dancing and of African culture.

In the first place, the importance and the active role of women in the carnivals of the Americas contrasts with traditional European customs, in which a woman's place was generally on

---

[7] Burke (1978), 187.

the balcony, observing (and sometimes throwing missiles at) the men below, rather than in the street, participating fully. Despite the practice of cross-dressing or the many references to reversal, the patriarchal world was not turned completely upside down at this time.

Indeed, the emphasis on drink and violence in the traditional European carnivals, as well as the composition of the carnival societies (dominated by young adult males), suggest that the events should be interpreted as – among other things – rituals for the affirmation of masculinity. There were other popular festivals in which women were 'on top', symbolically dominating men, like the Spanish feast of Santa Agueda described by the late Don Julio Caro Baroja, but this was not a major theme of the European carnival.[8]

In the New World, on the other hand, despite the transplantation of patriarchalism – described by Latin American writers from Gilberto Freyre to Gabriel García Marquez – women have long been more visible and more active in carnival. Thus an English officer in Trinidad in 1826 noted that 'a party of ladies, having converted themselves into a party of brigands, assailed me in my quarters.'[9] In Brazil, female participation in the *entrudo* was considered worthy of note by foreign visitors such as Thomas Lindley (1805), Henry Koster (1816), John Mawe (1822), Robert Walsh (1830), and Ferdinand Denis (1837).

Today, whether the role of women is passive or active, whether their function is to be viewed by men or to enact their own fantasies (or both), it is impossible to imagine a Brazilian carnival without an overwhelming female presence, including the *destaques*, symbolic figures on the floats; the *pastoras*, 'shepherdesses' dancing in front of or behind the floats; the *baianas*, middle-aged women in the traditional costume of Bahía; and finally the *porta-bandeira* or standard-bearer, whose dance with her male partner the *mestre-sala* counts for several points in the competition between samba schools in Rio. Carnival schools, clubs and 'blocks' usually have a female wing and a female as well as a male directorate.[10]

Linked to the more active role of women, the importance of

---

[8] Baroja (1965), 371–81; cf. Davis (1975), esp. 138ff.
[9] Quoted in Pearse (1955–6), 180.
[10] Simson (1991–2).

dancing makes the New World carnivals distinctive. Dance was not completely absent in Europe. Sword-dancing in particular occurred in traditional European carnivals. All the same, the dance did not have the same importance there as in Brazil (say) or in Trinidad, where the *calinda* or stick-dance has been a central part of the festivities from the early nineteenth century at the latest, or in New Orleans, which impressed a French visitor in 1802 because 'they dance everywhere.'[11]

The examples just cited are of male dances, but mixed dancing has also been important in the carnivals of the Americas since the nineteenth century. In early nineteenth-century Trinidad, men and women of the planter class danced the *belair*, the *bamboula* and the *ghouba*. The classic instance of mixed dancing is that of Brazil, in the age of the polka, dominant from 1850 to 1900, the age of the *maxixe*, from the 1870s to the 1910s, and the age of the samba, dominant from 1916 or thereabouts to our own time. In Rio, dancing was and is a most important part of the *desfile*, the carnival parade, which itself became a central part of the festivities from the mid-nineteenth century onwards. Not only the 'infantry' accompanying the floats, but many of the women displayed on the floats themselves dance the samba, despite the risk of falling.

Besides dancing in the streets, the Brazilian carnival has long included balls in private houses, clubs, hotels (starting with the Hotel Itália in Rio in 1840), and theatres (such as the Teatro São Pedro in Rio in 1844, or the Teatro São João in Salvador in the 1860s).[12] In other parts of Latin America, dancing has also been an important element in Carnival: in Buenos Aires, for example, and in Havana, where masked balls took place in the Tacón theatre from 1838 onwards.[13]

The View from Africa

Linked in turn to the dance is the place of African elements in carnival as in other Latin American festivities. To begin with these other festivities. The celebration of the feast of Corpus

[11] Hill (1972), 11; Kinser (1990), 22.
[12] Alencar (1965).
[13] Amuchástegui (1988), 158ff.; Ortiz (1954), 204.

Christi in colonial Brazil, in the province of Minas Gerais, for instance, included allegorical floats and dances by blacks with flags, drums and songs – all elements to be found later in Brazilian carnivals. The tradition of the *maracatu, cucumbi, congada* or 'kings of the Congo', the enthronement of black kings and queens in splendid costume on the feast of Our Lady of the Rosary, again in Minas Gerais, was also transferred to Carnival.[14]

The transition from the brotherhoods who organized such festivals to the later carnival societies and samba schools was an easy one.[15] Brotherhoods themselves probably attracted blacks in Minas, Bahía and elsewhere because they offered a substitute family for slaves uprooted from their homeland, and a form of social organization with parallels in West Africa, notably the secret societies. In similar fashion, when twentieth-century missionaries to Mozambique formed scout groups (*Patrulhas*), their success seems to have owed something to local traditions of sociability.[16]

The Africa from which slaves were transported to the New World was of course a cluster of cultures some of which were already interacting with the West and with Christianity. Take the case of the Congo, for example. Local rulers saw advantages in working with the missionaries and using the new doctrines and rituals to legitimate their power. Confraternities were founded. Christian festivals such as the feast of St James were celebrated not only by processions but by traditional African dances and combined with other festivals like the commemoration of the accession of Afonso, King of the Congo. While the missionaries believed that they had converted the Africans to Christianity, it is extremely likely, to say the least, that the people of the Congo saw themselves as incorporating exotic Western rituals into the local religion. The synthesis or syncretism between Christianity and African traditions so often noted in the cases of Brazil and Cuba had already begun in Africa itself.[17] Behind these rituals it is occasionally possible to glimpse elements of African tradition,

[14] Real (1967), xv; Meyer (1993), 161–74.
[15] Cf. Da Matta (1978).
[16] Mandelbaum (1989), 173.
[17] Thornton (1983); Hilton (1985), 50ff., 95ff.; Gray (1991), 13ff., 42ff.; MacGaffey (1986), 191–216; MacGaffey (1994), 254–9; cf. Balandier (1965), 39, 259, 264; Prins (1980).

such as the Nigerian festival of the queen, *Damurixá*.[18] Carnival itself did not exist in Africa, and to this day it has only taken root in a few regions (notably Cabo Verde and Réunion), but what Westerners might call the 'carnivalesque' was common.

Wherever and however they originated, Afro-American elements spread through the Brazilian carnival. In Rio in 1881, the allegorical float of the Democráticos, a white carnival society of high status, represented an African prince, Obá. If we try to escape what might be called the 'Riocentrism' of the majority of studies of Brazilian carnival and look at Olinda, Recife or Salvador, the survival or reconstruction of African traditions is even more obvious, long before the late twentieth-century movement of 're-Africanization' linked to black consciousness and black power. In Recife, for instance, a group of *maracatus*, led by a queen and vice-queen, is recorded to have participated in the carnival of 1872.[19]

The dance, whether religious or secular, was and may still be a more important art form in Africa than anywhere else. In East Africa, for example, there was the tradition of the *ngoma*, a dance which often took the form of a 'parade' or 'march past' by members of different dance associations, associations in which women played a prominent part. In late nineteenth-century Mombasa, these parades included floats reminiscent of 'the carnivals at Nice or at New Orleans', according to one British official.[20]

In West Africa, more relevant to the Americas since the majority of slaves came from that region, the dance was often closely associated with religious practices. The association between dance and religion was closer than in Europe, where there has been a long tradition of official hostility to dances in church or even on the occasion of religious festivals.[21] Among the Tallensi of West Africa, on the other hand, the anthropologist who knew them best reported that 'the dancing-ground is sacred.'[22] The dance was a ritual provoking loss of consciousness and the possession of the dancers by spirits or gods, as in the case of the Yoruba in Dahomey and Nigeria.

[18] Manuel Querino, quoted Risério (1981), 49.
[19] Real (1967), xvi-xvii; Fry (1988), 232–63; Risério (1981), 13, 17.
[20] Ranger (1975), 34, 167ff.
[21] Backman (1952).
[22] Fortes (1987), 51.

Possession, or 'spirit mediumship' as it is sometimes called, should not be regarded as a form of hysteria. As anthropologists have emphasized, it should be analysed as ritual or even as theatre. The possessed impersonate their particular spirit in much the same way as Carnival revellers enact the behaviour appropriate to their costume, their *fantasia*. Some of these spirits behave in a carnivalesque way: the *caboclo* spirits in *candomblé*, for example, male spirits who take over females and make their human vehicles smoke, drink and use bad language.[23] Drumming was central to these possession rituals. The drums were considered the voices of the gods, each god being associated with a distinctive rhythm.[24] Possession cults of this kind continue among blacks in the Americas, from the *vodun* of Haiti and the *santería* of Cuba to the *candomblé* of Brazil (which has particularly close links to Yoruba traditions), or its equivalent in Maranhão, the *tambor de mina*, the name emphasizing the beat of the drum.[25]

The central argument of this chapter is that these religious practices have made an important contribution to Afro-American carnivals. The place of drums in these carnivals is central in the cases of the *baterías* of Rio and the 'steel bands' of Trinidad (which replaced the traditional drums in the 1930s). The dances of the *candomblé* are sometimes compared with the carnival samba not only by observers but also by participants.[26] In Brazil, other religious practices were incorporated in Carnival via the *afoxé*, a word which means not only a musical instrument (a gourd rattle) and a dance performed by blacks, but also a *maracatu* or a procession of adepts of *candomblé*. The Brazilian composer and singer Gilberto Gil tells the story that when he was parading in the carnival of Salvador with the rest of his *afoxé* group, he once saw a middle-aged woman cross herself, apparently thinking that what she was watching was a religious procession.[27]

In the religious rituals described above, women have traditionally played an important part. The Hausa Bori possession cults, for example, were and are controlled by women. The so-called 'mother of the saint' (*mãe de santo, ialorixa*) remains the central

---

[23] Wafer (1991), 55–6.
[24] Leiris (1958); Verger (1969), 50–66.
[25] Mars (1946); Bastide (1958); Drewal (1989).
[26] Wafer (1991), 73–4; Omari (1994), 136.
[27] Bastide (1958), 248; Real (1967), 57; Risério (1981), 12, 52, 55–6.

figure in *candomblé*.[28] In Recife, the queens who lead the *maracatus* in the carnival are *mães de santo*.[29] To reinforce the hypothesis of the connection between African religion and American Carnival, it may be added that in Salvador, female spirits called *tobosa* ('girls') 'descended' at Carnival, in other words took possession of worshippers.[30] To speculate for a moment, I should like to suggest that the *baianas* so prominent in the carnival of Rio and other cities today, dignified ladies whirling in their long white dresses, are a secular version of the *mães do santo*. Indeed, the excitement and exaltation of Carnival, the 'vibrations' as the Brazilians call them, are a secular form of religious ecstasy.

Masks reveal other links between Africa and the Americas. They have an important role to play not only in Carnival but also in West African secret societies, such as the Poro of Liberia.[31] In Trinidad, one of the traditional carnival masks, the 'Moco Jumbie', has been traced back to religious practices in West Africa.[32] In Cuba, as in the Saturnalia of ancient Rome, the temporary liberty of slaves was central to the festival, which is said to have owed something to the African tradition of the Ekuaeansu. The blacks took to the streets of La Habana dressed as *congos* (again), *lucumíes*, *ararás* and *mandingas*.[33]

In Brazil in particular, Afro-American popular traditions are currently being studied with more attention than before by historians. At the same time they are receiving more emphasis in the carnivals themselves as part of the black consciousness movement. For example, *afoxé* groups such as the 'sons of Gandhi' (founded in 1949 but revived in the 1970s) play an important role in the carnival of Salvador.[34] In 1995, the Salvador carnival focused on Zumbi, leader of the rebel slave community of Palmares, in order to mark the tercentenary of his death.

Research on African elements in Carnival, like other aspects of black popular culture in colonial and nineteenth-century Brazil, has scarcely begun.[35] All the same, the elements mentioned above may be sufficient to launch the hypothesis that New World

---

[28] Landes (1947), 71ff., 142ff.
[29] Real (1967), 67.
[30] Bastide (1958), 194. On Umbanda and Carnival, Da Matta (1978), 136.
[31] Harley (1950); cf. Sieber (1962).
[32] Hill (1972), 12.
[33] Ortiz (1954), 210–11.
[34] Risério (1981), 52ff.
[35] Meyer (1993), 175–226; Soihet (1993).

carnivals are 'overdetermined', in the sense that they have emerged out of the encounter between two festive traditions, the European and the African. There is 'syncretism' in the precise sense of the temporary coexistence and interaction of elements from different cultures, just as there is 'anti-syncretism' in the sense of attempts to purify Carnival, first of its African elements (in the later nineteenth century), and more recently of its European ones.[36] There may also have been Amerindian elements in this compound, but if so it is difficult to identify them now (the use of Indian *fantasías* by blacks and whites is another matter).[37]

It looks as if there is some kind of cultural magnetism involved, an attraction between similar elements in the African and European traditions, just as there is a kind of circularity or reciprocal influence between elite and popular traditions.[38] For example, the mock combat appears to derive both from the dances associated with the cult of the Yoruba warrior-god Ogun and from the Iberian tradition of representing conflicts between 'Moors and Christians' in popular religious dramas or *autos*.[39] In 1816, the English visitor Henry Koster witnessed a Brazilian *entrudo* which included the 'christening of the king of the Moors' and a mock battle between Moors and Christians. The tradition of the *cucumbi* or 'kings of the Congo' owes something to the European tradition known in France as the *reinage*, in which men and women dressed as kings and queens ride to church in a cavalcade.[40] It may also follow African traditions. Again, carnival masks are related to two cultural traditions, the European and the African. The festivals thus exemplify what the Cuban sociologist and folklorist Fernando Ortiz, himself an enthusiast for carnival, called 'transculturation' (below, p. 208), in other words the reciprocal interaction between two cultures, as opposed to 'acculturation', in which the influence is supposed to be one-way.[41]

[36] Pye (1993); Stewart (1994).
[37] Real (1967), 84ff.
[38] Soihet (1993).
[39] Drewal (1989), 225; Baroja (1965), 174.
[40] Real (1967), 58; Hanlon (1993), 155.
[41] Ortiz (1952).

The Trajectories of Carnival

The trajectory of carnivals in the New World over the last two hundred years or so runs parallel to that of European carnivals between the sixteenth and the nineteenth centuries.[42] There have been four main stages in this process; participation, reform, withdrawal, and rediscovery. It must of course be remembered that the sources for the history of Carnival generally offer a vision 'from above', in which some popular activities are scarcely visible, but so far as the upper classes at least are concerned this model has its uses.

The stage of participation may be illustrated from Trinidad in the early nineteenth century, when (according to an English observer) 'high and low, rich and poor, learned and unlearned, all found masking suits for the carnival.' Another example from mid nineteenth-century Petrópolis, where the Brazilian court retired for the summer, is the Emperor Pedro II's enjoyment of the traditional *entrudo*, water-throwing and all.

The stage of reform was reached in Trinidad in the later nineteenth century, when some members of the ruling class went so far as to demand the complete abolition of Carnival.[43] In Brazil, from the 1830s onwards, criticisms of Carnival were regularly expressed. In 1844, Father Lopes Gama, the famous Recife journalist, noted the inconsistency between the 'madness' of the *entrudo* and the claim of Brazilians to participate in the progress of civilization.[44] By the late nineteenth century there was a campaign to replace the 'grosseiro e pernicioso entrudo' (as the *Jornal de Notícias* of Salvador called it in 1884) with something more 'rational', 'hygienic' and 'civilized' on the European model (as was remarked above, the Brazilian elite was apparently unaware of the importance of sex and violence in the European carnival tradition). These attempts at reform probably reached their climax in Rio in the age of prefect Francisco Pereira Passos, around 1900, when the carnival parades were transferred from Rua do Ouvidor in the heart of the city to avenues on the periphery where they could be controlled more easily. This attempt

[42] Burke (1978), 178ff., 207ff., 270ff., 281ff.; Queiroz (1978); cf. Pereira (1994), introduction.
[43] Pearse (1955–6), 187.
[44] Quoted in Real (1967), xii–xiii.

coincided with a public health campaign and a reconstruction of the city which provoked resistance and even riots.[45]

The language of 'civilization' versus 'barbarism' expressed masked white fears of the growing 'Africanization' of Carnival, fears expressed openly in letters to the Salvador newspaper the *Jornal de Notícias* in the first years of the twentieth century. For it was in the 1890s that black carnival clubs such as the Pândegos de Africa were founded in that city.[46] How successful the reform campaign was it is difficult to say. Maria Isaura Pereira de Queiroz has written of 'the domestication of an urban mass' in the carnival of Rio, but her concern with the central events of the festival needs to be balanced against the evidence for a more traditional and informal carnival in other parts of the city.[47]

That the reform was less than complete is suggested by the third stage, in other words the withdrawal from public participation on the part of the elites, who now organized their own festivities indoors, a 'closed carnival' replacing the old open one. In Trinidad, it was as early as the emancipation of the slaves in 1833 that the white elite 'withdrew from public participation' in Carnival, while the blacks 'appropriated' it, or at least became more visible, using the festivities to commemorate their emancipation and to mock the whites.[48] In Brazil both emancipation and withdrawal occurred half a century later. In Rio, in the words of the *Gazeta de Notícias* in 1890, 'the elegant carnival withdrew into ball-rooms, abandoning the streets to the poor devils.'[49] By contrast, in New Orleans the white clubs or 'krewes' have not withdrawn and continue to dominate the carnival. The parallel black groups like the Zulu Aid and Pleasure Club which once mocked the official festivities have now been incorporated into them.[50]

Brazil, like other parts of the New World, is now living through the fourth stage of the process, that of the rediscovery of popular culture, in particular Afro-American culture, on the part of the elites, including the 're-Africanization' of Carnival. There

[45] Pereira (1994), 39ff.
[46] Quoted in Fry et al. (1988), 236, 253–4.
[47] Queiroz (1992), 71–116; Zaluar (1978).
[48] Pearse (1955–6); Hill (1972), 23, 40, 43, 100.
[49] Quoted in Pereira (1994), 202.
[50] Contrast Edmondson (1955–6), 233–45, and Kinser (1990); cf. Da Matta (1978), 124–30.

has also been (at least in Recife) a return to the street on the part of the middle class, which had withdrawn to the closed world of clubs and hotels.[51] Needless to say, this fourth stage is linked to the commercialization of a festival which has become big business and in which television and record companies as well as tourist agencies (not to mention owners of gambling establishments and drug dealers) have become deeply involved.[52] In this respect as in others, modern Rio is the heir of nineteenth-century Nice and eighteenth-century Venice.

What makes American carnivals so different from European ones is essentially the African element. To return to Da Matta's idea of Carnival as a microcosm of Brazil, we might say that the festival both displays and dramatizes the interaction between different ethnic groups and subcultures.

[51] Real (1967), 158-9.
[52] Cavalcanti (1994).

II

Strengths and Weaknesses of the History of Mentalities

The history of mentalities is not easy to define to everyone's satisfaction. Carlo Ginzburg and the late Richard Cobb were and are often seen as leading practitioners of this approach, despite their denials that the history of mentalities was what they are doing. Even in France, where the tradition is the most self-conscious and the most continuous, the approach has undergone modifications in the fifty years which separate Marc Bloch from (say) Jacques Le Goff.

For the purposes of this essay the approach will be defined in terms of three distinctive features. In the first place, a stress on collective attitudes rather than individual ones, and the thought of ordinary people as well as that of formally educated elites. Secondly, an emphasis not so much on conscious thoughts or elaborated theories as on unspoken or unconscious assumptions, on perception, on the workings of 'everyday thought' or 'practical reason'. And finally, a concern with the 'structure' of beliefs as well as their content, in other words with categories, with metaphors and symbols, with how people think as well as what they think. In other words, to assert the existence of a difference in mentalities between two groups is to make a much stronger statement than merely asserting a difference in attitudes.[1]

---

[1] Critical surveys include Vovelle (1982); Gismondi (1985).

In all these respects the history of mentalities differs from other approaches to intellectual history, such as the American 'history of ideas', the traditional German *Geistesgeschichte*, and even the newer German *Begriffsgeschichte*.[2] It might be described as a historical anthropology of ideas. From Émile Durkheim onwards, sociologists and social anthropologists have been concerned with what they variously call the 'collective representations', 'modes of thought' or 'cognitive systems' of other cultures.[3] Durkheim's follower Lucien Lévy-Bruhl helped put the term 'mentality' into circulation with his study *La mentalité primitive* (1922), which argued that primitive peoples thought in a 'pre-logical' or 'mystical' way.

However, the problems raised by the study of mentalities are too important for even two disciplines to deal with, and they have been discussed in many more, including philosophy, psychology, economics, literature, the history of art, and the history of science (although participants in these debates have not always been aware of all the interdisciplinary ramifications).

For example, the so-called 'sociology of knowledge', represented by the essays of Karl Mannheim, for example, was independent of, but similar to, the work of the Durkheimians. In the 1920s, Mannheim studied what he called 'world-views', 'mental habits' or 'styles of thought', with their distinctive logics. His most famous example was the contrast between two opposite styles of thought in the early nineteenth century, associated with German conservative historicists and French liberal universalists.[4]

In the history of science, Abel Rey found 'les beaux ouvrages de M. Lévy-Bruhl' an inspiration for his work on scientific thought in antiquity.[5] Rey collaborated with Lucien Febvre and thus contributed to the development of the French 'mentalities' tradition. Again, there are similarities to the mentalities approach in the focus on 'epistemological obstacles' in the work of Gaston Bachelard (Rey's successor at the Sorbonne), and on 'epistemological breaks' in the work of his pupil Georges Canguilhem, who was in turn one of the teachers of Michel Foucault.[6]

Even closer to the mentalities approach was the work of the

---

[2] Koselleck (1972).
[3] Durkheim (1912); Evans-Pritchard (1937, 1940).
[4] Mannheim (1927), esp. 35–7, 191.
[5] Rey (1930), 434–5, 456–9.
[6] Bachelard (1947); Canguilhem (1955); Foucault (1961, 1966).

Polish microbiologist Ludwik Fleck (written in the 1930s, rediscovered in the 1970s) on 'thought communities' and what he
called (like Mannheim) their distinctive 'styles' of thought.[7] The
parallel with anthropology is clear, and the idea of an 'anthropology of science' or an 'anthropology of knowledge' is now
in circulation.[8] The point is to investigate 'changing pre-
suppositions, expectations, questions, methods, arguments, justi-
fications' rather than to focus attention on ideas in the narrow
sense.[9]

As we have seen (above, p. 14), an interest in these problems
goes back at least as far as the eighteenth century. Phrases such
as 'mode of thought', *manière de penser*, *Denkungsart* and so on
came into use, usually in the context of an encounter between
two cultures distant in space or time, the modern Western
European using these phrases to express a sense of distance from
'savages', the Middle Ages, and so on.

A systematic historical approach is rather more recent. It has
of course been associated with the French journal *Annales* since
the days of its founders Lucien Febvre and Marc Bloch, who
were much concerned with what they variously called 'historical
psychology' (*psychologie historique*), 'collective mentalities'
(*mentalités collectives*), 'conceptual apparatus' (*outillage mental*),
or, in the phrase they borrowed from Durkheim, 'collective representations' (*représentations collectives*). However, Bloch and
Febvre were not alone in their concern. Marcel Granet the sinolo-
gist and Georges Lefebvre the historian of the French Revolution
were already writing this kind of history in the 1930s.[10]

What they were doing was not even a French monopoly, for it
shaded into the cultural history practised by Johan Huizinga
(below, p. 184), whose *Waning of the Middle Ages*, first published in 1919, was concerned with collective attitudes, with the
history of feelings, and, most important, with what the author
called 'forms of thought' (*gedachtensvormen*), such as personification and symbolism. In this last respect Huizinga moved away
from Jacob Burckhardt and towards the social psychologist
Wilhelm Wundt, with whom he had once studied at Leipzig.

This chapter attempts an assessment of both the strengths and

---

[7] Fleck (1935); cf. Crombie (1994).
[8] Elkanah (1981); Vickers (1984).
[9] Crombie (1994), vol. 1, 7.
[10] Granet (1934); Lefebvre (1932).

the weaknesses of the history of mentalities, as practised in France in particular from the days of Bloch and Febvre to those of Duby, Le Goff, Vovelle and Le Roy Ladurie. In the last few years the term has been going out of fashion, to be replaced by 'representations' or 'the collective imagination' (*l'imaginaire social*).[11] In practice, however, the difference between the old history of mentalities and the new history of representations is not great enough for these reflections to have lost their relevance.

The first point to make about the history of mentalities is that something is needed to occupy the conceptual space between the history of ideas and social history, in order to avoid having to choose between an intellectual history with the society left out and a social history with the thought left out. The 'social history of ideas' practised by a historian of the Enlightenment, Peter Gay, was a step in this direction, but it remained on the intellectual side of the frontier. The 'social history of ideas' practised by a more recent historian of the Enlightenment, Robert Darnton, goes further; indeed Darnton uses the phrase more or less as a synonym for the history of mentalities.[12] One of the main points of this approach is to take more seriously than before the place of ideas in everyday social life. It is precisely for this reason that the Swedish historian Eva Österberg recently described her work as concerned with 'mentalities and other realities'.[13]

Consider the following recurrent problems in cultural history. Why is it that individuals from different cultures often find communication difficult? Why does one individual or group find absurd precisely what another takes for granted? How is it possible to be able to translate every word in a text from an alien (or even a half-alien) culture, yet to have difficulty in understanding the text? Because – so one is able to say if one adopts this approach to the past – there is a difference in mentality, in other words different assumptions, different perceptions, and a different 'logic' – at least in the philosophically loose sense of different criteria for justifying assertions – reason, authority, experience and so on. No wonder that a historian of the Middle Ages and an anthropologist have tried, independently, to revive the ideas of the French psychologist Jean Piaget in order to analyse

[11] Chartier (1988); Baczko (1984).
[12] Gay (1959), preface; Darnton (1990).
[13] Österberg (1991).

differences in mentality, following him in distinguishing 'pre-operatory' from 'operatory' thought and linking the latter to formal schooling.[14]

A classic example of the kind of problem for whose solution we need the concept of mentality – or something roughly like it – is that of the medieval ordeal, an example which has exercised educated Europeans from Montesquieu onwards. Trial by ordeal is easy enough to condemn in the name of reason, but it is difficult to explain historically without recourse to what Montesquieu called 'la manière de penser de nos pères' (in other words, mentality). A number of recent studies of the ordeal have adopted precisely this approach.[15] Again, in fields as far apart as economic history and the history of science, other scholars have found it impossible to solve their problems without invoking a concept like that of mentality, as opposed to a timeless rationality which usually turns out to have been defined ethnocentrically.

In the case of the economy, the Polish historian Witold Kula, in a brilliant account of the workings of the 'feudal system' in seventeenth- and eighteenth-century Poland, has demonstrated that it cannot be understood without taking into account the attitudes, values or mode of thought of the magnates who gained most from it.[16] Again, Edward Thompson's famous article on what he called the 'moral economy' of the English crowd suggested that food riots should be seen not as a simple response to hunger but as an expression of collective moral assumptions, a suggestion which was soon taken up and utilized in the study of rebellions in societies as distant as South East Asia.[17] There are obvious similarities between this approach to economic history and that of 'economic anthropology', which also stresses alternative rationalities, emphasizing, for example, the social function of what used to be called 'conspicuous waste' as a means of acquiring prestige and power.

In the history of science, too, recurrent attempts have been made to turn 'rationality' from an assumption into a problem, to abandon the simplistic distinction between the irrational 'magic' associated with the 'other' and the rational science associated

[14] Hallpike (1979), 12–40; Radding (1978).
[15] Brown (1975); cf. Morris (1975) and Radding (1979). Contrast Bartlett (1986).
[16] Kula (1962).
[17] Thompson (1971); Scott (1976); cf. Thompson (1991).

with 'us'. Hence the interest in collective 'styles of thought' already mentioned, invoked in order to supplement explanations of scientific innovation in terms of internal necessity or the achievement of individual geniuses.[18]

To defend, as well as describe, the approach it may be useful to cite four concrete examples from the early modern period where it seems particularly difficult to give a plausible account of certain beliefs without a concept like the idea of mentality or mode of thought.

(1) The idea of 'correspondences' between the seven planets, the seven metals, the seven days of the week, and so on.[19] Correspondences are neither identities nor similarities but seem to be somewhere in between, a middle category which seems to have parallels in other cultures, notably the Bororo (a tribe living in the Amazon region), who claimed to be macaws, and the Nuer, for whom 'a twin is a bird.'[20] The Bororo example was taken up by Lévy-Bruhl, who described the relationship between men and macaws in terms of 'mystical participation', a characteristic, so he suggested, of 'pre-logical' thought or 'primitive mentality'.

(2) The idea of the 'great chain', ladder or 'scale' of being, according to which it is better to live than to exist, better to feel than to live, better to think than to feel; in other words, better to be a tree than a stone, a horse than a tree, a human being than a horse.[21] The problem is that 'the complex system of analogies up and down the chain cannot be taken entirely literally, nor can it be understood as a mere convention, a useful and pleasing metaphor.'[22] The fact that this projection of the social hierarchy on to the cosmos has now come to seem quaint indicates a major change in Western mentality since the sixteenth century.

(3) Hence, to take a third example, the modern reader is likely to be somewhat puzzled by the following statement of Cardinal Bérulle's: 'L'état de l'enfance, état le plus vil et le plus abject de la nature humaine, après celui de la mort' ('The state of childhood,

[18] Crombie (1994).
[19] Tillyard (1943); cf. Foucault (1966), ch. 1.
[20] Evans-Pritchard (1956), 128f.; Crocker (1977).
[21] Lovejoy (1936).
[22] Walzer (1965), 156.

the most vile and abject state of human nature, after that of death').[23] The oddness is not – or not only – a function of the content of Bérulle's beliefs, of the fact that childishness has become more acceptable to adults than it seems to have been in the seventeenth century. It is the hierarchical arrangement, the structure of his beliefs, that we are likely to find most alien. It has also come to seem rather odd to describe death as an *état*. Yet personifications of abstractions were common enough in the medieval and early modern periods. Johan Huizinga, whose interest in personification has been mentioned already, once discussed a statement by St Francis to the effect that he was married to Lady Poverty. Huizinga suggested that this statement should not be taken either literally or metaphorically. Its logical status was somewhere in between.[24]

(4) Huizinga's suggestion may be helpful in interpreting a final example, which comes from the rebellion of the so-called 'red bonnets' in Brittany in 1675. The rebels expressed their demands in a document known as the 'peasant code'. One of its clauses runs as follows: 'It is forbidden to give refuge to the *gabelle* and her children, to give them anything to eat or anything they need; but on the contrary everyone is ordered to fire on her as one would on a mad dog' ('Il est défendu ... de donner retraite à la gabelle et à ses enfants, et de leur fournir ni à manger ni aucune commodité; mais au contraire, il est enjoint de tirer sur elle comme sur un chien enragé').[25] This 'gabelle' was of course the salt tax.

Some historians believe that the code is a forgery, precisely – one suspects – because they find this clause a stumbling block to credibility, although there is supporting evidence for the personification of the *gabelle*.[26] It is a scandal for historians who do not believe in differences in mentality. What could the rebels have meant? Whether or not the Breton peasants had a more archaic mentality than that of peasants elsewhere in France is a question I do not feel competent to answer. It is true that they employed

[23] Quoted in Snyders (1964), 194.
[24] Huizinga (1938), 162ff.
[25] Garlan and Nières (1975), 102.
[26] Le Braz (1922), 136ff.

personifications of death and plague as well as of the *gabelle*.[27] However, similar personifications can be found elsewhere in Europe. Even the notorious clause about giving the *gabelle* food differs only in degree of elaboration from the cry of some fifteenth-century Tuscans, 'Death to the tax' ('Muoia il catasto'); and this is a special case of a more common Italian slogan, 'Death to bad government' ('Muoia il malgoverno'). Is the injunction to be taken literally or metaphorically? Perhaps it is another statement which will not fit our own cultural categories of 'literal' and 'metaphorical', and so indicates an alien mentality.[28]

Faced with examples like these, historians need a concept like that of 'mentality' in order to avoid two opposite dangers. The first danger is that of dismissing the Breton peasants or Cardinal Bérulle as irrational or as unworthy of serious historical consideration. If a specific seventeenth-century attitude strikes us as odd, we have to remember that it was part of a belief system in which the different parts supported one another, making the central propositions virtually unfalsifiable. The second danger is that of sweeping the examples under the carpet, of assuming that seventeenth-century Frenchmen must 'really' have thought in the same way as we do, and so succumbing to what might be called 'premature empathy', an intellectual illness which was diagnosed some sixty years ago by Lévy-Bruhl (though Vico and Rousseau had been aware of it long before). Lévy-Bruhl offered his analysis precisely in order to replace the idea 'of substituting ourselves imaginatively for the primitives we are studying, and making them think as we would do if we were in their place', a diagnosis which has passed into British social anthropology under the name of the 'If I were a horse' problem.[29] The point is that to understand the behaviour of people in other cultures it is not sufficient to imagine oneself in their shoes, in their situation; it is also necessary to imagine their definition of the situation, to see it through their eyes. A similar point was made by Lucien Febvre in an essay which discussed the problem of what he called 'psychological anachronism'.[30]

The great strength of the idea of mentality is to make it possible to steer a course which avoids the two opposite hazards. If

[27] Croix (1981), 1067ff.
[28] Lloyd (1990).
[29] Lévy-Bruhl (1927), 15.
[30] Febvre (1938).

we replace it with some alternative concept, it seems reasonable to require the substitute to deal in a satisfactory way with examples of the kind which have just been discussed.

There is, of course, a case for replacing an approach which suffers from weaknesses and has had serious criticisms levelled against it. One objection, which is not infrequently heard in Britain, ought not to be taken too seriously; it is that the French treat mentalities as impersonal forces. In Britain it is obvious that there are no such forces, but only men thinking, as Herbert Butterfield put it. Or as Vivian Galbraith used to say, with provocative sexism, in his Oxford lectures in the 1950s, 'History is just chaps.' To the French, however (if I dare attempt an act of empathy with them), it is equally obvious that the term *mentalité* is not being used to describe a thing or a force, but rather to characterize the relation between beliefs, which is what makes them into a system. The beliefs are 'collective' only in the sense of being shared by individuals, not in the sense of standing outside them. The contrast between the British intellectual tradition of methodological individualism and the French tradition of holism is so strong, and goes back such a long way, that one is tempted to call the difference itself one between two different mentalities.

I shall be equally laconic, though not, I hope, cavalier, in response to the rather similar objection that historians of mentalities underestimate what human beings have in common. There is a sense (or level) at which human nature is always the same, but another level at which it is not. It is difficult to discuss differences in mentalities (or differences between cultures) without exaggerating their importance. I shall try to refer to differences in world-views without implying that different groups see the world in *completely* different ways.

There are, however, at least four more serious objections to the mentalities approach to intellectual history. They are usually presented in exaggerated form, but each contains a kernel of serious criticism.

(1) In the first place, to look for broad differences in mentalities encourages historians to treat attitudes they find alien as if they were homogeneous, to overestimate the degree of intellectual consensus in a given society in the past.[31] This is of course one of

---

[31] Gismondi (1985).

the classic objections to the concept of *Zeitgeist*, and to the traditional cultural history organized around it (*Geistesgeschichte*),
and the objection is only partially answered by saying that Hegel
(for example) did not treat seventeenth-century thought as homogeneous, but contrasted Francis Bacon (for instance) with his
contemporary Jacob Boehme. Bloch and Febvre (like Huizinga)
are not so far from traditional *Geistesgeschichte* as their use of
the new term 'mentality' might make one think. To write, as they
did on occasion, of 'the medieval Frenchman' or 'the sixteenth-
century Frenchman' as if there were no important variations in
attitude among the inhabitants of France in this period (male and
female, rich and poor, literate and illiterate, and so on) is seriously misleading.

There is no reason why a mentality should not be imputed to a
social class or other group rather than to a whole society, but this
tactic leads to similar problems on a lesser scale. From outside it
may seem reasonable enough to talk of, say, the 'legal mentality'
in seventeenth-century England, yet it cannot be assumed that all
lawyers had the same attitudes. We have to allow for individual
variation. Hence Carlo Ginzburg's famous study of Menocchio
the heretical miller from a village in Friuli, who compared the cosmos to a cheese with worms in it, was designed to undermine the
history of mentalities (though the author also employed his hero
as a spokesman, however eccentric, for traditional peasant culture, so that mentalities, thrown out of the door, came back in
again through the window).[32] Homogenization of beliefs is not a
necessary part of the approach. It is possible to follow Jacques Le
Goff and use the term 'mentality' to describe only the beliefs
which a given individual shares with a number of contemporaries,
limiting the approach to the investigation of common assumptions
rather than extending it to the whole of intellectual history.[33] In
practice, however, homogenization remains a danger.

(2) Linked to the problem of variation is the problem of change,
or variation over time. It is, in the words of a critic from within
the French tradition, Roger Chartier, 'the problem on which all
history of mentalities stumbles, that of the reasons for and

[32] Ginzburg (1976).
[33] Le Goff (1974).

modalities of the passage from one system to another'.[34] The
sharper the contrast between one mentality and another ('traditional' and 'modern', for example), the harder it is to explain
how change ever took place. The crucial idea here would seem to
be that of a 'system' of beliefs, a circle of thought in which each
part at once supports and is supported by the rest, making the
whole system impervious to falsification (a 'closed system' in the
words of the philosopher Karl Popper).[35]

A particularly clear example of circularity was studied by
Marc Bloch in his book about the belief that the rulers of France
and England had the power to cure skin disease by touching the
sufferer and pronouncing the formula, 'The king touches you,
God heals you.' Bloch pointed out that the same sufferers sometimes returned to be touched by the king on another occasion,
behaviour which shows both that the ritual had not worked and
that its failure to work had not destroyed the faith of the patient
in the remedy.[36] Another vivid example is the parallel account
given by Evans-Pritchard of the Zande belief in poison oracles.
'In this web of belief,' he wrote, 'every strand depends upon
every other strand, and a Zande cannot get out of its meshes
because it is the only world he knows.'[37] This notion of a system
of beliefs is at once a help and a hindrance to historians. If we do
not use it we cannot explain how ideas persist over the generations in the face of awkward empirical evidence, but if we do use
it we make it difficult for ourselves to understand change.

To put the point another way, it is all too easy to reify mentalities, to perceive them – in Fernand Braudel's famous metaphor –
as 'prisons' from which individuals cannot escape.[38] It is worth
stressing that this danger, acute in practice, is not one to which
historians of mentalities must inevitably succumb. In the case of
Italy, for instance, it is fascinating to see the gradual rise between
the thirteenth and seventeenth centuries of what has been called
the 'numerate mentality', revealed in practices like the spread and
elaboration of censuses as well as in private account-books.[39]
For an example of a change in the mentality of a group of

[34] Chartier (1988), 19–52.
[35] Popper (1934).
[36] Bloch (1924).
[37] Evans-Pritchard (1937), 194.
[38] Vovelle (1982); cf. Gismondi (1985), 211ff.
[39] Burckhardt (1860); Murray (1978), 180ff.

intellectuals over the relatively short term, one might point to the so-called 'scientific revolution' of the middle of the seventeenth century, notably to the so-called 'mechanization of the world picture' in which the shift from a view of the world as animate to a view of the cosmos as a vast machine was associated with a major change in ideas or assumptions about causality.[40] At much the same time, and among some of the same groups of people, there was a perceptible shift (even if it was less rapid and profound than used to be thought) from justifying statements by quoting authorities to justifying them by experience.[41] Again, the anthropologists Ernest Gellner and Robin Horton, elaborating ideas from Evans-Pritchard and Popper, have sketched out a general picture of change in modes of thought, emphasizing the importance of competition between theories and of awareness of alternatives to a given intellectual system.[42] In short, despite the force of this objection to the practice of past historians of mentalities, it can be and has been answered.

(3) Another serious objection to the history of mentalities is that it treats belief systems as autonomous. In other words, it is concerned with the relationship of beliefs with one another, to the exclusion of the relationship between beliefs and society. The objection must not be exaggerated. Neither Bloch's *Royal Touch* nor his colleague Febvre's *Problem of Unbelief* (which emphasized the impossibility of thinking all kinds of thought at all times) treated belief systems as completely independent of society. There remains a major difference in emphasis between two approaches to the history of thought. Historians of ideologies see thought as shaped (if not determined) by social forces, and they emphasize the cunning (conscious or unconscious) by which a particular view of the world is presented as natural, indeed the only possible one. Historians of mentalities by contrast see belief systems as relatively innocent and autonomous. The two approaches overlap but they do not coincide.[43]

(4) A still more serious objection to the mentalities approach is that it is built on evolutionism and more specifically, on the

---

[40] Dijksterhuis (1950); Blumenberg (1960).
[41] Dear (1985).
[42] Gellner (1974), ch. 8; Horton (1967, 1982).
[43] Vovelle (1982).

contrast between logical and pre-logical thought made by Lucien Lévy-Bruhl, foundations which have been undermined by later research. The importance of Lévy-Bruhl in the intellectual history of the early twentieth century still awaits adequate assessment. His critique of simple notions of empathy was a valuable one, and his own notion of 'pre-logical' thought was more subtle than some of his critics have realized.[44] He influenced thinkers as diverse as Ernst Cassirer, Jane Harrison, Johan Huizinga, and Ludwik Fleck. As remarked above, it was Lévy-Bruhl who launched the term *mentalité* in French in the 1920s. (In England, the word 'mentality' had been used as early as 1913, ironically enough by the anthropologist Bronislaw Malinowski in a letter to J. G. Frazer criticizing Durkheim's notion of 'the collective consciousness').[45] However, at the end of his life, Lévy-Bruhl abandoned his famous distinction between the 'pre-logical' and 'logical' mentalities. In any case, anthropologists as different as Evans-Pritchard and Lévi-Strauss have agreed to reject it, together with the evolutionist schema of which it formed a part.[46]

All the same, a rather simple contrast along roughly Lévy-Bruhlian lines, between two mentalities, can be found not only in the work of Febvre (and to a lesser extent in that of Bloch, always the most cautious of the two), but also in some of their successors, such as Jean Delumeau and Robert Muchembled. The last two historians have been criticized for attempting to explain peasant religion in early modern Europe almost entirely in negative terms, in terms of failure, anxiety and the constraints of a harsh environment. After all, it does seem rather implausible (as Wittgenstein once remarked with reference to Frazer) to treat an entire world-view as a mistake.[47] To describe an alien belief system as a failure is a gross form of ethnocentrism. Where do the criteria of success and failure come from if not from the speaker's own culture? Ethnocentrism is encouraged by the description of mentalities as 'traditional' and 'modern' (no less than 'primitive' and 'civilized', 'pre-logical' and 'logical'), since these dichotomies tend to slip into a contrast between Us and Them. The dichotomies elide the differences between (say) Chinese mandarins, Renaissance humanists and Breton peasants, all of

---

[44] Evans-Pritchard (1965), 78–99.
[45] Ackerman (1987), 267.
[46] Lévy-Bruhl (1949).
[47] Clark (1983), 75–6.

whose beliefs, since they are unlike ours, have to be described as 'traditional'.

All four criticisms of the approach come in different forms, more or less cogent, undermining the work of some historians of mentalities more effectively than others. However, all of them suggest the need to reformulate the approach to meet the objections. The remainder of this chapter will discuss three proposals for reformulation – a greater concern with interests, with categories and with metaphors.

Mentalities and Interests

In the days of Bloch and Febvre, Marxist historians did not have a credible alternative to the history of mentalities, because they dismissed ideas as mere 'superstructure' (or 'ideology' in a reductionist sense), and devoted their attention to economic history. Later Marxists, such as Edward Thompson and Raymond Williams, questioned the notion of 'superstructure', refined the notion of ideology, and revived alternative concepts such as cultural 'hegemony'. In these ways they moved closer to the idea of mentality. Lucien Febvre would have recognized Williams's concern with 'structures of feeling' as akin to his own interest in the history of emotions.[48]

What remains distinctive in the Marxian approach is the concern with interests, a concern which the classic history of mentalities lacked. Looking back on Marc Bloch's great book on the royal touch after more than seventy years, it has come to seem odd that he did not discuss in whose interest it was that the belief in the supernatural powers of kings should continue to exist. The question is a particularly important one for the early modern period, when the monarchy was under attack in the French and English civil wars, and more especially in the late seventeenth century. Charles II and Louis XIV were familiar with the ideas of the 'new science' of their day and they are unlikely to have believed in the virtues of their touch. Nevertheless, they continued the traditional practice, doubtless because they considered it in their interest to do so.

[48] Vovelle (1982).

More generally, historians of mentalities cannot afford to ignore the problems raised by students of ideologies, even if they do not deal with them in the same confident way as (say) the philosopher Louis Althusser. Some scholars who described themselves as historians of mentalities, notably Georges Duby and Michel Vovelle, began to concern themselves with these questions of interests, legitimation, and so on in the 1970s and early 1980s.[49] It is not easy to combine what might be described as the 'innocent' and the 'cynical' views of thought, but a synthesis may be possible along the lines of the study of the unconscious harmonizing of ideas with interests. Conflicts of interest make the unconscious conscious and the implicit explicit, and in this way they lead to change.

Paradigms and Schemata

The second proposal for the reform of the history of mentalities is a greater concern with categories, schemata, formulae, stereotypes or paradigms (the variety of terminology reveals the extent to which similar problems and insights have occurred in different fields and disciplines). In this area we may situate the work of Aby Warburg and Ernst Gombrich on art, of Thomas Kuhn on science, and of Michel Foucault on a variety of topics. The disciplinary and national contrasts between these scholars may make readers pause for a moment, but whatever their other differences, all four demonstrate an interest in categories and 'schemata', not only in the sense of recurrent themes or motifs but also in the structuring of thought.[50] Incidentally, all four scholars have drawn inspiration from one form or another of psychology. Like Bloch and Febvre, Warburg was interested in historical psychology even before his breakdown and subsequent treatment by Ludwig Binswanger. Gombrich and Kuhn acknowledged a debt to Gestalt psychology, while Foucault's studies of psychiatry are well known.

If the great stumbling block for the history of mentalities is, as suggested earlier, 'the reasons for and the modalities of the passage from one system to another', then there is an obvious case

---

[49] Duby (1979); Vovelle (1982).
[50] Warburg (1932); Gombrich (1960b); Kuhn (1962); Foucault (1966).

for taking up Kuhn's notion of an intellectual tradition or 'paradigm' which may absorb or resist change for long periods thanks to relatively minor 'adjustments', but will finally crack and allow a 'Gestalt switch' or intellectual 'revolution'. Kuhn's model of the process of intellectual change is an attractive one precisely because it is dynamic, concerned with a sequence.

The notion of paradigm is of course problematic even in the history of science, where it began. It becomes still more problematic if it is utilized in other intellectual fields.[51] As in the case of 'mentality', a paradigm must not be seen as a prison. It is something individuals use to make sense of their experience, yet at the same time it shapes their thinking. Despite these problems, the notion of paradigm can be and has been utilized with sensitivity, skill and caution – in studies of Renaissance humanism, for example, and of early modern political thought.[52]

Similar kinds of difficulty arise when one tries to work with the parallel notion of 'schema', which has already made its appearance in this book (above, pp. 39–41, 95–7). Schemata are amazingly long-lived on occasion, as Aby Warburg showed in his studies of the classical tradition, and Ernst Curtius (who was inspired by Warburg) in his work on *topoi* or commonplaces in European literature (the image of the world as a book, the *locus amoenus* or 'beautiful place', and so on).[53] All the same, these categories and stereotypes employed by individuals and groups to structure or interpret their experience of a changing world are themselves subject to change over the long term. The problem is to account for these changes. In his *Art and Illusion* (1960), the most creative and the best-known study to use the notion of the schema, Ernst Gombrich suggested that schemata are 'corrected' by artists by checking them against the natural world. However – as a reviewer was quick to point out – if the artist's view of nature is a product of the schemata, it is impossible to break out of the circle.[54] The same point might be made against Thomas Kuhn's view of perceived 'discrepancies' between paradigm and reality as leading to scientific revolutions.

A similar objection might be levelled against the idea of 'episteme', developed by Gaston Bachelard, Georges Canguilhem and

[51] Lakatos and Musgrave (1970); Hollinger (1980).
[52] Seigel (1968); Pocock (1972), 273–91.
[53] Curtius (1948).
[54] Arnheim (1962).

Michel Foucault, or against the idea of mental 'grids' or 'filters' employed by Foucault and some social anthropologists, filters which exclude some messages or aspects of reality while allowing others through.[55] These filters are more general, more abstract and perhaps more flexible than Warburg's 'schemata' but their function too is to assimilate different situations to one another in order to make them easier to understand. In other words, the greater the emphasis on system, the more difficult it is to explain change. One might regard this difficulty as the converse of the success of these models in explaining continuities, traditions and cultural reproduction. The cultural historian seems to be in a situation not unlike that of the physicists who view light as waves for some purposes and as particles for others.

All the same, it may be possible to say something about changes in the schemata. For example, one can focus on the displacement or migration of a given schema or stereotype from one object to another. After the discovery of America, for example, the traditional stereotypes of the 'monstrous races' (people with the heads of dogs, or with their faces in their stomachs and so on) did not disappear. They were relocated in this new world, as in the case of the Amazons (above, p. 140).[56] Again, the early modern stereotype of the witch (associated with sex orgies, the eating of babies, etc.) has been shown to have a long history. In the Middle Ages it was applied by the orthodox to heretics, and in ancient Roman times by pagans to Christians.[57]

To account for changes in the schemata or more generally in mentalities, it is probably necessary to combine external with internal approaches. A so-called 'belief system' may be viewed as a bundle of schemata, which generally support one another but may sometimes be in contradiction. A certain amount of contradiction is not difficult to live with, but once a certain critical threshold is passed, problems arise. Change might therefore be explained in terms of a combination of external 'forces' with 'allies' within the system, traitors within the gates of the fortress.

---

[55] Pike (1954); Foucault (1966); Douglas (1970).
[56] Wittkower (1942), 72–4; Friedman (1981), 197–207.
[57] Cohn (1975).

History of Metaphors

In the last paragraph I was driven to metaphor in the attempt to conceptualize conceptual change. The notions of 'schema' and 'system' may themselves be clarified if we look more closely at language, and especially at metaphor and symbol. Historians, like anthropologists and sociologists, are coming to recognize the importance of language in 'constituting' the reality they study.[58] Linguistics – notably the work of Antoine Meillet – was already influential on Febvre's history of mentalities, but a newer linguistics has something different to offer.

The relation between modes of communication and modes of thought has attracted much attention from both historians and anthropologists in the last generation.[59] Indeed, there is a danger that after many years of neglect, language has now been credited with too much power. Like Braudel's notion of mentalities as 'prisons', Nietzsche's idea of the 'prison-house of language' – developed by the American linguist Benjamin Whorf – is both reductionist and simplistic.[60] At the other extreme, at a time when it has become common to assume that reality is 'constructed' or 'constituted' by individuals and groups, the limits of that power to construct and the limits within which it operates need to be borne in mind. The world is not completely malleable.

However, if we are trying to describe the differences between mentalities, it seems useful to focus on recurrent metaphors, especially those which seem to structure thought. Obvious examples in the history of the West are the metaphor of the world as an organism (a 'body', an 'animal'), and the metaphor of the world as a machine, and the shift from one to the other in the course of the so-called 'scientific revolution' of the seventeenth century. The idea of the 'mechanization of the world picture' in the seventeenth century is a fruitful one which deserves a fuller, richer, wider treatment than it received in the famous book of that title published by the Dutch scholar E. J. Dijksterhuis in 1950. A similar point might be made about the decline of natural symbols like the 'body politic'. In the late Middle Ages, it was argued that a king had two bodies, his natural body, subject to decay

---

[58] Crick (1976).
[59] Goody (1977); Clanchy (1979); Eisenstein (1979).
[60] Jameson (1972); Whorf (1956).

and death, and his 'body politic', which was immortal. By the
seventeenth century, however, this argument was dismissed as
mere metaphor. A case might also be made for the decline in the
importance, if not in the employment, of personifications like the
gabelle, discussed above.[61]

The stress on dominant metaphors is especially valuable
because it is a means of liberating historians of mentalities from
the perils (if not the 'prison') of the binary system, the great divide
into traditional and modern. The point is not to suggest that a
given period be characterized in terms of one metaphor alone.
Seventeenth-century thinkers, for example, were fascinated not
only by the image of the machine but by the metaphor of law.
They spoke and wrote of the laws of nature and of the 'court' of
heaven, complete with its judges, advocates and so on. At times
they even enacted the metaphor. The Jansenists, for example,
many of whom came from the best legal families of the time, had
the habit of leaving written appeals to Christ on altars. 'In 1679 a
nun was buried with an *appel* to the Risen Saviour between her
hands, and forty days later, since that was the proper legal
interval, a *relief d'appel* was lowered into her tomb.'[62]

It is also necessary to ask whether there has been a decline of
metaphor, a reaction against metaphor, a gradual shift from a
more concrete to a more abstract mode of thought (associated
with literacy and numeracy), together with a greater interest in
the literal rather than the symbolic interpretation of texts, images
and events, a rise of 'literal-mindedness'. Like many other historians, I believe that a shift of this kind took place and would date
it – among the elites of Western Europe, at least – to the middle
of the seventeenth century. However, what happened might be
better redescribed not so much as a decline or abandonment of
metaphor as a change in the conception of metaphor, from objective 'correspondence' to mere subjective 'analogy'.[63]

The redescription is necessary to avoid the dangerous illusion
that we today think without the help of metaphors.[64] Historians
themselves make much more use of metaphors than they generally admit – metaphors of sickness and health, youth and old age,

---

[61] Kantorowicz (1957); cf. Archambault (1967); Starkey (1977).
[62] Knox (1950), 201.
[63] Hollander (1961), conclusion; Harris (1966); Vickers (1984); cf. Burke
(1993, 1997).
[64] Blumenberg (1960); Lakoff and Johnson (1980).

of rivers (the 'flow' of time), of buildings, of theatres, and so on.[65] The power of metaphor is coming to be taken seriously not only by linguists, philosophers and literary critics, but also by social anthropologists, who study its place in social life.[66] Historians of mentalities, who also study thought at the everyday level, have something important to gain by following their example. A case in point is that of the metaphor of purity, as enacted by nobles who refused to contaminate their blood by marrying commoners, dissident Christians who wanted to 'purify' the church, or communities who burned witches or expelled outsiders in campaigns of 'ethnic cleansing'.

It will be noted that of the three points discussed in the last few pages, the last, on metaphors, is concerned with an 'internalist' history of mentalities, in other words with the relation of beliefs to one another. The first, on interests, is concerned with an 'externalist' history, with the relation of beliefs to society. The second point, about categories, is concerned with both. Categories and schemata are ways of structuring thought. They are not neutral, however. They may be associated with interests, with attempts by some groups to control others, as has been suggested by the sociologists who have developed what they call 'labelling theory'. Give a witch a bad name and burn her. It is essential to any reformed or reformulated history of mentalities that it combine the insights of the internalist and externalist approaches.

Despite the renewal of the history of mentalities in the 1970s and 1980s by the appropriation and incorporation of concepts taken from other traditions, there has been a turn against it, even in France. A critique from outside, Geoffrey Lloyd's *Demystifying Mentalities* (1990), was rapidly translated into French and furnished with a more radical title suggesting that the moment had come to 'finish with' the approach, *Pour en finir avec les mentalités*. Today, historians of the *Annales* group, from Jacques Le Goff to Roger Chartier, are more likely to speak either of *représentations* or of *l'imaginaire social*.[67] The first is Durkheim's old term, though it now carries associations with American 'new historicism' and the Californian journal

---

[65] White (1973); Demandt (1978).
[66] Douglas (1970); Sapir and Crocker (1977).
[67] Chartier (1988), esp. ch. 1; cf. Boureau (1989).

Representations. The second is a difficult term to translate, but something like 'collective imagination' may approximate to it. It echoes a series of studies of the imagination by such theorists as Jacques Lacan, Louis Althusser, and Cornelius Castoriadis.

It would be unfair to suggest that current historians of representations or the collective imagination are simply carrying on the old firm under a new sign. Together with the word 'mentality' they have abandoned the misleading idea of 'pre-logical' thought. On the positive side, they show more interest than their predecessors in visual images. All the same, they continue to be preoccupied with the history of everyday thinking. For this reason, whatever term they use to describe their enterprise, they cannot avoid facing some of the same basic problems as their predecessors.

I2

Unity and Variety in Cultural History

Today, we are living through what has been called a 'cultural turn' in the study of humanity and society. 'Cultural studies' now flourish in many educational institutions, especially in the English-speaking world.[1] A number of scholars who would a decade or so ago have described themselves as literary critics, art historians or historians of science, now prefer to define themselves as cultural historians, working on 'visual culture', 'the culture of science', and so on. Political 'scientists' and political historians are exploring 'political culture', while economists and economic historians have turned their attention from production to consumption, and so to culturally shaped desires and needs. Indeed, in contemporary Britain and elsewhere, 'culture' has become an everyday term which ordinary people use when talking about their community or way of life.[2]

All the same, cultural history is not very firmly established, at least in an institutional sense. Come to that, it is not easy to answer the question, What is culture? It seems to be as difficult to define the term as to do without it. As we have seen in chapter 1, many varieties of 'cultural history' have been practised in different parts of the world since the late eighteenth century, when the term was originally coined in Germany (above, p. 2). In the last few years, cultural history has fragmented still further than

---

[1] Hall (1980); Turner (1990); Storey (1996).
[2] Baumann (1996), 4, 34.

before. The discipline of history is splitting into more and more subdisciplines, and most scholars prefer to contribute to the history of 'sectors' such as science, art, literature, education or historiography itself rather than writing about whole cultures. In any case, the nature, or at least the definition of cultural history is increasingly in dispute.

The moment seems a good one for taking stock and attempting to strike a balance. I begin here with a brief account of traditional cultural history, move on to the so-called 'new' cultural history, defined by contrast to the tradition, and end by discussing what is to be done now, whether we should opt for the new, return to the old, or attempt some kind of synthesis. Let me say once and for all that I make no claim to expertise in the whole of this enormous 'field'. Like other historians, I tend to work on a particular period (the sixteenth and seventeenth centuries) and on a particular region (Western Europe, especially Italy), as the case-studies in earlier chapters will have shown. In this final chapter, however, I shall be transgressing these spatial, temporal and disciplinary boundaries in the attempt to view cultural history (despite its internal divisions) as a whole.

Classical Cultural History and its Critics

In the middle of the nineteenth century, when Matthew Arnold was giving his lectures on 'Culture and Anarchy', and Jacob Burckhardt was writing his *Kultur der Renaissance in Italien*, the idea of culture seemed virtually self-explanatory. The situation was not so very different in 1926, when Johan Huizinga delivered his famous lecture, in Utrecht, on 'The Task of Cultural History'.

For all three scholars, 'culture' meant art, literature and ideas, 'sweetness and light' as Arnold described it, or in Huizinga's more prosaic but more precise formulation, 'figures, motifs, themes, symbols, concepts, ideals, styles and sentiments'.[3] The literature, ideas, symbols, sentiments and so on were essentially those to be found in the Western tradition, from the Greeks onwards, among elites with access to formal education. In short, culture was something which some societies had (or more

---

[3] Huizinga (1929); cf. Gilbert (1990), 46–80.

exactly, which some groups in some societies had), while others lacked it.

This is the 'opera house' conception of culture, as it has been labelled by an American anthropologist.[4] It underlies what might be called the 'classic' variety of cultural history, classic in the double sense that it emphasizes the classics, or the canon, of great works and also that it underlies a number of historical classics, notably Jacob Burckhardt's *Renaissance* (1860) and Johan Huizinga's *Waning of the Middle Ages* (1919), the second of these studies being in many ways an attempt both to imitate and to surpass the first. The difference between these works and specialized studies in the history of art, literature, philosophy, music and so on is their generality, their concern with all the arts and their relation to one another and to the 'spirit of the age'.

The two studies by Burckhardt and Huizinga – not to mention other distinguished works by the same authors – are marvellous books by great historians. Both writers had a gift for evoking the past and also for showing connections between different activities. All the same, I shall argue that their approach cannot or should not be the model for cultural history today, because it cannot deal satisfactorily with certain difficulties. Burckhardt and Huizinga themselves, unlike their followers, were at least intermittently aware of these difficulties, but for most of the time the classic approach is what they practised. This classical tradition of cultural history is open to at least five serious objections.

(1) It is suspended in the air, in the sense of ignoring (or at least placing little emphasis on) society – the economic infrastructure, the political and social structure, and so on. Burckhardt himself admitted in later life that his book had paid insufficient attention to the economic foundations of the Renaissance, while Huizinga discussed the late medieval preoccupation with death without relating it to the plagues which ravaged Europe from 1348 onwards. This general criticism was emphasized by the first scholars to criticize the classical model, the Marxists, or more exactly that fraction of the Marxists which took culture seriously.

In the 1940s and 1950s, three Central European refugees in England, Frederick Antal, Francis Klingender and Arnold

---

[4] Wagner (1975), 21.

Hauser, offered an alternative cultural history, a 'social history' of art and literature.[5] In the 1950s and 1960s, the studies of culture and society by Raymond Williams, Edward Thompson and others continued or reconstructed this tradition.[6] Thompson, for instance, objected to the location of popular culture in what he called the 'thin air' of meanings, attitudes and values, and attempted to situate it in 'its proper material abode', 'a working environment of exploitation and resistance to exploitation'.[7]

The alternative cultural history produced within this tradition has had much to say about the relation of what Marx called the cultural 'superstructure' to its economic 'base', though both Thompson and Williams were or became ill at ease with this metaphor.[8] They also showed a concern with what sociologists such as Max Weber have called the 'carriers' of culture. They viewed culture as a system of messages in which it is important to identify 'who says what to whom'. A view, incidentally, which was not and is not confined to Marxists.

In social anthropology, for example, the supporters of what is known as the 'pattern theory' of culture, a morphological approach not unlike that of (say) Huizinga, were criticized by the supporters of a functional theory of culture. One of the leaders of the functional school, Bronislaw Malinowski, took the example of a stick which might be used for digging, punting, walking or fighting. 'In each of these specific uses, the stick is embedded in a different cultural context; that is, put to different uses, surrounded with different ideas, given a different cultural value and as a rule designated by a different name.'[9]

(2) A second major criticism of classic cultural history is that it depends on the postulate of cultural unity or consensus. Some writers within the tradition liked to use the Hegelian term 'spirit of the age', *Zeitgeist*, but even when this phrase was not used the essential assumption remained. Thus Burckhardt wrote of 'the culture of the Renaissance', while Huizinga once advised cultural historians to search for 'the quality that unites all the cultural

[5] Antal (1947); Klingender (1947); Hauser (1951).
[6] Williams (1958, 1961); Thompson (1963).
[7] Thompson (1991), 7.
[8] Williams (1977).
[9] Malinowski (1931); cf. Singer (1968).

products of an age and makes them homogeneous'.[10] In similar fashion Paul Hazard entitled his study of late seventeenth-century intellectuals *The Crisis of the European Mind* (1935), while Perry Miller called his history of academic ideas in or near Harvard *The New England Mind* (1939). Arnold Toynbee took the idea of unity still more literally when he organized his comparative *Study of History* (1934–61) around twenty-six distinct 'civilizations'. The same idea or assumption underlay (indeed, underpinned) Oswald Spengler's massive volumes on the *Decline of the West* (1918–22).

The problem is that this postulate of cultural unity is extremely difficult to justify. Once again, it was the Marxists who took the lead in criticizing it. Thompson, for instance, remarked that 'the very term "culture", with its cosy invocation of consensus, may serve to distract attention from social and cultural contradictions.'[11] The same argument has been employed against social anthropologists working in the tradition of Émile Durkheim. Ironically enough, similar criticisms have been levelled by Ernst Gombrich against the Marxist historian Arnold Hauser as well as against Burckhardt, Huizinga and the art historian Erwin Panofsky for what he calls their Hegelian assumption of a 'spirit of the age' (above, p. 21), vividly illustrated in Panofsky's elegant essay *Gothic Architecture and Scholasticism* (1951).[12]

The problem is that cultural consensus or homogeneity is very difficult to discover. For example, the movement we call the Renaissance was a movement within elite culture, which is unlikely to have touched the peasant majority of the population. Even within the elite, there were cultural divisions at this time. Traditional Gothic art as well as the new Renaissance style continued to attract patrons. Antal went so far as to claim that the richly detailed and decorative art of Gentile da Fabriano expressed the world-view of the feudal nobility, while the simpler, more realistic art of Masaccio expressed that of the Florentine bourgeoisie. This contrast between two styles and two classes is much too simple, but the point that distinctions existed within the culture of the upper classes in fifteenth-century Florence deserves to be taken seriously.

[10] Huizinga (1929), 76.
[11] Thompson (1991), 6.
[12] Gombrich (1969).

In similar fashion, popular culture in early modern Europe, for instance, not only varied between one region and another but also took different forms in cities and villages, or among women and men. Even the culture of an individual may be far from homogeneous. The upper classes of early modern Europe may be described as 'bicultural' in the sense that they participated fully in popular culture as well as possessing a culture of their own which ordinary people did not share.[13] Again, in nineteenth-century Japan, some upper-class men, at least, began to live what has been called a 'double life', a life both Western and traditional, consuming two kinds of food, wearing two kinds of clothes, reading two kinds of books and so on.[14]

(3) A central notion in classic cultural history, taken over from the church, is that of 'tradition', the basic idea being that of handing over objects, practices and values from generation to generation. The complementary opposite of tradition was the idea of 'reception', the reception of Roman law, for instance, or that of the Renaissance outside Italy. In all these cases, it was widely assumed that what was received was the same as what was given: a cultural 'heritage' or 'legacy' (as in the titles of a once famous series of studies of *The Legacy of Greece*, *The Legacy of Rome*, and so on).

This assumption was undermined by the German Aby Warburg and his followers (pioneers in the 1920s of interdisciplinary 'cultural studies', or *Kulturwissenschaft*) in a series of remarkable monographs on the classical tradition in the Middle Ages and the Renaissance. They noted, for example, how the pagan gods 'survived' into medieval times only at the price of some remarkable transformations: Mercury, for instance, was sometimes represented as an angel, more often as a bishop.[15] Warburg was particularly interested in elements of tradition which he called 'schemata' or 'formulae', whether visual or verbal, which persisted over the centuries although their uses and applications varied.[16] The identification of stereotypes, formulae, commonplaces and recurrent themes in texts, images and performances and the study of their transformation have become an important part of the practice of

[13] Burke (1978), 23–64.
[14] Witte (1928); Seidensticker (1983).
[15] Warburg (1932); Seznec (1940).
[16] Warburg (1932), vol. 1, 3–58, 195–200

cultural history, witness the recent work on memory and travel discussed above (chapters 3 and 6).

Tradition, as a specialist on ancient India has put it, is subject to an inner conflict between the principles transmitted from one generation to another and the changing situations to which they are supposed to be applied.[17] To put the point another way, following the letter of tradition is likely to mean diverging from its spirit. No wonder that – as in the case of the disciples of Confucius (say), or Luther, the followers so often diverge from the founders. The façade of tradition may mask innovation.[18] As we have already seen, this point may be made about historiography itself. Ranke was not a Rankean, or Burckhardt a Burckhardtian, any more than Marx was a Marxist.

The idea of tradition has been subjected to a still more devastating critique by Eric Hobsbawm, who has argued that many practices which we regard as very old were actually invented relatively recently, many of them (in the case of Europe) between 1870 and 1914 in response to social change and to the needs of the increasingly centralized national states.[19] It might be suggested that Hobsbawm's distinction between invented and 'genuine' traditions is too sharp. Some degree of conscious or unconscious adaptation to new circumstances is a constant feature of the transmission of tradition, as Goody's example from West Africa (above, p. 58) illustrates more dramatically than most. All the same, Hobsbawm's challenge to cultural historians requires a response.

Given its ambiguities, one may well ask whether historians would not be better off if they abandoned the idea of tradition altogether. My own view is that it is virtually impossible to write cultural history without it, but that it is high time to abandon what might be called the traditional notion of tradition, modifying it to allow for adaptation as well as adoption, and drawing on the ideas of 'reception' theory, discussed below.

(4) A fourth criticism of classic cultural history is that the idea of culture implicit in this approach is too narrow. In the first place, it equates culture with high culture. In the last generation in

---

[17] Heesterman (1985), 10–25.
[18] Schwartz (1959).
[19] Hobsbawm and Ranger (1983), 263–307.

particular, historians have done a great deal to redress the balance and recover the history of the culture of ordinary people. However, even studies of popular culture often treat culture as a series of 'works', as examples of 'folksong', 'popular art', and so on. Anthropologists, on the other hand, have traditionally used the term 'culture' much more widely, to refer to the attitudes and values of a given society and their expression or embodiment in 'collective representations' (as Durkheim used to say) or 'practices', a term which has become associated with recent social theorists such as Pierre Bourdieu and Michel de Certeau. The ex-literary critics such as Raymond Williams and Richard Hoggart who founded British 'cultural studies' have moved in the same direction, from literary texts to popular texts and from popular texts to ways of life.

(5) The classical tradition of cultural history may also be criticized on the grounds that it is no longer appropriate or adequate for our time. Although the past does not change, history needs to be rewritten from generation to generation in order for that past to continue to be intelligible to a changing present. Classic cultural history was written for as well as about European elites. Today, on the other hand, the appeal of cultural history is wider and more diverse, geographically and socially. In some countries, this increasing appeal is associated with the rise of multidisciplinary courses under the umbrella of 'cultural studies'.

Classic cultural history emphasized a canon of great works within the European tradition, but the cultural historians of the late twentieth century are working in an age of decanonization. The well-publicized critique of the so-called 'canon' of great books in the USA and the ensuing 'culture wars' are only part of a much wider movement which has been labelled 'multiculturalism'.[20] Educated Westerners as well as Third World intellectuals are less and less at ease with the idea of a single 'great tradition' with a monopoly of cultural legitimacy. It is no longer possible for any of us to identify 'culture' with our own traditions.

We are living in an age of widespread discomfort with, if not rejection of, the so-called 'grand narrative' of the development of Western culture – the Greeks, the Romans, the Renaissance, the Discoveries, the Scientific Revolution, the Enlightenment, and so

[20] Bak (1993).

on, a narrative which can be used to legitimate claims to superiority on the part of Western elites.[21] There is equal discomfort with the idea of a literary, intellectual or artistic canon, or at least with the particular selection of texts or images which used to be presented as 'the' Great Books, Classics or Old Masters. Today, the process of 'canonization' and the social and political conflicts underlying it has become an object of study by cultural historians, but more for the light which it throws on the ideas and assumptions of the canonizers than on those of the canonized.[22]

What is to be done? To state my own view on an issue on which consensus seems at best to be somewhat remote, and at worst impossible, we should not abandon the study of the Renaissance and other movements in the 'high' culture of the West, which still have much to offer many people today despite the increasing cultural distance between late twentieth-century ideas and assumptions and those of the original audiences. Indeed, I should like to suggest that courses in 'cultural studies' would be much enriched if they were to make space for movements of this kind alongside contemporary popular culture. However, historians should write about these movements in a way which recognizes the value of other cultural traditions rather than regarding them as barbarism or absence of culture.

Anthropological History

Readers may be wondering whether the moral of the criticisms listed above is to abandon cultural history altogether. Perhaps this is the reason that the cultural studies movement – despite the example of one of its leaders, Raymond Williams – has been so little concerned with history (another reason might be the marginal position of cultural history in Britain). Yet it might well be argued that cultural history has become even more necessary than before in our age of fragmentation, specialization, and relativism. It is perhaps for this reason that scholars in other disciplines, from literary criticism to sociology, have been turning in

[21] Lyotard (1979); Bouwsma (1990), 348–65.
[22] Gorak (1991); Javitch (1991).

this direction. We seem to have been experiencing a rediscovery of the importance of symbols in history as well as in what used to be called 'symbolic anthropology'.

Another reaction to the criticisms might be to practise a different kind of cultural history. As we have seen, a number of Marxist historians and critics have attempted to do this. The work of Hauser, Antal, Thompson, Hobsbawm and Williams has already been mentioned, and it would not be difficult to extend the list to include Georg Lukács, Lucien Goldmann, and others. One might describe the work of these individuals as an alternative style of cultural history. Yet there remains something odd about the idea of a Marxist tradition of cultural history. To follow Marx was generally to affirm that culture was simply the 'superstructure', the icing on the cake of history. Marxists interested in the history of culture were in a marginal position which exposed them to attacks from two sides, from fellow-Marxists and from fellow-historians of culture. The reception of Edward Thompson's *The Making of the English Working Class* illustrates this point clearly enough.

A new style of cultural history, whether one calls it a second or a third style, has in fact emerged in the last generation, thanks in large part to ex-Marxists, or at least to scholars who once found some aspects of Marxism attractive. This approach is sometimes known as the 'new cultural history'.[23] Since novelty is a rapidly diminishing asset, it might be wiser to describe the new style in another way. One possibility is to speak of the 'anthropological' variety of history, since many of its practitioners (the present author among them) would confess to having learned much from anthropologists. They have also learned much from literary critics, like the 'new historicists' in the USA, who have adapted their methods of 'close reading' to the study of non-literary texts, such as official documents, and indeed to the study of 'texts' in inverted commas, from rituals to images.[24] Come to that, some anthropologists have learned from literary critics, as well as vice versa. Semiotics, the study of signs of all kinds, from poems and paintings to food and clothes, was the joint project of students of language and literature such as Roman Jakobson and Roland Barthes and anthropologists such as Claude Lévi-Strauss. Their

[23] Hunt (1989); cf. Chartier (1988).
[24] Greenblatt (1988a, 1988b).

concern with 'deep', unchanging structures of meaning diminished their appeal (to put it mildly) to historians, especially at first, but over the last generation or so the contribution of semiotics to the renewal of cultural history (the idea of a room or a meal as a system of signs, the awareness of oppositions and inversions, and so on) has become increasingly visible.

Despite the complex origins of the movement, 'anthropological history' may be a convenient label for it. It is clear enough that such history – like every style of history – is a child of our time, in this case a time of cultural clashes, multiculturalism and so on. For this very reason it has something to contribute to the study of the present as well as the past, viewing recent trends from the perspective of the long term.

Aby Warburg and Johan Huizinga already took an interest in anthropology at the beginning of the century, but today its influence among historians is much more pervasive than it was in their day. A substantial group of scholars now view the past as a foreign country, and like the anthropologists they see their task as one of interpreting the language of 'their' cultures, both literally and metaphorically. It was the British anthropologist Edward Evans-Pritchard who conceived of his discipline as a kind of translation from concepts of the culture being studied into those of the student's culture.[25] To employ the now famous distinction made by the anthropologist-linguist Kenneth Pike, it is necessary to move backwards and forwards between the 'emic' vocabulary of the natives of a culture, the insiders, and the 'etic' concepts of the outsiders who study them.

Cultural history is also a cultural translation from the language of the past into that of the present, from the concepts of contemporaries into those of historians and their readers. Its aim is to make the 'otherness' of the past both visible and intelligible.[26] This is not to say that historians should treat the past as completely alien. The dangers of treating another culture in this way have been made abundantly clear in the debate on 'orientalism', in other words the Western view (or views) of the East (or easts).[27]

Rather than thinking in terms of a binary opposition between Self and Other, as participants in cultural encounters have so

[25] Beidelman (1971); Lowenthal (1985); Pálsson (1993).
[26] Darnton (1984), 4; Pallares-Burke (1996).
[27] Said (1978).

often done, it may be more illuminating to try to think in terms of degrees of cultural distance. We could try to acquire a double vision, to see people in the past as unlike ourselves (in order to avoid the anachronistic imputation of our values to them), but at the same time as like us in their fundamental humanity.

The differences between the current anthropological model of cultural history and its predecessors, classical and Marxist, might be summed up in four points.

(1) In the first place, the traditional contrast between societies with culture and societies without culture has been abandoned. The decline of the Roman Empire, for instance, should not be viewed as the defeat of 'culture' by 'barbarism', but as a clash of cultures. Ostrogoths, Visigoths, Vandals and other groups had their own cultures (values, traditions, practices, representations, and so on). However paradoxical the phrase may seem, there was a 'civilization of the barbarians'. The assumption built into this third model is a cultural relativism as alien to the Marxists as it would have been to Burckhardt and Huizinga. Like anthropologists, the new cultural historians speak of 'cultures' in the plural. They do not assume that all cultures are equal in every respect, but they refrain from value judgements about the superiority of some over others, judgements which are inevitably made from the viewpoint of the historian's own culture and act as so many obstacles to understanding.

(2) In the second place, culture has been redefined along Malinowskian lines as comprising 'inherited artefacts, goods, technical processes, ideas, habits and values', or along Geertzian lines as 'the symbolic dimensions of social action'.[28] In other words, the meaning of the term has been extended to embrace a much wider range of activities than before – not only art but material culture, not only the written but the oral, not only drama but ritual, not only philosophy but the mentalities of ordinary people. Everyday life or 'everyday culture' is central to this approach, especially the 'rules' or conventions underlying everyday life, what Bourdieu calls the 'theory of practice' and the semiologist Jury Lotman, the 'poetics of everyday behaviour'.[29]

[28] Malinowski (1931), 621; Geertz (1973), 30.
[29] Bourdieu (1972); Lotman (1984); Frykman and Löfgren (1996).

Of course the process of learning how to be a medieval monk or a Renaissance noblewoman or a nineteenth-century peasant involved more than internalizing rules. As Bourdieu suggests, the learning process includes a more flexible pattern of responses to situations which – like the scholastic philosophers – he calls 'habitus'.[30] It might therefore be more accurate to use the term 'principle' rather than 'rule'.

In this wide sense, culture is now invoked in order to understand economic or political changes which had previously been analysed in a narrower, internal manner. For example, a historian of the decline of British economic performance between 1850 and 1980 explained it by 'the decline of the industrial spirit', linked to the gentrification of industrialists and ultimately to a revolution (or as the author calls it, a 'counter-revolution') in values.[31] For their part, political historians are making increasing use of the idea of 'political culture' to refer to attitudes, values and practices transmitted as part of the process of 'socializing' childen and taken for granted thereafter.

A striking example of a shift in this direction is the late F. S. L. Lyons, a political historian who entitled his last book *Culture and Anarchy in Ireland 1890–1939*. The point of the wry reference to Matthew Arnold was Lyons's conviction that Irish politics in that period could only be understood by taking into account 'the fact that at least four cultures have for the last three centuries been jostling each other in the island'. The dominant English culture coexisted and clashed with the Gaelic, Ulster Protestant, and Anglo-Irish cultures.[32]

(3) In the third place, the idea of 'tradition', central to the old cultural history, has been joined by a cluster of alternatives. One is the concept of cultural 'reproduction' launched in the 1970s by the French social theorists Louis Althusser and Pierre Bourdieu.[33] One advantage of this concept is to suggest that traditions do not continue automatically, out of inertia. On the contrary, as the history of education reminds us, it takes a great deal of effort to hand them down from generation to generation. The disadvantage of the term is that the idea of 'reproduction' suggests an

---

[30] Bourdieu (1972), 78–87.
[31] Wiener (1981).
[32] Lyons (1979).
[33] Althusser (1971); Bourdieu and Passeron (1970).

exact or even a mechanical copy, a suggestion which the history of education is far from confirming.[34] The idea of reproduction, like the idea of tradition, needs a counterpoise, such as the idea of reception.

The so-called 'reception theorists', among whom I include the Jesuit historian-anthropologist Michel de Certeau, have replaced the traditional assumption of passive reception by the new assumption of creative adaptation. They argue that 'the essential characteristic of cultural transmission is that whatever is transmitted changes.'[35] Adapting the doctrine of some Fathers of the church, who recommended Christians to 'despoil' pagan culture in the same way that the Israelites despoiled the treasures of the Egyptians, these theorists emphasize not handing down but 'appropriation'. Like the medieval scholastic philosophers, they argue that 'whatever is received is received according to the manner of the receiver' ('Quidquid recipitur, ad modum recipientis recipitur').[36] Their position implies a criticism of semiotics, or more exactly a historicization of semiotics, since it denies the possibility of finding fixed meanings in cultural artefacts.

In short, the stress has shifted from the giver to the receiver, on the grounds that what is received is always different from what was originally transmitted because receivers, consciously or unconsciously, interpret and adapt the ideas, customs, images and so on offered to them. The cultural history of Japan, for instance, offers many examples of what used to be called 'imitation', first of China and more recently of the West. This imitation is often so creative that a more accurate term for it might be 'cultural translation'. Thus Ch'an Buddhism was translated into Zen, and the Western novel domesticated by Natsume Soseki, who claimed to have written one of his stories 'in the manner of a haiku'.

The idea of reception may be linked to that of the schema, defined as a mental structure rather than in Warburg's sense of a visual or verbal topos. A schema can shape attitudes to the new, as in the case of the British travellers studied in chapter 6 above. The schema in this sense is sometimes described as a 'grid', a screen or a filter, which lets in some new elements but excludes

---

[34] Williams (1981), 181–205.
[35] Dresden (1975), 119ff.
[36] Jauss (1974); Certeau (1980); cf. Ricoeur (1981), 182–93.

others, thus ensuring that the messages which are received are different in some respects from the messages originally sent.[37]

(4) The fourth and last point is the reversal of the assumptions about the relation between culture and society implicit in the Marxist critique of classic cultural history. Cultural historians, like cultural theorists, have been reacting against the idea of the 'superstructure'. Many of them believe that culture is capable of resisting social pressures or even that it shapes social reality. Hence the increasing interest in the history of 'representations', and especially the story of the 'construction', 'invention' or 'constitution' of what used to be considered social 'facts' such as social class, nation, or gender. A number of recent books have the word 'invent' in their title, whether they deal with the invention of Argentina, Scotland, the people, or – as we have seen – of tradition.[38]

Associated with the interest in invention is the history of the collective imagination, *l'imaginaire social*, a new emphasis if not a new topic which crystallized in France partly in reponse to Michel Foucault's celebrated criticism of historians for what he called an 'impoverished' idea of the real which excluded what was imagined. This approach was effectively launched by two studies of the Middle Ages which appeared at much the same time, one concerned with this world and the other with the next, Georges Duby's *The Three Orders* (1979) and Jacques Le Goff's *Birth of Purgatory* (1981). The history of the imagination developed out of the history of collective mentalities, discussed in chapter 11 above. However, its practitioners pay more attention to visual sources, and also to the influence of traditional schemata on perception.

Historians were already producing studies of perception in the 1950s: images of the New World, for example, as a 'virgin land' or of Brazil as an earthly paradise, or the South Pacific as the home of noble or ignoble savages.[39] Indeed, Burckhardt and Huizinga were already aware that perception had a history. Burckhardt wrote of the rise of the view of the state as a 'work of

---

[37] Foucault (1971), 11; Ginzburg (1976).
[38] Hobsbawm and Ranger (1983); Morgan (1988); Pittock (1991); Shumway (1991).
[39] Smith (1950); Buarque de Holanda (1959); Smith (1960).

art', in other words as the result of planning, while Huizinga was interested in the influence of the romances of chivalry on the perception of social and political reality.[40] In their days, however, studies of this kind were viewed as marginal to the preoccupations of historians.

Today, on the other hand, what was once marginal has become central, and a number of traditional topics have been restudied from this viewpoint. Benedict Anderson, for instance, has rewritten the history of national consciousness in terms of what he calls 'imagined communities', noting the influence of fiction, as in the case of the Filipino José Rizal and his novel *Noli me tangere* (1887).[41] The continuing debate over the significance of the French Revolution is now particularly concerned with its place in the French 'political imagination'.[42] The history of witchcraft and demonology has also been studied as the history of the collective imagination, from the myth of the 'sabbath' to the projection of secret fears and desires onto individual scapegoats.[43] In short, the frontier between 'culture' and 'society' has been redrawn, and the empire of culture and of individual freedom has expanded.

Problems

How successful is the new cultural history? In my opinion, the approaches described above have been necessary ones. They are not simply a new fashion but responses to palpable weaknesses in earlier paradigms. This is not to say that all cultural historians should follow these approaches – it is surely better for a variety of styles of history to coexist than for one to gain a monopoly. In any case, reactions against the conventional wisdom have sometimes been pushed too far. For example, the current stress on the construction or invention of culture exaggerates human liberty as much as the older view of culture as the 'reflection' of society diminished that liberty. Invention is never free from constraints. One groups's invention or dream may be another group's prison. There are indeed revolutionary moments when the freedom to

---

[40] Burckhardt (1860), ch. 1; Huizinga (1919).
[41] Anderson (1983), 26–9.
[42] Furet (1984).
[43] Cohn (1975); Ginzburg (1990); Muchembled (1990); Clark (1996).

invent is at its maximum and everything seems possible, but these moments are followed by cultural 'crystallization'.

As so often happens in the history of disciplines, not to mention life in general, the attempt to solve some problems has raised others which are at least equally intractable. In order to highlight the continuing difficulties, it may be helpful to point to some of the weak points of two well-known recent examples of these new approaches. These books are among the most brilliant works of cultural history published in the last two or three decades. It is for this reason, as in the cases of Burckhardt and Huizinga, that their weaknesses are worth exploring.

In *The Embarrassment of Riches* (1987), a study of the Dutch Republic in the seventeenth century, Simon Schama invokes the names of Émile Durkheim, Maurice Halbwachs and Mary Douglas, and like these anthropologists he focuses on social values and their embodiment in everyday life. The Dutch Republic was a new nation, and Schama is concerned with the formation – if not the invention – of a new identity, expressed in the Dutch sense of themselves as a second Israel, a chosen people who had freed themselves from the yoke of the Spanish Pharaoh. He goes on to suggest that everyday life was influenced, or even shaped by this new identity. According to Schama, this is what accounts for the unusually sharp sense of privacy and domesticity in Holland, as well as for the cleanliness of Dutch houses, remarked upon by so many foreign travellers. They were showing the world, and especially the southern or Spanish Netherlanders, that they were different. For the first time, the obsessive cleanliness of Dutch housewives is presented as a part of Dutch history rather than remarked upon, as in the past, by historians on the way to more serious topics.

The weakness of this book, which it shares with the work of Burckhardt and Huizinga as well as with the Durkheimian anthropological tradition, is its emphasis on cultural unity. Schama dismisses views that regard culture as 'the outcrop of social class'. Unlike so many of the new cultural historians, he has not passed through a phase of sympathy with Marxism. He concentrates on what the Dutch had in common and has little to say about cultural contrasts or conflicts between regions or between religious or social groups. He interprets the obsession with cleanliness as a sign of Dutchness rather than as an attempt by middle-class townswomen to distinguish themselves from peasants or from their poorer urban neighbours. And yet, as recent work by a team of Dutch historians makes abundantly clear, contrasts and conflicts between rich and poor, urban and rural, and, not least, Catholic and Protestant were important in the history of the so-called 'United Provinces' in the seventeenth century.[44] The presence of an 'Orange' party in both cultures is not the only similarity between the northern Netherlanders in the seventeenth century and the northern Irish in the twentieth.

Carl Schorske's equally celebrated book is concerned with Vienna at the end of the nineteenth century, the Vienna of Arthur Schnitzler, Otto Wagner, Karl Lueger, Sigmund Freud, Gustav Klimt, Hugo von Hofmannsthal and Arnold Schoenberg. His many insights into the work of all these men, into the different arts they practised, and into their social milieu will have to be ignored here in order to concentrate attention on a single general problem, the tension between unity and variety. Schorske is well aware of the importance of subcultures in the polyglot imperial capital he chose to study. Indeed, he emphasizes the segregation of different groups of intellectuals and the fragmentation of culture, 'with each field proclaiming independence of the whole, each part in turn falling into parts'.[45] In similar fashion, his own study is divided into seven essays on different aspects of the culture of *fin de siècle* Vienna – literature, architecture, politics, psychoanalysis, painting, and music.

Fragmentation was doubtless a deliberate choice on the author's part. It is at least symbolically appropriate for a study of modernism.[46] It also responds to the author's concern 'to respect the historical development of each constituent branch of modern culture (social thought, literature, architecture etc.), rather than to hide the pluralized reality behind homogenizing definitions'.[47] The rejection of facile assumptions about the *Zeitgeist* and the willingness to take internal development seriously is one of the many virtues of this study.

Schorske is also interested in the 'cohesion' of the different 'cultural elements' described in his various chapters, and their relation to a shared political experience, 'the crisis of a liberal

---

[44] Schama (1987); Boekhorst et al. (1992).
[45] Schorske (1981), xxvii, xix.
[46] Cf. Roth (1994a); Roth (1994b), 3–4.
[47] Schorske (1981), xix–xx.

polity'. Indeed, his book carries the subtitle, 'politics and culture'. In this way he tries to hold the balance between 'internalist' and 'externalist' explanations of cultural change. In practice, however, politics receives a chapter of its own, like painting and music. Connections are implied, but they are not always made explicit, at least not at any length. The final paragraphs discuss only Schoenberg and Kokoschka. The author has chosen not to write a concluding chapter which might have attempted to tie the threads together. Such a choice deserves to be respected whether it is dictated by modesty, honesty or the desire to leave readers free to draw their own conclusions. All the same, this renunciation is in a sense a flight from responsibility. The *raison d'être* of a cultural historian is surely to reveal connections between different activities. If this task is impossible, one might as well leave architecture to the historians of architecture, psychoanalysis to the historians of psychoanalysis, and so on.

The essential problem for cultural historians today, as I see it at any rate, is how to resist fragmentation without returning to the misleading assumption of the homogeneity of a given society or period. In other words, to reveal an underlying unity (or at least, underlying connections) without denying the diversity of the past. For this reason it may be useful to draw attention to a body of recent and distinguished work on the history of cultural encounters.

The Encounter Model

In the last few years, cultural historians have been taking increasing interest in encounters, and also in cultural 'clash', 'conflict', 'contest', or 'invasion', not to forget or minimize the destructive aspects of these contacts.[48] For their part, historians of discovery or colonialism have begun to look at the cultural as well as the economic social and political consequences of European expansion.

It would of course be unwise to treat these encounters as if they happened between two cultures, falling back into the language of cultural homogeneity and treating cultures as objectively bounded entities (individuals may have a strong sense of

---

[48] Axtell (1985); Bitterli (1986); Lewis (1995).

boundary, but in practice the frontiers are crossed again and again). The point to emphasize here is the relatively new interest in the way in which the parties involved perceived, understood, or indeed failed to understand one another. More than one recent monograph has emphasized mistranslation and the 'mistaken identity' between concepts in two cultural systems, a misunderstanding which may well have aided the process of coexistence. A dialogue of the deaf is still a kind of dialogue.[49] For example, in Africa and elsewhere Christian missionaries have often assumed that they 'converted' the local population, since in their view the acceptance of the jealous God of the Christians necessarily involved the rejection of other religions. On the other hand, as some Africanists have suggested, some of the converts may have been interested in appropriating certain spiritual techniques in order to incorporate them into the local religious system (above, p. 154). It is difficult to say who was manipulating whom, but it is at least clear that the different parties to the encounter were operating with different definitions of the situation.[50]

In some remarkable books, historical anthropologists have attempted to reconstruct the 'vision of the vanquished', the way in which the Caribs perceived Columbus, the Aztecs Cortés, or the Incas Pizarro.[51] The example which has given rise to most debate concerns the encounter between the Hawaiians and Captain Cook and his sailors. The art historian Bernard Smith studied European perceptions of the encounter along the lines of Aby Warburg's histories of schemata. The anthropologist Marshall Sahlins then tried to reconstruct the views of the Hawaiians. He noted that Cook arrived at the moment of the year when the Hawaiians expected their god Lono, and argued that his arrival was perceived as an epiphany of the god, thus assimilating the extraordinary new event, the arrival of strangers, into the cultural order. The argument has been challenged, and the debate continues.[52] In a similar fashion, Western sinologists, long concerned with the ways in which European missionaries and diplomats perceived the Chinese, have begun to think seriously about the manner in which the Chinese perceived the

[49] Lockhart (1994), 219; MacGaffey (1994), 259–60.
[50] Smith (1960); Prins (1980); McGaffey (1986), 191–216; cf. Hilton (1985).
[51] Portilla (1959); Wachtel (1971); Hulme (1987); Clendinnen (1992).
[52] Smith (1960); Sahlins (1985); Obeyesekere (1992); Sahlins (1995).

Westerners.[53] It has been argued, for instance, that in China the Virgin Mary was assimilated to the indigenous goddess of mercy, Kuan Yin, while in Mexico she was assimilated to the goddess Tonantzin, thus producing the hybrid Madonna of Guadalupe.[54]

Although I am a European historian of Europe, as earlier chapters will have made abundantly clear, I have cited these examples from Asia, Africa, America and Australia for two reasons. In the first place, some of the most exciting current research in cultural history has been taking place on the frontiers – on the frontiers of the subject, on the frontiers of Europe. In the second place, this work on frontiers may serve as an inspiration for the rest of us. If no culture is an island, not even Hawaii or Britain, it should be possible to make use of the encounter model to study the history of our own culture, or cultures, which we should view as various rather than homogeneous, multiple rather than singular. Encounters and interactions should therefore join the practices and representations which Chartier has described as the principal objects of the new cultural history. After all, as Edward Said recently remarked, 'The history of all cultures is the history of cultural borrowing.'[55]

The history of empires offers clear examples of cultural interaction. The historian Arnaldo Momigliano wrote a book on the limits of Hellenization, the interaction between Greeks, Romans, Celts, Jews and Persians inside and outside the Roman Empire.[56] When the so-called 'barbarians' invaded that empire, a process of cultural interaction took place which included not only the Romanization of the invaders but also the reverse, the 'Gothicization' of the Romans. In the late medieval or the early modern period, one might examine the frontier between the Ottoman Empire and Christendom in this way.

For example, a study has been made of religious interaction – or as the author put it, 'transferences' – at an unofficial level, such as the pilgrimages by Muslims to the shrines of Christian saints and vice versa. Art historians have studied the common material culture of the frontier, for example the use of the Turkish scimitar by Polish troops. Historians of literature have

[53] Gernet (1982); Spence (1990).
[54] Boxer (1975), ch. 4; Lafaye (1974).
[55] Said (1993), 261.
[56] Momigliano (1975).

compared the epic heroes on both sides of the border, the Greek Digenes Akritas, for example, and the Turkish Dede Korkut. In short, the frontier zone, whether Muslim or Christian, had much in common, in contrast to the rival centres of Istanbul and Vienna.[57]

A similar point might be made about medieval Spain. From the time of Américo Castro in the 1940s onwards, some historians have emphasized the symbiosis or *convivencia* of Spanish Jews, Christians, and Muslims, the cultural exchanges between them. For example, Jewish scholars were fluent in Arabic, and Hebrew poetry was inspired by the Arabic lyric. As on the eastern European border, the warriors on both sides used similar equipment and seem to have had similar values. The material culture of the 'Mozarabs' (Christians under Muslim rule) and the 'Mudejars' (Muslims under Christian rule) combined elements from both traditions. Some Catholic churches (like some synagogues) were built in the Muslim style, with horseshoe arches, tiles, and geometrical decoration on doors and ceilings. It is generally impossible to say whether pottery and other artefacts in the 'Hispano-Mauresque' style was made by or for Christians or Muslims, the repertoire of themes being a common one.[58]

Exchanges also took place in the domains of language and literature. Many people were bilingual. Some wrote Spanish in the Muslim script and others Arabic in the Roman alphabet. Some people used two names, one Spanish and one Arabic, which suggests that they had two identities. Romances of chivalry written in a similar style were popular on both sides of the religious frontier (above, chapter 9). Some lyrics switch from Spanish to Arabic within a single line. 'Que faray Mamma? Meu l'habib est' ad yana!' ('What shall I do, mother? My lover is at the door!'). The most spectacular examples of symbiosis come from the practices of popular religion. As was the case on the Ottoman–Habsburg border, there were shrines, such as that of San Ginés, which attracted devotion from Muslims and Christians alike.[59]

The cultural history of other nations might be written in terms

[57] Hasluck (1929); Angyal (1957); Mankowski (1959); Inalcik (1973), 186–202.
[58] Terrasse (1932, 1958).
[59] Castro (1948); Stern (1953); Galmés de Fuentes (1967); MacKay (1976); Mann et al. (1992).

of encounters between regions, such as north and south in Italy, France, or even England. In the case of colonial north America, David Fischer has identified four regional cultures or 'folkways' carried by four groups of immigrants, the East Anglians to Massachusetts, the Southerners to Virginia, the Midlanders to the Delaware and the Borderers to the 'Back Country'. Styles of language and building, as well as political and religious attitudes, remained distinct for centuries.[60]

This example suggests the possibility of a still more ambitious enterprise, that of studying cultural history as a process of interaction between different subcultures, between male and female, urban and rural, Catholic and Protestant, Muslim and Hindu, and so on. Each group defines itself in contrast to the others, but creates its own cultural style – as in the case of British youth groups in the 1970s, for example – by appropriating items from a common stock, and assembling them into a system with a new meaning.[61]

The sociological concept of 'subculture', which implies diversity within a common framework, and the concept of 'counter-culture', which implies an attempt to invert the values of the dominant culture, deserve to be taken more seriously by cultural historians than they are at present.[62] Working with the concept of subculture has the advantage of making certain problems more explicit than before. Does the subculture include every aspect of the life of its members, or only certain domains? Is it possible to belong to more than one subculture at a time? Was there more in common between two Jews, one of whom was Italian, or two Italians, one of whom was Jewish?[63] Is the relation between the main culture and the subculture one of complementarity or conflict?

Social classes as well as religions might be analysed as subcultures. The late Edward Thompson was a severe critic of the view of culture as community which privileged shared meanings over conflicts of meaning. Ironically enough, he has himself been criticized for the communitarian model of workers' culture underlying his famous *Making of the English Working-Class*. We might attempt to go beyond this communitarian model with the help of

---

[60] Fischer (1989).
[61] Hebdige (1979).
[62] Yinger (1960); Clarke (1974); Clarke et al. (1975).
[63] Bonfil (1990).

Pierre Bourdieu, whose ethnography of contemporary France has stressed the extent to which the bourgeoisie and the working class have each defined themselves by contrast to the other.[64] In similar fashion, in a book which is or should be exemplary for historians, two Swedish ethnologists have placed the making of the Swedish middle class in the context of its members' struggle to differentiate themselves from both the nobility and the working class in cultural domains such as attitudes to time and space, dirt and cleanliness.[65] Solidarity within a group is usually strongest at the moment of sharpest conflict with outsiders. In this way cultural historians might contribute to the reintegration of history in an age of hyperspecialization when it has been broken into national, regional and disciplinary fragments.[66]

Consequences

In the case of cultural encounters the perception of the new in terms of the old, described in the last section, generally proves impossible to sustain over the long term. The new experiences first threaten and then undermine the old categories. The traditional 'cultural order' – as the American anthropologist Marshall Sahlins calls it – sometimes cracks under the strain of the attempt to assimilate them.[67] The next stage varies from culture to culture along a spectrum ranging from assimilation to rejection via adaptation and resistance, like the resistance to Protestantism in the Mediterranean world discussed by Fernand Braudel.[68] Why members of some cultures should be particularly interested in novelty or in the exotic is a question as fascinating as it is difficult to answer. The argument that more integrated cultures are relatively closed, while open and receptive cultures have less integration, runs the danger of circularity but has at least the virtue of presenting the problem from the receiver's point of view.[69] The paragraphs which follow will concentrate on receptivity at the expense of resistance.

The consequences of encounters between cultures were first

[64] Thompson (1963); Bourdieu (1979).
[65] Frykman and Löfgren (1979).
[66] Cf. Kammen (1984); Bender (1986).
[67] Sahlins (1981) 136–56.
[68] Braudel (1949), part 2, ch. 6, section 1.
[69] Ottenberg (1959); Schneider (1959).

studied systematically by scholars from New World societies where the encounters had been particularly dramatic. At the beginning of the century, North American anthropologists, including the German emigré Franz Boas, described the changes in American Indian cultures as a result of contact with white culture in terms of what they called 'acculturation', the adoption of elements from the dominant culture. A pupil of Boas, Melville Herskovits, defined acculturation as a more comprehensive phenomenon than diffusion and tried to explain why some traits rather than others were incorporated into the accepting culture.[70] This emphasis on the selection or screening of traits has proved illuminating. For example, in the case of the Spanish conquest of Mexico and Peru, it has been noted that the Indians adopted cultural elements from the 'donor culture' for which there were no local equivalents. It has also been argued that after a few years the adoption of new elements declines. A phase of appropriation is followed by cultural 'crystallization'.[71]

At this point, students of culture, beginning with specialists in the history of religion in the ancient Mediterranean world, have often spoken of 'syncretism'. Herskovits was particularly interested in religious syncretism, for instance the identification between traditional African gods and Catholic saints in Haiti, Cuba, Brazil and elsewhere. Another pupil of Boas, Gilberto Freyre, interpreted the history of colonial Brazil in terms of what he called the formation of 'a hybrid society', or the 'fusion' of different cultural traditions.[72] At least one historian of the Renaissance, Edgar Wind, employed the term 'hybridization' to describe the interaction of pagan and Christian cultures. His point was to reject a one-way analysis of the secularization of Renaissance culture, arguing that 'hybridization works both ways.' For example, 'a Madonna or a Magdalen could be made to resemble a Venus,' but on the other hand 'Renaissance art produced many images of Venus which resemble a Madonna or a Magdalen.'[73]

In similar fashion, the Cuban sociologist Fernando Ortiz argued that the term 'acculturation' should be replaced by 'transculturation' on the grounds that both cultures were changed as

---

[70] Herskovits (1938); cf. Dupront (1966).
[71] Foster (1960), 227–34; Glick (1979), 282–4.
[72] Freyre (1933); Herskovits (1937, 1938).
[73] Wind (1958), 29.

the result of their encounters, not just the so-called 'donor'. Ortiz was one of the first to suggest that we should speak of the American discovery of Columbus.[74] A good example of this kind of reverse acculturation in which the conquerors are conquered is that of the 'Creoles', the men and women who were of European origin but were born in the Americas and became, in the course of time, more and more American in their culture and consciousness.[75]

The assimilation of Christian saints to non-Christian gods and goddesses such as the West African Shango, the Chinese Kuan Yin, and the Nahuatl Tonantzin has its analogies in Europe. As Erasmus pointed out, a similar process had taken place in early Christian times, where saints like St George were assimilated to gods and heroes like Perseus. 'Accommodation' was the traditional term used to describe this process in the sixteenth century (as in the early church), when Jesuit missionaries to China and India, for instance, attempted to translate Christianity into the local cultural idioms by presenting it as compatible with many of the values of the mandarins and the brahmins.

Preoccupation with this problem is natural in a period like ours marked by increasingly frequent and intense cultural encounters of all kinds. A great variety of terms are used in different places and different disciplines to describe the processes of cultural borrowing, appropriation, exchange, reception, transfer, negotiation, resistance, syncretism, acculturation, enculturation, inculturation, interculturation, transculturation, hybridization (*mestizaje*), creolization, and the interaction and interpenetration of cultures. Following the revival of interest in the Mudejar art mentioned above (itself related to an increasing awareness of the Muslim world today), some Spaniards now speak of a process of 'mudejarism' in their cultural history.[76] Some of these new terms may sound exotic, and even barbarous. Their variety bears eloquent witness to the fragmentation of today's academic world. They also reveal a new conception of culture as *bricolage*, in which the process of appropriation and assimilation is not marginal but central.

Conceptual as well as empirical problems remain. The idea of

[74] Ortiz (1940), introduction.
[75] Brading (1991); Alberro (1992).
[76] Burns (1977); Goytisolo (1986).

'syncretism', for example, has been used to describe a range of situations, from cultural 'mixing' to synthesis. To use the term so loosely raises, or more exactly obscures, a number of problems.[77]

Among these problems is that of the intentions of the agents, of their interpretations of what they are doing, the emic point of view (above, p. 193). For example, in the case of the interaction between Christianity and African religions, we have to consider various scenarios. African rulers, as we have seen, may well have seen themselves as incorporating new elements into their traditional religion. In the case of the 'syncretism' of the African slaves in the Americas, their identification between St Barbara and Shango, for instance, they may well have been following the defensive tactics of conforming outwardly to Christianity while retaining their traditional beliefs. In the case of religion in contemporary Brazil, on the other hand, 'pluralism' might be a better term than syncretism, since the same people may participate in the practices of more than one cult, just as patients may seek cures from more than one system of medicine.

To return to 'traditional' language, individuals may have access to more than one tradition and choose one rather than another according to the situation, or appropriate elements from both to make something of their own. From the 'emic' point of view, what the historian needs to investigate is the logic underlying these appropriations and combinations, the local reasons for these choices. It is for this reason that some historians have been studying the responses of individuals to encounters between cultures, especially those who changed their behaviour – whether we call them 'converts', from the perspective of their new culture, or 'renegades', from the point of view of their old one. The point is to study these individuals – Christians who turned Muslim in the Ottoman Empire, or Englishmen who turned Indian in North America – as extreme and especially visible cases of response to the situation of encounter and to focus on the ways in which they reconstructed their identity.[78] The complexities of the situation are well illustrated by the study of a group of Brazilian blacks, descendants of slaves, who returned to West Africa because they considered it their home, only to find that the locals perceived them as Americans.[79]

---

[77] Apter (1991).
[78] Axtell (1985); Scaraffia (1993).
[79] Carneiro da Cunha (1985).

From outside, on the other hand, these people are examples of the general process of 'syncretism'. It has been suggested that we confine the use of this term to the 'temporary coexistence' of elements from different cultures, distinguishing it from a true 'synthesis'.[80] But how long is 'temporary'? Can we assume that synthesis or integration necessarily triumphs in the long term? In our time it is difficult not to be struck by movements of anti-syncretism or dis-integration, campaigns for the recovery of 'authentic' or 'pure' traditions.[81]

The concept of cultural 'hybridity' and the terms associated with it are equally problematic.[82] It is all too easy to slide (as Freyre, for instance, often did) between discussions of literal and metaphorical miscegenation, whether to sing the praises of cross-fertilization or to condemn the 'bastard' or 'mongrel' forms of culture which emerge from this process. Is the term 'hybridization' supposed to be descriptive or explanatory? Are new forms supposed to emerge by themselves in the course of a cultural encounter, or are they the work of creative individuals?

Linguistics offers another way of approaching the consequences of cultural encounters.[83] The meeting of cultures, as of languages, might be described in terms of the rise first of pidgin, a form of language reduced to essentials for the purpose of intercultural communication, and then of creole. 'Creolization' describes the situation when a pidgin develops a more complex structure as people begin to use it as their first language and for general purposes. Linguists argue that what was once perceived simply as error, as 'broken' English or 'kitchen' Latin, ought to be regarded as a variety of language with its own rules. A similar point might be made about (say) the language of architecture on the frontier between cultures.

In some contexts, the best linguistic analogy might be a 'mixed language' like the *media lengua* of Ecuador, in which Spanish vocabulary is combined with Quechua syntax, or the 'macaronic' Latin discussed in chapter 8 above. During the Renaissance, for example, the ornaments of one architectural style (the classical) were sometimes superimposed on the structures of another (the Gothic). In other contexts, a better analogy might be that of the

---

[80] Pye (1993).
[81] Stewart (1994).
[82] Young (1995).
[83] Glick (1979), 277–81; Hannerz (1992), 264–6.

bilinguals who 'switch' between one language and another according to the situation. As we have seen in the case of some nineteenth-century Japanese, it is possible for people to be bicultural, to live a double life, to switch from one cultural code to another.

To return to the situation today. Some observers are impressed by the homogenization of world culture, the 'Coca-Cola effect', though they often fail to take into account the creativity of reception and the renegotiation of meanings discussed earlier in the chapter. Others see mixing or hear pidgin everywhere. A few believe they can discern a new order, the 'creolization of the world'.[84] One of the great students of culture in our century, the Russian scholar Mikhail Bakhtin, used to emphasize what he called 'heteroglossia', in other words the variety and conflict of tongues and points of view out of which, so he suggested, new forms of language and new forms of literature (notably the novel) have developed.[85]

We have returned to the fundamental problem of unity and variety, not only in cultural history but in culture itself. It is necessary to avoid two opposite oversimplifications; the view of culture as homogeneous, which is blind to differences and conflicts, and the view of culture as essentially fragmented, which fails to take account of the ways in which all of us create our individual or group mixes, syncretisms or syntheses. The interaction of subcultures sometimes produces a unity of apparent opposites. Shut your eyes for a moment and listen to a South African speaking. It is not easy to tell whether the speaker is black or white. It is worth asking whether the black and white cultures of South Africa share other common features, despite their contrasts and conflicts, thanks to centuries of interaction.

For an outsider, whether historian or anthropologist, the answer to the question is surely 'Yes'. The similarities appear to outweigh the differences. To insiders, however, the differences probably outweigh the similarities. This point about differences in perspective is probably valid for many cultural encounters. It follows that a cultural history centred on encounters should not be written from one viewpoint alone. In the words of Mikhail

---

[84] Hannerz (1987); cf. Friedman (1994), 195–232.
[85] Bakhtin (1981).

Bakhtin, such a history has to be 'polyphonic'. In other words, it has to contain within itself a variety of tongues and points of view, including those of victors and vanquished, men and women, insiders and outsiders, contemporaries and historians.

Bibliography

Ackerman, Robert (1987) *J. G. Frazer*, Cambridge

Acton, William (1691) *A New Journal of Italy*, London

Addison, Joseph (1705) *Remarks on Several Parts of Italy*, rpr. in his *Works*, 4 vols, London 1890, vol. 1, 356–538

Alatas, Syed H. (1977) *The Myth of the Lazy Native: a Study of the Image of the Malays, Filipinos and Javanese from the Sixteenth to the Twentieth Century and its Function in the Ideology of Colonial Capitalism*, London

Alberro, Solange (1992) *Les Espagnols dans le Mexique colonial: histoire d'une acculturation*, Paris

Alencar, Edgar de (1965) *O Carnaval Carioca através da musica*, 2nd edn, Rio de Janeiro

Allport, Gordon W. and L. Postman (1945) 'The Basic Psychology of Rumour', rpr. in *The Process and Effect of Mass Communication*, ed. Wilbur Schramm, Urbana 1961, 141–55

Alsop, Joseph (1982) *The Rare Art Traditions*, London

Althusser, Louis (1971) *Lenin and Philosophy*, London

Amalvi, Christian (1984) 'Le 14–Juillet', in Nora, vol. 1, 421–72

Amuchástegui, A. J. Pérez (1988) *Mentalidades argentinas*, Buenos Aires

Amyraut, Moyse (1665) *Discours sur les songes divines dont il est parlé dans l'Écriture*, Saumur

Anderson, Benedict (1983) *Imagined Communities*, 2nd edn London 1991

Angyal, Andreas (1957) 'Die Welt der Grenzfestungen: Ein Kapitel aus der südosteuropäische Geistesgeschichte des 16. und 17. Jhts', *Südost Forschungen* 16, 311–42

Anselmo, A. J. (1926) *Bibliografia das obras impressas em Portugal no século xvi*, Lisbon

Antal, Frederick (1947) *Florentine Painting and its Social Background*, London

Apte, Michael (1985) *Humor and Laughter: an Anthropological Approach*, Ithaca

Apter, Andrew (1991) 'Herskovits's Heritage: Rethinking Syncretism in the African Diaspora', *Diaspora* 1, 235–60

Arantes, Antonio Augusto (1982) *O Trabalho e a Fala*, São Paulo

Archambault, Paul (1967) 'The Analogy of the Body in Renaissance Political Literature', *Bibliothèque d'Humanisme et Renaissance* 29, 21–53

Arens, W. (1979) *The Man-Eating Myth*, New York

Ariès, Philippe (1960) *Centuries of Childhood*, English trans. London 1962

Arnheim, Rudolf (1962) 'Review of Gombrich', *Art Bulletin* 44, 75–9

Arthos, John (1968) *Milton and the Italian Cities*, London

Ashmole, Elias (1966) *Diary*, ed. C. H. Josten, 5 vols, Oxford

Axtell, James (1985) *The Invasion Within: the Contest of Cultures in Colonial North America*, New York

Azpilcueta, Martín de (1582) *El silencio ser necessario en el choro*, Rome

Bachelard, Gaston (1947) *La formation de l'esprit scientifique*, Paris

Backman, E. Louis (1952) *Religious Dances in the Christian Church and in Popular Medicine*, London

Baczko, Bronislaw (1984) *Les imaginaires sociaux*, Paris

Bak, Hans, ed. (1993) *Multiculturalism and the Canon of American Culture*, Amsterdam

Bakhtin, Mikhail M. (1929) *Problems of Dostoyevsky's Poetics*, English trans. Manchester 1984

Bakhtin, Mikhail M. (1965) *Rabelais and his World*, English trans. Cambridge, Mass. 1968

Bakhtin, Mikhail M. (1981) 'From the Prehistory of Novelistic Discourse', in his *The Dialogic Imagination*, Austin, 41–83

Balandier, Georges (1965) *Daily Life in the Kingdom of the Kongo*, English trans. London 1968

Barasch, Moshe (1987) *Giotto and the Language of Gestures*, Cambridge, Mass.

Barnes, John (1947) 'The Collection of Genealogies', *Rhodes–Livingstone Journal* 5, 48–55

Baroja, Julio Caro (1965) *El Carnaval*, Madrid

Barolsky, Paul (1978) *Infinite Jest: Wit and Humor in Italian Renaissance Art*, New York

Baron, Hans (1955) *The Crisis of the Early Italian Renaissance*, Princeton

Bartlett, Frederick C. (1932) *Remembering: a Study in Experimental and Social Psychology*, Cambridge

Bartlett, Robert (1986) *Trial by Fire and Water: the Medieval Judicial Ordeal*, Oxford

Bastide, Roger (1958) *Le candomblé de Bahia*, Paris

Bastide, Roger (1966) 'The Sociology of the Dream', in *The Dream and Human Societies*, ed. Gustav E. von Grunebaum and Roger Caillois, Berkeley and Los Angeles, 199–212

Bastide, Roger (1970) 'Mémoire collective et sociologie du bricolage', *Année Sociologique*, 65–108

Battisti, Eugenio (1962) *L'antirinascimento*, Milan

Batts, Michael S. (1987) *A History of Histories of German Literature*, New York

Baumann, Gerd (1996) *Contesting Culture: Discourses of Identity in Multi-ethnic London*, London

Baxandall, Michael (1972) *Painting and Experience in Fifteenth-Century Italy*, Oxford

Beccaria, Gian Luigi (1968) *Spagnolo e spagnoli in Italia*, Turin

Beidelman, Thomas O., ed. (1971) *The Translation of Cultures*, London

Bell, Desmond (1986) 'The Traitor within the Gates', *New Society*, 3 Jan., 15–17

Bellori, Giovan Pietro (1672) *Le vite*, ed. Evelina Borea, Turin 1976

Bender, Thomas (1986) 'Wholes and Parts: the Need for Synthesis in American History', *Journal of American History* 73, 120–36

Bennassar, Bartolomé (1967) *Valladolid au siècle d'or*, The Hague

Bennassar, Bartolomé and Lucile Bennassar (1989) *Les chrétiens d'Allah*, Paris

Benz, Ernest (1969) *Die Vision*, Stuttgart

Beradt, Charlotte (1966) *Das Dritte Reich des Traums*, Munich

Berger, Philippe (1987) *Libro y lectura en la Valencia del Renacimiento*, 2 vols, Valencia

Bernardi, Claudio (1990) *La drammaturgia della settimana santa in Italia*, Milan

Besançon, Alain (1971) *Histoire et expérience du moi*, Paris

Birdwhistell, Ray L. (1970) *Kinesics and Context: Essays on Body-Motion Communication*, Philadelphia

Bishko, Charles J. (1963) 'The Castilian as Plainsman', in *The New World Looks at its History*, ed. Archibald R. Lewis and T. F. McGann, Austin, 47–65

Bitossi, Carlo (1976) 'Andrea Spinola. Elaborazione di un "manuale" per la classe dirigente', in Costantini et al. (1976), 115–75

Bitterli, Urs (1986) *Cultures in Conflict*, English trans. Cambridge 1989

Black, Jeremy (1985) *The British and the Grand Tour*, London

Blackbourn, David (1993) *Marpingen: Apparitions of the Virgin Mary in Bismarckian Germany*, Oxford

Bloch, Marc (1924) *The Royal Touch*, English trans. London 1973

Bloch, Marc (1925) 'Mémoire collective, tradition et coutume', *Revue de Synthèse Historique* 40, 73–83

Blumenberg, Hans (1960) *Paradigmen zu einer Metaphorologie*, Bonn

Blunt, John J. (1823) *Vestiges of Ancient Manners*, London

Boekhorst, Pieter, Peter Burke and Willem Frijhoff, eds (1992) *Cultuur en maatschappij in Nederland 1500–1850*, Meppel

Bogucka, Maria (1983) 'Le geste dans la vie de la noblesse polonaise aux 16e, 17e et 18e siècles', *Revue d'Histoire Moderne et Contemporaine* 30, 3–15

Bonfil, Robert (1990) *Rabbis and Jewish Communities in Renaissance Italy*, New York

Bonifacio, Giovanni (1616) *L'arte de' cenni*, Vicenza

Bonora, Ettore and Mario Chiesa, eds (1979) *Cultura letteraria e tradizione popolare in Teofilo Folengo*, Milan

Borromeo, Carlo (1758) *Instructiones Pastorum*, Augsburg

Borsellino, Nino (1973) *Gli anticlassicisti del '500*, Rome and Bari

Bourdieu, Pierre (1972) *Outlines of a Theory of Practice*, English trans. Cambridge 1977

Bourdieu, Pierre (1979) *Distinction*, English trans. London 1984

Bourdieu, Pierre and Jean-Claude Passeron (1970) *Reproduction in Education, Society and Culture*, English trans. Beverly Hills 1977

Boureau, Alain (1989) 'Propositions pour une histoire restreinte des mentalités', *Annales ESC* 44, 1491–1504

Bouwsma, William J. (1990) *A Usable Past*, Berkeley

Boxer, Charles R. (1975) *Mary and Misogyny*, London

Brading, David (1991) *The First America*, Cambridge

Brandes, Stanley (1980) *Metaphors of Masculinity*, New York

Braudel, Fernand (1949) *The Mediterranean and the Mediterranean World in the Age of Philip II*, English trans. London 1972–3

Braun, Lucien (1973) *Histoire de l'histoire de la philosophie*, Paris

Braun, Rudolf and David Gugerli (1993) *Macht des Tanzes – Tanz der Mächtigen: Hoffeste und Herrschaftszeremoniell, 1550–1914*, Munich

Bredekamp, Horst (1985) *Vicino Orsini und der heilige Wald von Bomarzo*, 2 vols, Worms

Bremmer, Jan and Herman Roodenburg, eds (1991) *A Cultural History of Gesture*, Cambridge

Brewer, John (1995) 'Culture as Commodity: 1660–1800', in *The Consumption of Culture 1600–1800*, ed. Ann Bermingham and John Brewer, London, 341–61

Brizzi, Gian Paolo (1976) *La formazione della classe dirigente nel '600–'700*, Bologna

[Bromley, William] (1692) *Remarks made in Travels through France and Italy*, rpr. London 1693

[Bromley, William] (1702) *Several Years' Travels*, London

Bronzini, Giovanni Battista (1966) *Tradizione di stile aedico dai cantari al Furioso*, Florence

Brown, Horatio ed., (1864) *Calendar of State Papers, Venetian*, 14 vols, London

Brown, Peter (1975) 'Society and the Supernatural', *Daedalus*, Spring, 133–47

Brown, Peter M. (1967) 'Aims and Methods of the Second *Rassettatura* of the Decameron', *Studi Secenteschi* 8, 3–40

Bruford, W. H. (1962) *Culture and Society in Classical Weimar*, Cambridge

Buarque de Holanda, Sergio (1959) *Visões de Paraíso*, Rio de Janeiro

Buckley, Anthony (1989) 'We're Trying to Find our Identity: Uses of History among Ulster Protestants', in *History and Ethnicity*, ed. Elizabeth Tonkin et al., New York, 183–97

Burckhardt, Jacob (1860) *Civilization of the Renaissance in Italy*, English trans. 1878, latest edn Harmondsworth 1990

Burke, Peter (1972) *Culture and Society in Renaissance Italy*, London

Burke, Peter (1978) *Popular Culture in Early Modern Europe*, 2nd edn Aldershot 1994

Burke, Peter (1982) 'Le roi comme héros populaire', *History of European Ideas* 3, 267–71

Burke, Peter (1984) 'How to be a Counter-Reformation Saint', in *Religion and Society in Early Modern Europe*, ed. Kaspar von Greyerz, London, 45–55, rpr. in Burke (1987), 48–62

Burke, Peter (1987) *Historical Anthropology of Early Modern Italy: Essays on Perception and Communication*, Cambridge

Burke, Peter (1991) 'Tacitism, Scepticism and Reason of State', in *The Cambridge History of Political Thought 1450–1700*, ed. James H. Burns, Cambridge

Burke, Peter (1992) *The Fabrication of Louis XIV*, New Haven

Burke, Peter (1993) 'The Rise of Literal-Mindedness', *Common Knowledge* 2, 108–21

Burke, Peter (1995) *The Fortunes of the Courtier*, Cambridge

Burke, Peter (1996) 'The Myth of 1453: Notes and Reflections', in *Querdenken: Dissens und Toleranz im Wandel der Geschichte: Festschrift Hans Guggisberg*, ed. Michael Erbe et al., Mannheim, 23–30

Burke, Peter (1997) 'The Demise of Royal Mythologies', in *Iconography, Propaganda and Legitimation*, ed. Allan Ellenius, Oxford

Burnet, Gilbert (1686) *Some Letters*, Amsterdam

Burns, Robert I. (1977) 'Mudejar History Today', *Viator* 8, 127–43

Butterfield, Herbert (1931) *The Whig Interpretation of History*, London

Butterfield, Herbert (1955) *Man on his Past*, Cambridge

Câmara Cascudo, Luis de (c.1974) *História dos nossos gestos*, São Paulo

Camporesi, Piero (1976) *La maschera di Bertoldo*, Turin

Canguilhem, Georges (1955) *La formation du concept de réflexe aux 17e et 18e siècles*, Paris

Caraffa, Ferrante (1880), 'Memorie', *Archivio Storico per le Provincie Napolesane* 5, 242–61

Cardano, Girolamo (1557) *De rerum varietate*, Basle

Carlton, Charles (1987) *Archbishop William Laud*, London
Carneiro da Cunha, Manuela (1985) *Negros, estrangeiros: os escravos libertos e sua volta à Africa*, São Paulo
Carstairs, G. Morris (1957) *The Twice-Born*, London
Carvajal, Gaspar de (1955) *Relación del nuevo descubrimento del famoso río Grande de las Amazonas*, ed. J. Hernández Millares, Mexico City and Buenos Aires
Castaneda, Carlos (1968) *The Teachings of Don Juan: a Yaqui Way of Knowledge*, rpr. Harmondsworth 1970
Castro, Américo (1948) *The Structure of Spanish History*, English trans. Princeton 1954
Cavalcanti, Maria Laura Viveiros de Castro (1994) *Carnaval Carioca*, Rio de Janeiro
Cebà, Ansaldo (1617) *Il cittadino di repubblica*, Genoa
Cebà, Ansaldo (1623) *Lettere*, Genoa
Certeau, Michel de (1980) *The Practice of Everyday Life*, English trans. Berkeley 1984
Chadwick, W. Owen (1957) *From Bossuet to Newman*, 2nd edn Cambridge 1987
Chambers, David and Brian Pullan, eds (1992) *A Documentary History of Venice*, Oxford
Chaney, Edward (1985) *The Grand Tour and the Great Rebellion*, Geneva
Chartier, Roger (1987) *The Cultural Uses of Print in Early Modern France*, Princeton
Chartier, Roger (1988) *Cultural History between Practices and Representations*, Cambridge
Chastel, André (1961) *Art et humanisme à Florence au temps de Laurent le Magnifique*, Paris
Chastel, André (1986) 'Gesture in Painting: Problems of Semiology', *Renaissance and Reformation* 10, 1–22
Chevalier, Maxime (1976) *Lectura y lectores en la España de los siglos xvi y xvii*, Madrid
Chiaramonti, Scipione (1625) *De conjectandis cuiusque moribus et latitantibus animi affectibus semiotike moralis, seu de signis*, Venice
Christian, William (1981) *Apparitions in Late Medieval Spain*, Princeton
Cian, Vittorio (1887) 'Un episodio della storia della censura in Italia nel secolo xvi: l'edizione spurgata del *Cortegiano*', *Archivio Storico Lombardo* 14, 661–727
Clanchy, Michael T. (1979) *From Memory to Written Record*, London
Clark, Alfred J. (1921) Appendix to Margaret Murray, *The Witch-Cult in Western Europe*, Oxford
Clark, Stuart (1983) 'French Historians and Early Modern Popular Culture', *Past and Present* 100, 62–99
Clark, Stuart (1997) *Thinking with Demons*, Oxford

Clarke, John et al. (1975) 'Subcultures, Culture and Class', in *Resistance Through Rituals*, ed. S. Hall and Tony Jefferson, rpr. London 1976, 9–74

Clarke, Michael (1974) 'On the Concept of Sub-culture', *British Journal of Sociology* 25, 428–41

Clendinnen, Inga (1992) *Aztecs*, Cambridge

Cohen, Tom V. (1988) 'The Case of the Mysterious Coil of Rope', *Sixteenth-Century Journal* 19, 209–21

Cohn, Norman (1975) *Europe's Inner Demons*, London

Cohn, Samuel K. (1988) *Death and Property in Siena*, Baltimore

Comparato, Vittorio I. (1979) 'Viaggatori inglesi in Italia', *Quaderni Storici* 42, 850–86

Connerton, Paul (1989) *How Societies Remember*, Cambridge

Copenhaver, Brian (1978) 'The Historiography of Discovery in the Renaissance: the Sources and Composition of Polydore Vergil's *De Inventoribus Rerum*', *Journal of the Warburg and Courtauld Institutes* 41, 192–214

Corbin, Alain (1982) *The Foul and the Fragrant*, English trans. Leamington 1986

Coryat, Thomas (1611) *Crudities*, rpr. London 1978

Costantini, Claudio (1978) *La Repubblica di Genova nell'età moderna*, Turin

Costantini, Claudio et al. (1976) *Dibattito politico e problemi di governo a Genova nella prima metà del seicento*, Florence

Cozzi, Gaetano (1958) *Il doge Niccolò Contarini*, Venice and Rome

Crick, Malcolm (1976) *Explorations in Language and Meaning*, London

Croce, Benedetto (1895) 'I Lazzari', rpr. in his *Aneddoti*, vol. 3, Bari 1954, 198–211

Crocker, Jon C. (1977) 'My Brother the Parrot', in *The Social Use of Metaphor*, ed. James D. Sapir and J. C. Crocker, Philadelphia

Croix, Alain (1981) *La Bretagne aux 16e et 17e siècles*, 2 vols, The Hague

Crombie, Alistair C. (1994) *Styles of Thinking in the European Tradition*, 3 vols, London

Crouzet, Michel (1982) *Stendhal et l'italianité: essai de mythologie romantique*, Paris

Crummey, Robert O. (1970) *The Old Believers and the World of Antichrist*, Madison

Cunha, Euclides da (1902) *Revolt in the Backlands*, English trans. Chicago 1944

Curtius, Ernst R. (1948) *European Literature and the Latin Middle Ages*, English trans. New York 1953

Da Matta, Roberto (1978) *Carnaval, malandros e herois*, Rio de Janeiro

D'Andrade, Roy (1961) 'Anthropological Studies of Dreams', in

220   Bibliography

Psychological Anthropology, ed. Francis L. K. Hsu, Homewood, Ill., 296–307
Darnton, Robert (1971) 'The Social History of Ideas', rpr. in his *The Kiss of Lamourette*, London 1990, 219–52
Darnton, Robert (1984) *The Great Cat Massacre*, New York
Darnton, Robert (1995) *The Forbidden Best-Sellers of Pre-revolutionary France*, New York
Davis, John (1973) *Land and Family in Pisticci*, London
Davis, Natalie Z. (1975) 'Women on Top', in her *Society and Culture in Early Modern France*, Cambridge 1987, 124–51
Davis, Natalie Z. (1987) *Fiction in the Archives*, Cambridge
Dear, Peter (1985) 'Totius in Verba: Rhetoric and Authority in the Early Royal Society', *Isis* 76, 145–61
Della Casa, Giovanni (1558) *Il Galateo*, Florence
Del Torre, Michelangelo (1976) *Le origini moderne della storiografia filosofica*, Florence
Demandt, Alexander (1978), *Metaphern für Geschichte*, Munich
De' Seta, Cesare (1981) 'L'Italia nello specchio del Grand Tour', in his *Architettura ambiente e società a Napoli nel '700*, Turin, 127–263
Diacon, Todd A. (1991) *Millenarian Vision, Capitalist Reality: Brazil's Contestado Rebellion, 1912–6*, Durham N.C.
Dickens, A. Geoffrey and John Tonkin (1985) *The Reformation in Historical Thought*, Cambridge, Mass.
Dijksterhuis, Eduard J. (1950) *The Mechanization of the World Picture*, English trans. Oxford 1961
Dinzelbacher, Peter (1981) *Vision und Visionslitteratur im Mittelalter*, Stuttgart
Dodds, Eric R. (1951) *The Greeks and the Irrational*, Berkeley and Los Angeles
Dodds, Eric R. (1965) *The Age of Anxiety*, Cambridge
Douglas, Mary (1970) *Natural Symbols*, London
Douglas, Mary (1980) 'Maurice Halbwachs', rpr. in her *In the Active Voice*, London 1982, 255–71
Dresden, Sem (1975) 'The Profile of the Reception of the Italian Renaissance in France', in *Itinerarium Italicum*, ed. Heiko Oberman and Thomas A. Brady, Leiden, 119–89
Drewal, Margaret Thompson (1989) 'Dancing for Ogun in Yorubaland and in Brazil', in *Africa's Ogun: Old World and New*, ed. Sandra T. Barnes, Bloomington, 199–234
Duby, Georges (1979) *The Three Orders*, English trans. Chicago 1980
Dürer, Albrecht (1956) *Schriftliche Nachlass*, vol. 1, ed. Hans Rupprich, Berlin
Dupront, Alphonse (1966) *L'acculturazione*, Turin
Durand, Gilbert (1948) *Les structures anthropologiques de l'imaginaire*, Paris

Durkheim, Émile (1912) *The Elementary Forms of the Religious Life*, English trans. 1915, rpr. New York 1961

Dutton, Paul (1994) *The Politics of Dreaming in Carolingian Europe*, Lincoln, Nebr.

Edelstein, Leon (1967) *The Idea of Progress in Classical Antiquity*, Baltimore

Edmondson, Munro S. (1955–6) 'Carnival in New Orleans', *Caribbean Quarterly* 4, 233–45

Eggan, Dorothy (1952) 'The Manifest Content of Dreams', *American Anthropologist* 54, 469–85

Eggan, Dorothy (1966) 'Hopi Dreams in Cultural Perspective', in *The Dream and Human Societies*, ed. Gustav E. von Grunebaum and Roger Caillois, Berkeley and Los Angeles, 237–66

Eisenstein, Elizabeth E. (1979) *The Printing Press as an Agent of Change*, Cambridge

Elias, Norbert (1939) *The Civilizing Process*, English trans. Oxford 1994

Elkanah, Yehuda (1981) 'A Programmatic Attempt at an Anthropology of Knowledge', in *Sciences and Cultures*, ed. Everett Mendelsohn and Y. Elkanah, Dordrecht, 1–76

Entwistle, William J. (1939) *European Balladry*, Oxford

Erikson, Erik H. (1968) 'In Search of Gandhi', *Daedalus* 695–729

Escarpit, Robert (1958) 'Histoire de l'histoire de la littérature', in *Histoire des littératures*, ed. Raymond Queneau, vol. 3, Paris, 1749–813

Evangelisti, Claudia (1992) 'Libelli famosi: processi per scritte infamanti nella Bologna di fine '500', *Annali della Fondazione Einaudi* 26, 181–237

Evans-Pritchard, Edward E. (1937) *Witchcraft, Oracles and Magic among the Azande*, Oxford

Evans-Pritchard, Edward E. (1940) *The Nuer*, Oxford

Evans-Pritchard, Edward E. (1956) *Nuer Religion*, Oxford

Evans-Pritchard, Edward E. (1965) *Theories of Primitive Religion*, Oxford

Evelyn, John (1955) *Diary*, ed. E. S. de Beer, 5 vols, Oxford

Febvre, Lucien (1938) 'History and Psychology', trans. in *A New Kind of History*, ed. Peter Burke, London 1973, ch. 1

Fentress, James and Chris Wickham (1992) *Social Memory*, Oxford

Fenzi, E. (1966) 'Una falsa lettera del Cebà e il Dizionario Politico-Filosofico di Andrea Spinola', *Miscellanea di Storia Ligura* 4, 111–65

Ferguson, Wallace K. (1948) *The Renaissance in Historical Thought*, Cambridge, Mass.

Fermor, Sharon (1993) 'Movement and Gender in Sixteenth-Century Italian Painting', in *The Body Imaged*, ed. Kathleen Adler and Marcia Pointon, Cambridge, 129–46

Ferreira, Jerusa Pires (1979) *Cavalaria em cordel*, Rio de Janeiro

Firth, Raymond (1934) 'The Meaning of Dreams', rpr. in his *Tikopia Ritual and Belief*, London 1967, 162–73

Fischer, David H. (1989) *Albion's Seed: Four British Folkways in America*, New York

Fleck, Ludwik (1935) *Genesis and Development of a Scientific Fact*, English trans. Chicago 1979

Foglietta, Uberto (1559) *Della repubblica di Genova*, Rome

Foisil, Madeleine (1970) *La révolte des nu-pieds*, Paris

Fontes, Anna (1987) 'Pouvoir (du) rire. Théorie et pratique des facéties aux 15e et 16e siècles: des facéties humanistes aux trois recueils de L. Domenichi', *Réécritures* 3, Paris, 9–100

Fortes, Meyer (1987) *Religion, Morality and the Person*, Cambridge

Foster, George (1960) *Culture and Conquest: America's Spanish Heritage*, Chicago

Foucault, Michel (1961) *Madness and Civilization*, English trans. New York 1965

Foucault, Michel (1966) *The Order of Things*, English trans. London 1970

Foucault, Michel (1971) *L'ordre du discours*, Paris

Frankl, Paul (1960) *The Gothic: Literary Sources and Interpretations through Eight Centuries*, Princeton

Frank-van Westrienen, Anna (1983) *De Groote Tour*, Amsterdam

Freud, Sigmund (1899) *The Interpretation of Dreams*, English trans. London 1960

Freud, Sigmund (1905) *Jokes and their Relation to the Unconscious*, English trans. 1913, rev. edn New York 1965

Freud, Sigmund (1929) 'Some Dreams of Descartes: Letter to M. Leroy', in *Works*, vol. 21, London 1961, 203–4

Freyre, Gilberto (1933) *The Masters and the Slaves*, English trans. New York 1940

Friedlaender, Walter (1955) *Caravaggio Studies*, Princeton

Friedman, John B. (1981) *The Monstrous Races in Medieval Art and Thought*, Cambridge, Mass.

Friedman, Jonathan (1994) *Cultural Identity and Global Process*, London

Fry, Peter, Sérgio Carrara and Ana Luiza Martins-Costa (1988) 'Negros e brancos no carnaval da Velha República', in *Escravidão e invenção da liberdade*, ed. João José Reis, São Paulo, 232–63

Frye, Northrop (1959) *Anatomy of Criticism*, New York

Frykman, Jonas and Orvar Löfgren (1979) *Culture Builders*, English trans. New Brunswick 1987

Frykman, Jonas and Orvar Löfgren, eds (1996) *Force of Habit: Exploring Everyday Culture*, Lund

Fumaroli, Marc (1980) *L'âge de l'éloquence: rhétorique et res literaria de la Renaissance au seuil de l'époque classique*, Geneva

Furet, François (1984) 'La Révolution dans l'imaginaire politique français', *Le Débat* 30, 173–81

Fussell, Paul (1975) *The Great War and Modern Memory*, Oxford

Gaeta, Franco (1961) 'Alcuni considerazioni sul mito di Venezia', *Bibliothèque d'Humanisme et Renaissance* 23, 58–75

Galbraith, John K. (1958) *The Affluent Society*, 2nd edn Harmondsworth 1962

Galmés de Fuentes, Alvaro (1967) *El libro de las batallas*, Oviedo

Garber, Jörn (1983) 'Von der Menschheitsgeschichte zur Kulturgeschichte', in *Kultur zwischen Bürgertum und Volk*, ed. Jutta Held, Berlin, 76–97

García, Carlos (1617) *La oposición y conjunción de los dos grandes luminares de la tierra, o la antipatia de franceses y españoles*, ed. M. Bareau, Edmonton 1979

Garlan, Yvon and Claude Nières, eds (1975) *Les révoltes bretonnes de 1675*, Paris

Gay, Peter (1959) *The Party of Humanity*, New York

Geertz, Clifford (1973) *The Interpretation of Cultures*, New York

Gellner, Ernest (1974) *Legitimation of Belief*, Cambridge

Gernet, Jacques (1982) *China and the Christian Impact*, English trans. Cambridge 1985

Gilbert, Felix (1990) *History: Politics or Culture?* Princeton

Gilman, Stephen (1960–3) 'Bernal Díaz del Castillo and *Amadís de Gaula*', in *Studia Philologica, Homenaje a Damas Alonso*, 3 vols, Madrid, vol. 2, 99–114

Ginzburg, Carlo (1966) *The Night Battles*, English trans. London 1983

Ginzburg, Carlo (1976) *Cheese and Worms*, English trans. London 1981

Ginzburg, Carlo (1978) 'Titian, Ovid and Sixteenth-Century Codes for Erotic Illustration', rpr. in his *Myths, Emblems, Clues*, London 1990, 77–95

Ginzburg, Carlo (1990) 'Deciphering the Sabbath', in *Early Modern European Witchcraft*, ed. Bengt Ankarloo and Gustav Henningsen, Oxford, 121–38

Gismondi, Michael A. (1985) 'The Gift of Theory', *Social History* 10, 211–30

Glick, Thomas F. (1979) *Islamic and Christian Spain in the Early Middle Ages*, Princeton

Góes, Fred de (1982), *O país do Carnaval Elétrico*, São Paulo

Goethe, Johan Wolfgang von (1951) *Italienische Reise*, ed. H. von Einem, Hamburg

Goldwasser, Maria Júlia (1975), *O Palácio do Samba*, Rio de Janeiro

Gombrich, Ernst H. (1960a) 'Vasari's *Lives* and Cicero's *Brutus*', *Journal of the Warburg and Courtauld Institutes* 23, 309–21

Gombrich, Ernst H. (1960b) *Art and Illusion*, London

Gombrich, Ernst H. (1969) 'In Search of Cultural History', rpr. in his *Ideals and Idols*, London 1979, 25–59

Gombrich, Ernst H. (1984) 'Architecture and Rhetoric in Giulio

Romano's Palazzo del Te', in his *New Light on Old Masters*, Oxford 1986, 161–70

Goody, Jack (1977) *The Domestication of the Savage Mind*, Cambridge

Gorak, Jan (1991) *The Making of the Modern Canon: Genesis and Crisis of a Literary Idea*, London

Gossman, Lionel (1968) *Medievalism and the Ideologies of the Enlightenment*, Baltimore

Gothein, Eberhard (1889) *Die Aufgaben der Kulturgeschichte*, Leipzig

Goubert, Pierre (1982) *The French Peasantry in the Seventeenth Century*, English trans. Cambridge 1986

Goulemot, Jean-Marie (1986) 'Histoire littéraire et mémoire nationale', *History and Anthropology* 2, part 2, 225–35

Goytisolo, Juan (1986) 'Mudejarism Today', English trans. in his *Saracen Chronicles*, London 1992, ch. 1

Graf, Arturo (1916) 'Un buffone di Leone X', in his *Attraverso il '500*, Turin, 365–90

Graham, Loren, Wolf Lepenies and Peter Weingart (1983) *Functions and Uses of Disciplinary Histories*, Dordrecht

Graham, Sandra L. (1988) *House and Street: the Domestic World of Servants and Masters in Nineteenth-Century Rio de Janeiro*, Cambridge

Granet, Marcel (1934) *La pensée chinoise*, Paris

Gray, Richard (1991) *Black Christians and White Missionaries*, New Haven

Grayson, Cecil (1959) *A Renaissance Controversy, Latin or Italian?* Oxford

Greenblatt, Stephen (1988a) *Shakespearean Negotiations: the Circulation of Social Energy in Renaissance England*, Oxford

Greenblatt, Stephen, ed. (1988b) *Representing the English Renaissance*, Berkeley and LA

Grendi, Edoardo (1987) *La repubblica dei genovesi*, Bologna

Grendler, Paul (1969) *Critics of the Italian World*, Madison

Grendler, Paul (1977) *The Roman Inquisition and the Venetian Press, 1540–1605*, Princeton

Grendler, Paul (1988) *Schooling in Renaissance Italy: Literacy and Learning 1300–1600*, Baltimore

Griffith, Richard, Otoya Miyagi and Akira Tago (1958) 'Typical Dreams', *American Anthropologist* 60, 1173–9

Grinten, Evert van der (1952) *Enquiries into the History of Art-Historical Writing*, Delft

Grove's Dictionary of Music and Musicians (1980) ed. S. Sadie, 20 vols, London

Grudin, Robert (1974) 'The Jests in Castiglione's *Il Cortegiano*', *Neophilologus* 58, 199–204

Gruzinski, Serge (1988) *The Conquest of Mexico*, English trans. Cambridge 1993

Guazzo, Stefano (1574) *La civil conversazione*, ed. Amedeo Quondam, 2 vols, Modena 1993

Guénée, Bernard (1976–7) 'Temps de l'histoire et temps de la mémoire au Moyen Age', rpr. in his *Politique et histoire au Moyen Age*, Paris 1981, 253–63

Guerri, Domenico (1931) *La corrente popolare nel Rinascimento*, Florence

Gundersheimer, Werner (1966) *Louis Le Roy*, Geneva

Gurevich, Aaron Y. (1984) 'Two Peasant Visions', rpr. in his *Historical Anthropology of the Middle Ages*, Cambridge 1992, 50–64

Haase, Roland (1933) *Das Problem des Chiliasmus und der Dreissig-Jährigen Krieg*, Leipzig

Habermas, Jürgen (1962) *The Structural Transformation of the Public Sphere*, English trans. Cambridge 1989

Haitsma Mulier, Eco O. G. (1980) *The Myth of Venice*, Assen

Halbwachs, Maurice (1925) *Les cadres sociaux de la mémoire*, Paris

Halbwachs, Maurice (1941) *La topographie légendaire des évangiles en terre sainte: étude de mémoire collective*, Paris

Halbwachs, Maurice (1950) *The Collective Memory*, English trans. New York 1980

Hale, John R. (1954) *England and the Italian Renaissance*, 2nd edn London 1963

Hall, Calvin S. (1951) 'What People Dream About', *Scientific American*, May, 60–9

Hall, Stuart (1980) 'Cultural Studies: Two Paradigms', rpr. in Storey (1996), 31–48

Hallowell, A. Irving (1966) 'The Role of Dreams in Ojibwa Culture', in *The Dream and Human Societies*, ed. Gustav E. von Grunebaum and Roger Caillois, Berkeley and Los Angeles,

Hallpike, Christopher R. (1979) *The Foundations of Primitive Thought*, Oxford

Hanlon, Gregory (1993) *Confession and Community in Seventeenth-Century France*, Philadelphia

Hannerz, Ulf (1987) 'The World in Creolization', *Africa* 57, 546–59

Hannerz, Ulf (1992) *Cultural Complexity*, New York

Harbsmeier, Michael (1982) 'Reisebeschreibungen als mentalitäts-geschichtliche Quellen', in *Reiseberichte als Quellen europäischer Kulturgeschichte*, ed. Antoni Mączak and Hans Jürgen Teuteberg, Wolfenbüttel, 1–32

Harley, George W. (1950) *Masks as Agents of Social Control in North-East Liberia*, Cambridge, Mass.

Harris, Victor (1966) 'Allegory to Analogy in the Interpretation of Scriptures', *Philological Quarterly* 45, 1–23

Haskell, Francis (1993) *History and its Images*, New Haven

Hasluck, Frederick W. (1929) *Christianity and Islam under the Sultans*, 2 vols, Oxford

Hauser, Arnold (1951) *The Social History of Art*, 2 vols, London

Hay, Denys (1952) *Polydore Vergil*, Oxford
Headley, John M. (1963) *Luther's View of Church History*, New Haven
Hebdige, Dick (1979) *Subculture: the Meaning of Style*, London
Heers, Jacques (1961) *Gênes au xve siècle: activité économique et problèmes sociaux*, Paris
Heesterman, Johannes C. (1985) *The Inner Conflict of Traditions*, Chicago
Heger, E. (1932) *Die Anfänge der neueren Musikgeschichtschreibung um 1770 bei Gerbert, Burney und Hawkins*, rpr. Baden-Baden 1974
Heikamp, Detlev (1969) 'Les merveilles de Pratolino', *L'Oeuil* 171, 16–27
Heinz, Günther (1972) 'Realismus und Rhetorik im Werk des Bartolomeo Passarotti', *Jahrbuch Kunsthistorisches Sammlung in Wien* 68, 153–69
Herskovits, Melville J. (1937) 'African Gods and Catholic Saints in New World Negro Belief', *American Anthropologist* 39, 635–43
Herskovits, M. J. (1938) *Acculturation: a Study of Culture Contact*, New York
Hervey, Mary (1921) *The Life, Correspondence and Collections of Thomas Howard, Earl of Arundel*, Cambridge
Herzfeld, Michael (1985) *The Poetics of Manhood: Contest and Identity in a Cretan Mountain Village*, Princeton
Hill, Errol (1972) *The Trinidad Carnival*, Austin
Hilton, Anne (1985) *The Kingdom of Kongo*, Oxford
Hobsbawm, Eric J. (1959) *Primitive Rebels*, Manchester
Hobsbawm, Eric J. and Terence O. Ranger, eds (1983) *The Invention of Tradition*, Cambridge
Hofmann, Christine (1985) *Das Spanische Hofzeremoniell von 1500–1700*, Frankfurt
Hollander, John (1961) *The Untuning of the Sky*, Princeton
Hollinger, David A. (1980) 'T. S. Kuhn's Theory of Science and its Implications for History', in *Paradigms and Revolutions*, ed. Gary Gutting, Notre Dame, 195–222
Horton, Robin (1967) 'African Traditional Thought and Western Science', *Africa*, 155–86
Horton, Robin (1982) 'Tradition and Modernity Revisited', in *Rationality and Relativism*, ed. Martin Hollis and Steven Lukes, Oxford, 201–60
Howard, Deborah (1975) *Jacopo Sansovino: Architecture and Patronage in Renaissance Venice*, New Haven
Huizinga, Johan (1919) *Autumn of the Middle Ages*, English trans. Chicago 1995
Huizinga, Johan (1929) 'The Task of Cultural History', English trans. in *Men and Ideas*, New York 1960, 17–76
Huizinga, Johan (1938) *Homo Ludens*, English trans. London 1970

Hulme, Peter (1987) *Colonial Encounters*, London
Hulme, Peter (1994) 'Tales of Distinction', in *Implicit Understandings*, ed. Stuart B. Schwartz, Cambridge, 157–97
Hunt, Lynn, ed (1989) *The New Cultural History*, Berkeley
Huntington, Archer M, ed. (1905) *Catalogue of the Library of F. Columbus*, New York
Huppert, George (1970) *The Idea of Perfect History*, Urbana
Hutton, Patrick H. (1993) *History as an Art of Memory*, Hanover and London
Ife, Barry W. (1985) *Reading and Fiction in Golden Age Spain*, Cambridge
Iggers, Georg G. (1982) 'The University of Göttingen 1760–1800 and the Transformation of Historical Scholarship', *Storia della Storiografia* 2, 11–36
Impey, Oliver and Arthur Macgregor, eds (1985) *The Origins of Museums: the Cabinet of Curiosities in Sixteenth- and Seventeenth-Century Europe*, Oxford
Inalcik, Halil (1973) *The Ottoman Empire: the Classical Age, 1300–1600*, London
Irving, Washington (1824) *Tales of a Traveller*, 2 vols, Paris
Jaeger, Werner (1933) *Paideia*, vol. 1, English trans. Oxford 1939
Jameson, Fredric (1972) *The Prison-House of Language*, Princeton
Jardine, Nicholas (1984) *The Birth of History and Philosophy of Science*, Cambridge
Jauss, Hans-Robert (1974) *Toward an Aesthetic of Reception*, English trans. Minneapolis 1982
Javitch, Daniel (1991) *Proclaiming a Classic: the Canonization of the Orlando Furioso*, Princeton
Jorio, Andrea di (1832) *La mimica degli antichi investigata nel gestire napoletano*, rpr. Naples 1964
Josselin, Ralph (1976) *Diary*, ed. Alan D. Macfarlane, London
Joutard, Philippe (1976) *La Sainte-Barthélemy: ou les résonances d'un massacre*, Neuchâtel
Jung, Carl Gustav (1928) 'General Aspects of Dream Psychology', in his *Collected Works*, vol. 8, London 1960, 237–80
Jung, Carl Gustav (1930) 'Dream-Analysis in its Practical Application', in his *Modern Man in Search of a Soul*, London 1933, 1–31
Jung, Carl Gustav (1945) 'On the Nature of Dreams', in his *Collected Works*, vol. 8, London 1960, 281–300
Kagan, Richard L. (1990) *Lucrecia's Dreams: Politics and Prophecy in Sixteenth-Century Spain*, Berkeley
Kammen, Michael (1984) 'Extending the Reach of American Cultural History', rpr. in his *Selvages and Biases*, Ithaca 1987, 118–53
Kantorowicz, Ernst H. (1957) *The King's Two Bodies*, Princeton
Kaplan, Steven L., ed. (1984) *Understanding Popular Culture*, Berlin
Kelley, Donald R. (1970) *Foundations of Modern Historical*

Scholarship: Language, Law and History in the French Renaissance, New York

Kelley, Donald R. and Richard H. Popkin, eds (1991) *The Shapes of Knowledge from the Renaissance to the Enlightenment*, Dordrecht

Kessler, Johan (1540) *Sabbata*, ed. T. Schiess, Leipzig 1911

Kidder, Daniel (1845) *Sketches of Residence and Travels in Brazil*, 2 vols, New York

Kinser, Samuel (1990) *Carnival American Style: Mardi Gras at New Orleans and Mobile*, Chicago

Klaniczay, Gábor (1984) 'Shamanistic Elements in Central European Witchcraft', rpr. in his *The Uses of Supernatural Power*, Cambridge 1990, 151–67

Klingender, Francis (1947) *Art and the Industrial Revolution*, London

Knowlson, James R. (1965) 'The Idea of Gesture as a Universal Language', *Journal of the History of Ideas* 26, 495–508

Knox, Dilwyn (1989) 'On Immobility', in *Begetting Images*, ed. Mary B. Campbell and Mark Rollins, New York, 71–87

Knox, Dilwyn (1990) 'Ideas on Gesture and Universal Languages *c*.1550–1650', in *New Perspectives on Renaissance Thought*, ed. John Henry and Sarah Hutton, London, 101–36

Knox, Dilwyn (1995) 'Erasmus' *De Civilitate* and the Religious Origins of Civility in Protestant Europe', *Archiv für Reformationsgeschichte* 86, 7–47

Knox, Ronald (1950) *Enthusiasm*, Oxford

Kohl, Benjamin G. and Ronald G. Witt, eds (1978) *The Earthly Republic: Italian Humanists on Government and Society*, Philadelphia

Koselleck, Reinhart (1972) '*Begriffsgeschichte* and Social History', rpr. in his *Futures Past*, 1979, English trans. Cambridge, Mass. 1985, 73–91

Koselleck, Reinhart (1979) 'Terror and Dream', in his *Futures Past*, English trans. Cambridge, Mass. 1985, 213–30

Kris, Ernst (1953) *Psychoanalytic Explorations in Art*, London

Kroeber, Alfred L. and Clyde Kluckhohn (1952) *Culture: a Critical Review of Concepts and Definitions*, rpr. New York 1963

Kuhn, Thomas S. (1962) *The Structure of Scientific Revolutions*, Chicago

Kula, Witold (1962) *Economic Theory of the Feudal System*, English trans. London 1976

Lafaye, Jacques (1974) *Quetzlcóatl and Guadalupe: the Formation of Mexican National Consciousness, 1531–1813*, English trans. Chicago 1976

Lakatos, Imre and A. Musgrave, eds (1970) *Criticism and the Growth of Knowledge*, London

Lakoff, George and Mark Johnson (1980) *Metaphors We Live By*, Chicago

Landes, Ruth (1947) *The City of Women*, rpr. New York 1996

Lanza, Maria (1931) 'Un rifacitore popolare di leggende cavalleresche', *Il Folklore Italiano* 6, 134–45

Larivaille, Paul (1980) *Pietro Aretino fra Rinascimento e Manierismo*, Rome

Larsen, Sidsel S. (1982) 'The Glorious Twelfth: the Politics of Legitimation in Kilbroney', in *Belonging*, ed. Anthony P. Cohen, London, 278–91

Lassels, Richard (1654) 'Description of Italy', in Chaney (1985), 147–231

Lassels, Richard (1670) *A Voyage of Italy*, rpr. London 1698

Laud, William (1847–60) *Works*, 7 vols, Oxford

Lavin, Irving (1983) 'Bernini and the Art of Social Satire', *History of European Ideas* 4, 365–78

Lazard, Sylvie (1993) 'Code de comportement de la jeune femme en Italie au 14e siècle', in *Traités de savoir-vivre italien*, ed. Alain Montandon, Clermont, 7–23

Lazzaro, Claudia (1990) *The Italian Renaissance Garden*, New Haven

Le Braz, Anatole (1922) *La légende de la mort*, 4th edn, Paris

Lefebvre, Georges (1932) *The Great Fear*, English trans. London 1973

Le Goff, Jacques (1971) 'Dreams in the Culture and Collective Psychology of the Medieval West', English trans. in his *Time, Work and Culture in the Middle Ages*, Chicago 1980, 201–4

Le Goff, Jacques (1974) 'Mentalities', English trans. in *Constructing the Past*, ed. Jacques Le Goff and Pierre Nora, Cambridge 1985, 166–80

Le Goff, Jacques (1982) 'Les gestes de St Louis', in *Mélanges Jacques Stiennon*, Paris, 445–59

Le Goff, Jacques (1983) 'Christianity and Dreams', English trans. in his *The Medieval Imagination*, Chicago 1988, 193–231

Le Goff, Jacques (1984) 'The Dreams of Helmbrecht the Elder', in his *The Medieval Imagination*, Chicago 1988, 232–42

Le Goff, Jacques (1985) 'Gestures in Purgatory', English trans. in his *The Medieval Imagination*, Chicago 1988, 86–92

Le Goff, Jacques (1988) *Histoire et mémoire*, Paris

Leiris, Michel (1958) *La possession et ses aspects théatraux chez les Éthiopiens de Gondar*, Paris

Leonard, Irving A. (1933) *Romances of Chivalry in the Spanish Indies*, Berkeley

Leonard, Irving A. (1949) *Books of the Brave*, Cambridge, Mass.

Leopoldi, José Savio (1978) *Escola da Samba, ritual e sociedade*, Rio de Janeiro

Lercari, Giovanni Battista (1579) *Le discordie e guerre civili dei genovesi nell'anno 1575*, Genoa 1857

Le Roy Ladurie, Emmanuel (1979) *Carnival*, English trans. London 1980

Levine, Joseph M. (1977) *Dr Woodward's Shield*, Berkeley

230   Bibliography

Levine, Robert M. (1992) *Vale of Tears: Revisiting the Canudos Massacre in North-East Brazil, 1893–7*, Berkeley and Los Angeles
Levinson, Leonard L. (1972) *Bartlett's Unfamiliar Quotations*, London
Lévi-Strauss, Claude (1955) *Tristes tropiques*, English trans. London 1973
Lévy-Bruhl, Lucien (1927) *La mentalité primitive*, Paris
Lévy-Bruhl, Lucien (1949) *Notebooks*, English trans. Oxford 1975
Lewis, Bernard (1995) *Cultures in Conflict: Christians, Muslims and Jews in the Age of Discovery*, New York
Lincoln, Jackson S. (1935) *The Dream in Primitive Cultures*, London
Linger, Daniel Touro (1992) *Dangerous Encounters: Meanings of Violence in a Brazilian City*, Stanford
Lipking, Lawrence (1970) *The Ordering of the Arts*, Princeton
Lippe, Rudolf zu (1974) *Naturbeherrschung am Menschen*, Frankfurt
Llosa, Mário Vargas (1969) 'Carta de batalla por *Tirant lo Blanc*', rpr. as introduction to *Tirant lo Blanc*, Madrid 1970, 9–41
Lloyd, Geoffrey (1990) *Demystifying Mentalities*, Cambridge
Lockhart, James (1994) 'Sightings: Initial Nahua Reactions to Spanish Culture', in *Implicit Understandings*, ed. Stuart Schwartz, Cambridge, 218–48
Lopez, Roberto (1952) 'Économie et architecture médiévales', *Annales: Économies, Sociétés, Civilisations* 7, 433–8
Lord, Albert B. (1960) *The Singer of Tales*, Cambridge, Mass.
Lotman, Jurij M. (1984) 'The Poetics of Everyday Behaviour in Eighteenth-Century Russia', in *The Semiotics of Russian Culture*, ed. Ann Shukman, Ann Arbor, 231–56
Lovejoy, Arthur O. (1936) *The Great Chain of Being*, Cambridge, Mass.
Lowenthal, David (1985) *The Past is a Foreign Country*, Cambridge
Lucchi, Piero (1982) 'Leggere scrivere e abbaco', in *Scienze, credenze occulte, livelli di cultura*, ed. Paola Zambelli, Florence, 101–20
Luck, Georg (1958) '*Vir Facetus*: a Renaissance Ideal', *Studies in Philology* 55, 107–21
Luzio, Alessandro and Rodolfo Renier (1891) 'Buffoni, nani e schiavi dei Gonzaga ai tempi d'Isabella d'Este', *Nuova Antologia* 118, 618–50; 119, 112–46
Lyons, Francis S. L. (1979) *Culture and Anarchy in Ireland, 1890–1939*, Oxford
Lyotard, Jean-François (1979) *The Post-Modern Condition*, English trans. Manchester 1984
Macdonagh, Oliver (1983) *States of Mind*, London
Macfarlane, Alan D. (1970) *The Family Life of Ralph Josselin*, Cambridge
MacGaffey, Wyatt (1986) *Religion and Society in Central Africa*, Chicago
MacGaffey, Wyatt (1994) 'Dialogues of the Deaf: Europeans on the

Atlantic Coast of Africa', in *Implicit Understandings*, ed. Stuart B. Schwartz, Cambridge, 249–67

MacKay, Angus (1976) 'The Ballad and the Frontier in Late Medieval Spain', *Bulletin of Hispanic Studies* 52, 15–33

MacKay, Angus (1977) *Spain in the Middle Ages: From Frontier to Empire*, London

MacKenney, Richard (1987) *Tradesman and Traders: the World of the Guilds in Venice and Europe, c.1250–c.1650*, London

McLaughlin, Martin (1988) 'Histories of Literature in the Quattrocento', in *The Languages of Literature in Renaissance Italy*, ed. Peter Hainsworth et al., Oxford, 63–80

Mączak, Antoni (1978) *Travel in Early Modern Europe*, English trans. Cambridge 1995

Mączak, Antoni and Hans Teuteberg, eds (1982) *Reiseberichte als Quellen europäischer Kulturgeschichte*, Wolfenbüttel

Malaguzzi Valeri, Francesco (1913–23) *La corte di Lodovico il Moro*, 4 vols, Milan

Malinowski, Bronislaw (1931) 'Culture', in *Encyclopaedia of the Social Sciences*, vol. 4, rpr. New York 1948, 621–45

Mandelbaum, JonnaLynn K. (1989) *The Missionary as a Cultural Interpreter*, New York

Mankowski, Tadeusz (1959) *Orient w Polskiej Kulturze Artystycznej*, Wroclaw

Mann, Vivian et al., eds (1992) *Convivencia: Jews, Muslims and Christians in Medieval Spain*, New York

Mannheim, Karl (1927) *Conservatism: a Contribution to the Sociology of Knowledge*, English trans. London 1986

Marín, Francisco Rodríguez (1911) *Franciso Pacheco Maestro de Velázquez*, Madrid

Marquand, Allan (1922) *Andrea della Robbia and his Atelier*, 2 vols, Princeton

Mars, Louis (1946) *La crise de possession dans le Vaudou*, Port-au-Prince

Martin, Jean-Clément (1987) *La Vendée et la France*, Paris

Martin, John (1987) 'Popular Culture and the Shaping of Popular Heresy in Renaissance Venice', in *Inquisition and Society in Early Modern Europe*, ed. Stephen Haliczer, London, 115–28

[Martyn, Thomas] (1787) *The Gentleman's Guide in his Tour through Italy*, London

Marwick, Max (1964) 'Witchcraft as a Social Strain-Gauge', *Australian Journal of Science* 26, 263–8

Masini, Eliseo (1621) *Il Sacro Arsenale*, rpr. Rome 1665

Mauss, Marcel (1935) 'The Techniques of the Body', English trans. in *Economy and Society* 2 (1973), 70–88

Maxwell, Gavin (1956) *God Protect Me from My Friends*, London

Mazzotti, Giuseppe (1986) *The World at Play in Boccaccio's 'Decameron'*, Princeton

Meinhold, Peter (1967) *Geschichte der kirchlichen Historiographie*, Freiburg and Munich

Melisch, Stephan (1659) *Visiones Nocturnae*, English trans. *Twelve Visions*, London 1663

Meyer, Marlyse (1993) *Caminhos do Imaginário no Brasil*, São Paulo

Michalek, Boleslaw (1973) *The Modern Cinema of Poland*, Bloomington

Michéa, René (1939) 'Goethe au pays des *lazaroni*', in *Mélanges Jules Legras*, Paris, 47–62

Miller, Patricia Cox (1994) *Dreams in Late Antiquity*, Princeton

Molmenti, Pompeo (1879) *Storia della Venezia nella vita privata*, 3 vols, new edn Bergamo 1927–9

Momigliano, Arnaldo D. (1963) 'Pagan and Christian Historiography in the Fourth Century', rpr. in his *Essays in Ancient and Modern Historiography*, Oxford 1977, 107–26

Momigliano, Arnaldo D. (1975) *Alien Wisdom: the Limits of Hellenism*, Cambridge

Montaigne, Michel de (1992) *Journal*, ed. François Rigolot, Paris

Montandon, Alain, ed. (1995) *Les espaces de la civilité*, Mont-de-Marsan

Monteiro, Duglas Teixeira (1974) *Os errantes do novo século*, São Paulo

Monter, E. William (1969) *Calvin's Geneva*, New York

Moore, John (1781) *A View of Society and Manners in Italy*, Dublin

Morgan, Edmund S. (1988) *Inventing the People*, New York

Morris, Colin (1975) '*Judicium Dei*', in *Church, Society and Politics*, ed. Derek Baker, Oxford, 95–111

Morris, Desmond (1977) *Manwatching: a Field Guide to Human Behaviour*, London

Morris, Desmond et al. (1979) *Gestures: Their Origins and Distribution*, London

Moryson, Fynes (1617) *An Itinerary*, rpr. Amsterdam 1971

Muchembled, Robert (1990) 'Satanic Myths and Cultural Reality', in *Early Modern European Witchcraft*, ed. Bengt Ankarloo and Gustav Henningsen, Oxford, 139–60

Muir, Edward (1981) *Civic Ritual in Renaissance Venice*, Princeton

Muir, Edward and Guido Ruggiero, eds (1990) *Sex and Gender*, Baltimore

Mulkay, Michael (1988) *On Humour*, Cambridge

Murray, Alexander (1978) *Reason and Society in the Middle Ages*, Oxford

Niedermann, Joseph (1941) *Kultur: Werden und Wandlungen des Begriffs von Cicero bis Herder*, Florence

Nipperdey, Thomas (1981) 'Der Kölner Dom als Nationaldenkmal', rpr. in his *Nachdenken über die deutsche Geschichte*, Munich 1986, 156–71

Nora, Pierre, ed. (1984–92), *Les lieux de mémoire*, 7 vols, Paris

Norton, Frederick J. and Edward Wilson (1969) *Two Spanish Chapbooks*, Cambridge

Obeyesekere, Gananath (1992) *The Apotheosis of Captain Cook*, Princeton

Österberg, Eva (1991) *Mentalities and Other Realities*, Lund

Omari, Mikelle Smith (1994) 'Candomblé', in *Religion in Africa*, ed. Thomas D. Blakeley et al., London, 135–59

Ortalli, Gherardo (1993) 'Il giudice e la taverna', in *Gioco e giustizia nell'Italia di Comune*, ed. Gherardo Ortalli, Treviso and Rome, 49–70

Ortiz, Fernando (1940) *Cuban Counterpoint: Tobacco and Sugar*, English trans. New York 1947

Ortiz, Fernando (1952) 'La transculturación blanca de los tambores de los negros', rpr. in his *Estudios etnosociológicos*, Havana 1991, 176–201

Ortiz, Fernando (1954) 'Los viejos carnavales habaneros', rpr. in his *Estudios etnosociológicos*, Havana 1991, 202–11

Ottenberg, Simon (1959) 'Ibo Receptivity to Change', in *Continuity and Change in African Cultures*, ed. William Bascom and Melville J. Herskovits, Chicago, 130–43

Owen, Stephen (1986) *Remembrances*, Cambridge, Mass.

Ozouf, Mona (1984) 'Le Panthéon', in Nora, vol. 1, 139–66

Pallares-Burke, Maria Lúcia (1996) *Nísia Floresta, O Carapuceiro e Outras Ensaios de Tradução Cultural*, São Paulo

Pallavicino, Giulio (1975) *Inventione di scriver tutte le cose accadute alli tempi suoi (1583–1589)*, ed. Edoardo Grendi, Genoa

Pálsson, Gísli (1993) *Beyond Boundaries: Understanding, Translation and Anthropological Discourse*, Oxford

Panofsky, Erwin (1939) *Studies in Iconology*, New York

Paoli, Ugo E. (1959) *Il latino maccheronico*, Padua

Parker, Richard G. (1991) *Bodies, Pleasures and Passions*, Boston

Paschetti, Bartolommeo (1583) *Le bellezze di Genova*, Genoa

Pearse, Andrew (1955–6) 'Carnival in Nineteenth-Century Trinidad', *Caribbean Quarterly* 4, 175–93

Peloso, Silvano (1984) *Medioevo nel sertão*, Rome

Pereira, Leonardo Affonso de Miranda (1994) *O Carnaval das Letras*, Rio de Janeiro

Phillips, Henry (1980) *The Theatre and its Critics in Seventeenth-Century France*, Oxford

Piccolomini, Alessandro (1539) *La Rafaella*, rpr. Milan 1969

Pike, Kenneth L. (1954) *Language in Relation to a Unified Theory of the Structure of Human Behaviour*, rev. edn The Hague and Paris 1967

Pittock, Joan H. (1973) *The Ascendancy of Taste*, London

Pittock, Murray (1991) *The Invention of Scotland*, London

Plaisance, Michel (1972) 'La structure de la beffa dans le Cene d'A. F.

Grazzini', in Rochon, 45–98
Pocock, John G. A. (1972) *Politics, Language and Time*, London
Pocock, John G. A. (1975) *The Machiavellian Moment*, Princeton
Poleggi, Ennio (1968) *Strada Nuova*, Genoa
Poleggi, Ennio (1969) 'Genova e l'architettura di villa nel secolo xvi', *Bollettino Centro Andrea Palladio* 11, 231–40
Popper, Karl (1934) *The Logic of Scientific Discovery*, English trans. London 1959
Portilla, Miguel León- (1959) *Visión de los vencidos*, Mexico City
Prandi, Stefano (1990) *Il cortegiano ferrarese*, Florence
Pratt, Mary Louise (1992) *Imperial Eyes: Travel Writing and Transculturation*, London
Pred, Alan (1986) *Place, Practice and Structure*, Cambridge
Price, Simon R. F. (1986) 'The Future of Dreams: From Freud to Artemidorus', *Past and Present* 113, 3–37
Prins, Gwyn (1980) *The Hidden Hippopotamus*, Cambridge
Propp, Vladimir (1976) 'Ritual Laughter in Folklore', in his *Theory and History of Folklore*, Manchester 1984
Pye, Michael (1993) *Syncretism v Synthesis*, Cardiff
Queiroz, Maria Isaura Pereira de (1978), 'Évolution du Carnaval Latino-Américain', *Diogène* 104, 53–69
Queiroz, Maria Isaura Pereira de (1992) *Carnaval brasileiro*, São Paulo
Quondam, Amedeo (1982) 'L'accademia', in *Letteratura Italiana*, ed. Alberto Asor Rosa, Turin, vol. 1, 823–98
Rackham, Bernard (1952) *Italian Maiolica*, 2nd edn London 1963
Radding, Charles M. (1978) 'The Evolution of Medieval Mentalities', *American Historical Review* 83, 577–97
Radding, Charles M. (1979) 'Superstition to Science', *American Historical Review* 84, 945–69
Radin, Paul (1936) 'Ojibwa and Ottawa Puberty Dreams', in *Essays in Anthropology Presented to Alfred L. Kroeber*, ed. Robert H. Lowie, Berkeley, 233–64
Rajna, Pio (1872) *Ricerche intorno ai Reali di Francia*, Bologna
Rak, Michele (1971) *La parte istorica: storia della filosofia e libertinismo erudito*, Naples
Ranger, Terence O. (1975) *Dance and Society in Eastern Africa 1890–1970: the Beni Ngoma*, London
Rassem, Mohammed and Justin Stagl, eds (1980) *Statistik und Staatsbeschreibung in der Neuzeit*, Paderborn
Ray, John (1673) *Observations Topographical, Moral and Physiological*, London
Raymond, John (1648) *An Itinerary*, London
Real, Katarina (1967) *O Folclore no Carnaval de Recife*, 2nd edn Recife 1990
Rebora, Piero (1936) 'Milano in Shakespeare e negli scrittori inglesi del suo tempo', in *Civiltà italiana e civiltà inglese*, Florence, 209–27

Reik, Theodor (1920) 'Uber kollektives Vergessen', *International Zeitschrift für Psychanalyse* 6, 202–15

Reusch, Franz H., ed. (1886) *Die 'indices librorum prohibitorum' des sechszehnten Jahrhunderts*, Tübingen

Rey, Abel (1930) *La science orientale avant les grecs*, Paris

Richardson, Brian (1994) *Print Culture in Renaissance Italy*, Cambridge

Ricoeur, Paul (1981) *Hermeneutics and the Human Sciences*, Cambridge, 182–93

Risério, António (1981), *Carnaval Ijexá*, Salvador

Robertson, Clare (1992) *'Il Gran Cardinale': Alessandro Farnese, Patron of the Arts*, New Haven and London

Rochon, André, ed. (1972) *Formes et significations de la beffa*, Paris

Rochon, André, ed. (1975) *Formes et significations de la beffa*, vol. 2, Paris

Rodini, Robert J. (1970) *A. F. Grazzini*, Madison

Rogers, Samuel (1956) *Italian Journal*, ed. John R. Hale, London

Rosa, João Guimarães (1956) *Grande Sertão: Veredas*, São Paulo

Roth, Michael S., ed. (1994a) 'Performing History: Modernist Contextualism in Carl Schorske's Fin-de-Siècle Vienna', *American Historical Review* 99, 729–45

Roth, Michael S., ed. (1994b) *Rediscovering History*, Stanford

Rotunda, Dominic P. (1942) *Motif-Index of the Italian Novella in Prose*, Bloomington

Rousso, Henry (1987) *The Vichy Syndrome*, English trans. Cambridge, Mass. 1991

Rubiès, Joan Pau (1995) 'Instructions for Travellers', *History and Anthropology*, 1–51

Rubin, Patricia L. (1995) *Giorgio Vasari: Art and History*, New Haven

Ruggiero, Guido (1993) *Binding Passions: Tales of Magic, Marriage and Power at the End of the Renaissance*, New York

Sahlins, Marshall (1981) *Historical Metaphors and Mythical Realities*, Ann Arbor

Sahlins, Marshall (1985) *Islands of History*, Chicago

Sahlins, Marshall (1995) *How 'Natives' Think*, Chicago

Said, Edward (1978) *Orientalism*, London

Said, Edward (1993) *Culture and Imperialism*, 2nd edn New York 1994

Sallmann, Jean-Michel, ed. (1992) *Visions indiennes, visions baroques: les métissages de l'inconscient*, Paris

Samuel, Raphael (1994) *Theatres of Memory*, London

San Carlo e il suo tempo (1986), Rome

Sánchez, Alberto (1958) 'Los libros de caballerías en la conquista de América', *Anales Cervantinos* 7, 237–60

Sapegno, Maria Serena (1993) '*Storia della letteratura italiana* di

Girolamo Tiraboschi', in *Letteratura Italiana: Le Opere*, ed. Alberto Asor Rosa, vol. 2, Turin, 1161–95

Sapir, James D. and Jon C. Crocker, eds (1977) *The Social Use of Metaphor*, Philadelphia

Savelli, Rodolfo (1981) *La repubblica oligarchica: legislazione, istituzioni e ceti a Genova nel '500*, Milan

Scaraffia, Lucetta (1993) *Rinnegati: per una storia dell'identità occidentale*, Rome and Bari

Schäfer, Dietrich (1891) *Geschichte und Kulturgeschichte*, Jena

Schama, Simon (1987) *The Embarrassment of Riches*, London

Schmitt, Jean-Claude (1981) 'Gestus/Gesticulatio', in *La lexicographie du latin médiéval*, Paris, 377–90

Schmitt, Jean-Claude (1990) *La raison des gestes dans l'occident médiéval*, Paris

Schneider, Harold K. (1959) 'Pakot Resistance to Change', in *Continuity and Change in African Cultures*, ed. William Bascom and Melville J. Herskovits, Chicago, 144–67

Schorske, Carl E. (1980) *Fin-de-Siècle Vienna: Politics and Culture*, Cambridge

Schudson, Michael (1992) *Watergate: How We Remember, Forget and Reconstruct the Past*, paperback edn New York 1993

Schwartz, Benjamin (1959) 'Some Polarities in Confucian Thought', in *Confucianism in Action*, ed. David S. Nivison and Arthur F. Wright, Stanford, 50–62

Scott, James C. (1976) *The Moral Economy of the Peasant: Rebellion and Subsistence in South East Asia*, New Haven

Screech, Michael M. (1979) *Rabelais*, London

Seeberg, Erich (1923) *Gottfried Arnold*, Meerane

Seidensticker, Edward (1983) *Low City, High City: Tokyo from Edo to the Earthquake, 1867–1923*, Harmondsworth

Seigel, Jerrold E. (1968) *Rhetoric and Philosophy in Renaissance Humanism*, Princeton

Sells, A. Lytton (1964) *The Paradise of Travellers*, London

Sennett, Richard (1977) *The Fall of Public Man*, Cambridge

Sewall, Samuel (1878), *Diary*, Boston

Seznec, Jean (1940) *The Survival of the Pagan Gods*, English trans. New York 1953

Sharp, Cecil (1907) *English Folksong*, London

Sharp, Samuel (1766) *Travels*, London

Shumway, Nicolas (1991) *The Invention of Argentina*, Berkeley

Sieber, Roy (1962) 'Masks as Agents of Social Control', rpr. in *The Many Faces of Primitive Art*, ed. Douglas Fraser, Englewood Cliffs 1966, 257–62

Simson, Olga Rodrigues de Moraes von (1991–2) 'Mulher e Carnaval: mito e realidade', *Revista de História* 125–6, 7–32

Singer, Milton (1968) 'The Concept of Culture', in *International*

Encyclopaedia of the Social Sciences, ed. D. L. Sills, New York, vol. 3, 527–43

Skippon, Philip (1732) 'An Account of a Journey', in *A Collection of Voyages*, ed. A. and J. Churchill, 6 vols, London, vol. 6, 485–694

Slater, Candace (1982) *Stories on a String: the Brazilian Literatura de Cordel*, Berkeley

Smith, Bernard (1960) *European Vision and the South Pacific*, 2nd edn New Haven 1985

Smith, Henry N. (1950) *Virgin Land*, Cambridge, Mass.

Snyders, Georges (1964) *La pédagogie en France aux 17e et 18e siècles*, Paris

Sodré, Nelson Werneck (1966) *Historia da imprensa no Brasil*, São Paulo

Soihet, Raquel (1993) 'Subversão pelo Riso: Reflexões sobre Resistência e Circularidade Cultural no Carnaval Carioca (1890–1945)', Tese de Prof. Titular, UFF, Rio de Janeiro

Sorrentino, Andrea (1935) *La letteratura italiana e il Sant'Ufficio*, Naples

Spence, Jonathan (1990) *The Question of Hu*, London

Spicer, Joaneath (1991) 'The Renaissance Elbow', in Bremmer and Roodenburg, 84–128

Spinola, Andrea (1981) *Scritti scelti*, ed. Carlo Bitossi, Genoa

Stagl, Justin (1980) 'Die Apodemik oder "Reisekunst" als Methodik der Sozialforschung vom Humanismus bis zur Aufklärung', in Rassem and Stagl, 131–202

Stagl, Justin (1990) 'The Methodizing of Travel in the Sixteenth Century: a Tale of Three Cities', *History and Anthropology* 4, 303–38

Starkey, David (1977) 'Representation through Intimacy', in *Symbols and Sentiments*, ed. Ioan M. Lewis, London and New York, ch. 10

Stern, Samuel M., ed. (1953) *Les chansons mozarabes*, Palermo

Stewart, Charles, ed. (1994) *Syncretism/anti-Syncretism*, London

Storey, John, ed. (1996) *What is Cultural Studies?* London

Stoye, John W. (1952) *English Travellers Abroad 1604–67*, rev. edn New Haven 1989

Swedenborg, Emmanuel (1744) *Journal of Dreams*, English trans. Bryn Athyn 1918

Tacchella, Lorenzo (1966) *La riforma tridentina nella diocesi di Tortona*, Genoa

Tafuri, Manfredo (1969) *Jacopo Sansovino e l'architettura del '500 a Venezia*, Padua

Tanturli, Giuliano (1976) 'Le biografie d'artisti prima del Vasari', in *Il Vasari storiografo e artista*, Florence

Taviani, Francesco (1969) *La commedia dell'arte e la società barocca*, Rome

Terrasse, Henri (1932) *L'art hispano-mauresque des origines au 13e siècle*, Paris

Terrasse, Henri (1958) *Islam d'Espagne: une rencontre de l'Orient et de l'Occident*, Paris

Tesauro, Emmanuele (1654) *Il cannocchiale aristotelico*, rpr. Turin 1670

Theweleit, Klaus (1977) *Male Fantasies*, English trans., 2 vols, Cambridge 1987–9

Thomas, Henry (1920) *Spanish and Portuguese Romances of Chivalry*, Cambridge

Thomas, Keith V. (1977) 'The Place of Laughter in Tudor and Stuart England', *Times Literary Supplement*, 21 Jan.

Thompson, Edward P. (1963) *The Making of the English Working Class*, London

Thompson, Edward P. (1971) 'The Moral Economy of the English Crowd', rpr. in Thompson (1991), 185–258

Thompson, Edward P. (1991) *Customs in Common*, 2nd edn Harmondsworth 1993

Thompson, Paul (1978) *The Voice of the Past*, 2nd edn Oxford 1988

Thompson, Stith (1955–8) *Motif-Index of Folk Literature*, 6 vols, Copenhagen

Thornton, John K. (1983) *The Kingdom of the Kongo*, Madison

Tillyard, Eustace M. W. (1943) *The Elizabethan World Picture*, London

Tindall, William Y. (1934) *John Bunyan, Mechanick Preacher*, New York

Tomalin, Margaret (1982) *The Fortunes of the Warrior Maiden in Italian Literature*, Ravenna

Trexler, Richard (1980) *Public Life in Renaissance Florence*, New York

Trompf, Garry W. (1979) *The Idea of Historical Recurrence in Western Thought from Antiquity to the Reformation*, Berkeley

Turler, Hieronymus (1574) *De arte peregrinandi*, rpr. Nuremberg 1591; English trans. *The Traveller*, 1575, rpr. Gainesville 1951

Turner, Graeme (1990) *British Cultural Studies*, 2nd edn London 1996

Turner, Victor (1983), 'Carnaval in Rio', in *The Celebration of Society*, ed. F. E. Manning, Bowling Green, 103–24

Vansina, Jan (1961) *Oral Tradition*, English trans. London 1965; rev. version, *Oral Tradition as History*, Madison 1985

Varese, Claudio, ed. (1955) *Prosatori volgari del Quattrocento*, Milan and Naples

Verger, Pierre (1969) 'Trance and Convention in Nago-Yoruba Spirit Mediumship', in *Spirit Mediumship and Society in Africa*, ed. John Beattie and John Middleton, London, 50–66

Veryard, Ellis (1701) *An Account of a Journey*, London

Vickers, Brian (1984) 'Analogy v Identity', in *Occult and Scientific Mentalities in the Renaissance*, ed. Brian Vickers, Cambridge, 95–163

Vovelle, Michel (1982) *Ideologies and Mentalities*, English trans. Cambridge 1990

Wachtel, Nathan (1971) *The Vision of the Vanquished*, English trans. Hassocks 1977

Wafer, Jim (1991) *The Taste of Blood: Spirit Possession in Brazilian Candomblé*, Philadelphia

Wagner, Roy (1975) *The Invention of Culture*, 2nd edn Chicago 1981

Walzer, Michael (1965) *The Revolution of the Saints*, Cambridge, Mass.

Warburg, Aby (1932) *Gesammelte Schriften*, 2 vols, Leipzig and Berlin

Warner, W. Lloyd (1959) *The Living and the Dead*, New Haven

Watt, Ian and Jack Goody (1962–3) 'The Consequences of Literacy', *Comparative Studies in Society and History* 5, 304–45

Weber, Eugen (1976) *Peasants into Frenchmen*, London

Wellek, René (1941) *The Rise of English Literary History*, Chapel Hill

Welsford, Enid (1935) *The Fool*, London

White, Christopher (1995) *Thomas Howard, Earl of Arundel*, Malibu

White, Hayden V. (1973) *Metahistory*, Baltimore

White, Lynn (1962) *Medieval Technology and Social Change*, Oxford

Whorf, Benjamin L. (1956) *Language, Thought and Reality*, Cambridge, Mass.

Wickham, Chris J. (1985) 'Lawyer's Time: History and Memory in Tenth- and Eleventh-Century Italy', in *Studies in Medieval History Presented to R. H. C. Davis*, ed. Henry Mayr-Harting and Robert I. Moore, London, 53–71

Wiener, Martin J. (1981) *English Culture and the Decline of the Industrial Spirit, 1850–1980*, Cambridge

Williams, Raymond (1958) *Culture and Society*, London

Williams, Raymond (1961) *The Long Revolution*, London

Williams, Raymond (1977) *Marxism and Literature*, Oxford

Williams, Raymond (1981) *Culture*, London

Wilson, Monica Hunter (1951) 'Witch-Beliefs and Social Structure', rpr. in *Witchcraft and Sorcery*, ed. Max Marwick, Harmondsworth 1970, 252–63

Wind, Edgar (1958) *Pagan Mysteries in the Renaissance*, Oxford

Witte, Johannes (1928) *Japan zwischen zwei Kulturen*, Leipzig

Wittkower, Rudolf (1942) 'Marvels of the East: a Study in the History of Monsters', rpr. in *Allegory and the Migration of Symbols*, London 1977, 45–74

Wittkower, Rudolf (1967) 'Francesco Borromini, his Character and Life', rpr. in *Studies in the Italian Baroque*, London 1975, 153–66

Wolf, Eric (1956) 'Aspects of Group Relations in a Complex Society: Mexico', *American Anthropologist* 58, 1065–78

Woodhouse, John, ed. (1982) 'Avvertimenti necessari per i cortegiani', *Studi Secenteschi* 23, 141–61

Wotton, Henry (1907) *Letters and Papers*, ed. Logan P. Smith, Oxford

Yates, Frances (1966) *The Art of Memory*, London

Yinger, John M. (1960) 'Contraculture and Subculture', *American Sociological Review*, 25, 625–35

Young, Robert J. C. (1995) *Colonial Desire: Hybridity in Theory, Culture and Race*, London

Zaluar, Alba (1978) 'O Clóvis ou a Criatividade Popular num Carnaval Massificado', *Cadernos do CERU*, Rio de Janeiro, 50–63

Index

academies, 91, 115, 120
acculturation, 158, 207
Acton, William, English traveller, 103, 106–8
Addison, Joseph, English writer, 72, 99–100, 103, 105, 108–9, 123, 127
Adelung, Johan Christoph, German cultural historian, 2, 16, 18, 20
Adriani, Gianbattista, Florentine scholar, 6–7
Africa, 41, 49, 58, 153–8, 202
Agrippa, Heinrich, German humanist, 72
Althusser, Louis, French philosopher, 195
Alting, Heinrich, German theologian, 9
Amado, Jorge, Brazilian novelist, 134, 143, 148
Amazons, 140
amnesia, structural or social, 54, 56–8
anachronism, 19, 169
Anderson, Benedict, British/Irish/American historian and anthropologist, 198
Andrade, Mario da, Brazilian writer, 148
Andrade, Oswald de, Brazilian writer, 142
Antal, Frederick, Hungarian art historian, 185, 187
anthropology, 24–5, 78, 82, 86, 94, 149, 155, 163–4, 169, 174, 186, 191–3
Arcimboldo, Giuseppe, Milanese painter, 80
Aretino, Pietro, Tuscan writer, 80, 83, 88, 134–5
Ariosto, Ludovico, Italian poet, 125–7, 133–4, 140
Arlotto, Tuscan priest and jester, 80, 88–9, 92
Arnold, Gottfried, German church historian, 9–10
Arnold, Matthew, English critic, 184, 195
Arriaga, Rodriguez de, Spanish theologian, 9
art, history of, 5–7

Arundel, Thomas Howard Earl of, English traveller, 98, 103–4
Ashmole, Elias, English astrologer, 30–5
astronomy, history of, 12–13

Bacon, Francis, English philosopher, 17, 64, 95, 106
Bakhtin, Mikhail, Russian cultural theorist, 77–8, 86–7, 93, 100, 129, 132, 211–12
Banchieri, Adriano, Italian monk and writer, 92
Bandello, Matteo, Lombard writer, 83, 85, 88
Barbaro, Francesco, Venetian patrician and humanist, 69
Baron, Hans, American historian, 119
baroque, cultural movement, 91
Barros, João de, Portuguese humanist, 138
Bartlett, Frederick, English psychologist, 44, 49
Bastide, Roger, French anthropologist, 48
Battisti, Eugenio, Italian art historian, 130
Baudouin, François, French humanist, 11–12
Bedell, William, English traveller, 75
Bellarmine, Robert, Italian Jesuit, 68, 89
Bembo, Pietro, Venetian humanist, 4, 135
benandanti, 40–1
Bentley, Richard, English scholar, 19
Berger, Peter, social psychologist, 58
Besançon, Alain, French historian, 29
Bettinelli, Saverio, Italian scholar, 18
biculturality, 130, 186
Birdwhistell, Ray, American specialist in 'Kinesics', 62
Bisaccioni, count Maiolino, Italian writer, 100–1

biting the finger, 63
Blackbourn, David, British historian, 37
Bloch, Marc, French historian, 44–5, 164,
 172, 175
Boas, Franz, German anthropologist, 207
Boboli gardens, Florence, 80
Boccaccio, Giovanni, Florentine writer, 82–3,
 88–9, 125
Boccalini, Traiano, Italian political theorist,
 72, 98, 131–2
Bomarzo, 80–1
Bonifacio, Giovanni, Veronese lawyer, 60, 62,
 67
Borgia, Cesare, Italian prince, 85
Bororo Indians, 48, 167
Borromeo, Carlo, archbishop of Milan, 68,
 76, 89
Borromini, Francesco, Italian architect, 65
Bossuet, Jacques-Bénigne, French churchman,
 9
Bourdieu, Pierre, French anthropologist, 95,
 194–5, 206
Braudel, Fernand, French historian, 172, 206
Brazil, 48–9, 61, 141–61, 207, 209
Bromley, William, English traveller, 103,
 105–7, 109
Brunelleschi, Filippo, Florentine architect, 83
Bruni, Leonardo, Tuscan humanist, 3–4, 18
Bunyan, John, English religious writer, 39–40
Burckhardt, Jacob, Swiss historian, 21, 79, 83,
 85, 184–5, 197–8
Burnet, Gilbert, Scottish bishop and traveller,
 75, 100, 105–7, 109–10
Burney, Charles, English historian of music, 8
Butterfield, Herbert, English historian, 1, 170

California, 139
Cambiaso, Luca, Genoese painter, 115
Camões, Luis de, Portuguese poet, 138
cannibals, 95
canon, of great works, 190–1
Caravaggio, Lombard painter, 71, 85
Cardano, Girolamo, Italian physician, 40
caricature, 91
Carné, Marcel, French film director, 148
carnival, 84, 98, 101, 117, 145, 148–61
carnivalesque, 129–30, 155–6
Casaubon, Isaac, French scholar, 5
Castellesi, Adriano, Roman humanist, 4
Castiglione, Baldassare, Lombard writer,
 65–6, 70, 81–2, 89–90, 113, 134
Cebà, Ansaldo, Genoese patrician writer, 90,
 116, 119–20
Cellini, Benvenuto, Florentine sculptor, 36–7
censorship, 57–8, 88
Certeau, Michel de, French Jesuit
 anthropologist, 196
Charlemagne, 141
Charles I, King of England, 31, 33–4

Charles II, King of England, 33, 175
Chartier, Roger, French historian, 171
chemistry, history of, 13
Chiaramonti, Scipione, Italian semiotician, 62
chivalry, 15, 132–4, 136–47
Cicero, Marcus Tullius, Roman orator and
 politician, 3, 6, 43, 69, 71
civic spirit, 112, 118–19
classes, social, 199, 205
Columbus, Christopher, 122, 139
Comenius (Komensky), Jan Amos, Czech
 scholar, 37
commonplaces, 24, 26, 36–7, 39–41, 46,
 49–52, 74, 94–5, 104, 177
Comnena, Anna, Byzantine princess, 43
Condorcet, marquis de, French *philosophe*
 and historian, 20–1
Congo, 154
Conselheiro, Antonio, Brazilian holy man and
 rebel leader, 146
constructivism, viii, 51, 97, 179, 198
Cook, Captain James, English sailor, 202
Cortese, Paolo, Roman humanist, 70
Coryat, Thomas, English traveller, 75, 96,
 101–6
Courtin, Antoine, French writer on manners,
 65
Craxi, Benito, Italian prime minister, 151
creoles, 208
creolization, 210–11
Cresolles, Louis de, French Jesuit, 11
Croce, Giulio Cesare, Bolognese poet, 91, 126
crossed legs, 65, 71
cultural borrowing, 203
cultural crystallization, 52, 199, 207
cultural distance, 87, 92, 95, 97–100, 106,
 164, 194
cultural encounters, 158, 164, 193, 201–6
cultural order, 206
cultural pluralism, 55, 209
cultural relativism, 45–6, 61, 194
cultural reproduction, 195–6
cultural studies, 190–1
cultural translation, 97, 139, 151, 193, 196
cultural turn, 183
cultural unity, 186–7, 199
culture: as communication, 61; concept of,
 1–2; decline of, 17–18; pattern dream,
 24–5; political, 195; popular, 16, 124–35,
 188; reproduction, 27; and society,
 18–19; as totality, 19–20; wars, 190,
 201

Da Matta, Roberto, Brazilian anthropologist,
 145, 149, 161
dance, 67, 70–2, 153, 155
Darnton, Robert, American historian, 77, 79,
 93, 165
Dekker, Thomas, English dramatist, 102

Della Casa, Giovanni, Italian writer, 67, 70–1, 81, 90
Della Porta, Giovanni Battista, Neapolitan dramatist and scientist, 70
Delumeau, Jean, French historian, 174
Diaz, Bernal, Spanish soldier and chronicler, 139
disciplines, history of, 11–14
distance, cultural, 87, 92, 95, 97–100, 106
doctrine, history of, 8–10
Dodds, Eric R., British classical scholar, 29
Domenichi, Ludovico, Italian editor, 80, 88
Doria, Andrea, Genoese patrician and admiral, 114–5
Doria, Paolo Matteo, Neapolitan nobleman, 73
dreams, 23–42
Dryden, John, English poet, 5, 20
Duby, Georges, French historian, 197
Dürer, Albrecht, German artist, 36
Durkheim, Émile, French sociologist, 44, 55, 58, 149, 163, 187

Eggan, Dorothy, American anthropologist, 26, 31
Eichhorn, Johan Gottfried, German cultural historian, 2, 20
Elias, Norbert, German sociologist, 73–4, 77, 87–90, 92
emic and etic, 193
Erasmus, Desiderius, Dutch humanist, 98
Estève, Pierre, French scholar, 12–13, 20
Estienne, Henri, French Calvinist printer, 75
Evans-Pritchard, Edward, British social anthropologist, 172, 193
Evelyn, John, English virtuoso, 63, 92, 98, 103, 105–8

façades, Italy as land of, 100, 109
Fauchet, Claude, French humanist, 4
Febvre, Lucien, French historian, 164, 169
Félibien, André, French scholar, 7
Firenzuola, Angelo, Italian writer, 66–7
Fischer, David H., American historian, 205
Fish, Stanley, American literary critic, 56
Fleck, Ludwik, Polish microbiologist, 164
Florence, 77–93, 112
Foglietta, Oberto, Genoese humanist, 115, 117
Folengo, Teofilo, Italian poet, 132–3
Fontenelle, Bernard de, French scholar, 14–15, 20
forgery, 19–20
Forkel, Johan Nicolaus, German historian of music, 8
formulae, 96, 107, 114, 134, 188
Forster, E. Morgan, English novelist, 95
Foucault, Michel, French theorist, 1, 23, 73–4, 163, 176–8, 197

France, 53, 57, 64–5
Frazer, James G., British anthropologist, 174
Freind, John, English scholar, 12
Freud, Sigmund, 24, 28, 35, 52, 58, 61, 78
Freyre, Gilberto, Brazilian historian, 207
frontiers, 147
Frye, Northrop, Canadian critic, 144
Fussell, Paul, American critic, 49–50

Galbraith, John Kenneth, American economist, 113
Galbraith, Vivian Hunter, English historian, 170
Gama, Lopes, Brazilian priest and journalist, 159
García, Carlos, Spanish writer, 65
gardens, 80–1, 84, 130–1
Geertz, Clifford, American anthropologist, 149, 194
Genoa, 61, 96, 112–23
Gerbert, Martin, Swiss historian of music, 8
gesture, 60–76
Ghiberti, Lorenzo, Florentine sculptor, 5
Giberti, Gianmatteo, bishop of Verona, 68
Gil, Gilberto, Brazilian composer and singer, 148, 156
Ginzburg, Carlo, Italian historian, 40–1, 61, 125, 162, 171
Giraldi Cinthio, Gianbattista, Italian writer, 90
Gmelin, J. F., German scholar, 13
Gombrich, Ernst H., art historian, 6, 21, 49, 176–7, 187
Gonja, 58
Goody, Jack, British social anthropologist, 58
Grazzini, Antonfrancesco, Florentine writer, 82–3, 88, 90, 92, 129
Guazzo, Stefano, Italian writer, 67, 70
Guicciardini, Francesco, Florentine historian, 102, 119
Guicciardini, Ludovico, Florentine writer, 88
Guizot, François, French politician and historian, 21

Habermas, Jürgen, German social theorist, 111
habitus, 68, 195
Halbwachs, Maurice, French sociologist, 44–5, 48
Hawaii, 202
Hawkins, John, English historian of music, 8
Hegel, Georg Wilhelm Friedrich, German philosopher, 21
Heidelberg, 57
Henri III, King of France, 126
Henry, Robert, British historian, 18–19
Herbert, Edward, of Cherbury, English traveller, 102
Herder, Johann Gottfried, German thinker, 16, 20–1

Hobsbawm, Eric J., British historian, 55, 146, 189
Hopi Indians, 26, 27, 31
Huet, Pierre-Daniel, French scholar, 5
Huizinga, Johan, Dutch historian, 164, 168, 184–5, 193, 197–8
Hurd, Richard, English scholar, 14–15
hybridization, of cultures, 207, 210

ideas, history of, 11
identity, 48–9, 54, 83, 199
ideology, 175
Ignatius Loyola, Spanish saint, 138
inquisition, 40–1, 63, 88, 104–5
insults, 63
invention, 55, 189, 197
Ireland, 53–5
Irving, Washington, American writer, 76
Italy, 60–135

Jaeger, Werner, German classical scholar, 42
James, Henry, American novelist, 97
Japan, 27, 188, 196
jokes, 77–93
Jorio, Andrea di, Neapolitan scholar, 62
Josselin, Ralph, English clergyman, 30–5
Jung, Carl Gustav, Swiss psychologist, 24
Junius, Franciscus, Dutch humanist, 7

Kessler, Johan, Swiss Protestant pastor, 50
Koselleck, Reinhart, German historian, 23
Krafft, Jens, Danish scholar, 15
Kuhn, Thomas, American historian of science, 59, 176–7
Kula, Witold, Polish historian, 166

La Curne de Sainte-Palaye, Jean-Baptiste de, French scholar, 15
language, history of, 3–5, 19
La Popelinière, Henri Voisin de, French historian, 11
Lassels, Richard, English traveller, 65–6, 92, 99, 103, 106–8, 115
Laud, William, archbishop of Canterbury, 29–35
law, history of, 11–12, 20
lazzaroni, 96
Leclerc, Daniel, French scholar, 12
legitimation, 55, 58
Le Goff, Jacques, French historian, 23, 29, 60, 171, 197
Leonard, Irving, American scholar, 141
Le Roy, Louis, French humanist, 17
Le Roy Ladurie, Emmanuel, French historian, 117
Lévi-Strauss, Claude, French anthropologist, 48
Lévy-Bruhl, Lucien, French philosopher, 163, 167, 169, 174

Lincoln, Jackson S., American anthropologist, 24
Lipsius, Justus, Dutch humanist, 95
Lloyd, Geoffrey, British scholar, 181
Locke, John, English philosopher, 14
Lopez, Roberto, American historian, 113
Lord, Albert, American Slavist, 49
Loredan, Gianfrancesco, Venetian patrician writer, 80, 91
Louis XII, King of France, 53
Louis XIII, King of France, 53
Louis XIV, King of France, 57, 175
Lovejoy, Arthur, American historian of ideas, 11
Lucian, Greek satirist, 37, 116, 134
Luther, Martin, 50, 58, 98
luxury, 119
Lyons, Francis S. L., Irish historian, 195

Machiavelli, Niccolò, 85, 116
Maimbourg, Louis, French historian, 9
Mainardi, Arlotto, Tuscan priest and jester, 80, 88–9, 92
Malinowski, Bronislaw, Polish social anthropologist, 58, 174, 186, 194
Mander, Karel van, Dutch painter-writer, 6
Mannheim, Karl, Hungarian sociologist, 163
Martini, Gianbattista, Italian historian of music, 8
Marxism, 175, 185–7, 192
Massinger, Philip, English dramatist, 102
mathematics, history of, 13
Matthias Corvinus, King of Hungary, 51, 53
Mauss, Marcel, French anthropologist, 62
medicine, history of, 12
Melisch, Stephan, Silesian visionary, 37–9
memory, 43–59
mentalities, history of, 14–16, 44, 97
metaphor, 167–8, 179–81
Michelet, Jules, French historian, 21
Milan, 101–10
Milton, John, English poet, 102
modes of thought, see mentalities
Momigliano, Arnaldo, Italian historian, 203
Montaigne, Michel de, French essayist, 63, 84, 96, 126
Montesquieu, Charles de, French theorist, 15, 166
Montucla, Jean Étienne, French scholar, 13, 17, 20
Moore, John, British traveller, 76
Morhof, Daniel, German scholar, 4
Morison, Fynes, English traveller, 68, 101–4, 107
Morris, Desmond, English ethologist, 62
Muchembled, Robert, French historian, 174
Mundy, Peter, English traveller, 103, 107
music, history of, 7–8

myth, 24, 26–7, 39, 51; as charter, 58–9; and identity, 54; of Italy, 100–1; of the lazy native, 95; of the monstrous races, 140; of Venice, 117; of the witches' sabbath, 198

Naples, 96, 127
nationalism, 55
Nora, Pierre, French historian, 46–7
novel, history of, 5
Nyakyusa people, 41

Ojibwa Indians, 25, 36, 42
oral history, 46
oral poetry, 49, 126–7, 133, 143
oral tradition, 47, 51–2, 131
ordeals, 166
Ortiz, Fernando, Cuban sociologist, 158, 207
Österberg, Eva, Swedish historian, 165
otherness, 79, 193

Pallavicino, Giulio, Genoese patrician, 114
Panofsky, Erwin, German art historian, 187
Pasquier, Étienne, French humanist lawyer, 4, 20
Philip II, King of Spain, 118
philosophy, history of, 10–11
Piaget, Jean, French psychologist, 165
Piccolomini, Alessandro, Sienese writer, 66–7
Pike, Kenneth, American linguist, 193
Poland, 53–4
Pope, Alexander, English poet, 5
Portugal, 138–9
positivism, historical, viii, 22, 51, 97
possession cults, 155–6
Pratolini, Vasco, Italian novelist, 92–3
privacy, 95, 111–23, 199
Procopius, Byzantine historian, 43
Propp, Vladimir, Russian folklorist, 82, 89
psychology, historical, 164
Pushkin, Aleksandr, Russian writer, 29, 56

Quakers, 61
Queiroz, Maria Isaura Pereira de, Brazilian sociologist, 149, 160
Quevedo, Francisco, Spanish poet, 118

Rabelais, François, French writer, 129, 132
Radin, Paul, American anthropologist, 25, 42
Raimondi, Marcantonio, Italian engraver, 128
Ranke, Leopold von, German historian, 21
Ray, John, English botanist and traveller, 99, 103, 106–8, 110
Raymond, John, English traveller, 103, 105–6
re-enactment, 51, 55
relativism, historical, 45–6, 61, 194
Rey, Abel, historian of science, 163
rhetoric, history of, 11
Richardson, Tony, English film director, 54

rituals, 48–9, 82, 89, 112
Robertson, William, Scottish historian, 15
Rogers, Samuel, English poet, 97
Romano, Giulio, Italian artist, 80, 135
Rosa, João Guimarães, Brazilian writer, 143
Russia, 29, 56, 61, 101

Sahlins, Marshall, American anthropologist, 202, 206
saints, 51–2
Sallust, Roman historian, 113, 116
Sandrart, Joachim von, German painter-writer, 6
Sarpi, Paolo, Venetian friar-historian, 98
satire, history of, 5
Schama, Simon, British historian, 199–200
schemata, 24, 26, 36–7, 39–41, 46, 49–52, 95–7, 100–1, 176–8, 188, 196
Schmitt, Jean-Claude, French historian, 64
Schorske, Carl, American historian, 200–1
science, history of, 12–13, 163–4, 166–7, 177
Sebastian, King of Portugal, 51, 53, 139, 146
Selden, John, English scholar, 14
semiotics, 192–3
Sennett, Richard, American sociologist, 111
Settala, Manfredo, Lombard virtuoso, 108
Sewall, Samuel, New England judge, 30–5
Shakespeare, William, quoted, 43, 63
Sharp, Samuel, English traveller, 96
Sheen, Fulton, American bishop, quoted, 54
Sicily, 145
Skippon, Philip, English traveller, 63, 75, 101, 103, 108, 110
Soviet Encyclopaedia, 57–8
space: and memory, 48–9; public and private, 111–23
Spain, 53, 65, 72–3, 114, 118, 136–8, 204
Sparta, 122
spies, 103–5
Spinola, Ambrogio, Genoese patrician and soldier, 115
Spinola, Andrea, Genoese patrician, 61, 119–22
Stendhal (Henri Beyle), French writer, 76
stereotypes, 24, 26, 36–7, 39–41, 46, 49–52, 74, 94–7, 100–1, 140, 176–8
sub-cultures, 205
Sweden, 49
Swedenborg, Emmanuel, Swedish theologian, 28, 39
Switzerland, 122
symbols, 26, 28, 33, 35–6, 39, 42, 47, 167–8, 179, 192
Symonds, Richard, English traveller, 103
syncretism, 154, 158, 207, 209–10

Tasso, Torquato, Italian poet, 98, 115, 127, 140
taxation, and heroism, 53

Teresa of Avila, Spanish saint, 138
Tesauro, Emmanuele, Italian rhetorician, 91
theatre, 67
Thomas, Keith, British historian, 77
Thompson, Edward P., English historian, 166,
    186–7, 205
Thompson, Stith, American folklorist, 83
Tiraboschi, Girolamo, Italian scholar, 5
Toledo, Pedro de, Spanish viceroy of Naples,
    72
Toynbee, Arnold, English historian, 187
tradition, 55, 188–9
transculturation, 158, 207
translation, see cultural translation
travellers, 63, 94–110
Trexler, Richard, American historian, 122
Turler, Hieronymus, German traveller, 72, 95

Valla, Lorenzo, Roman humanist, 3, 11, 19
Vansina, Jan, Belgian anthropologist-
    historian, 47
Vargas Llosa, Mário, Peruvian novelist, 137,
    146
Vasari, Giorgi
    128–9
Vegio, Matteo
Vendée, peasa
Venice, 101, 1
Vergil, Polydo
Veryard, Elias

105–6, 108
Vico, Gianbattista, Neapolitan philosopher of
    history, 11, 13–15
visions, 37–40
Vives, Juan Luis, Spanish humanist, 16, 137
Voltaire, François Arouet de, French
    philosophe, 17, 20

Wajda, Andrzej, Polish film director, 54
Walpole, Horace, English virtuoso, 6, 18–19
Warburg, Aby, German cultural historian,
    176–7, 188, 193
Warton, Thomas, English scholar, 5, 15–16,
    19
Wedgwood, C. Veronica, English historian, 29
William III, King of England, 51–2, 54
Williams, Raymond, British critic, 175, 186,
    190
Winckelmann, Johan Joachim, German art
    historian, 7, 18
Wind, Edgar, German art historian, 207
witches, 40–1, 178, 198
women, 40–1, 64, 66, 69, 71, 82, 87, 90, 126,
    143, 151–3, 156–7,
    n diplomat, 98, 104
    psychologist, 164

    0